ATLAS

OF

ANOTHER AMERICA

AN

ARCHITECTURAL FICTION

PARK BOOKS

ATLAS

OF

ANOTHER AMERICA

BEING A DESCRIPTION OF

FREEDOMLAND,

A TWENTY-FIRST CENTURY SETTLEMENT SCHEME FOR THE AMERICAN NATION

IN THE

GRAND AGRARIAN DEMOCRATIC TRADITION

OF

MR. THOMAS JEFFERSON

BUT ALSO TAKING INTO CONSIDERATION THE CURRENT ECONOMIC AND POLITICAL ORDER;

COMPRISING
A COMPLETE GRAPHIC DISCOURSE ON THE DESIGNED ESTABLISHMENT OF THE SETTLEMENT
INCLUDING DETAILED PLANS
OF THE

128 UNIQUE NEIGHBORHOOD FARM ESTATES.

WITH

AN APPENDIX

CONTAINING DOCUMENTS PERTINENT TO THE ORIGINS OF FREEDOMLAND
INCLUDING

"ATYPICAL PLANS,"
A MEDITATION ON THE AMERICAN DREAM, HOUSES, AND THE COLLAPSE OF THE ECONOMY,
"SUPERMODEL HOMES,"
IN WHICH THE AUTHOR RECOUNTS HIS TOUR THROUGH THE MODEL HOMES OF MR. DAVID WEEKLEY,
"SIX TYPICAL PLANS,"
AN ANALYSIS OF THE HOMES OF THE NATION'S GREATEST BUILDERS
&
"NOTES ON FREEDOMLAND,"
CONSTITUTING OPINIONS AND REMARKS ON THE NATURE AND CONTEXT OF THE WORK.

WITH AN AFTERWORD
BY ALBERT POPE

AND
A POSTSCRIPT,
"NEW HOMES FOR AMERICA"

BY KEITH KRUMWIEDE

ZURICH
2016

Birds Inspect the Plans of Freedomland
after *The Concert of Birds,* 1670
Melchior d'Hondecoeter

FREEDOMLAND

IN WHICH THE OBJECT IN VIEW IS TO UNITE,
IN A BETTER MANNER THAN HAS HITHERTO BEEN DONE
AND WITH A TASTE FOUNDED IN OUR VERY NATURE
WITH ECONOMY AND UTILITY,

AMERICAN HOMES

SO AS TO COMBINE ARCHITECTURAL FITNESS WITH PICTURESQUE EFFECT
IN THE SERVICE OF BUILDING COMMUNITIES
CONNECTED TO OUR NOBLE PAST AND PREPARED FOR AN UNCERTAIN FUTURE.

A DISCOURSE CONCERNING THE DESIGNED ESTABLISHMENT OF

FREEDOMLAND

Neither wou'd we have it thought a labour so tedious, as 'tis generally fancy'd, to establish in this manner a Colony, which may become not only an advantage, but a glory to the Nation: We have Prospects before us most attractive, and unprecedented, in the three tempting Points wealth, safety, and liberty: Benefits, like these, can never fail of drawing Numbers of Inhabitants from Every Corner: And, Men once got together, 'tis as easy to dispose them regularly, and with due Regard to Order, Beauty, and the Comforts of Society, as to leave them to the Folly of fixing at Random, and destroying their Interest by indulging their Humour; So that we have more than ordinary Cause to expect, that in a very short Time, we shall be able to present the solid life its self, as now we give the shadow only, in the following Explanation.

—Sir Robert Mountgomery, *A Discourse Concerning the design'd Establishment of a New Colony to the South of Carolina in the Most delightful Country of the Universe*, 1717.

Having been required by the times to draw up a detailed plan for the general improvement of American housing in the aftermath of the great financial crisis and its effect upon our collective confidence in the correctness of our living patterns, I humbly submit the following proposal.

We begin our description as did Sir Robert Mountgomery in describing his fabled proposal for the Margravate of Azilia: "You must suppose a level, dry, and fruitful Tract of Land, in some fine Plain or Valley" that, having been surveyed as part of the great parceling of America according to the methods set forth in the Land Ordinance of 1785, is continuously gridded into square townships of six miles per side, each containing thirty-six one-mile square sections of 640 acres.

This grid, the framework for Thomas Jefferson's vision of a rural democratic society of citizen farmers, but also a great game board of rampant real estate speculation, provides the underlying structure for Freedomland, a new settlement model that reconciles resurgent dreams for an agrarian urbanism with long-habituated domestic appetites, it now being fully established by learned persons, and increasingly acknowledged by laypersons, that our current settlement patterns are both unlovely and unsustainable. Freedomland is premised, then, on the following irrefutable truths: that local farming is good, being that it provides better food and makes better use of our increasingly limited resources than commercial agriculture; that urban living is also good, improving as it does the health, happiness, and prosperity of the populace; and that the majority of Americans, the veracity of the above notwithstanding, still aspire to the material and spatial luxuries represented by the detached single-family house as it is most resplendently found in the suburbs.

The plan of Freedomland results from the subdivision of a typical survey township into four equal squares, three miles to each side. The northwest and southeast quadrants are established as new towns and further subdivided to form thirty-six square sections of 160 acres each, excepting that area dedicated to the town's primary roads which divide them at intervals of one half mile. As in the original survey townships, these sections are numbered, "beginning with the number one in the northeast section and proceeding west and east alternately through the township with progressive numbers, until the thirty-six be completed." The two remaining quadrants are preserved in—or if necessary restored to—their natural state as unencumbered retreats for the pleasure of the townspeople.

One survey township divided to form two towns and two natural preserves is the absolute minimum area necessary for the establishment of Freedomland. If this plan is aggregated to form a group larger than a single 36 square mile survey township, then a checkerboard layout results, in a like manner to that proposed by Mr. Jefferson, producing, at the grand scale, an alternating arrangement of town and country. There is no maximum limit to such an aggregation except for any geographical or political obstacles that may arise to thwart the just and proper extension of the settlement by the townspeople.

The four sections at the center of each town are occupied by a civic core comprised of the infrastructures necessary to the maintenance and preservation of the community. Whereas the original Land Ordinance reserved section 16, at the center of every township, for the use of education, in Freedomland—it being recognized that the choices in means and methods of education are best left to individual families—the central squares are rightly devoted to more pressing and universal needs: The waste square, an ever-growing, manicured pyramid of refuse, rises slowly in section 16; the water square, a circular reservoir nearly one half mile in diameter, occupies section 15; the energy square, a forest of 20 by 20-foot solar panels, powers the town from section 21; and the market square, anchored in section 22 by a ten-acre big box of community and commerce, provides a venue for public assembly as well as access to those products and services not produced through the prodigious industry of the townspeople.

The thirty-two remaining sections are quartered by roads secondary to those abovementioned to form four equal parcels of 40 acres, less the dimension of the roads by which they are divided and served. The 128 individual neighborhood farm estates thus established, each an independent self-governing community, are further divided into four 10-acre squares of which three are dedicated to agricultural pursuits, while the dwellings are located on the fourth. In this manner, fully three quarters of every town in Freedomland shall remain open, green, and free of buildings.

Each neighborhood estate in Freedomland is comprised of between eight and sixty-four houses, with all those within any particular estate being one just like the next and in this manner ensuring a cohesiveness of identity and consistency of character such that property values are protected and community values are promoted. Whereas architects have proven themselves disinclined, or perhaps just ill-prepared, to deliver designs desired by a majority of the American people, the houses in Freedomland are built according to designs carefully selected from among the best produced by the country's greatest builders—designs that have proven to be highly popular with persons possessed of the most discriminating taste and therefore certain to attract the finest type of citizen. Depending upon the number of houses and the particular manner in which they are arranged, a neighborhood of houses may take on the character of either a large villa or a small village. Families are thus able to select the estate that most closely matches their spatial, stylistic, and, consequently, social preferences, thereby affording them a life among like-minded neighbors with a shared sense of duty and purpose.

It being well known that people, by their very nature, are equally desirous of the pleasures of novelty as they are needful of the comforts of familiarity, Freedomland seeks to offer both in due time. Taking advantage of the increasingly short life span of our houses—and in a manner similar to crop rotation—the entire estate, including the dwellings, which are dismantled and rebuilt, rotates counterclockwise every twenty years, completing a full rotation after eighty years. This has the positive effect of providing each resident, at regular intervals, with a new home that is exactly the same as their old home. As each estate rotates, this has the further beneficial consequence of producing an ever-changing prospect of built and open space throughout the town. Although the debris produced as a result of the dismantling and rebuilding will, in the early years, likely contribute to the rapid growth of the pyramid of waste at the center of each town, it is expected that the spirit of competition naturally occurring in a free society will, as it has in the past, stimulate advances in home building technology that cause the materials and methods employed in the ongoing re-creation of Freedomland to become ever lighter and more efficient. Such advances will allow each town to more sustainably pursue its cyclical regeneration, signaling to its neighbors its deep commitment to the stability and endurance of our beloved nation.

It is hoped that this description, concise though it may be, is sufficient to describe the sublime structure of Freedomland, its natural and rightful connection to the foundational principles of our great country, and its superiority to our current modes of settlement.

THE COMPLETE DRAWINGS OF THE SUBLIME SETTLEMENT OF

FREEDOMLAND

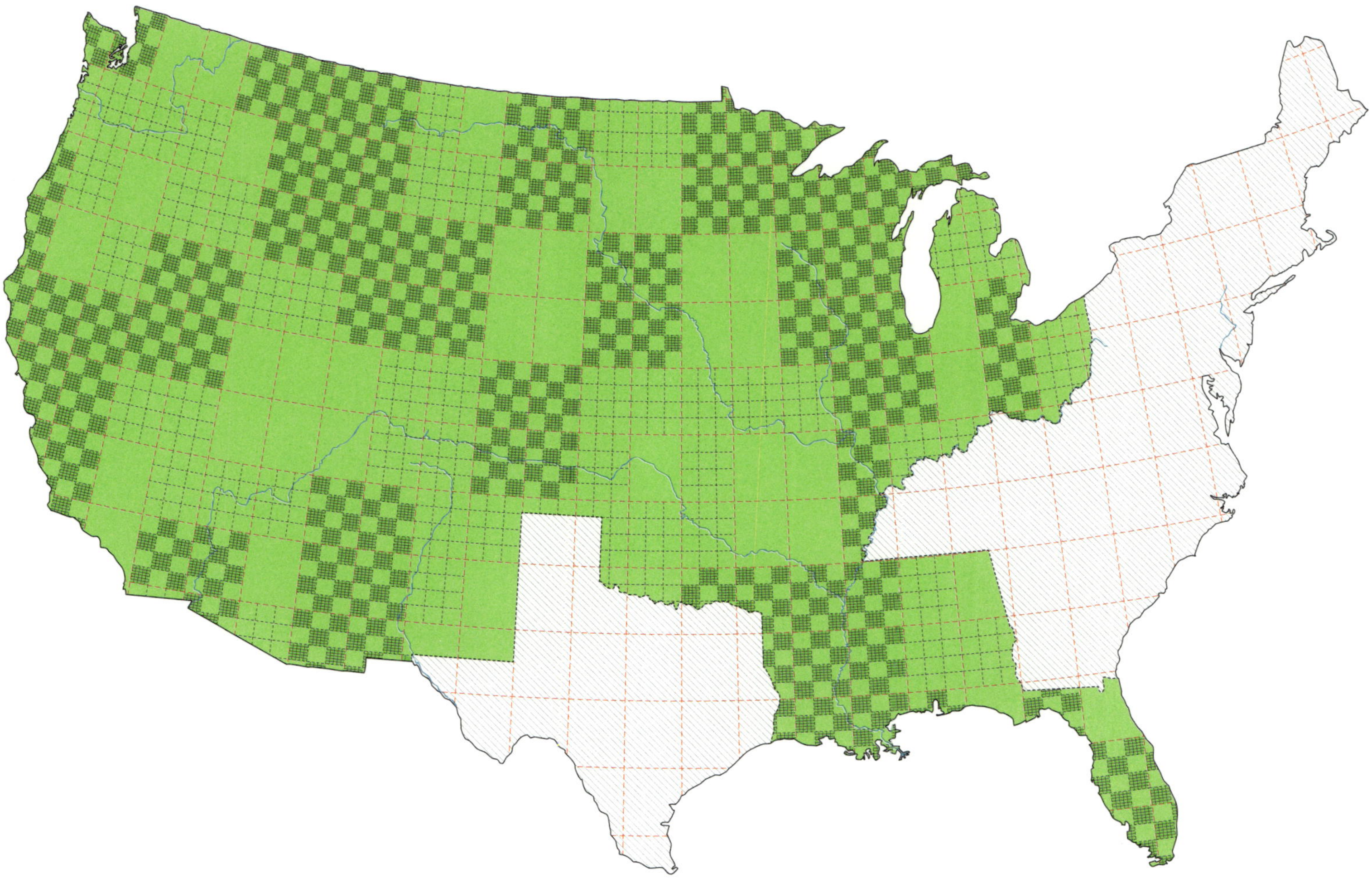

The Surveying of America

Resulting from a method first proposed by Thomas Jefferson, the Public Land Survey System (PLSS) governs the manner in which public domain lands in the United States are surveyed and apportioned. The system was first established with the passage of the Land Ordinance of 1785, "an ordinance for ascertaining the mode of disposing of Lands in the Western Territory," and subsequently refined by the Northwest Ordinance of 1787—also known as the Freedom Ordinance—which established the public domain and enshrined the concept of the fee simple ownership of land. Under the Land Ordinance, a rectangular survey system was established, dividing "the territory into townships of six miles square, by lines running due north and south, and other crossing these at right angles, as near may be, . . ."

The Survey Township

According to the 1785 ordinance, "the townships . . . shall be marked by subdivisions into lots of one mile square, or 640 acres, in the same direction as the external lines, and numbered from 1 to 36." In 1796 it was further set forth that the "sections shall be numbered, respectively, beginning with number one in the northeast section, and proceeding west and east alternately, through the township, with progressive numbers till the thirty-sixth be completed." The survey townships, tied as they are to our country's origins, are the foundational unit of Freedomland, and the lands so surveyed constitute the maximum extent of its expansion.

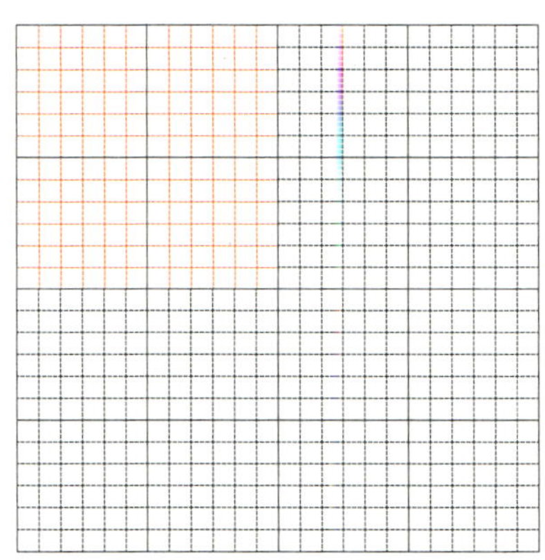

Take, for instance, the checker board for a plan. Let the black squares only be building squares, and the white ones be left open, in turf and trees. . . . The atmosphere of such a town would be like that of the country . . .

—Thomas Jefferson, from a letter to C.F. Volney, 1805.

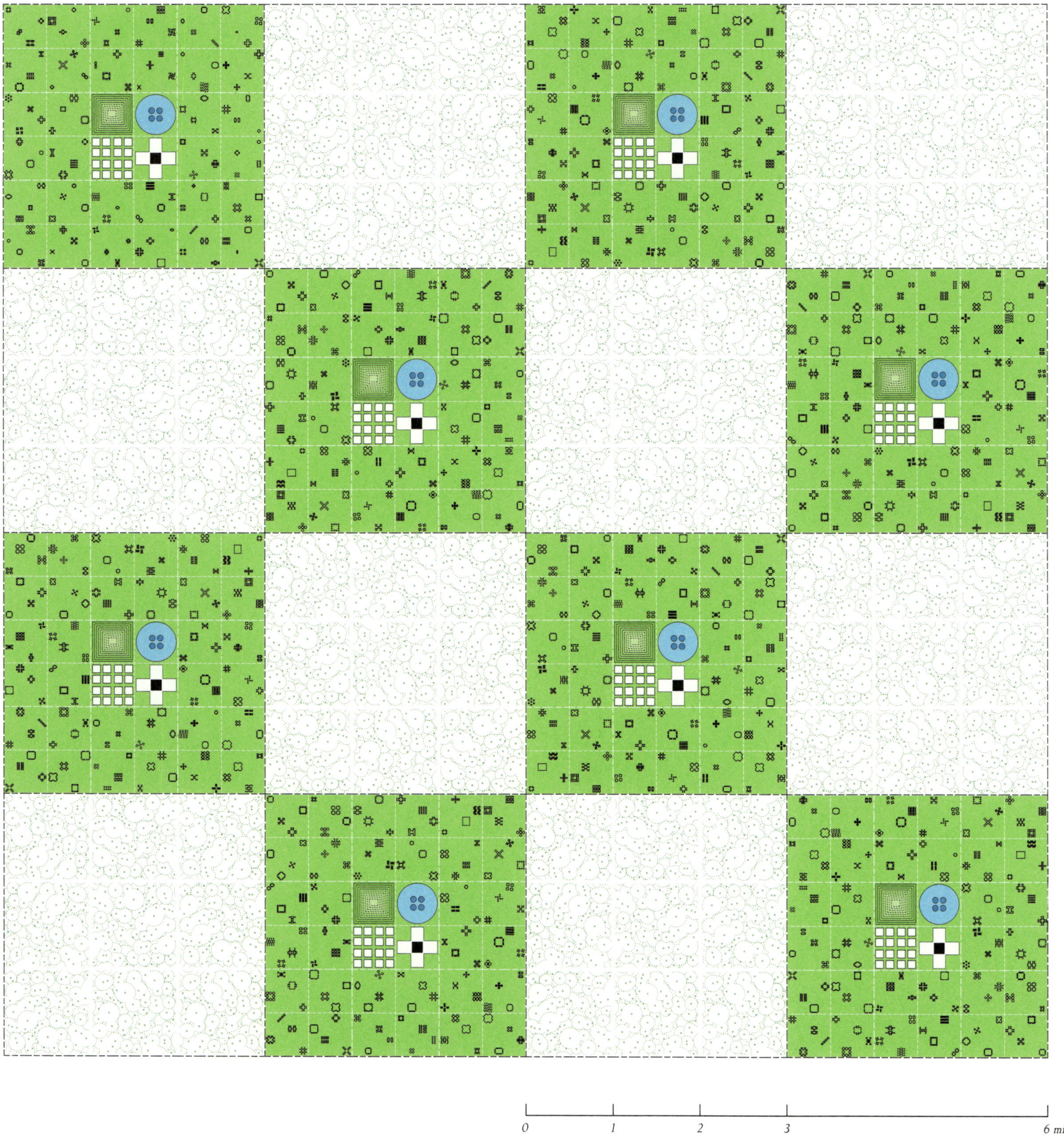

Checkerboard Logic

The subdivision of the original survey townships, along with their propagation across the territories previously apportioned for settlement, results in an alternating pattern of inhabited and unspoiled land similar to that of a checkerboard.

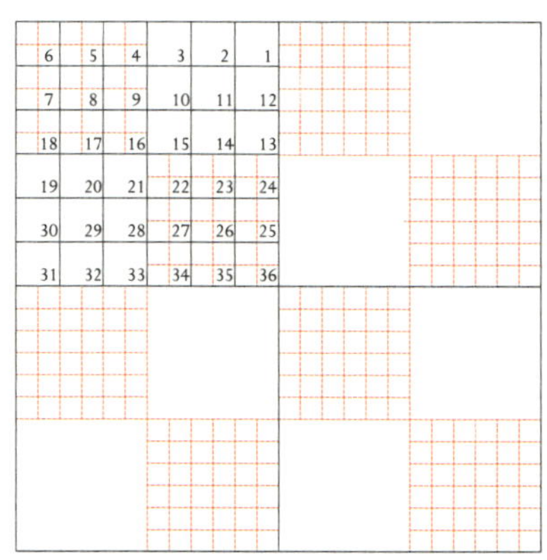

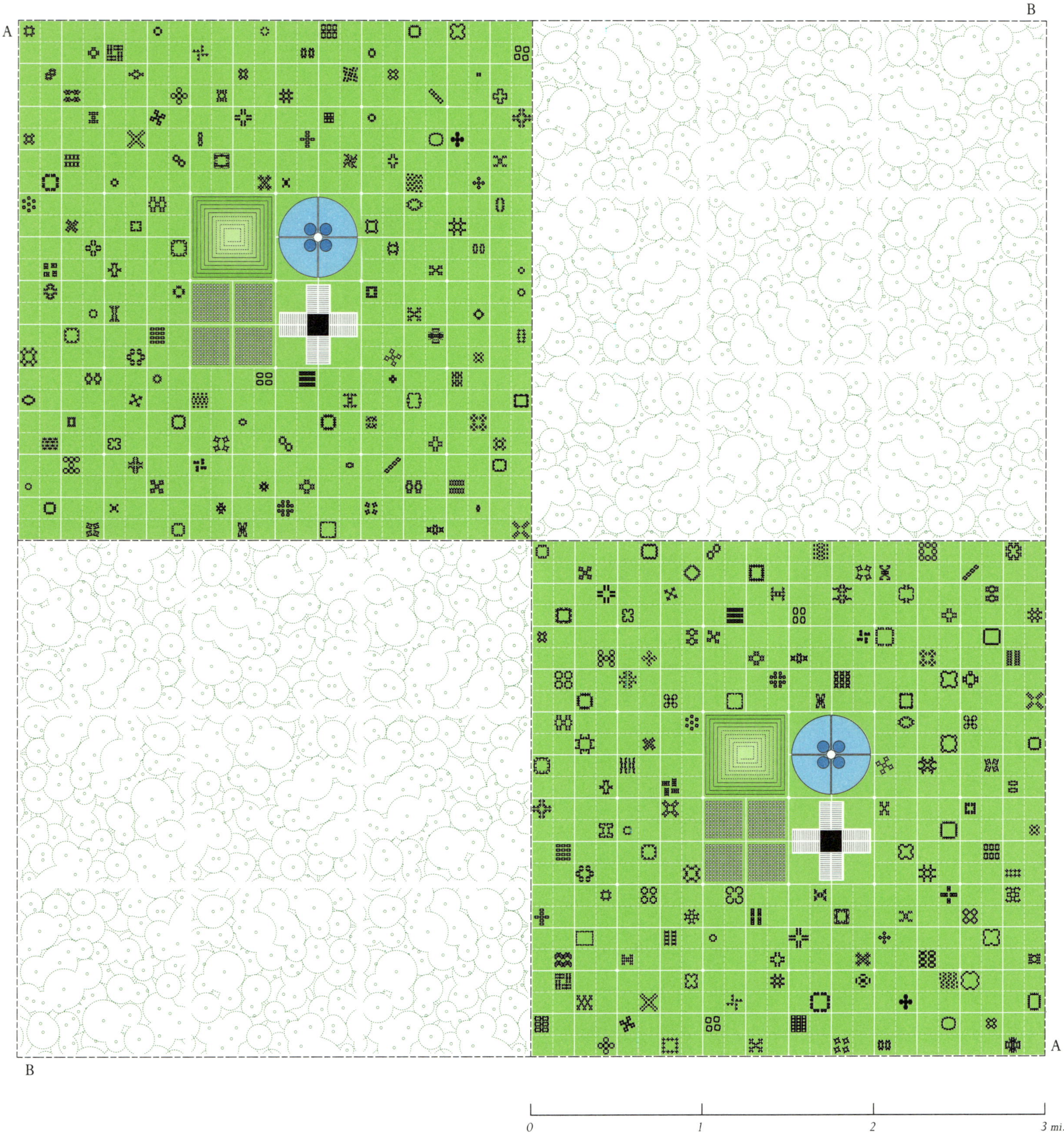

Quartering of Survey Township

In Freedomland each 6 by 6-mile survey township—numbered according to the PLSS, as shown in the diagram to the right—is quartered, producing four squares, each three miles on a side. The northwest and southeast quadrants are each occupied by an independent town, while the other two squares shall remain undeveloped as natural preserves and hunting grounds accessible for the benefit of all the township's people. This four-square unit is the absolute minimum size required for the establishment of Freedomland.

A. Town

B. Country

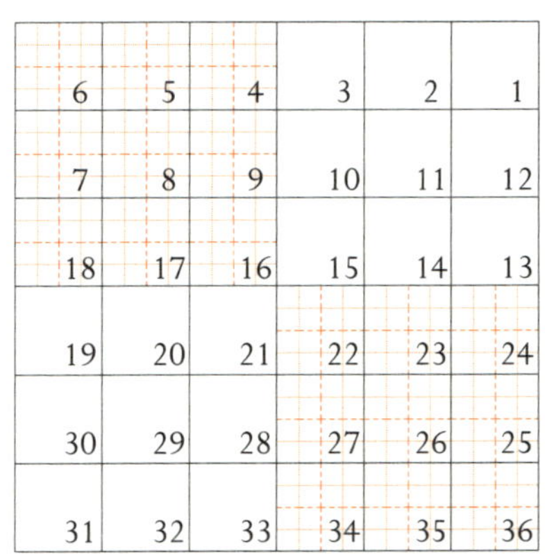

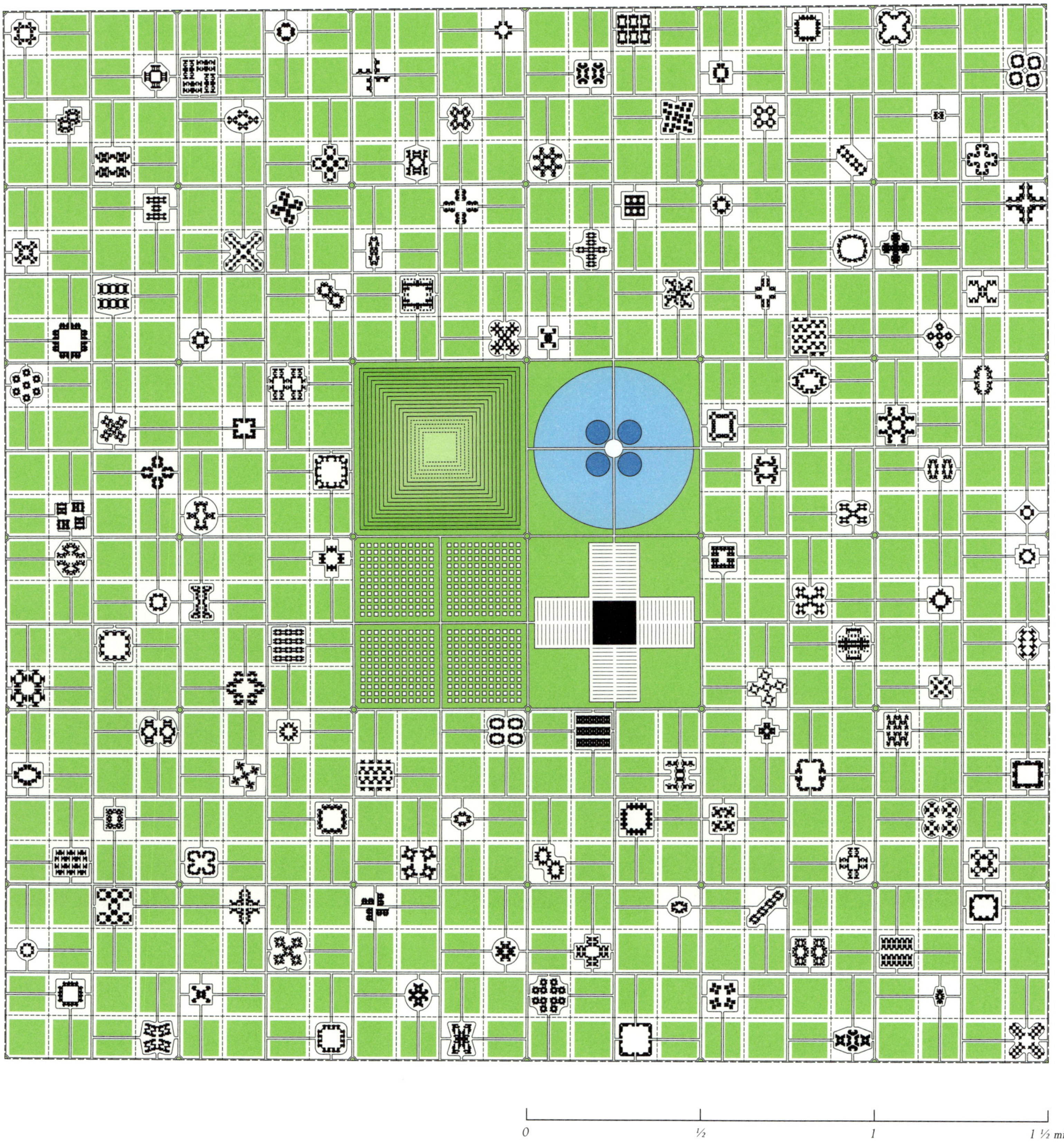

Town Organization

In Freedomland, the 3 by 3-mile town sites created by the quartering of a survey township are subdivided into thirty-six half-mile square sections and are numbered in a like manner to that of the original survey townships. The four squares at the center of each new township constitute the infrastructural heart of the town. The thirty-two remaining 160-acre sections are quartered, after the method provided for in the PLSS, in which each section could be further subdivided into quarter sections to produce 128 40-acre parcels.

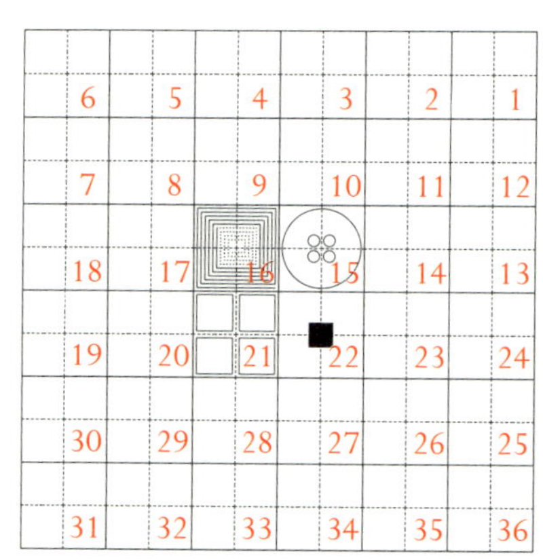

A View of Freedomland
after *Meadows near Greifswald,* 1822
Caspar David Friedrich

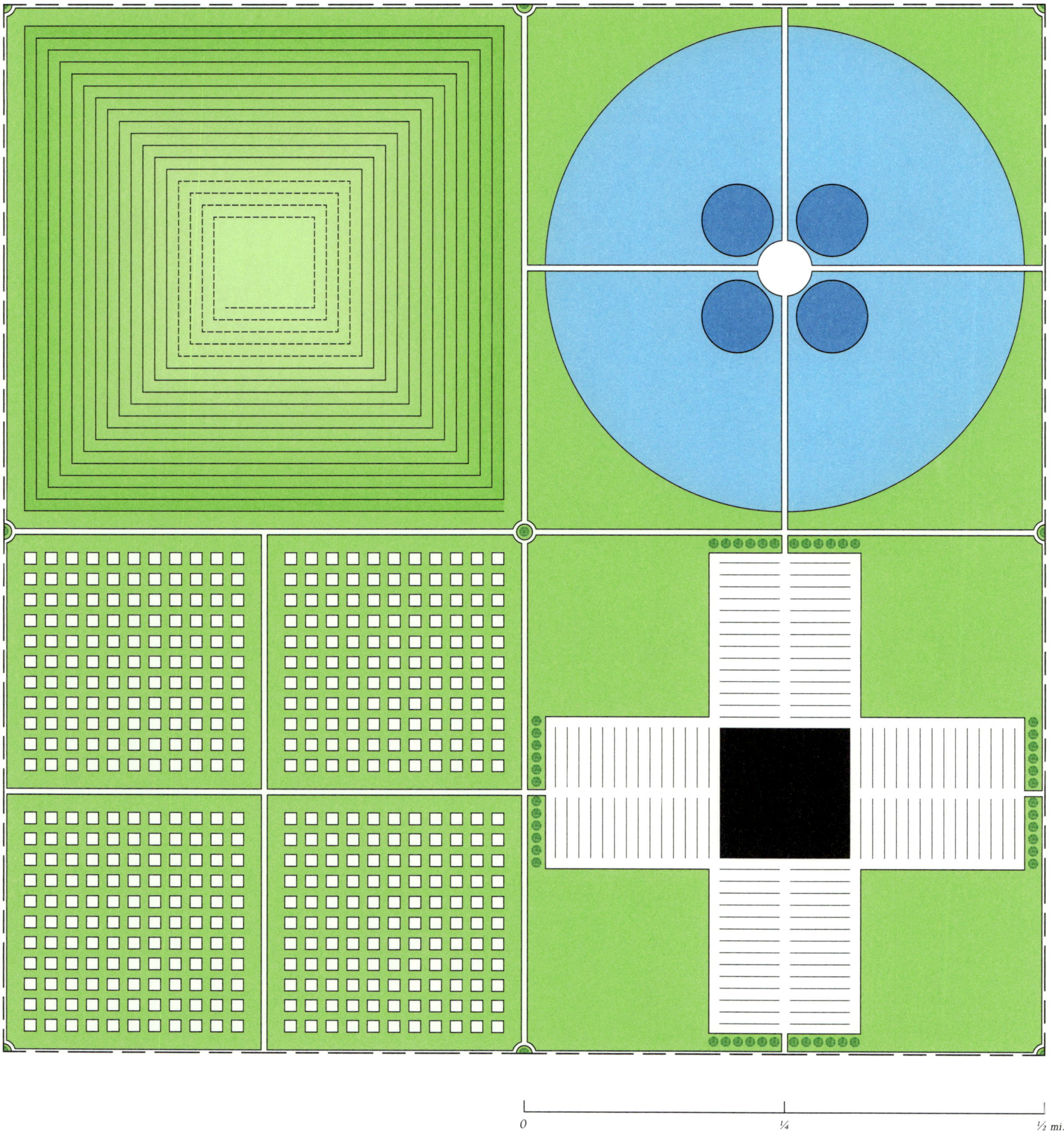

The Infrastructural Civic Core

An infrastructural civic core occupies the four central squares of each town in Freedomland. The waste square, an ever-growing, manicured pyramid of refuse, rises slowly in section 16; the water square, a circular reservoir nearly one half-mile in diameter, occupies section 15; the energy square, a forest of 20 by 20-foot solar panels, powers the town from section 21; and the market square, located in section 22 and anchored by a 10-acre big box of exchange and interaction, provides a venue for public assembly as well as access to those products and services not sourced locally. The four corners of the market square are reserved for the joint recreational use of the townspeople.

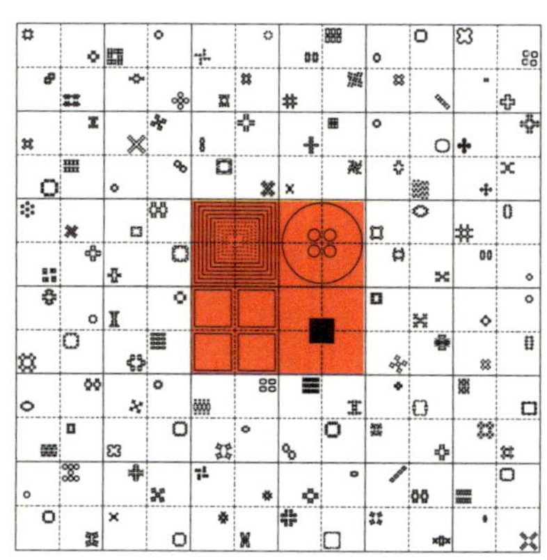

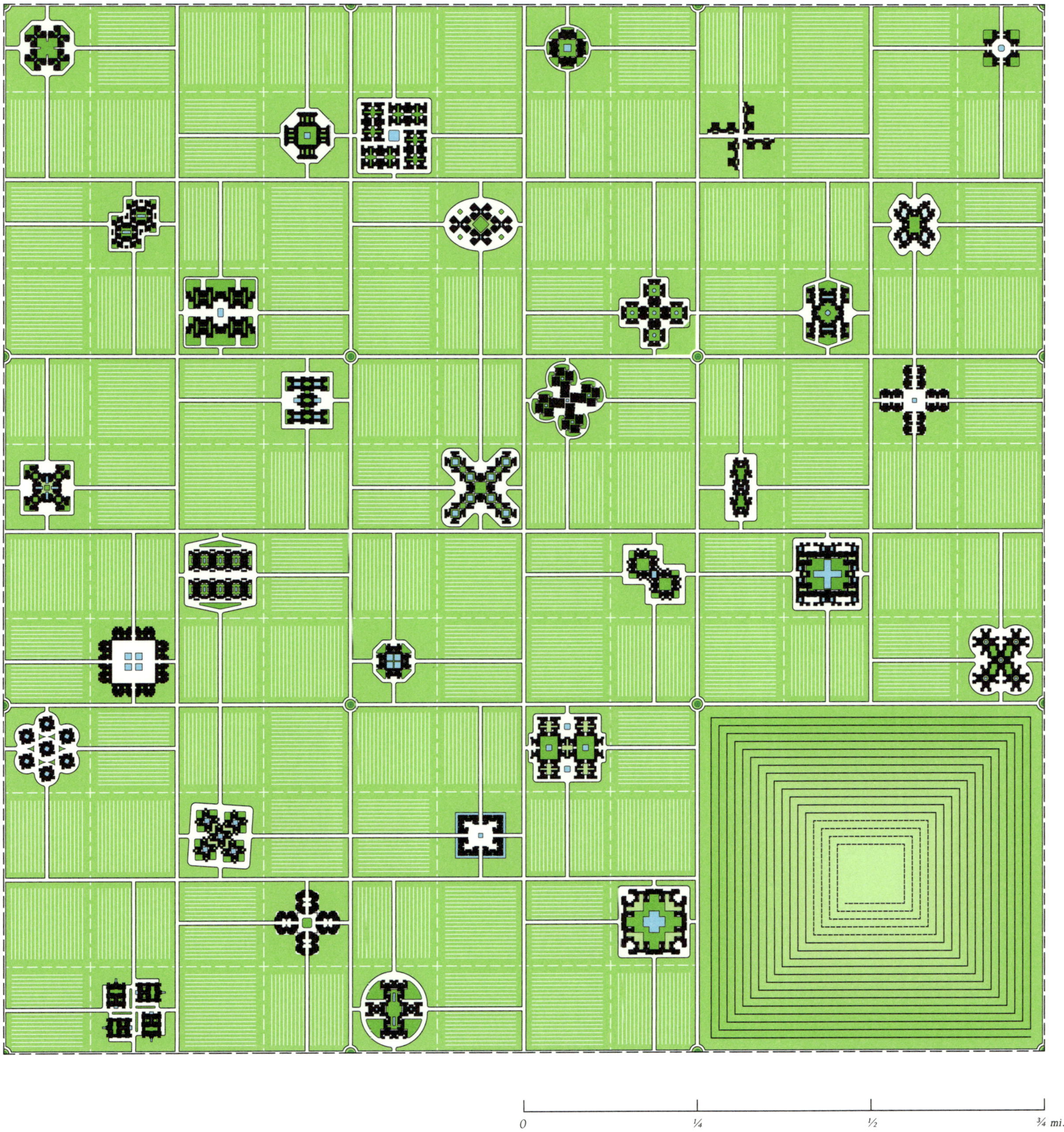

Nine Sections in the Town's Northwest Quadrant

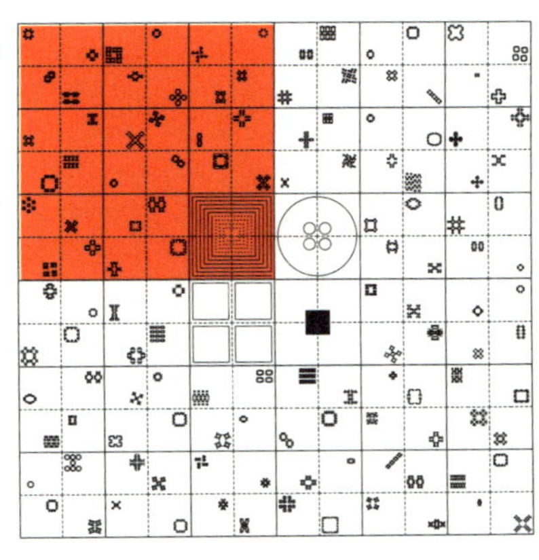

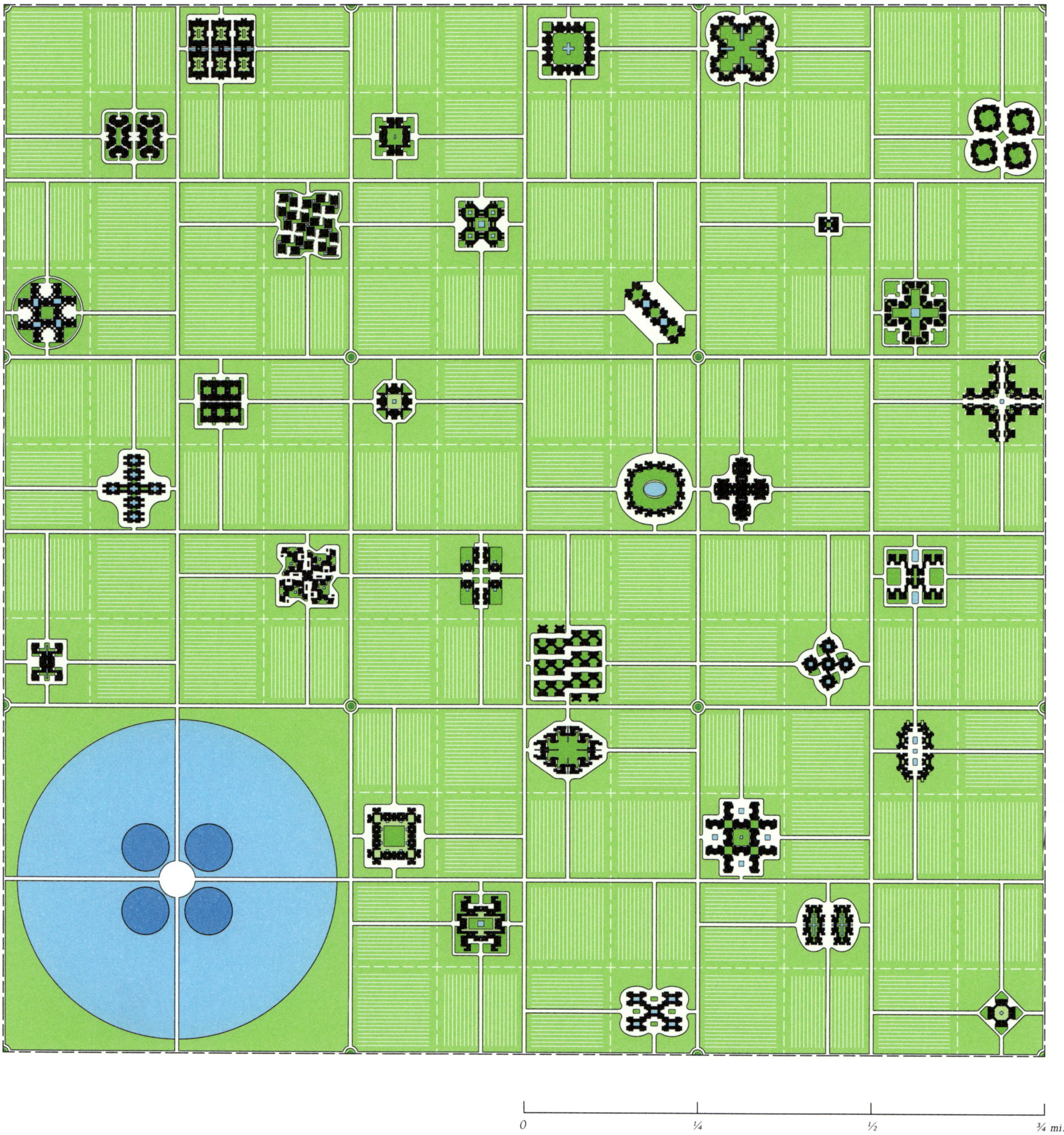

Nine Sections in the Town's Northeast Quadrant

In each of the town's four primary quadrants the eight sections outside of the infrastructural core are subdivided into four 40-acre neighborhood farm estates. Each estate is composed of between eight and sixty-four houses. Every house in any particular estate is identical and was selected from the plan catalogs of the nation's greatest domestic builders. Operations common to the siting of these plans in their "natural" suburban habitat (namely reflection and rotation) are utilized here to produce tighter, "urban" groupings. These neighborhoods, depending upon the number of houses employed and their particular arrangement, give the impression of being either small villages or large villas.

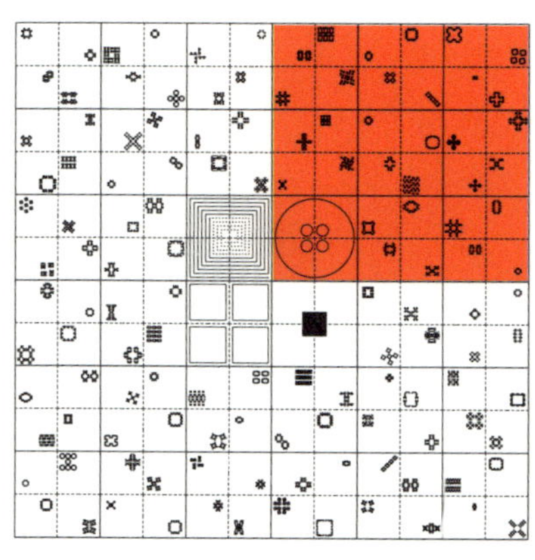

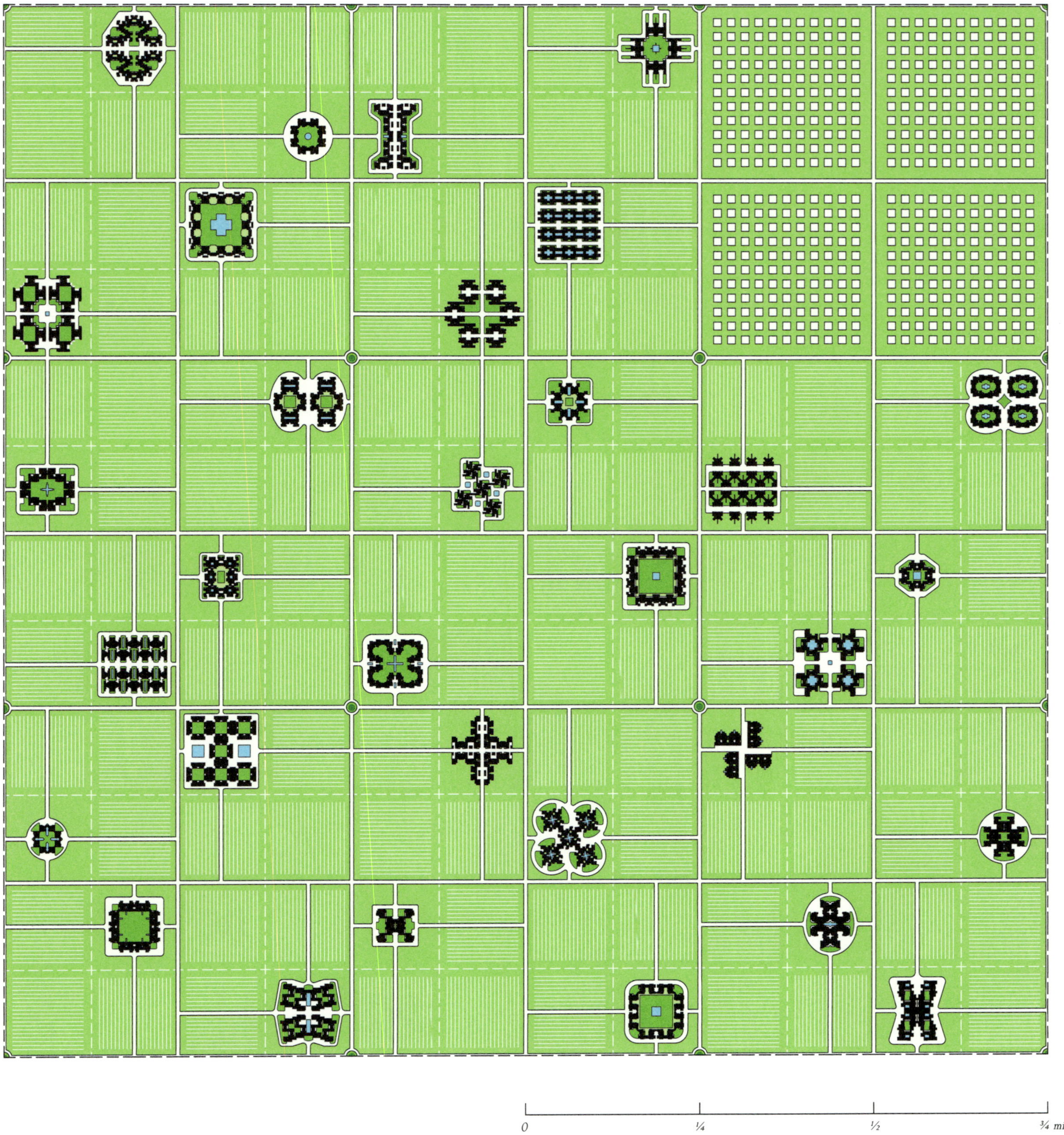

Nine Sections in the Town's Southwest Quadrant

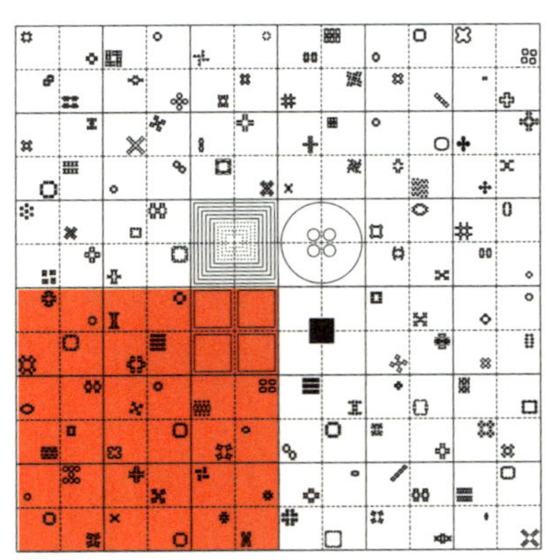

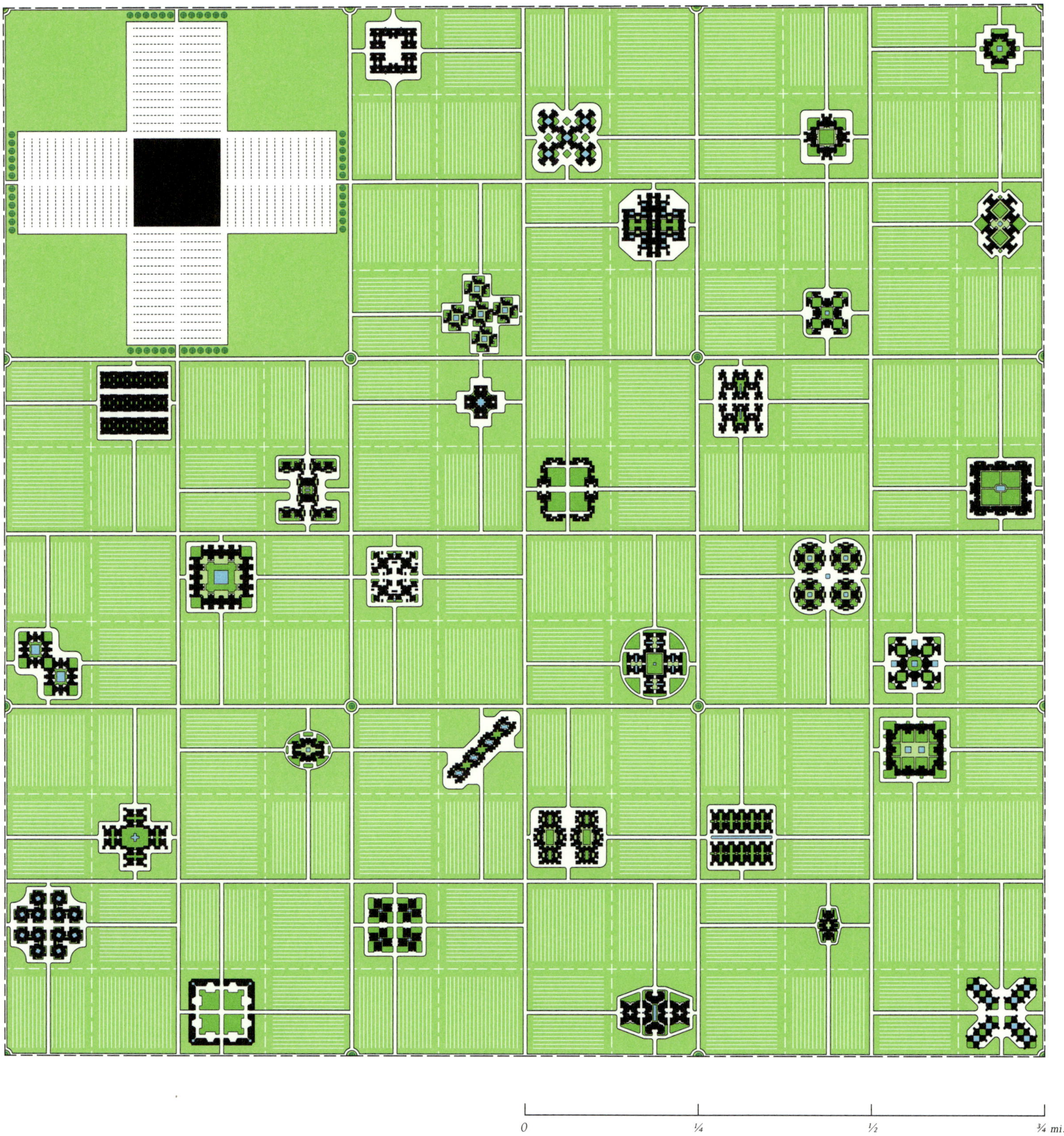

Nine Sections in the Town's Southeast Quadrant

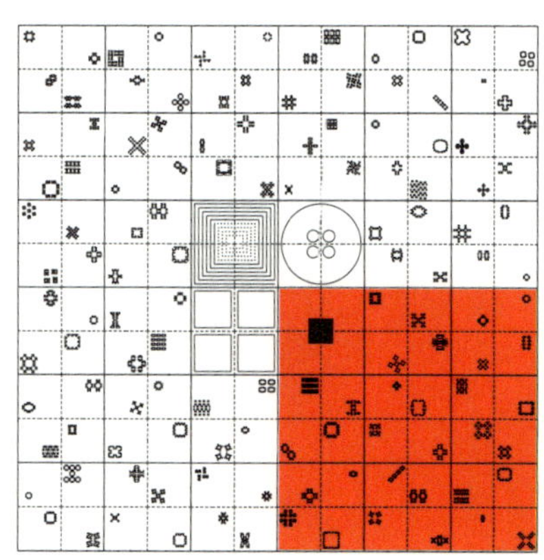

Finally, there seem to be but three Ways for a Nation to acquire Wealth. The first is by War, as the Romans did, in plundering their conquered Neighbours. This is Robbery. The second by Commerce, which is generally Cheating. The third by Agriculture, the only honest Way, wherein Man receives a real Increase of the Seed thrown into the Ground, in a kind of continual Miracle, wrought by the Hand of God in his Favour, as a Reward for his innocent Life and virtuous Industry.

—Benjamin Franklin, "Positions to be Examined, Concerning National Wealth," 1769.

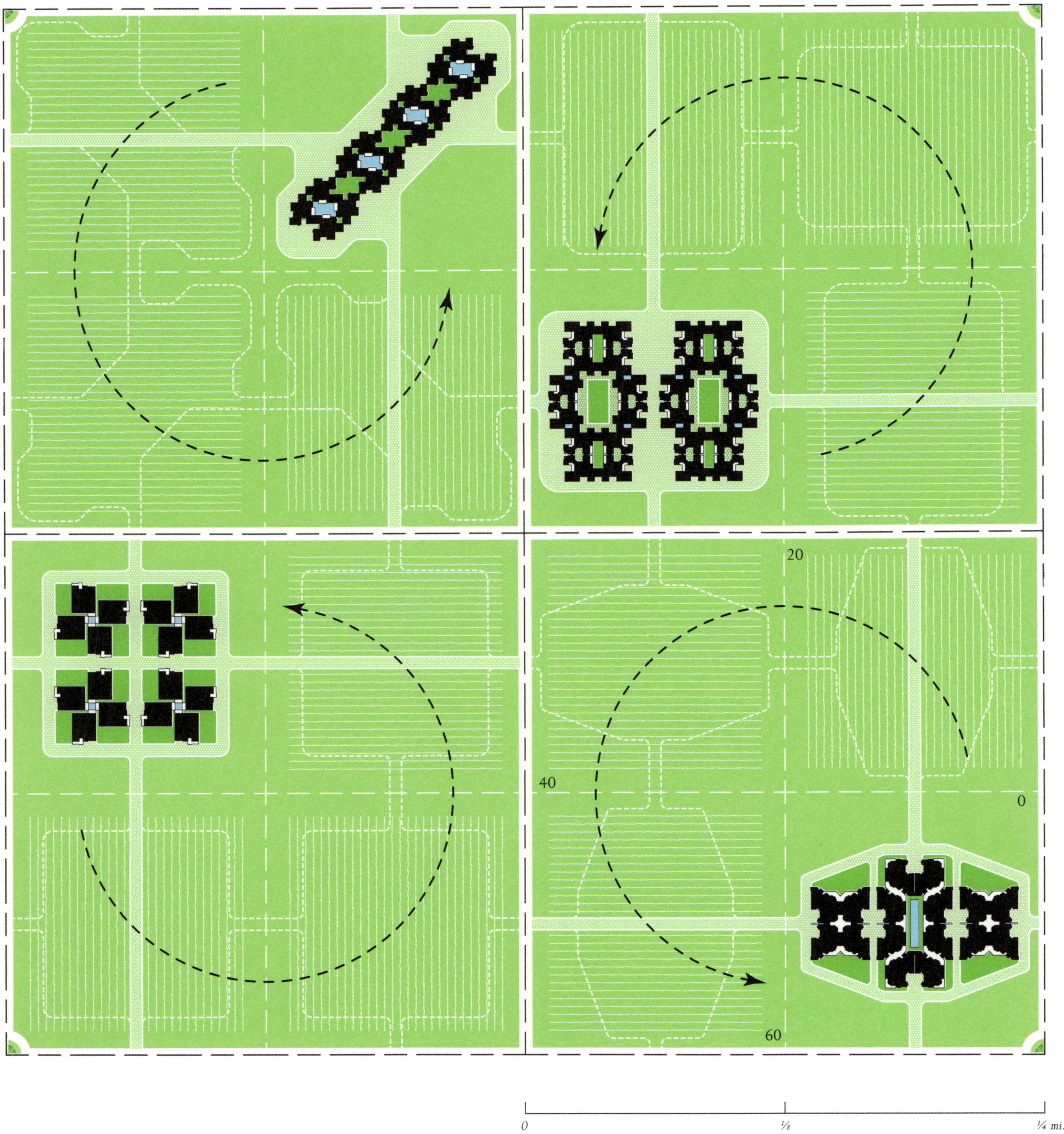

Farming and the Rotation of the Houses

Each half-mile square (160 acre) section is comprised of four 40-acre neighborhood farm estates. Of the four 10-acre quadrants in each estate, three are dedicated to the cultivation of crops, while the residents' dwellings occupy the fourth. In a manner similar to the practice of crop rotation each neighborhood is dismantled and rebuilt on the adjacent quadrant every twenty years following a counterclockwise rotational scheme. This has the benefit of fulfilling the American desire for perpetual newness in their houses, thereby making a virtue of the abbreviated life span of our houses. Every eighty years the neighborhood makes one full rotation on its parcel. The selection and cultivation of crops is the responsibility of each individual estate. It is expected that some residents will engage others in both the construction of their homes and the cultivation of their lands.

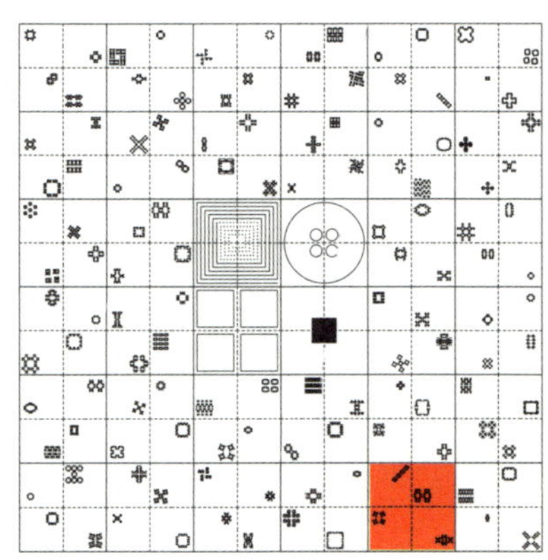

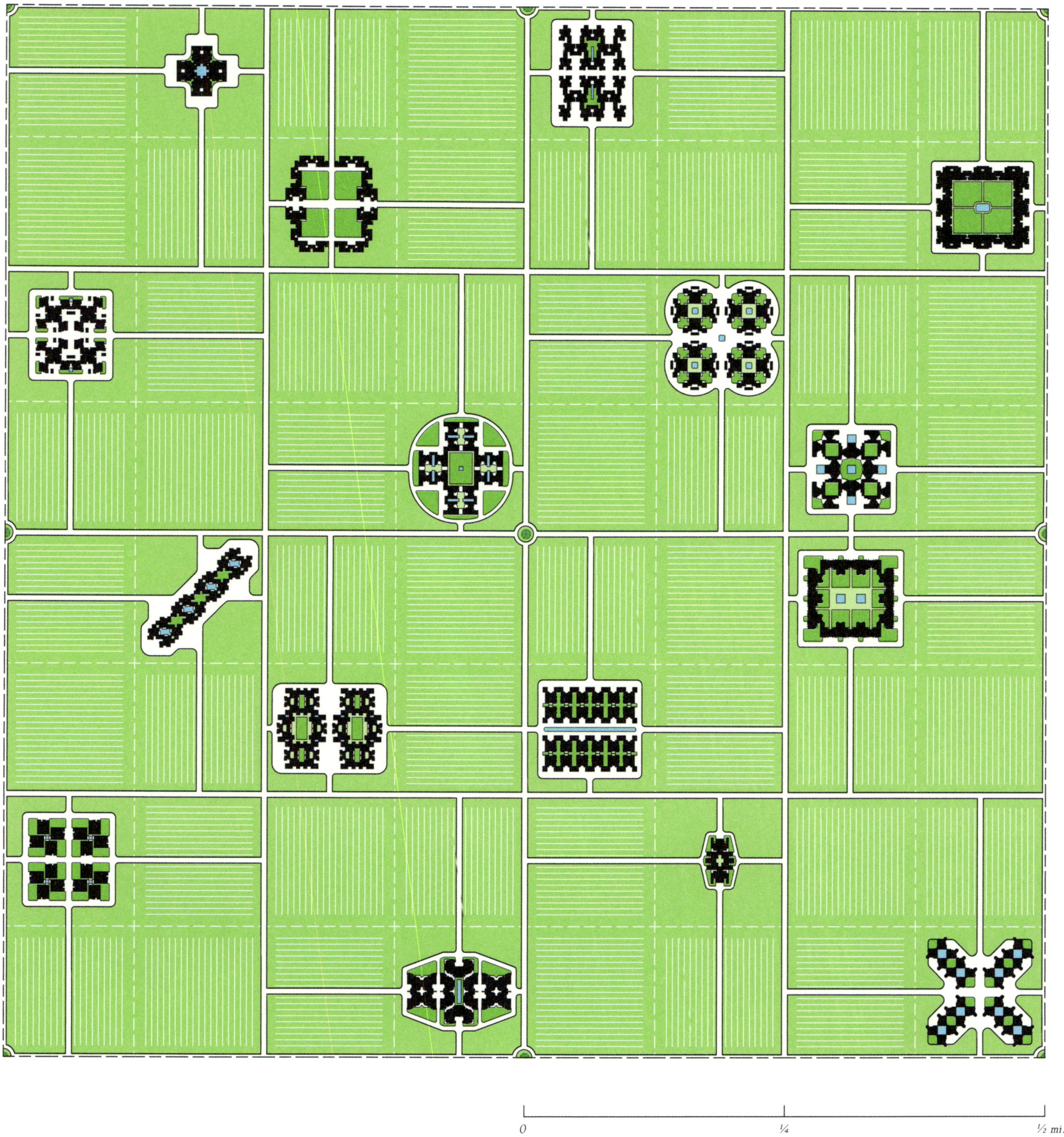

Year 0

Sections 25, 26, 35, and 36

As the estates of Freedomland rotate on a twenty-year cycle, an ever-changing prospect of built and open space is produced in the town. In year zero, shown here, the estates in the four sections at the southeast corner of town are distributed evenly across an agrarian landscape. The drawings on the following pages describe the changing arrangement generated by the rotational rule and demostrate its beneficial consequences.

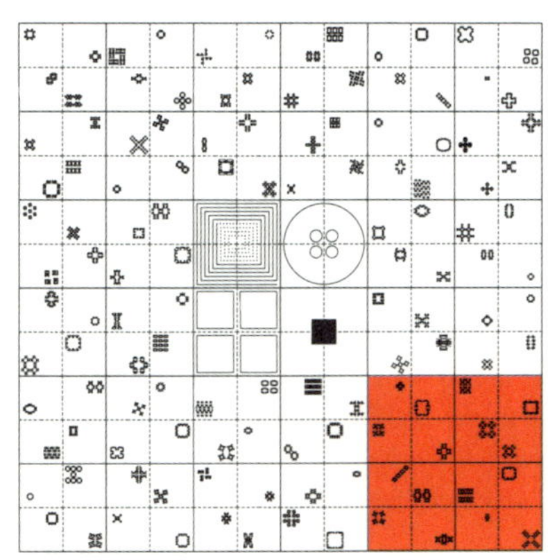

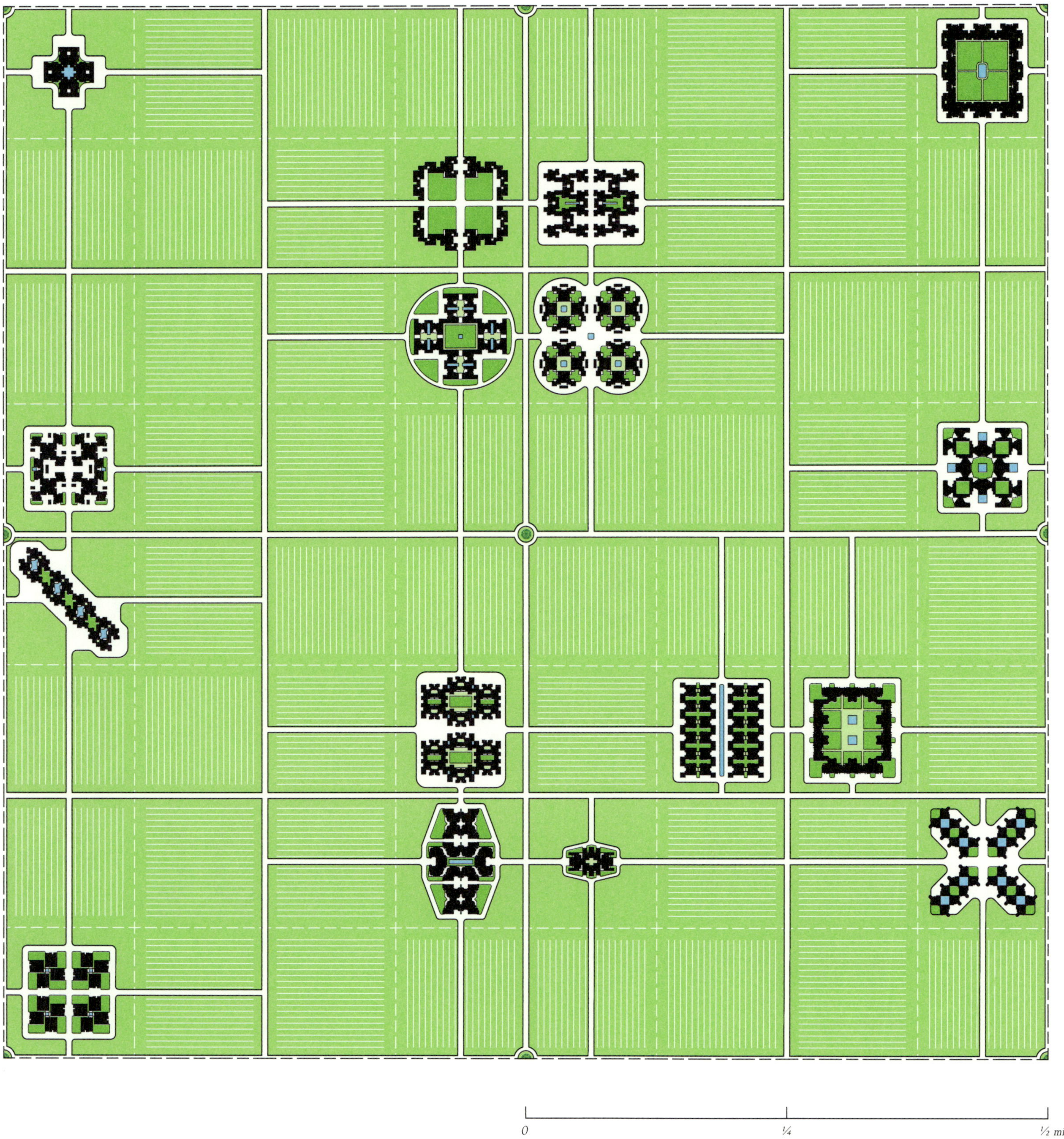

Year 20

Sections 25, 26, 35, and 36

As the position of the estates change with each successive twenty-year rotation, Freedomland is transformed and the townspeople's prospects refreshed. Here, in year twenty, as several estates converge at intersections of the grid, village-like clusters appear, along with the opportunity for new neighborly associations.

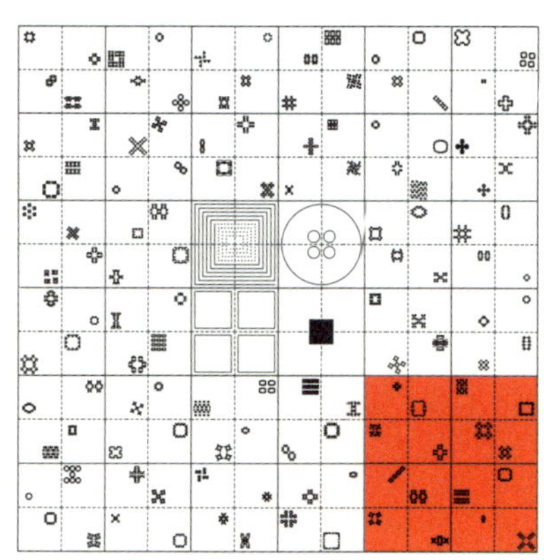

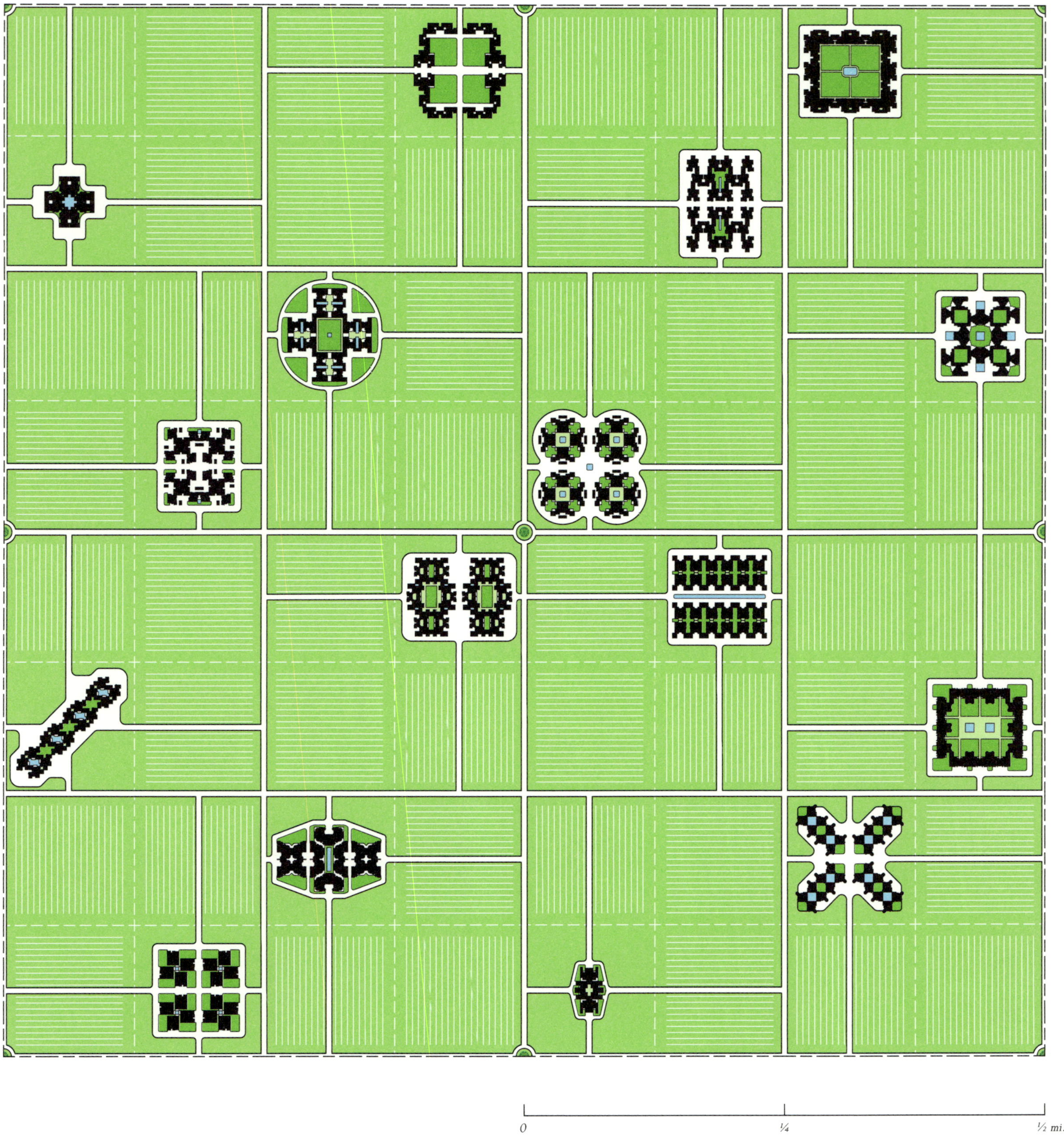

Year 40

Sections 25, 26, 35, and 36

Following the next rotation in year forty, the estates are once again dispersed—more or less evenly—across a rural landscape.

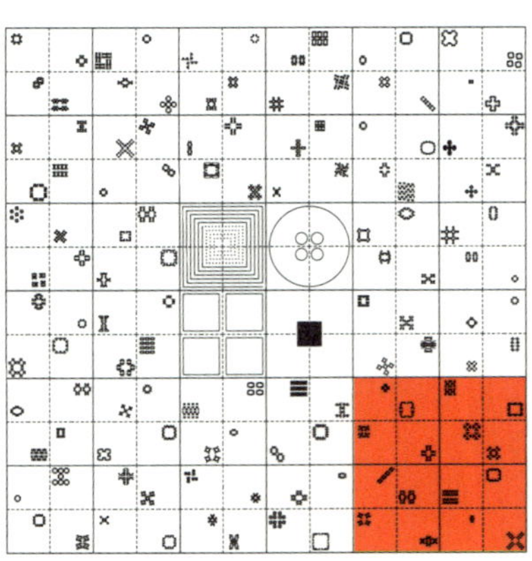

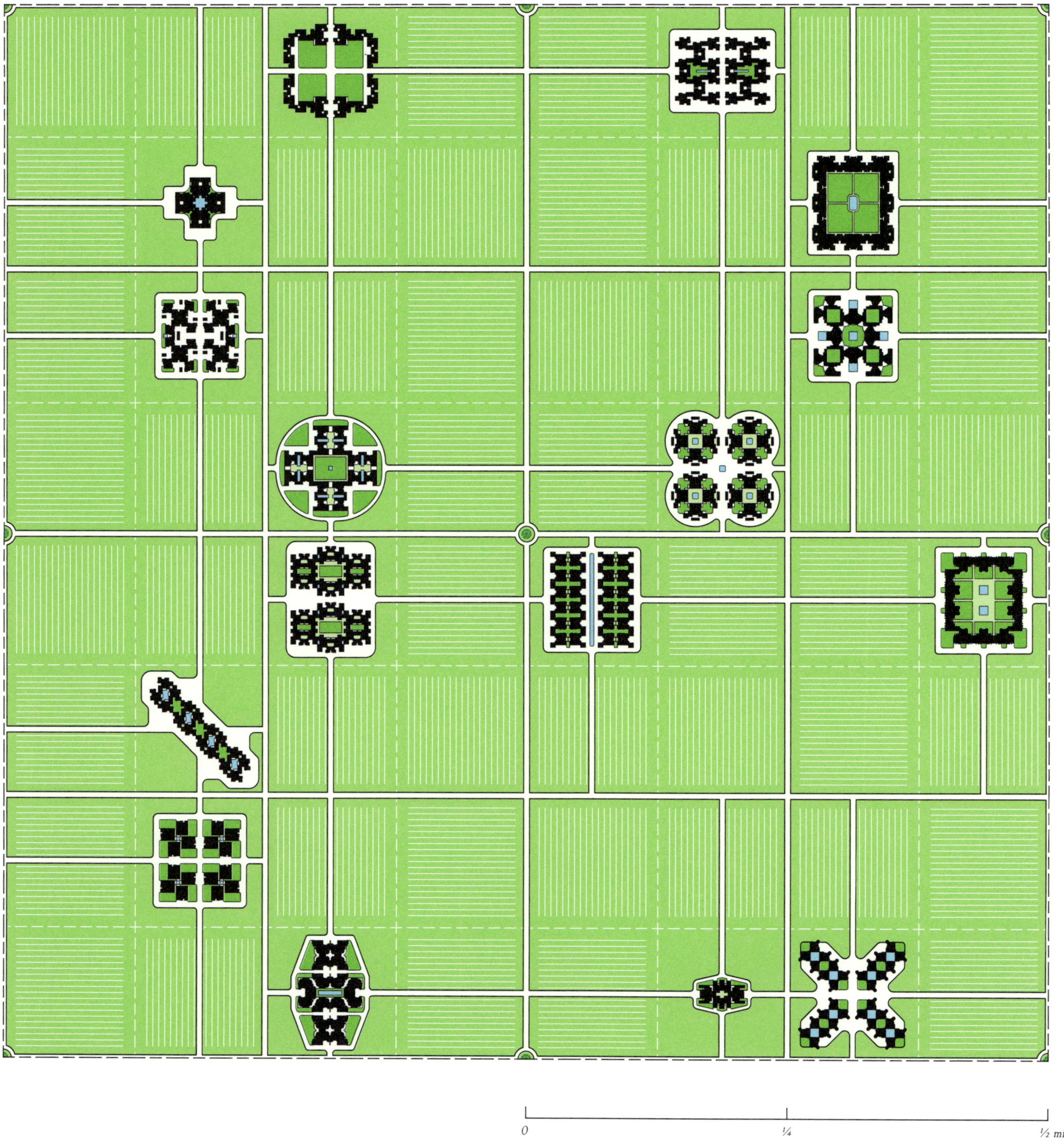

Year 60

Sections 25, 26, 35, and 36

In year sixty, Freedomland is transformed yet again, as some of the roads—now lined with estates—are reborn as rural boulevards.

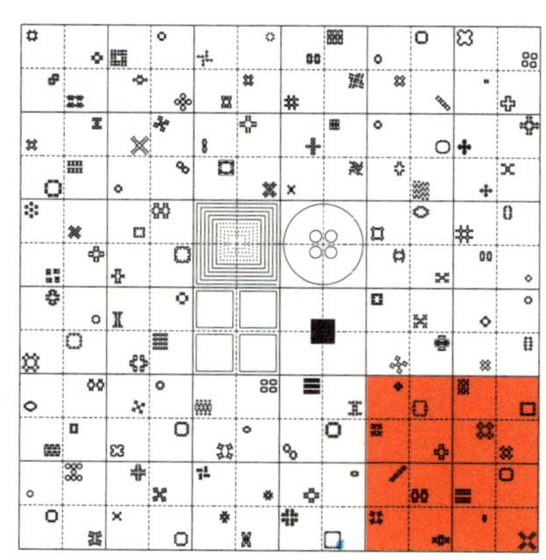

A CATALOG OF THE ESTATES OF

FREEDOMLAND

Section	Quadrant	Estate
Section 1	NE	Elysian Fields
	NW	Cuadratos d'Azilia
	SW	Brook Farm Manor
	SE	Bastide de Buck
Section 2	NE	La Grande Place des Petit
	NW	Swackhamer Grange
	SW	Hotel Sphinx
	SE	Astral Plains
Section 3	NE	A Suburban Set
	NW	Smiley's Acres
	SW	Rancho El Goodo
	SE	Levittown the Younger
Section 4	NE	Gessel Manor
	NW	Durusoy Landing
	SW	Platz der Pope
	SE	Equipe de Dix Village
Section 5	NE	The Citadel at Filarete Fields
	NW	Hamilton Holdings
	SW	Seltzer Springs
	SE	Casa di Branzi
Section 6	NE	Bellew Green
	NW	Happy Valley
	SW	Langford's Pine Valley Estates
	SE	Rudoph's Reserve
Section 7	NE	LK Vineyards
	NW	Brough of Birsay
	SW	Garageland
	SE	Estate of Mind
Section 8	NE	Ville d'Anelle
	NW	Citizen Farms
	SW	La Quinta de Zeiger
	SE	Sharmen's Overlook
Section 9	NE	La Croix Brillante
	NW	Habitat
	SW	Palazzo del Popolo di Otto Totti
	SE	Neo-Palladian Acres
Section 10	NE	Il Super Studios
	NW	A Model Modern Paradise
	SW	Riley's Safe House
	SE	Huge Acres
Section 11	NE	Cirque de Besançon
	NW	Fresca
	SW	Bald Bend
	SE	Bloomersbury
Section 12	NE	Via Varner
	NW	Exodus Landing
	SW	Garden Homes
	SE	Les Jois des Jeunes
Section 13	NE	Robin Hood Gardens
	NW	Casa Grande del Cultivo
	SW	Walden 8
	SE	New Haven
Section 14	NE	Davies Lawn and Tennis Club
	NW	Subdivision Square
	SW	Nishikado Palace
	SE	Shadrach Woods
Section 15	NE	Water
	NW	Water
	SW	Water
	SE	Water
Section 16	NE	Waste
	NW	Waste
	SW	Waste
	SE	Waste
Section 17	NE	Estate del Suzanne
	NW	The Quarters at Narkomfin Castle
	SW	CityLAB Center for Practical Utopias
	SE	Schloss von Sibelius
Section 18	NE	The Villas at Broad Acres
	NW	A Little Garden City
	SW	Nadaville
	SE	New Ark
Section 19	NE	Du Flumadon
	NW	Finio Farms
	SW	Rancho Riata
	SE	The Palace (of Don Barthelmismo)
Section 20	NE	The New Era Union
	NW	Atria Romano Accipitris
	SW	Wazeone Woods
	SE	Yostville
Section 21	NE	Energy
	NW	Energy
	SW	Energy
	SE	Energy
Section 22	NE	Market
	NW	Market
	SW	Market
	SE	Market
Section 23	NE	The Little Hamlet
	NW	Acri Anonimi
	SW	The Villas at Pek Park
	SE	Bayt el Kadi
Section 24	NE	Maison Tres McDermott
	NW	A Chateau
	SW	Martin-Hall-in-the-Meadows
	SE	Casa de Campo
Section 25	NE	Blithedale Hall
	NW	Siedlung der Zimmer
	SW	Il Quadrato di Quattro Quadrati
	SE	Raja Mahal
Section 26	NE	Maisons Dom-ino
	NW	La Villa Radieuse
	SW	The Independent Group
	SE	Hopeloos Stad
Section 27	NE	Supermodel Homes
	NW	Homestead
	SW	The Estates at Satter Fields
	SE	La Ville Bourgeoise
Section 28	NE	RAMSALAND
	NW	Kubo Verde
	SW	Subtopian Acres
	SE	Palais du Kern
Section 29	NE	Le Ville Rotunda
	NW	Levy's Landing
	SW	Lyon's Gate at Freedomland
	SE	Le Domaine de la Durand
Section 30	NE	Banham's Bottom
	NW	Somewhere Meadows
	SW	Marigold Springs
	SE	Pellitshker Plotz
Section 31	NE	The Nine Squares
	NW	Samuelsville
	SW	The Big House at Fourier Forest
	SE	Gage's Glorious Gay Gardens
Section 32	NE	Atypical Plans
	NW	Eupepsia Farms
	SW	The Reserve at Freedomland
	SE	Linda Court
Section 33	NE	Topolobampo
	NW	Monticello Manor Homes
	SW	Wilson Estates at Outterbridge Park
	SE	Fort Goodwill
Section 34	NE	The Colony
	NW	The Sanctuary
	SW	Shangri-La
	SE	Really New Harmony
Section 35	NE	Leroy's
	NW	Palats Soren
	SW	Village Green Preservation Villas
	SE	Pleiades Prospect
Section 36	NE	Parallelogram Park
	NW	Animal Farm
	SW	Cockaigne Hall
	SE	La Ville Radieuse

The Estates of Freedomland

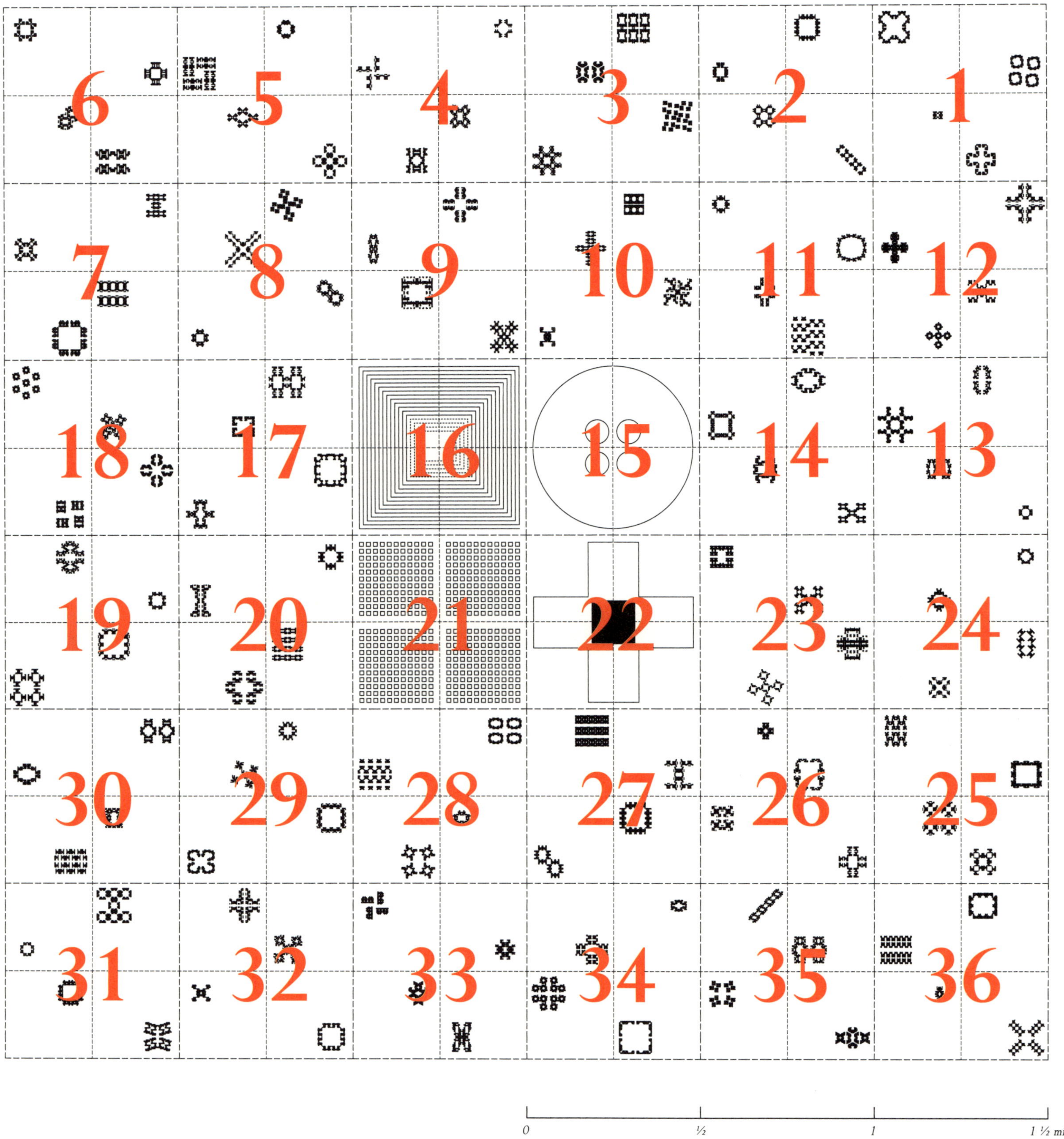

6 5 4 3 2 1
7 8 9 10 11 12
18 17 16 15 14 13
19 20 21 22 23 24
30 29 28 27 26 25
31 32 33 34 35 36
0 ½ 1 1 ½ mi.

A Traveler Approaches Elysian Fields, Freedomland
after *The Road in the Rye,* 1881
Grigoriy Myasoyedov

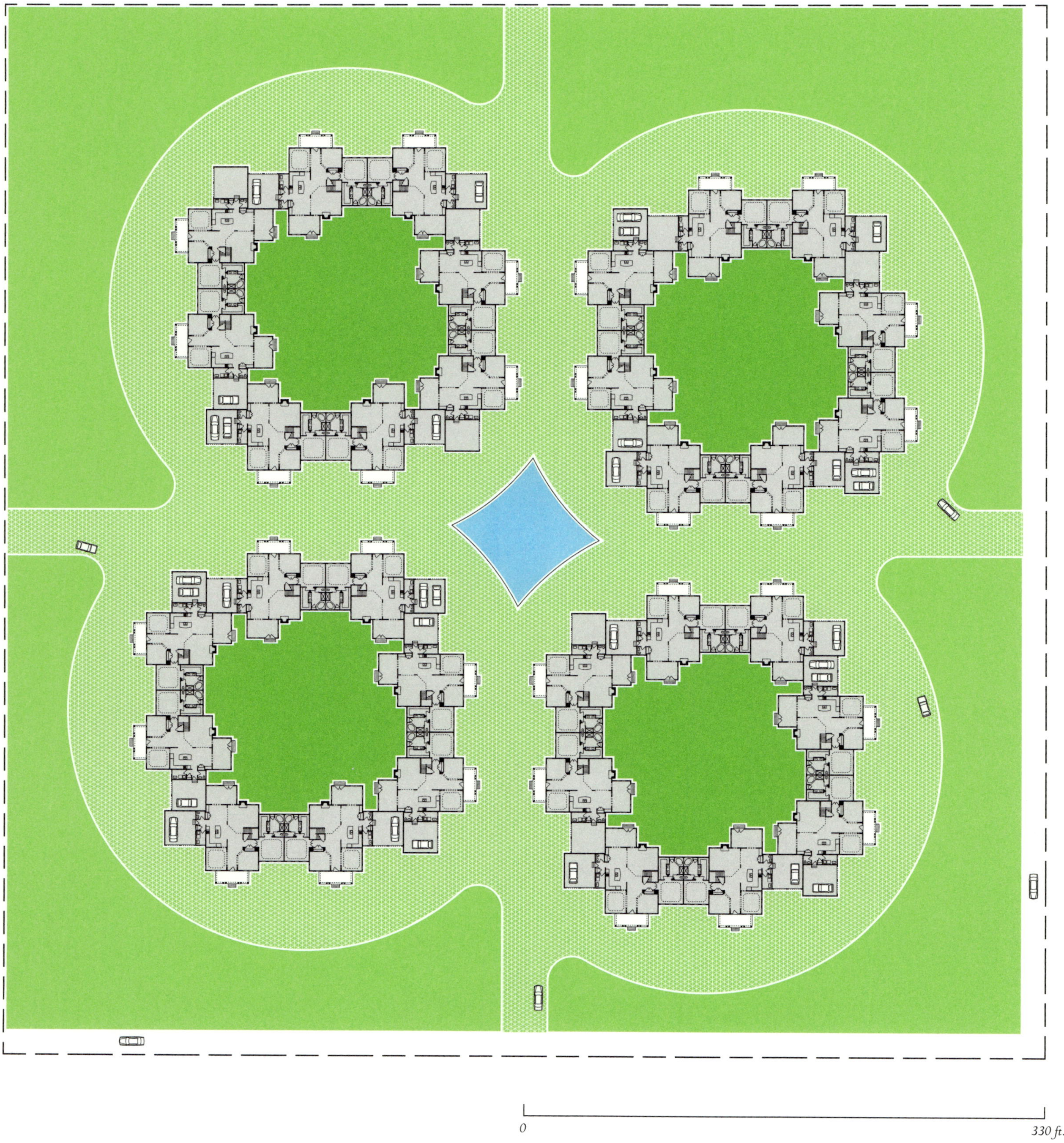

Elysian Fields
SE 1/4 NE 1/4 Section 1

32 Houses
114,688 Square Feet
160 Bedrooms
128 Full Bathrooms
32 Half Bathrooms

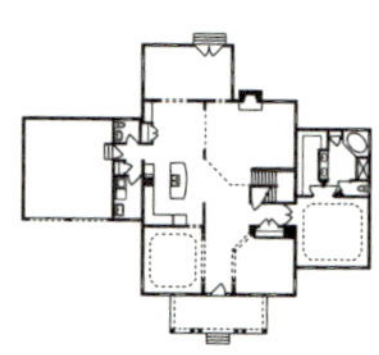

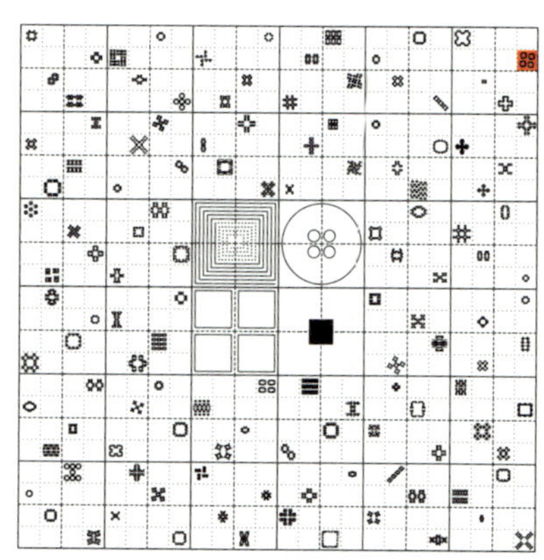

Ryland Homes, The Parson, 3584 sq. ft., Delaware

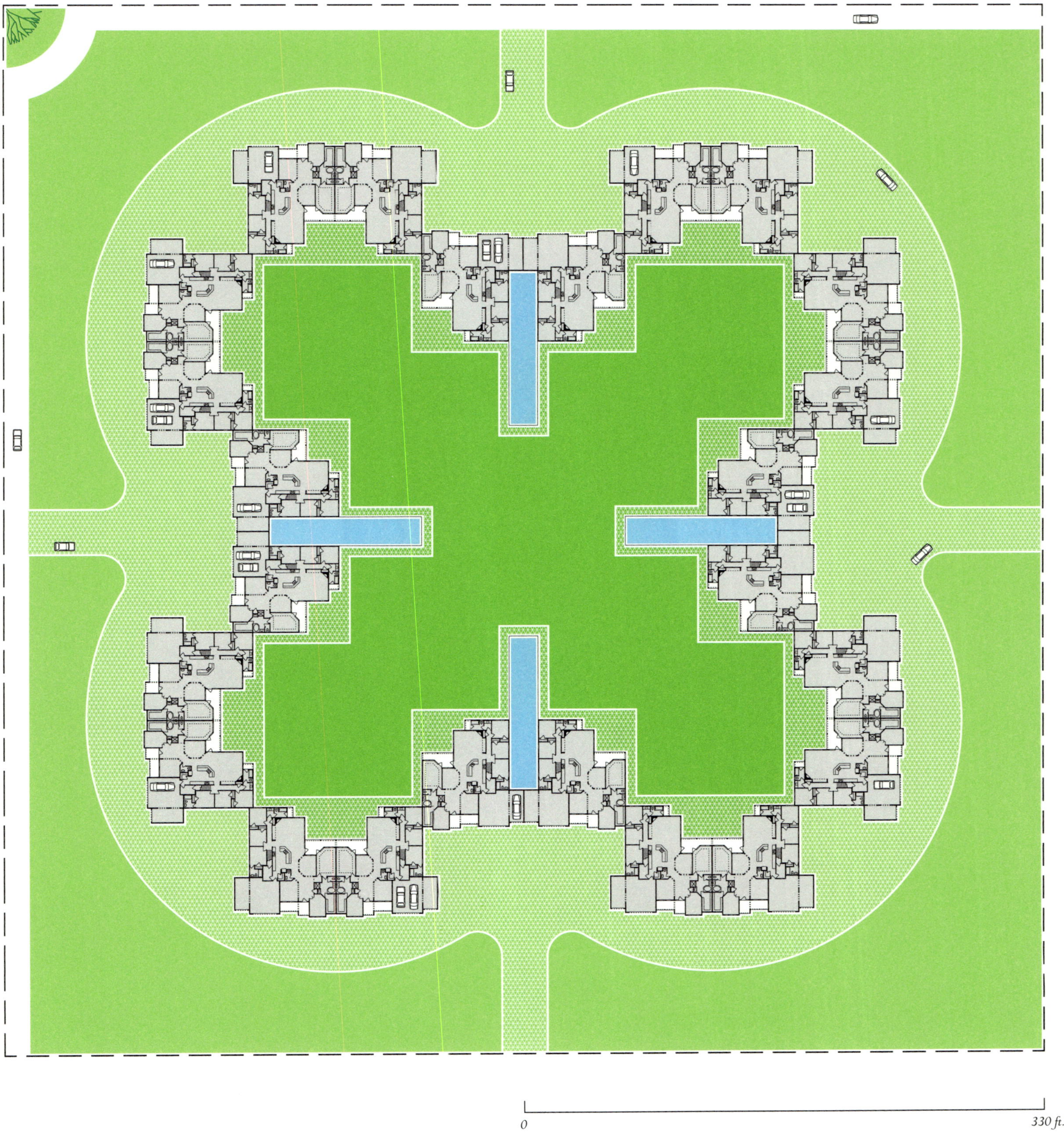

Cuadrados d'Azilia
NW 1/4 NW 1/4 Section 1

24 Houses
87,384 Square Feet
96 Bedrooms
72 Full Bathrooms
24 Half Bathrooms

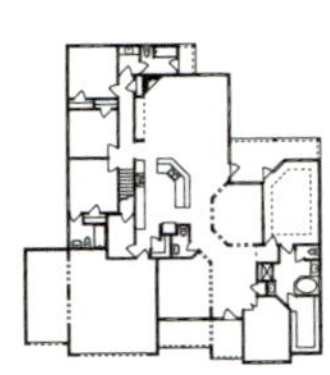

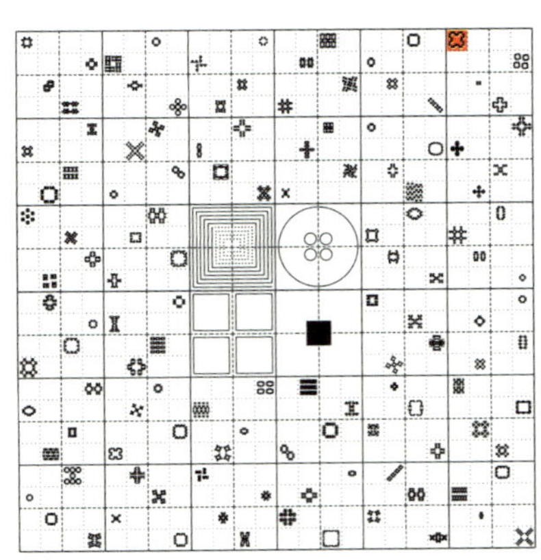

Pulte Homes, Monet, 3641 sq. ft., Texas

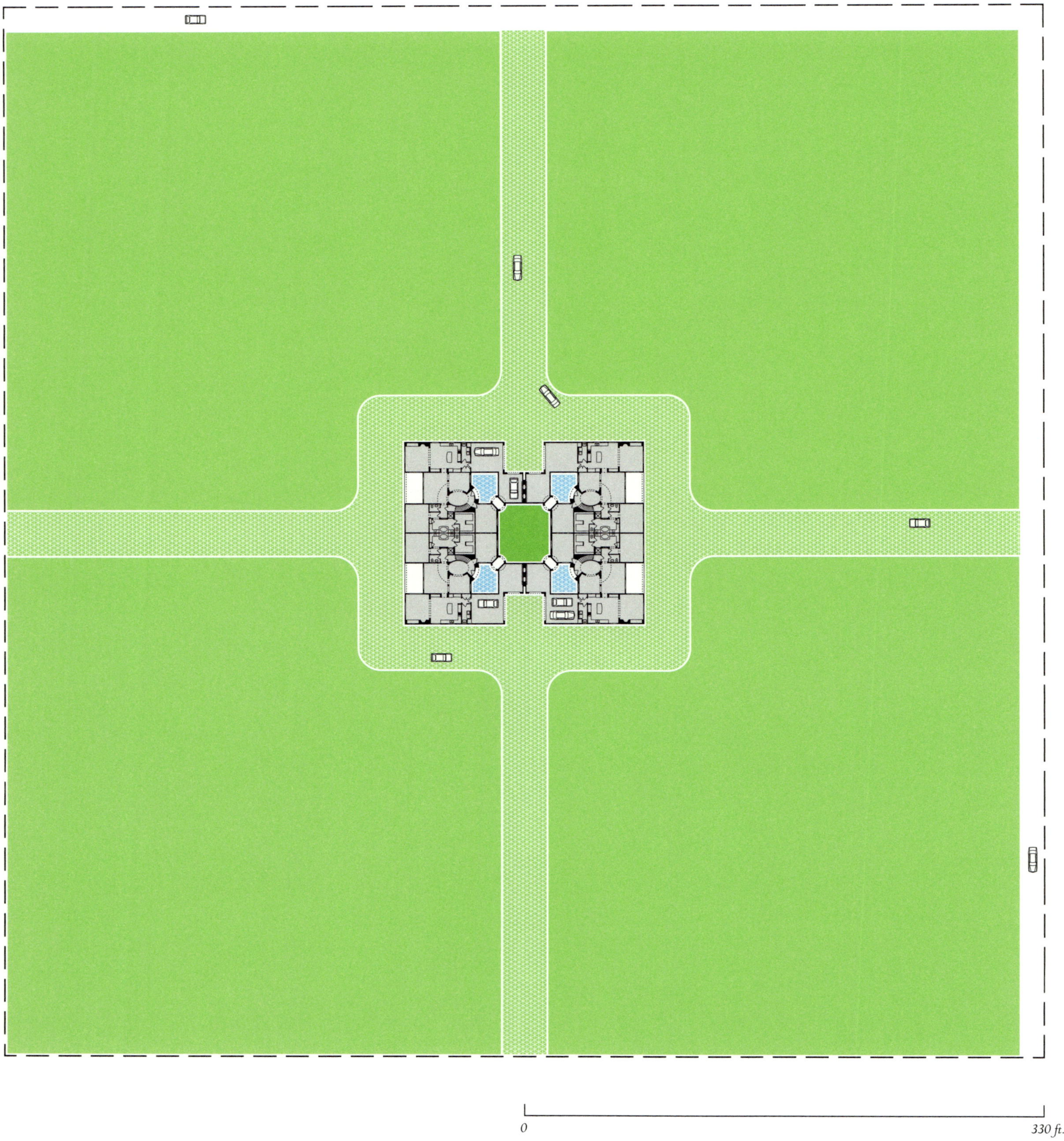

Brook Farm Manor

NE 1/4 SW 1/4 Section 1

4 Houses
16,252 Square Feet
16 Bedrooms
12 Full Bathrooms
4 Half Bathrooms

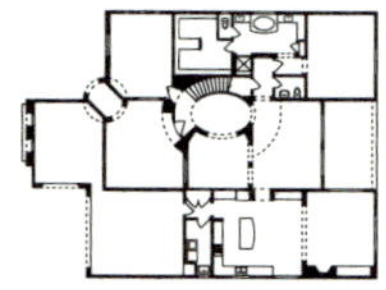

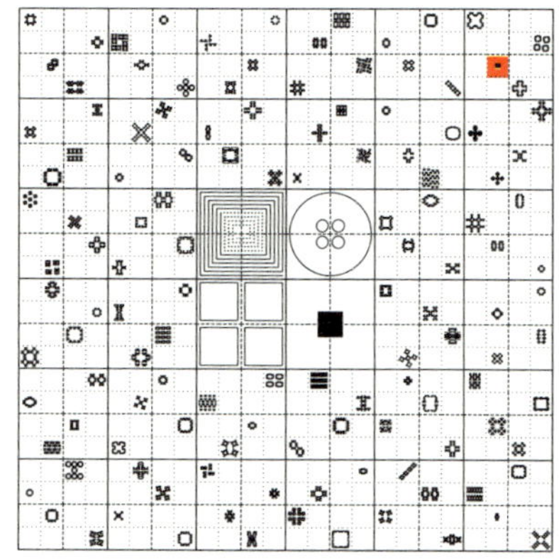

Del Webb, Mirasol, 4063 sq. ft., Arizona

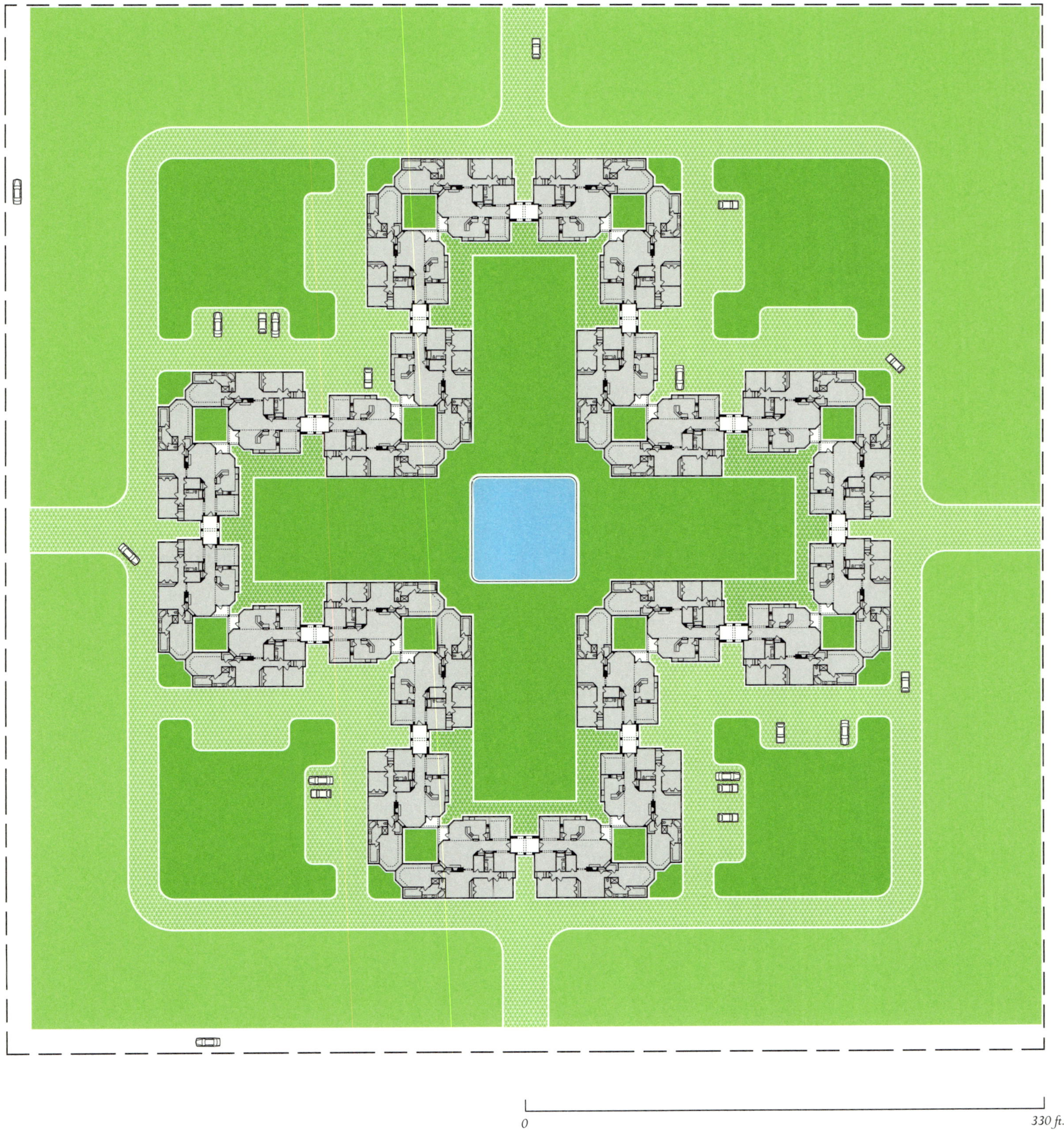

Bastide de Buck

SW 1/4 SE 1/4 Section 1

24 Houses
58,128 Square Feet
72–96 Bedrooms
48 Full Bathrooms
0 Half Bathrooms

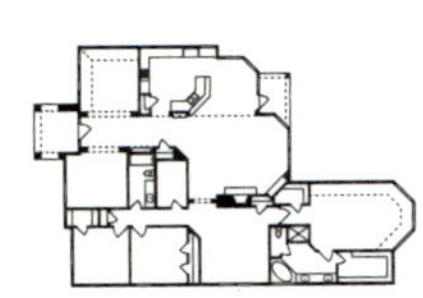

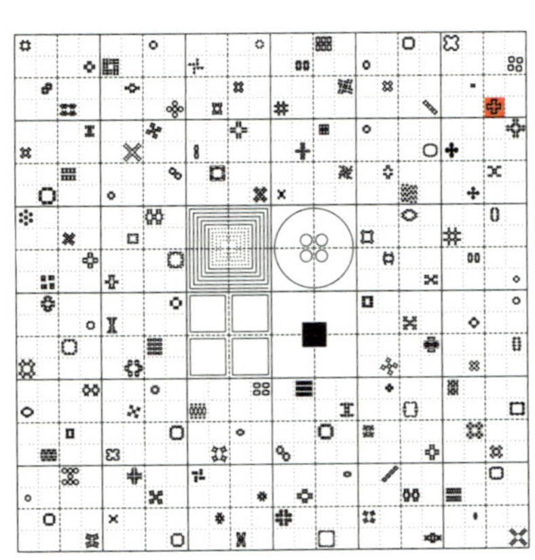

Beazer Homes, The Muirfield, 2422 sq. ft., Texas

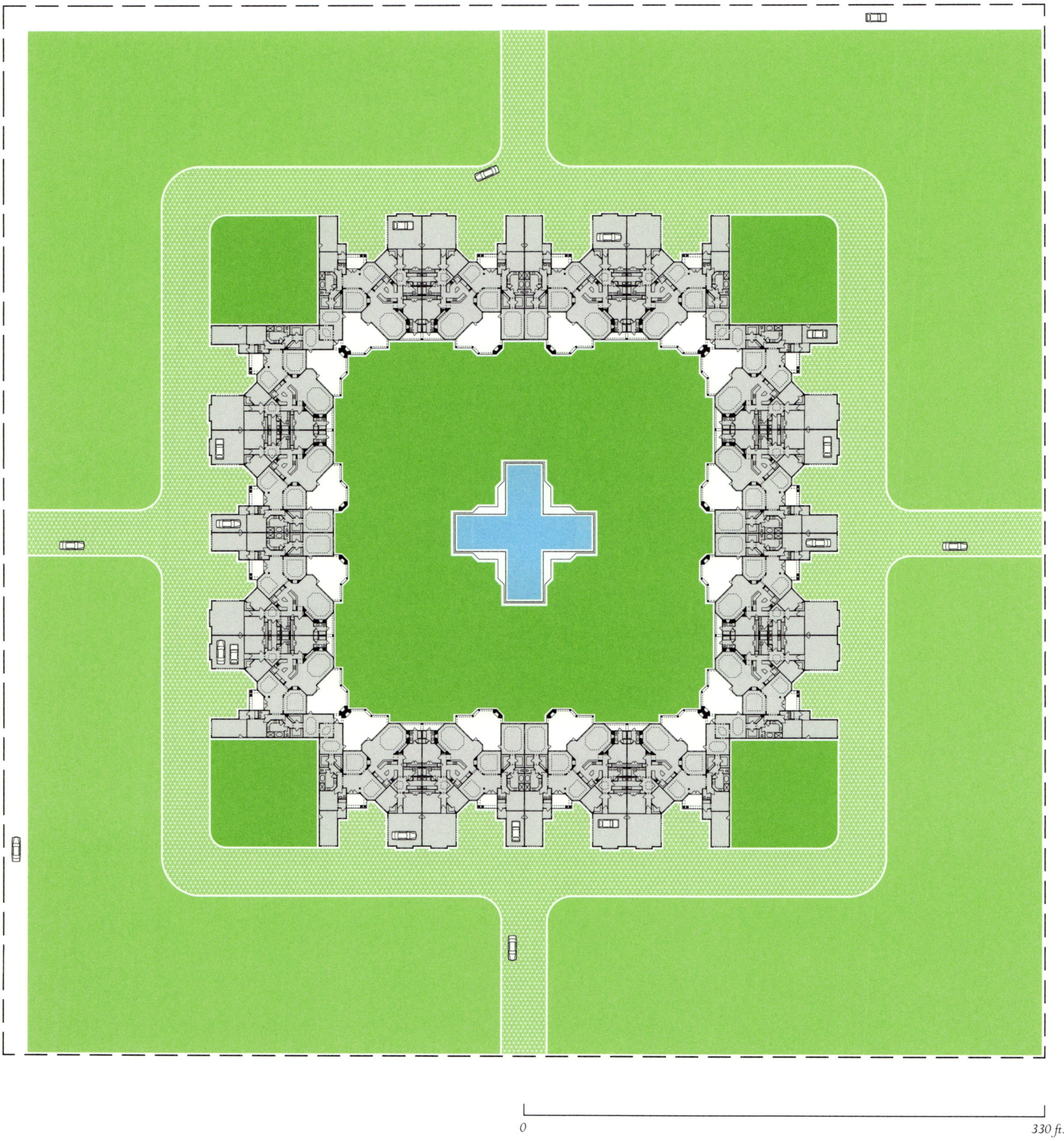

La Grande Place des Petit

NW 1/4 NE 1/4 Section 2

16 Houses
51,568 Square Feet
64 Bedrooms
48 Full Bathrooms
16 Half Bathrooms

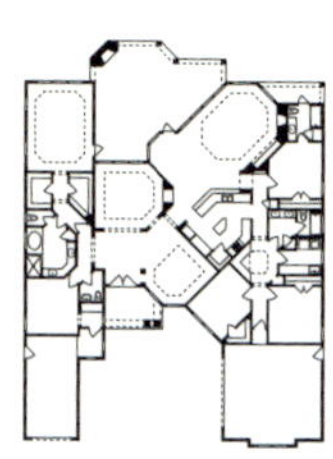

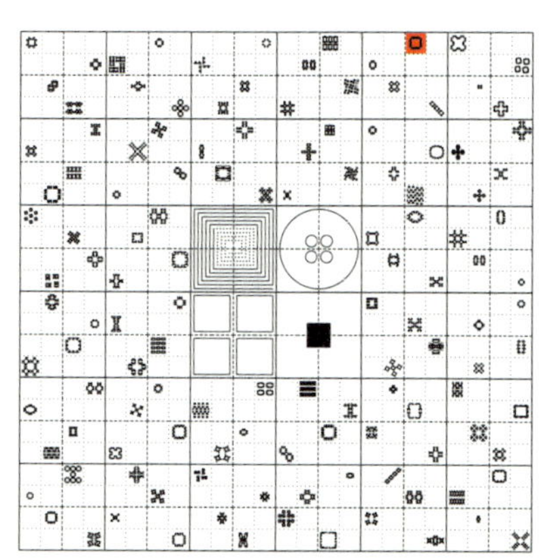

Ryland Homes, Suffolk, 3223 sq. ft.Florida

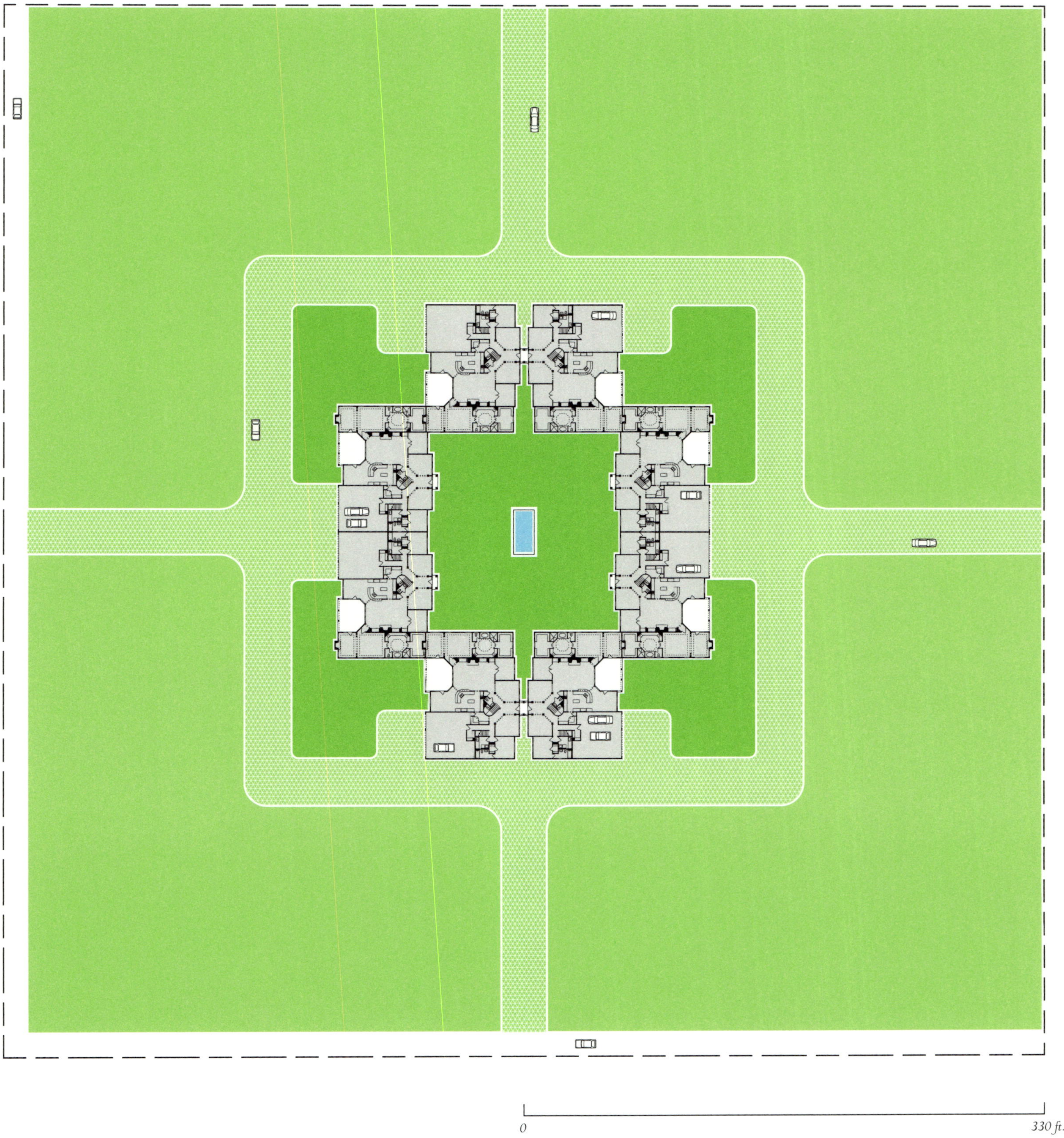

Swackhamer Grange

SW 1/4 NW 1/4 Section 2

8 Houses
44,568 Square Feet
40 Bedrooms
40 Full Bathrooms
8 Half Bathrooms

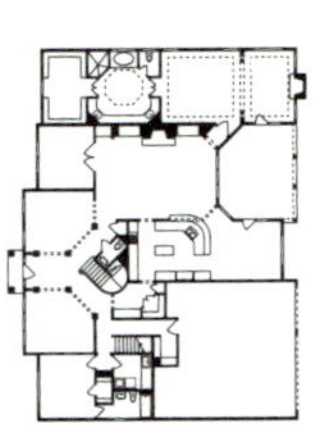

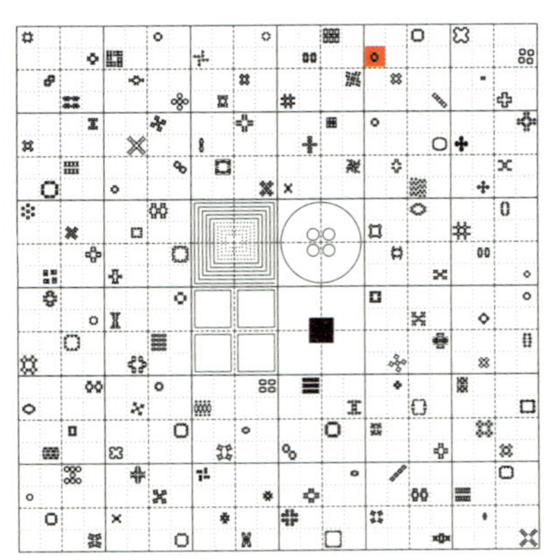

Beazer Homes, Versailles, 5571 sq. ft., Tennessee

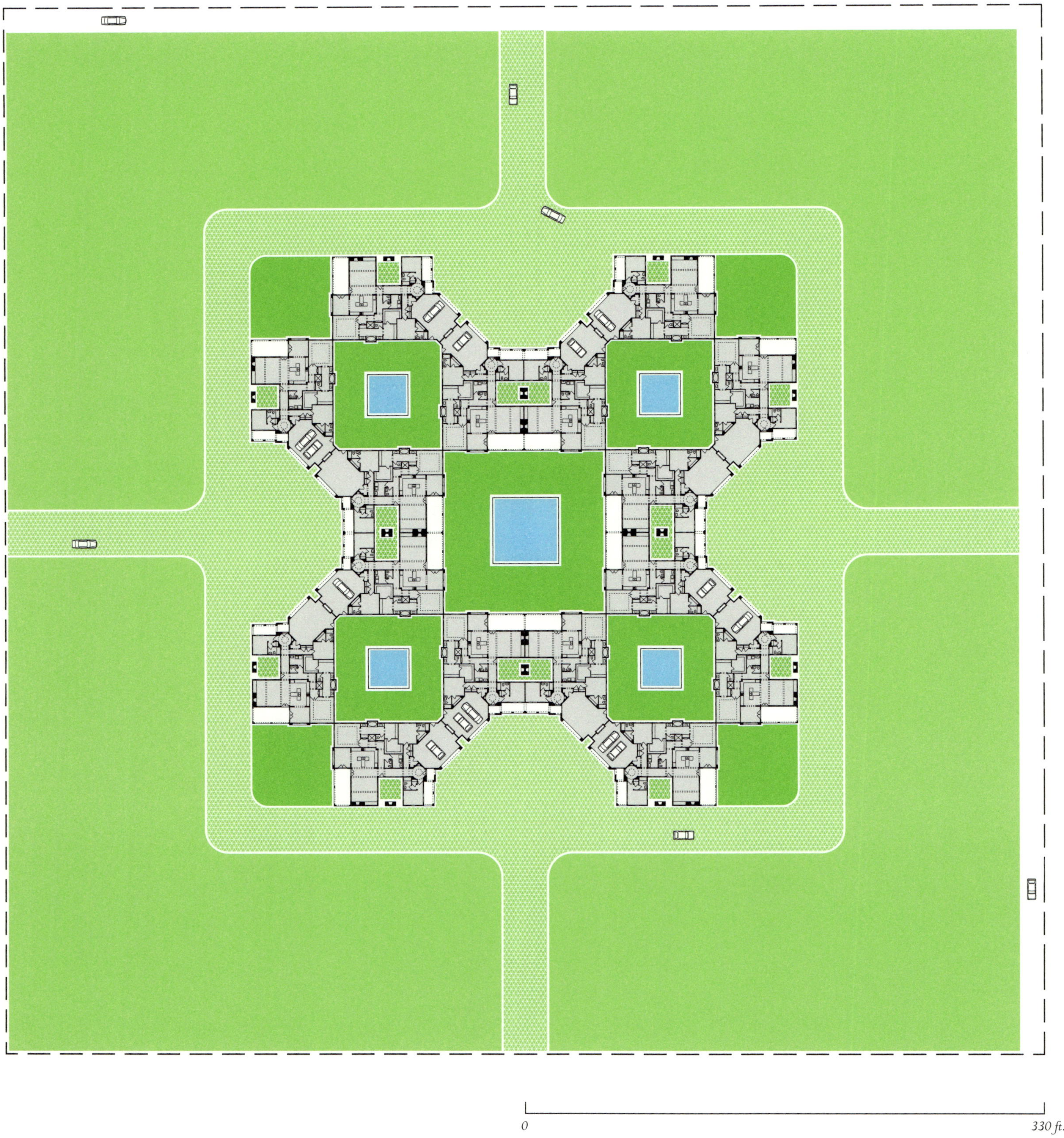

Hotel Sphinx

NE 1/4 SW 1/4 Section 2

16 Houses
43,008 Square Feet
48 Bedrooms
48 Full Bathrooms
16 Half Bathrooms

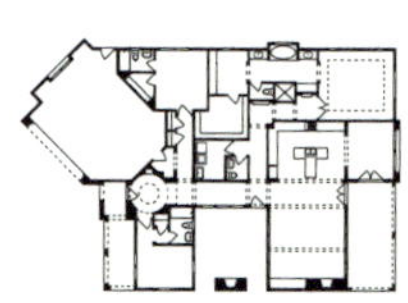

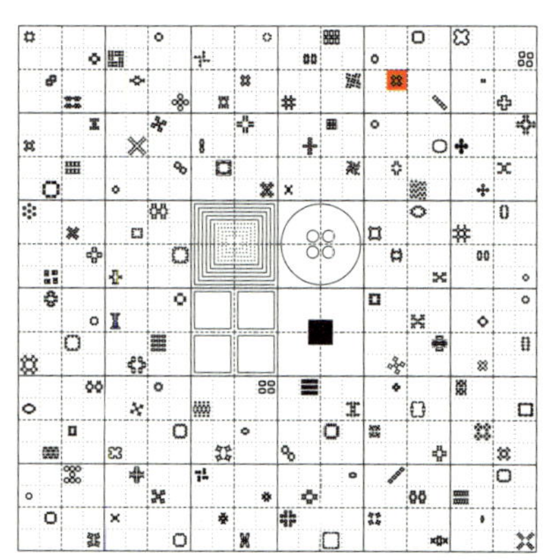

Maracay Homes, Plan 2011 - Angelico, 2688 sq. ft., Arizona

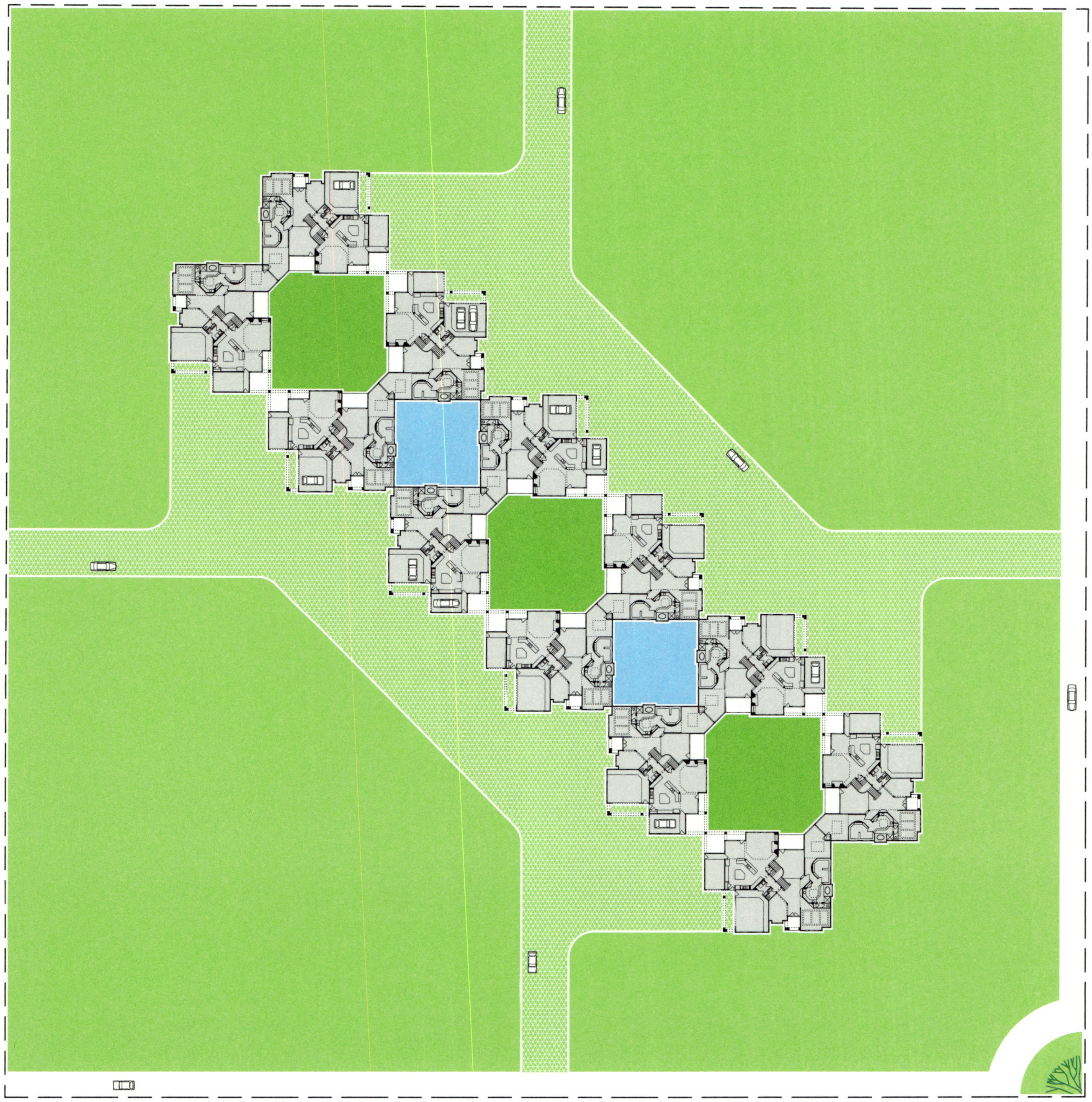

0 330 ft.

Astral Plains

SE 1/4 SE 1/4 Section 2

12 Houses
53,520 Square Feet
48–60 Bedrooms
36–48 Full Bathrooms
12 Half Bathrooms

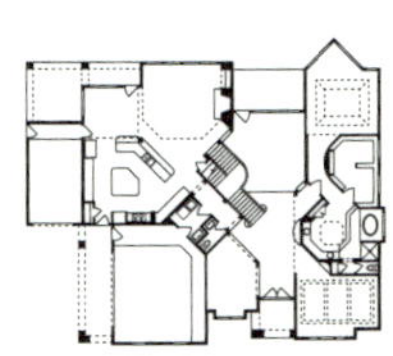

David Weekley Homes, The Kramer, 4460 sq. ft., Texas

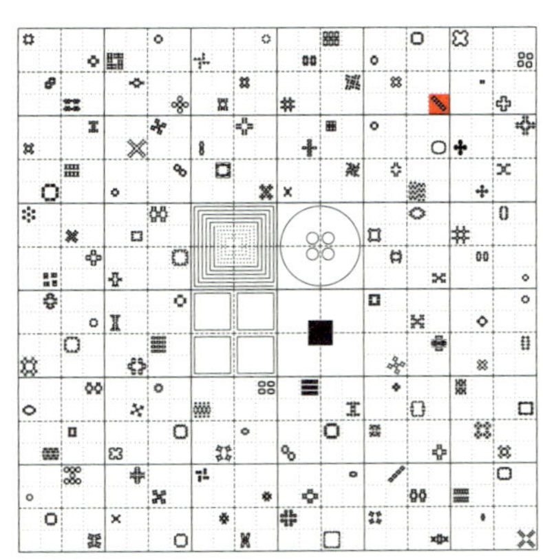

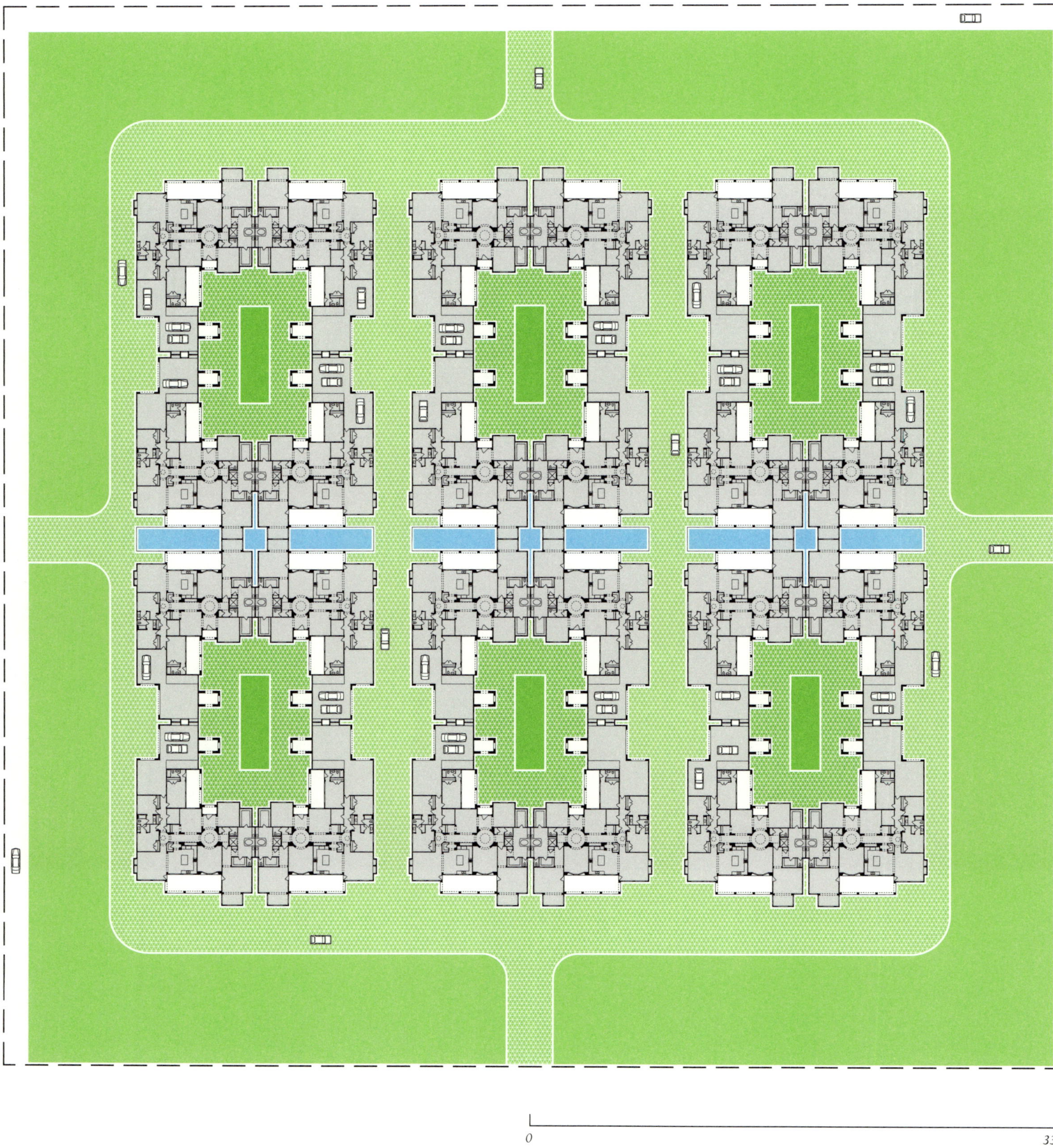

A Suburban Set

NW 1/4 NE 1/4 Section 3

24 Houses
101,208 Square Feet
96 Bedrooms
72 Full Bathrooms
24 Half Bathrooms

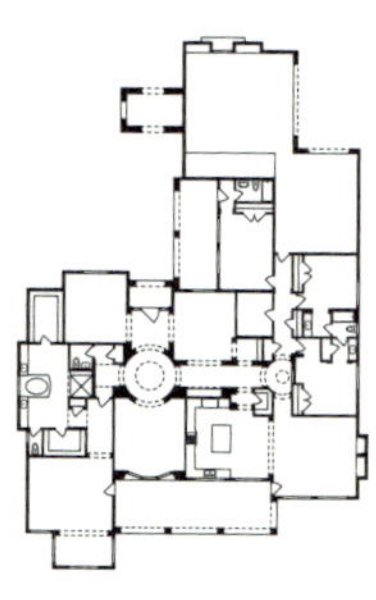

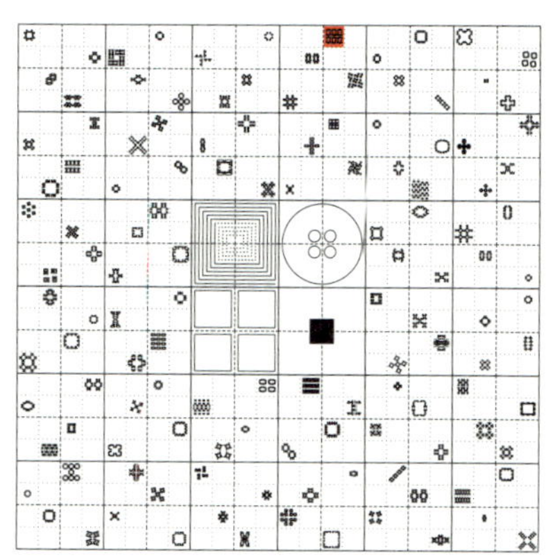

Meritage Homes, Residence 4 at Mirabel, 4217 sq. ft., Arizona

A Solitary Farmer Works Smiley's Acres, Freedomland
after *The Veteran in a New Field,* 1865
Winslow Homer

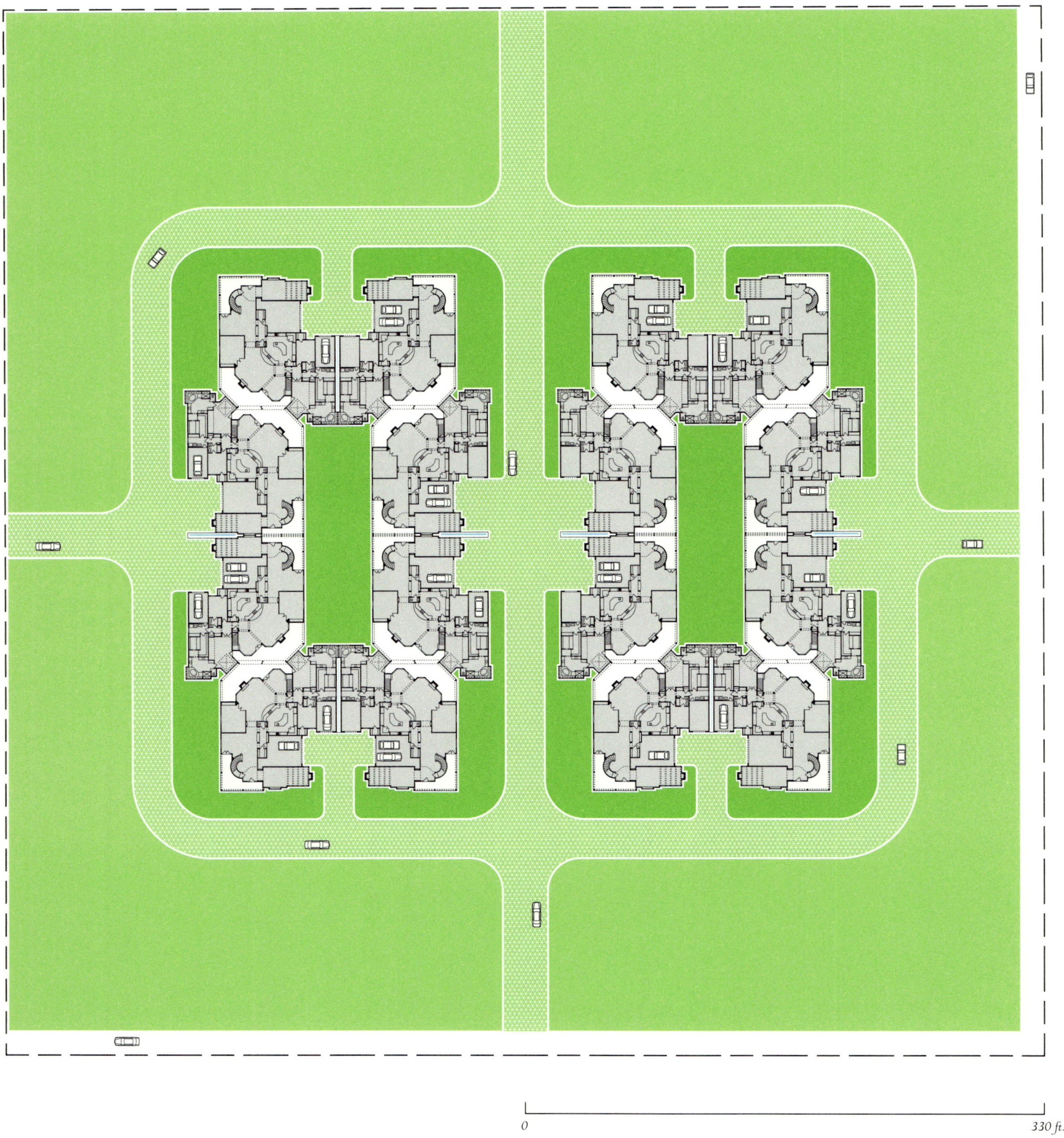

Smiley's Acres
SE 1/4 NW 1/4 Section 3

16 Houses
96,000 Square Feet
80 Bedrooms
80 Full Bathrooms
16 Half Bathrooms

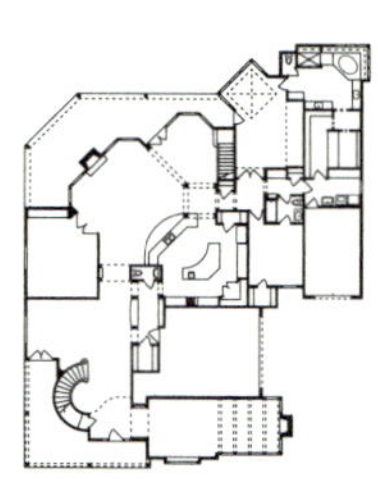

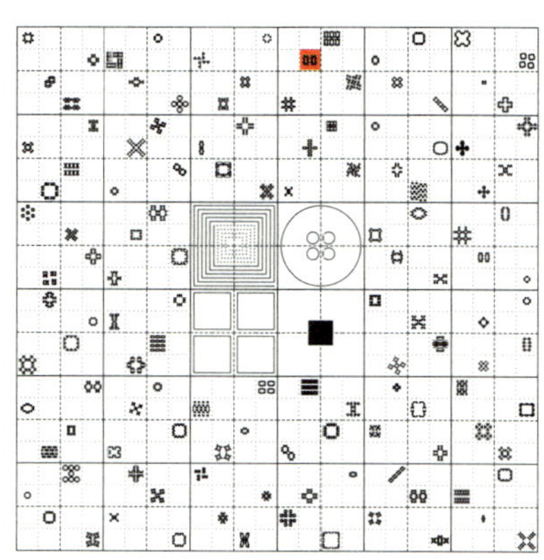

Meritage Homes, The Chalet, 6000 sq. ft., Texas

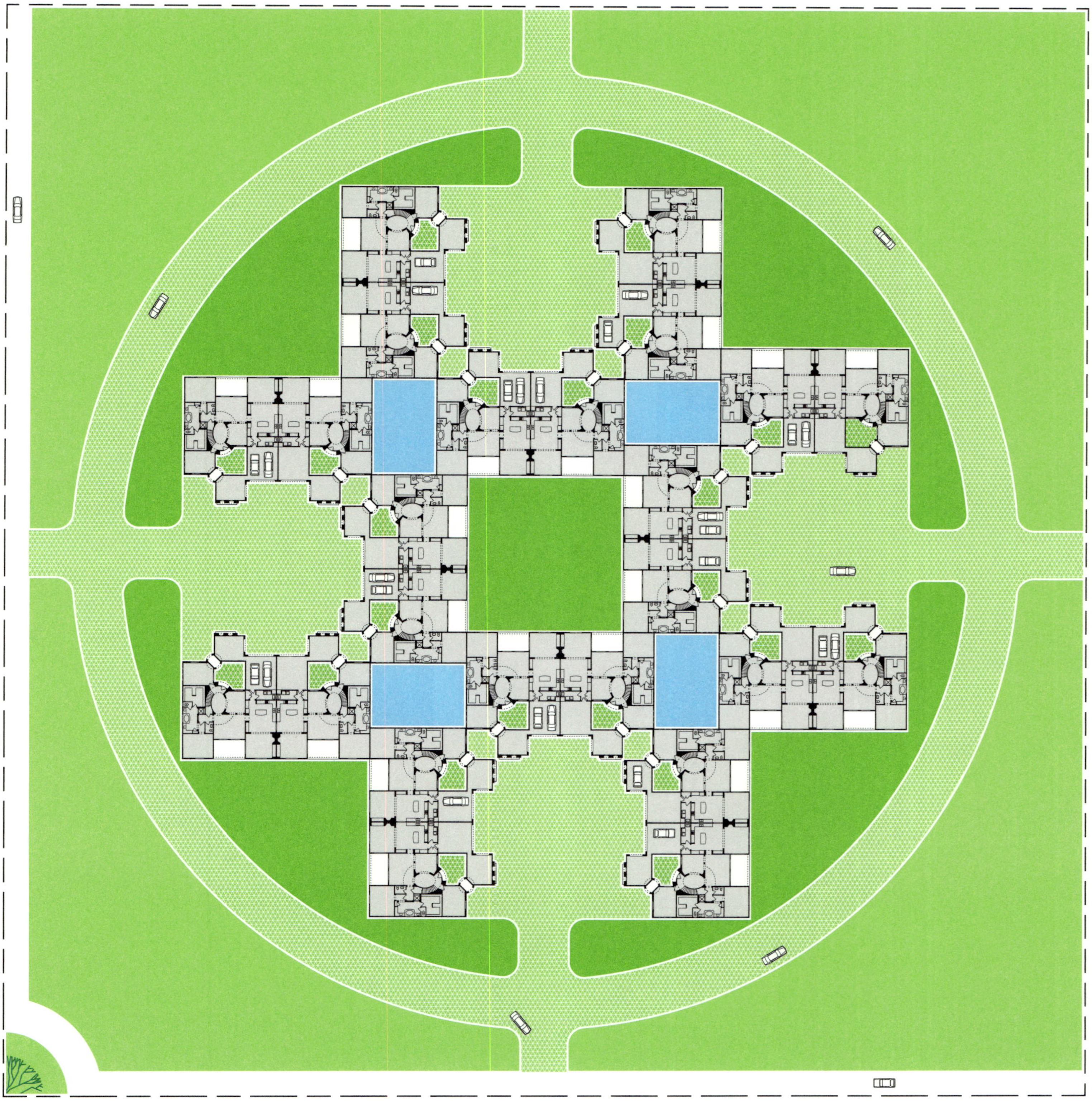

Rancho el Goodo

SW 1/4 SW 1/4 Section 3

24 Houses
97,512 Square Feet
96 Bedrooms
72 Full Bathrooms
24 Half Bathrooms

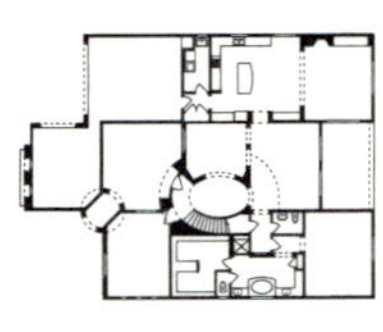

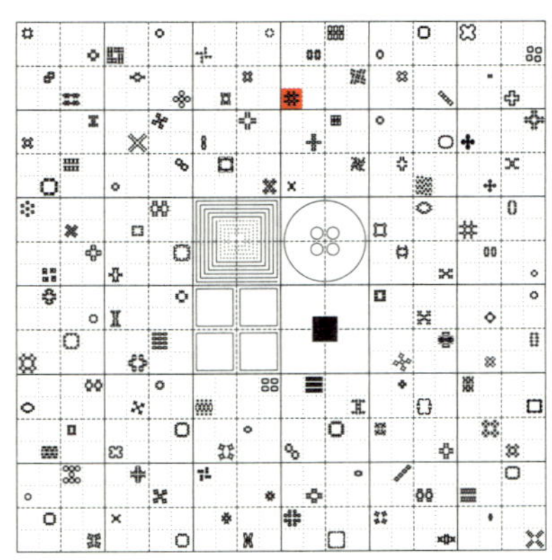

Del Webb, Mirasol, 4063 sq. ft., Arizona

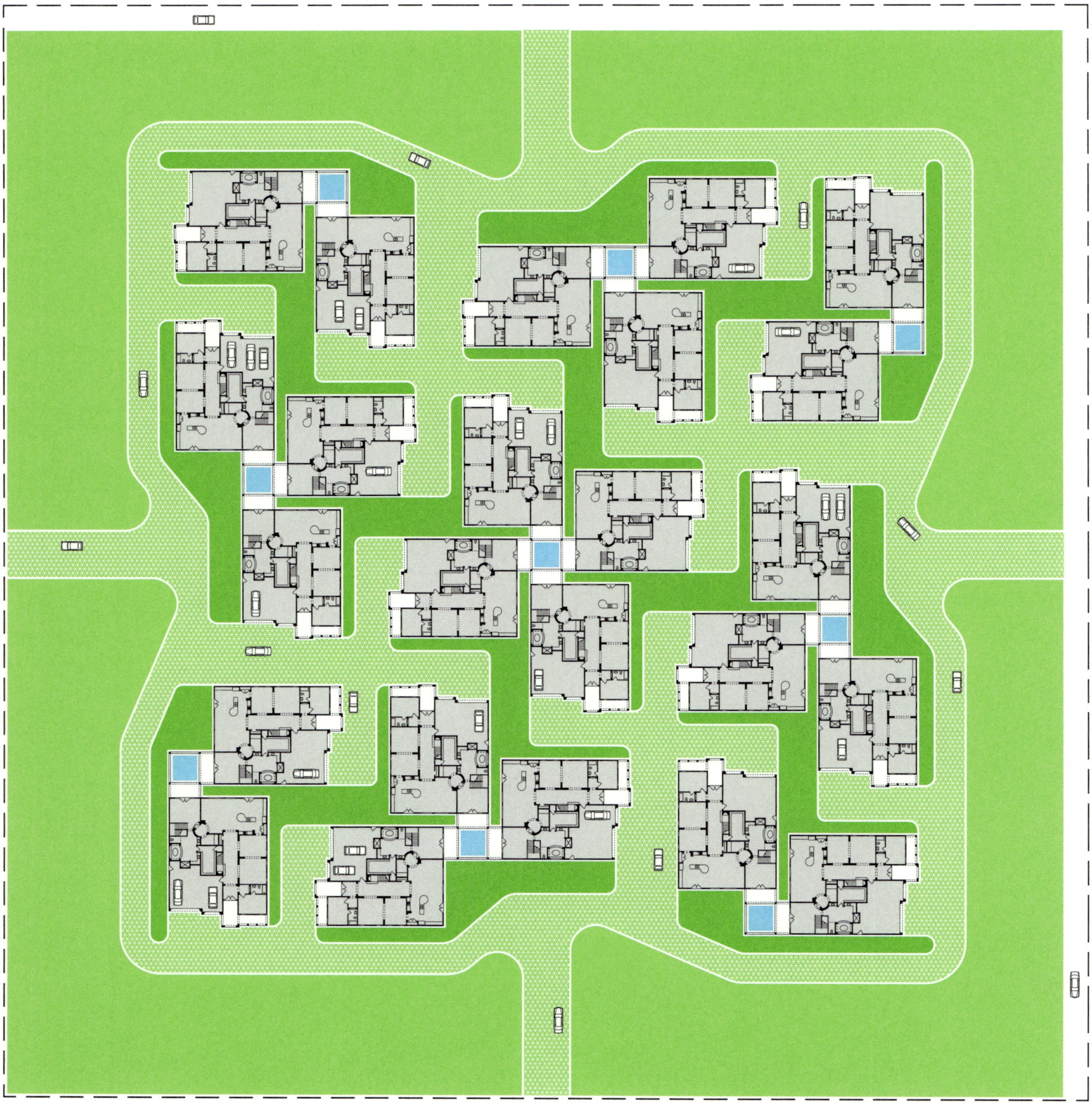

Levittown the Younger

NE 1/4 SE 1/4 Section 3

24 Houses
114,000 Square Feet
144–168 Bedrooms
96 Full Bathrooms
24 Half Bathrooms

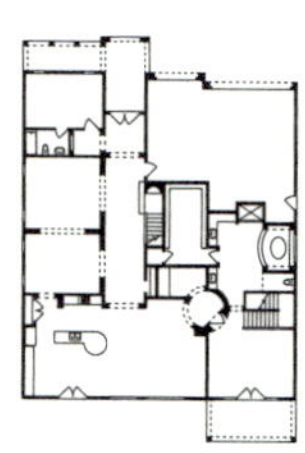

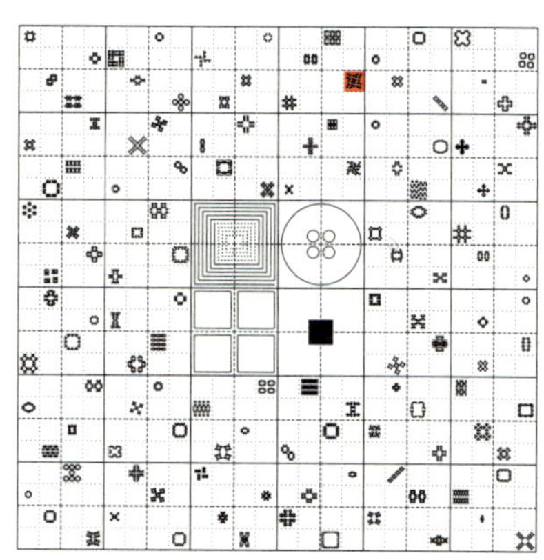

Richmond American Homes, Picasso, 4750 sq. ft., Arizona

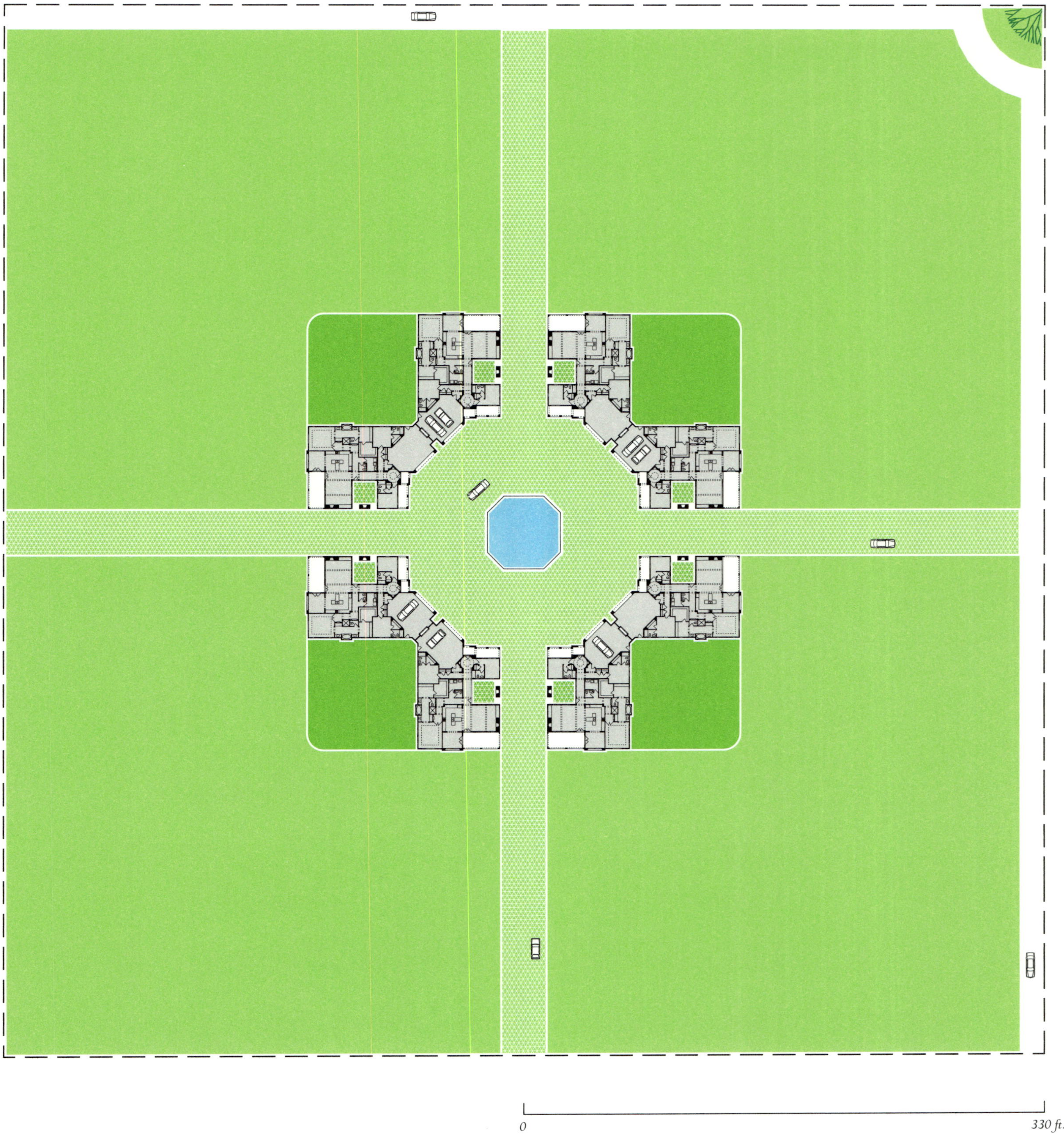

Gessel Manor

NE 1/4 NE 1/4 Section 4

8 Houses
21,504 Square Feet
24 Bedrooms
24 Full Bathrooms
8 Half Bathrooms

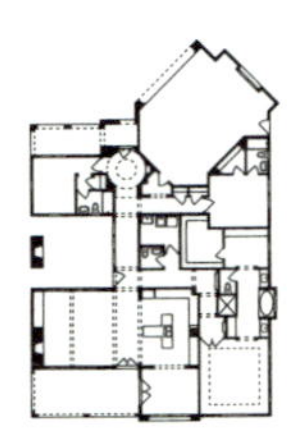

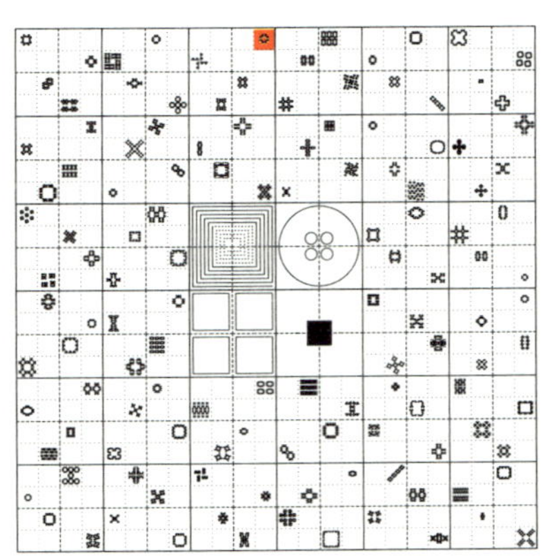

Maracay Homes, Plan 2011- Angelico, 2688 sq. ft., Arizona

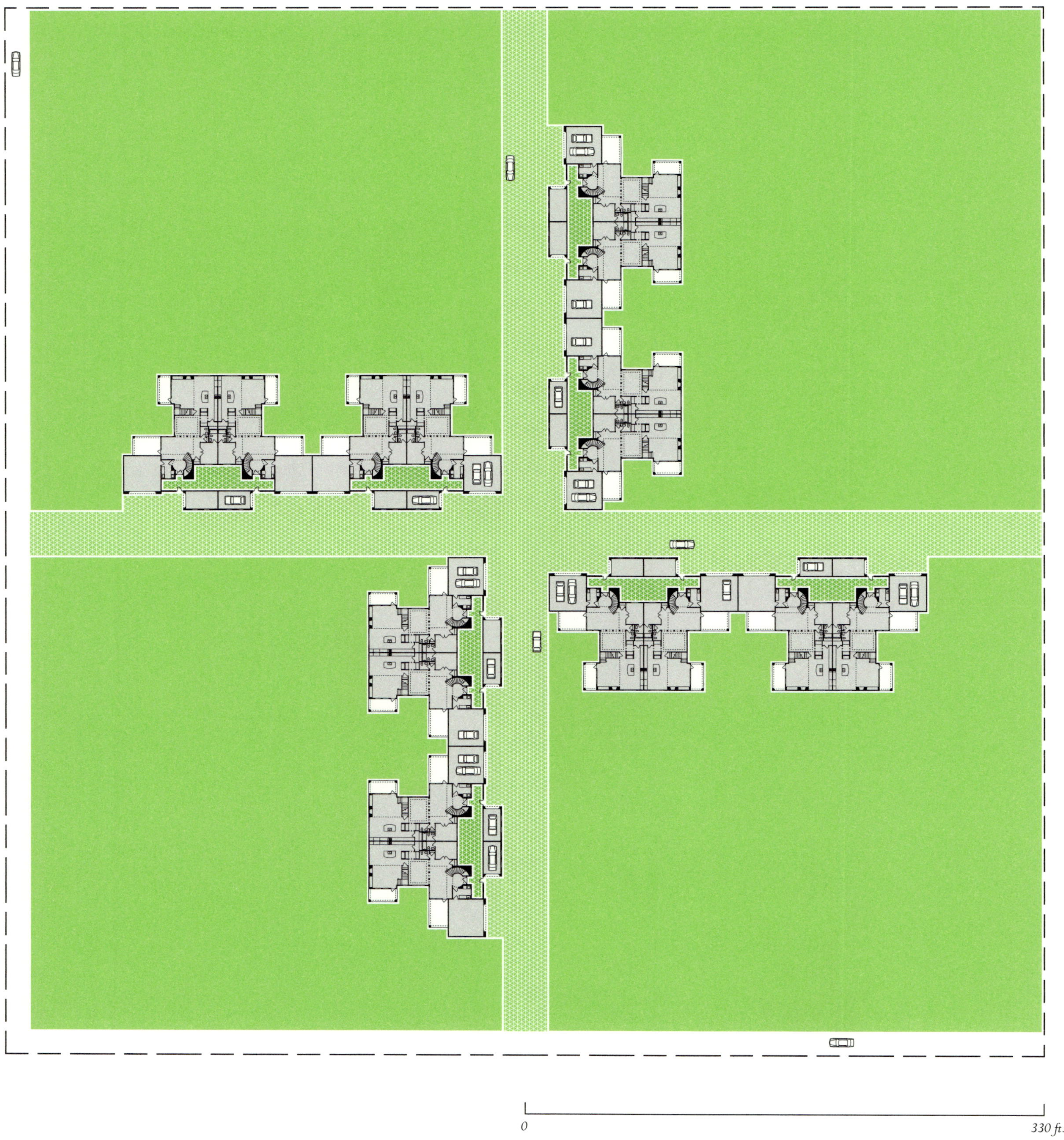

Durusoy Landing

SW 1/4 NW 1/4 Section 4

16 Houses
60,800 Square Feet
48–80 Bedrooms
64 Full Bathrooms
16 Half Bathrooms

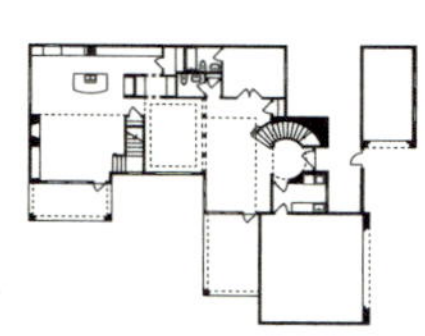

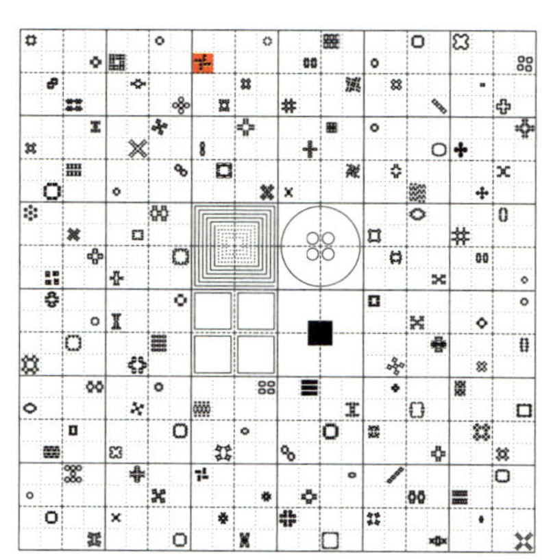

Pulte Homes, The Provence, 3800 sq. ft., Nevada

An Awkward Moment at Platz der Pope, Freedomland
after *A Plate of Cakes,* circa 1890
Jehan Georges Vibert

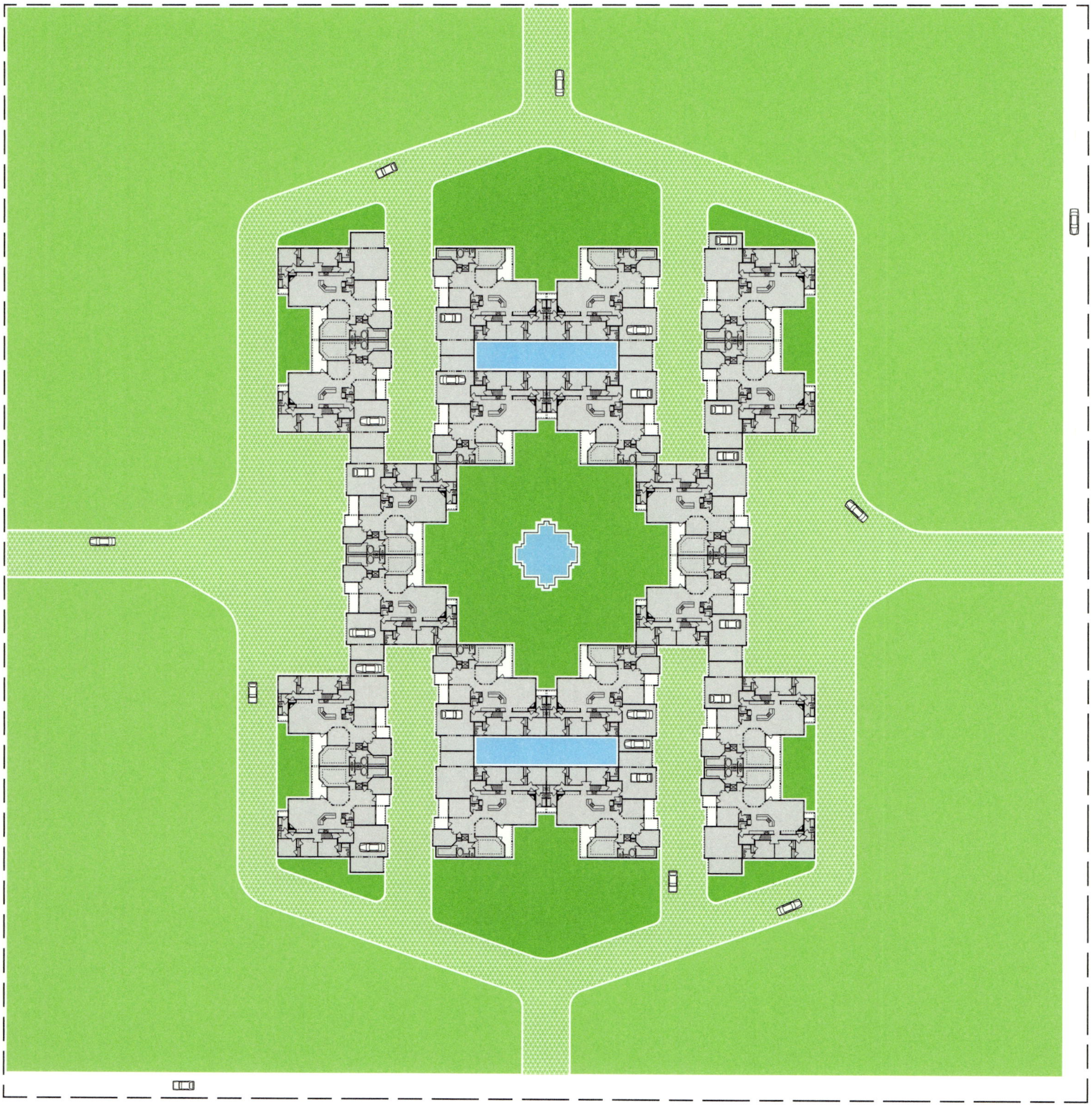

Platz der Pope

SE 1/4 SW 1/4 Section 4

20 Houses
72,820 Square Feet
80 Bedrooms
60 Full Bathrooms
20 Half Bathrooms

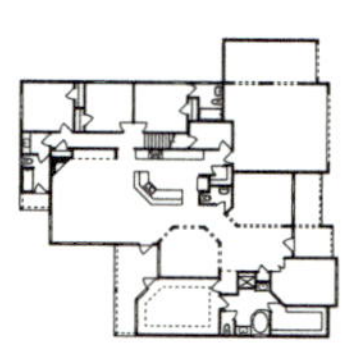

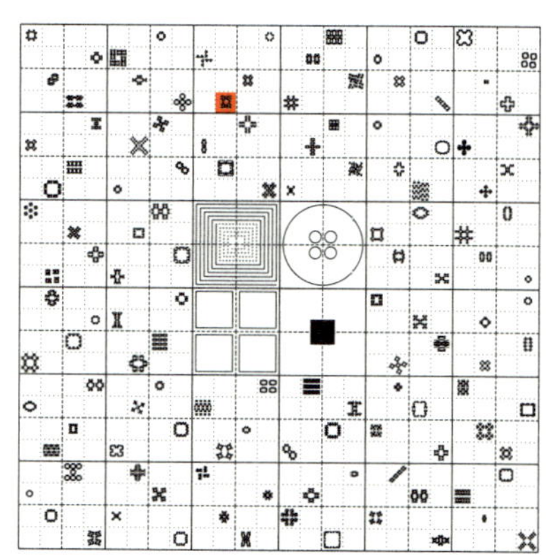

Pulte Homes, Monet, 3641 sq. ft., Texas

Equipe de Dix Village
NW 1/4 SE 1/4 Section 4

16 Houses
74,000 Square Feet
64 Bedrooms
64 Full Bathrooms
16 Half Bathrooms

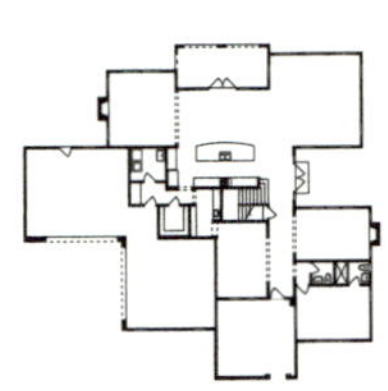

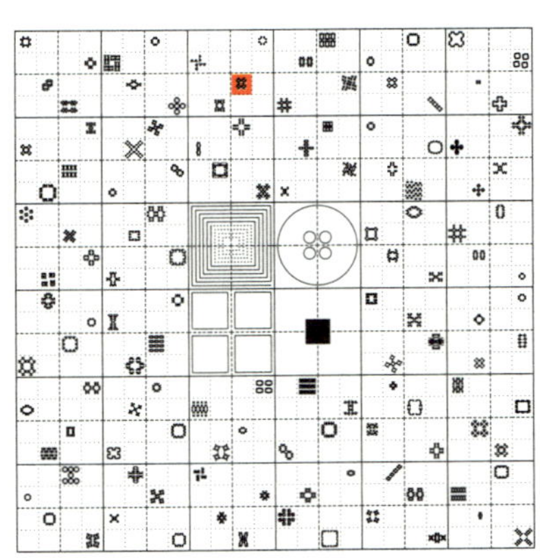

Shea Homes, Plan 2 at Maravilla, 4625 sq. ft., California

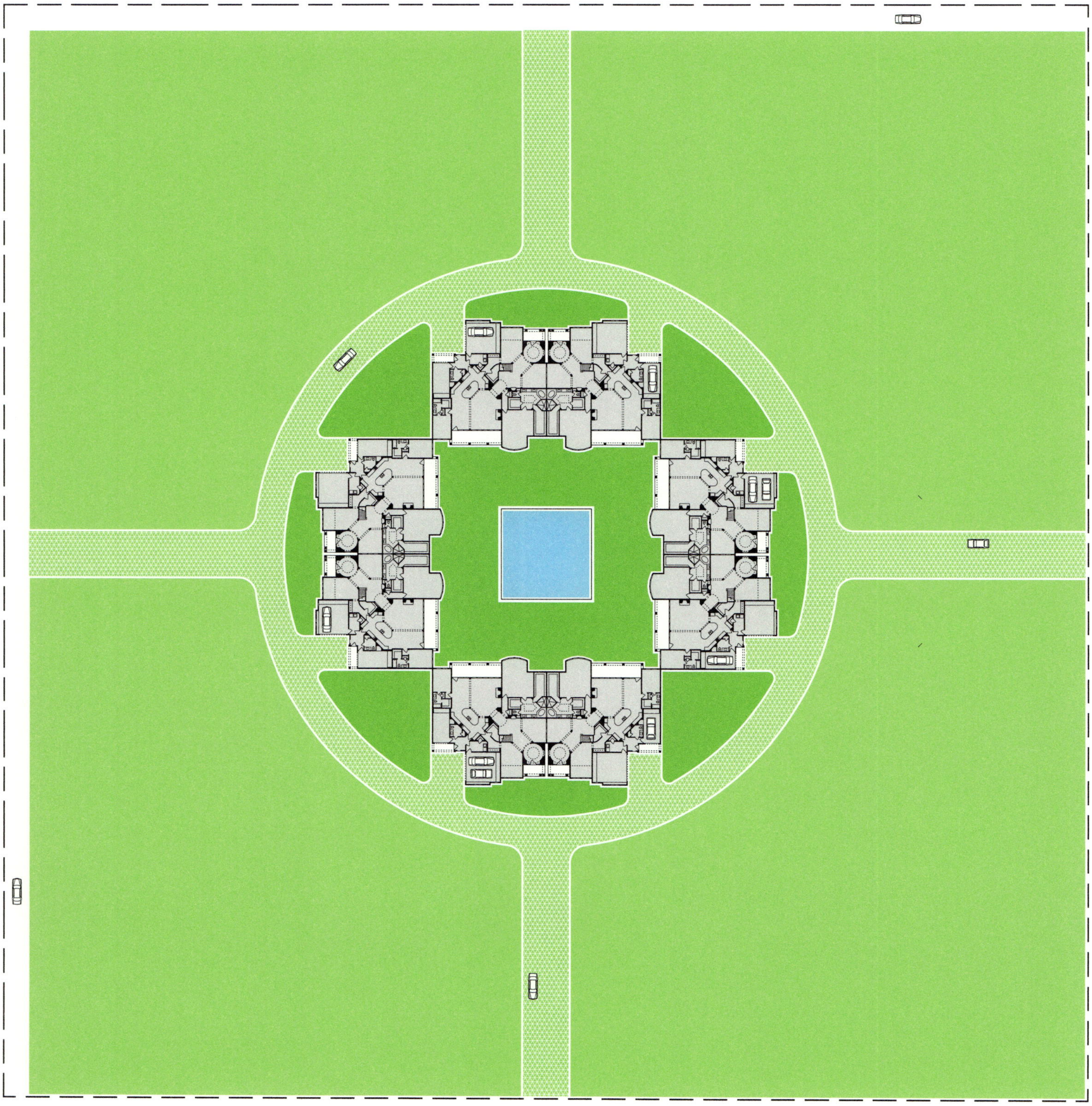

The Citadel at Filarete Fields

NW 1/4 NE 1/4 Section 5

8 Houses
56,008 Square Feet
48 Bedrooms
40 Full Bathrooms
8 Half Bathrooms

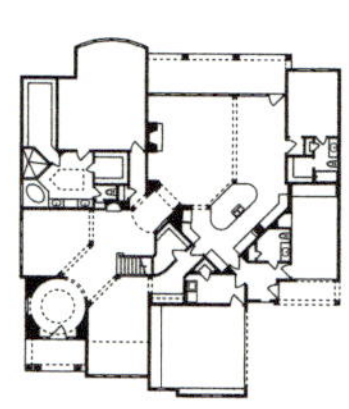

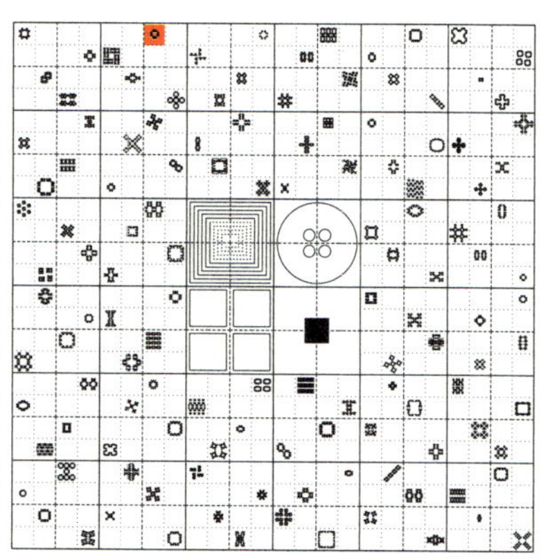

Perry Homes, Plan 7001W, 7001 sq. ft., Texas

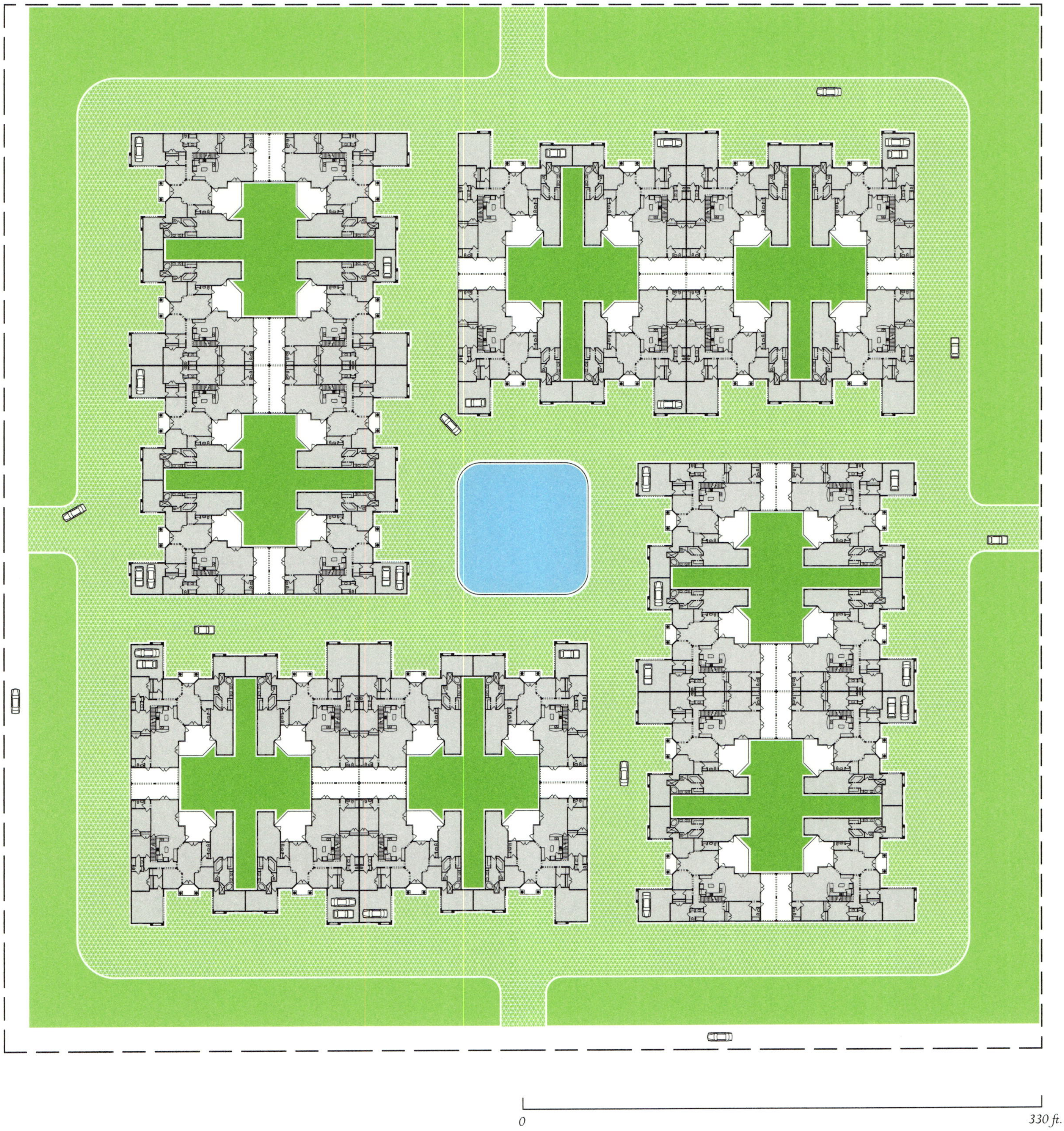

Hamilton Holdings

SW 1/4 NW 1/4 Section 5

32 Houses
111,200 Square Feet
128–160 Bedrooms
128 Full Bathrooms
32 Half Bathrooms

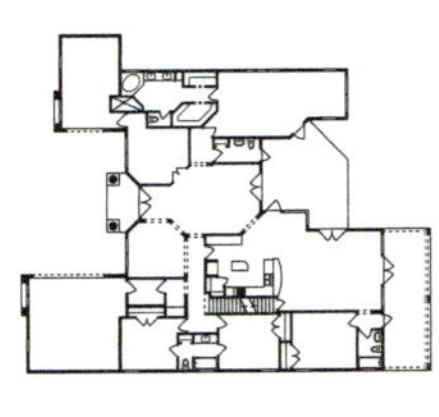

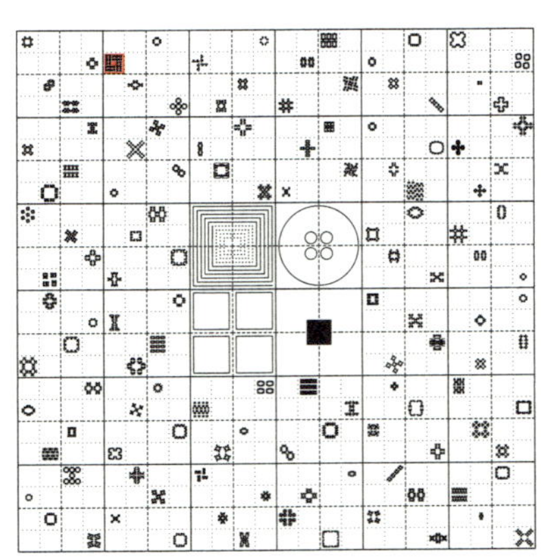

Ryland Homes, Charleston II, 3475 sq. ft., Florida

Seltzer Springs

NE 1/4 SW 1/4 Section 5

16 Houses
38,752 Square Feet
48–64 Bedrooms
32 Full Bathrooms
0 Half Bathrooms

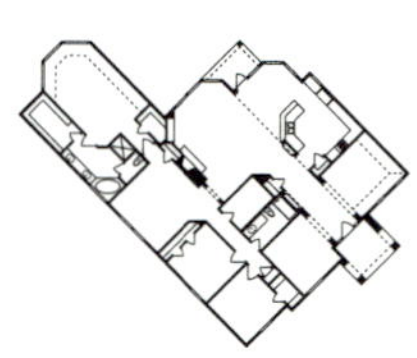

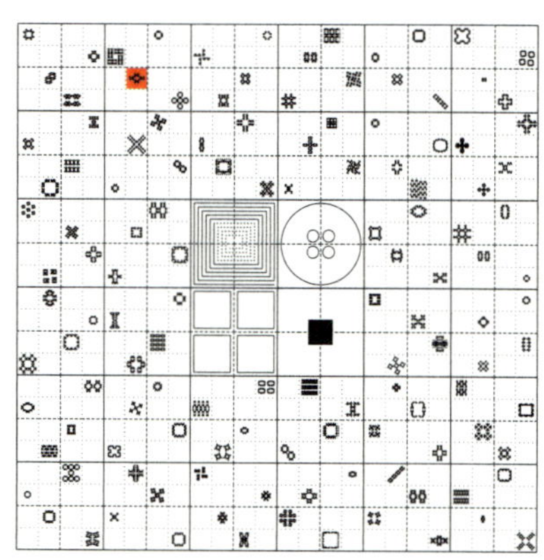

Beazer Homes, The Muirfield, 2422 sq. ft., Texas

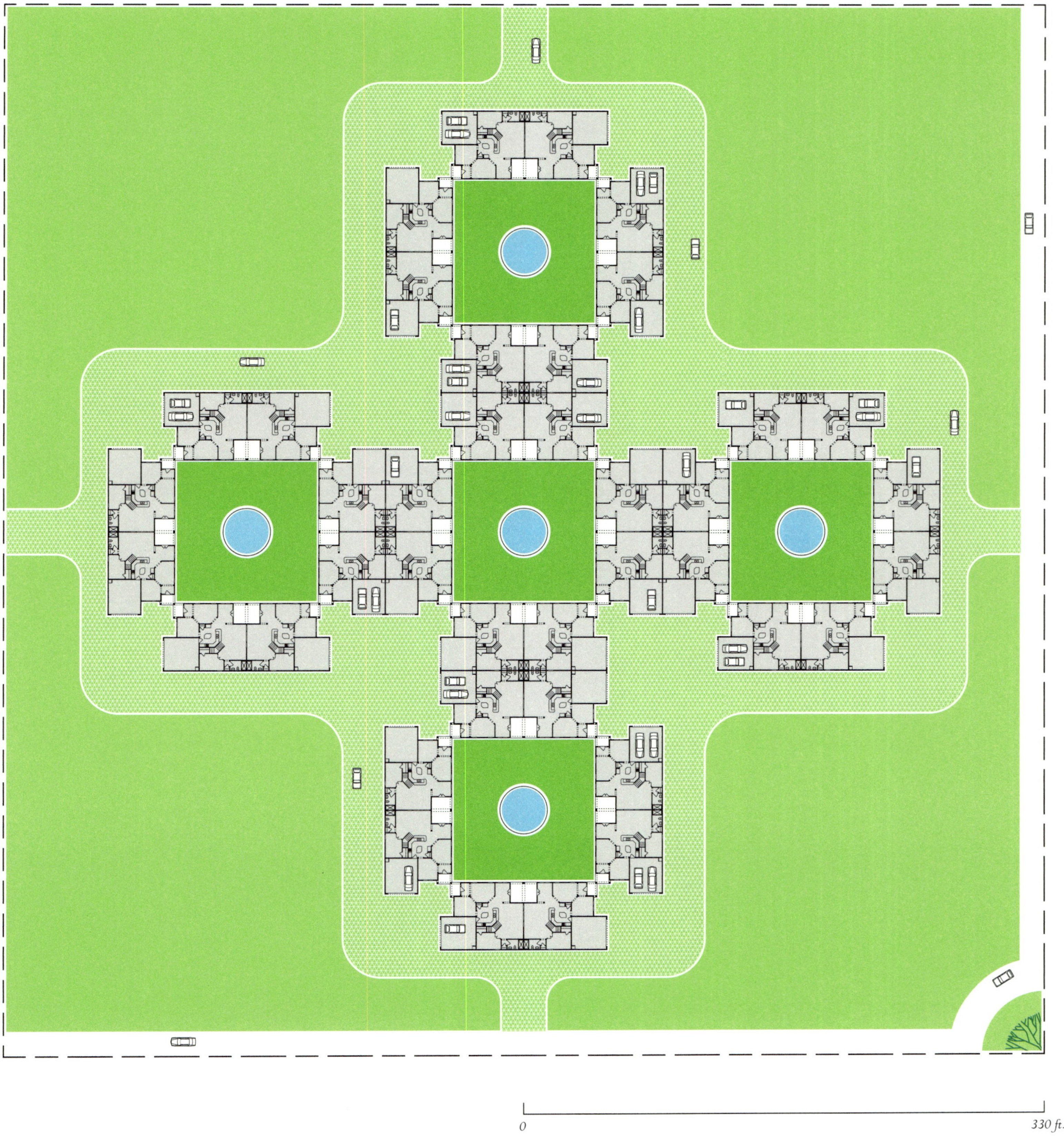

Casa di Branzi
SE 1/4 SE 1/4 Section 5

40 Houses
120,600 Square Feet
120–160 Bedrooms
120 Full Bathrooms
0 Half Bathrooms

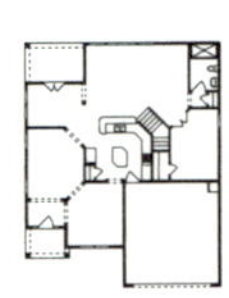

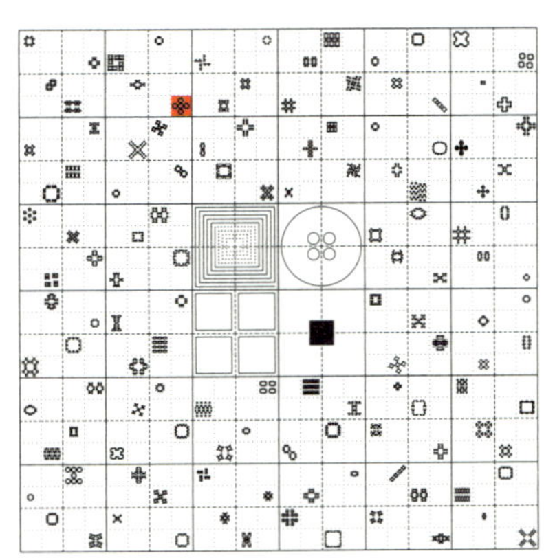

Beazer Homes, Terrace, 3015 sq. ft., Nevada

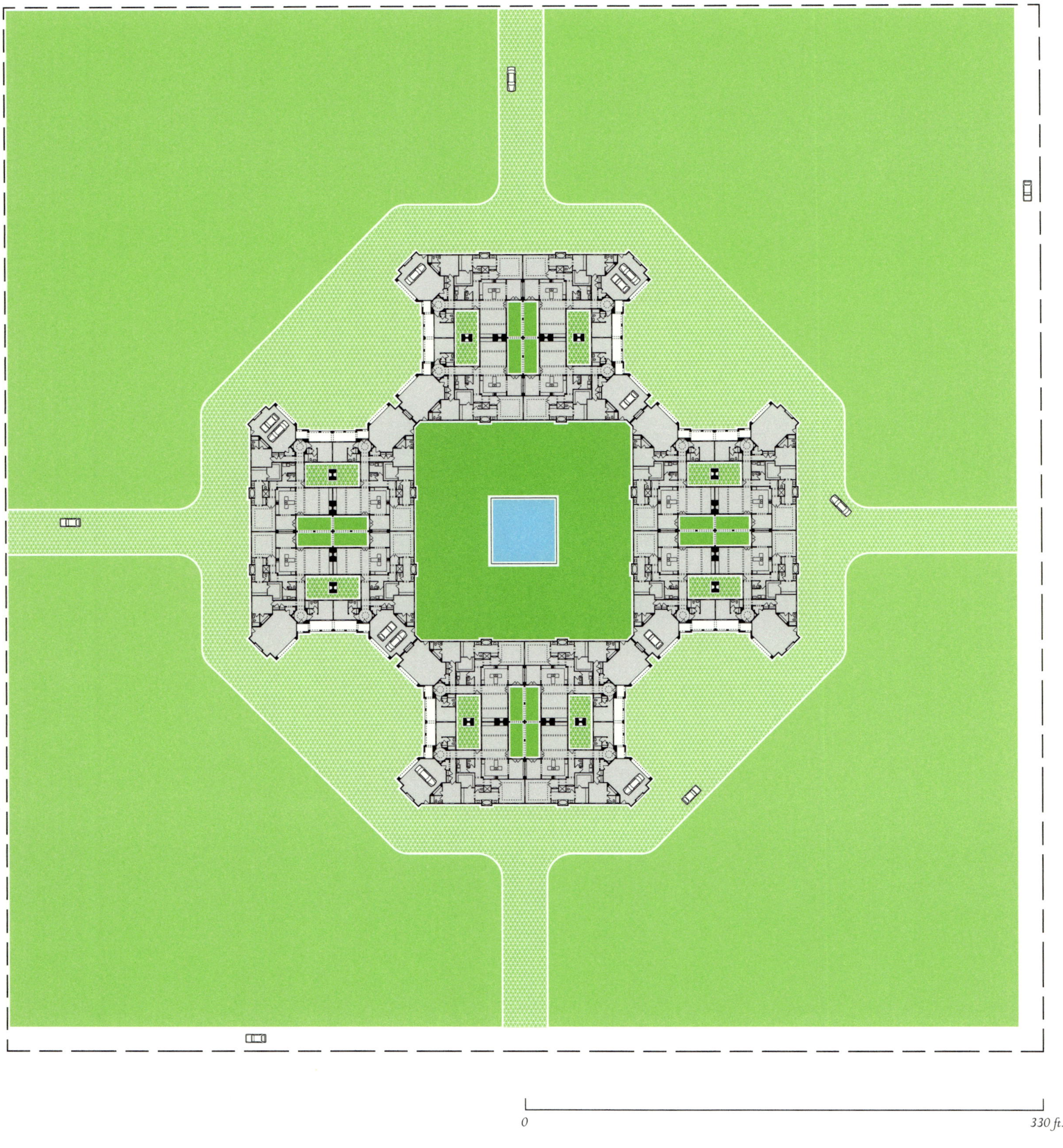

Bellew Green

SE 1/4 NE 1/4 Section 6

16 Houses
43,008 Square Feet
48 Bedrooms
48 Full Bathrooms
16 Half Bathrooms

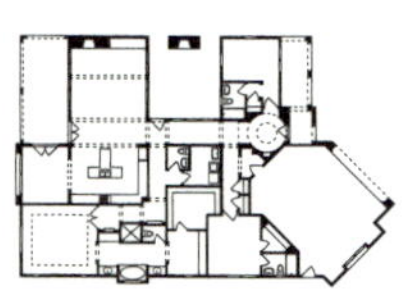

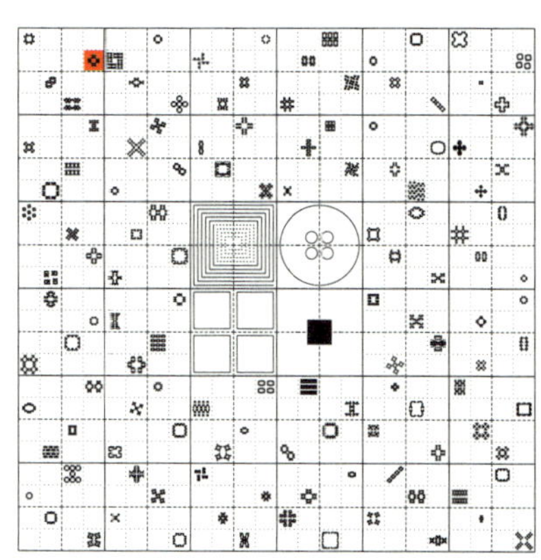

Maracay Homes, Plan 2011- Angelico, 2688 sq. ft., Arizona

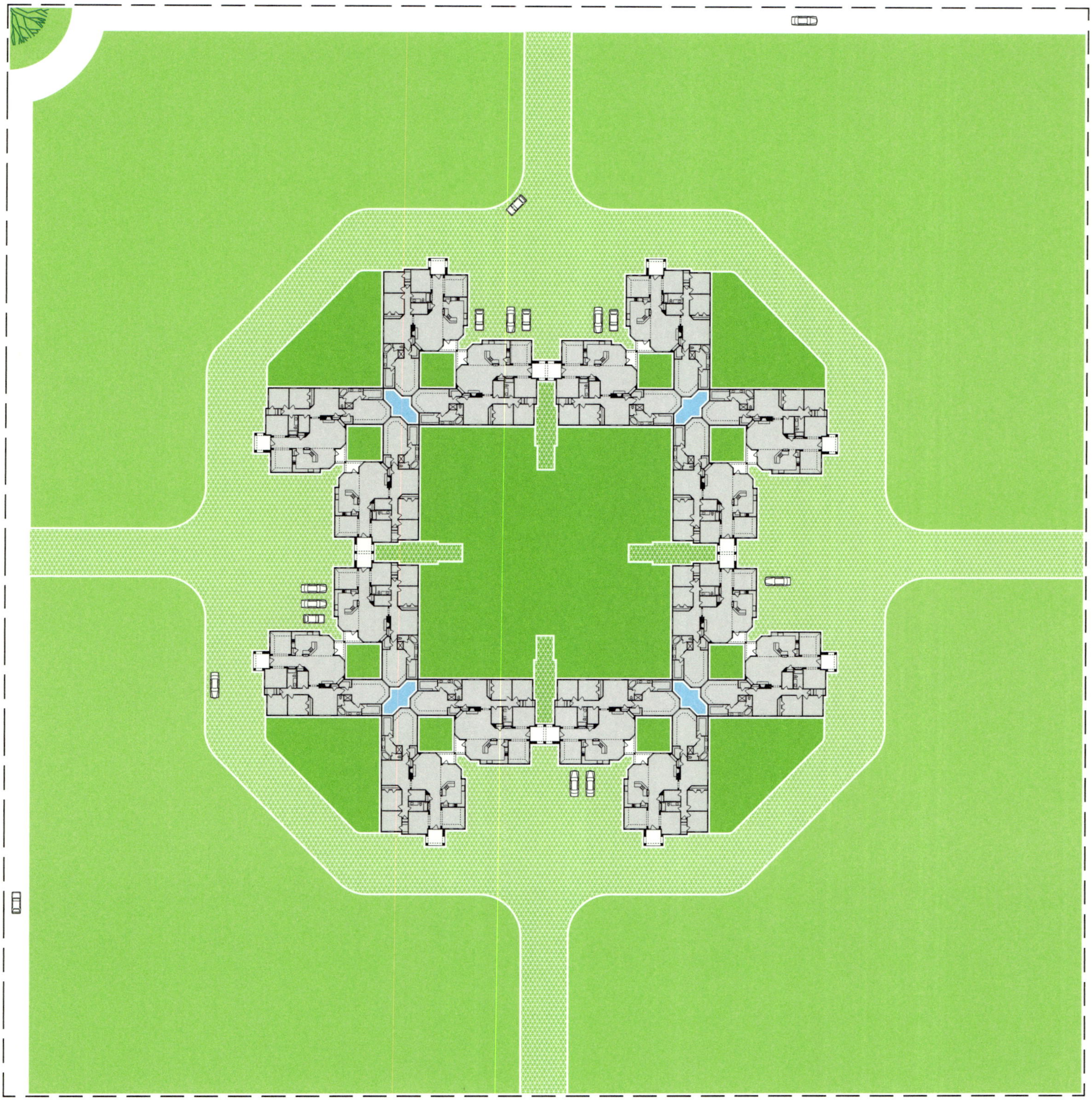

Happy Valley

NW 1/4 NW 1/4 Section 6

16 Houses
38,752 Square Feet
48–64 Bedrooms
32 Full Bathrooms
0 Half Bathrooms

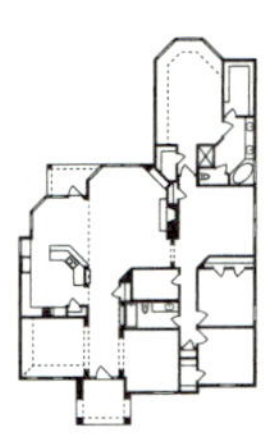

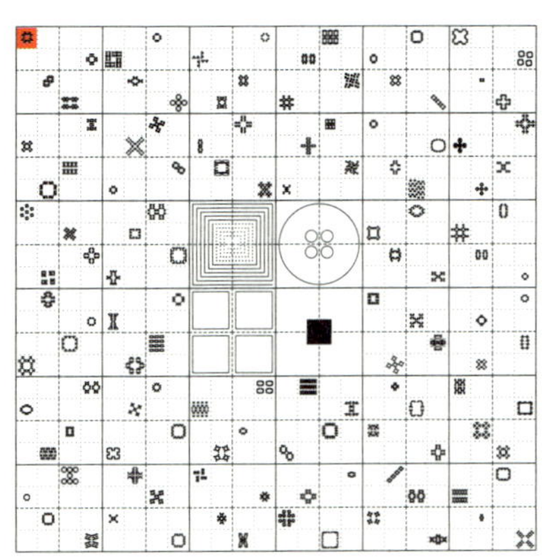

Beazer Homes, The Muirfield, 2422 sq. ft., Texas

Laundry Day at Happy Valley, Freedomland
after *Laundry at the Edge of a River,* 1882
Emilio Sanchez-Perrier

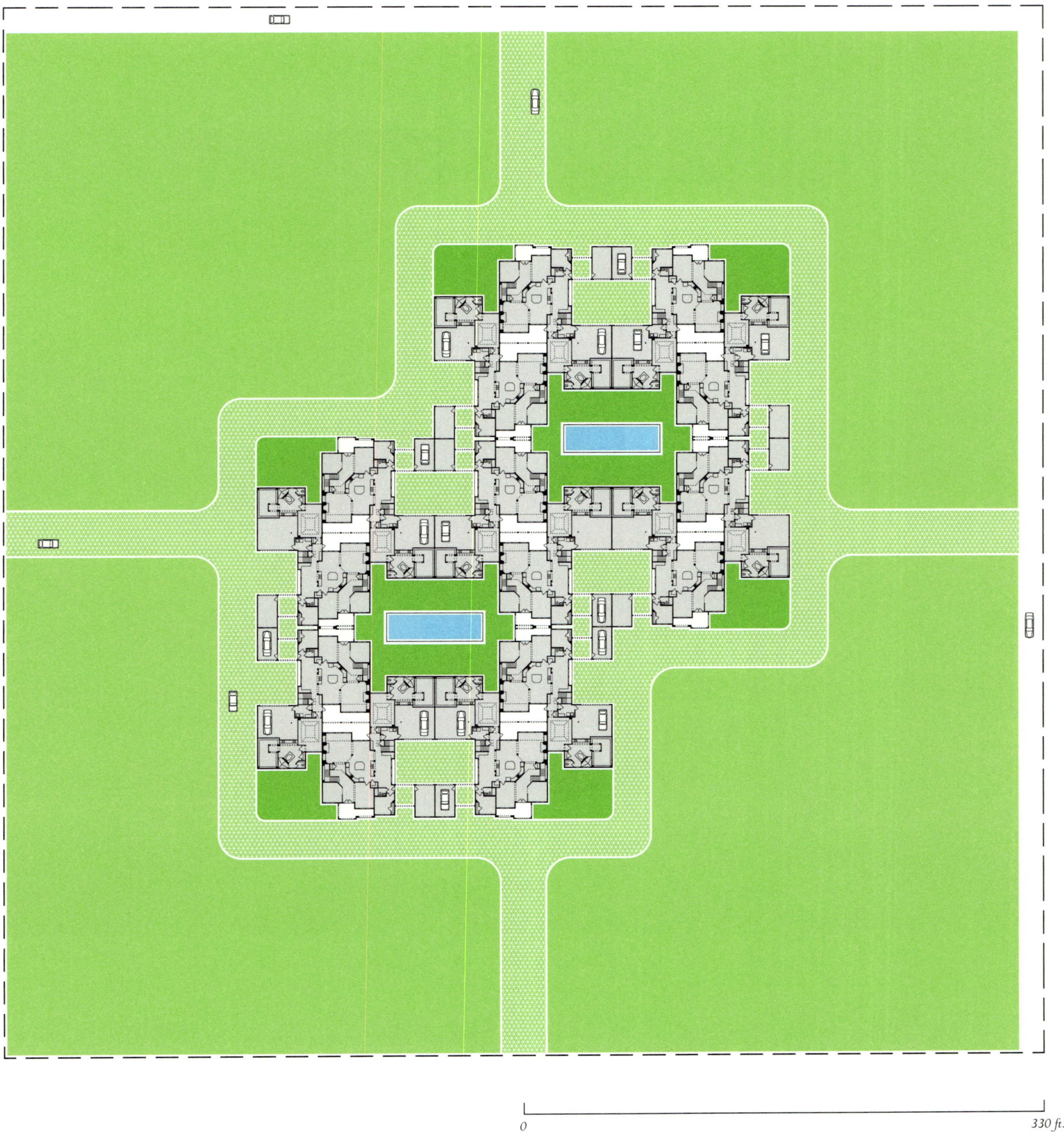

Langford's Pine Valley Estates

NE 1/4 SW 1/4 Section 6

14 Houses
79,184 Square Feet
70 Bedrooms
70 Full Bathrooms
14 Half Bathrooms

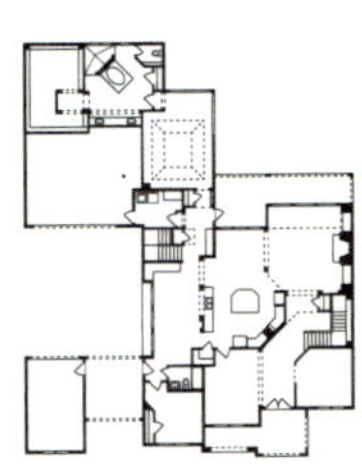

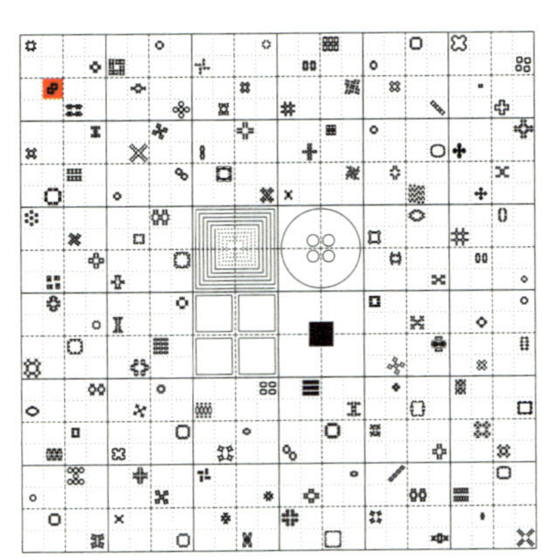

David Weekley Homes, McKeon, 5656 sq. ft., Texas

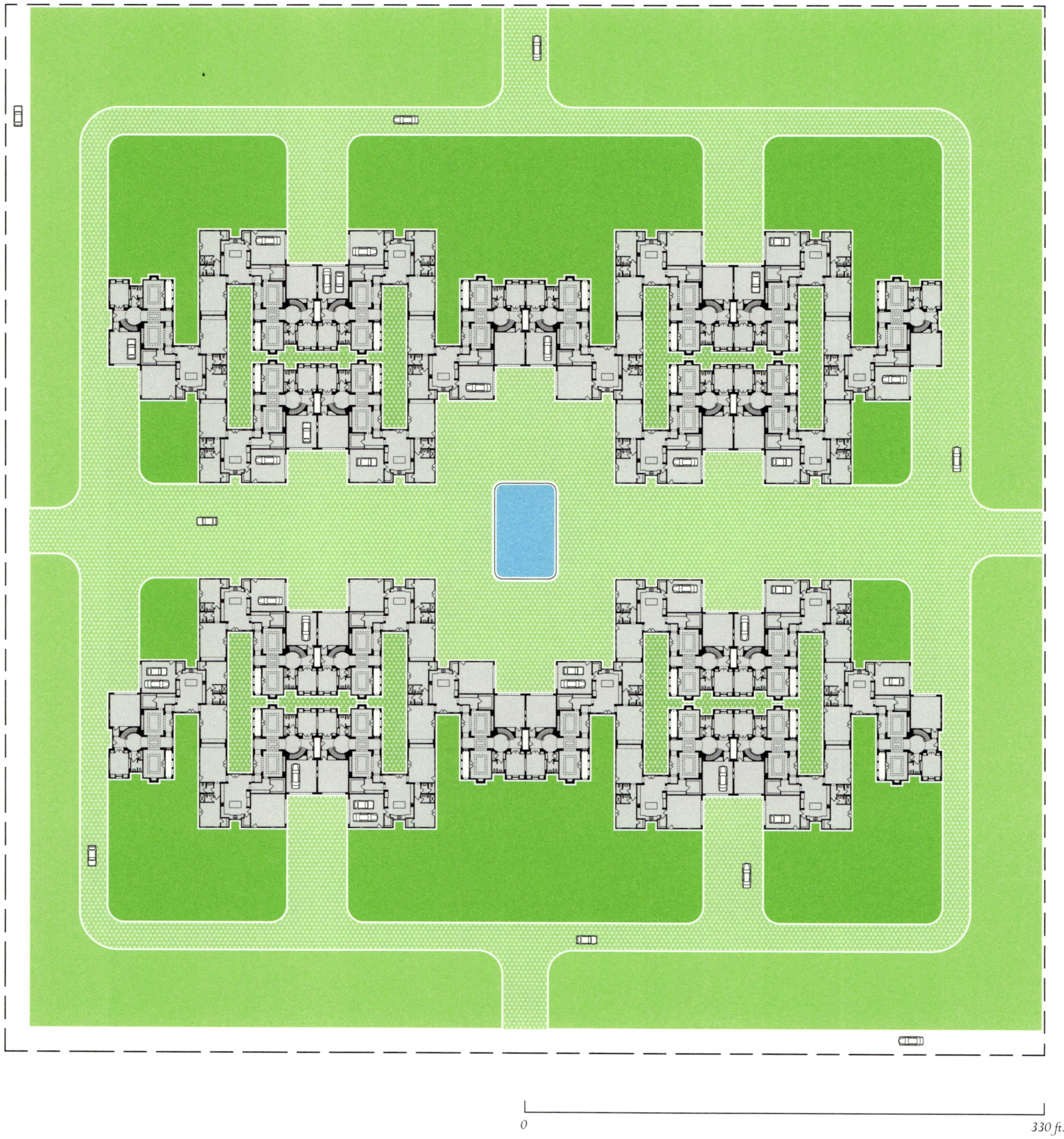

Rudolph's Reserve
SW 1/4 SE 1/4 Section 6

24 Houses
157,392 Square Feet
120 Bedrooms
120 Full Bathrooms
48 Half Bathrooms

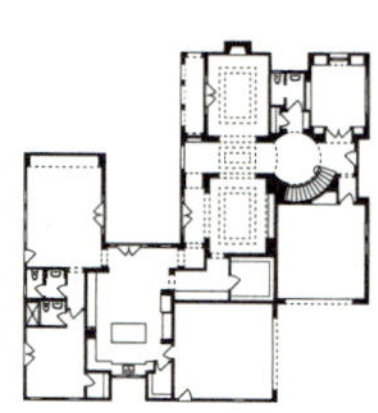

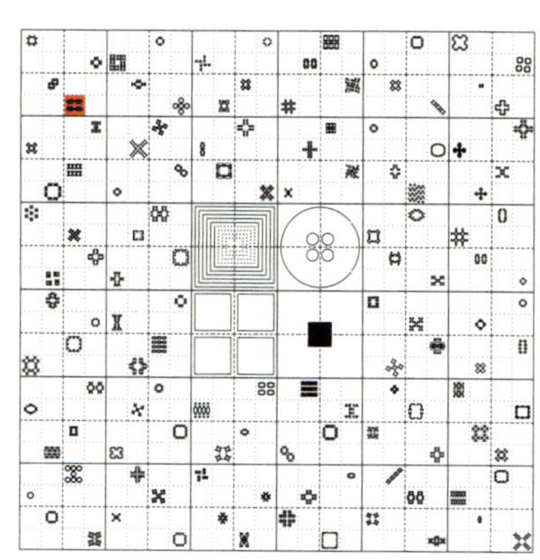

KB Home, The Stratford, 6558 sq. ft., California

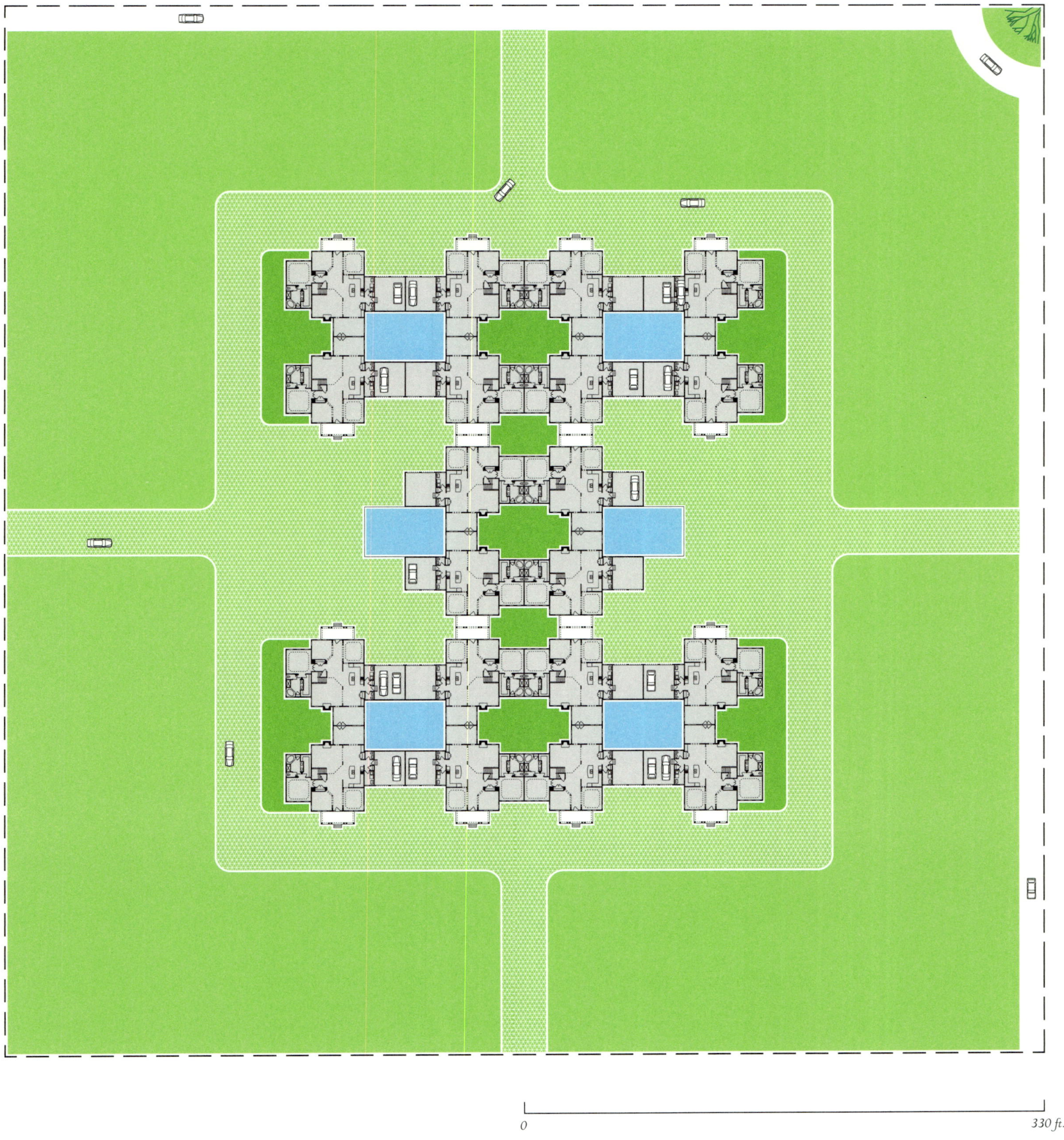

LK Vineyards

NE 1/4 NE 1/4 Section 7

20 Houses
71,680 Square Feet
100 Bedrooms
80 Full Bathrooms
20 Half Bathrooms

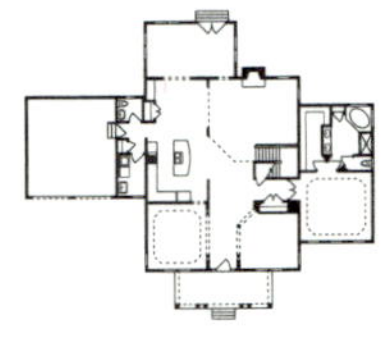

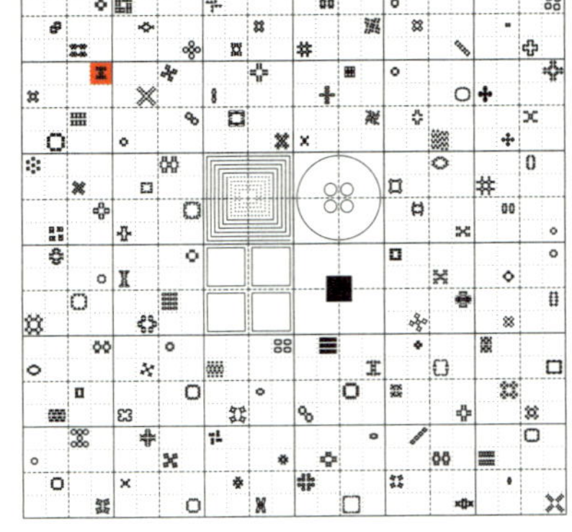

Ryland Homes, The Parson, 3584 sq. ft., Delaware

Brough of Birsay
SW 1/4 NW 1/4 Section 7

16 Houses
58,256 Square Feet
64 Bedrooms
48 Full Bathrooms
16 Half Bathrooms

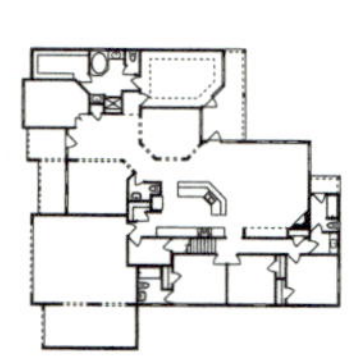

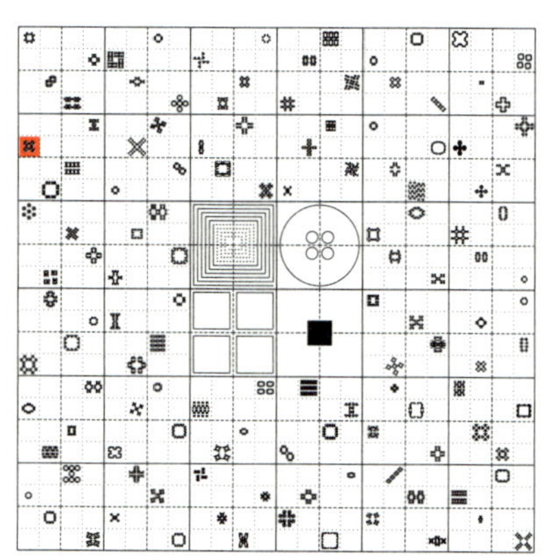

Pulte Homes, Monet, 3641 sq. ft., Texas

Market Day in Garageland, Freedomland
after *Market Scene on a Quay,* 1635–1640
Frans Snyders

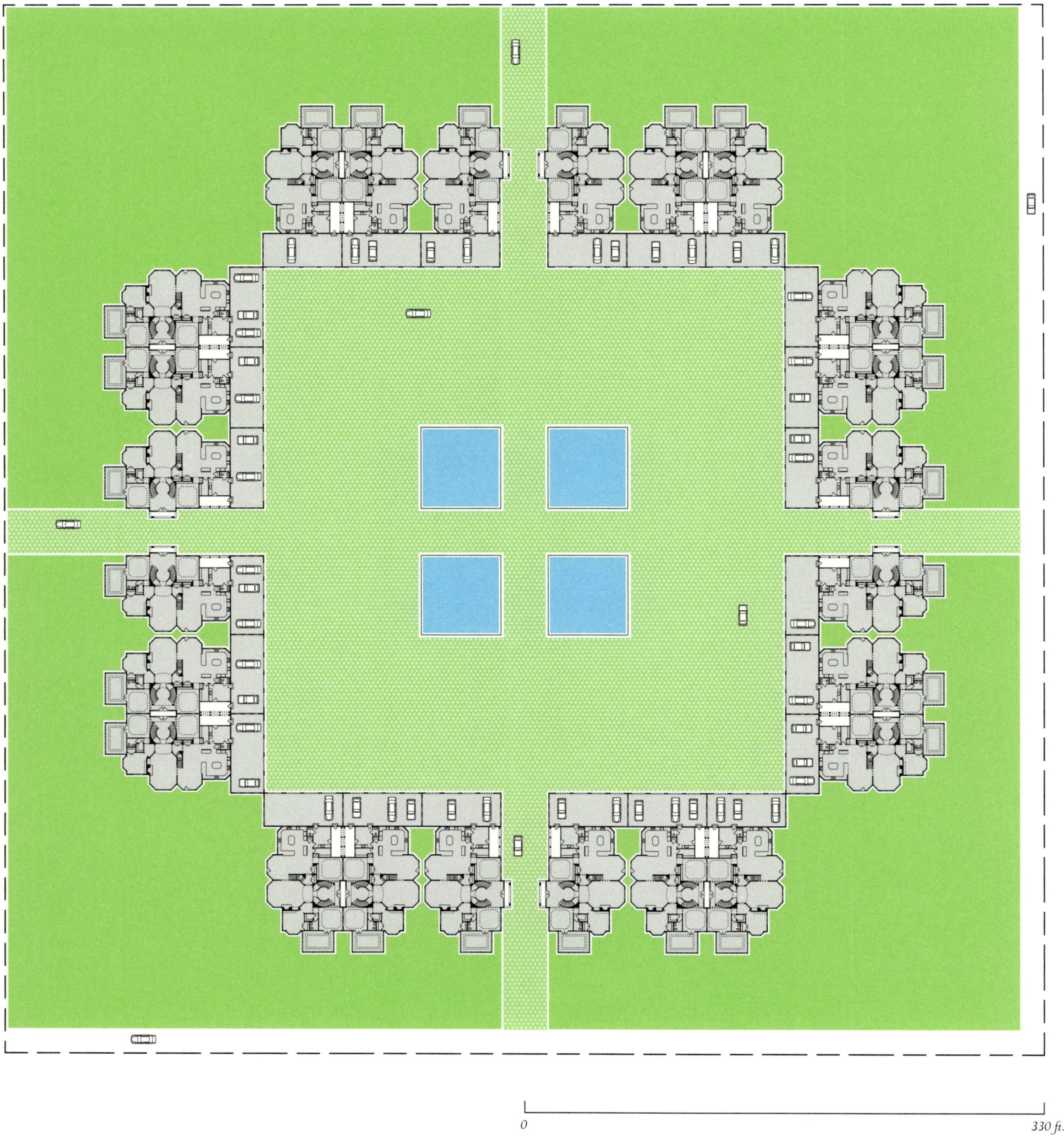

Garageland

SE 1/4 SW 1/4 Section 7

24 Houses
127,800 Square Feet
96 Bedrooms
96 Full Bathrooms
48 Half Bathrooms

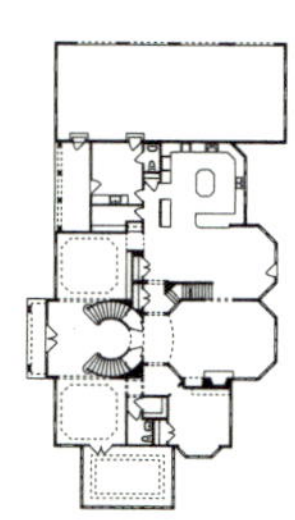

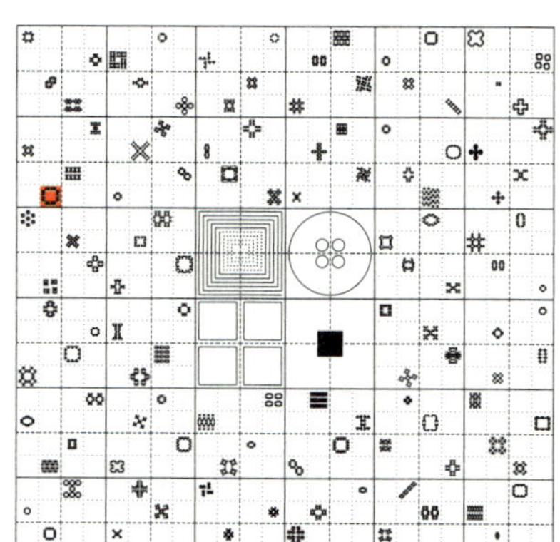

K. Hovnanian Homes, The Tara, 5325 sq. ft., Maryland

Estate of Mind

NW 1/4 SE 1/4 Section 7

32 Houses
121,600 Square Feet
96–160 Bedrooms
128 Full Bathrooms
32 Half Bathrooms

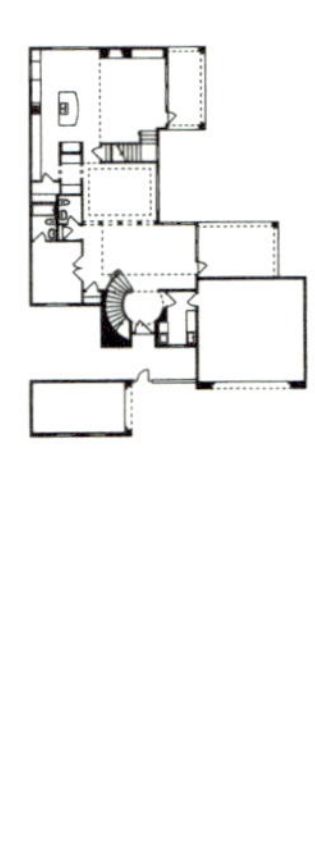

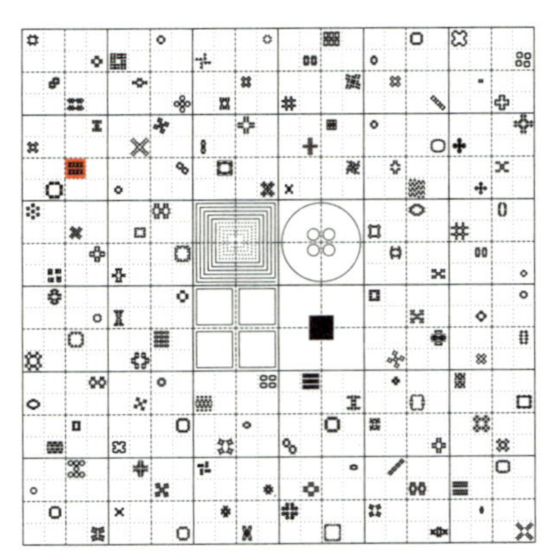

Pulte Homes, The Provence, 3800 sq. ft., Nevada

0 330 ft.

Ville d'Anelle

NW 1/4 NE 1/4 Section 8

20 Houses
95,000 Square Feet
120–140 Bedrooms
80 Full Bathrooms
20 Half Bathrooms

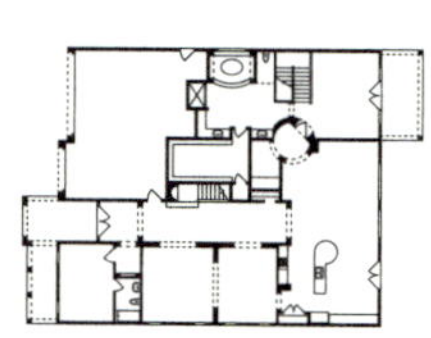

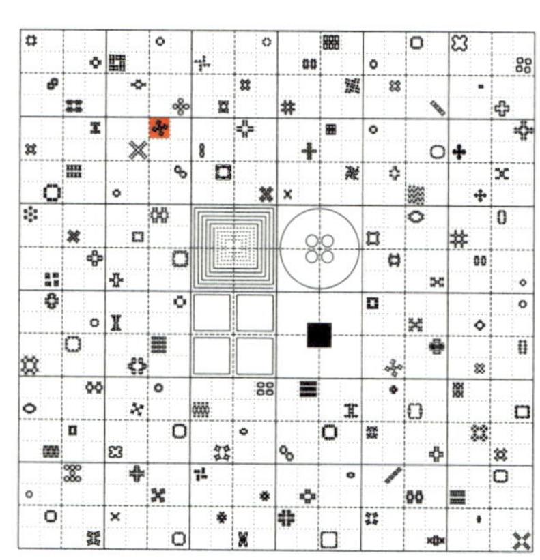

Richmond American Homes, Picasso, 4750 sq. ft., Arizona

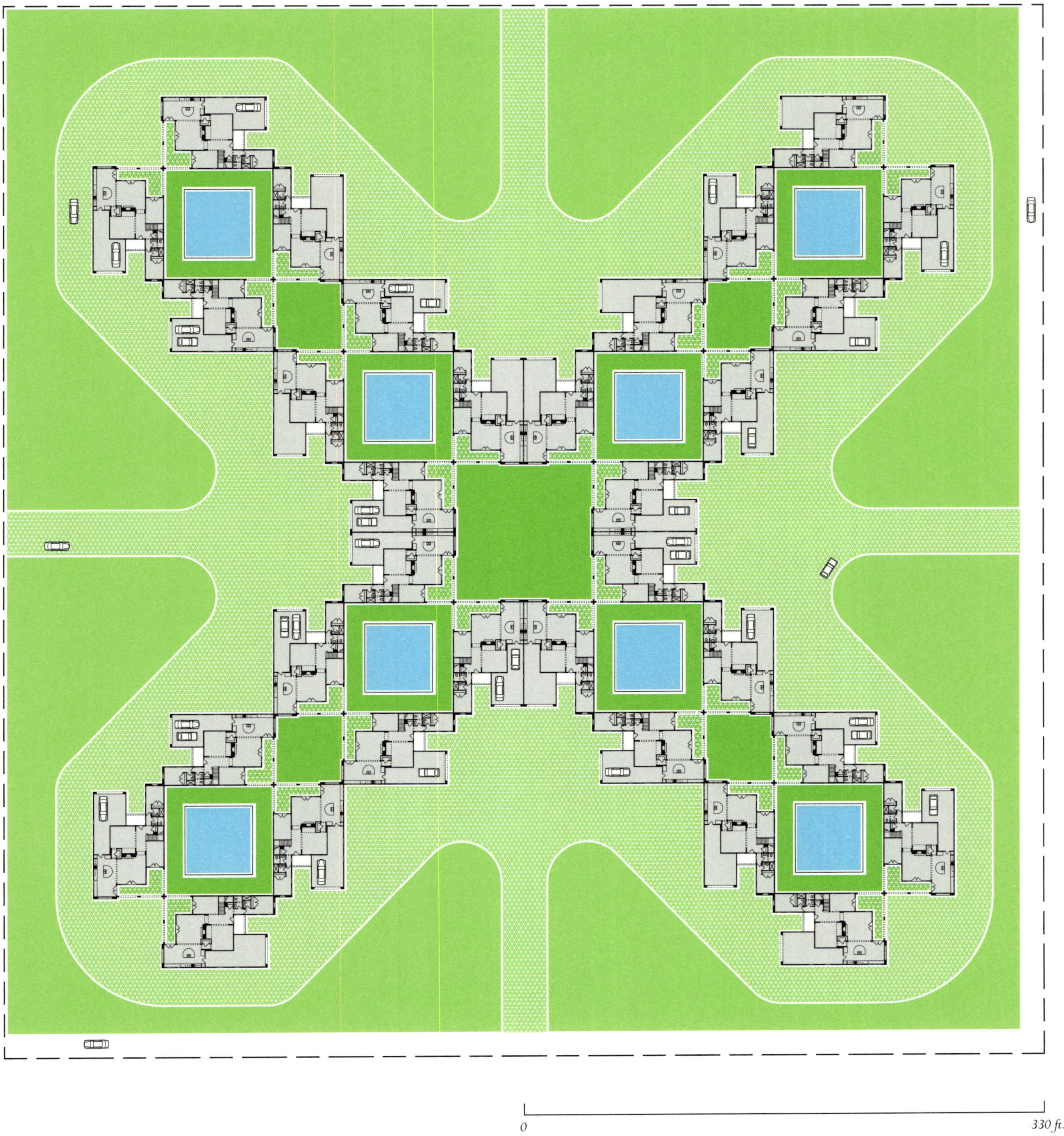

Citizen Farms

SE 1/4 NW 1/4 Section 8

32 Houses
124,544 Square Feet
160 Bedrooms
128 Full Bathrooms
32 Half Bathrooms

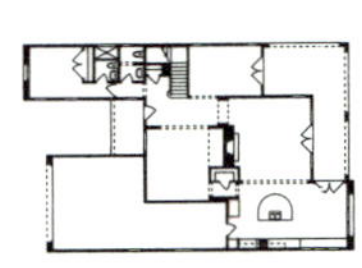

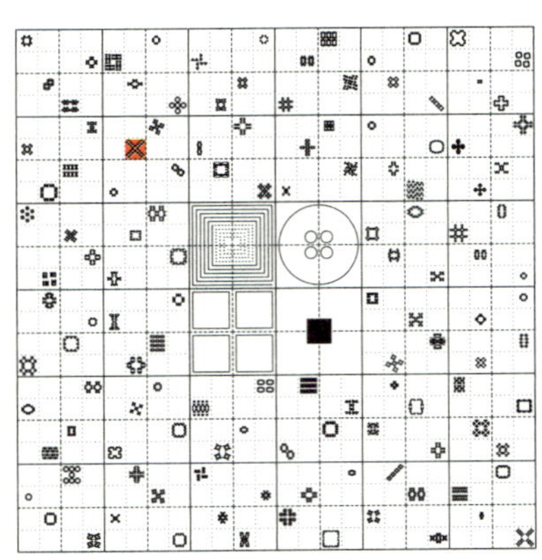

Shea Homes, Plan 4 at Vista Vallerta, 3892 sq. ft., California

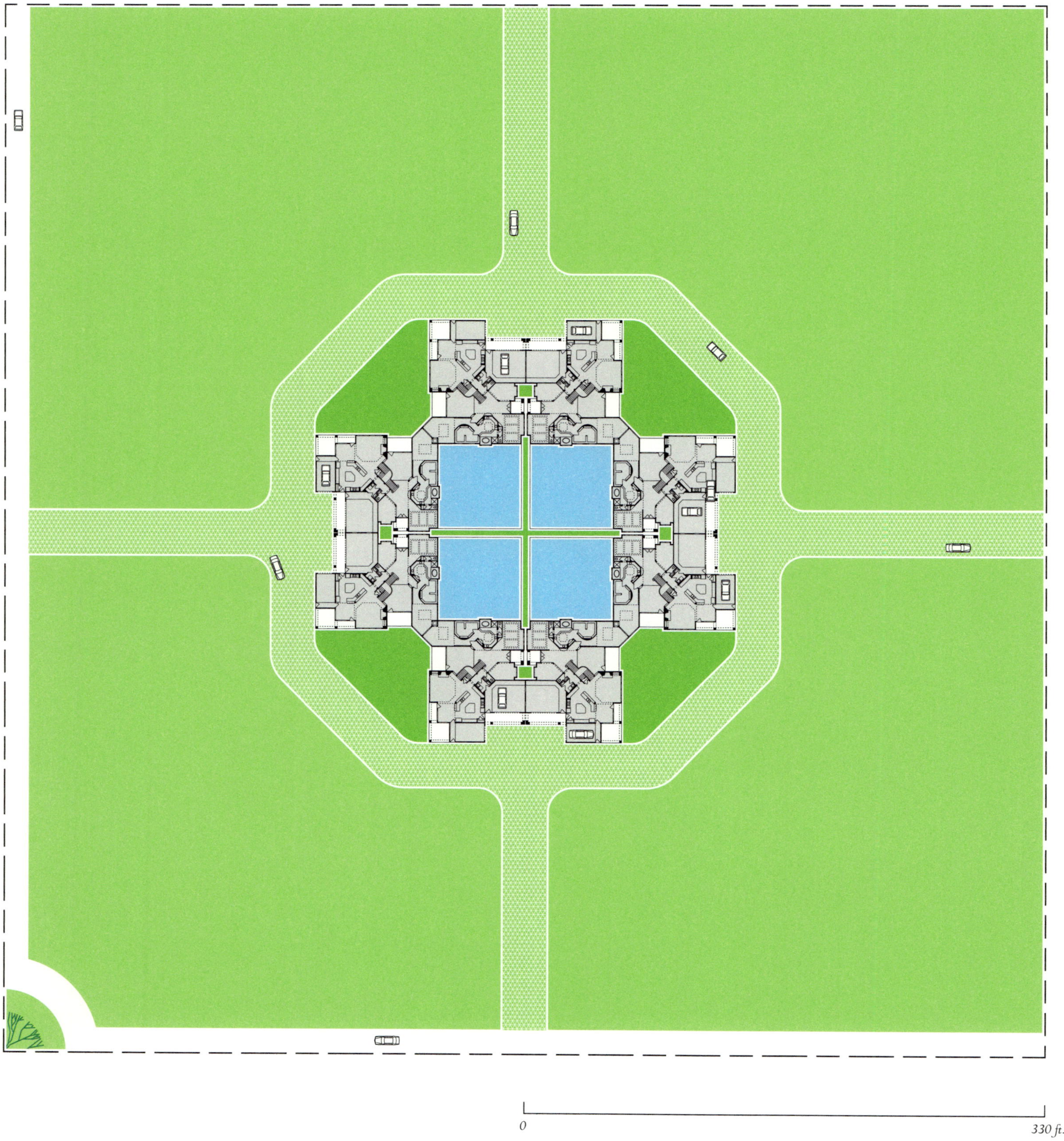

La Quinta de Zeiger

SW 1/4 SW 1/4 Section 8

8 Houses
35,680 Square Feet
32–40 Bedrooms
24–32 Full Bathrooms
8 Half Bathrooms

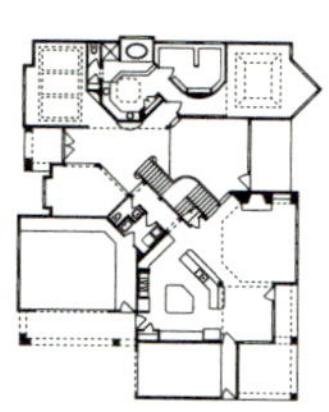

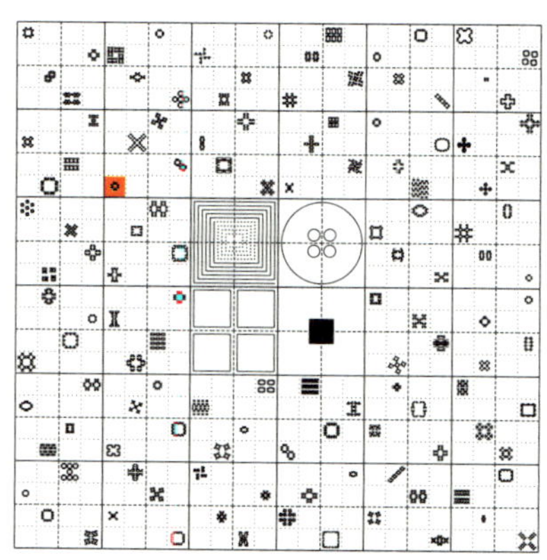

David Weekley Homes, The Kramer, 4460 sq. ft., Texas

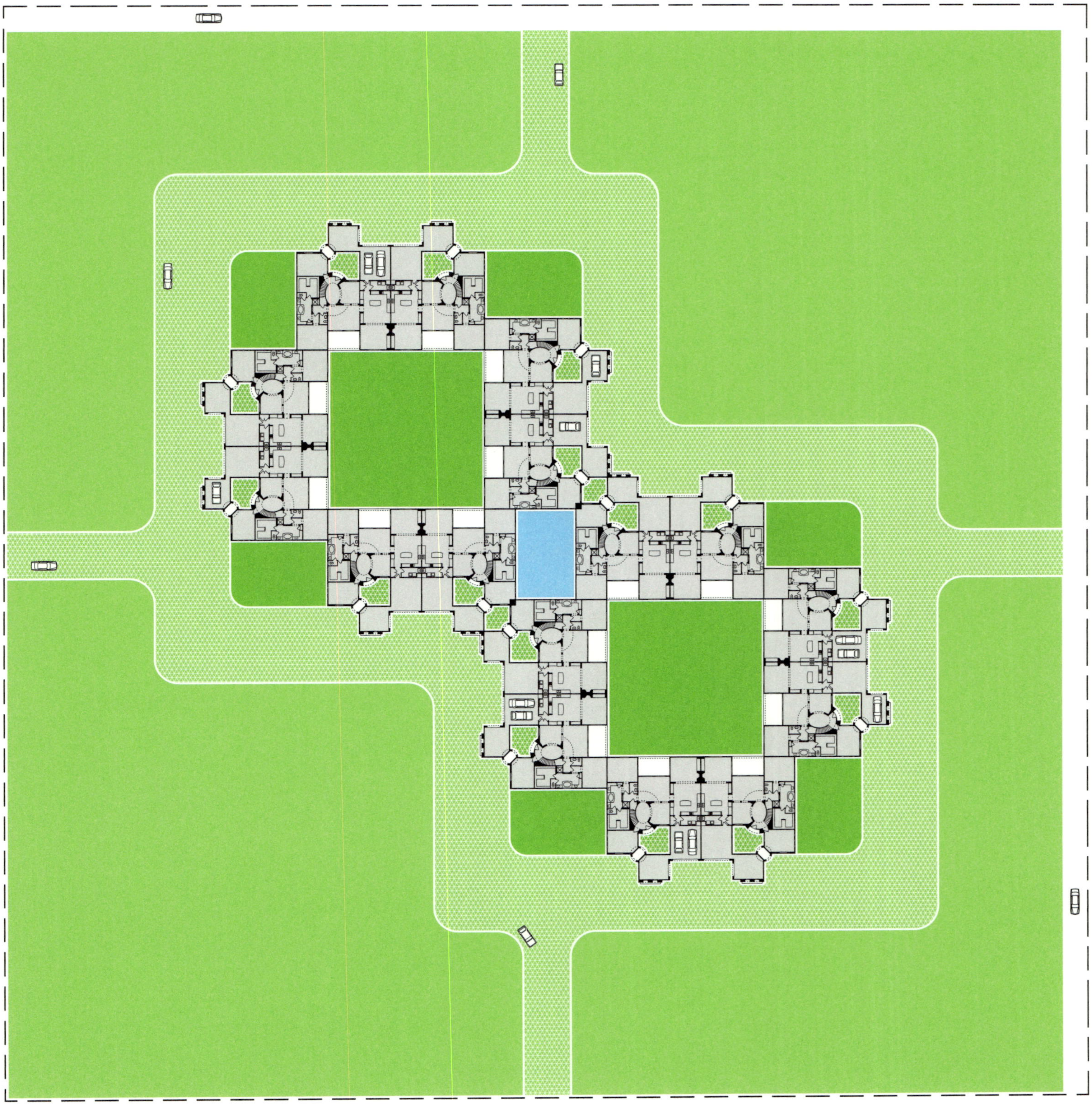

Scharmen's Overlook
NE 1/4 SE 1/4 Section 8

16 Houses
65,008 Square Feet
64 Bedrooms
48 Full Bathrooms
16 Half Bathrooms

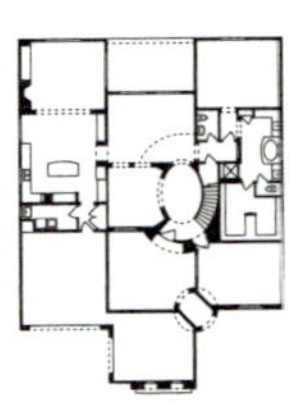

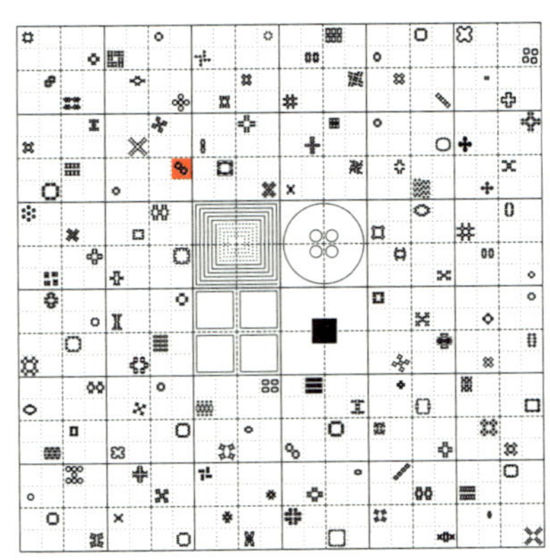

Del Webb, Mirasol, 4063 sq. ft., Arizona

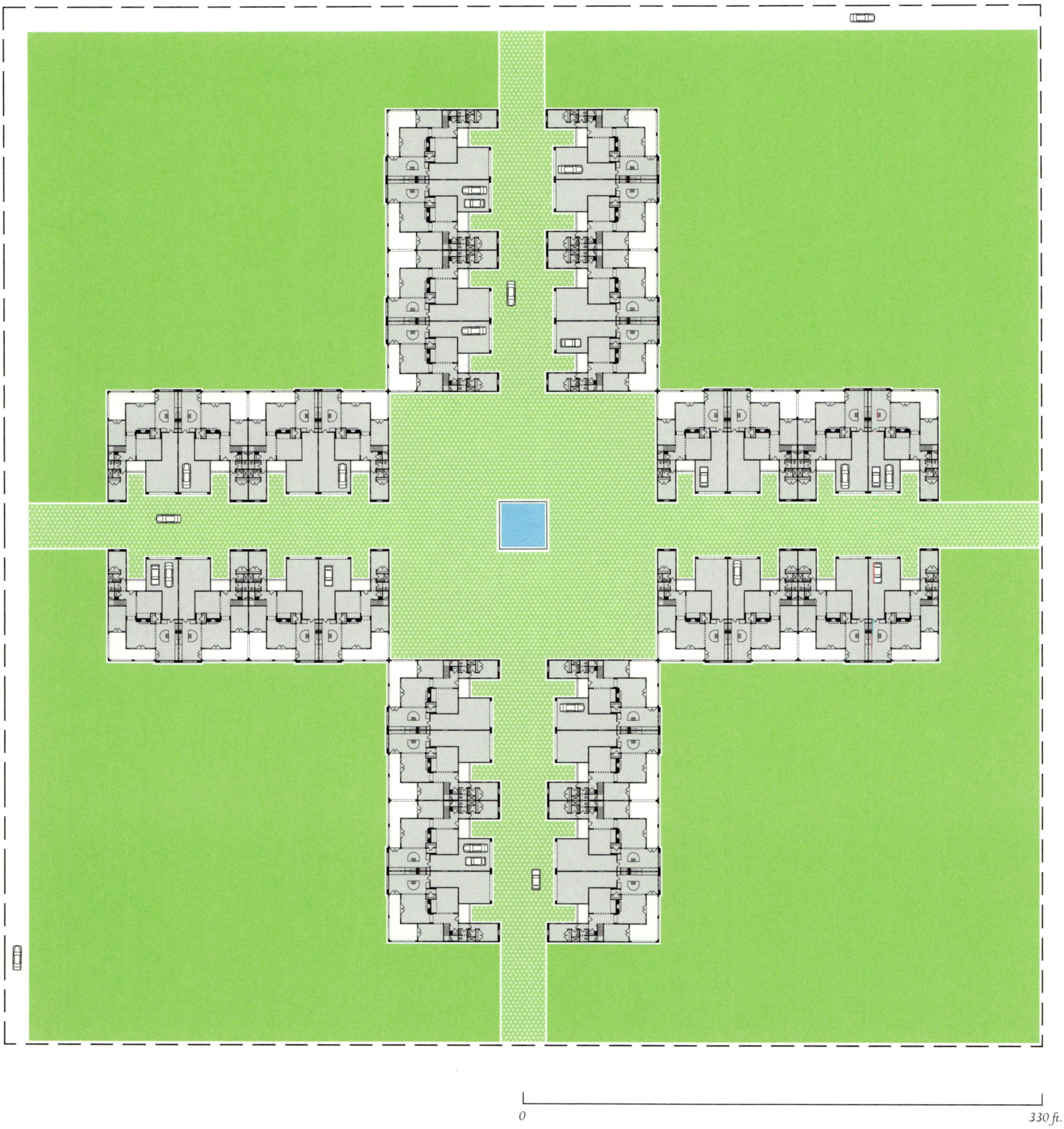

La Croix Brillante

NW 1/4 NE 1/4 Section 9

32 Houses
124,544 Square Feet
160 Bedrooms
128 Full Bathrooms
32 Half Bathrooms

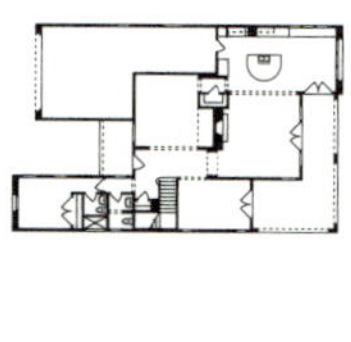

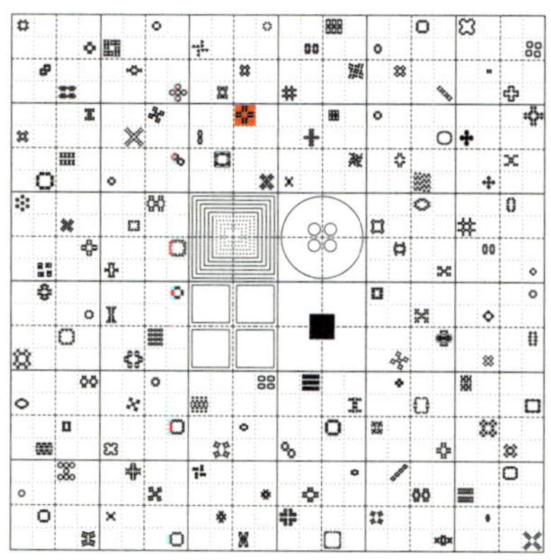

Shea Homes, Plan 4 at Vista Vallerta, 3892 sq. ft., California

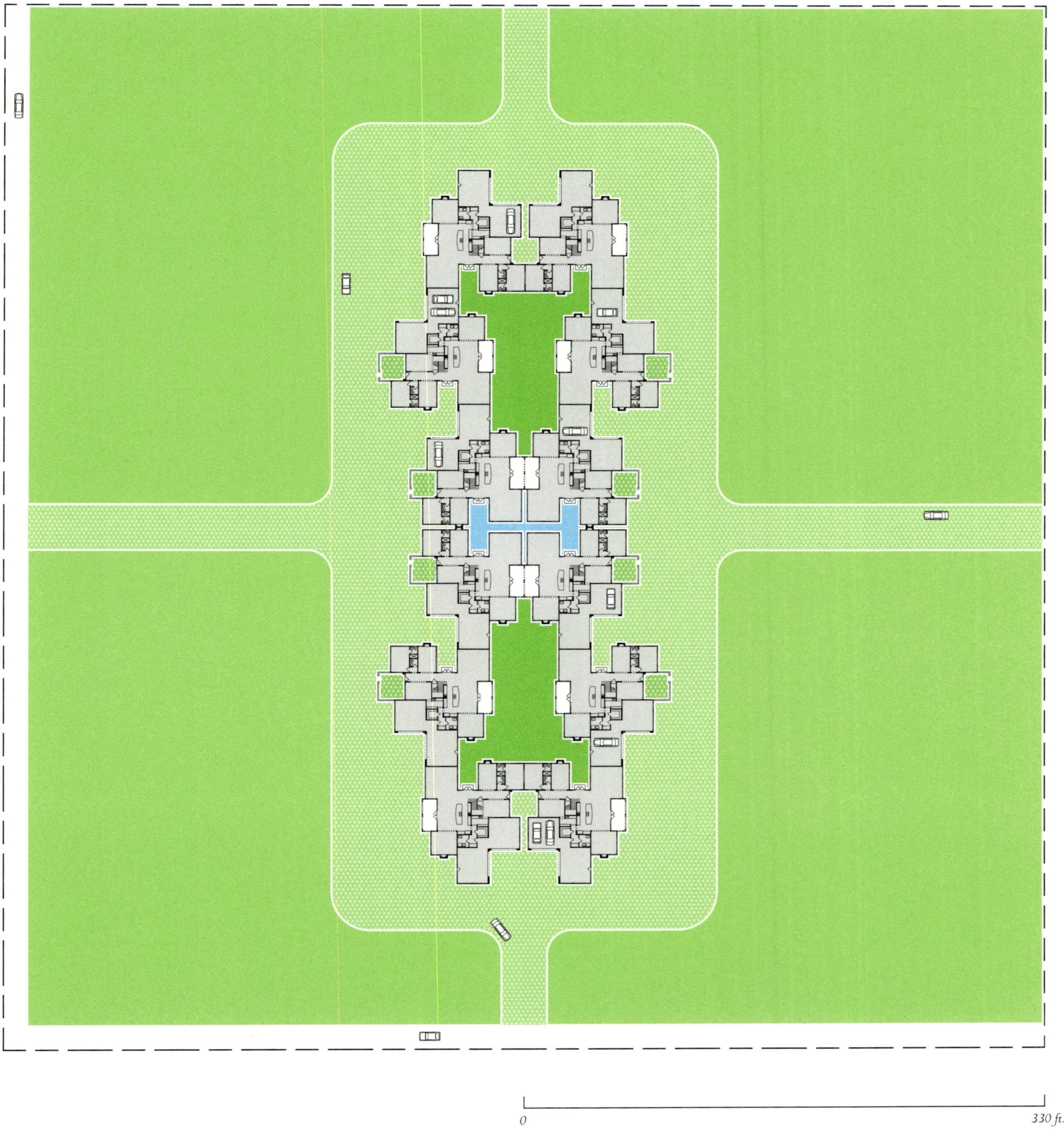

Habitat

SW 1/4 NW 1/4 Section 9

12 Houses
55,500 Square Feet
48 Bedrooms
48 Full Bathrooms
24 Half Bathrooms

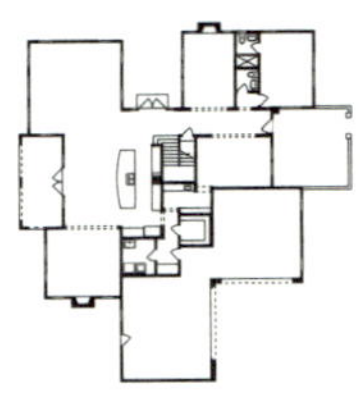

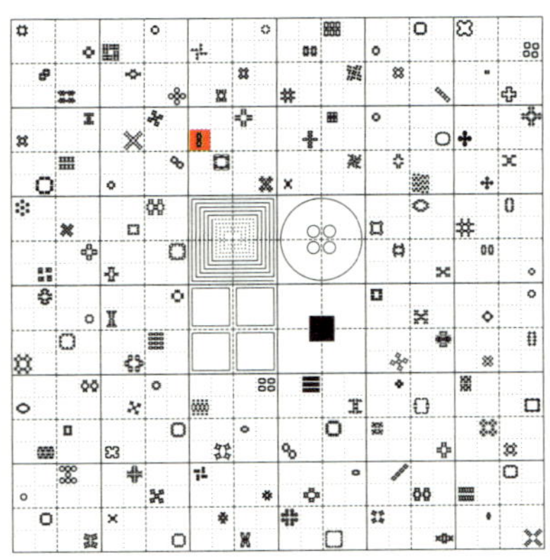

Shea Homes, Plan 2 at Maravilla, 4625 sq. ft., California

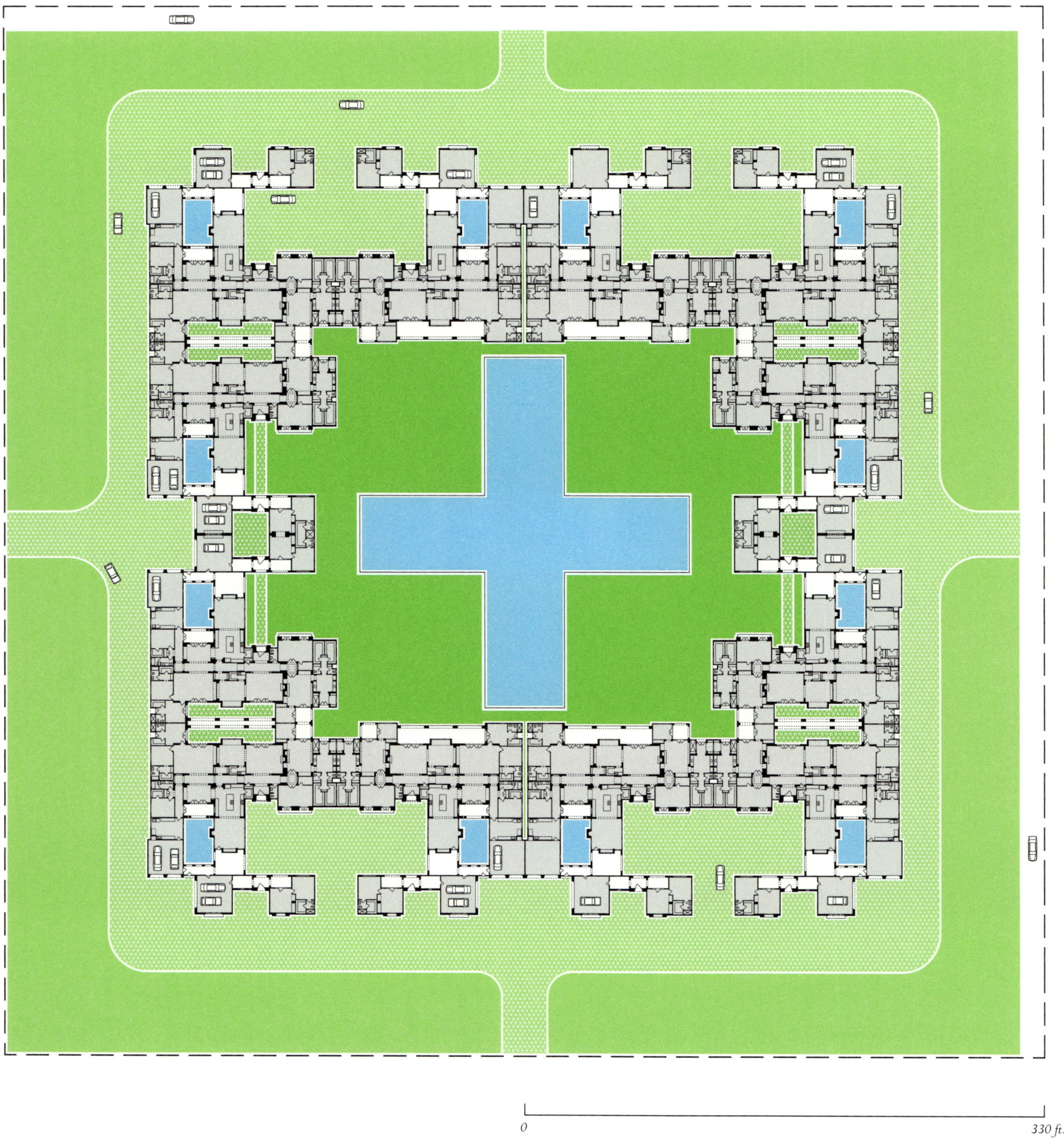

Palazzo del Popolo di Otto Totti
NE 1/4 SW 1/4 Section 9

12 Houses
73,200 Square Feet
60–72 Bedrooms
60–72 Full Bathrooms
12 Half Bathrooms

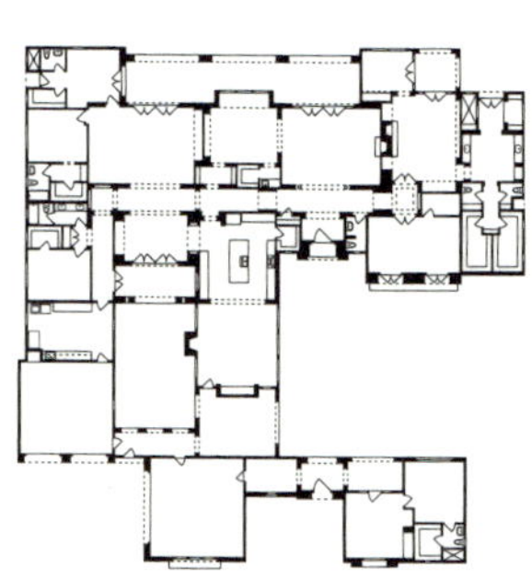

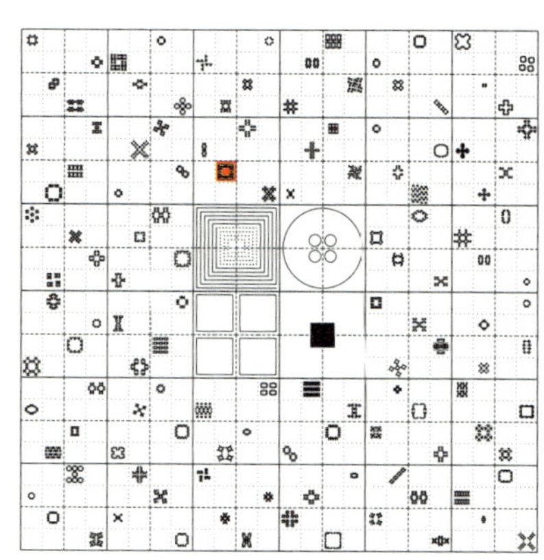

Toll Brothers, The Terreno, 6100 sq. ft., Arizona

Gathering Flowers near Neo-Palladian Acres, Freedomland
after *Girl in a Field,* 1857
Ludwig Knaus

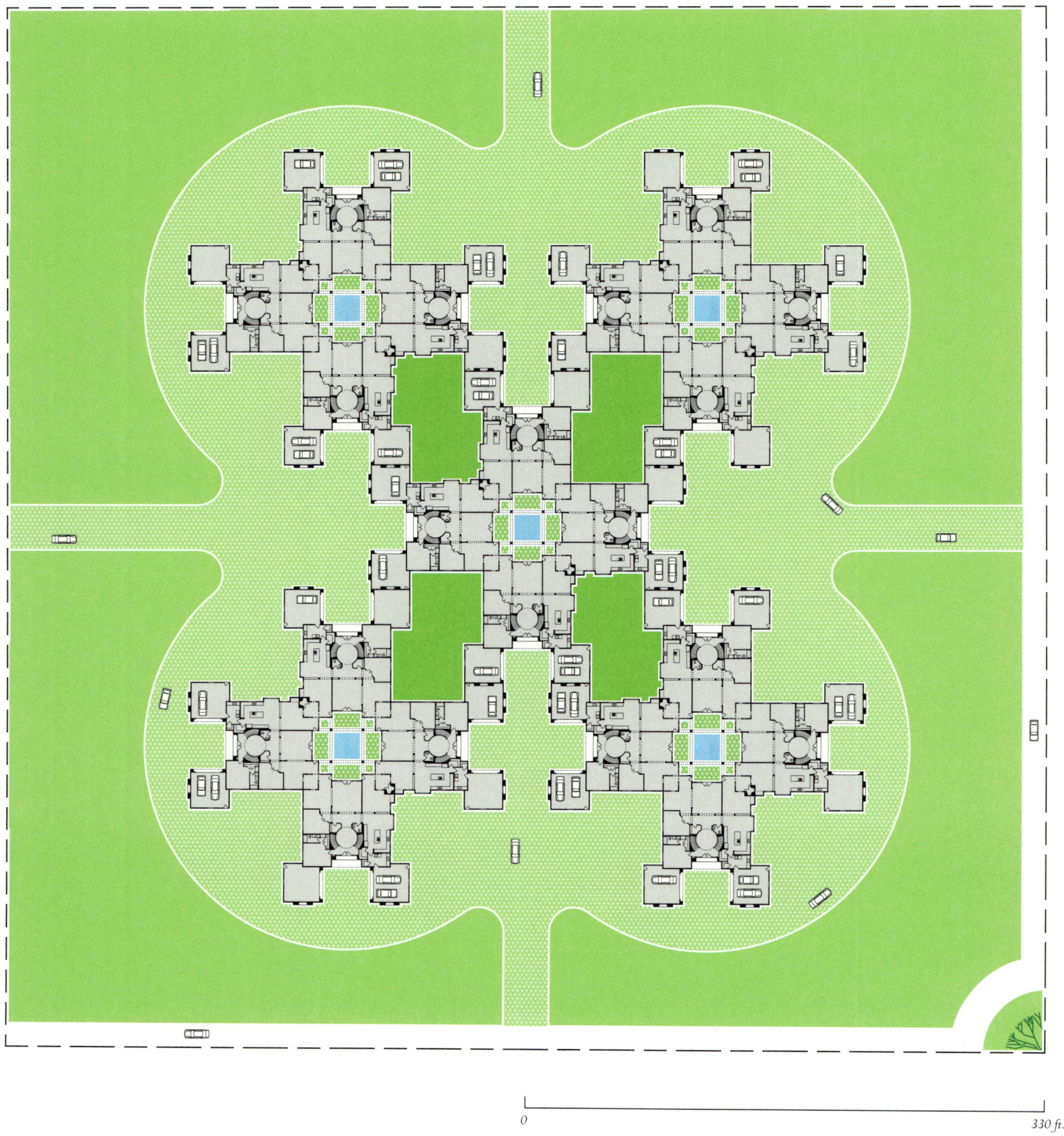

Neo-Palladian Acres

SE 1/4 SE 1/4 Section 9

20 Houses
102,500 Square Feet
80–100 Bedrooms
80 Full Bathrooms
20 Half Bathrooms

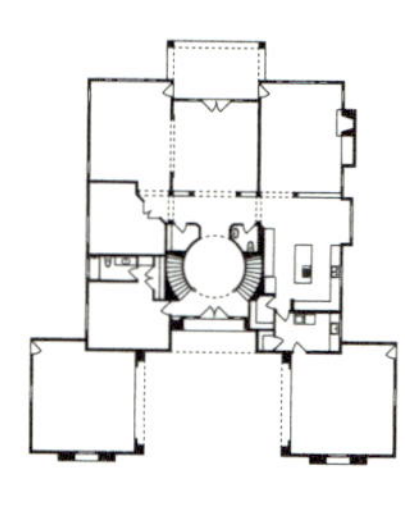

Toll Brothers, The Mirador, 5125 sq. ft., Arizona

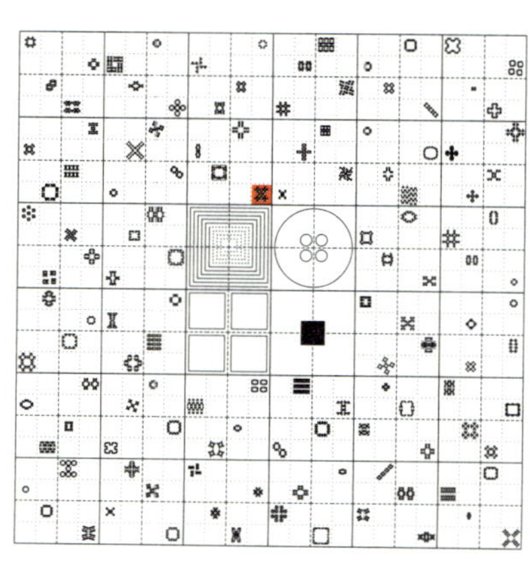

Il Super Studios

NW 1/4 NE 1/4 Section 10

24 Houses
58,128 Square Feet
72–96 Bedrooms
48 Full Bathrooms
0 Half Bathrooms

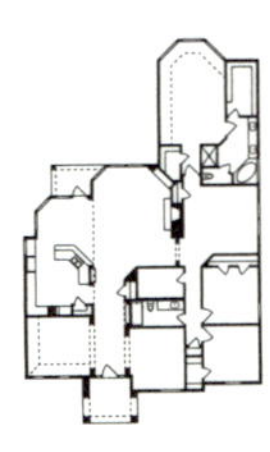

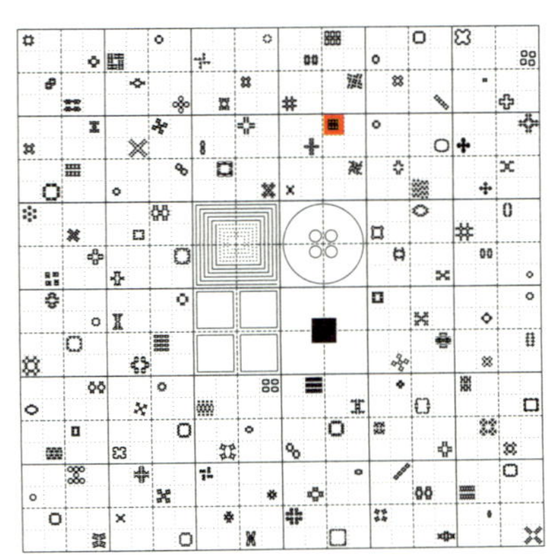

Beazer Homes, The Muirfield, 2422 sq. ft., Texas

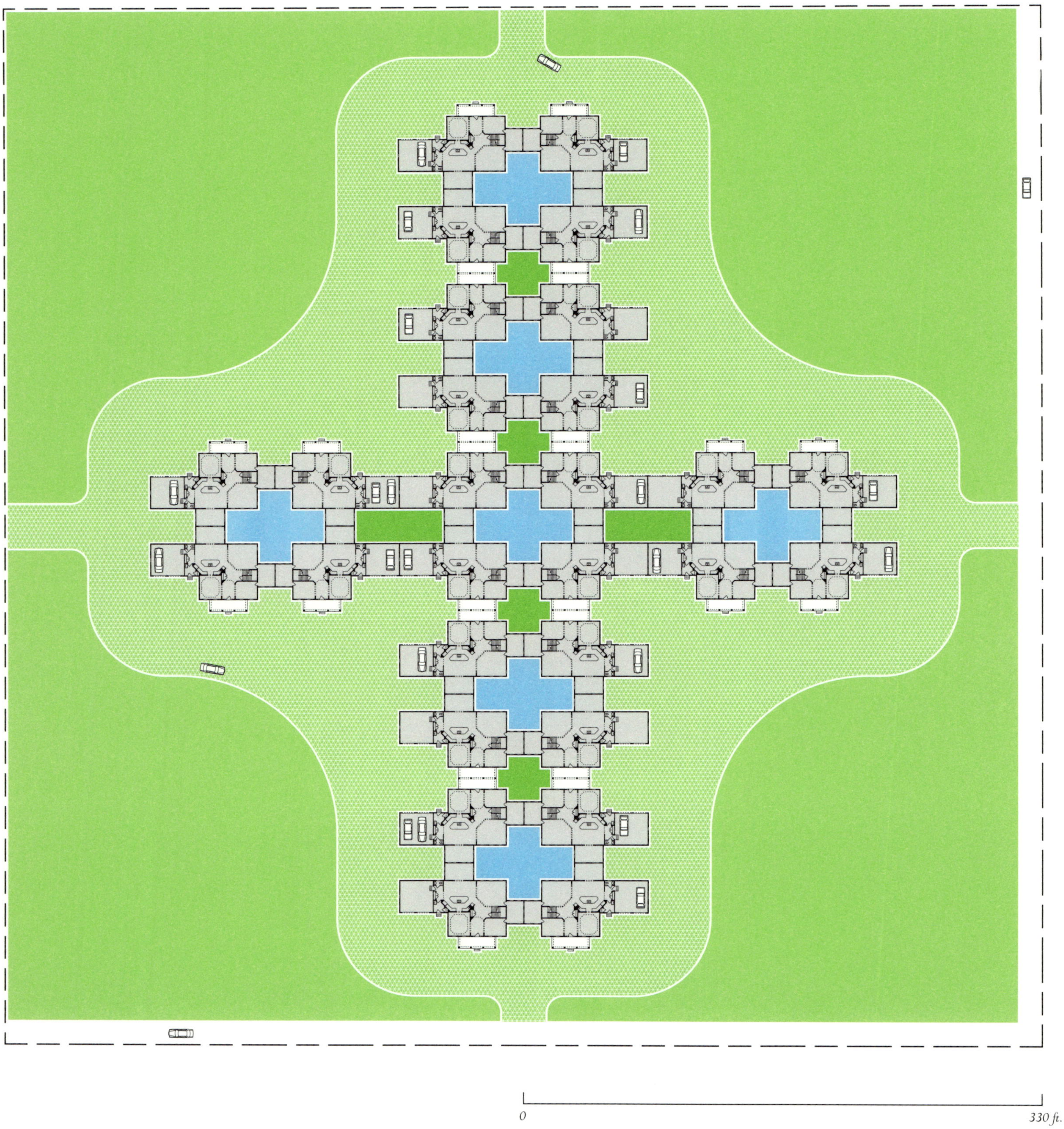

A Model Modern Paradise

SE 1/4 NW 1/4 Section 10

28 Houses
103,684 Square Feet
84 Bedrooms
56 Full Bathrooms
28 Half Bathrooms

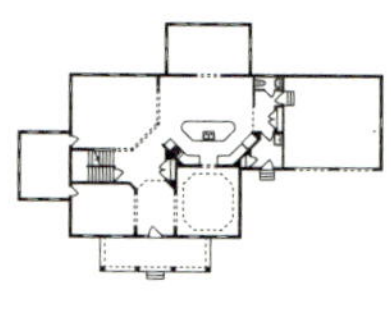

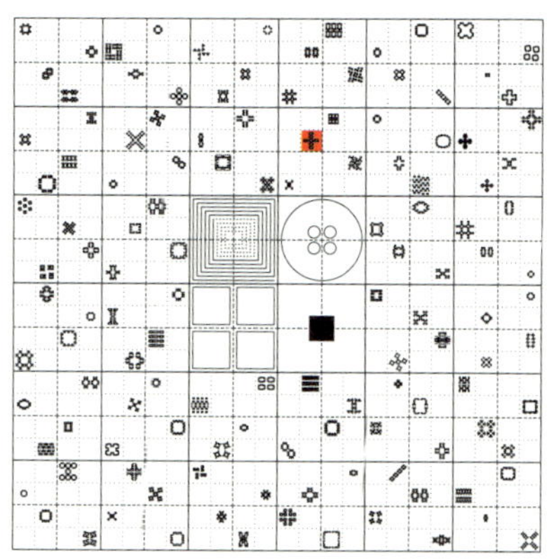

Ryland Homes, The Wye, 3703 sq. ft., Delaware

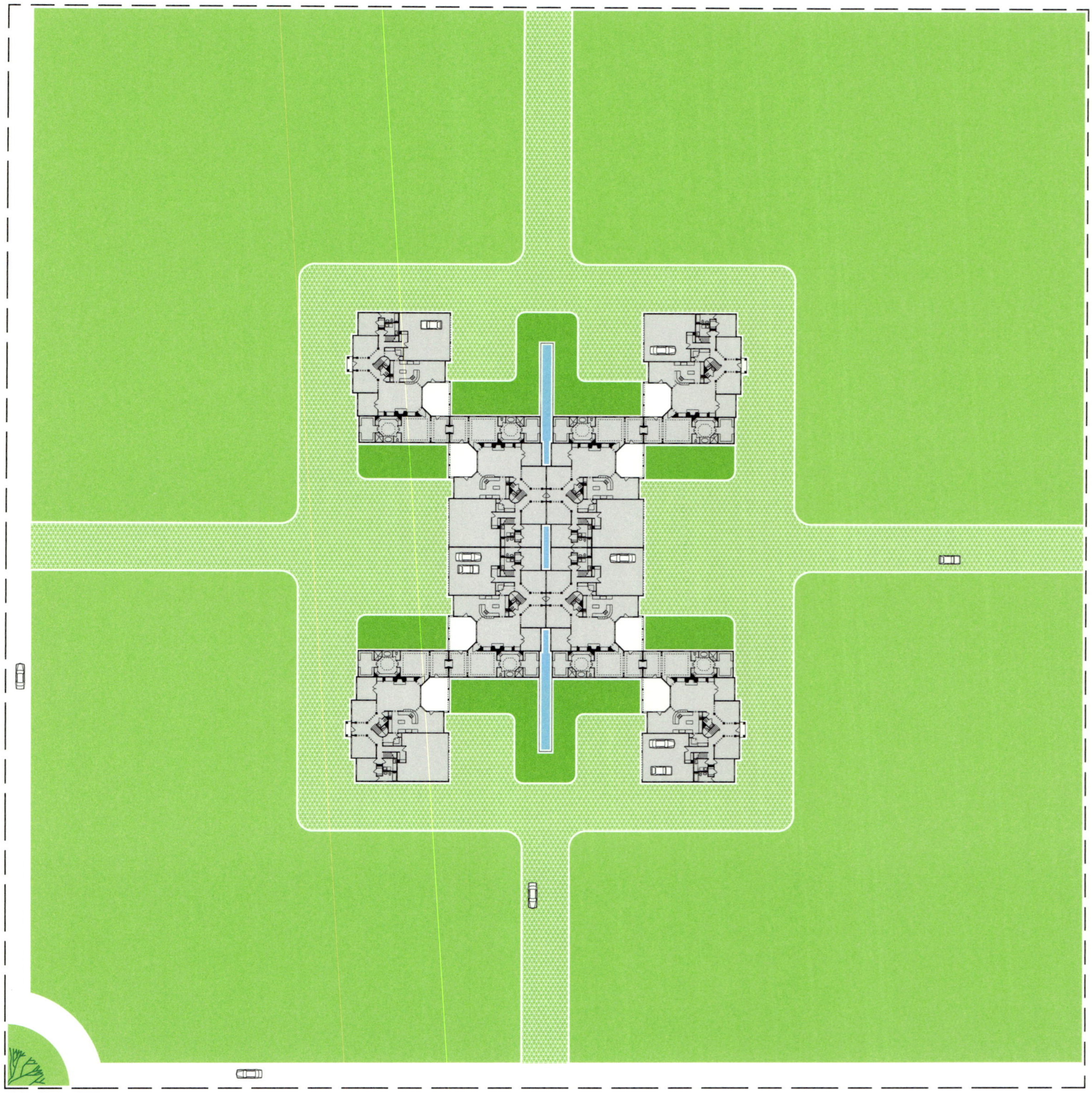

Riley's Safe House

SW 1/4 SW 1/4 Section 10

8 Houses
44,568 Square Feet
40 Bedrooms
40 Full Bathrooms
8 Half Bathrooms

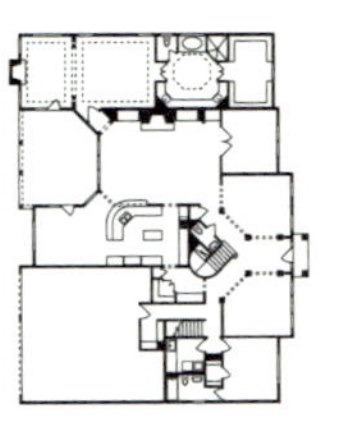

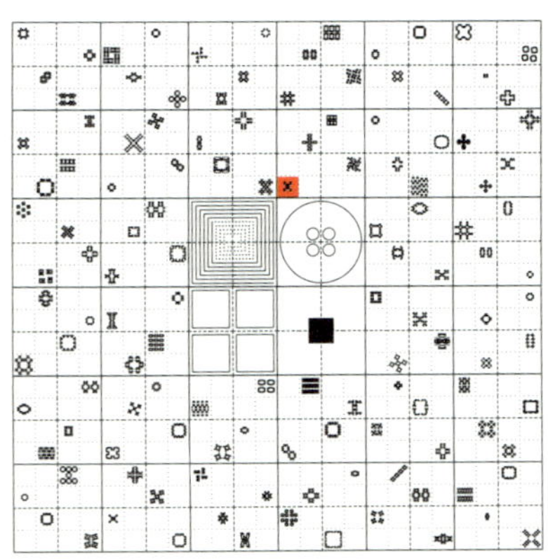

Beazer Homes, Versailles, 5571 sq. ft., Tennessee

Huge Acres

NE 1/4 SE 1/4 Section 10

20 Houses
113,120 Square Feet
100 Bedrooms
100 Full Bathrooms
20 Half Bathrooms

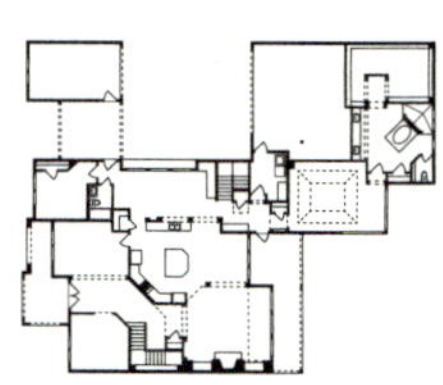

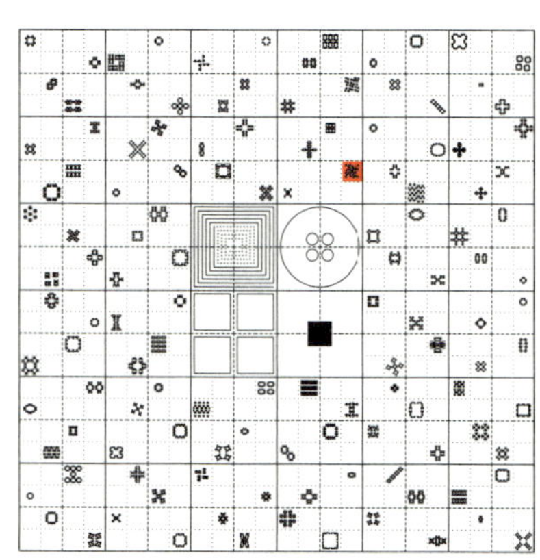

David Weekley Homes, McKeon, 5656 sq. ft., Texas

High in the air, soaring over an ocean of verdure, I assemble all the powers. I am going to apportion the earth. I will endow it with the brilliance that the sun, at its apogee, refuses to those countries darkened by the cold shadows of the north. I will revive the marvelous fields of the most august antiquity. There I will sow the seeds of the arts; I will develop their resources to ensure the happiness of mankind.

—Claude Nicolas Ledoux, *Architecture Considered in Relation to Art, Mores, and Legislation*, 1804.

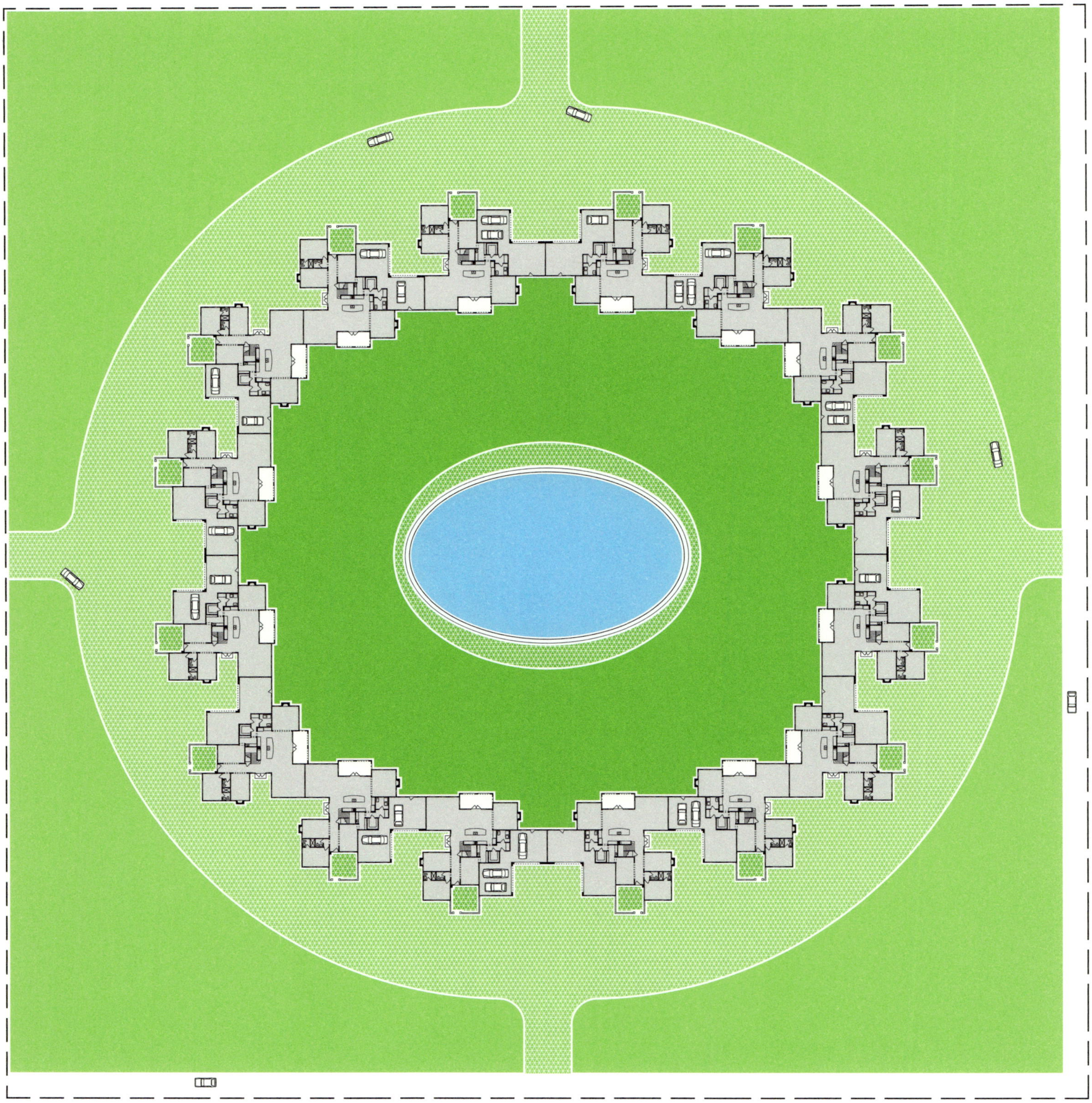

Cirque de Besançon

SE 1/4 NE 1/4 Section 11

16 Houses
74,000 Square Feet
64 Bedrooms
64 Full Bathrooms
32 Half Bathrooms

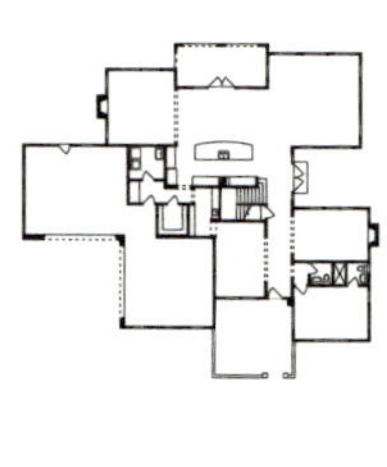

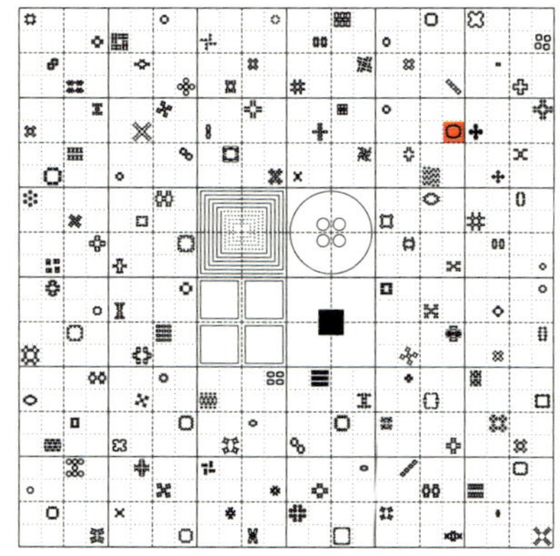

Shea Homes, Plan 2 at Maravilla, 4625 sq. ft., California

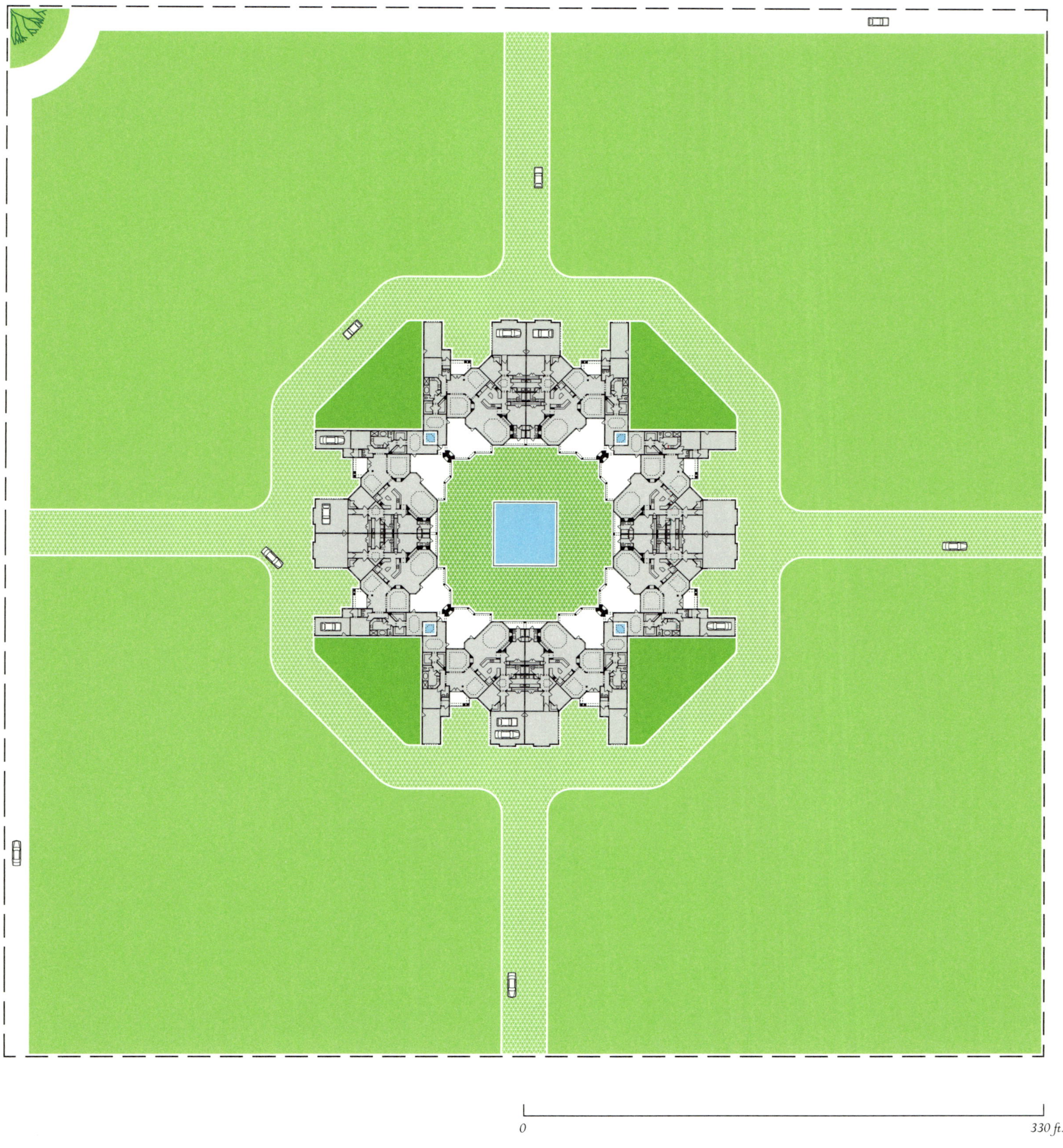

Fresca

NW 1/4 NW 1/4 Section 11

8 Houses
25,784 Square Feet
32 Bedrooms
24 Full Bathrooms
8 Half Bathrooms

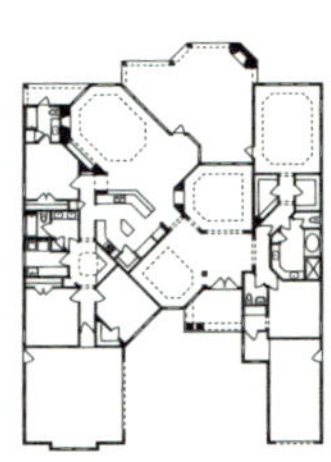

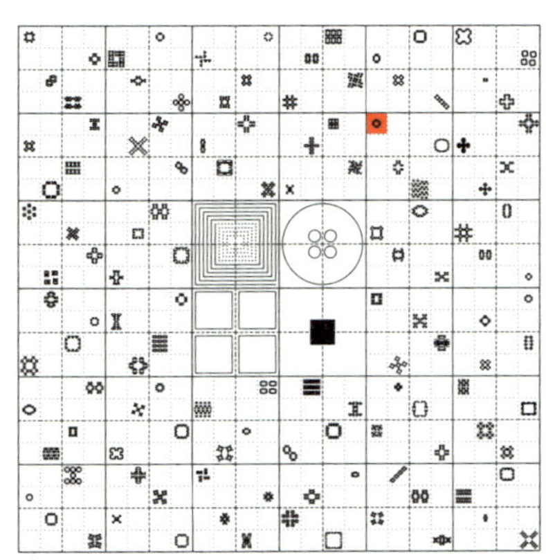

Ryland Homes, Suffolk, 3223 sq. ft., Florida

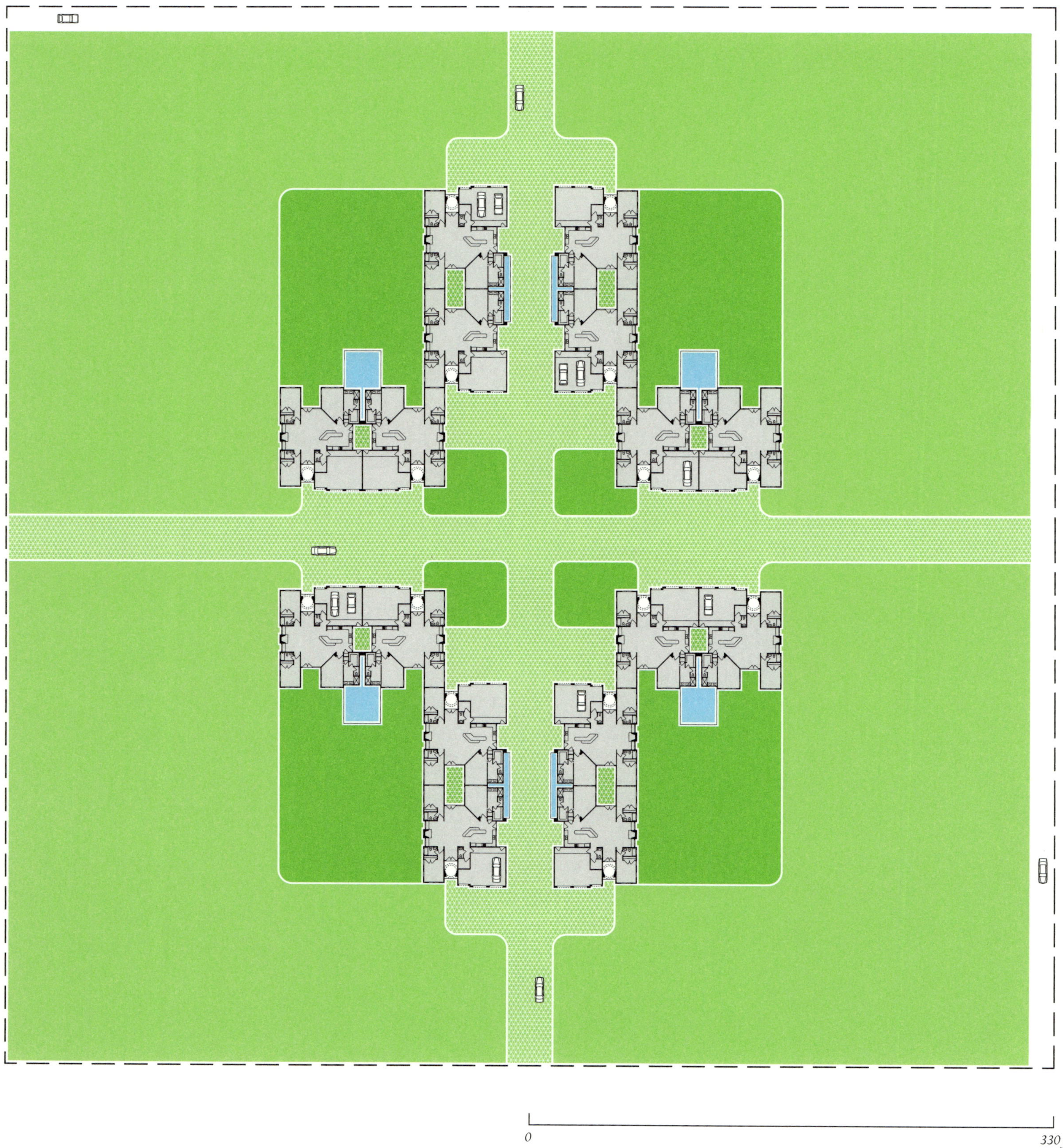

Bald Bend

NE 1/4 SW 1/4 Section 11

16 Houses
33,392 Square Feet
48 Bedrooms
48 Full Bathrooms
16 Half Bathrooms

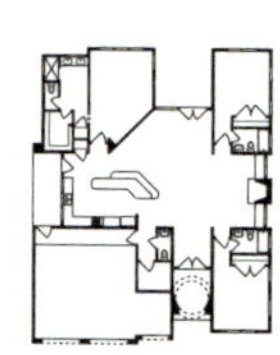

Avatar Homes, Valderama, 2087 sq. ft., Arizona

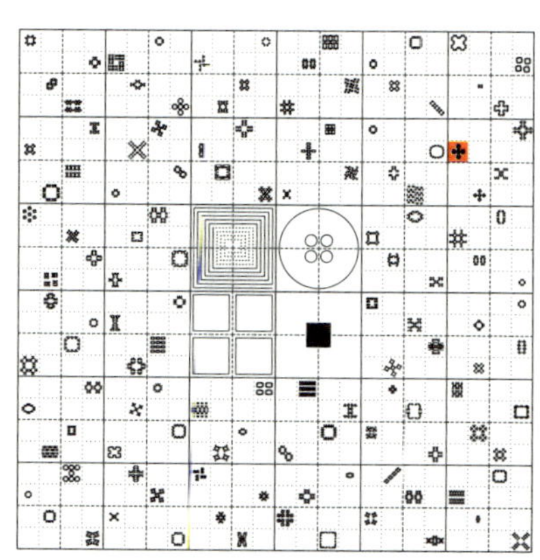

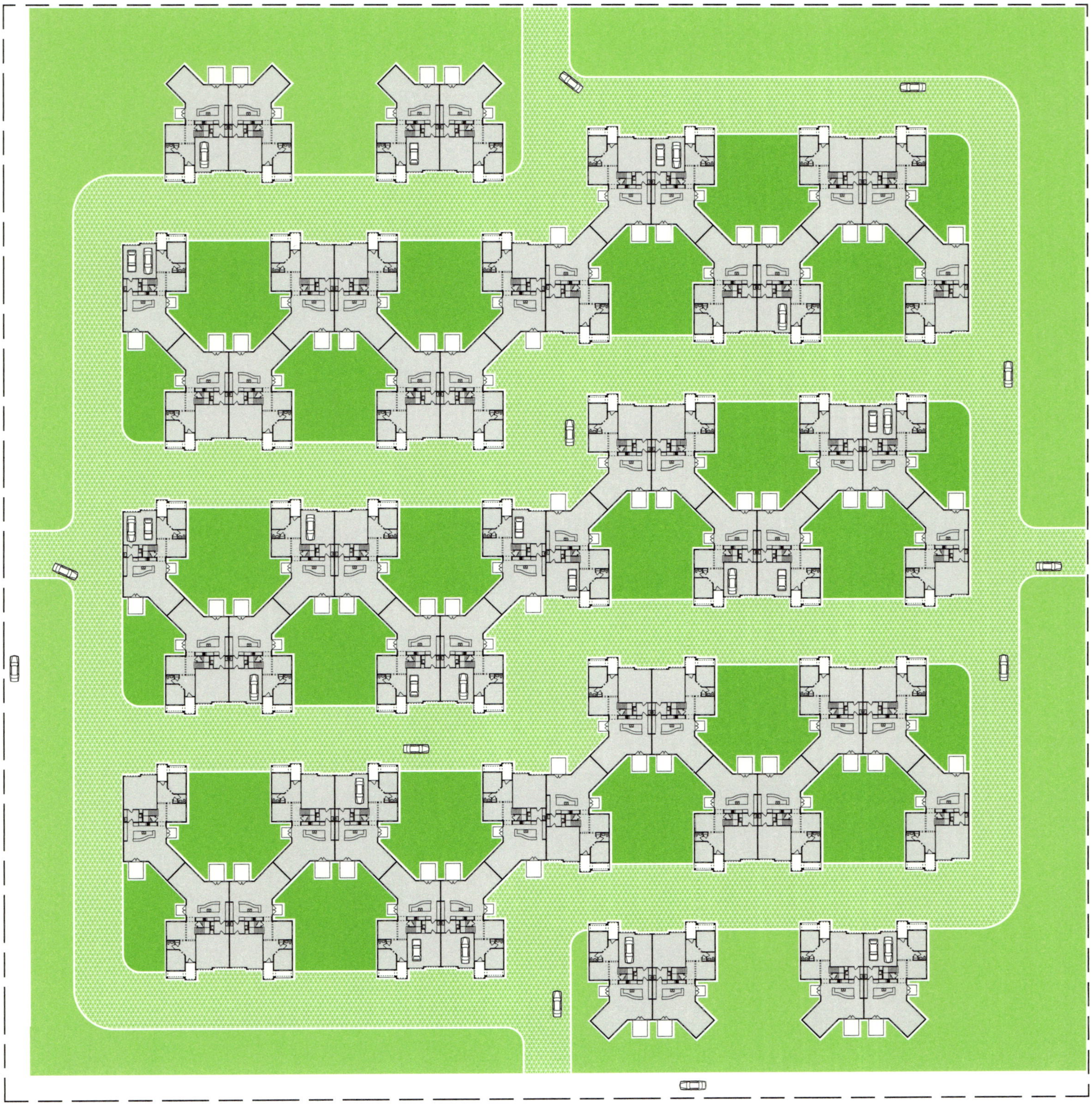

Bloomersbury

SW 1/4 SE 1/4 Section 11

56 Houses
181,328 Square Feet
168–224 Bedrooms
112–168 Full Bathrooms
0–56 Half Bathrooms

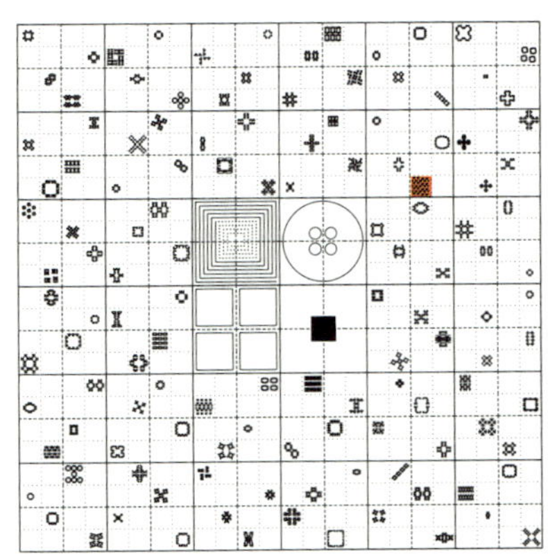

KB Home, Garden Plan 3238, 3238 sq. ft., California

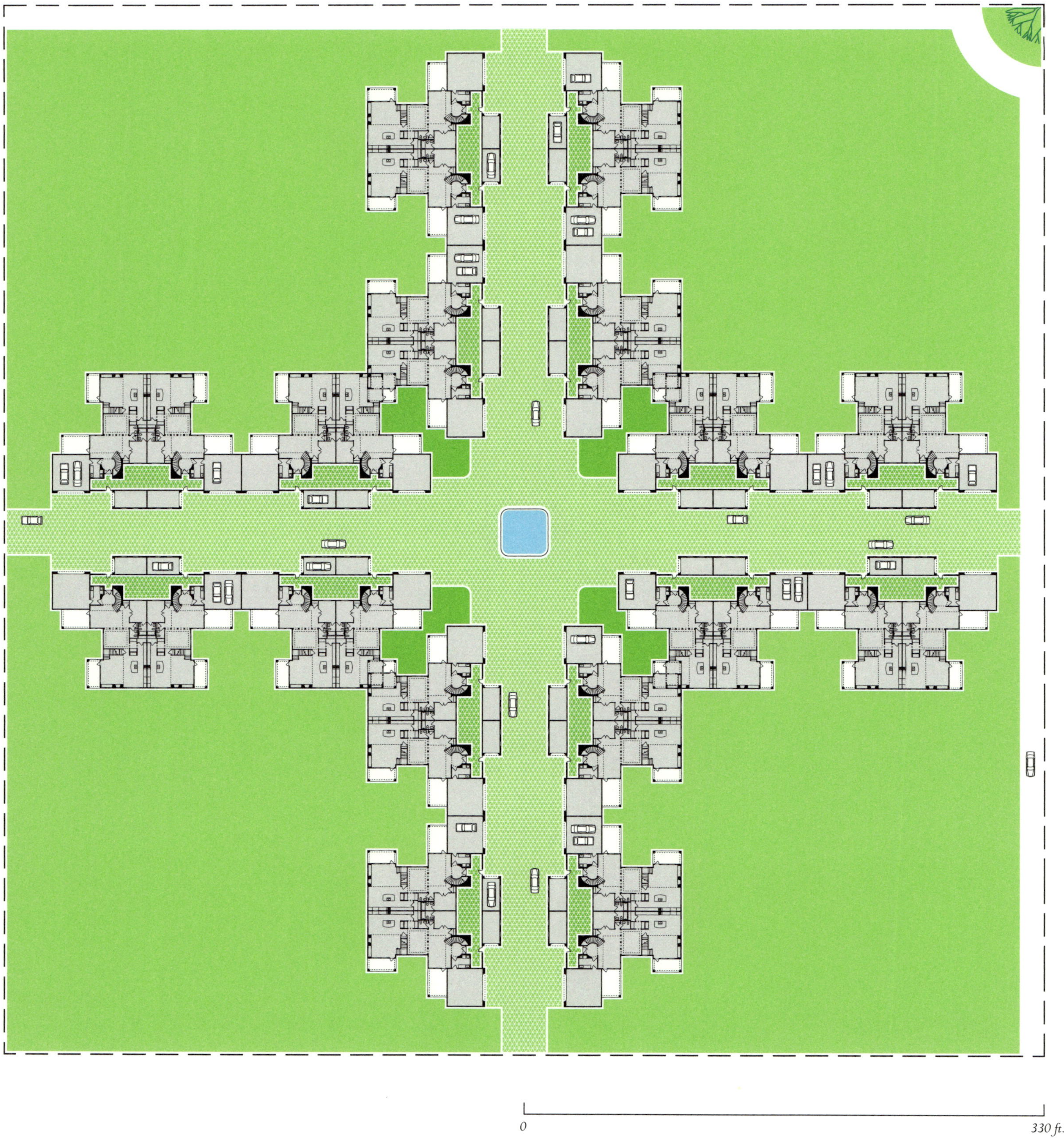

Via Varner

NE 1/4 NE 1/4 Section 12

32 Houses
121,600 Square Feet
96–160 Bedrooms
128 Full Bathrooms
32 Half Bathrooms

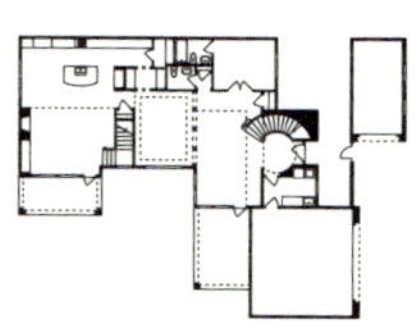

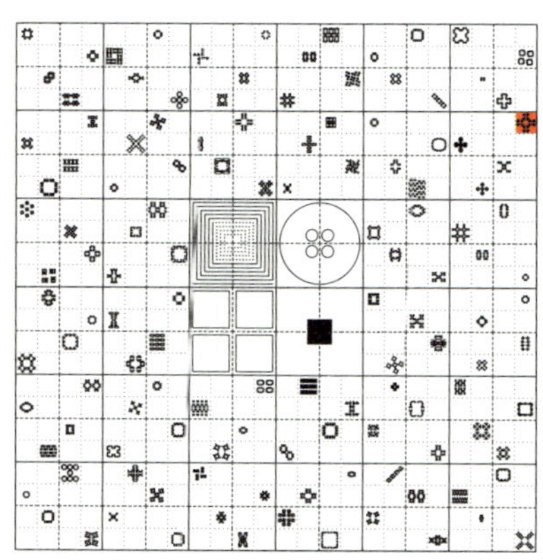

Pulte Homes, The Provence, 3800 sq. ft., Nevada

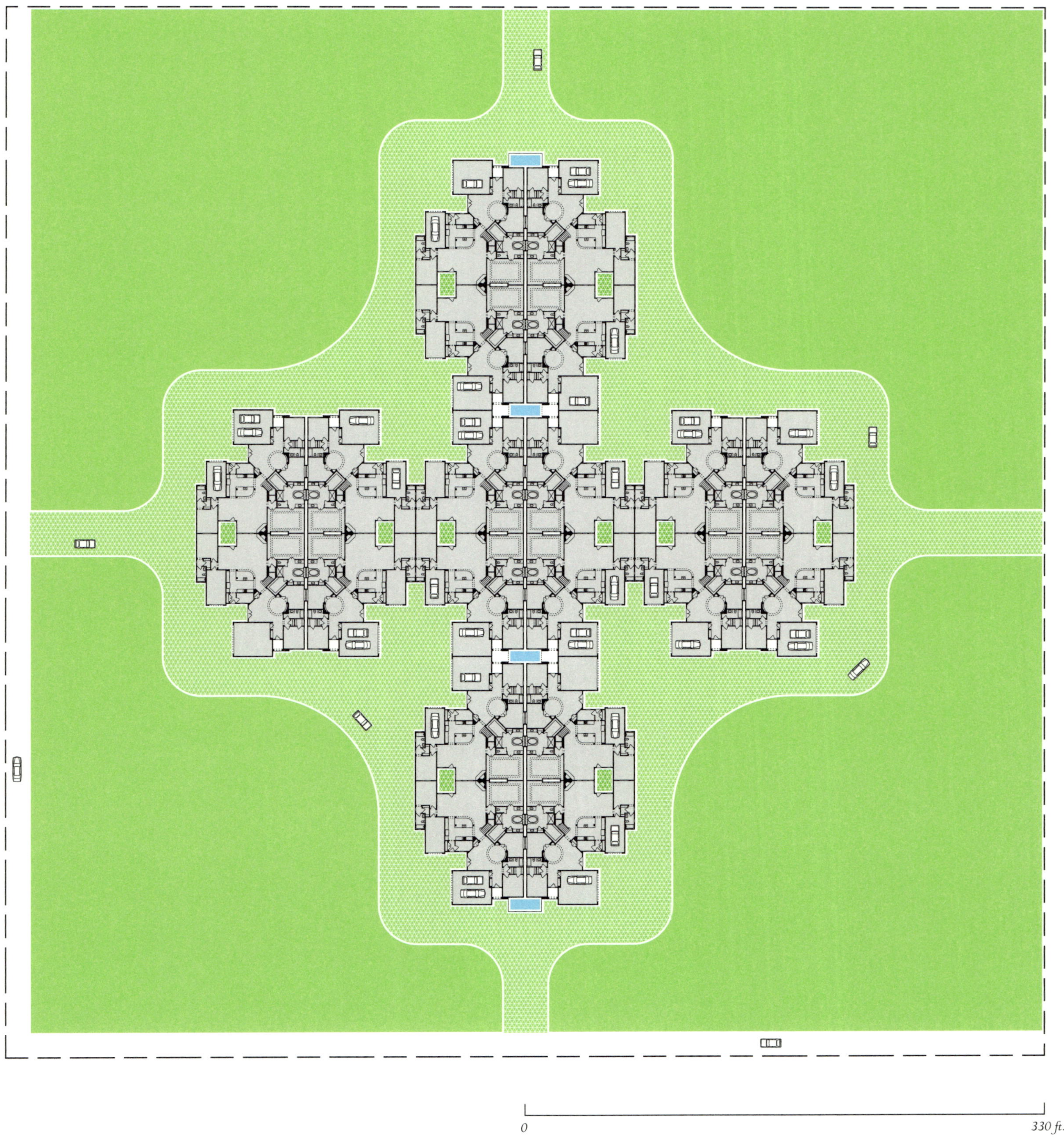

Exodus Landing

SW 1/4 NW 1/4 Section 12

20 Houses
60,860 Square Feet
80 Bedrooms
80 Full Bathrooms
0 Half Bathrooms

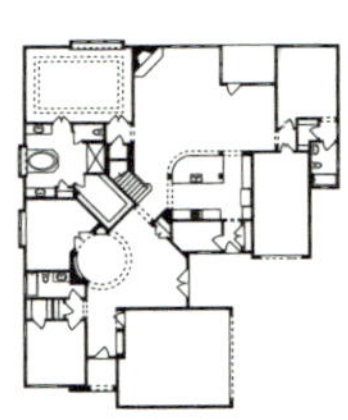

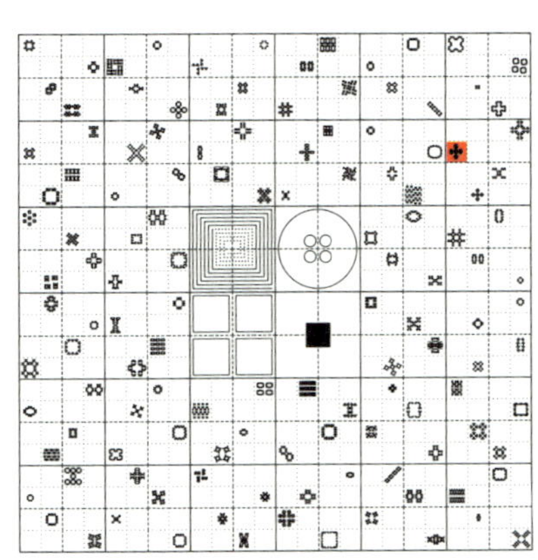

K. Hovnanian Homes, Bellvue VIII, 3043 sq. ft., Texas

A Voluntary Stroll near Exodus Landing, Freedomland
after *A Sunday Stroll,* 1841
Carl Spitzweg

Garden Homes

SE 1/4 SW 1/4 Section 12

20 Houses
74,060 Square Feet
60 Bedrooms
40 Full Bathrooms
20 Half Bathrooms

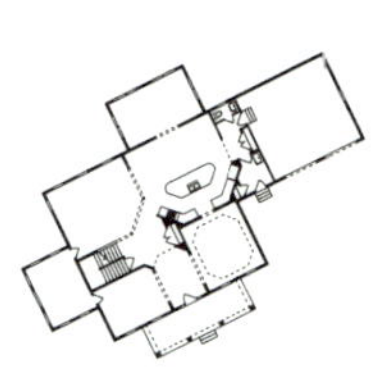

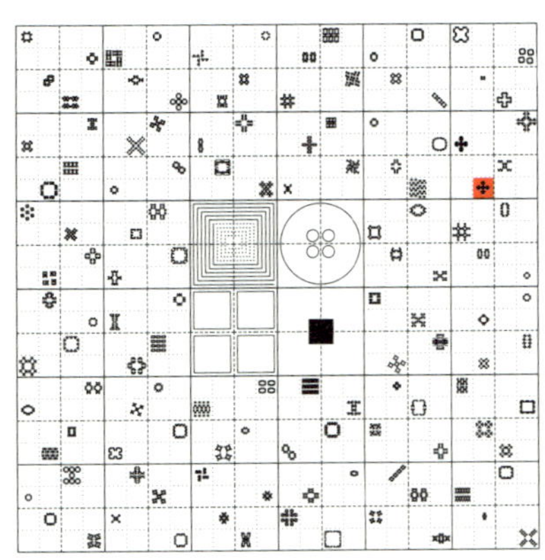

Ryland Homes, The Wye, 3703 sq. ft., Delaware

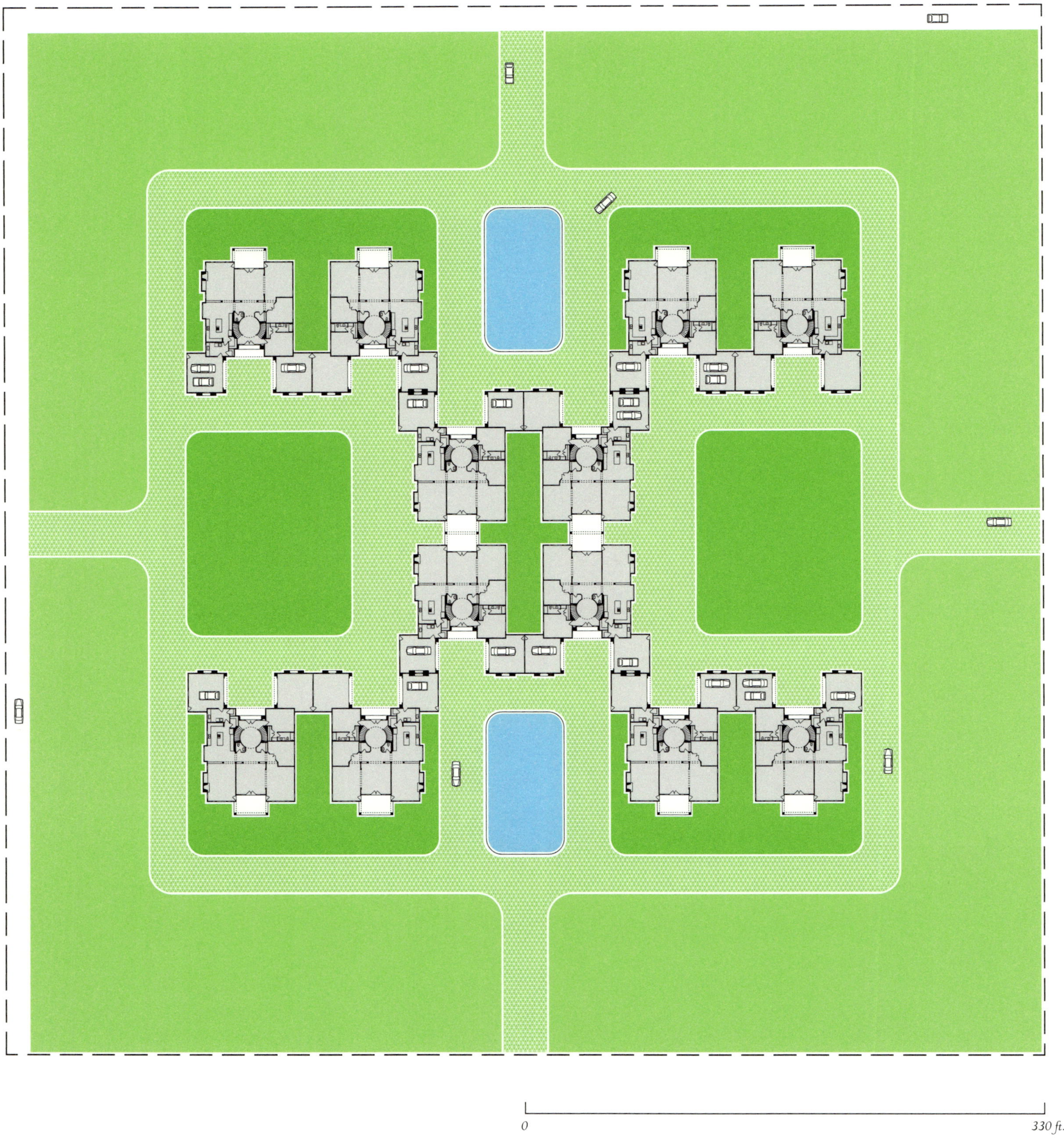

Les Joie des Jeunes
NW 1/4 SE 1/4 Section 12

12 Houses
61,500 Square Feet
48–60 Bedrooms
48 Full Bathrooms
12 Half Bathrooms

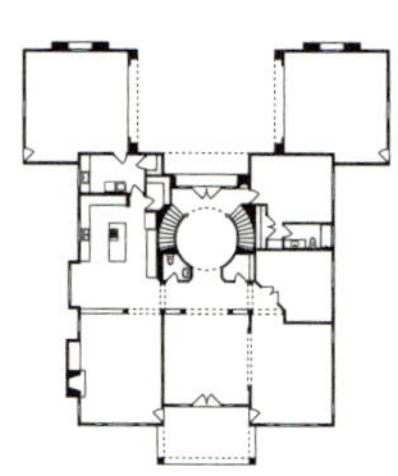

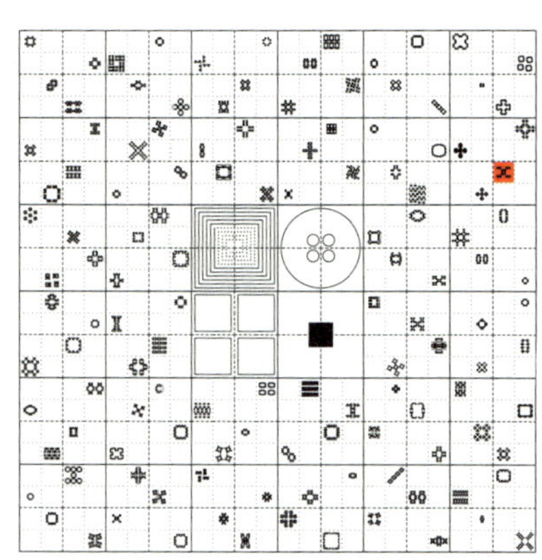

Toll Brothers, The Mirador, 5125 sq. ft., Arizona

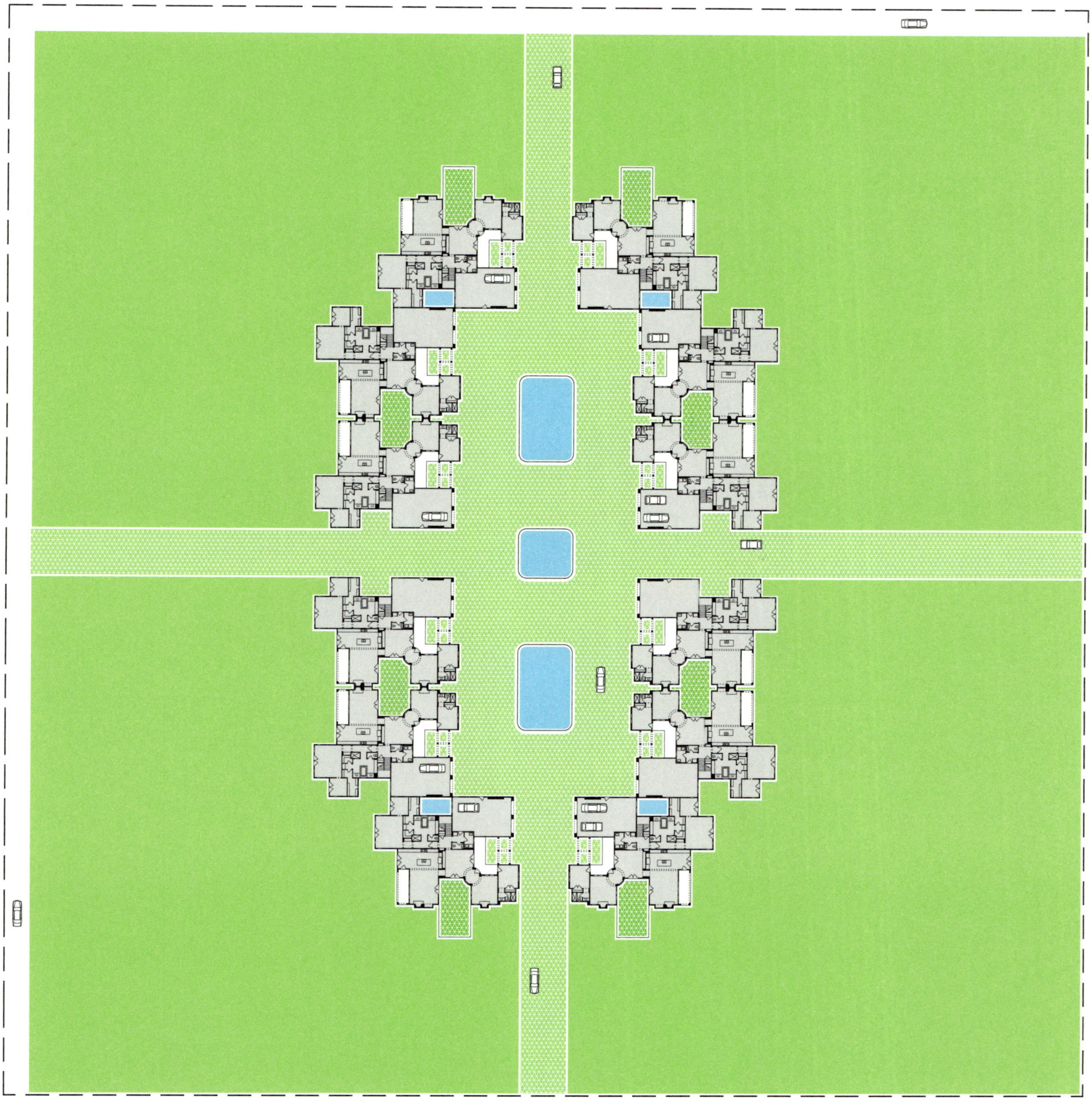

0 330 ft.

Robin Hood Gardens

NW 1/4 NE 1/4 Section 13

12 Houses
73,464 Square Feet
60 Bedrooms
60 Full Bathrooms
12 Half Bathrooms

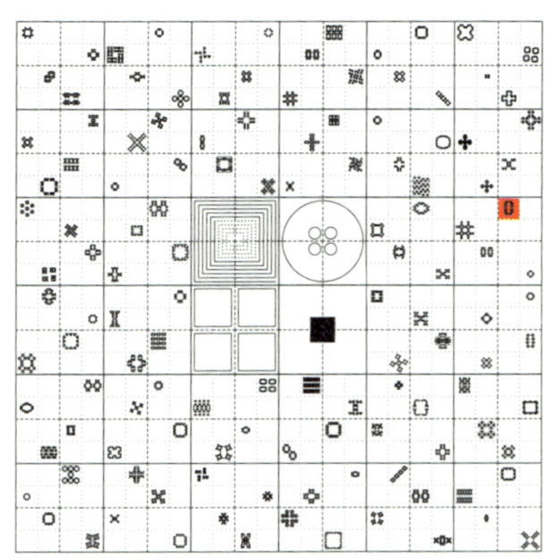

Standard Pacific Homes, Residence 1H, 6122 sq. ft., California

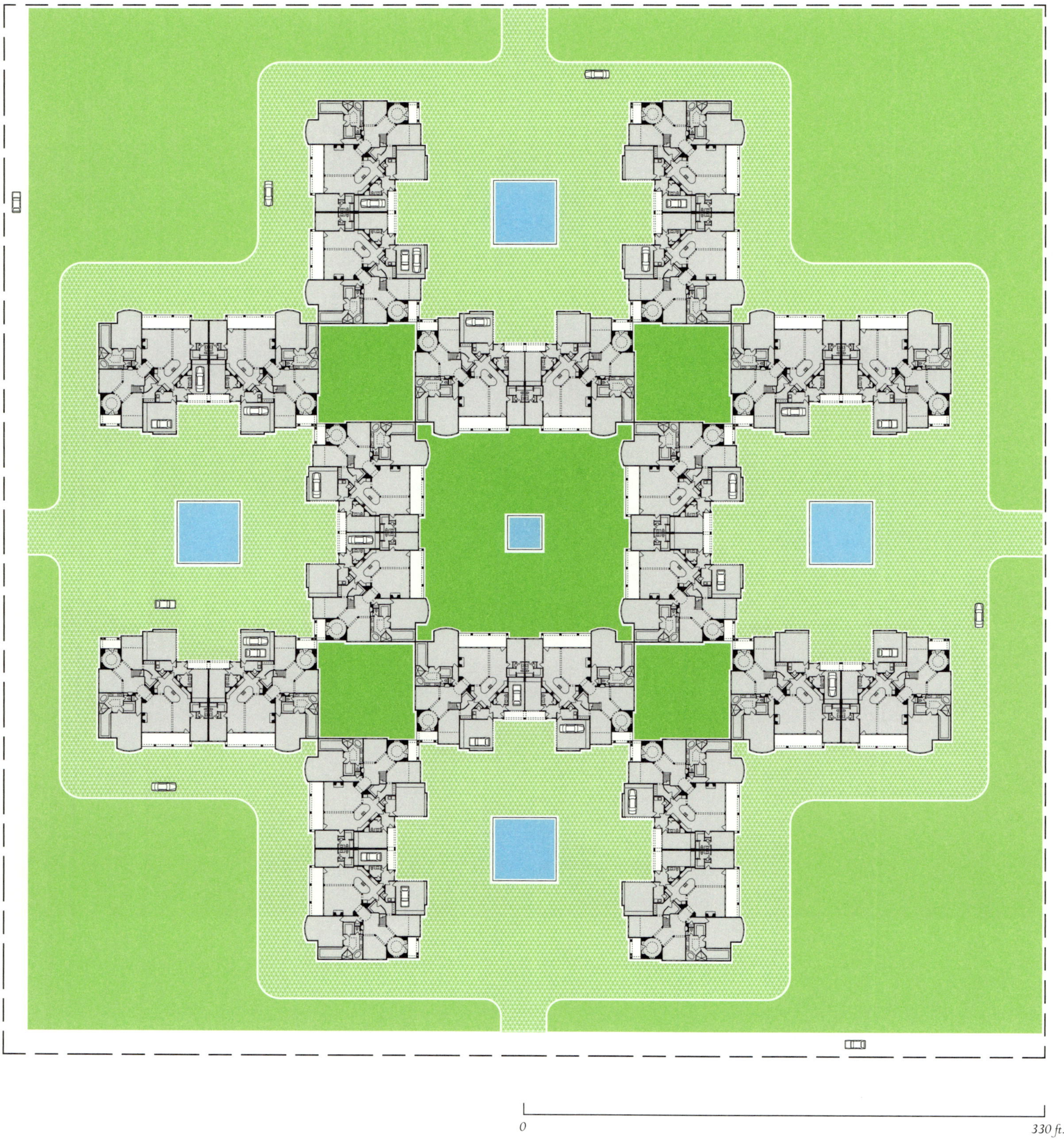

Casa Grande del Cultivo

SW 1/4 NW 1/4 Section 13

24 Houses
168,024 Square Feet
144 Bedrooms
120 Full Bathrooms
24 Half Bathrooms

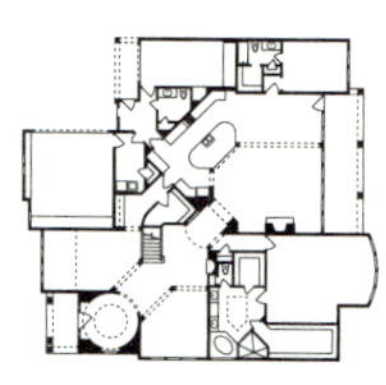

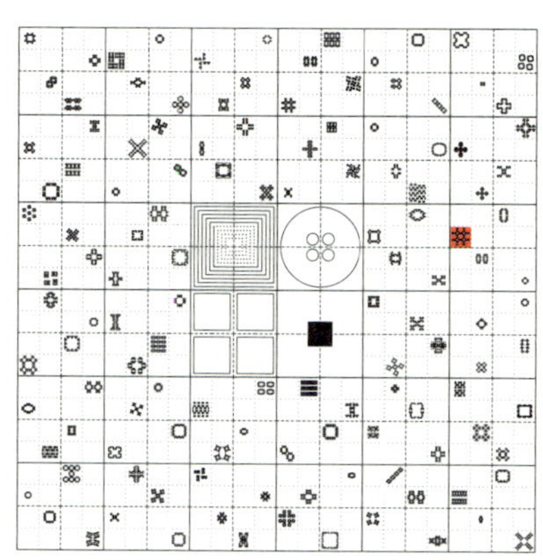

Perry Homes, Plan 7001W, 7001 sq. ft., Texas

Hunting at the Edge of Freedomland
after *Duck Shooting*, 1852
Arthur Fitzwilliam Tait

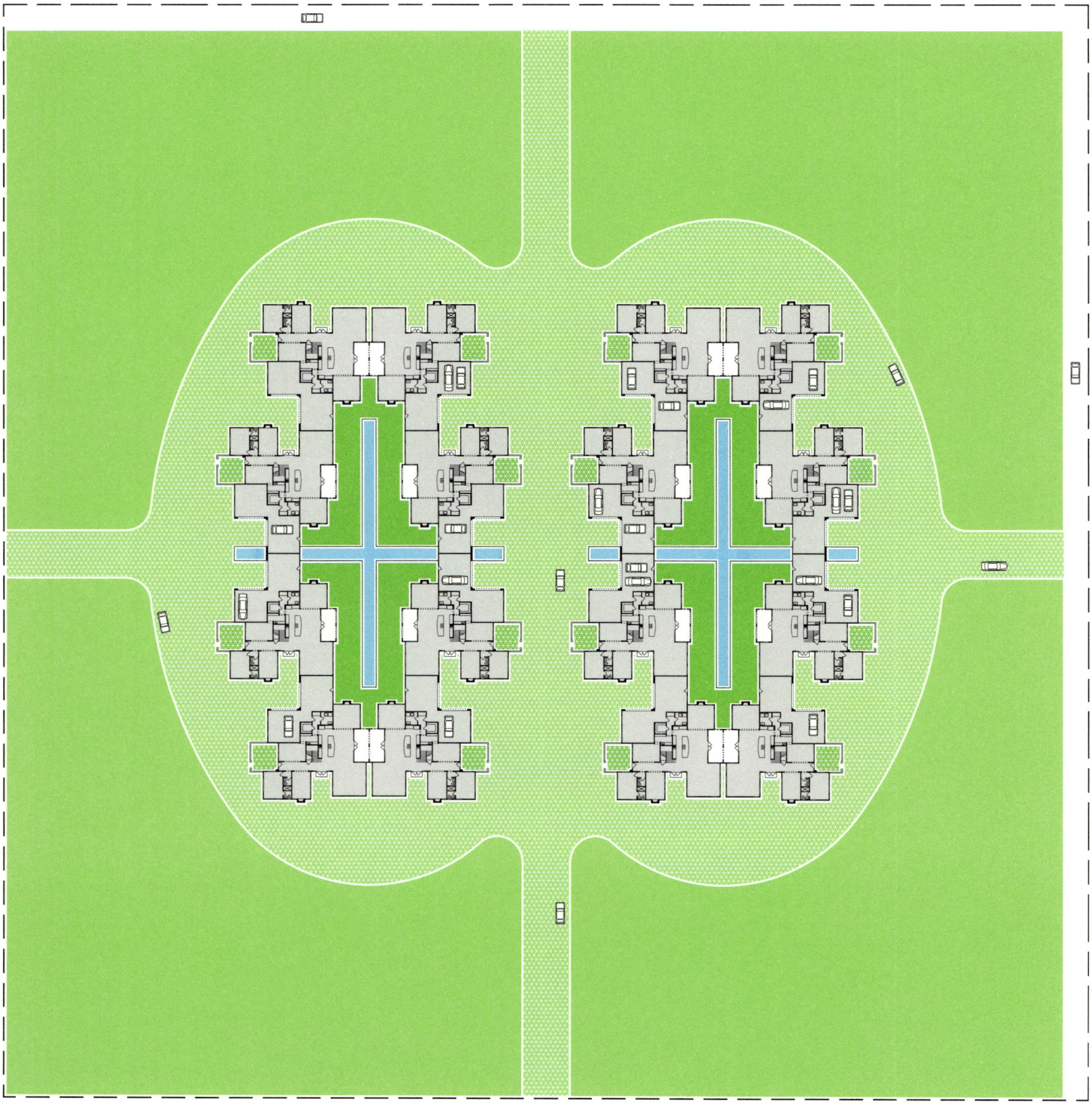

Walden 8

NE 1/4 SW 1/4 Section 13

16 Houses
74,000 Square Feet
64 Bedrooms
64 Full Bathrooms
16 Half Bathrooms

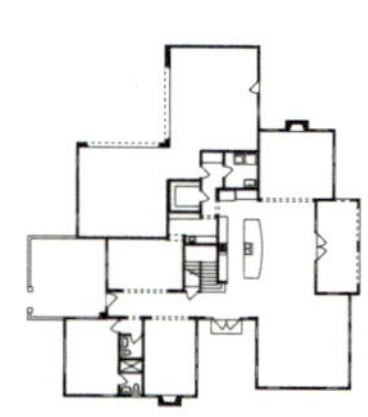

Shea Homes, Plan 2 at Maravilla, 4625 sq. ft., California

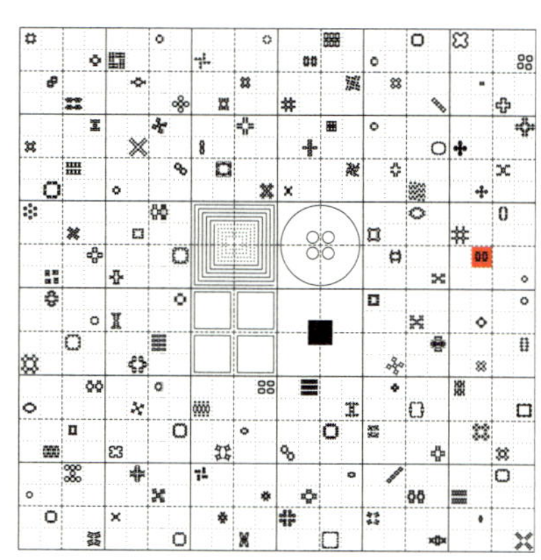

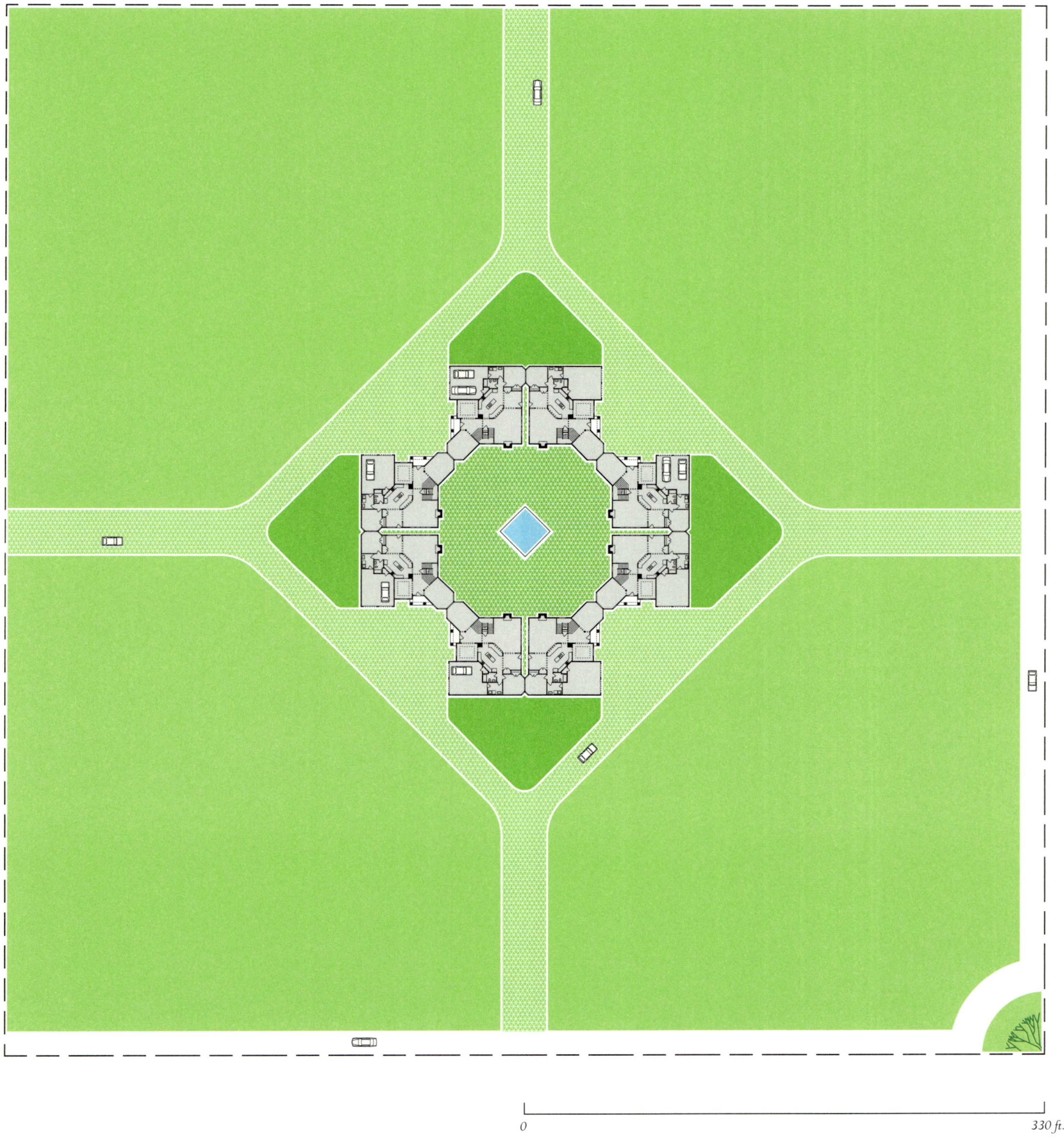

New Haven

SE 1/4 SE 1/4 Section 13

8 Houses
26,880 Square Feet
32 Bedrooms
24 Full Bathrooms
0 Half Bathrooms

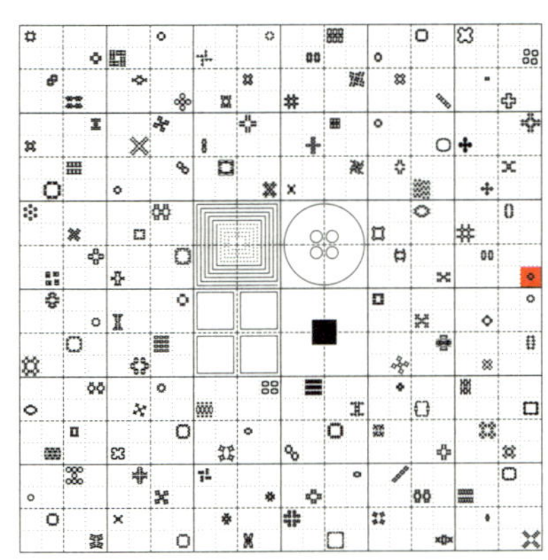

Centex Homes, The Wellington, 3360 sq. ft., Georgia

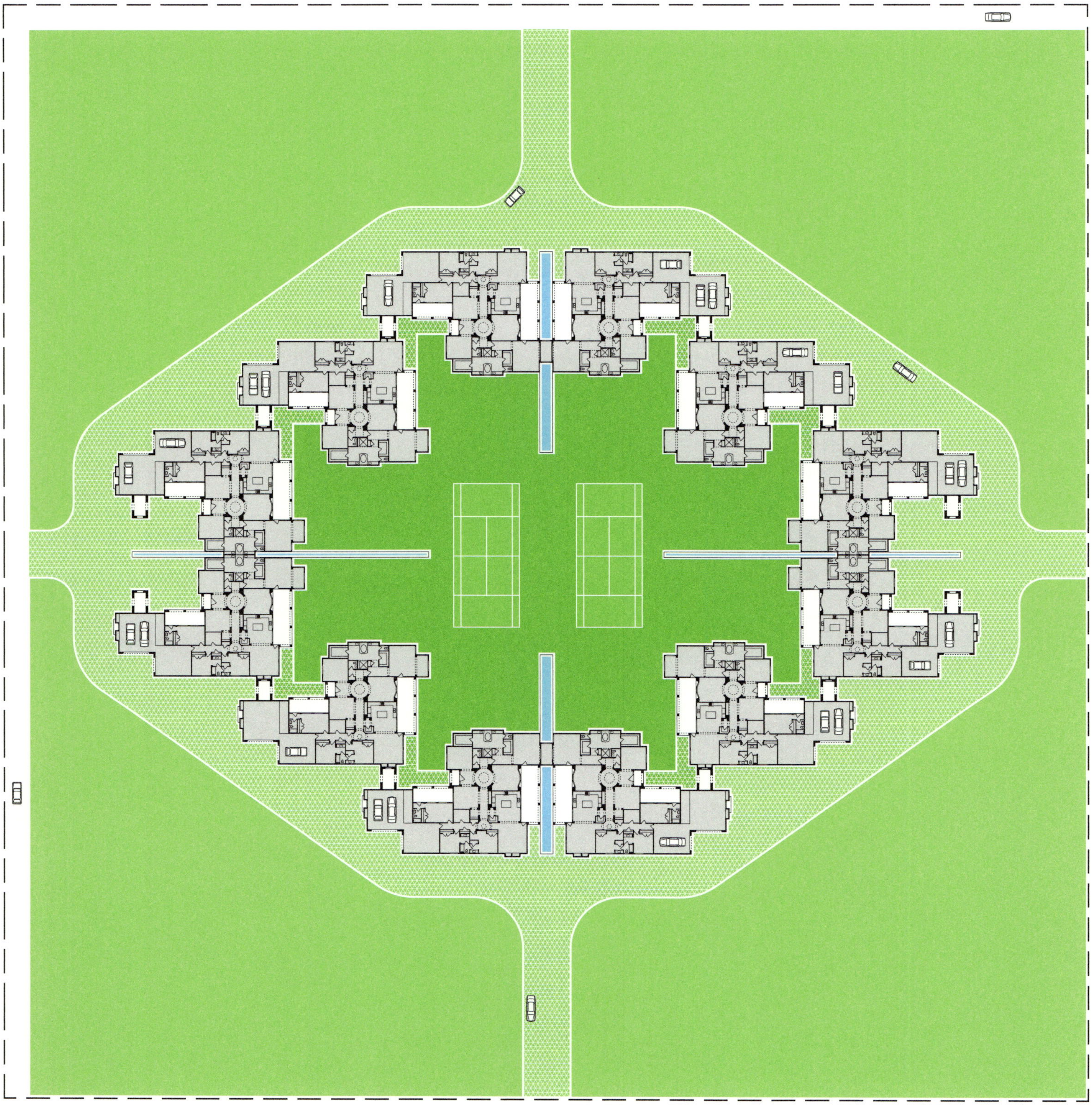

0 330 ft.

Davies Lawn and Tennis Club

NW 1/4 NE 1/4 Section 14

12 Houses
50,504 Square Feet
48 Bedrooms
36 Full Bathrooms
12 Half Bathrooms

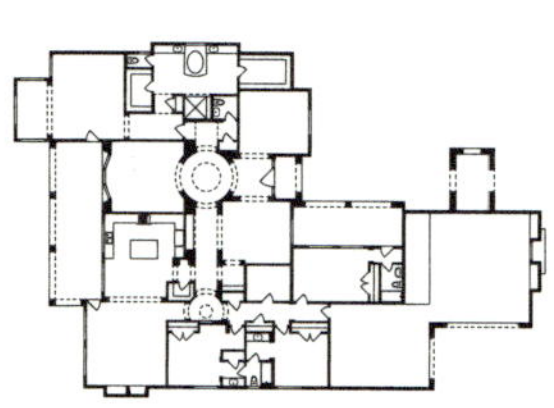

Meritage Homes, Residence 4 at Mirabel, 4217 sq. ft., Arizona

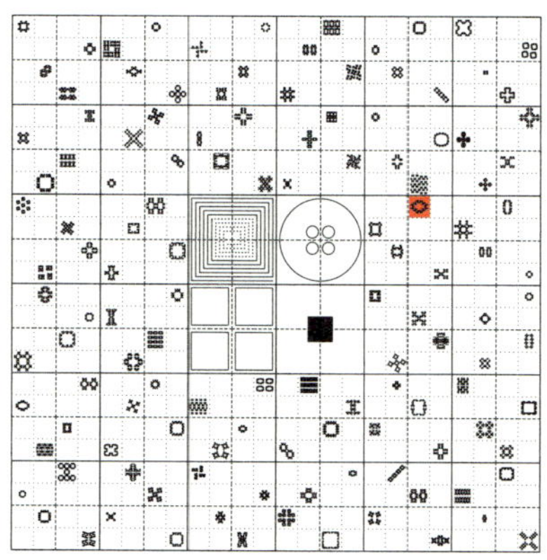

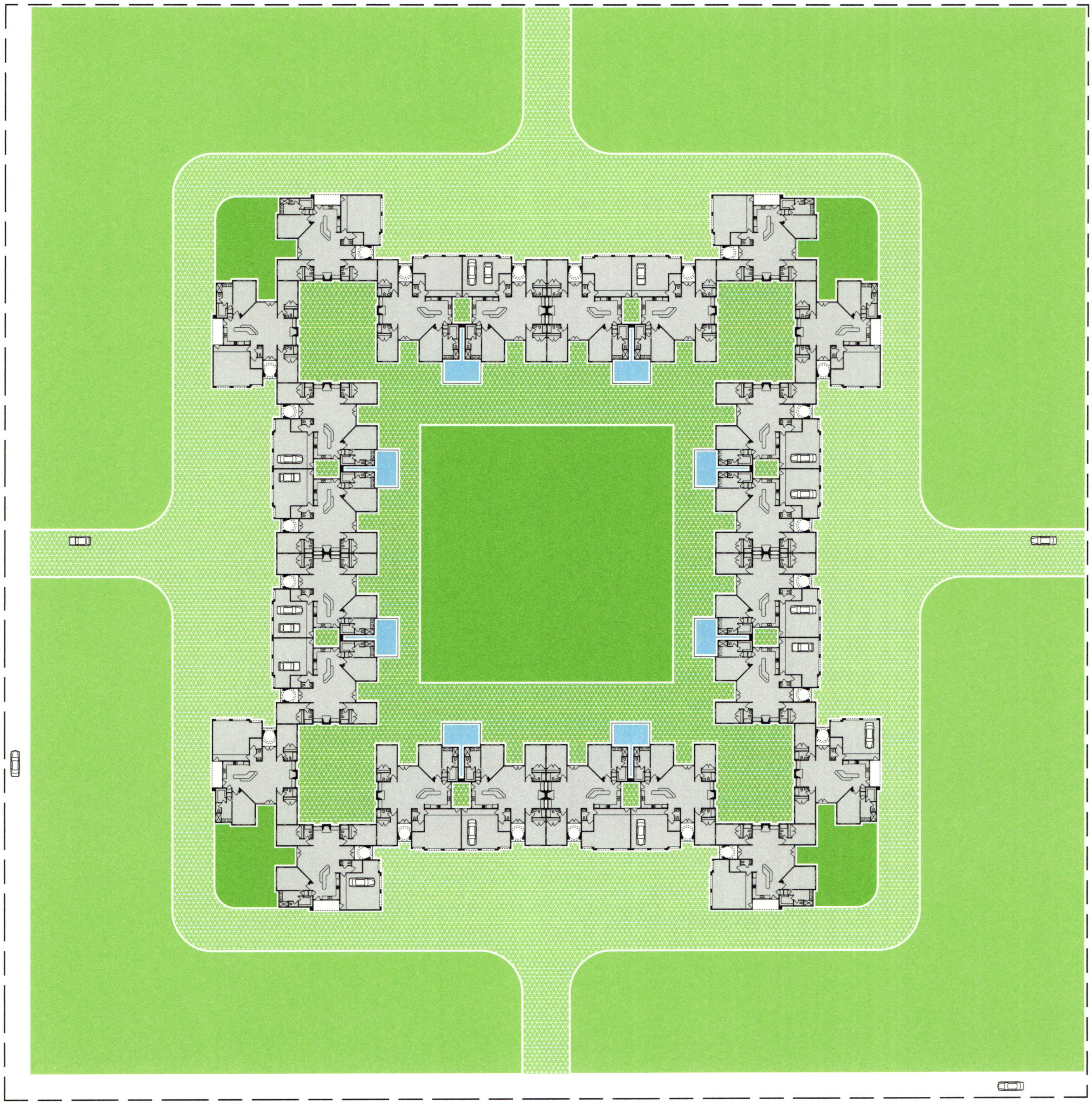

0 330 ft.

Subdivision Square

SW 1/4 NW 1/4 Section 14

24 Houses
50,088 Square Feet
72 Bedrooms
72 Full Bathrooms
24 Half Bathrooms

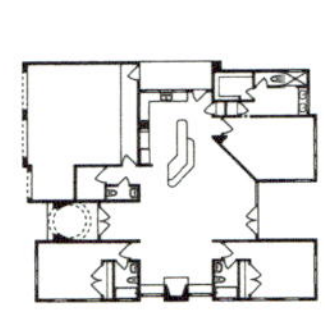

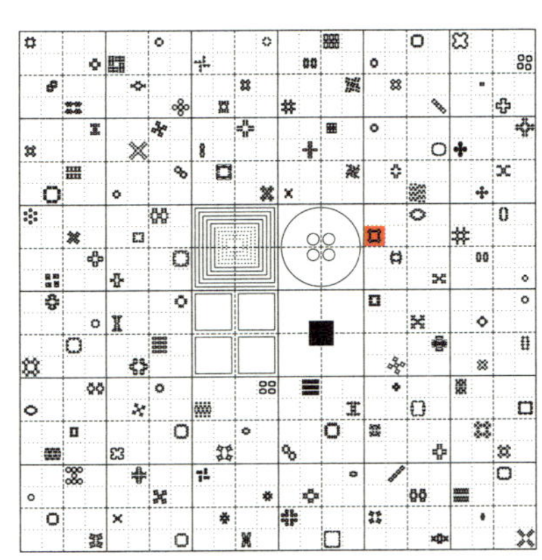

Avatar Homes, Valderama, 2087 sq. ft., Arizona

Nishikado Palace

NE 1/4 SW 1/4 Section 14

16 Houses
104,928 Square Feet
80 Bedrooms
80 Full Bathrooms
32 Half Bathrooms

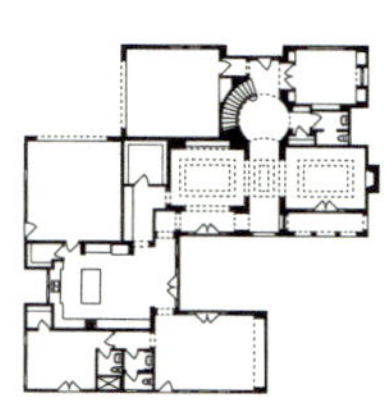

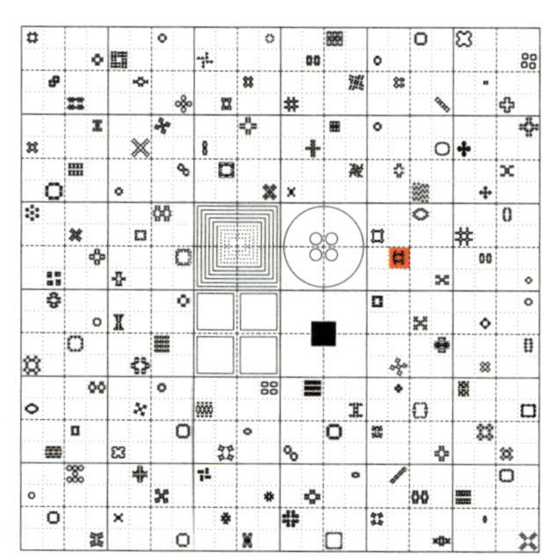

KB Home, The Stratford, 6558 sq. ft., California

Shadrach Woods

SE 1/4 SE 1/4 Section 14

20 Houses
71,680 Square Feet
100 Bedrooms
80 Full Bathrooms
20 Half Bathrooms

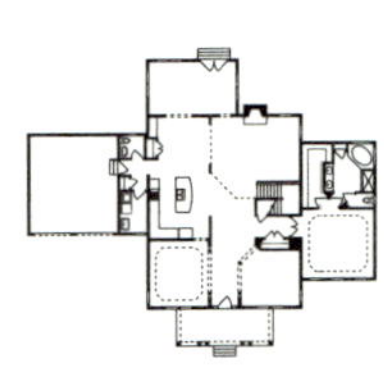

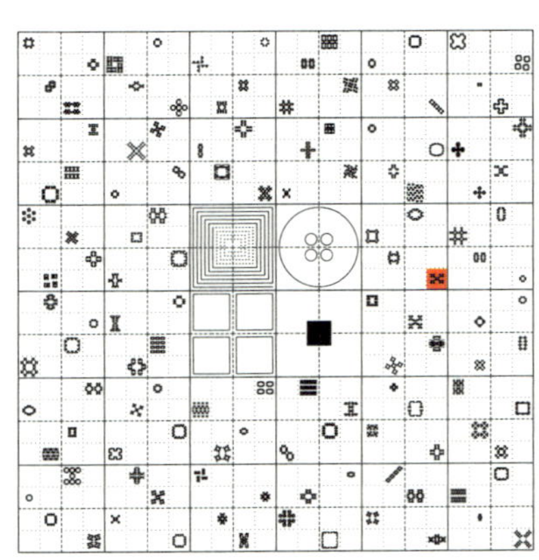

Ryland Homes, The Parson, 3584 sq. ft., Delaware

Mr and Mrs Andrews of Shadrach Woods, Freedomland
after *Mr and Mrs Andrews,* 1749
Thomas Gainsborough

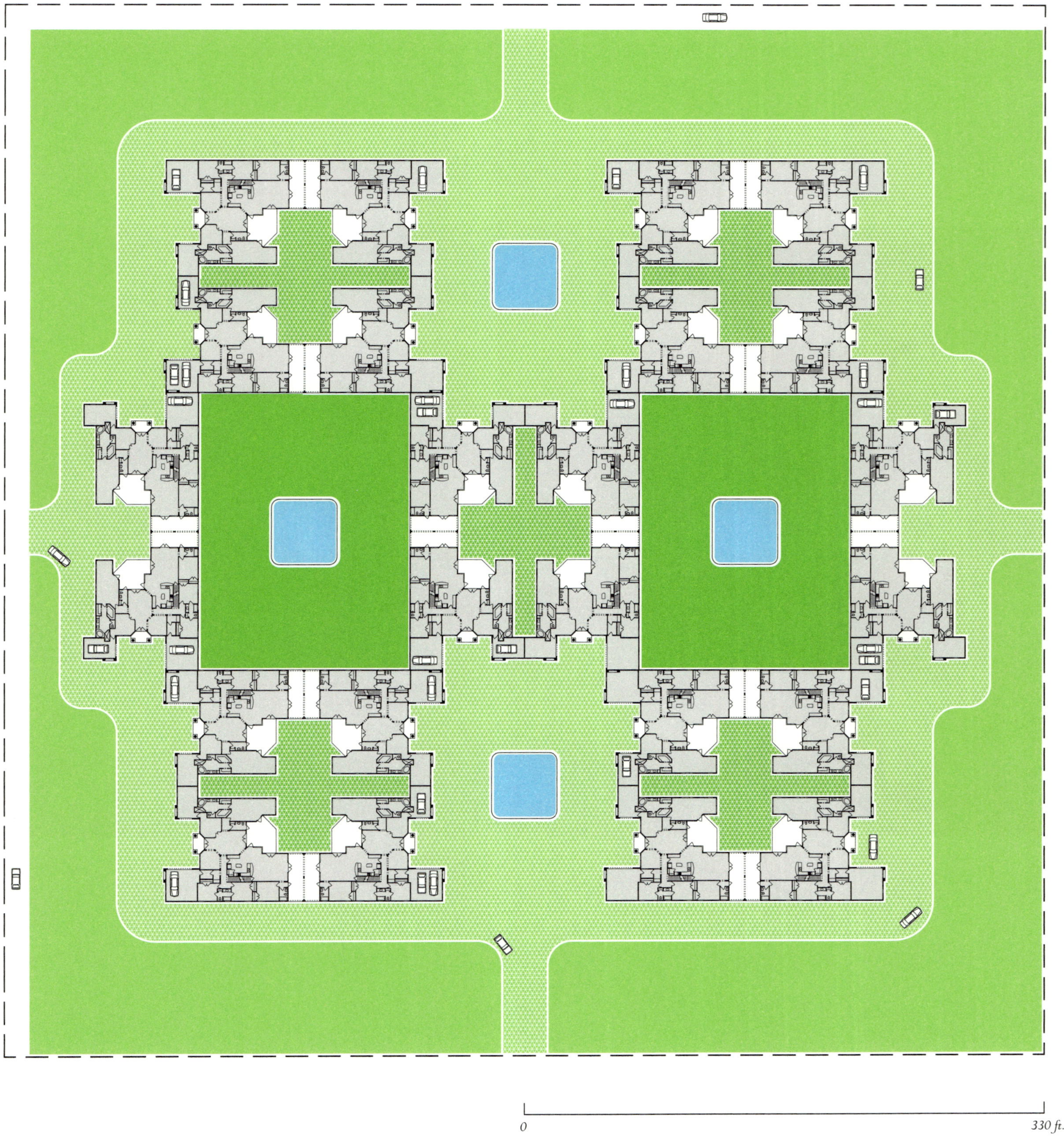

Estate del Suzanne

NW 1/4 NE 1/4 Section 17

24 Houses
83,400 Square Feet
96–120 Bedrooms
96 Full Bathrooms
24 Half Bathrooms

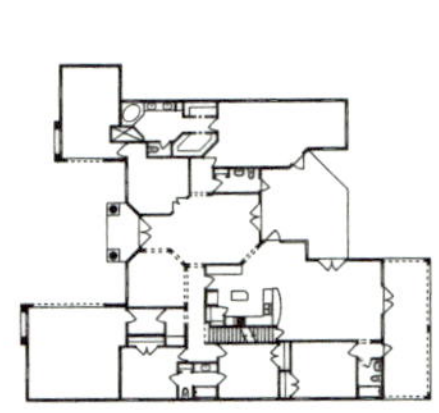

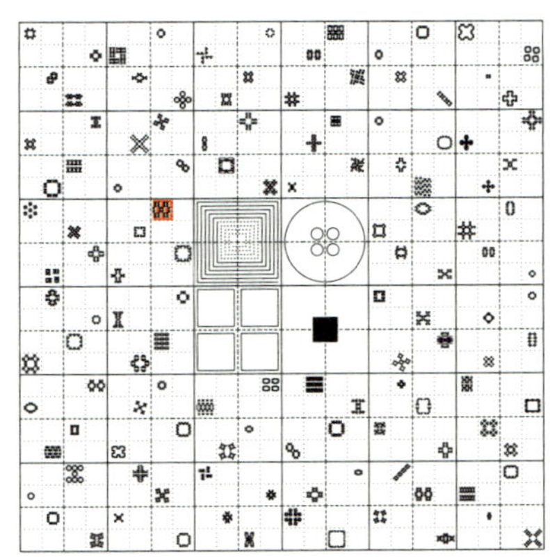

Ryland Homes, Charleston II, 3475 sq. ft., Florida

The Quarters at Narkomfin Castle

SE 1/4 NW 1/4 Section 17

12 Houses
36,516 Square Feet
48 Bedrooms
48 Full Bathrooms
0 Half Bathrooms

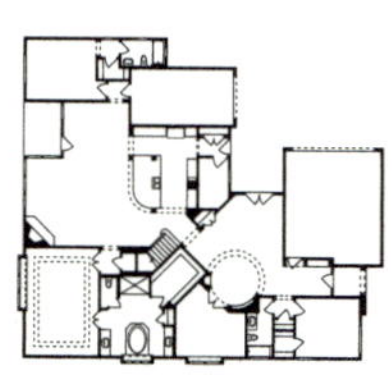

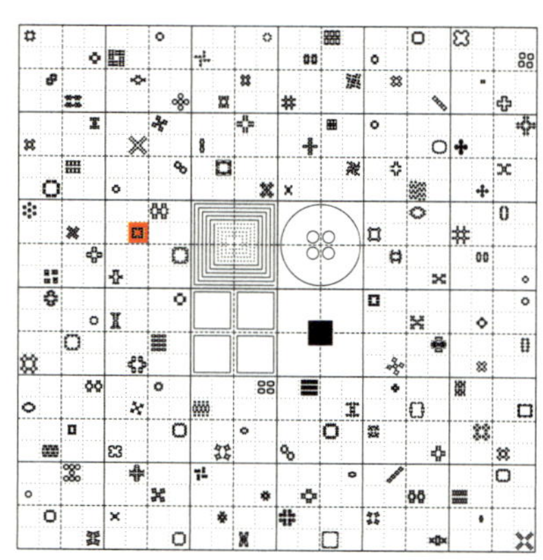

K. Hovnanian Homes, Bellvue VIII, 3043 sq. ft., Texas

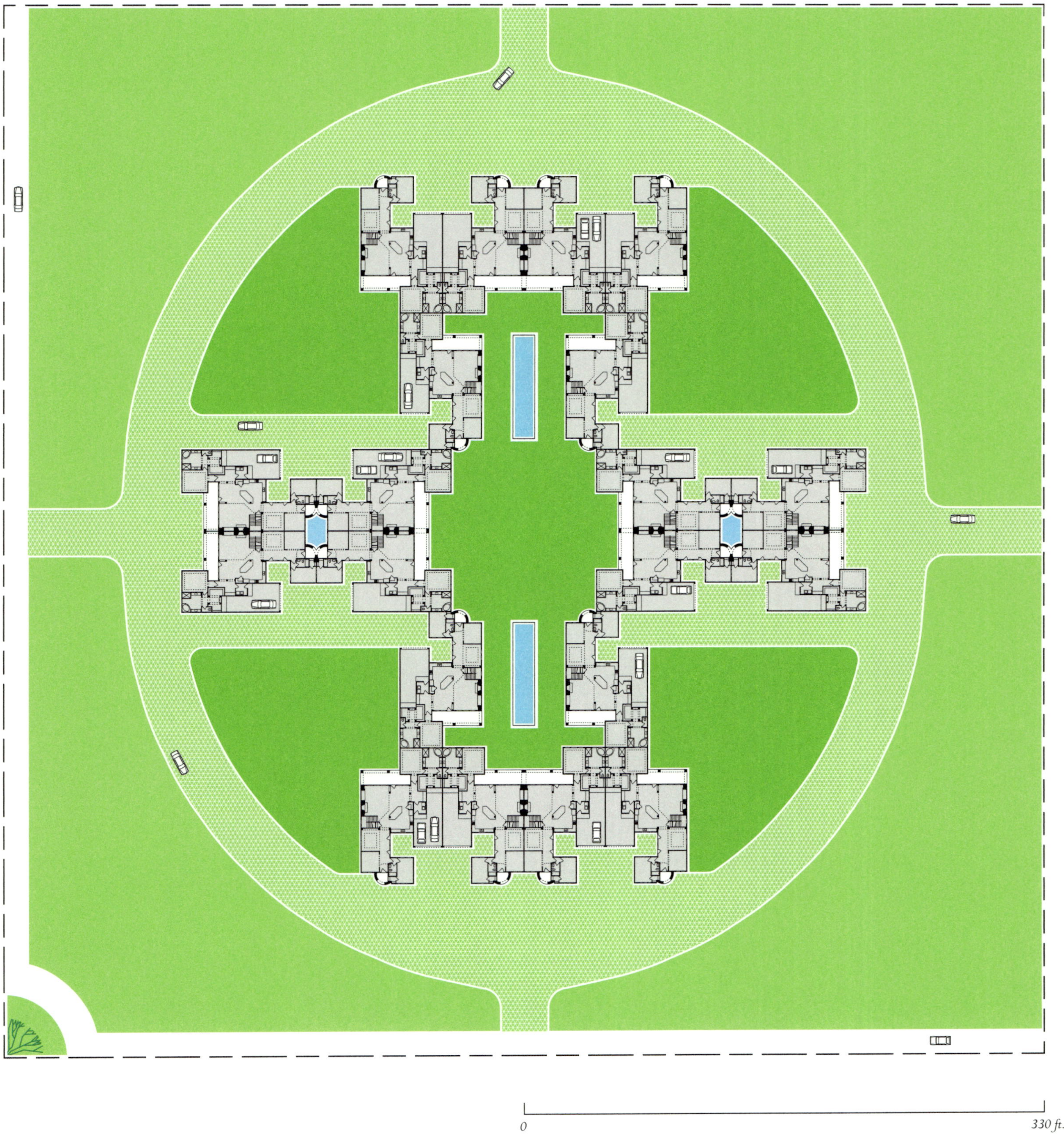

CityLAB Center for Practical Utopias

SW 1/4 SW 1/4 Section 17

20 Houses
74,160 Square Feet
100 Bedrooms
80 Full Bathrooms
20 Half Bathrooms

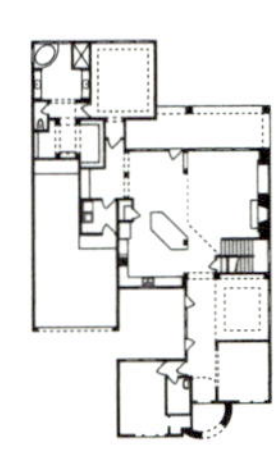

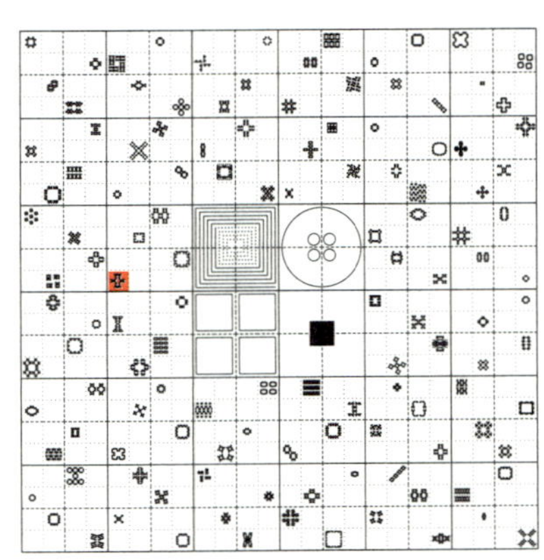

David Weekley Homes, The Palladio, 3708 sq. ft., Texas

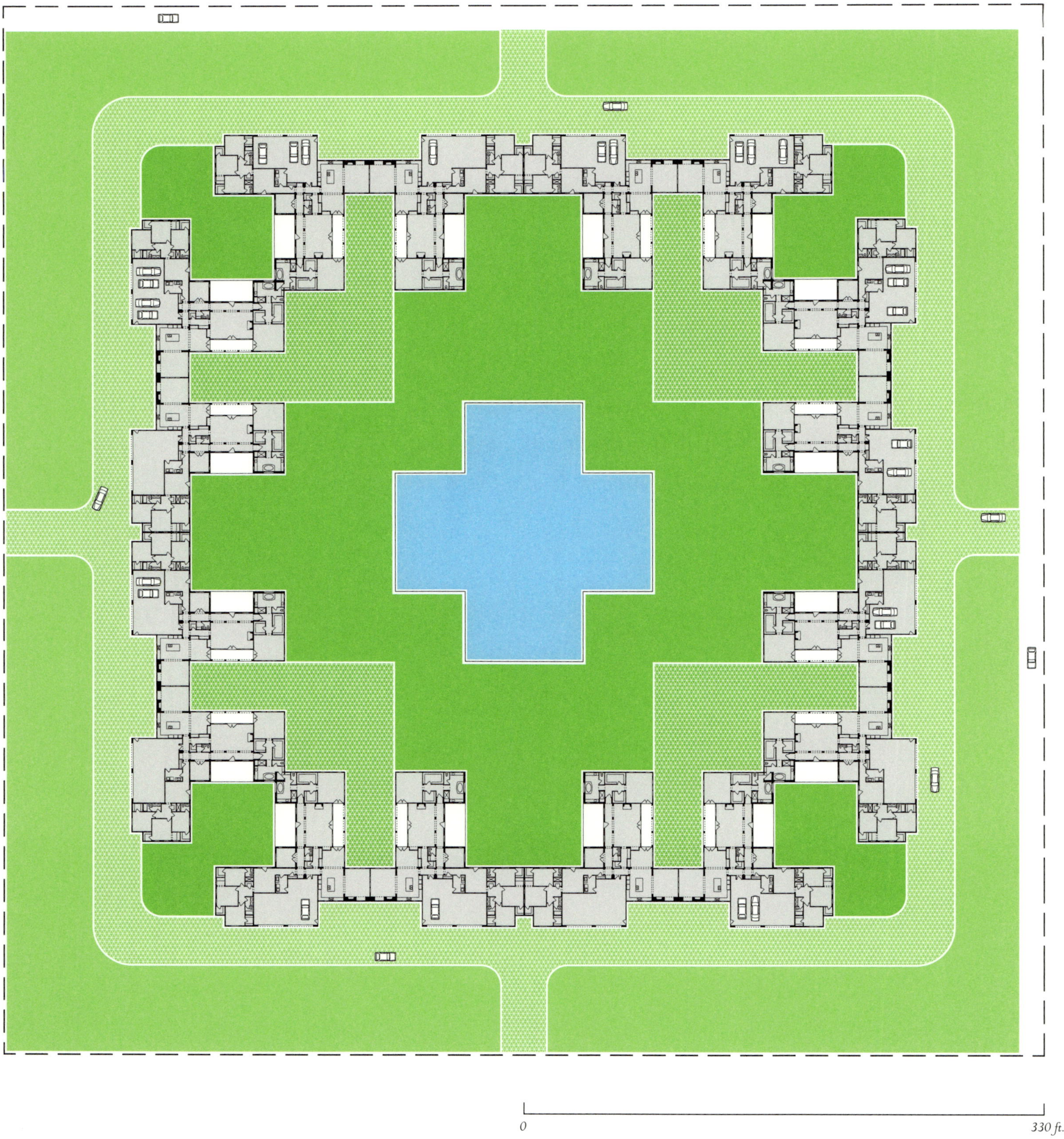

Schloss von Sibelius
NE 1/4 SE 1/4 Section 17

16 Houses
66,816 Square Feet
64 Bedrooms
48 Full Bathrooms
16 Half Bathrooms

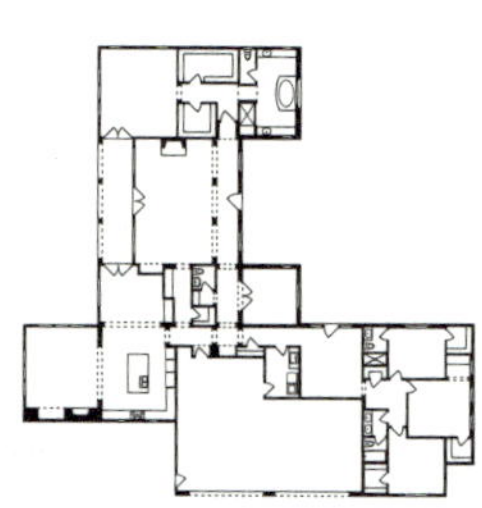

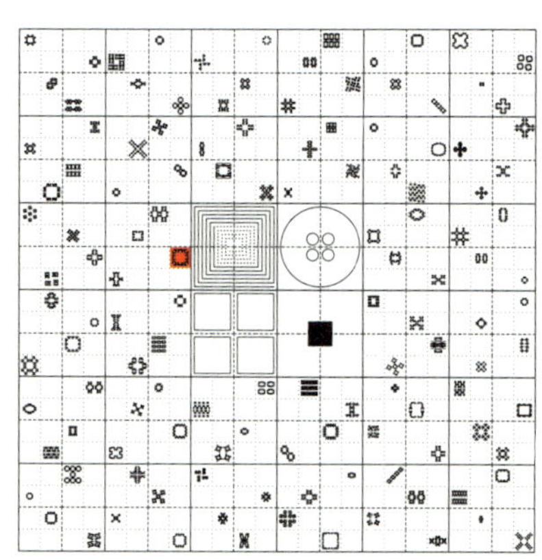

Pulte Homes, The Appaloosa, 4176 sq. ft., California

The broad acre city . . . is the inevitable municipality of the future. . . . We live now in cities of the past, slaves of the machine and of traditional building. We cannot solve our living and transportation problems by burrowing under or climbing over, and why should we? We will spread out . . .

—Frank Lloyd Wright, *The Disappearing City,* 1932.

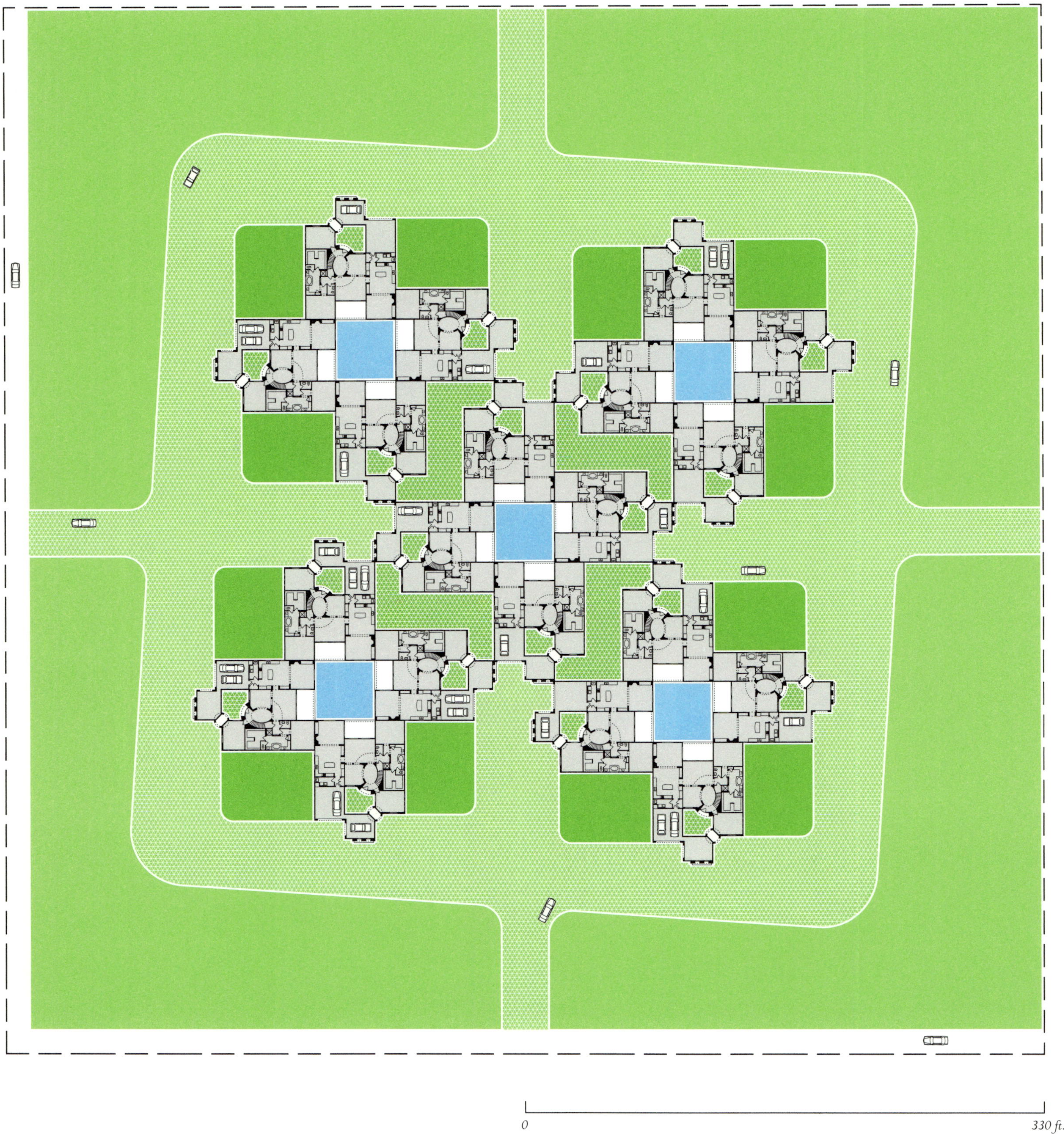

The Villas at Broad Acres
SW 1/4 NE 1/4 Section 18

20 Houses
81,260 Square Feet
80 Bedrooms
60 Full Bathrooms
20 Half Bathrooms

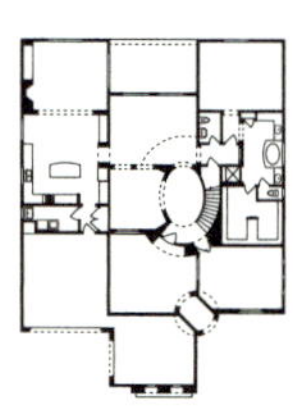

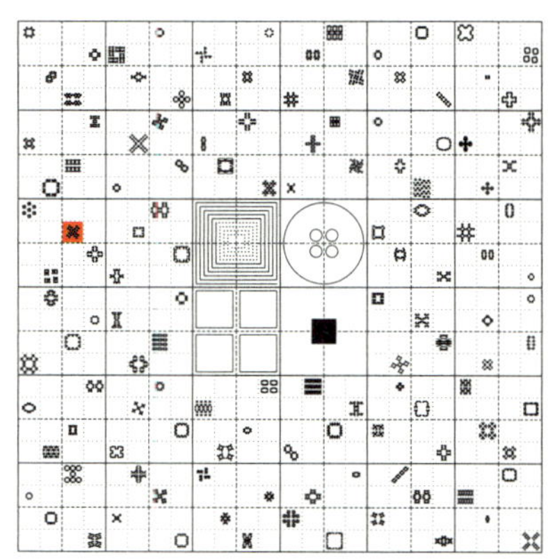

Del Webb, Mirasol, 4063 sq. ft., Arizona

A Little Garden City

NW 1/4 NW 1/4 Section 18

28 Houses
103,684 Square Feet
84 Bedrooms
56 Full Bathrooms
28 Half Bathrooms

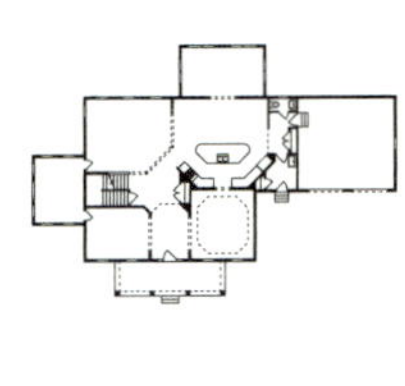

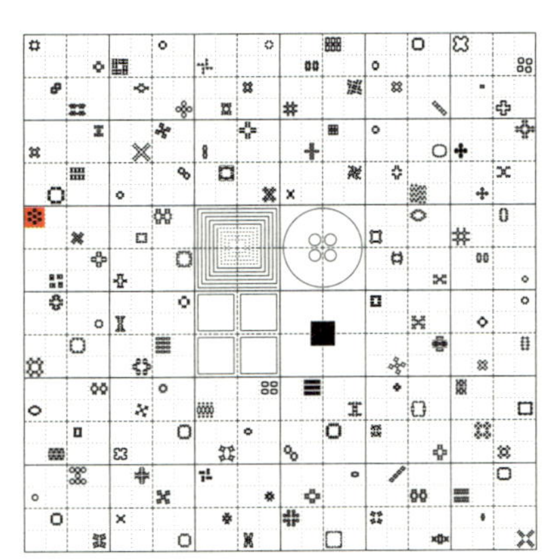

Ryland Homes, The Wye, 3703 sq. ft., Delaware

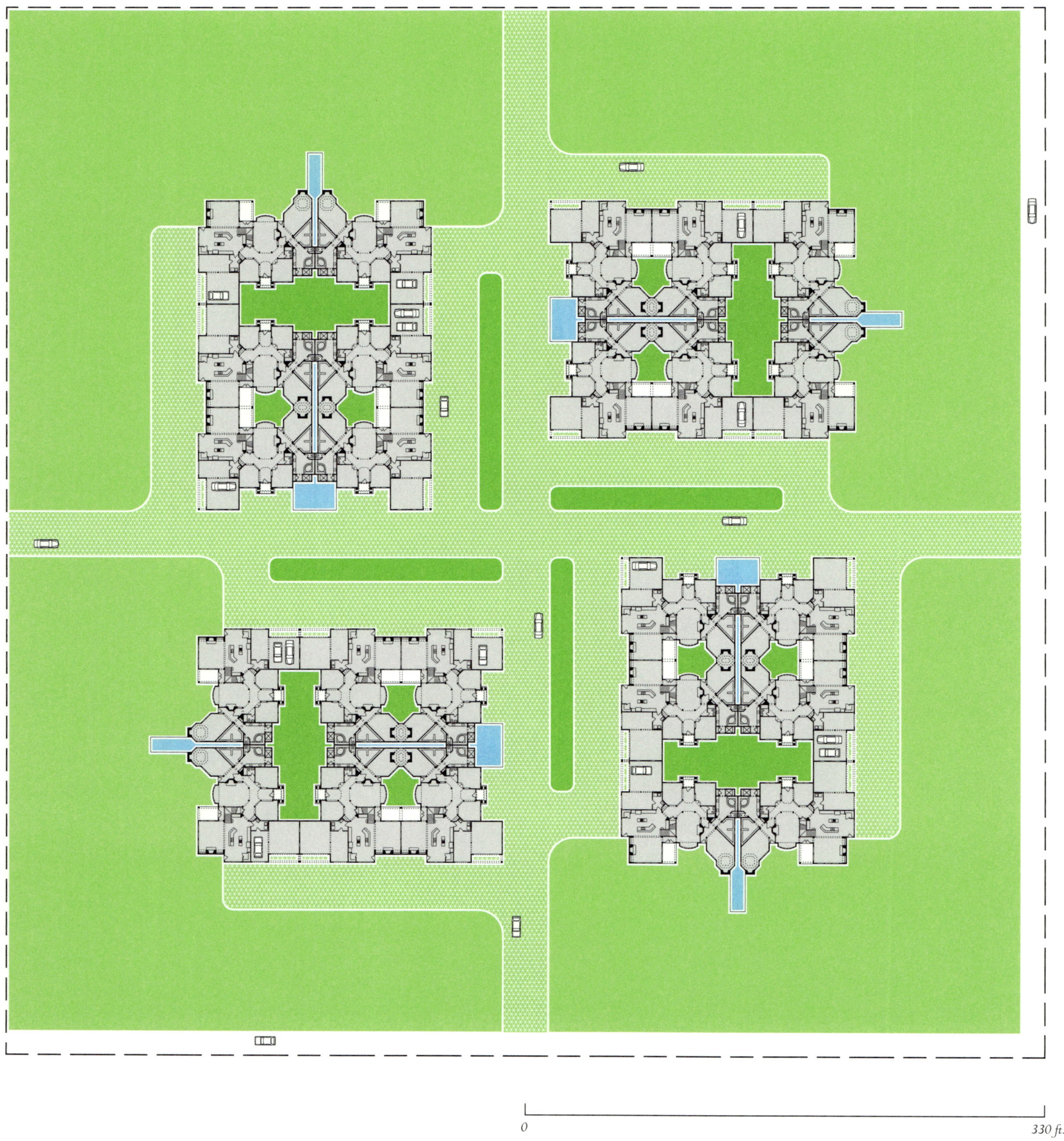

Nadaville

SE 1/4 SW 1/4 Section 18

24 Houses
102,840 Square Feet
96–120 Bedrooms
96 Full Bathrooms
24 Half Bathrooms

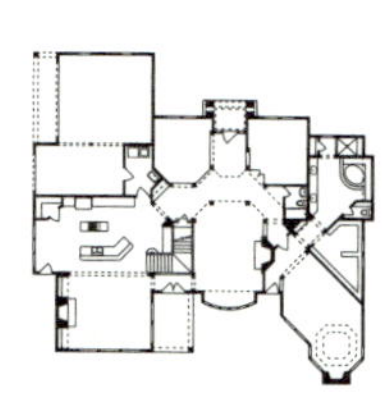

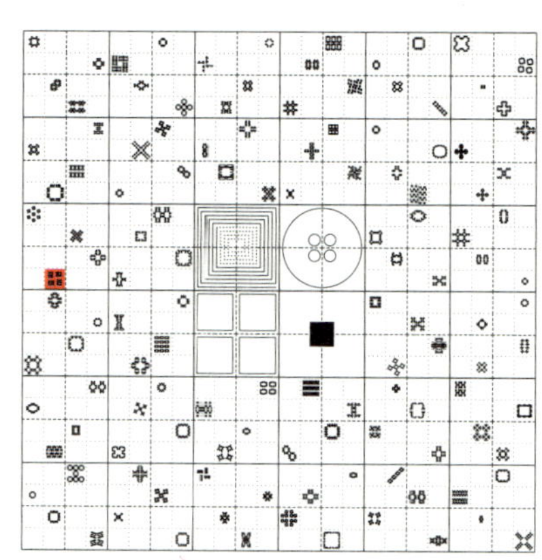

David Weekley Homes, The Lynnhaven, 4285 sq. ft., Texas

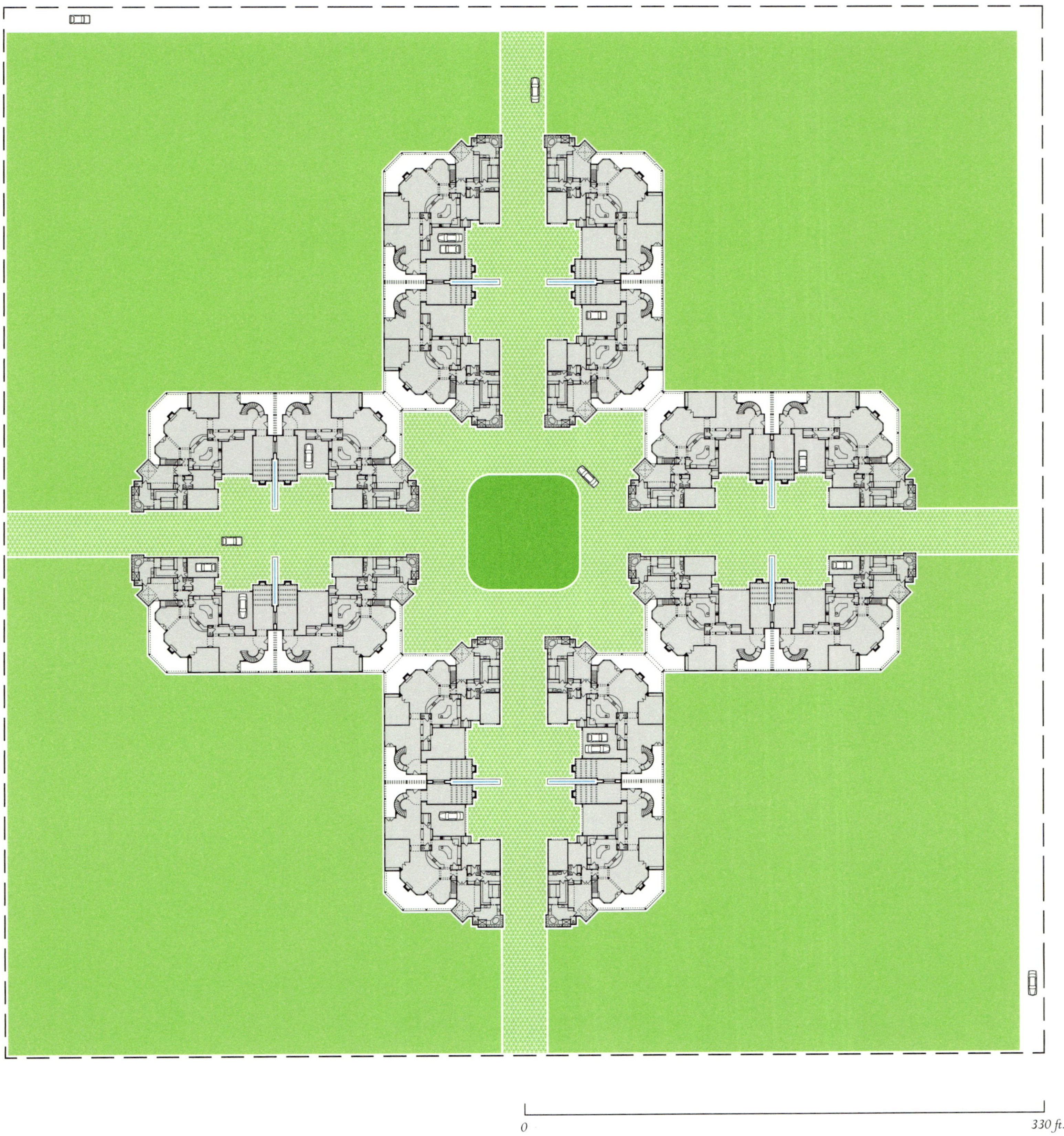

New Ark

NE 1/4 SE 1/4 Section 18

16 Houses
96,000 Square Feet
80 Bedrooms
80 Full Bathrooms
16 Half Bathrooms

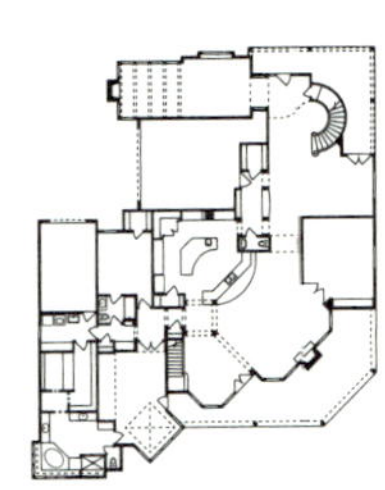

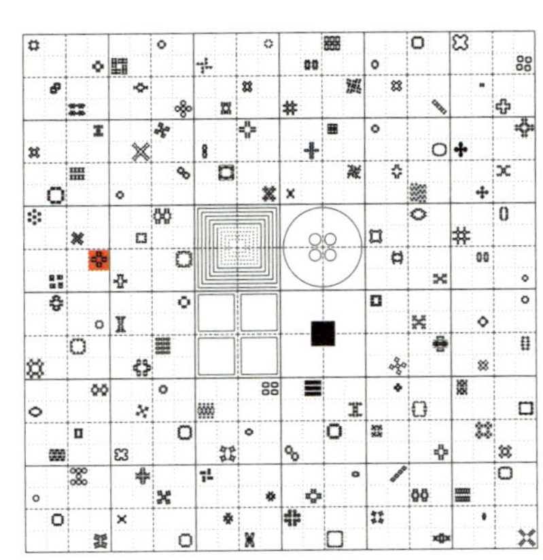

Meritage Homes, The Chalet, 6000 sq. ft., Texas

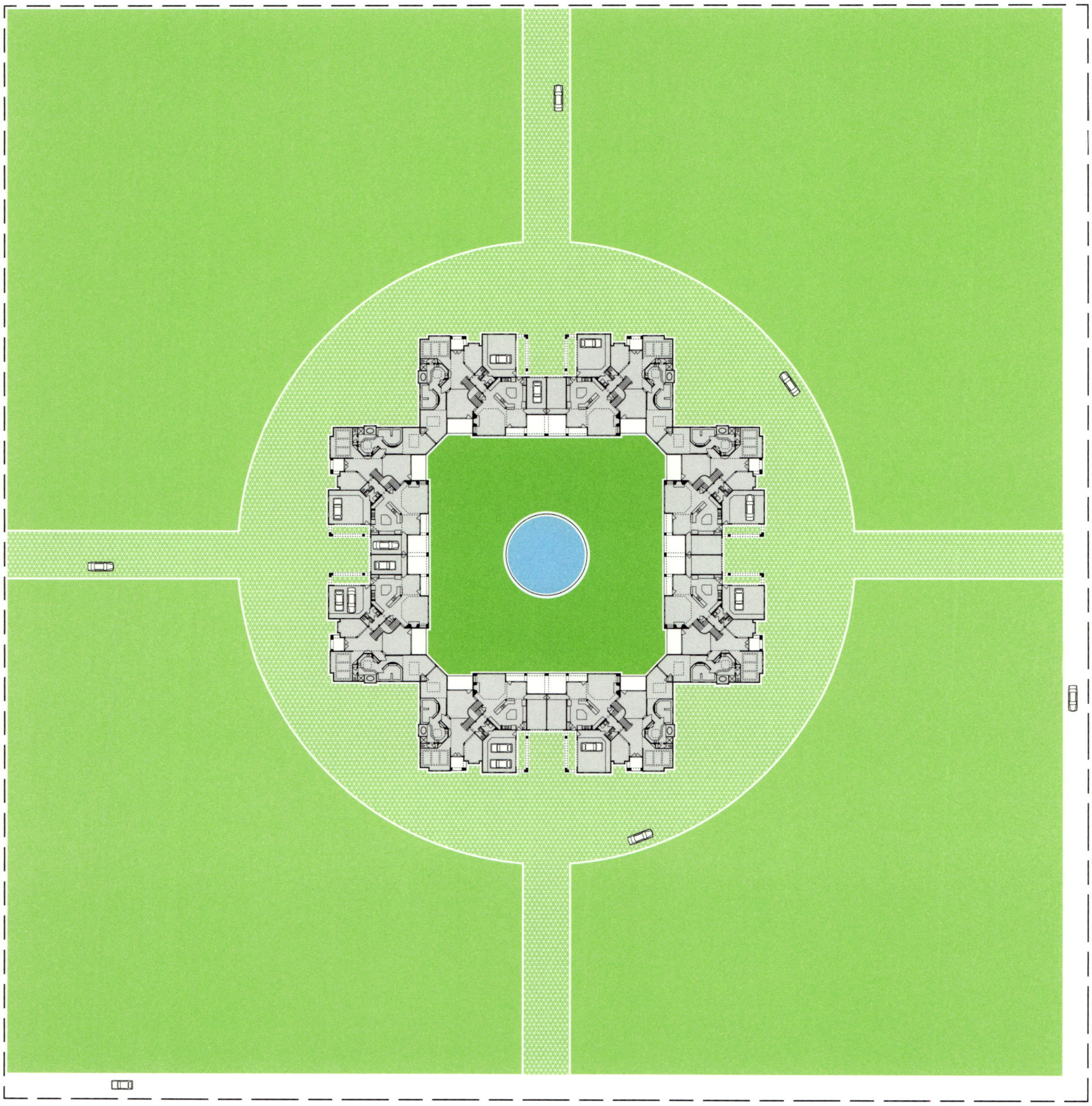

Du Flumadon

SE 1/4 NE 1/4 Section 19

8 Houses
35,680 Square Feet
32–40 Bedrooms
24–32 Full Bathrooms
24 Half Bathrooms

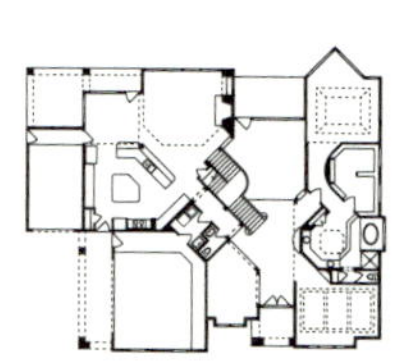

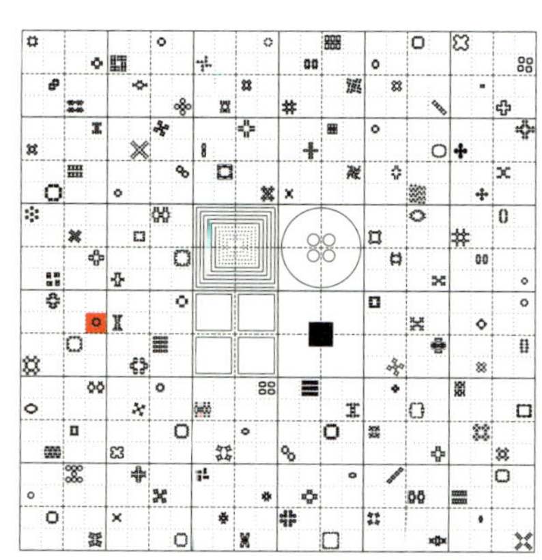

David Weekley Homes, The Kramer, 4460 sq. ft., Texas

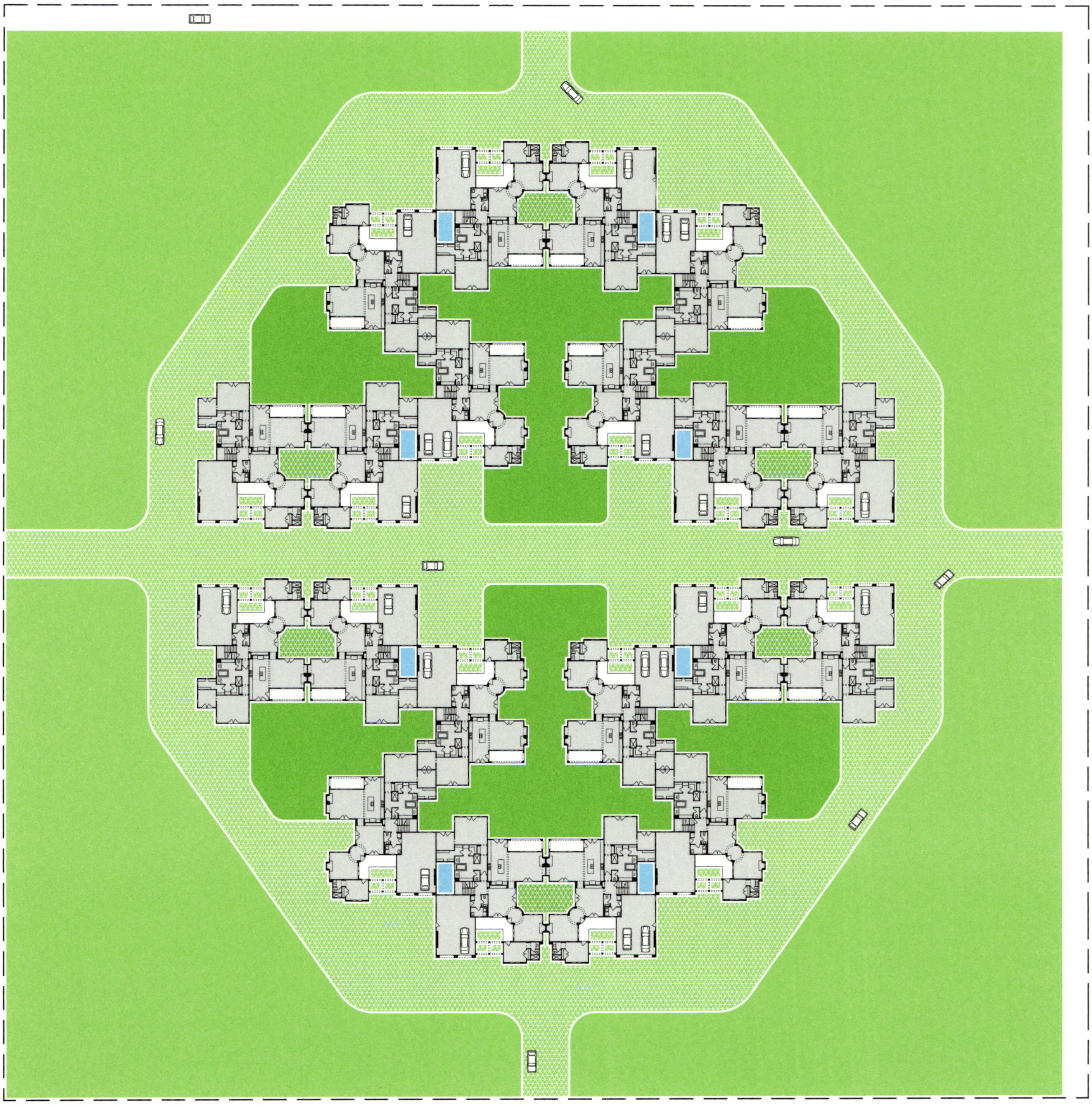

0 330 ft.

Finio Farms

NE 1/4 NW 1/4 Section 19

20 Houses
122,440 Square Feet
100 Bedrooms
100 Full Bathrooms
20 Half Bathrooms

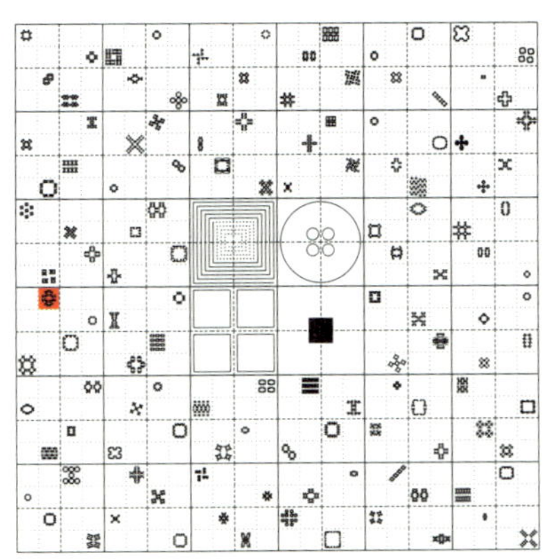

Standard Pacific Homes, Residence 1H, 6122 sq. ft., California

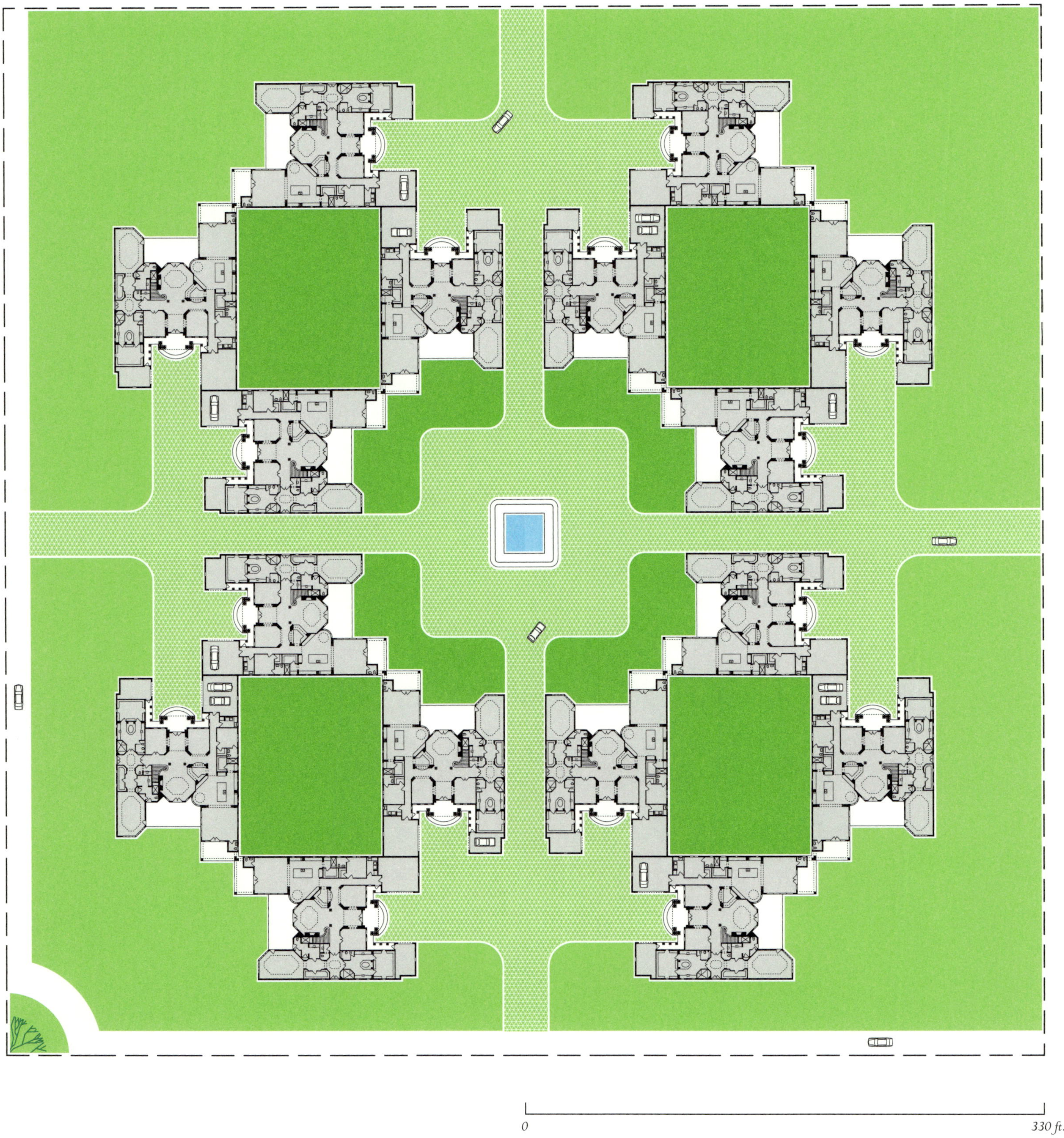

Rancho Riata

SW 1/4 SW 1/4 Section 19

16 Houses
126,480 Square Feet
80 Bedrooms
96 Full Bathrooms
32 Half Bathrooms

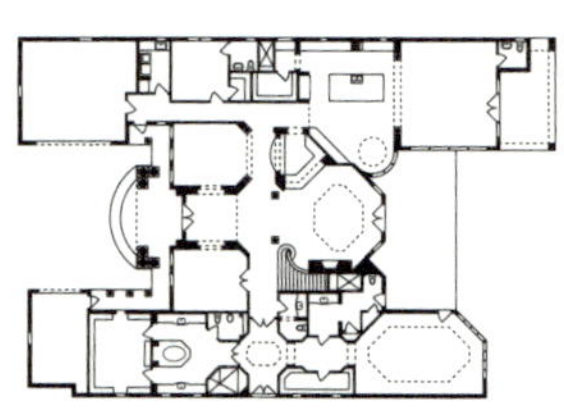

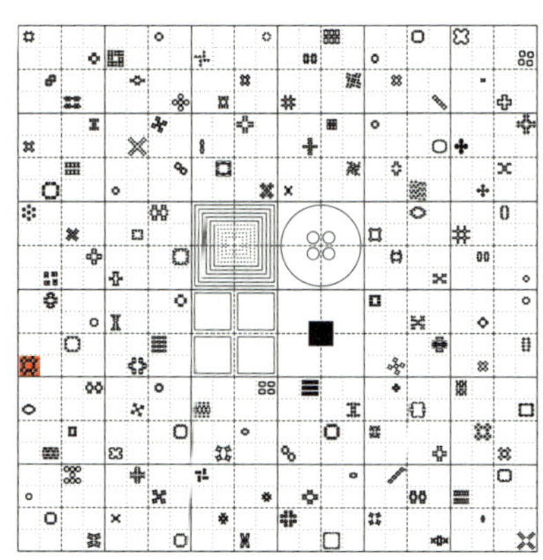

Taylor Morrison Homes, Casa del Playa, 7905 sq. ft., Florida

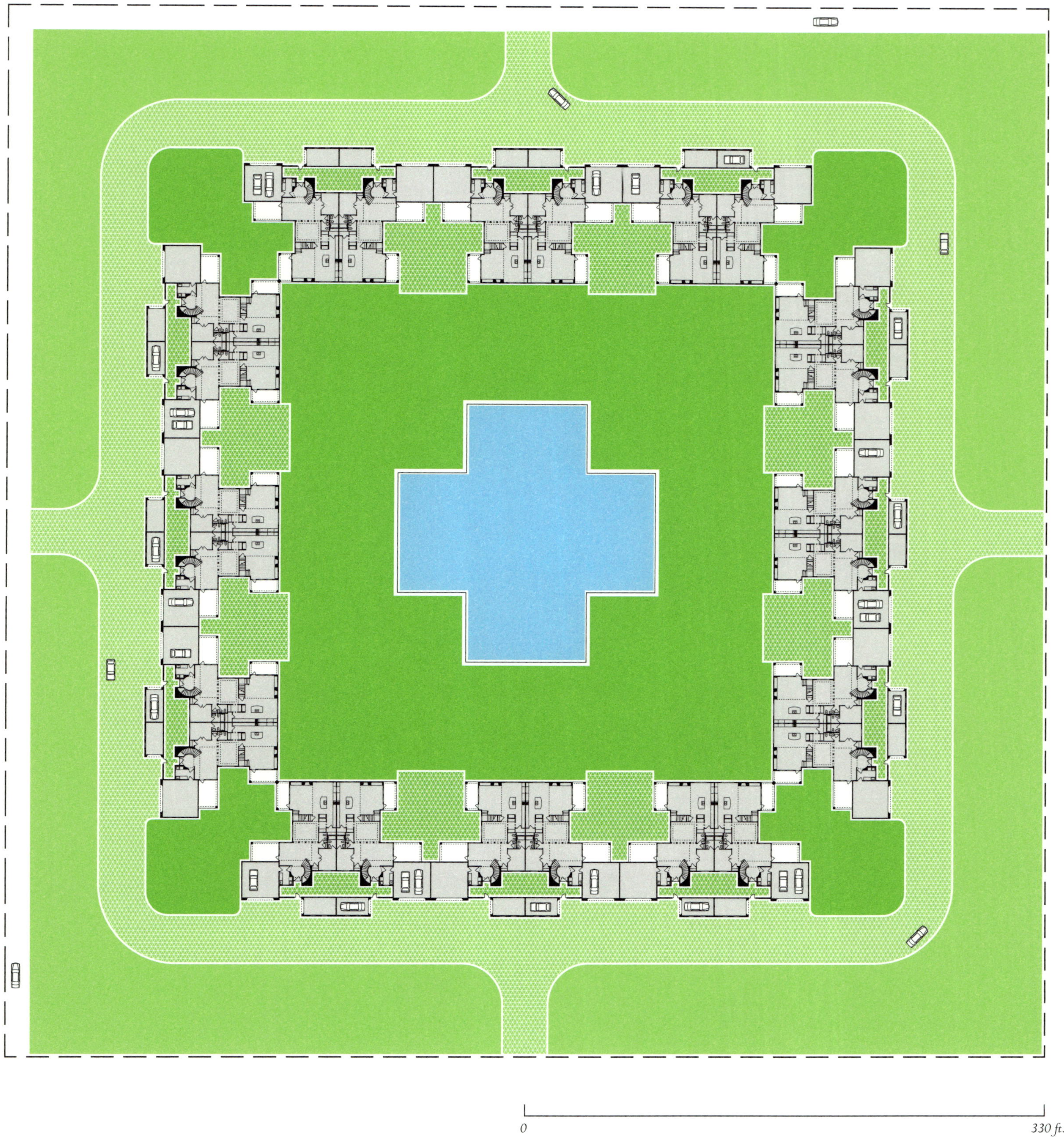

The Palace (of Don Barthelmismo)
NW 1/4 SE 1/4 Section 19

24 Houses
91,200 Square Feet
72–120 Bedrooms
96 Full Bathrooms
24 Half Bathrooms

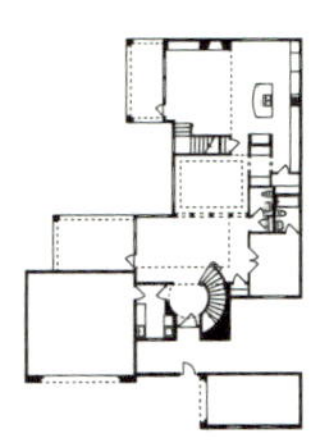

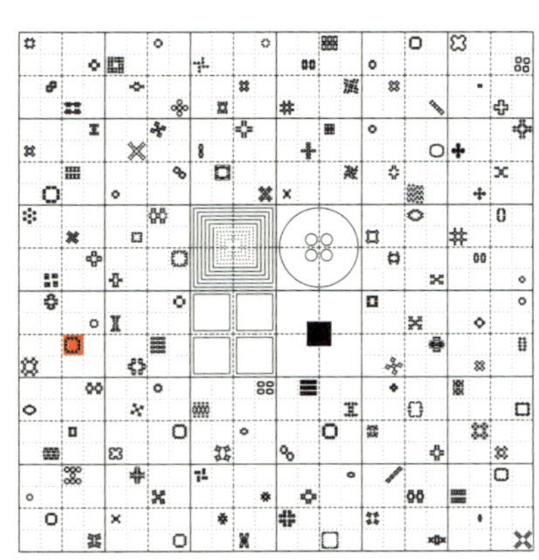

Pulte Homes, The Provence, 3800 sq. ft., Nevada

Don Barthelmismo Meets with Workers at The Palace, Freedomland
after *Capital and Labour,* 1874
Henry Stacy Marks

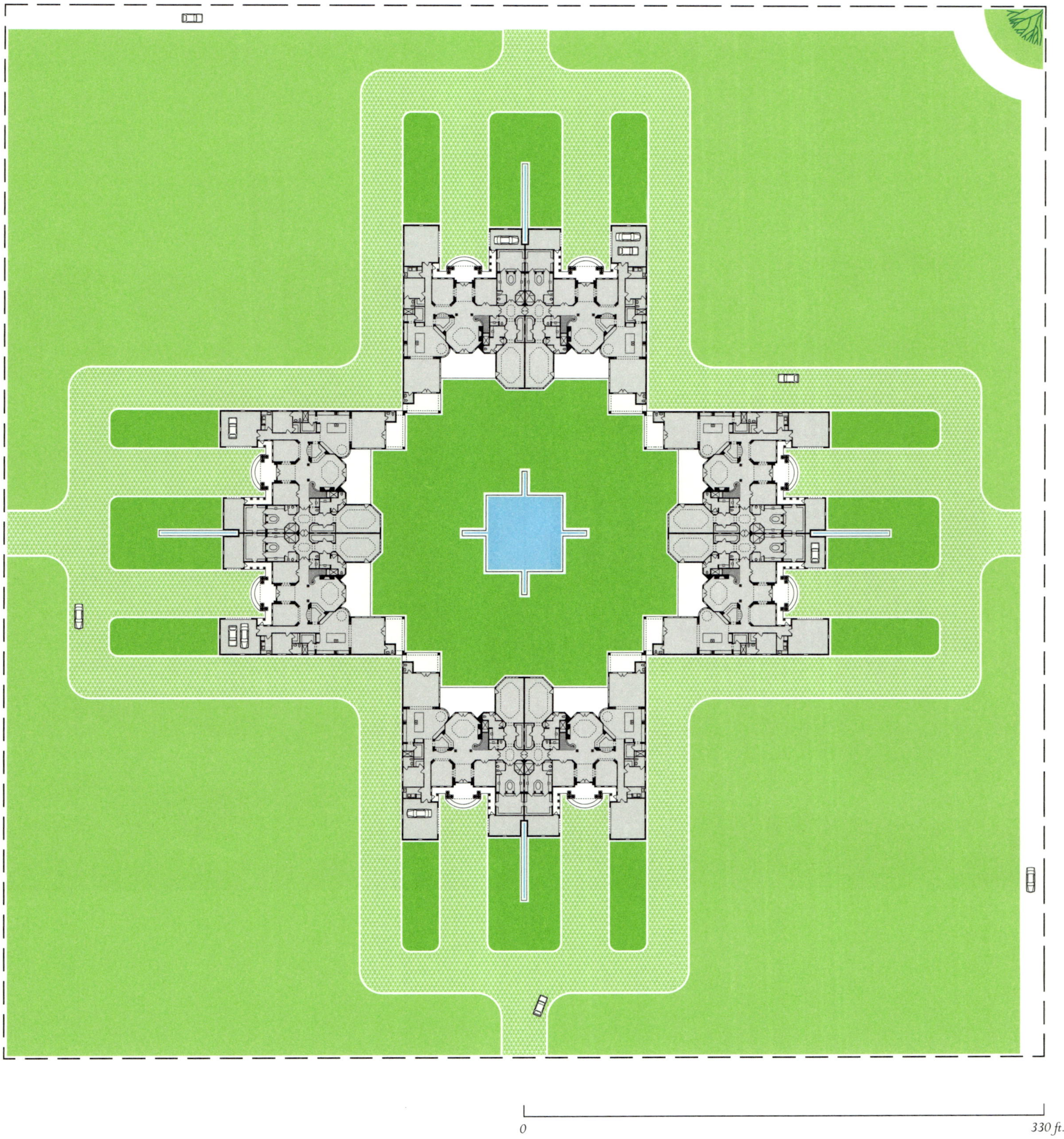

The New Era Union

NE 1/4 NE 1/4 Section 20

8 Houses
63,240 Square Feet
40 Bedrooms
48 Full Bathrooms
16 Half Bathrooms

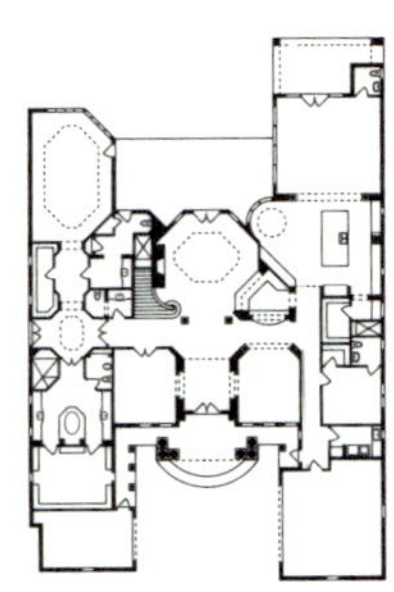

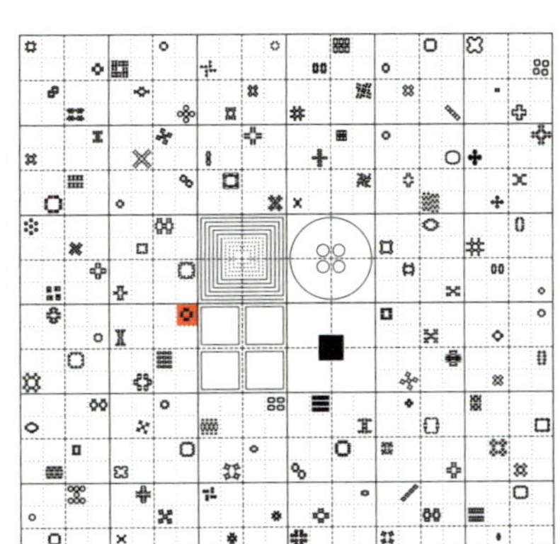

Taylor Morrison Homes, Casa del Playa, 7905 sq. ft., Florida

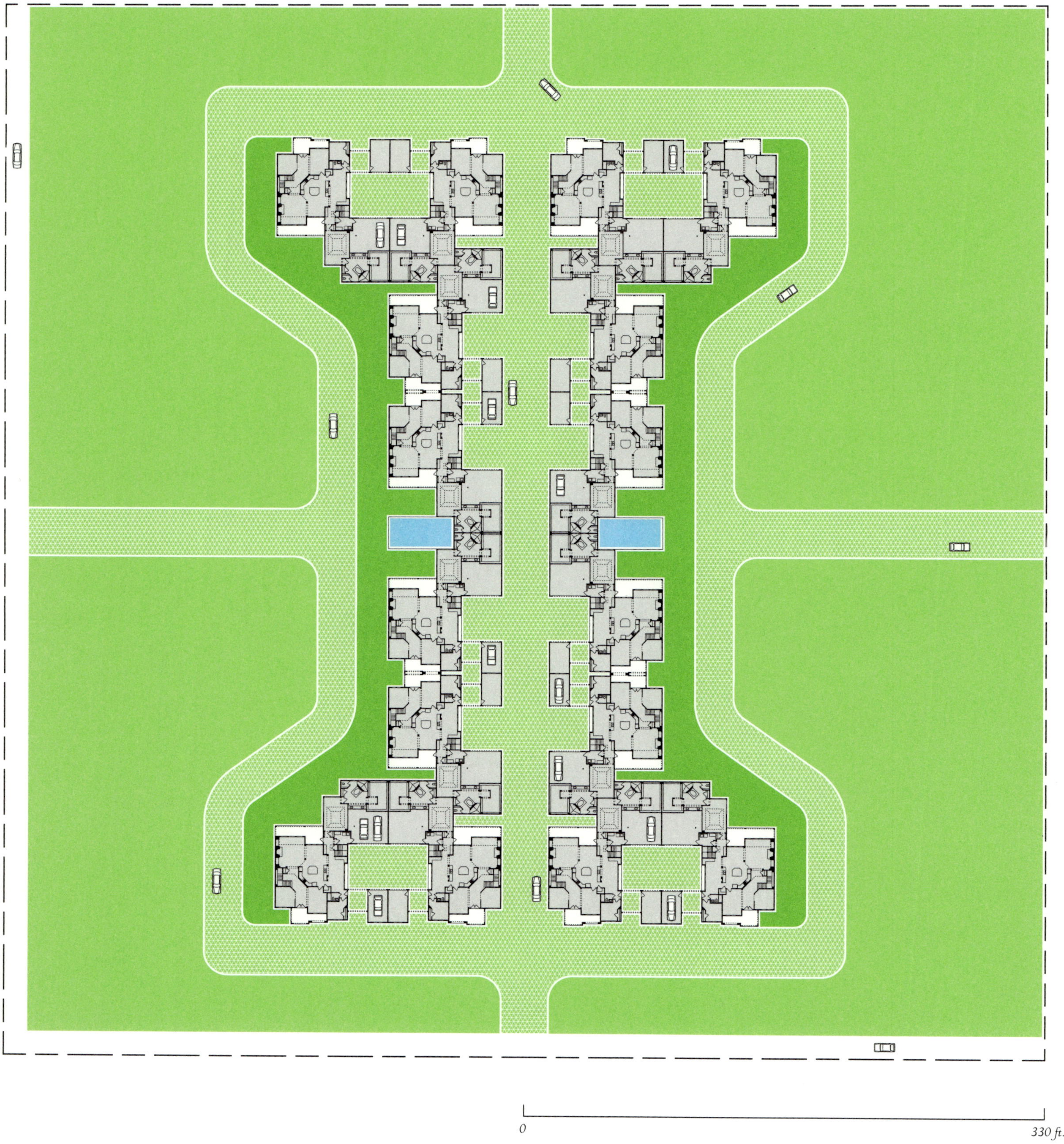

Atria Romano Accipitris

SW 1/4 NW 1/4 Section 20

16 Houses
90,496 Square Feet
80 Bedrooms
80 Full Bathrooms
16 Half Bathrooms

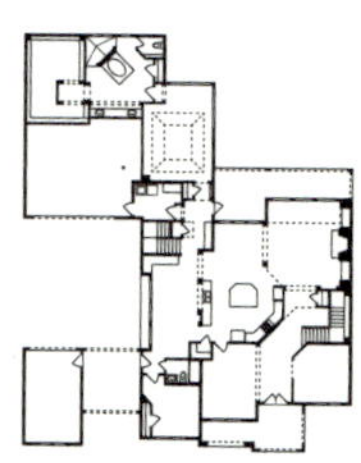

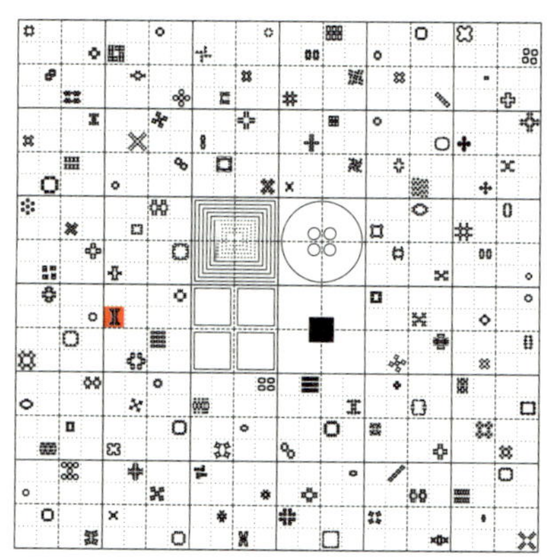

David Weekley Homes, McKeon, 5656 sq. ft., Texas

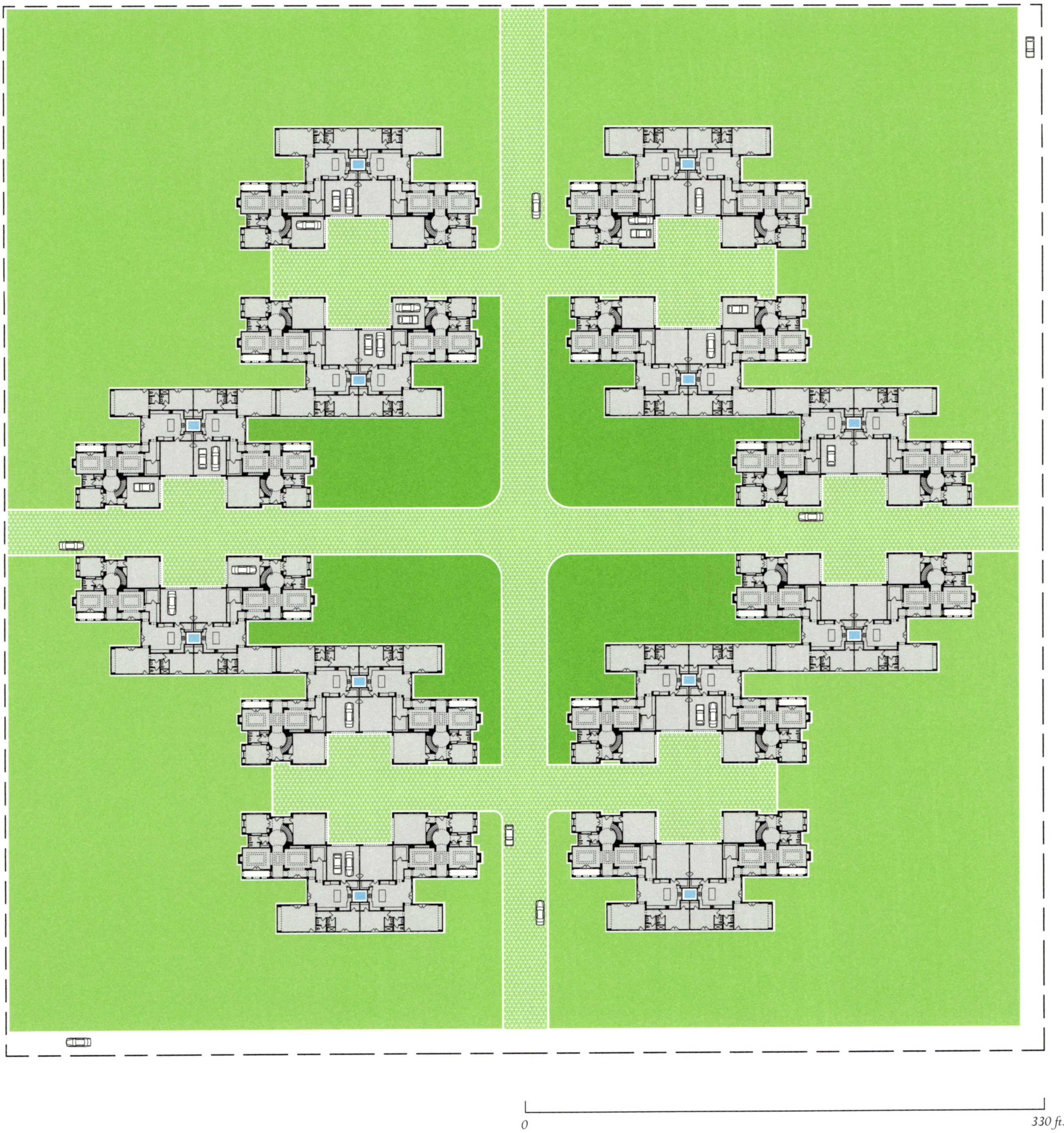

Wazeone Woods

SE 1/4 SW 1/4 Section 20

24 Houses
157,392 Square Feet
120 Bedrooms
120 Full Bathrooms
48 Half Bathrooms

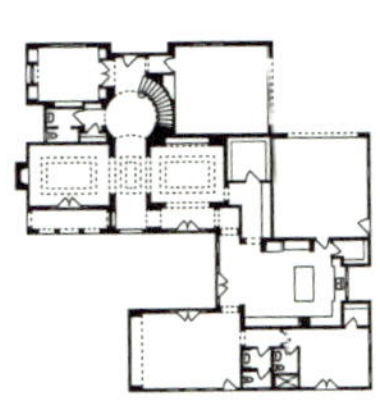

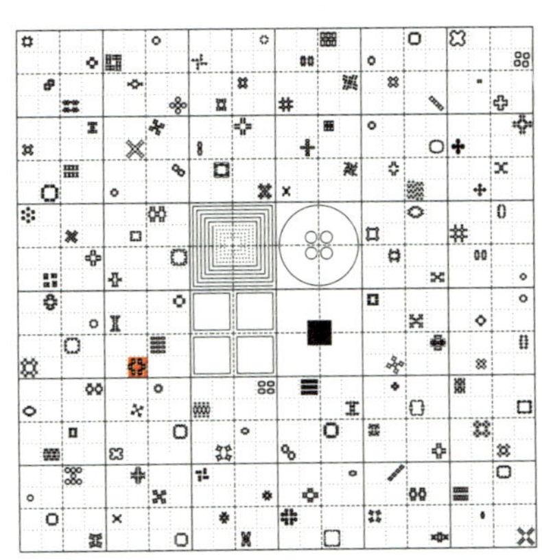

KB Home, The Stratford, 6558 sq. ft., California

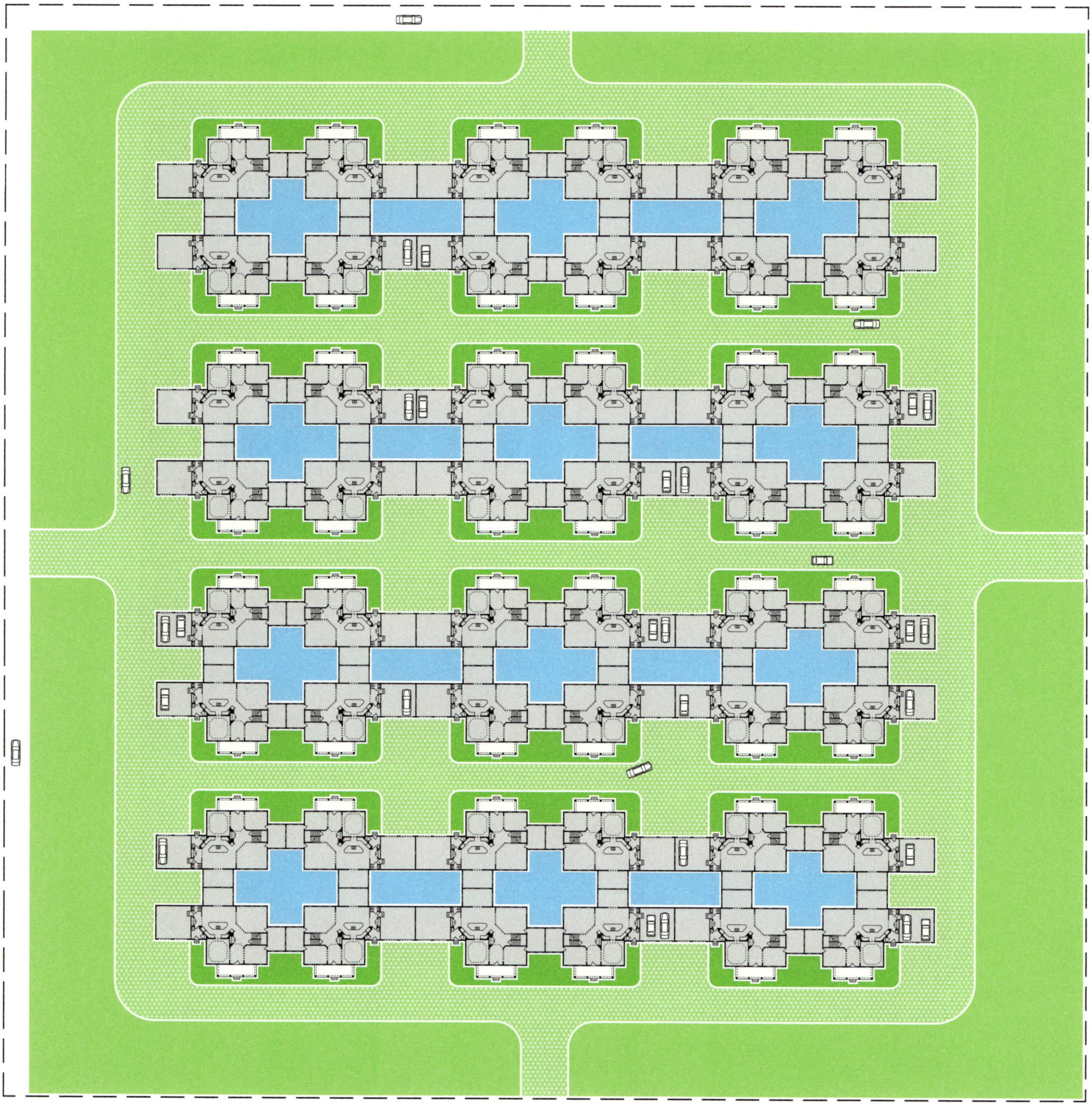

Yostville

NW 1/4 SE 1/4 Section 20

48 Houses
177,744 Square Feet
144 Bedrooms
96 Full Bathrooms
48 Half Bathrooms

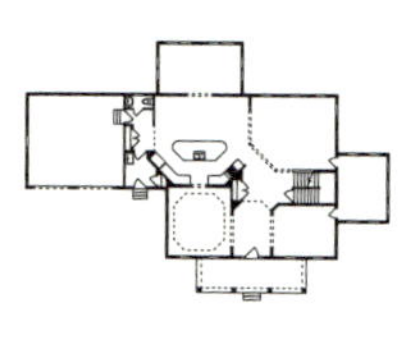

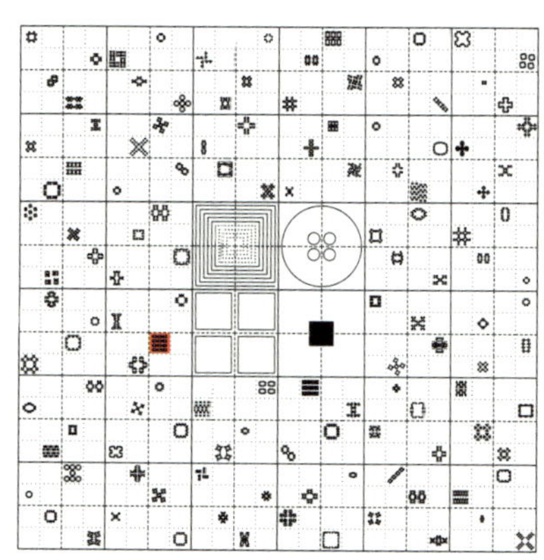

Ryland Homes, The Wye, 3703 sq. ft., Delaware

A Portrait of Madame Déficit at the Little Hamlet, Freedomland
after *Maria Carolina of Austria, Queen of Naples,* circa 1768
Anton Raphael Mengs

The Little Hamlet

SW 1/4 NE 1/4 Section 23

20 Houses
85,700 Square Feet
80–100 Bedrooms
80 Full Bathrooms
20 Half Bathrooms

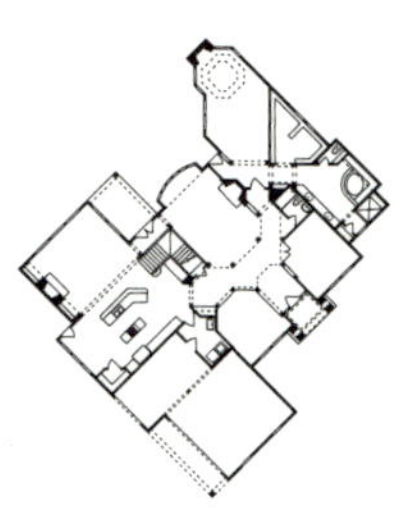

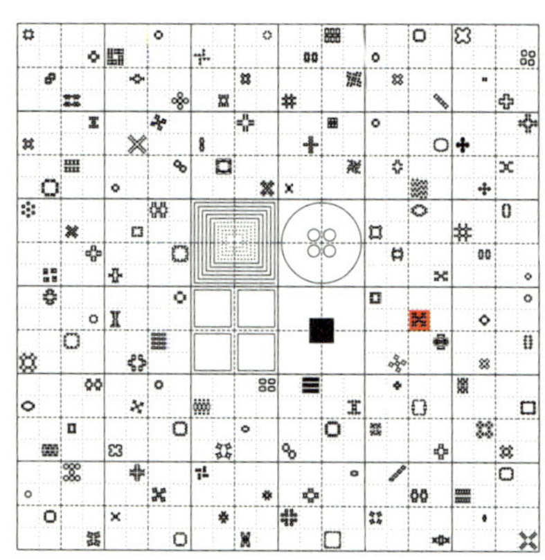

David Weekley Homes, The Lynnhaven, 4285 sq. ft., Texas

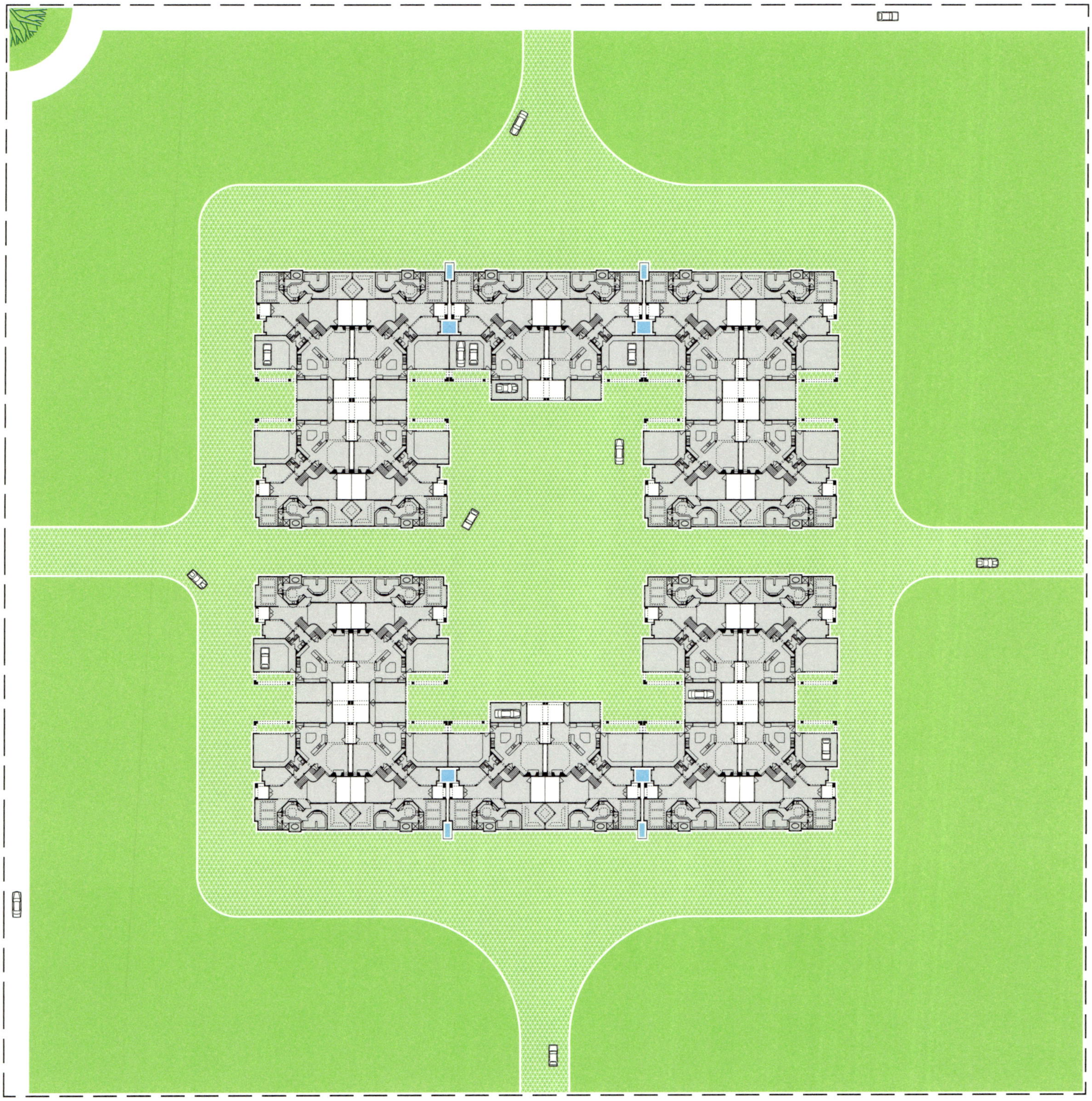

Acri Anonimi

NW 1/4 NW 1/4 Section 23

20 Houses
89,200 Square Feet
80–100 Bedrooms
60–80 Full Bathrooms
20 Half Bathrooms

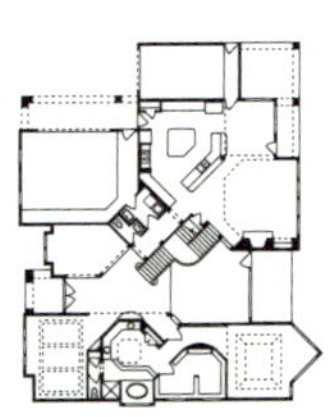

David Weekley Homes, The Kramer, 4460 sq. ft., Texas

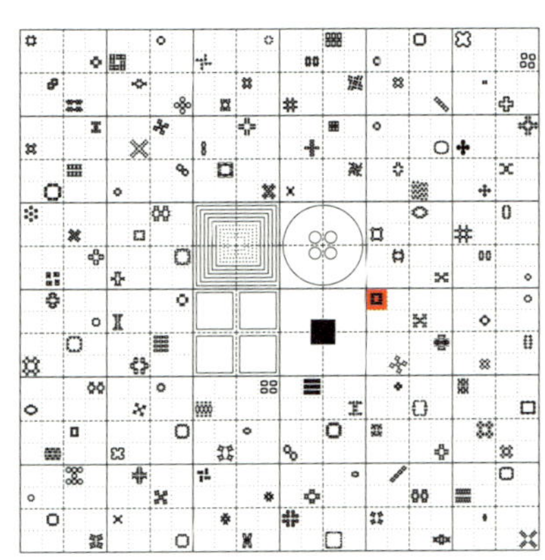

The Villas at Pek Park
SE 1/4 SW 1/4 Section 23

20 Houses
76,000 Square Feet
60–100 Bedrooms
80 Full Bathrooms
20 Half Bathrooms

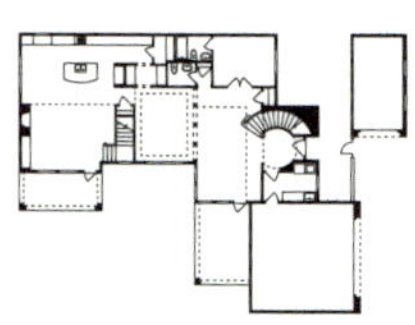

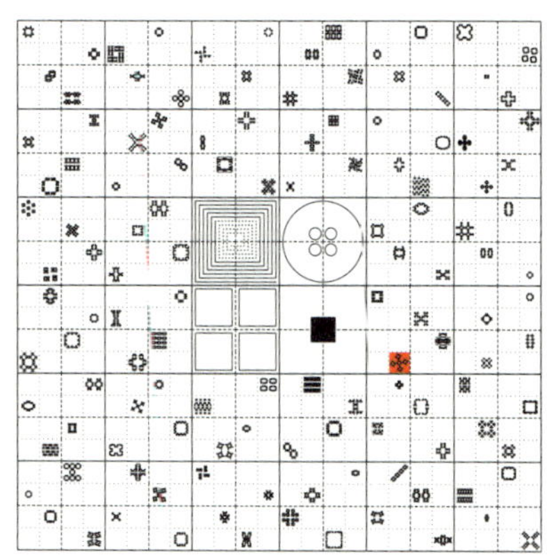

Pulte Homes, The Provence, 3800 sq. ft., Nevada

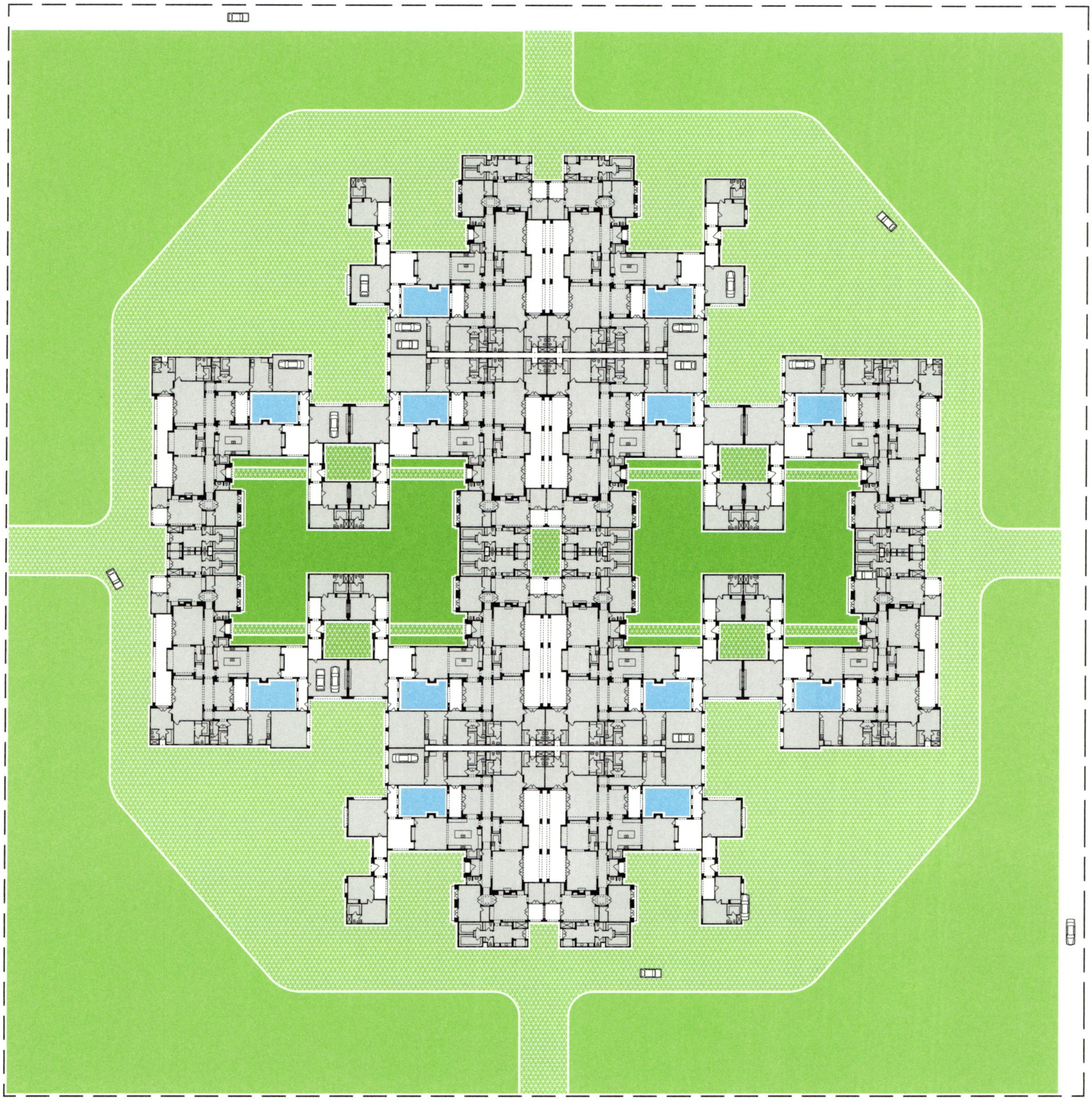

Bayt el Kadi

NE 1/4 SE 1/4 Section 23

12 Houses
73,200 Square Feet
60–72 Bedrooms
60–72 Full Bathrooms
12 Half Bathrooms

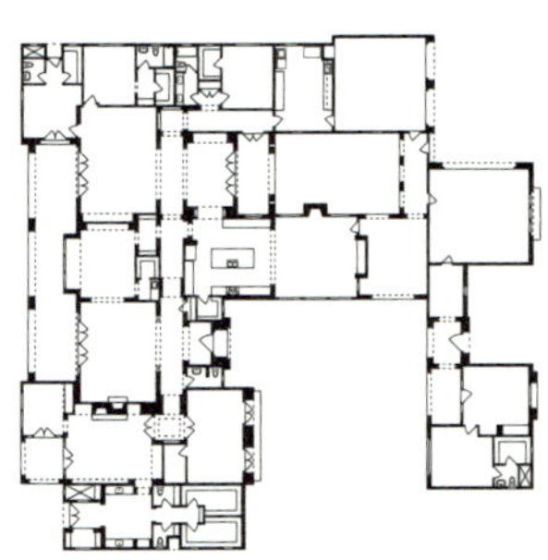

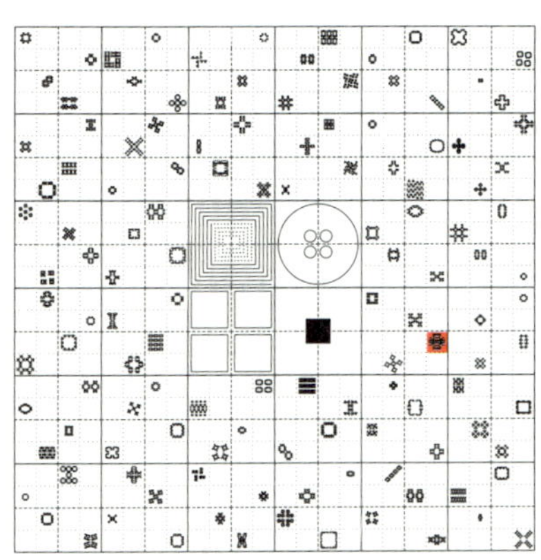

Toll Brothers, The Terreno, 6100 sq. ft., Arizona

Maison Tres McDermott

NW 1/4 NE 1/4 Section 24

8 Houses
28,928 Square Feet
32 Bedrooms
24 Full Bathrooms
8 Half Bathrooms

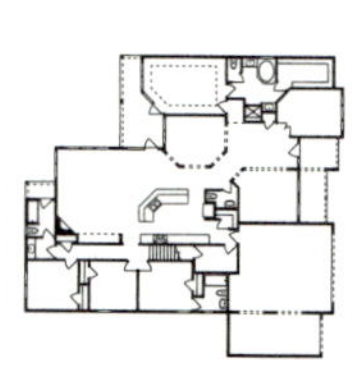

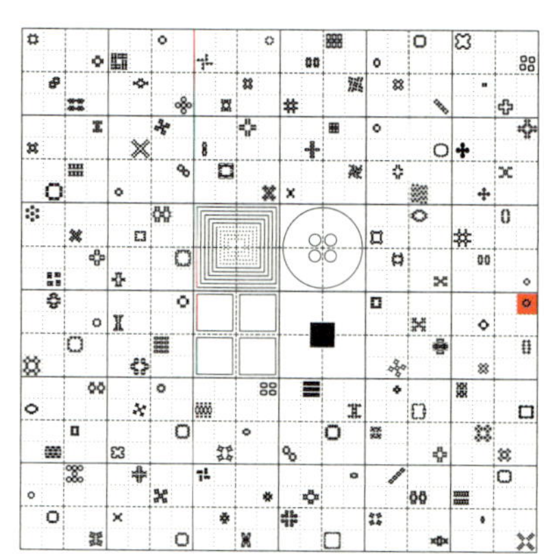

Pulte Homes, The Monet, 3616 sq. ft., Texas

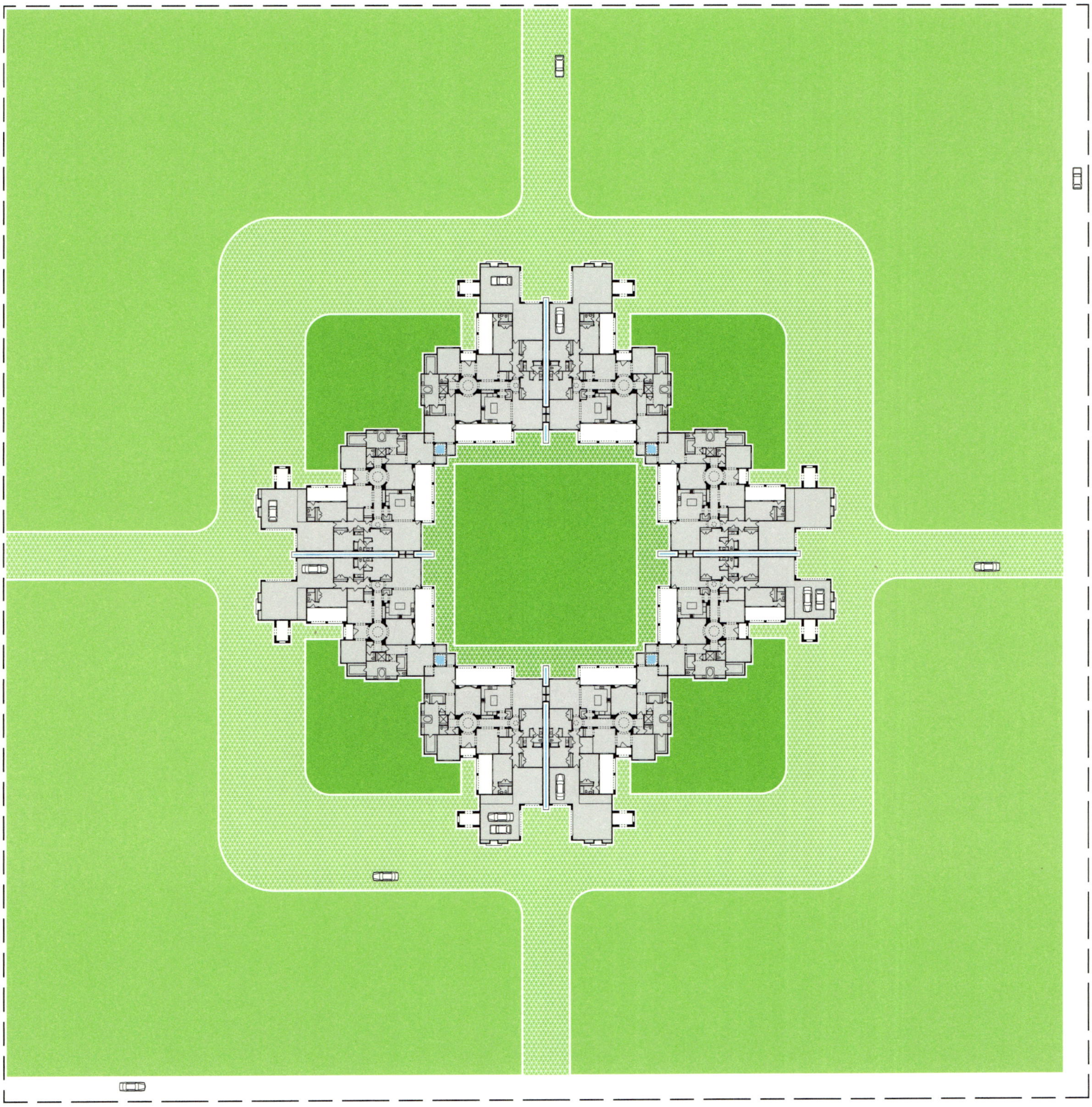

A Chateau

SE 1/4 NW 1/4 Section 24

8 Houses
33,736 Square Feet
24 Bedrooms
16 Full Bathrooms
8 Half Bathrooms

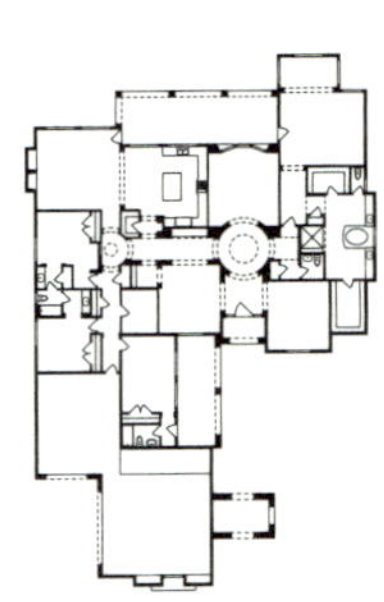

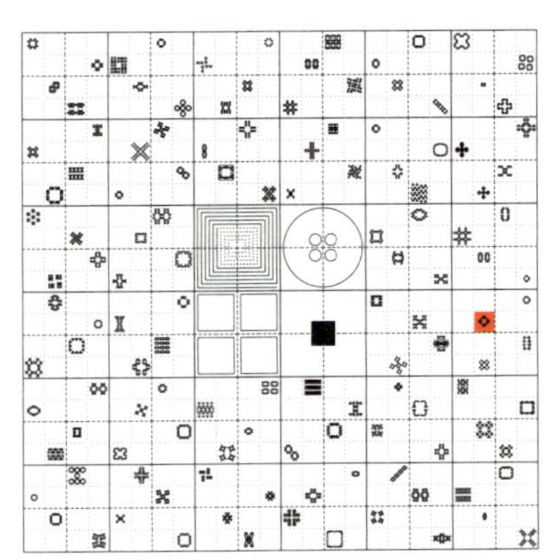

Meritage Homes, Residence 4 at Mirabel, 4217 sq. ft., Arizona

The Mowers at A Chateau, Freedomland
after *The Mowers,* 1887
Grigoriy Myasoyedov

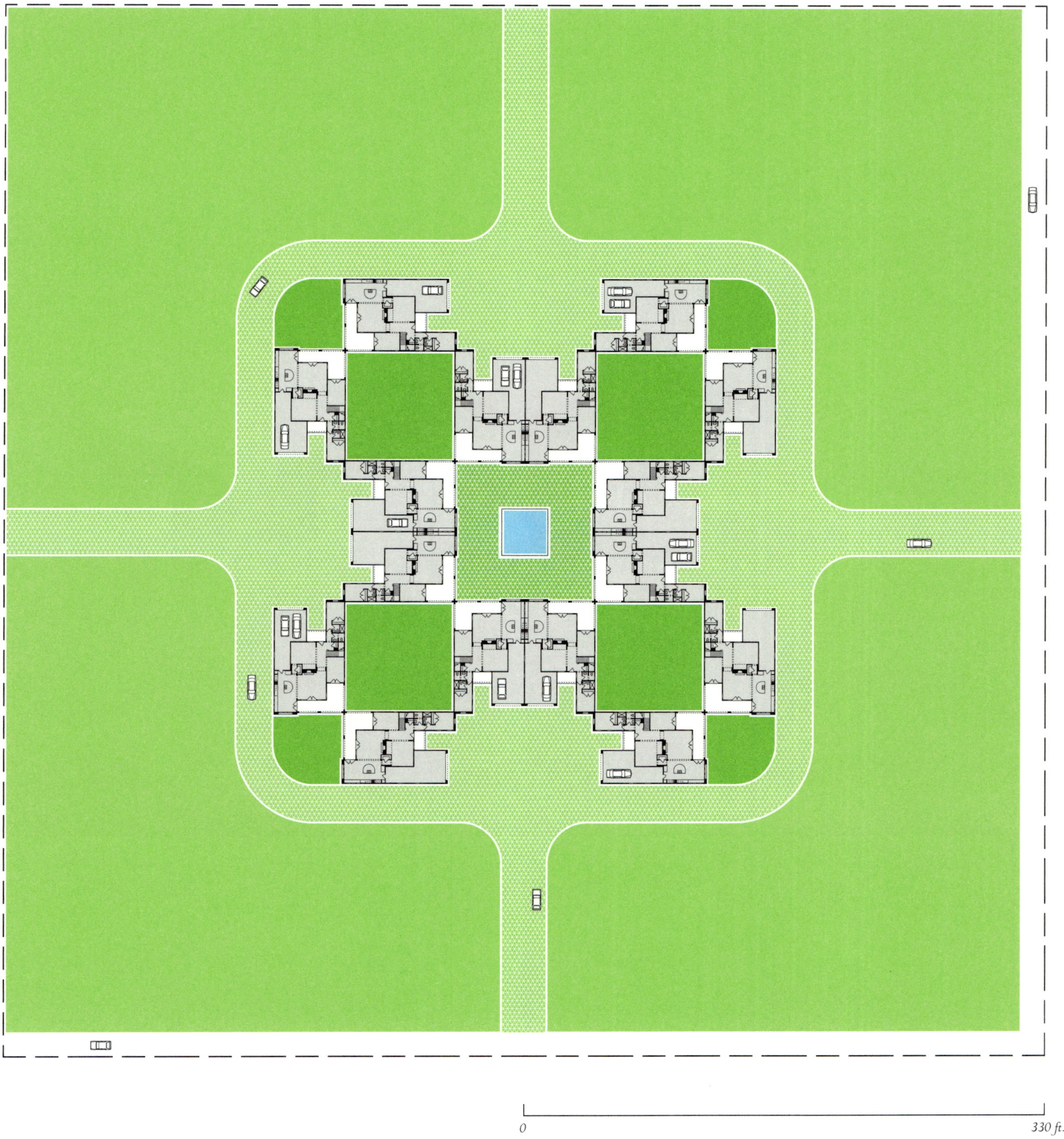

Martin-Hall-in-the-Meadows

SE 1/4 SW 1/4 Section 24

16 Houses
62,272 Square Feet
80 Bedrooms
64 Full Bathrooms
16 Half Bathrooms

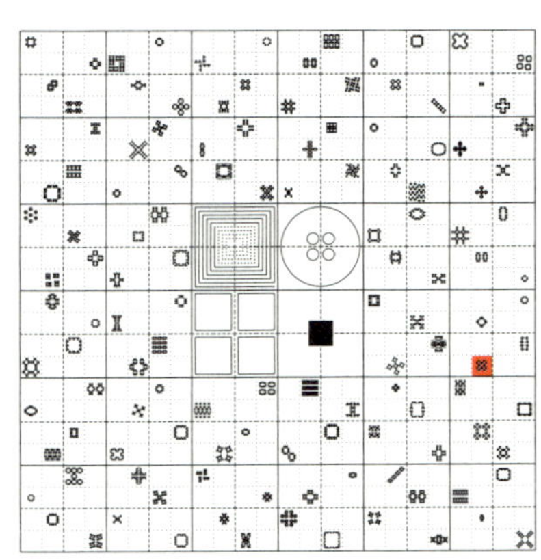

Shea Homes, Plan 4 at Vista Vallerta, 3892 sq. ft., California

Casa de Campo

NE 1/4 SE 1/4 Section 24

8 Houses
63,240 Square Feet
40 Bedrooms
48 Full Bathrooms
16 Half Bathrooms

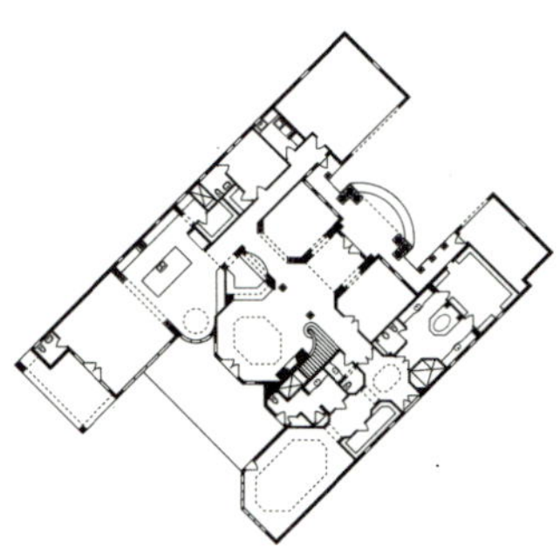

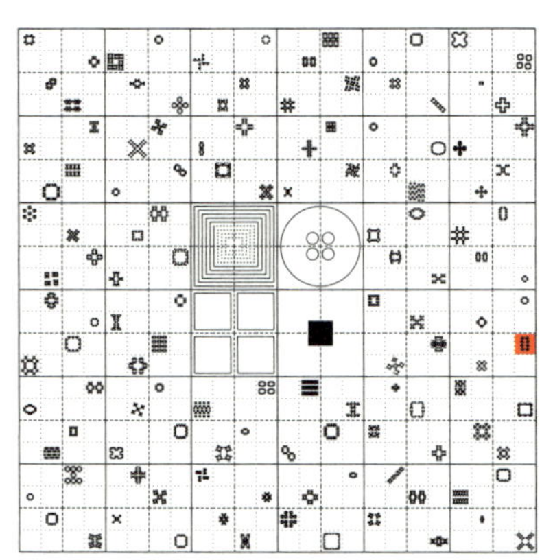

Taylor Morrison Homes, Casa del Playa, 7905 sq. ft., Florida

A Romance Begins at Blithedale Hall, Freedomland
after *John And Sophia Musters Riding At Colwick Hall,* 1777
George Stubbs

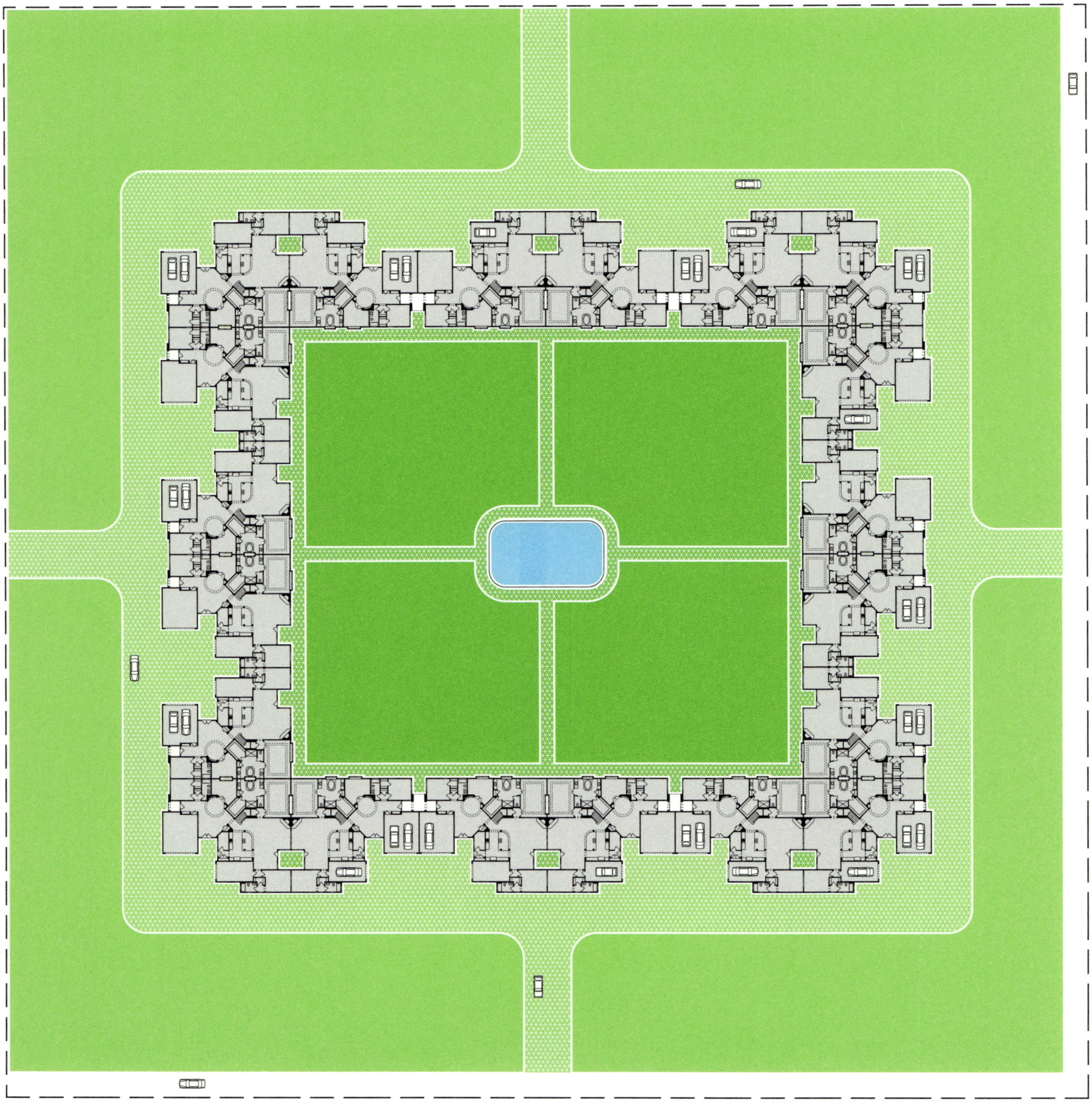

Blithedale Hall

SE 1/4 NE 1/4 Section 25

20 Houses
60,860 Square Feet
80 Bedrooms
80 Full Bathrooms
0 Half Bathrooms

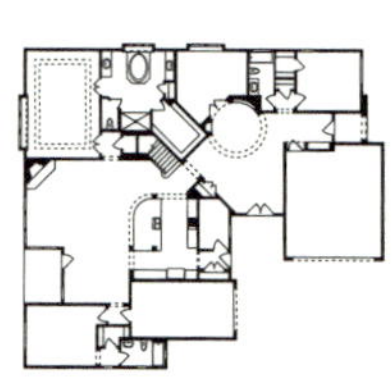

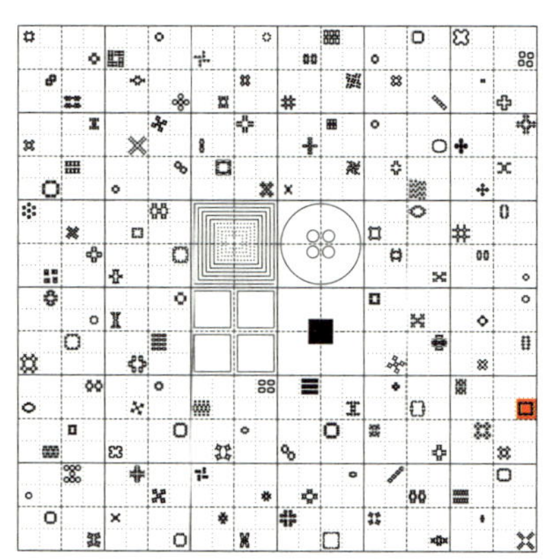

K. Hovnanian Homes, Bellvue VIII, 3043 sq. ft., Texas

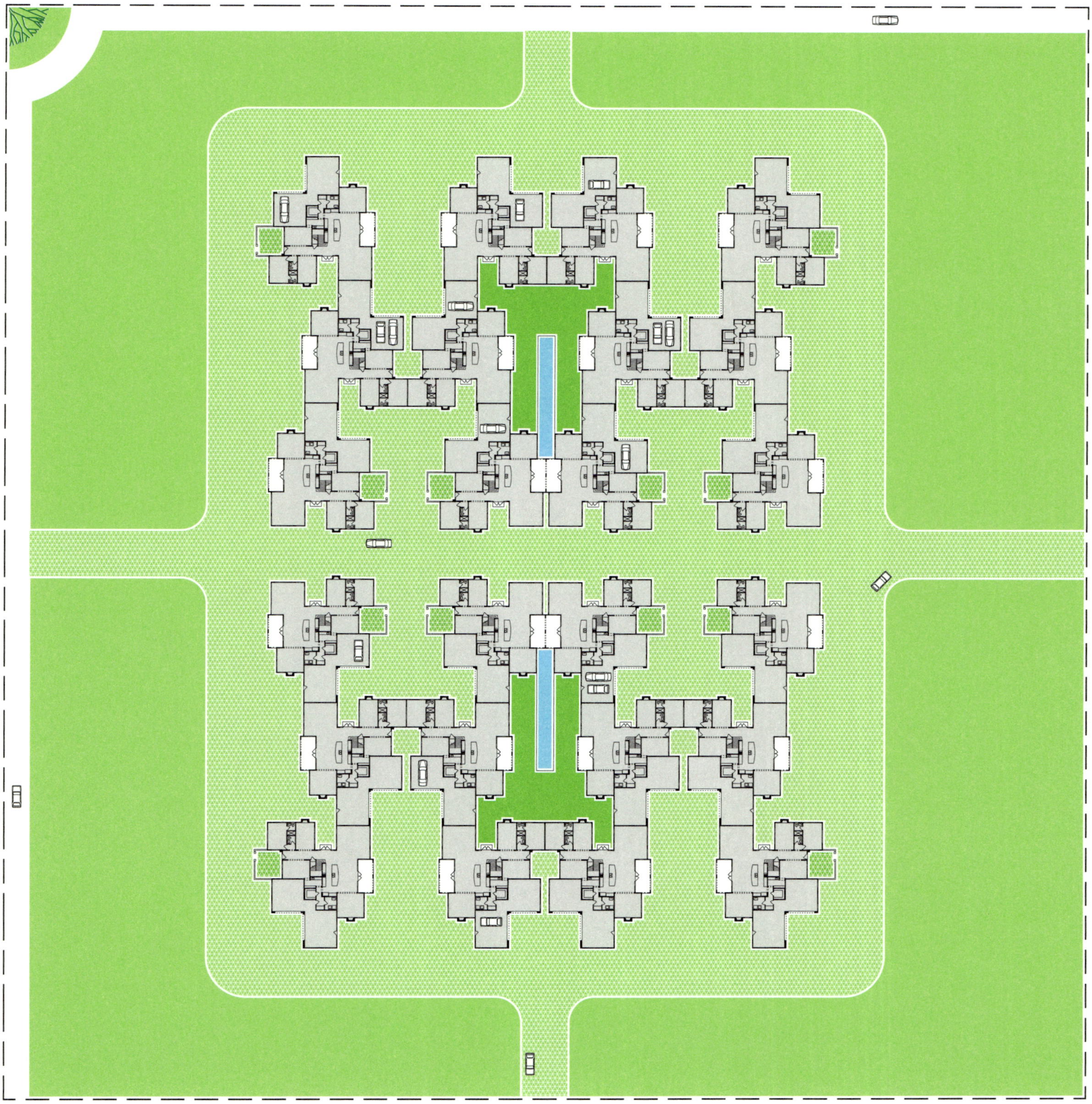

Eine Siedlung der Zimmer

NW 1/4 NW 1/4 Section 25

24 Houses
111,000 Square Feet
96 Bedrooms
96 Full Bathrooms
24 Half Bathrooms

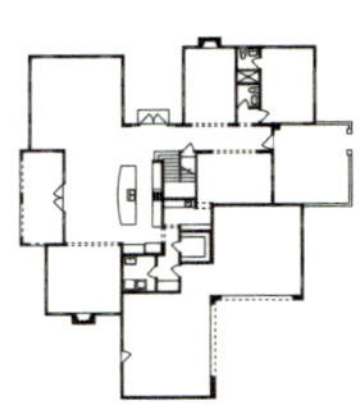

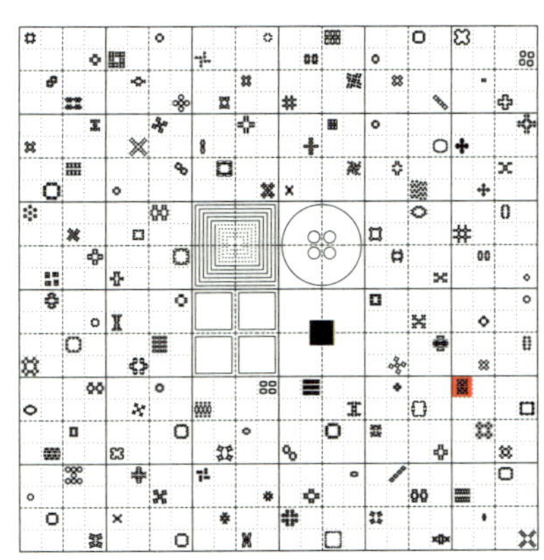

Shea Homes, Plan 2 at Maravilla, 4625 sq. ft., California

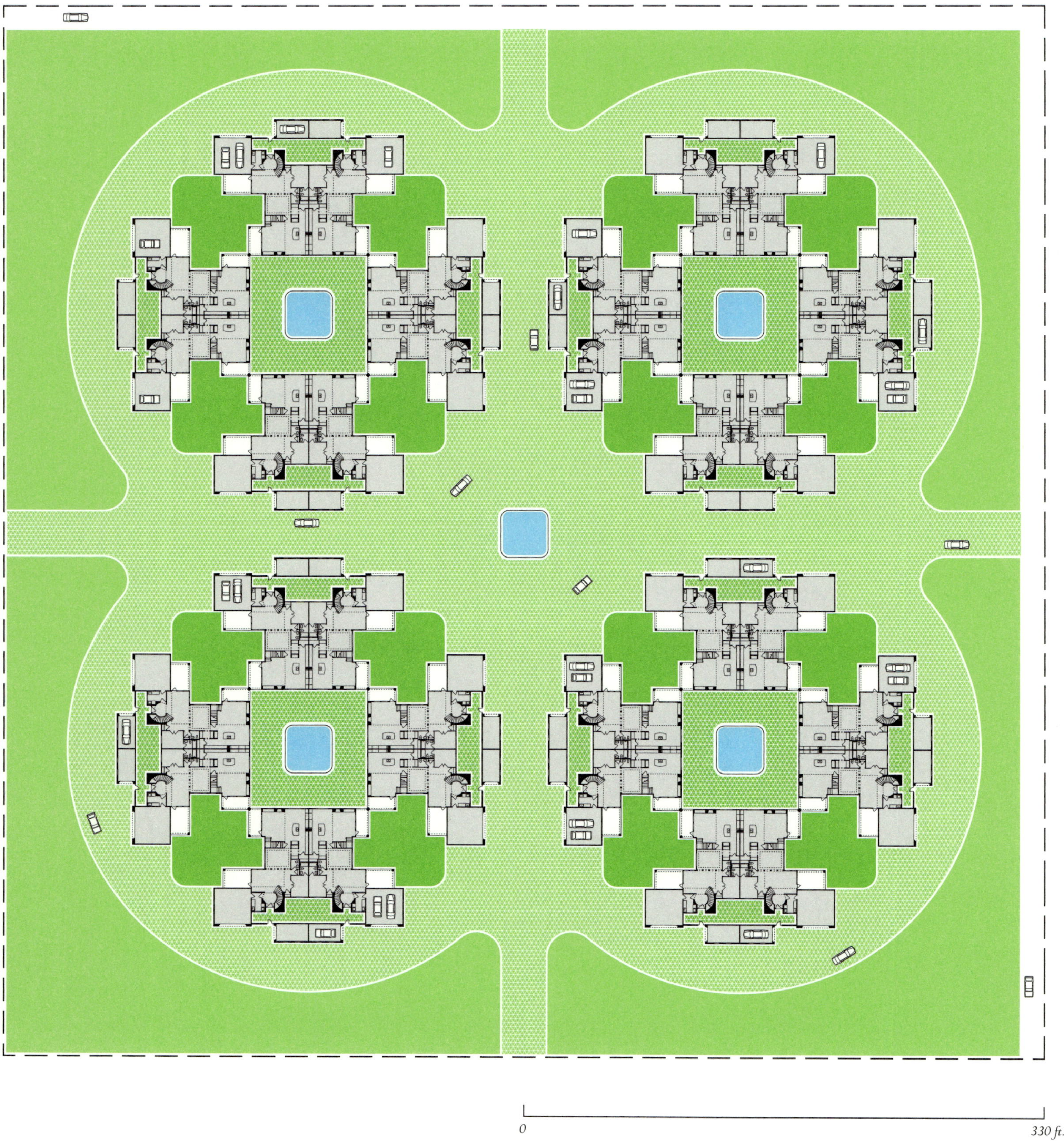

Il Quadrato di Quattro Quadrati

NE 1/4 SW 1/4 Section 25

32 Houses
121,600 Square Feet
96–160 Bedrooms
128 Full Bathrooms
32 Half Bathrooms

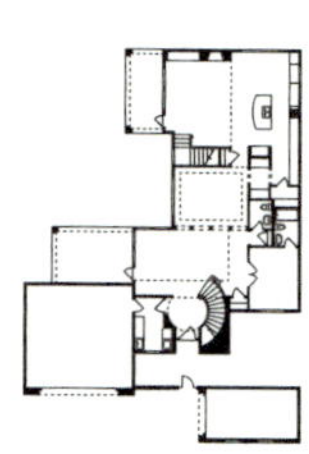

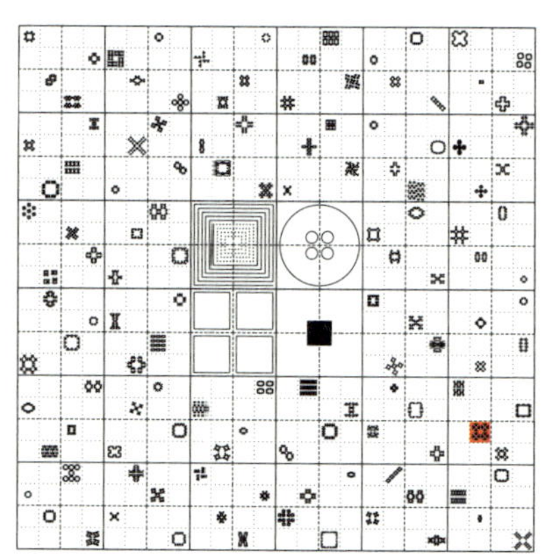

Pulte Homes, The Provence, 3800 sq. ft., Nevada

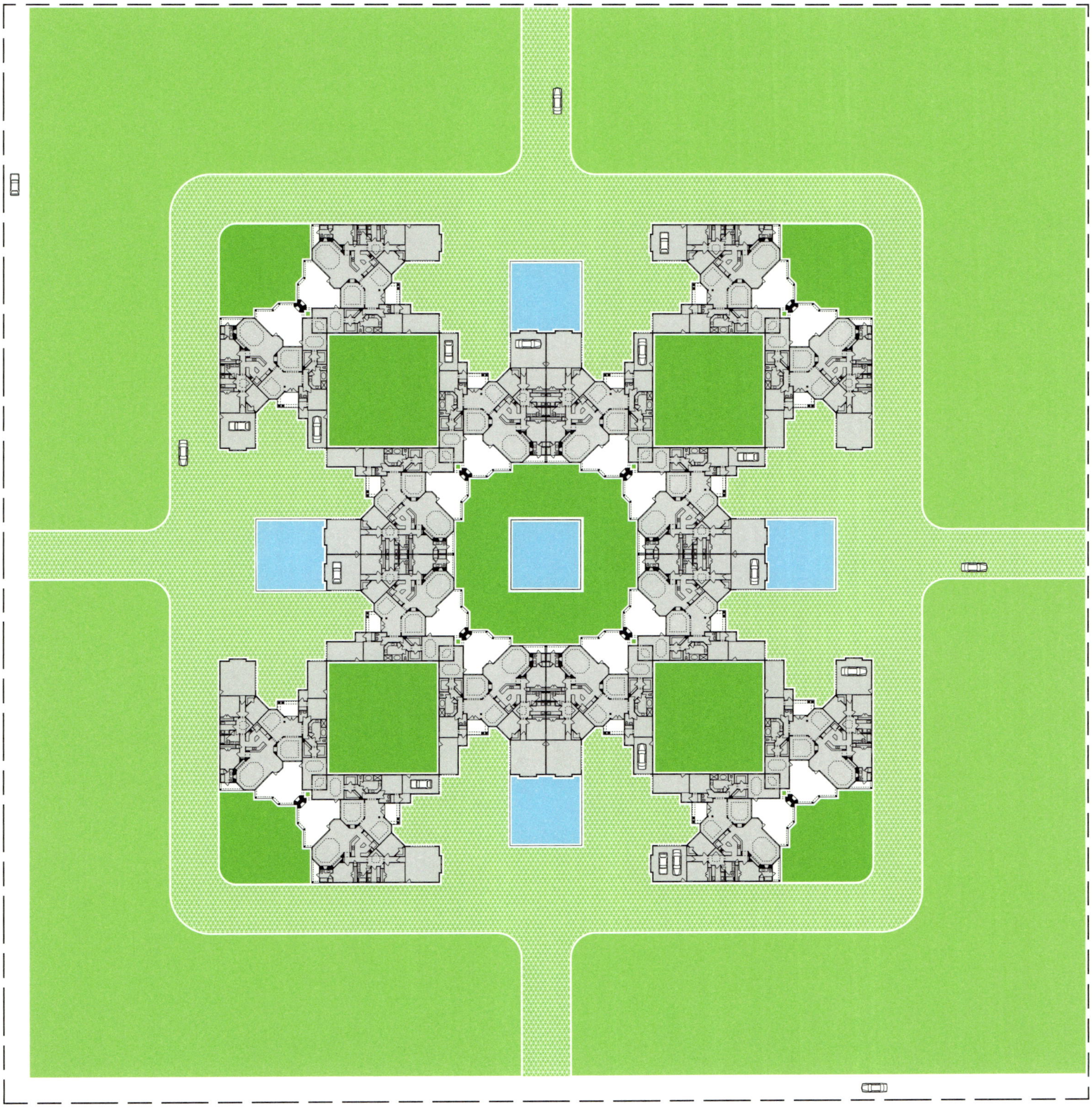

Raja Mahal

SW 1/4 SE 1/4 Section 25

16 Houses
51,568 Square Feet
64 Bedrooms
48 Full Bathrooms
16 Half Bathrooms

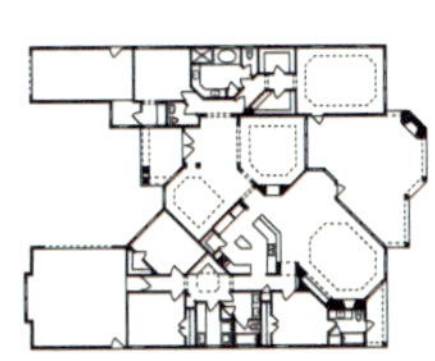

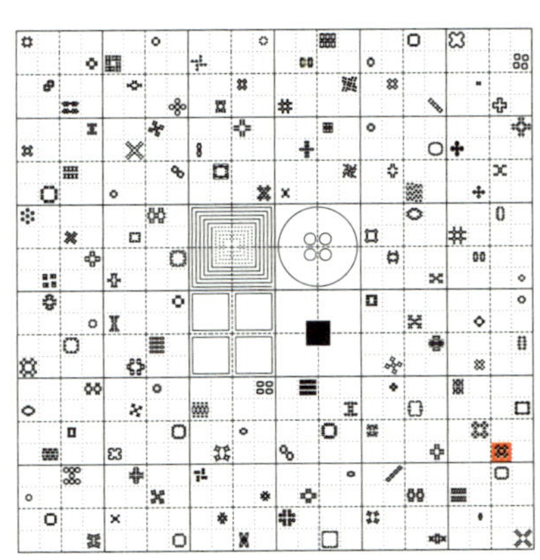

Ryland Homes, Suffolk, 3223 sq. ft., Florida

Maisons Dom-ino

SW 1/4 NE 1/4 Section 26

20 Houses
74,160 Square Feet
100 Bedrooms
80 Full Bathrooms
20 Half Bathrooms

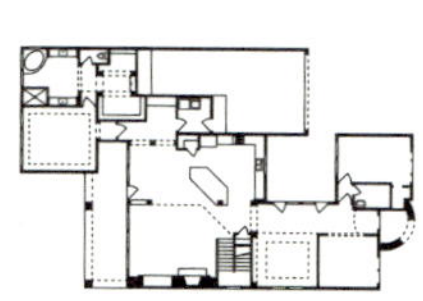

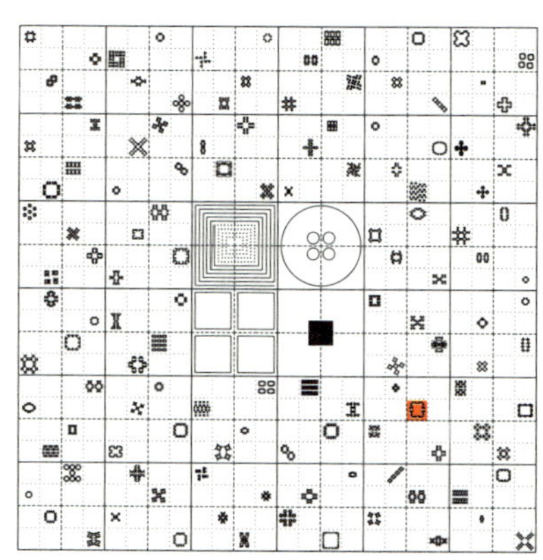

David Weekley Homes, The Palladio, 3708 sq. ft., Texas

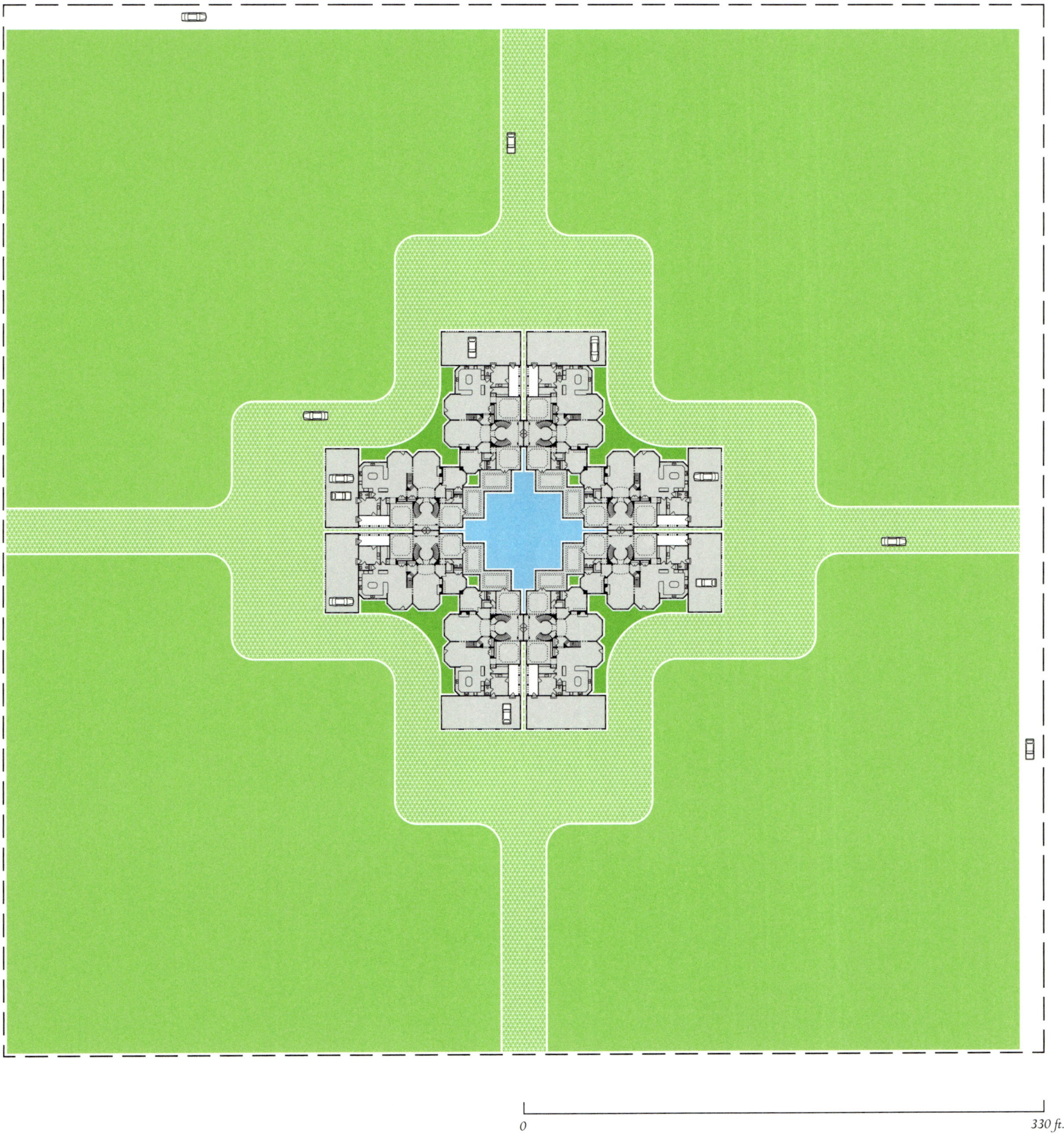

La Villa Radieuse

NE 1/4 NW 1/4 Section 26

8 Houses
42,600 Square Feet
32 Bedrooms
32 Full Bathrooms
16 Half Bathrooms

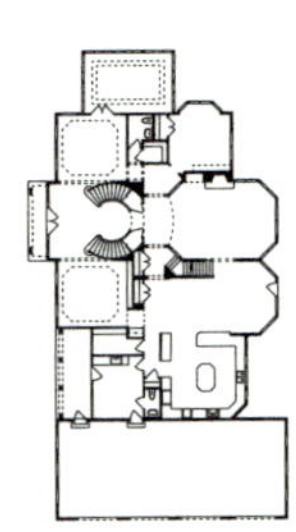

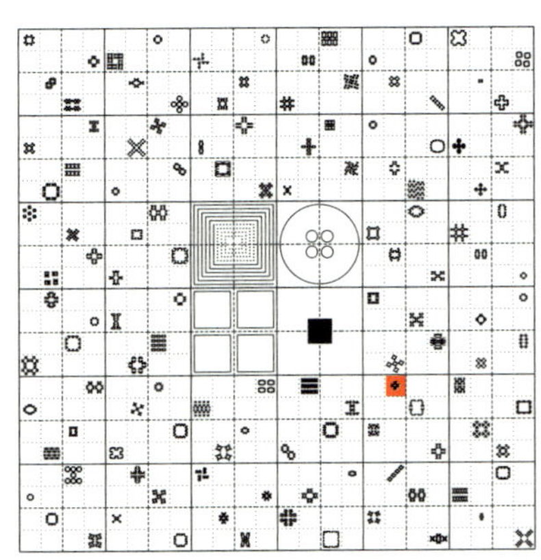

K. Hovnanian Homes, The Tara, 5325 sq. ft., Maryland

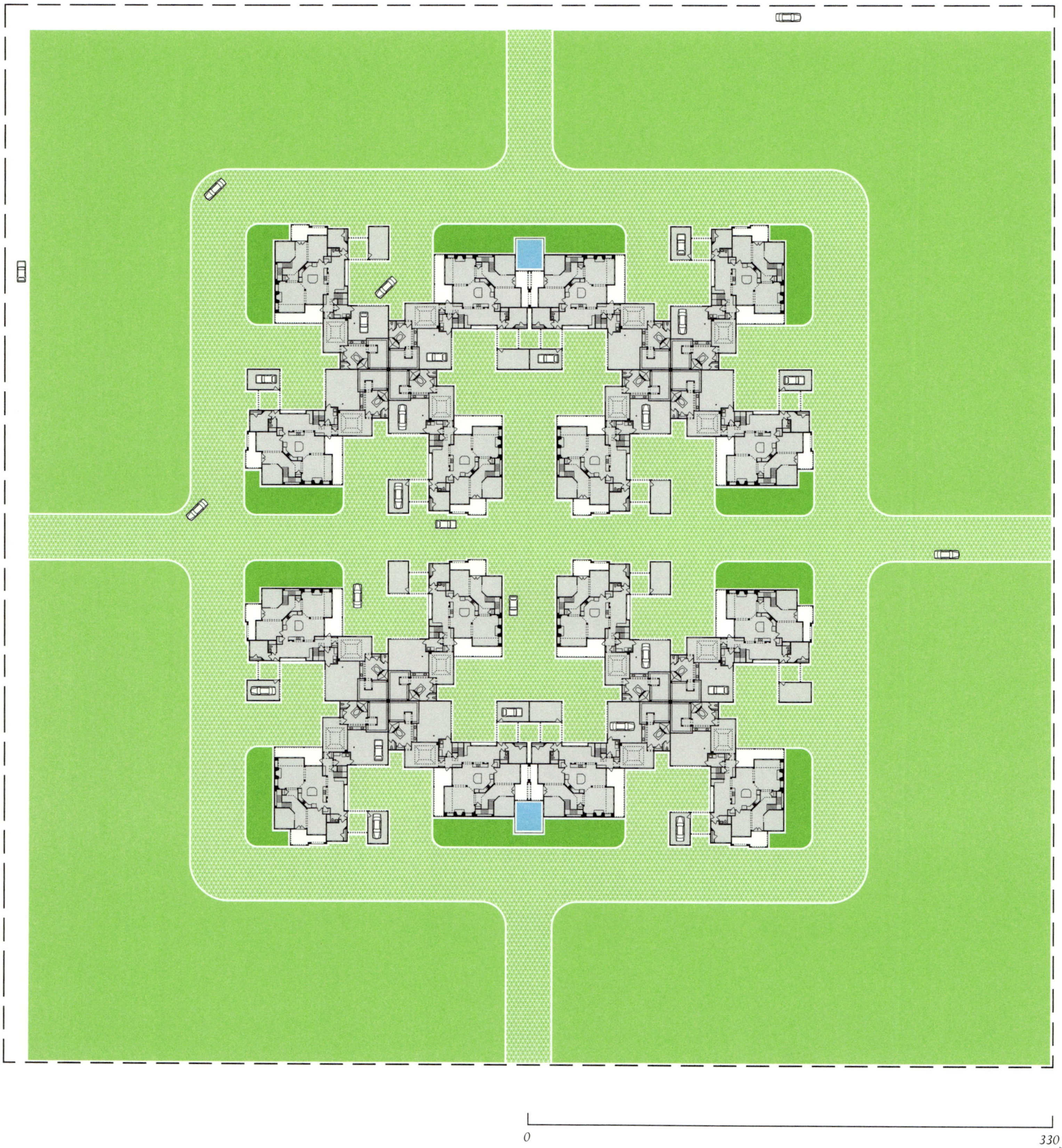

The Independent Group

NW 1/4 SW 1/4 Section 26

16 Houses
90,496 Square Feet
80 Bedrooms
80 Full Bathrooms
16 Half Bathrooms

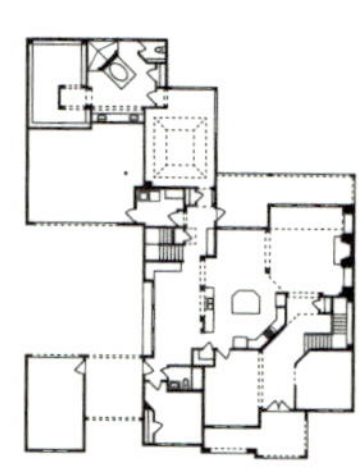

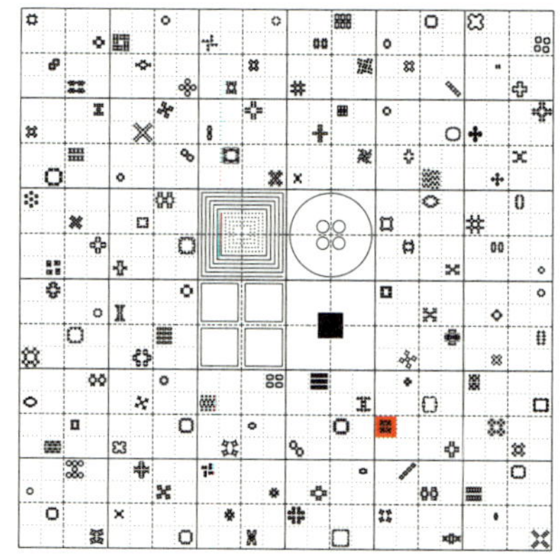

David Weekley Homes, McKeon, 5656 sq. ft., Texas

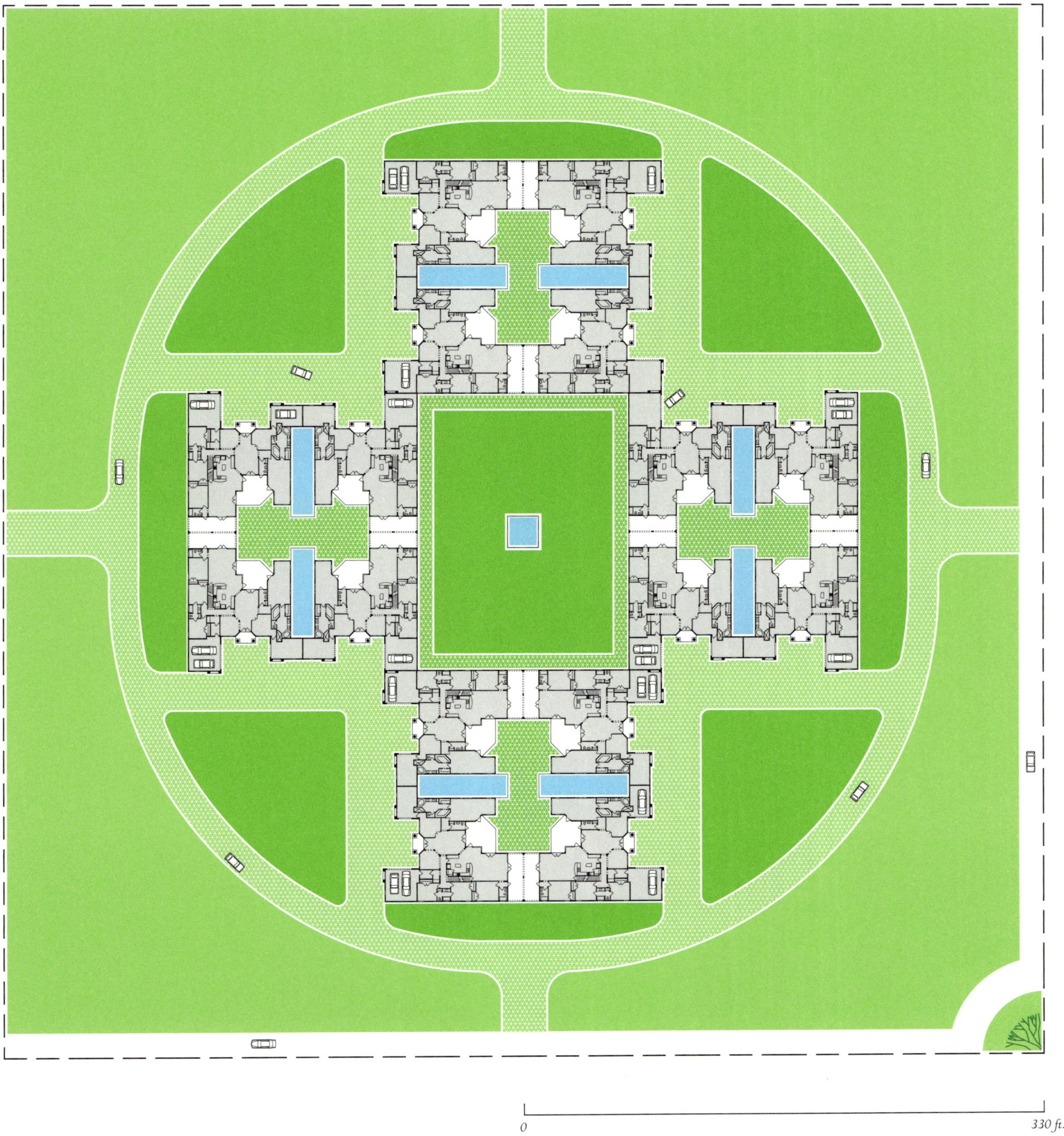

Hopeloos Stad

SE 1/4 SE 1/4 Section 26

16 Houses
55,600 Square Feet
64–80 Bedrooms
64 Full Bathrooms
16 Half Bathrooms

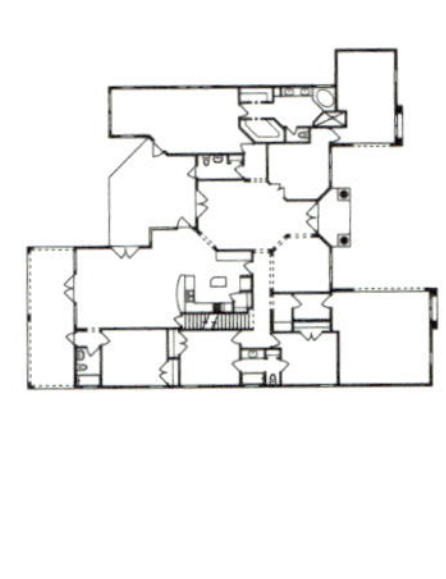

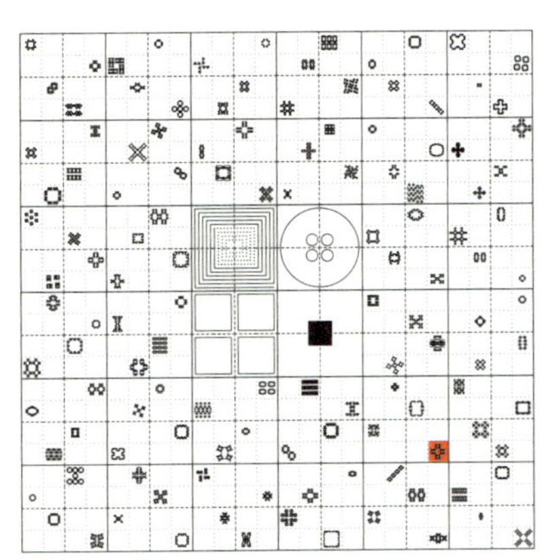

Ryland Homes, Charleston II, 3475 sq. ft., Florida

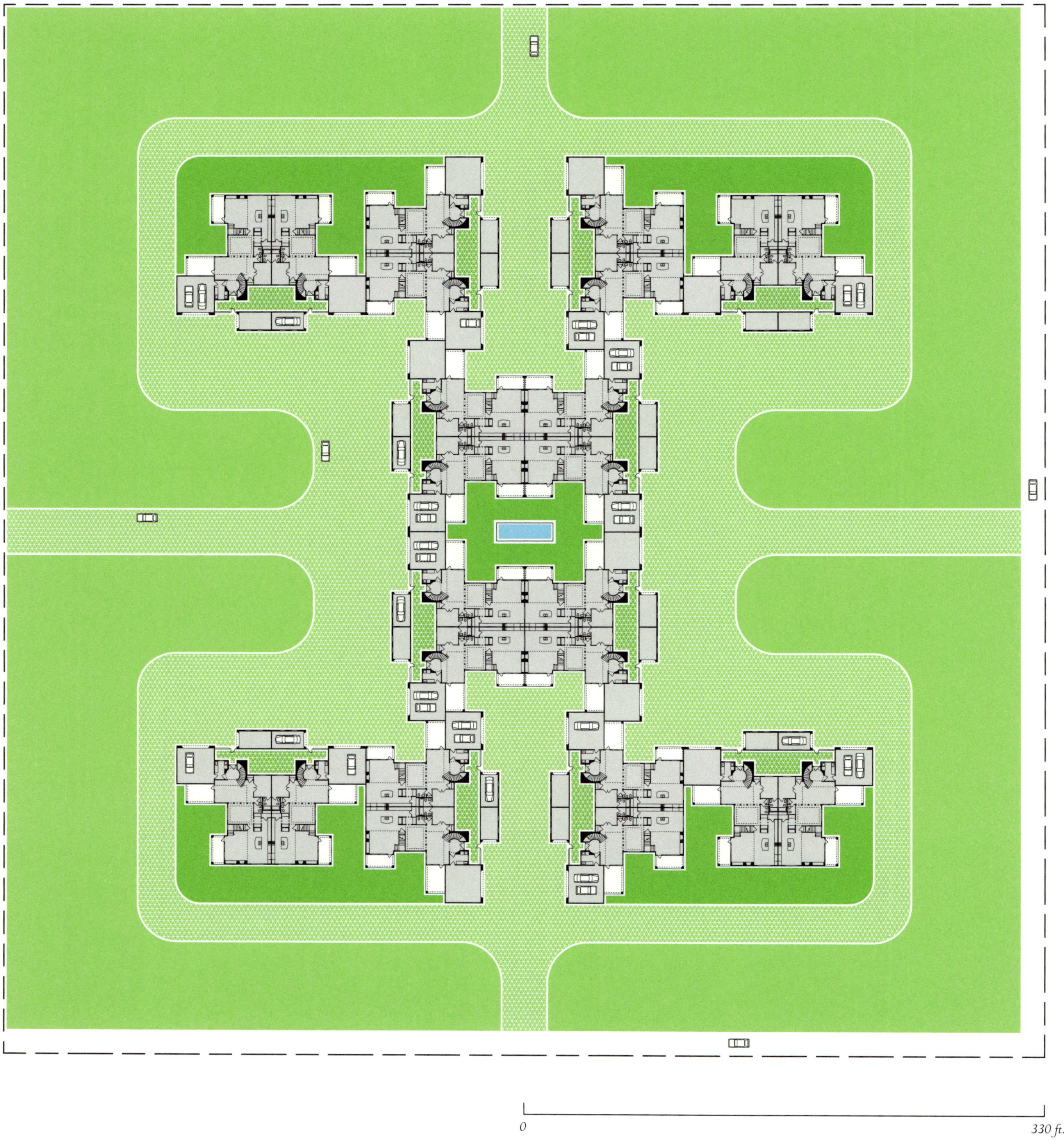

Supermodel Homes

SE 1/4 NE 1/4 Section 27

24 Houses
91,200 Square Feet
72–120 Bedrooms
96 Full Bathrooms
24 Half Bathrooms

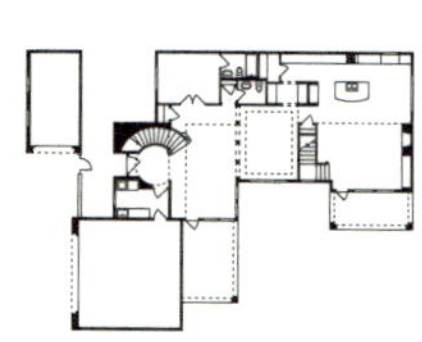

Pulte Homes, The Provence, 3800 sq. ft., Nevada

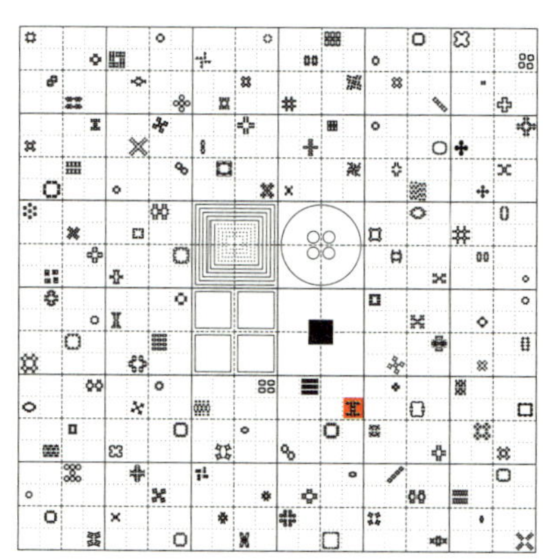

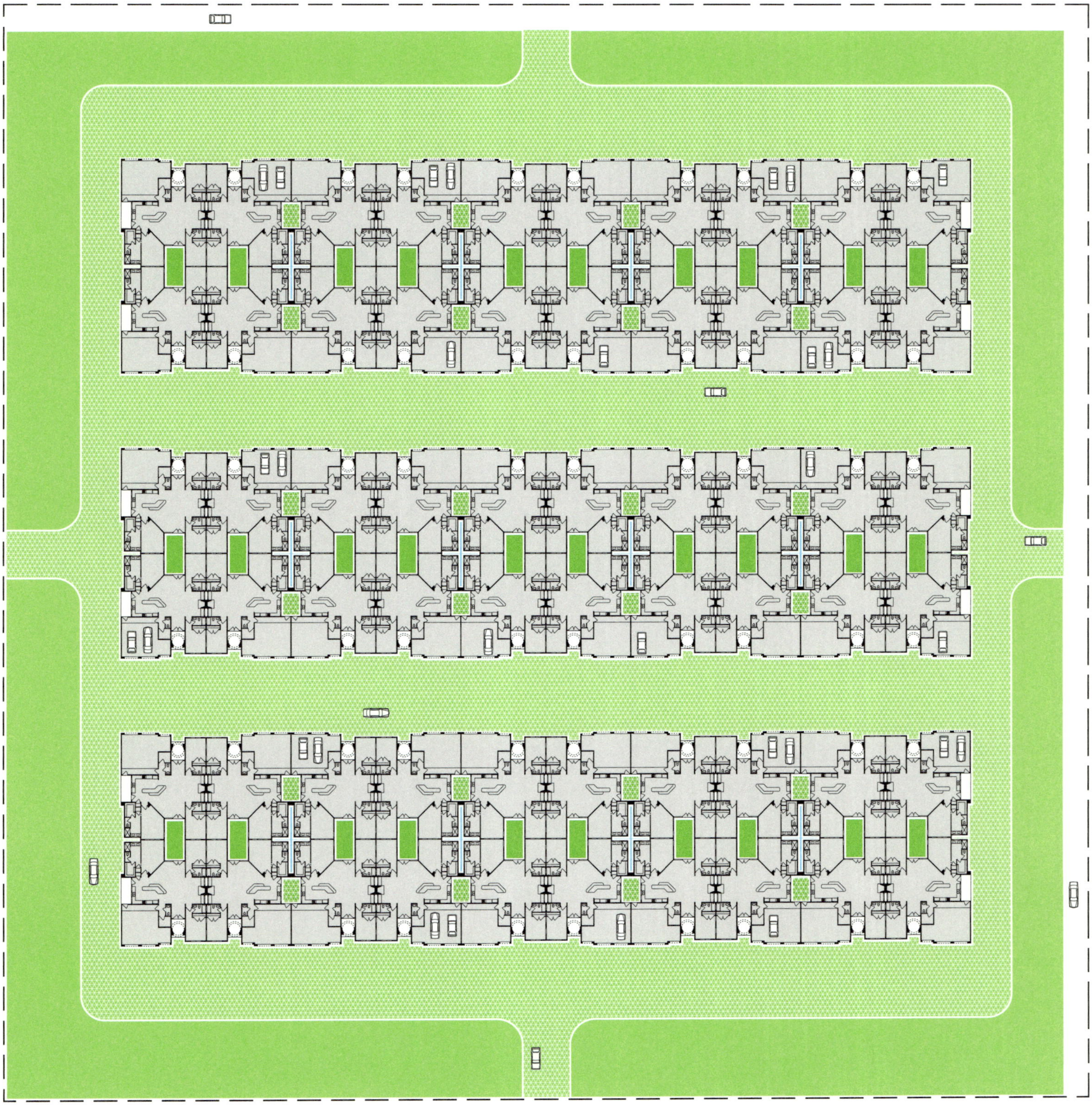

Homestead

NE 1/4 NW 1/4 Section 27

60 Houses
125,220 Square Feet
180 Bedrooms
180 Full Bathrooms
60 Half Bathrooms

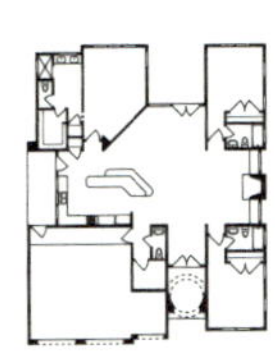

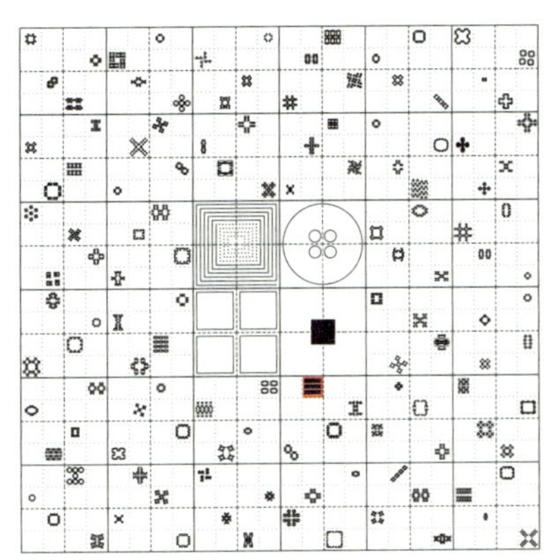

Avatar Homes, Valderama, 2087 sq. ft., Arizona

A Good Shepherd, Freedomland
after *Sainte Genevieve,* 1887
Charles Sprague Pearce

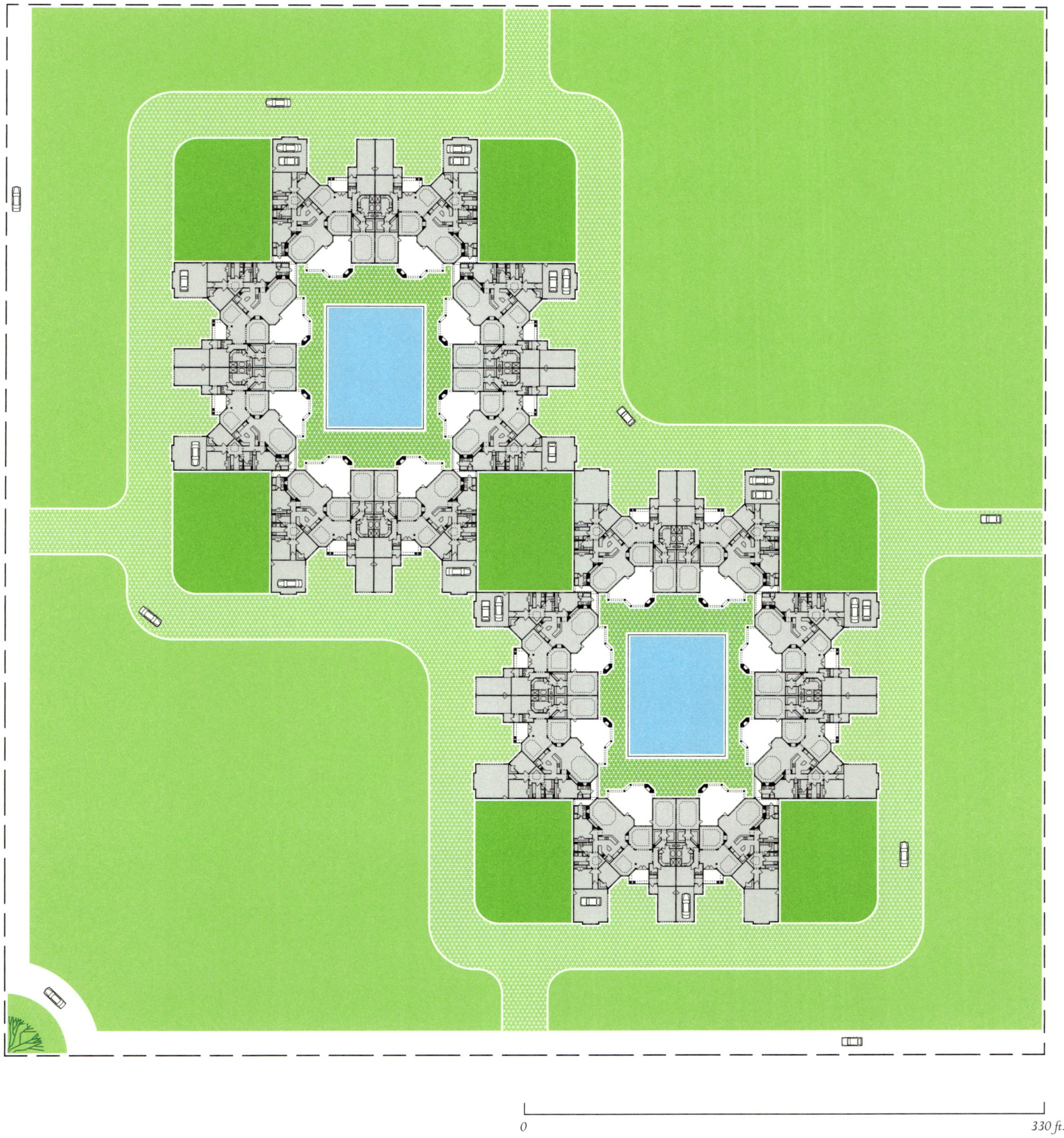

The Estates at Satter Fields
SW 1/4 SW 1/4 Section 27

16 Houses
51,568 Square Feet
64 Bedrooms
48 Full Bathrooms
16 Half Bathrooms

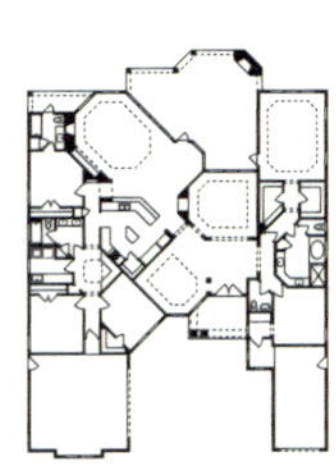

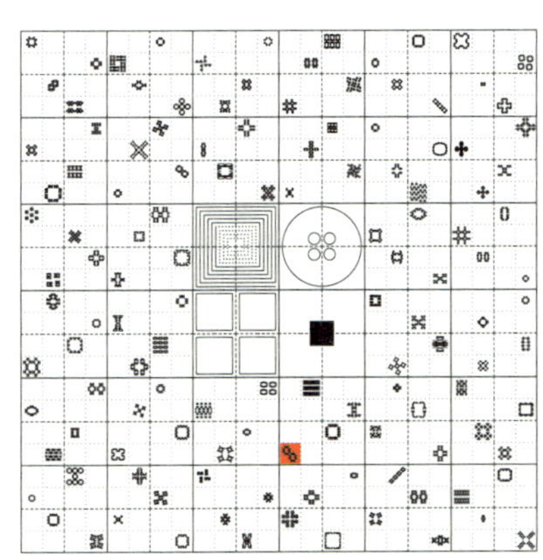

Ryland Homes, Suffolk, 3223 sq. ft., Florida

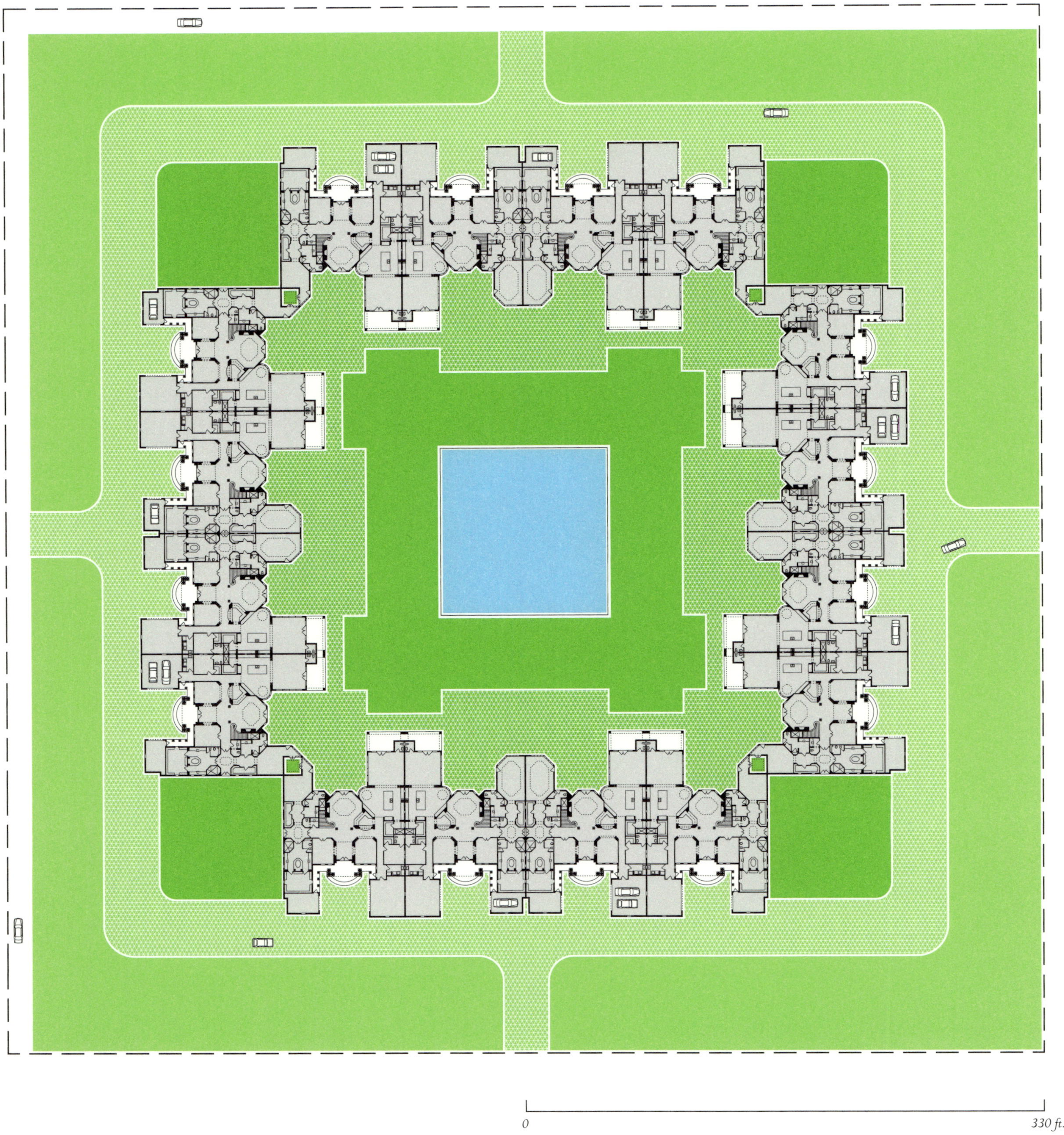

La Ville Bourgeoise

NW 1/4 SE 1/4 Section 27

16 Houses
126,480 Square Feet
80 Bedrooms
96 Full Bathrooms
32 Half Bathrooms

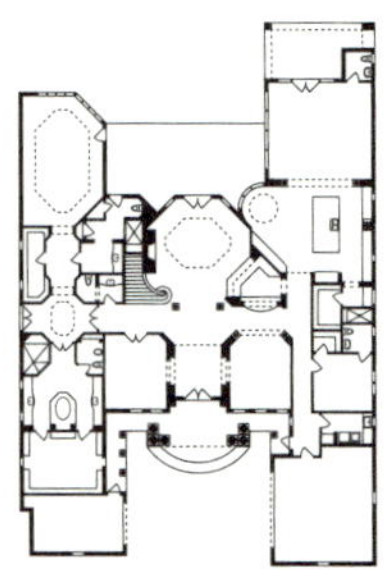

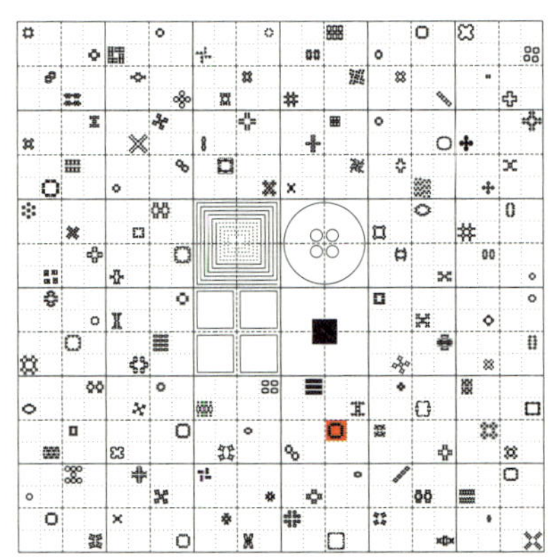

Taylor Morrison Homes, Casa del Playa, 7905 sq. ft., Florida

RAMSALAND

NE 1/4 NE 1/4 Section 28

32 Houses
114,688 Square Feet
160 Bedrooms
128 Full Bathrooms
32 Half Bathrooms

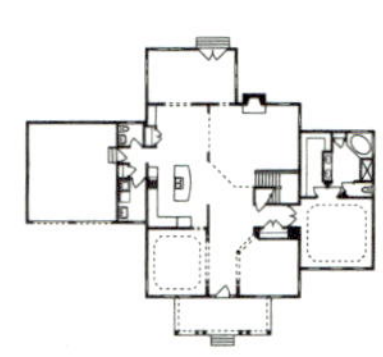

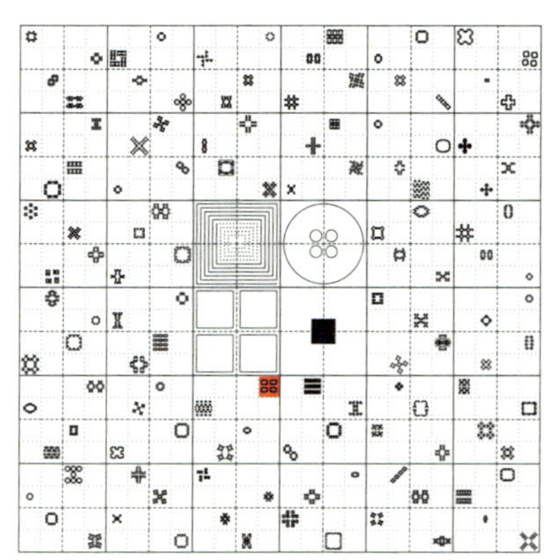

Ryland Homes, The Parson, 3584 sq. ft., Delaware

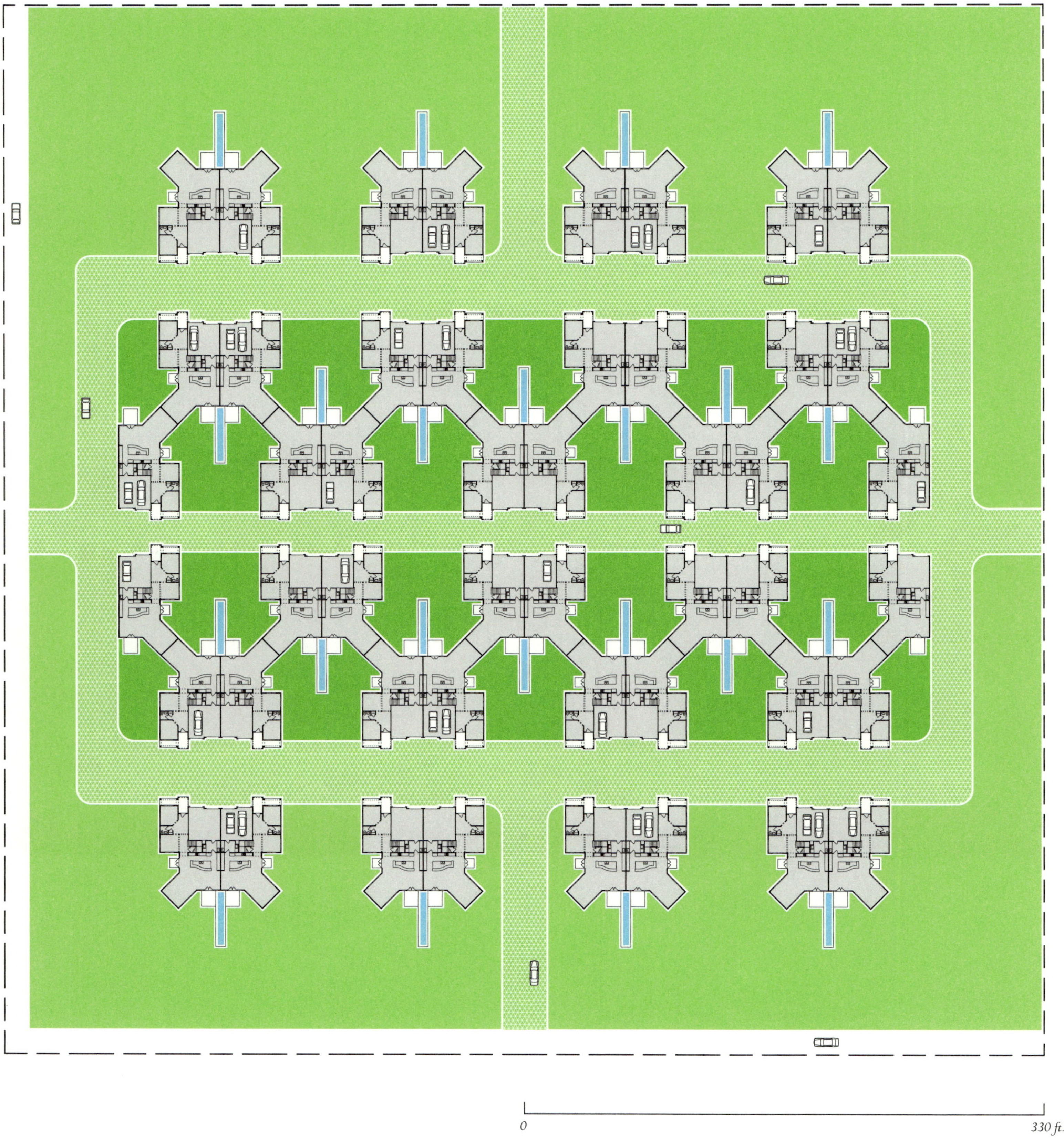

Kubo Verde

SW 1/4 NW 1/4 Section 28

48 Houses
154,424 Square Feet
144–192 Bedrooms
96–144 Full Bathrooms
0–48 Half Bathrooms

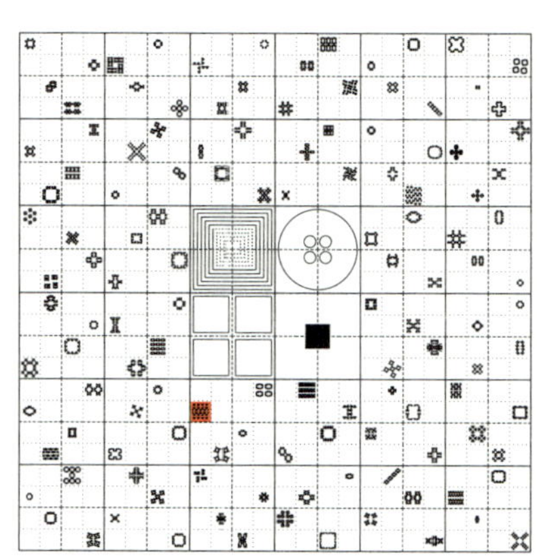

KB Home, Garden Plan 3238, 3238 sq. ft., California

Returning from the Hunt to Subtopian Acres, Freedomland
after *Portrait of a Family in a Landscape,* 1641
Albert Cuyp

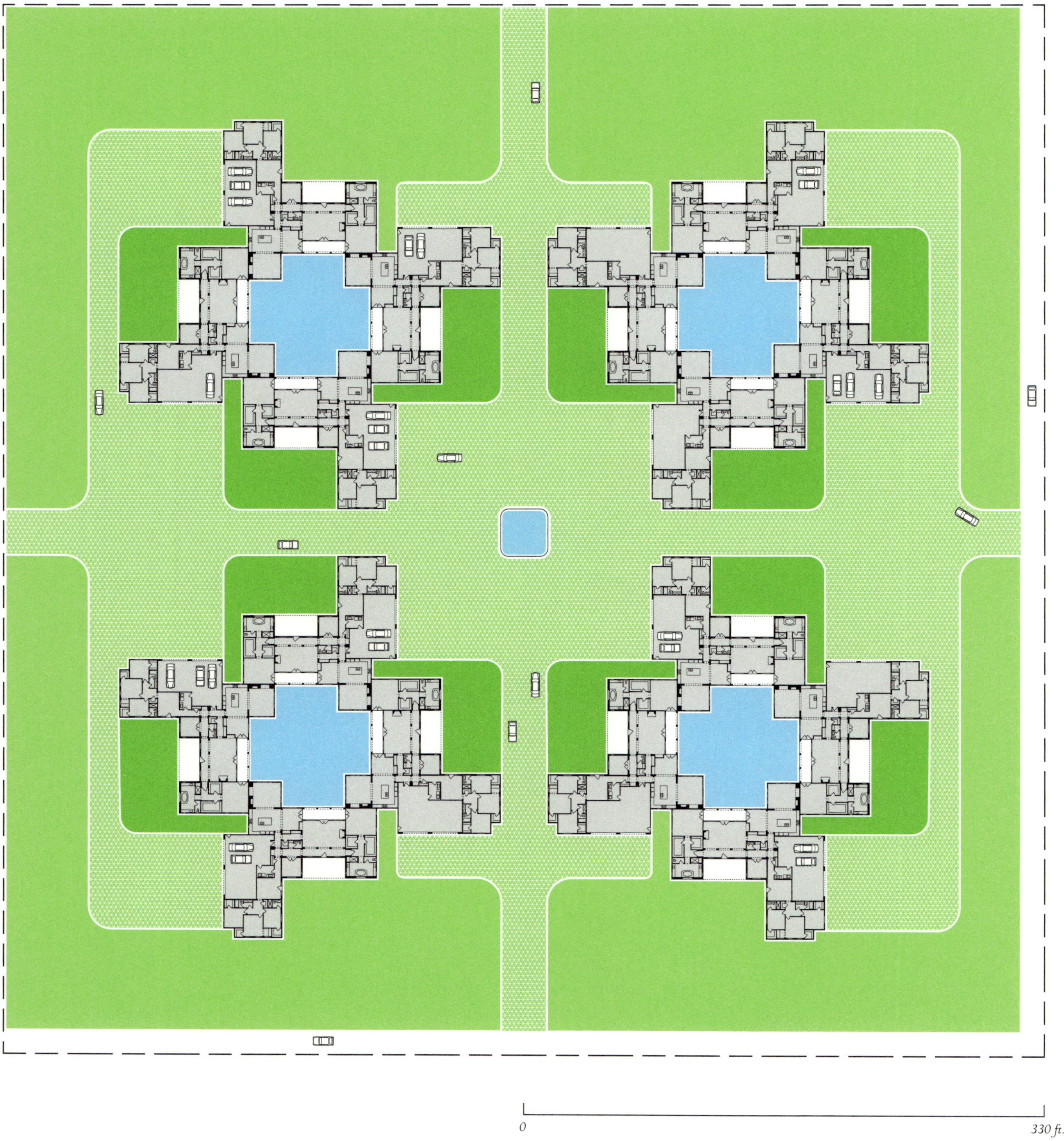

Subtopian Acres
SE 1/4 SW 1/4 Section 28

16 Houses
66,816 Square Feet
64 Bedrooms
48 Full Bathrooms
16 Half Bathrooms

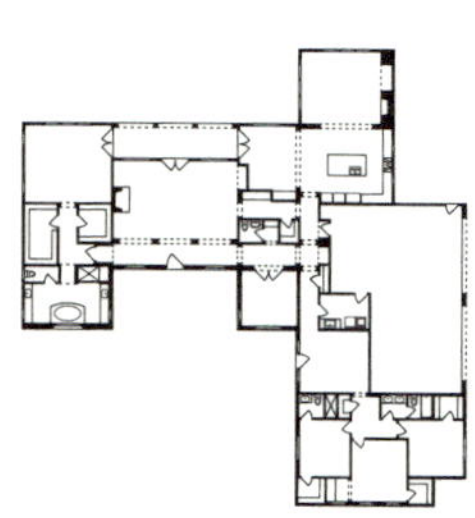

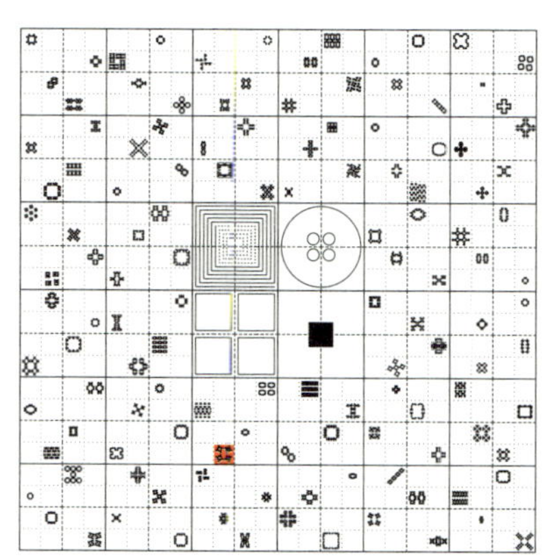

Pulte Homes, The Appaloosa, 4176 sq. ft., California

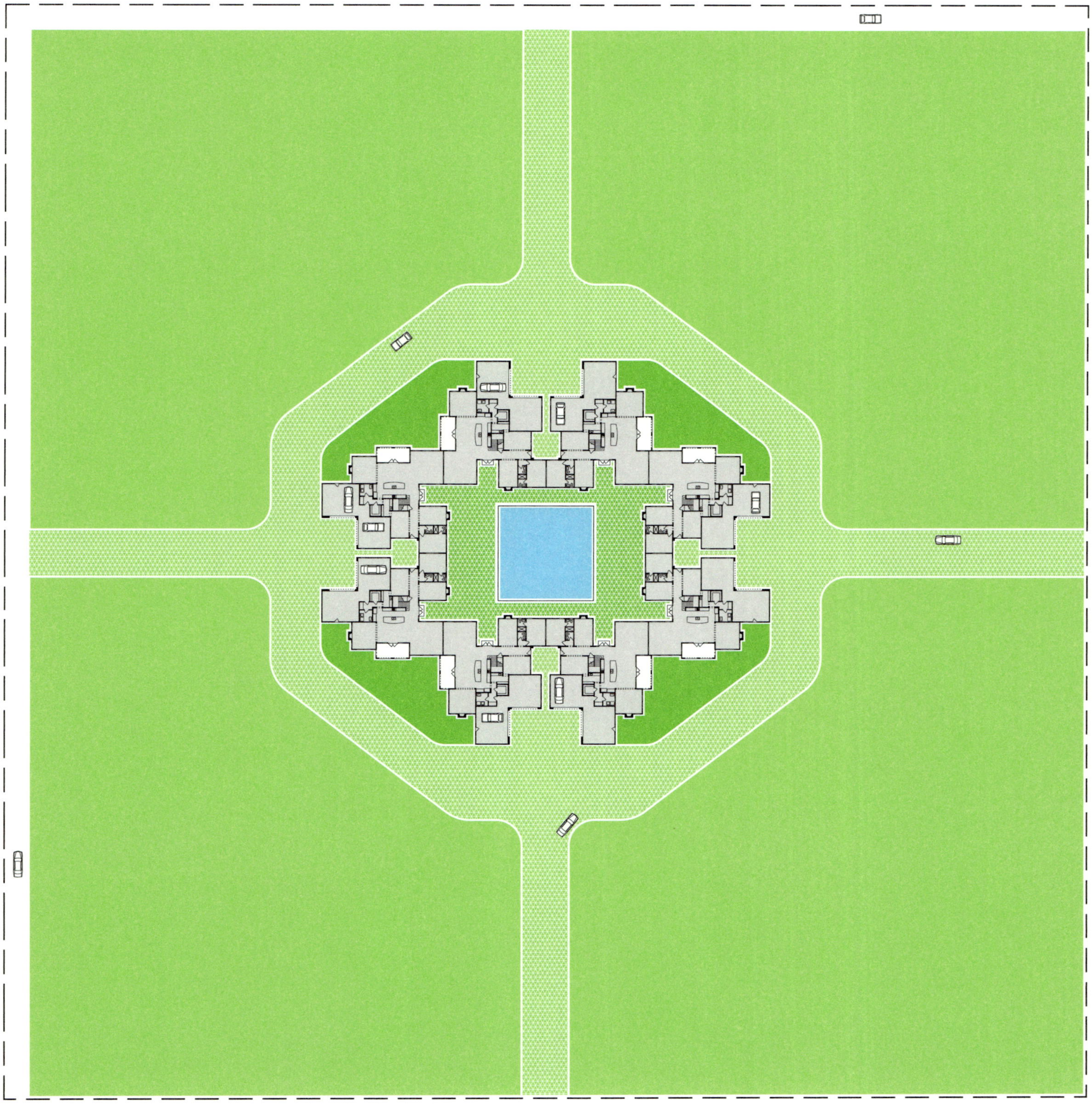

Palais du Kern

NW 1/4 SE 1/4 Section 28

8 Houses
37,000 Square Feet
32 Bedrooms
32 Full Bathrooms
8 Half Bathrooms

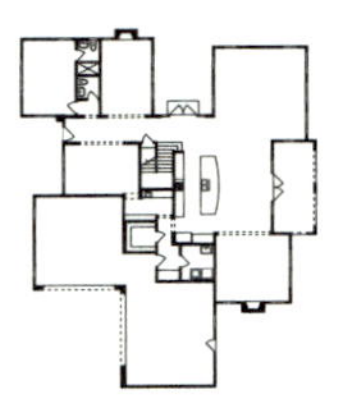

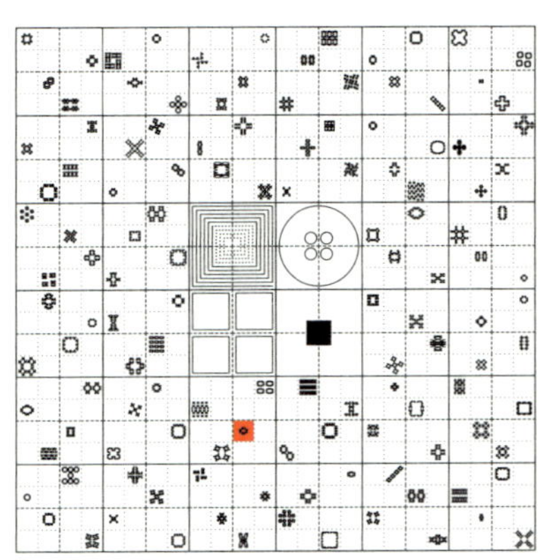

Shea Homes, Plan 2 at Maravilla, 4625 sq. ft., California

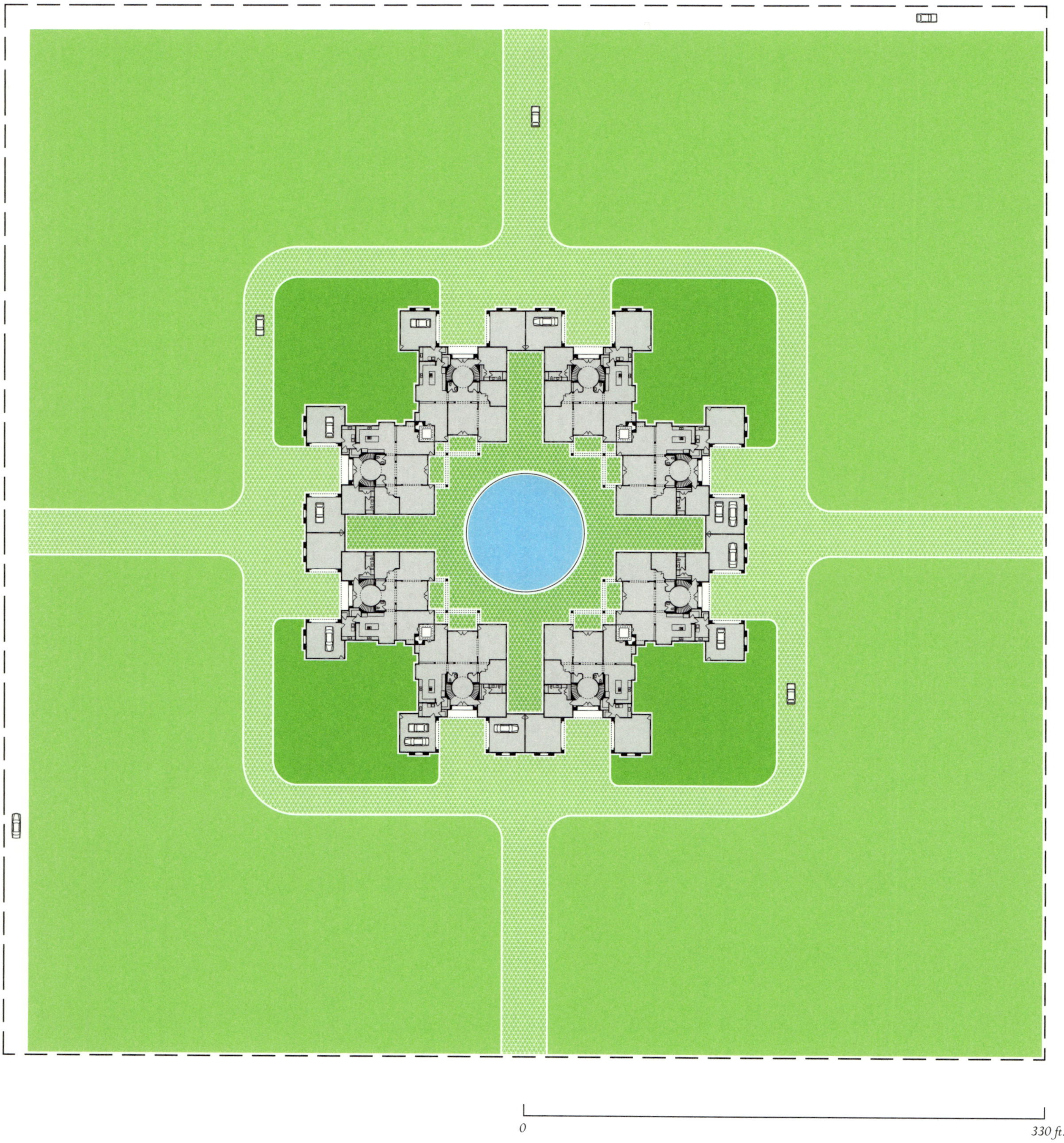

Le Ville Rotunda

NW 1/4 NE 1/4 Section 29

8 Houses
41,000 Square Feet
32–40 Bedrooms
32 Full Bathrooms
8 Half Bathrooms

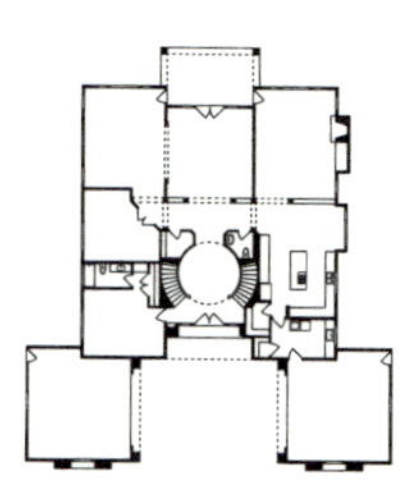

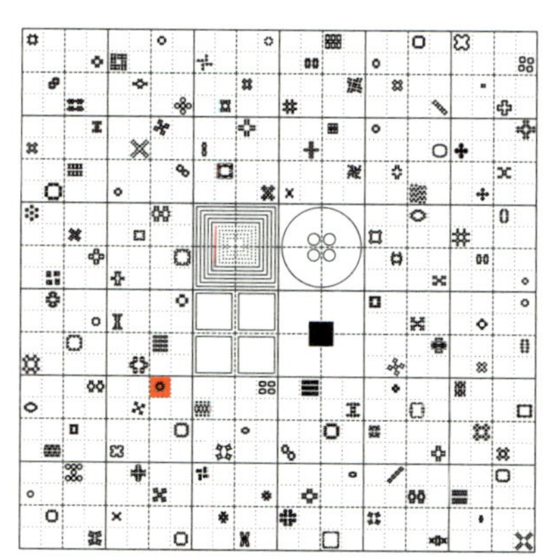

Toll Brothers, The Mirador, 5125 sq. ft., Arizona

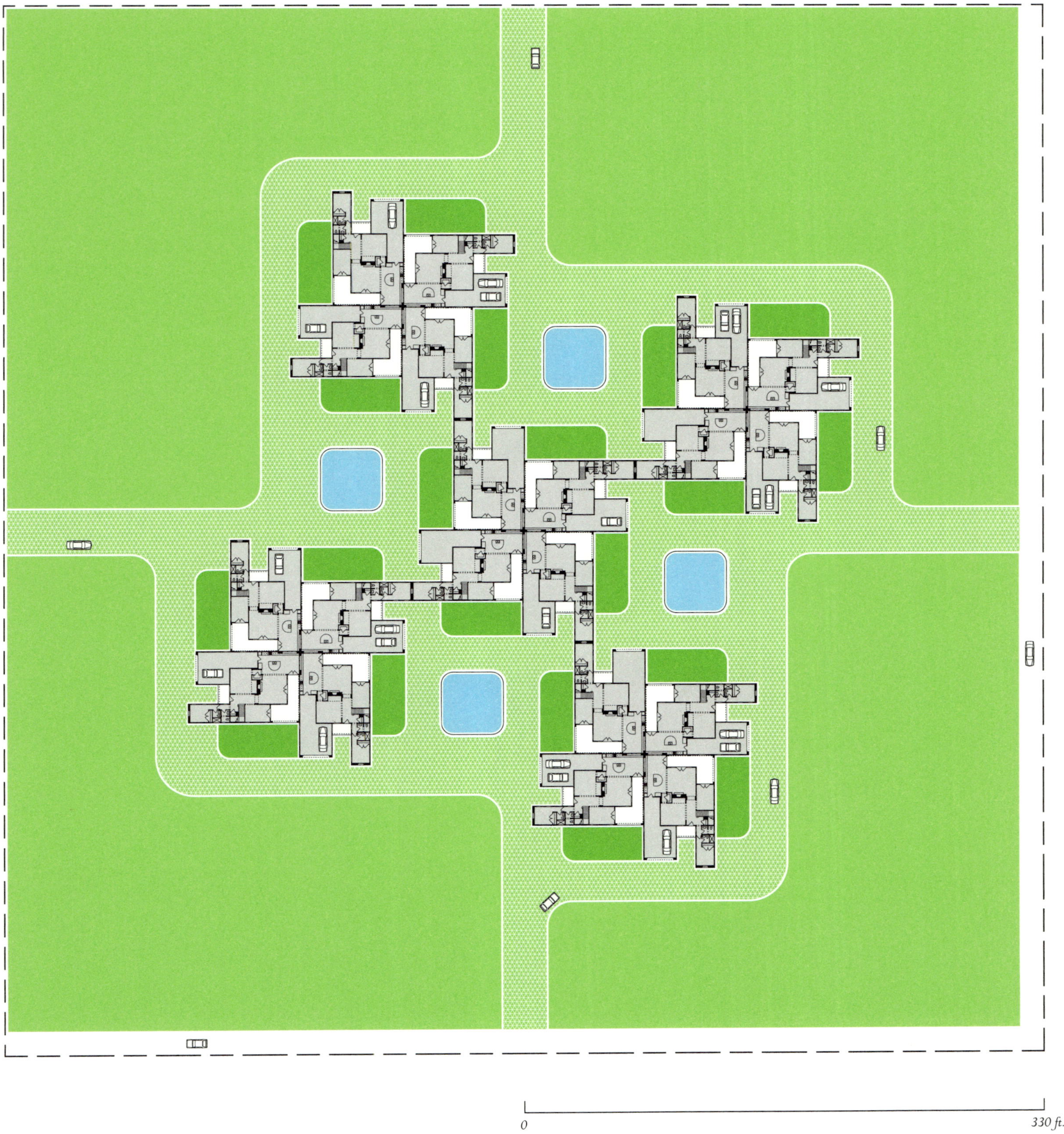

Levy's Landing

SE 1/4 NW 1/4 Section 29

20 Houses
77,840 Square Feet
100 Bedrooms
80 Full Bathrooms
20 Half Bathrooms

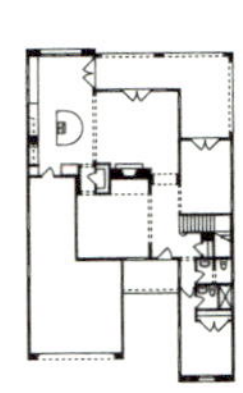

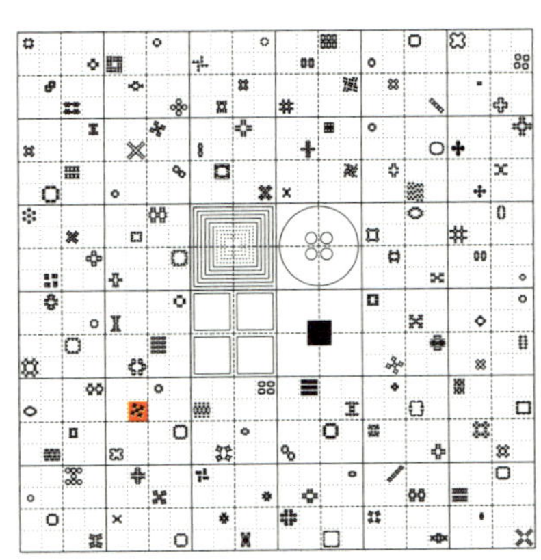

Shea Homes, Plan 4 at Vista Vallerta, 3892 sq. ft., California

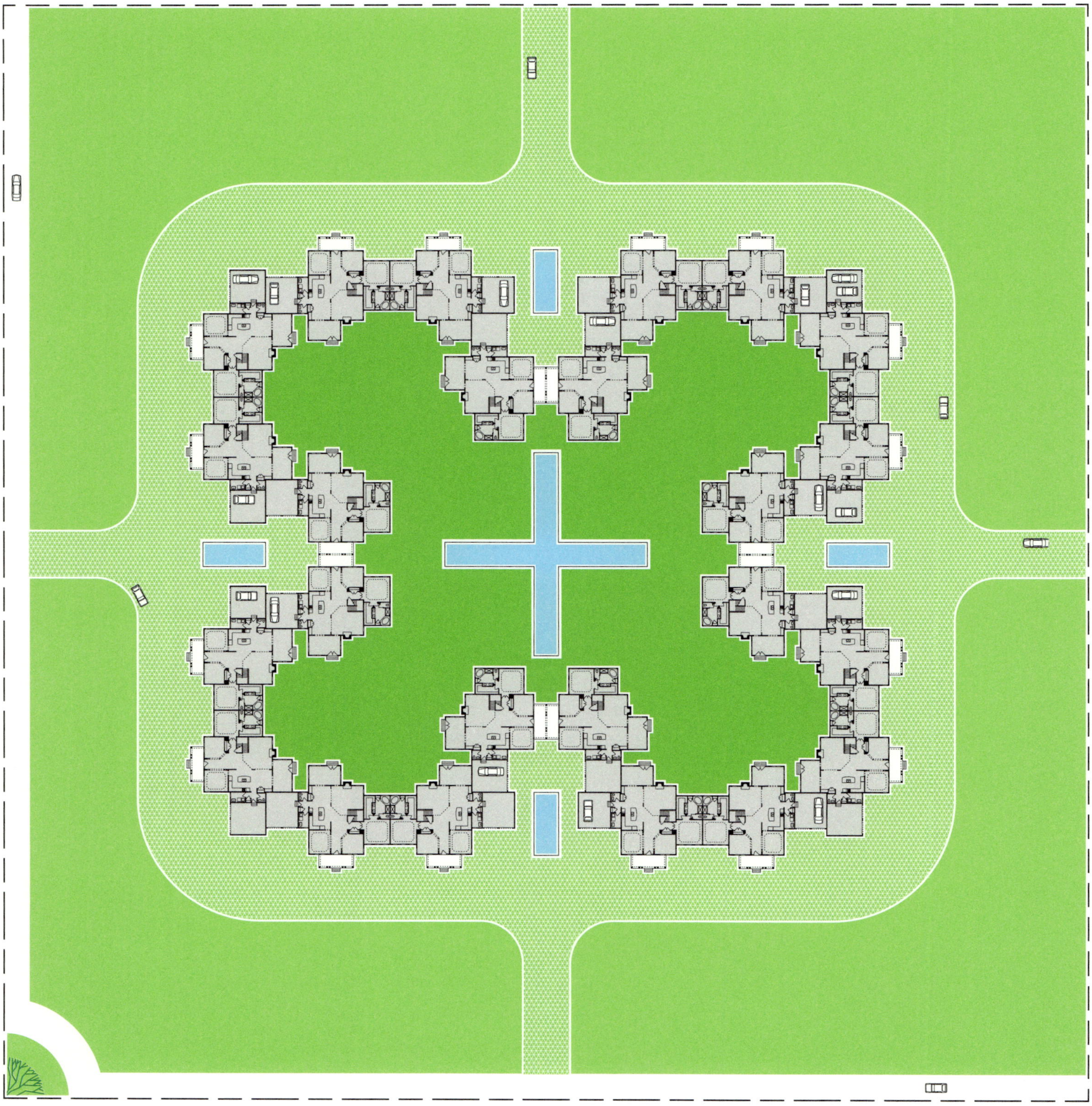

0 330 *ft.*

Lyon's Gate at Freedomland
SW 1/4 SW 1/4 Section 29

24 Houses
86,016 Square Feet
120 Bedrooms
96 Full Bathrooms
24 Half Bathrooms

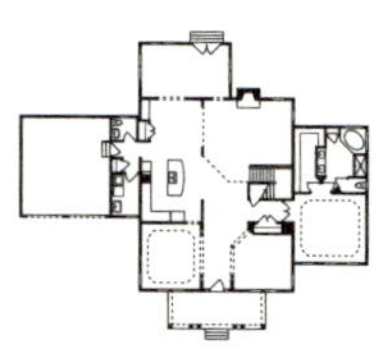

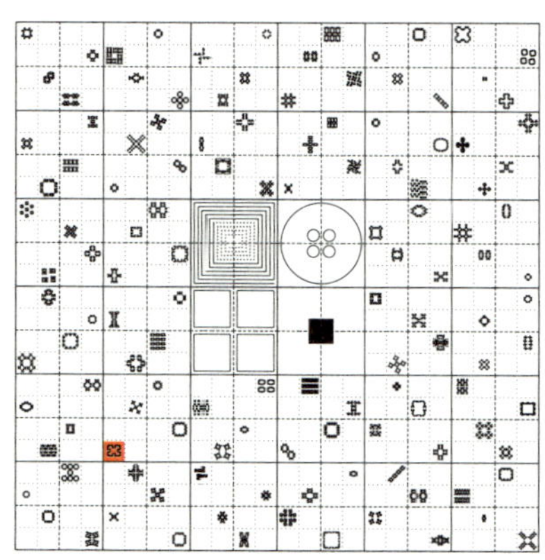

Ryland Homes, The Parson, 3584 sq. ft., Delaware

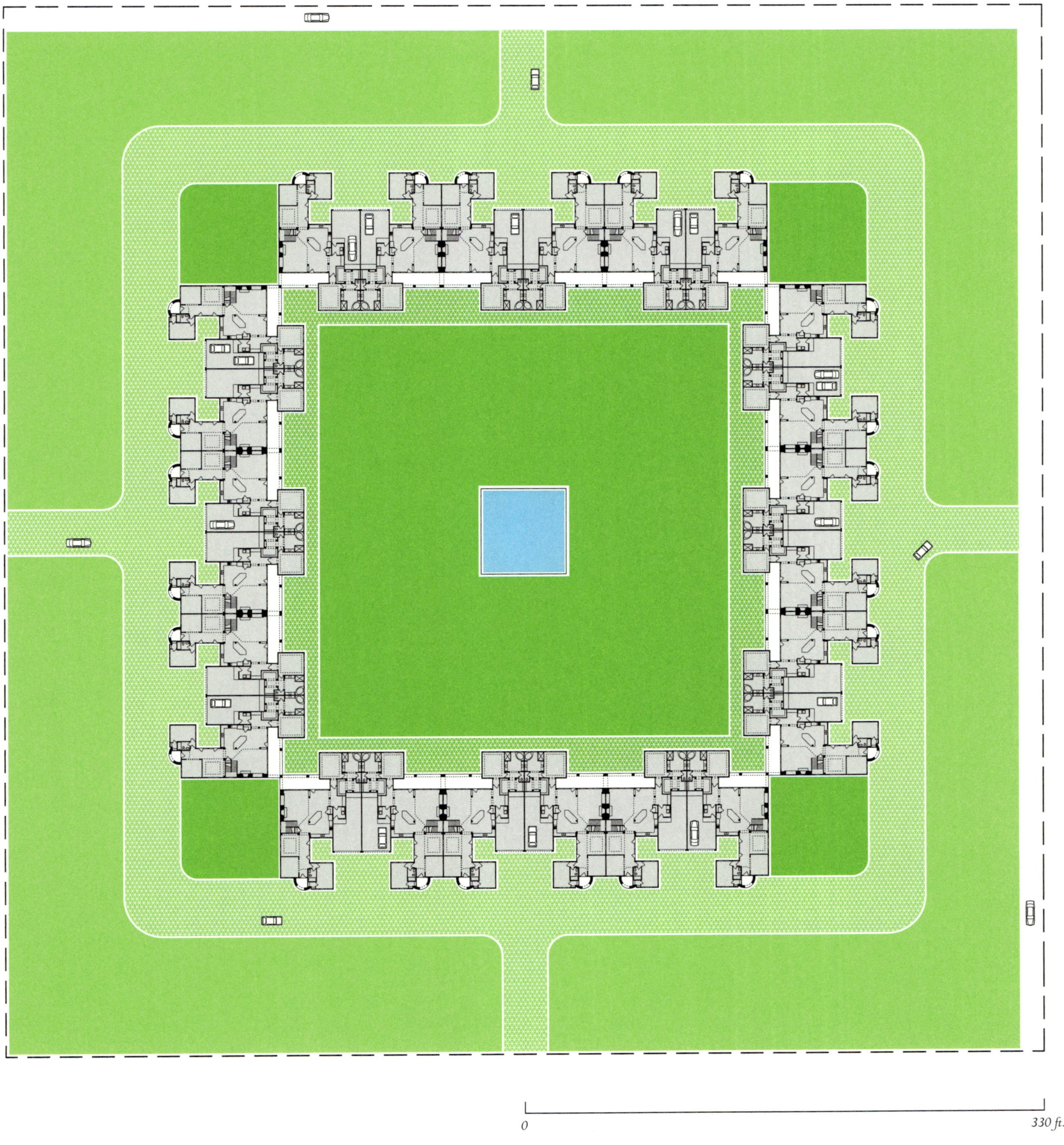

Le Domaine de la Durand

NE 1/4 SE 1/4 Section 29

24 Houses
88,992 Square Feet
120 Bedrooms
96 Full Bathrooms
24 Half Bathrooms

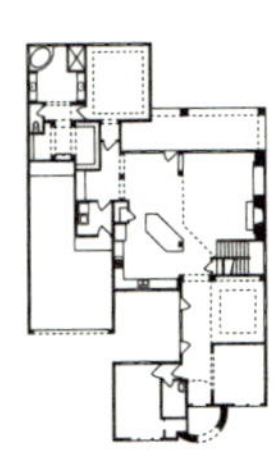

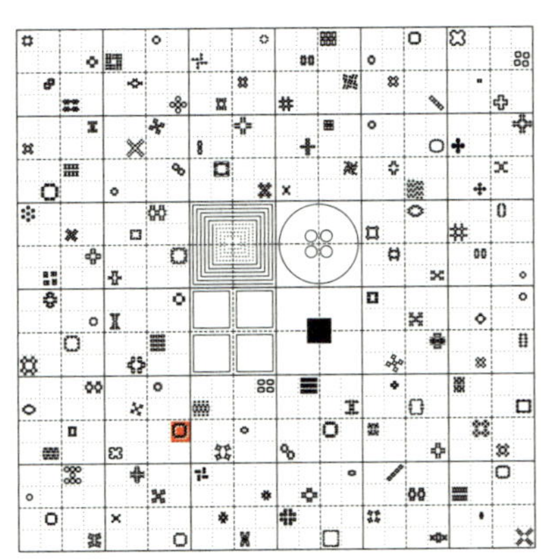

David Weekley Homes, The Palladio, 3708 sq. ft., Texas

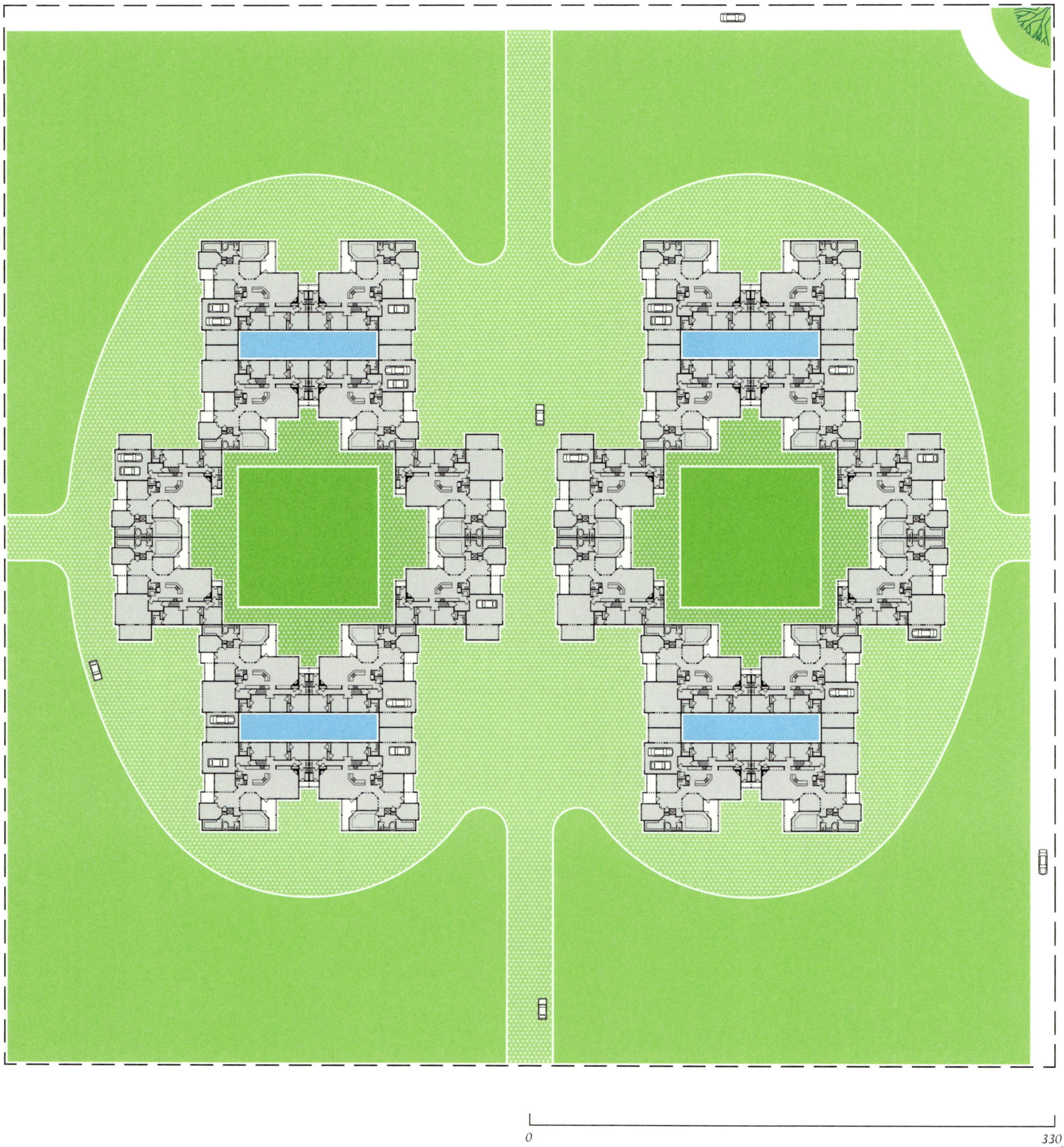

Banham's Bottom

NE 1/4 NE 1/4 Section 30

24 Houses
87,384 Square Feet
96 Bedrooms
72 Full Bathrooms
24 Half Bathrooms

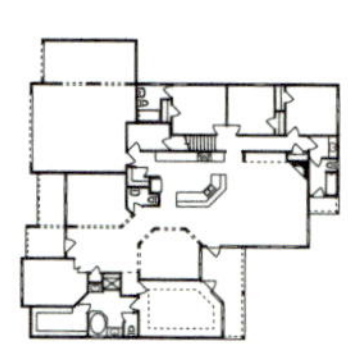

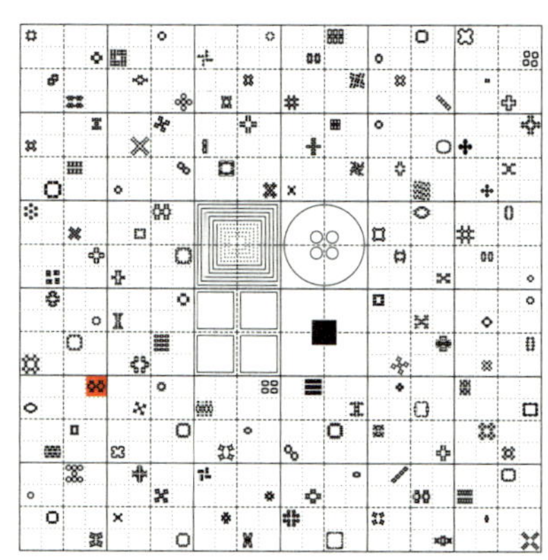

Pulte Homes, Monet, 3641 sq. ft., Texas

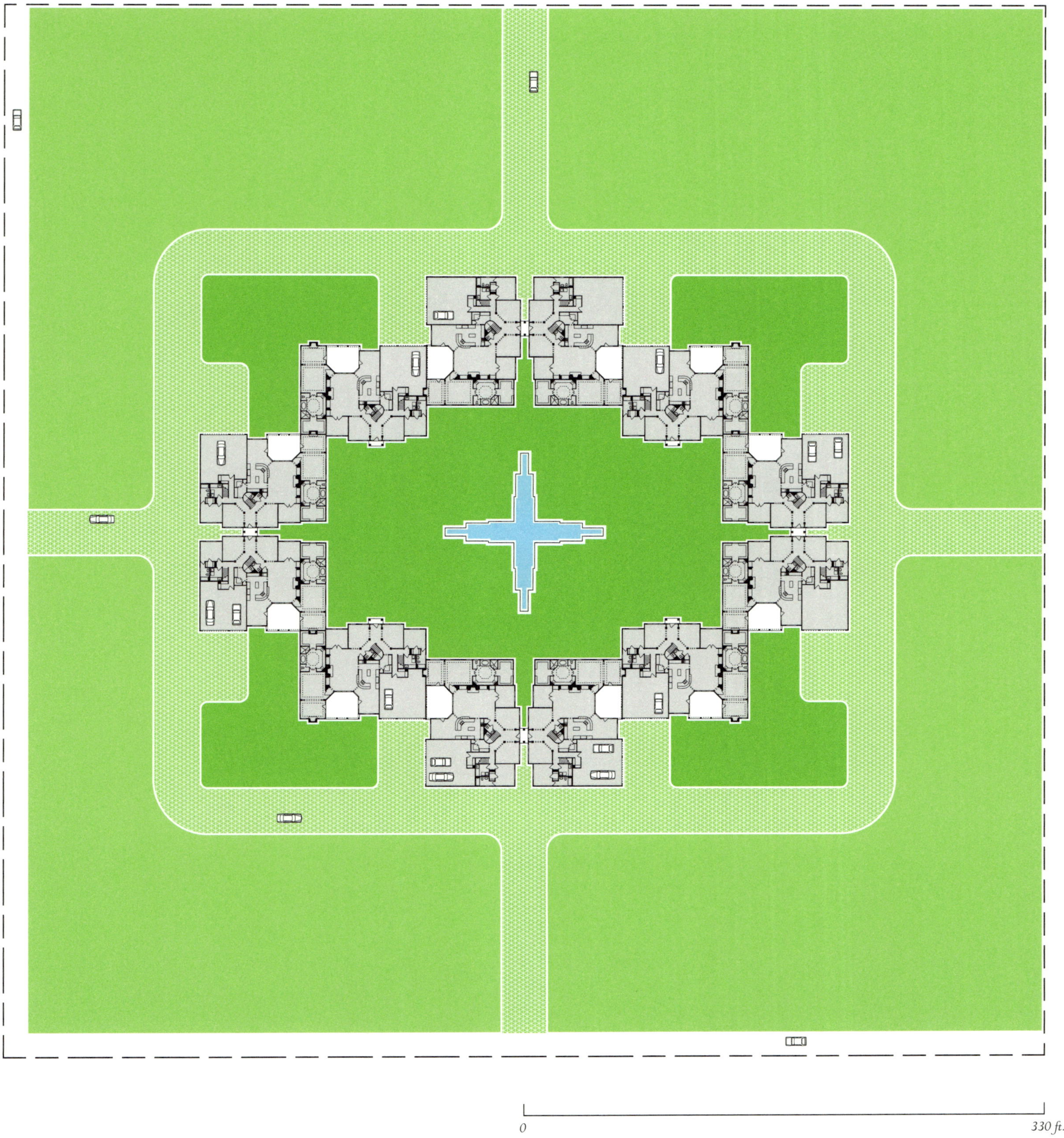

Somewhere Meadows

SW 1/4 NW 1/4 Section 30

12 Houses
66,852 Square Feet
60 Bedrooms
60 Full Bathrooms
12 Half Bathrooms

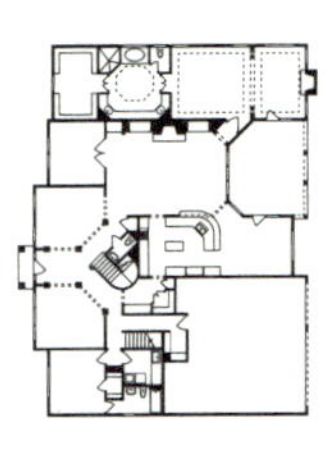

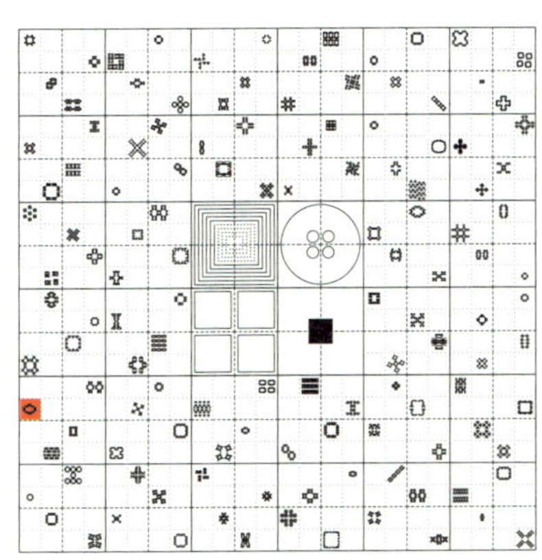

Beazer Homes, Versailles, 5571 sq. ft., Tennessee

Riding out from Freedomland
after *Lord Rivers Coursing at Newmarket with His Friends,* 1818
Jacques-Laurent Agasse

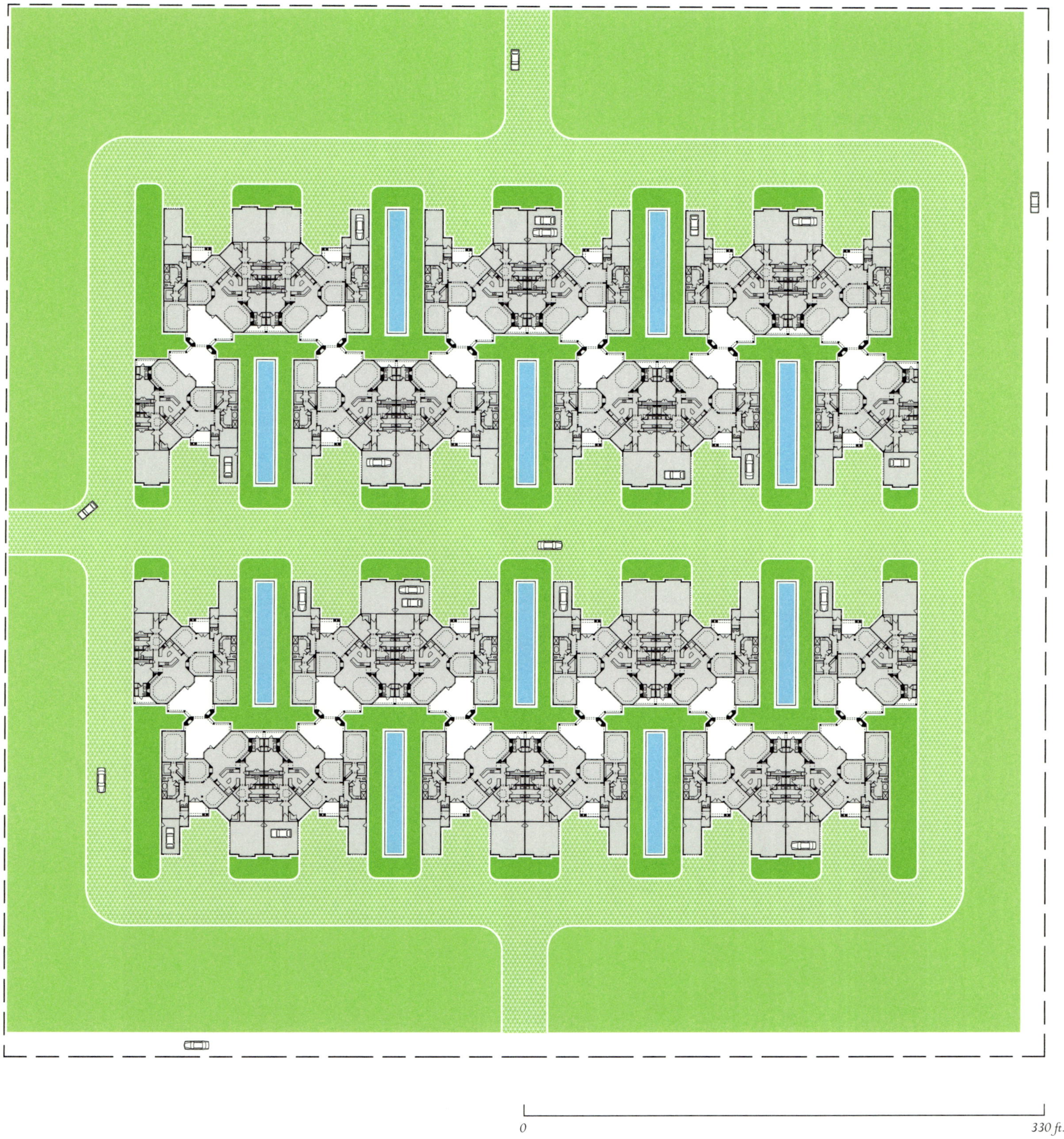

Marigold Springs

SE 1/4 SW 1/4 Section 30

24 Houses
73,464 Square Feet
96 Bedrooms
72 Full Bathrooms
24 Half Bathrooms

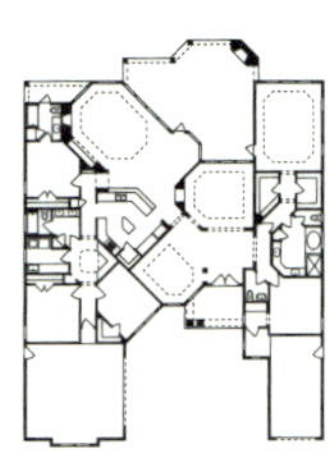

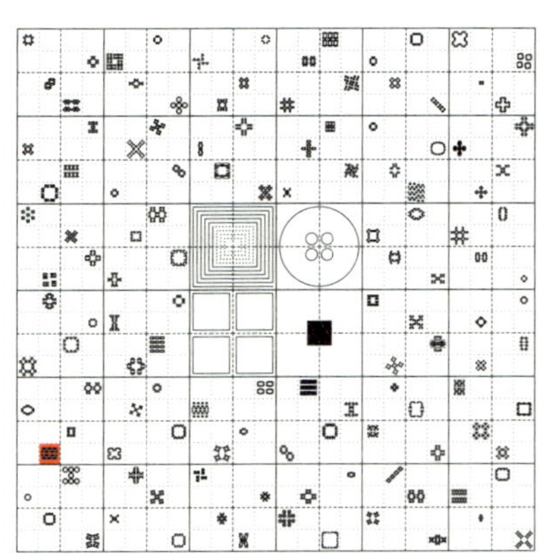

Ryland Homes, Suffolk, 3223 sq. ft., Florida

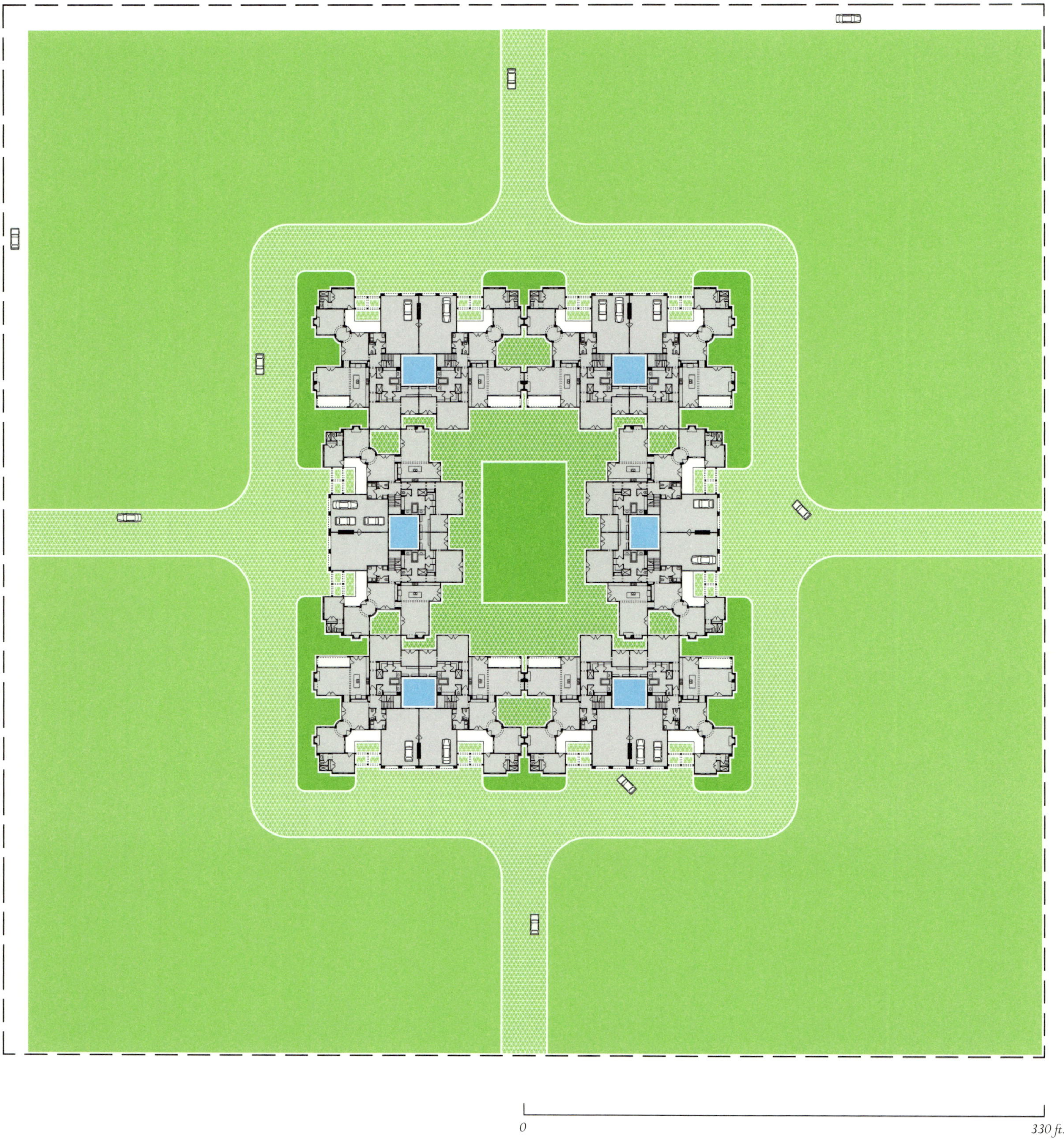

Pellitshker Plotz

NW 1/4 SE 1/4 Section 30

12 Houses
73,464 Square Feet
60 Bedrooms
60 Full Bathrooms
12 Half Bathrooms

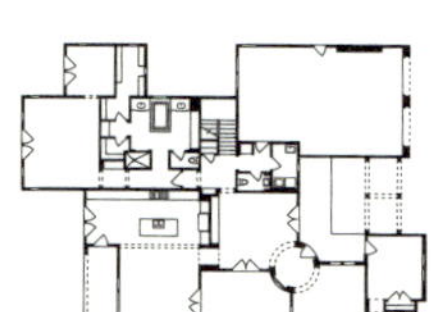

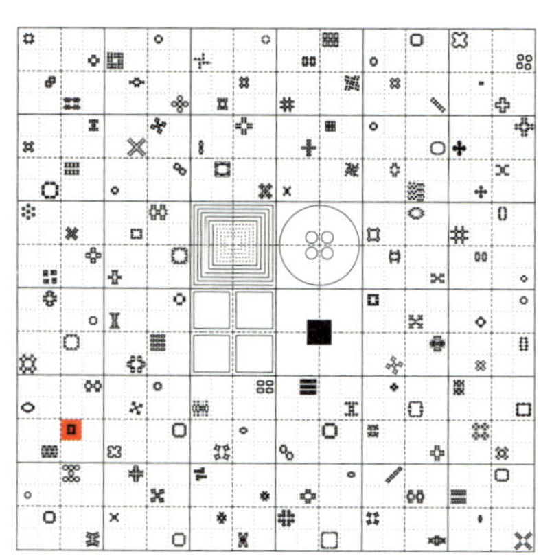

Standard Pacific Homes, Residence 1H, 6122 sq. ft., California

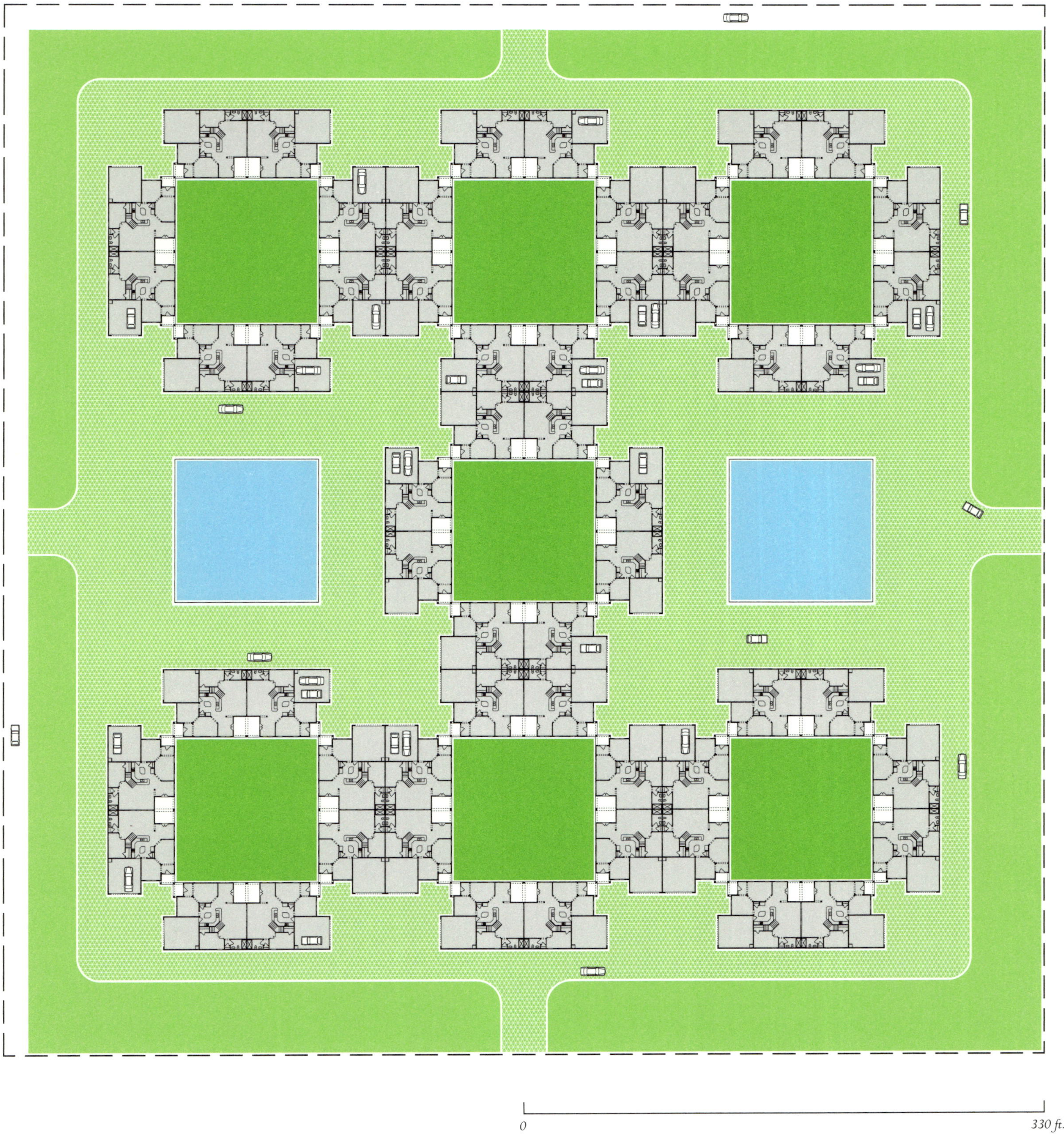

The Nine Squares

NW 1/4 NE 1/4 Section 31

56 Houses
168,840 Square Feet
168–224 Bedrooms
168 Full Bathrooms
56 Half Bathrooms

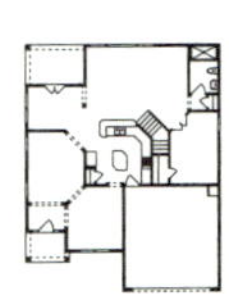

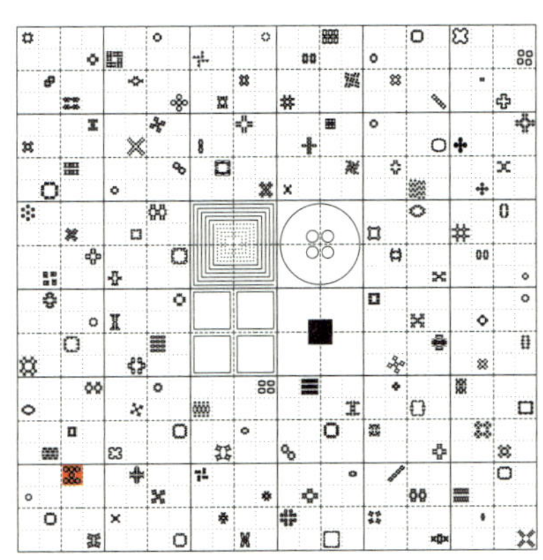

Beazer Homes, Terrace, 3015 sq. ft., Nevada

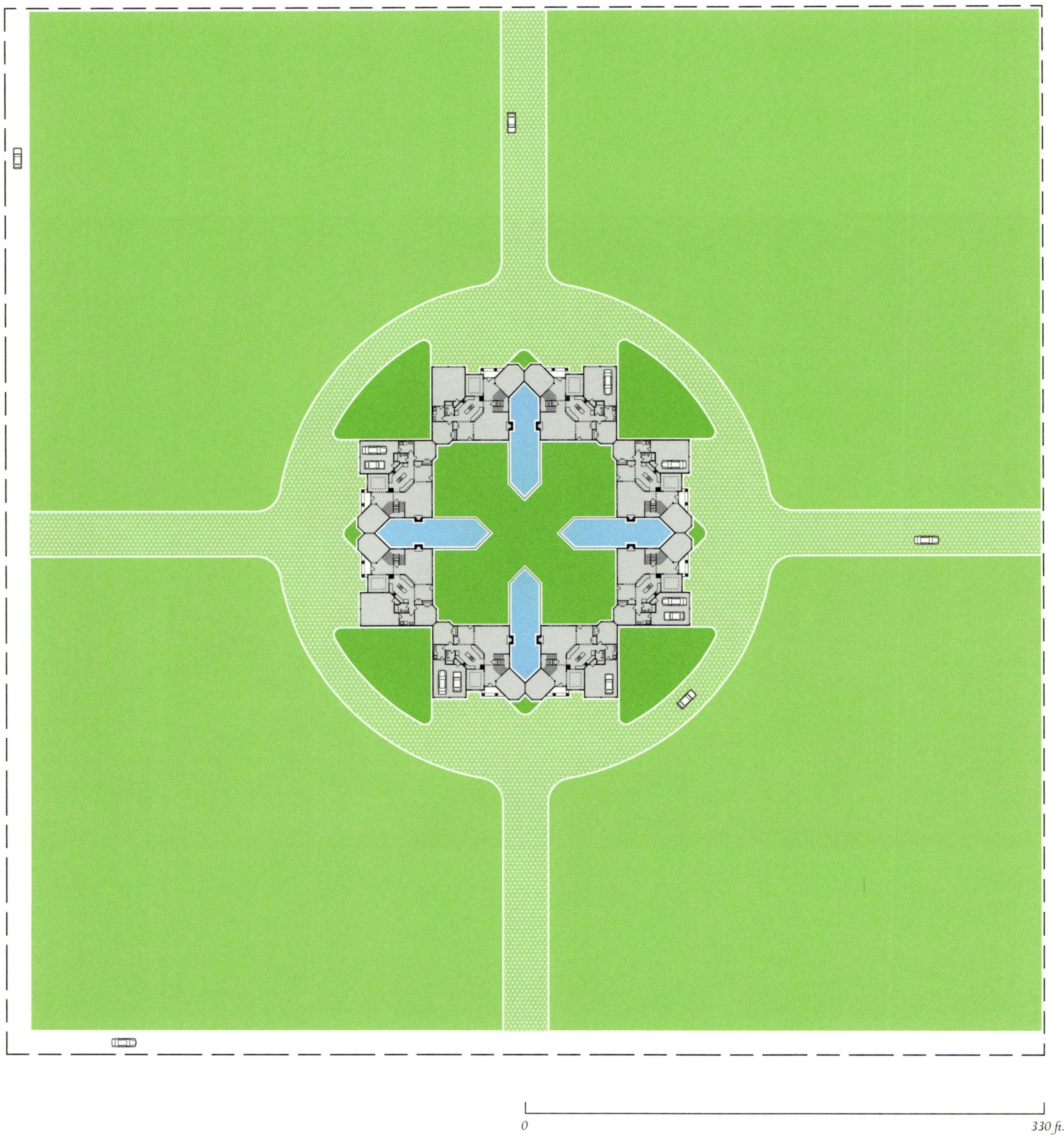

Samuelsville

SW 1/4 NW 1/4 Section 31

8 Houses
26,880 Square Feet
32 Bedrooms
24 Full Bathrooms
0 Half Bathrooms

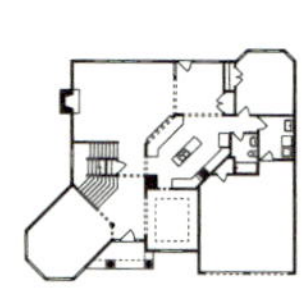

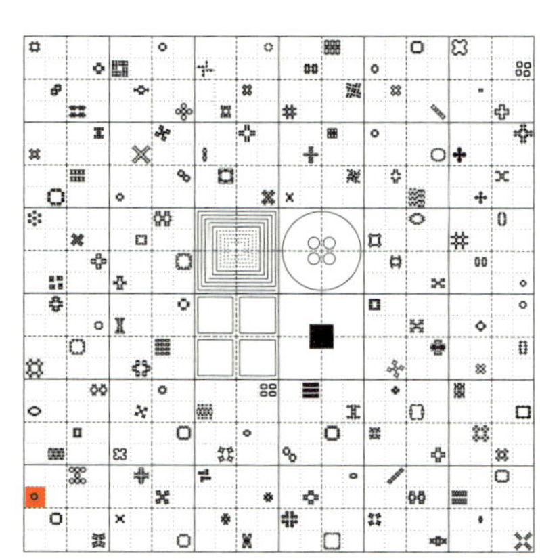

Centex Homes, The Wellington, 3360 sq. ft., Georgia

A Crowd Gathers in Fourier Forest near Freedomland
after *The Preaching of St. John the Baptist,* 1601–1604
Pieter Brueghel the Younger

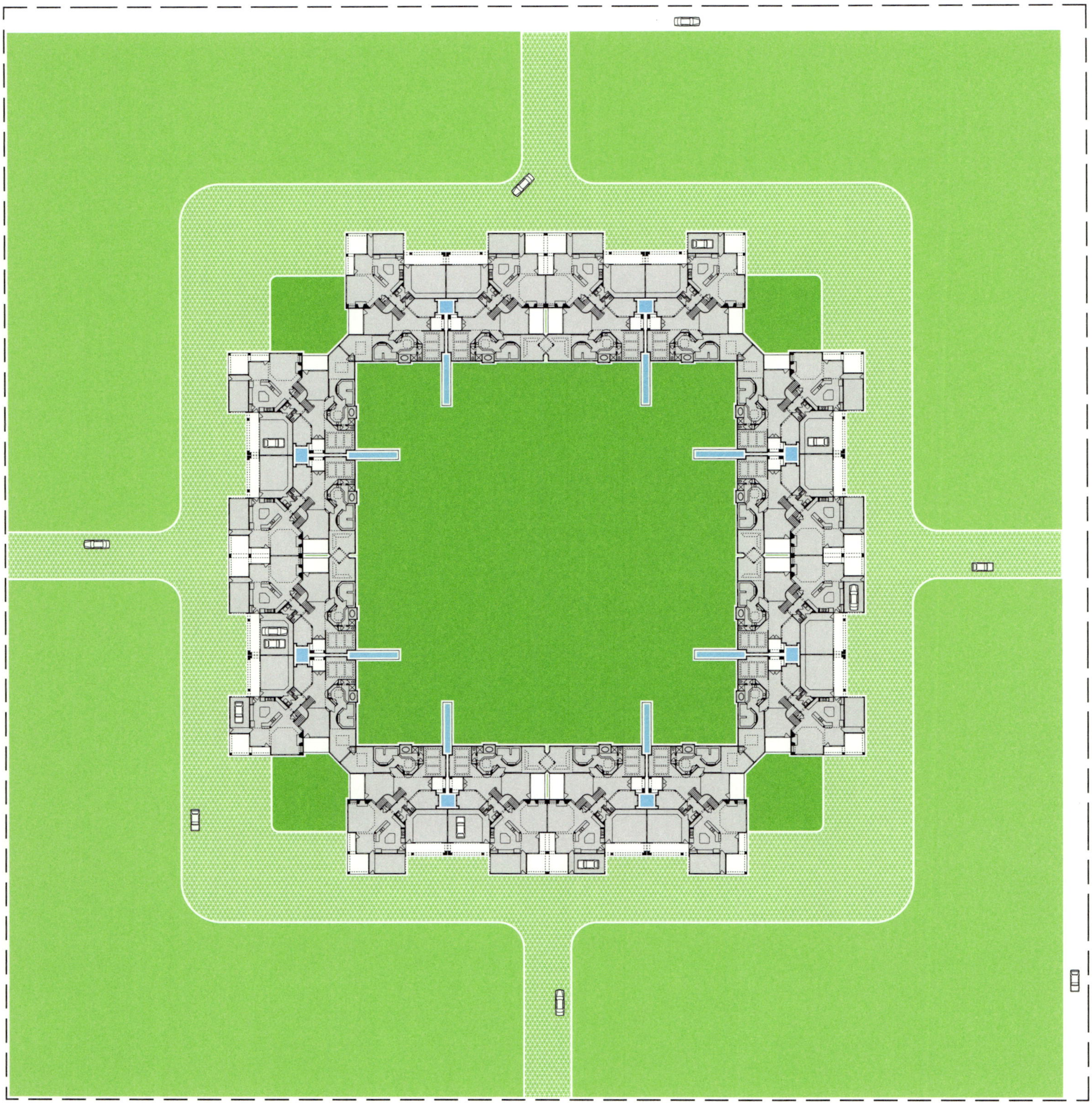

The Big House at Fourier Forest

NE 1/4 SW 1/4 Section 31

16 Houses
71,360 Square Feet
64–80 Bedrooms
48–64 Full Bathrooms
16 Half Bathrooms

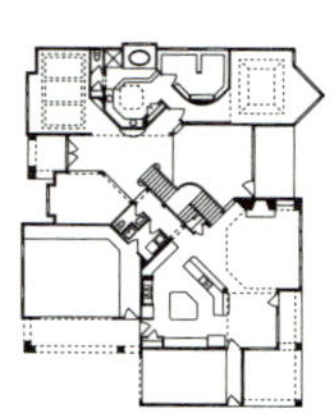

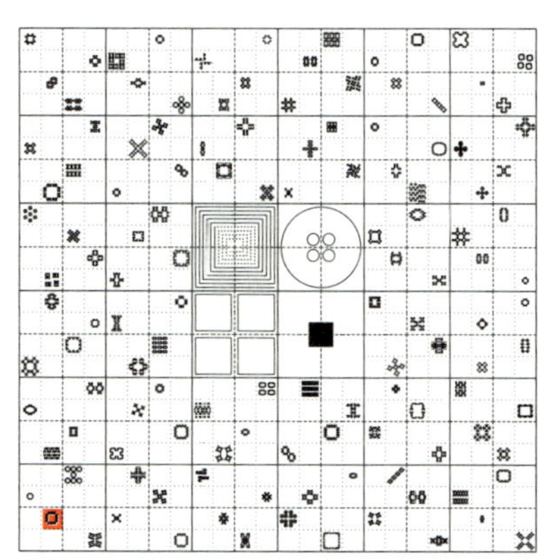

David Weekley Homes, The Kramer, 4460 sq. ft., Texas

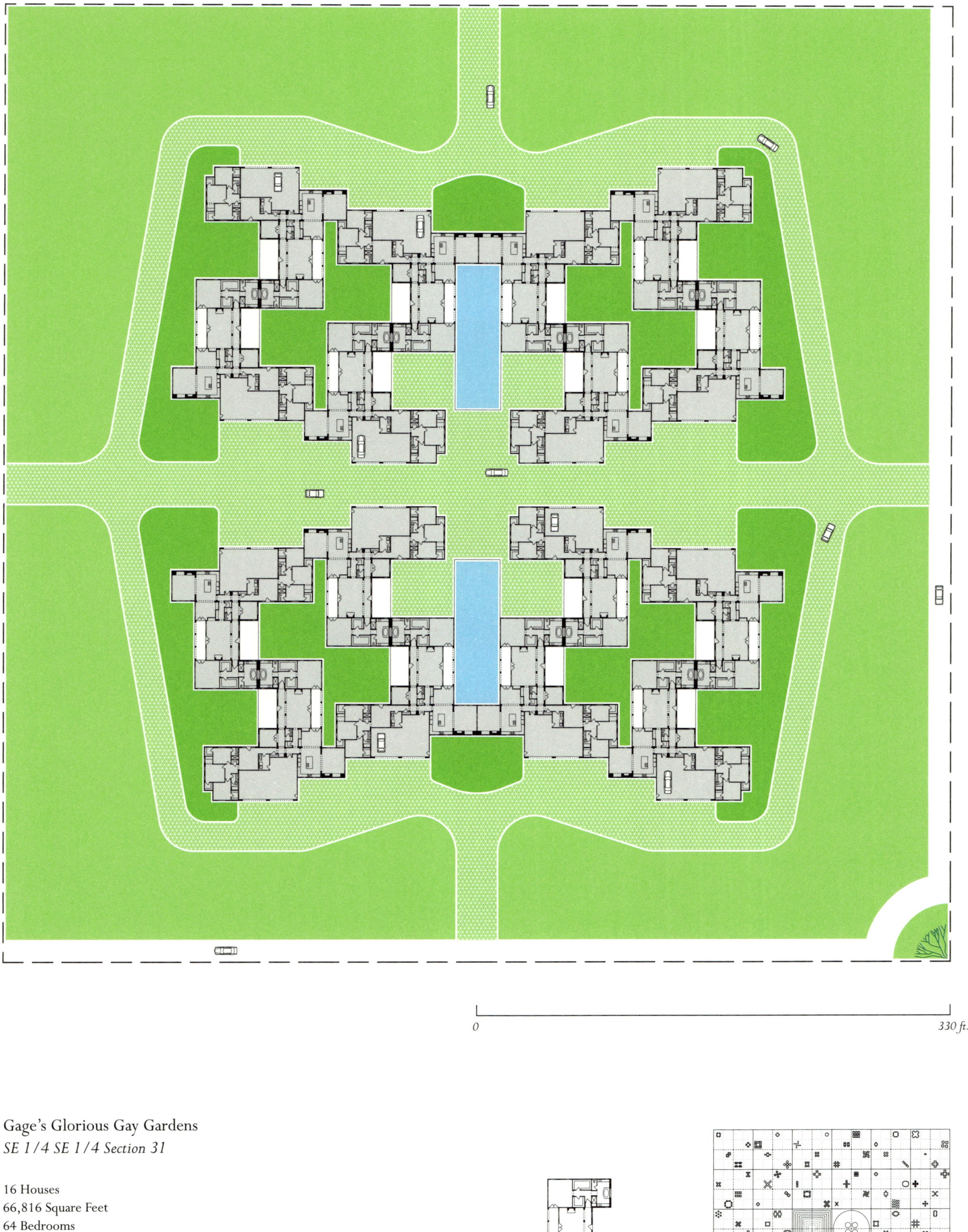

Gage's Glorious Gay Gardens

SE 1/4 SE 1/4 Section 31

16 Houses
66,816 Square Feet
64 Bedrooms
48 Full Bathrooms
16 Half Bathrooms

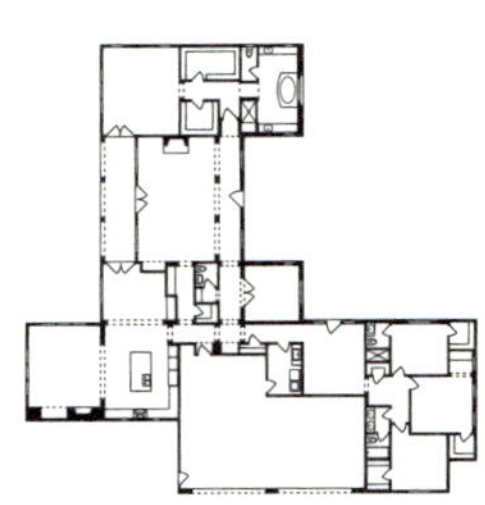

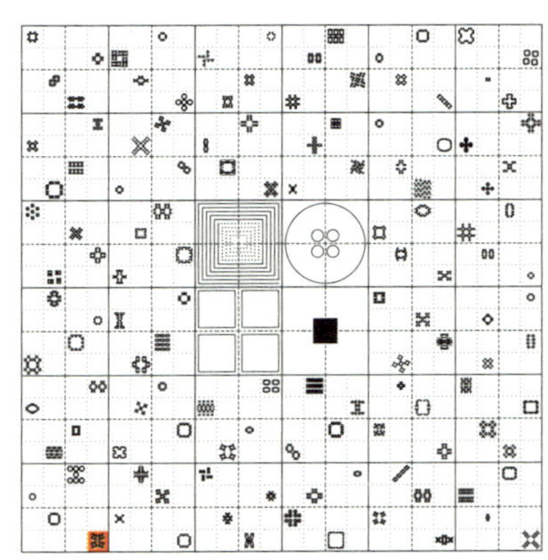

Pulte Homes, The Appaloosa, 4176 sq. ft., California

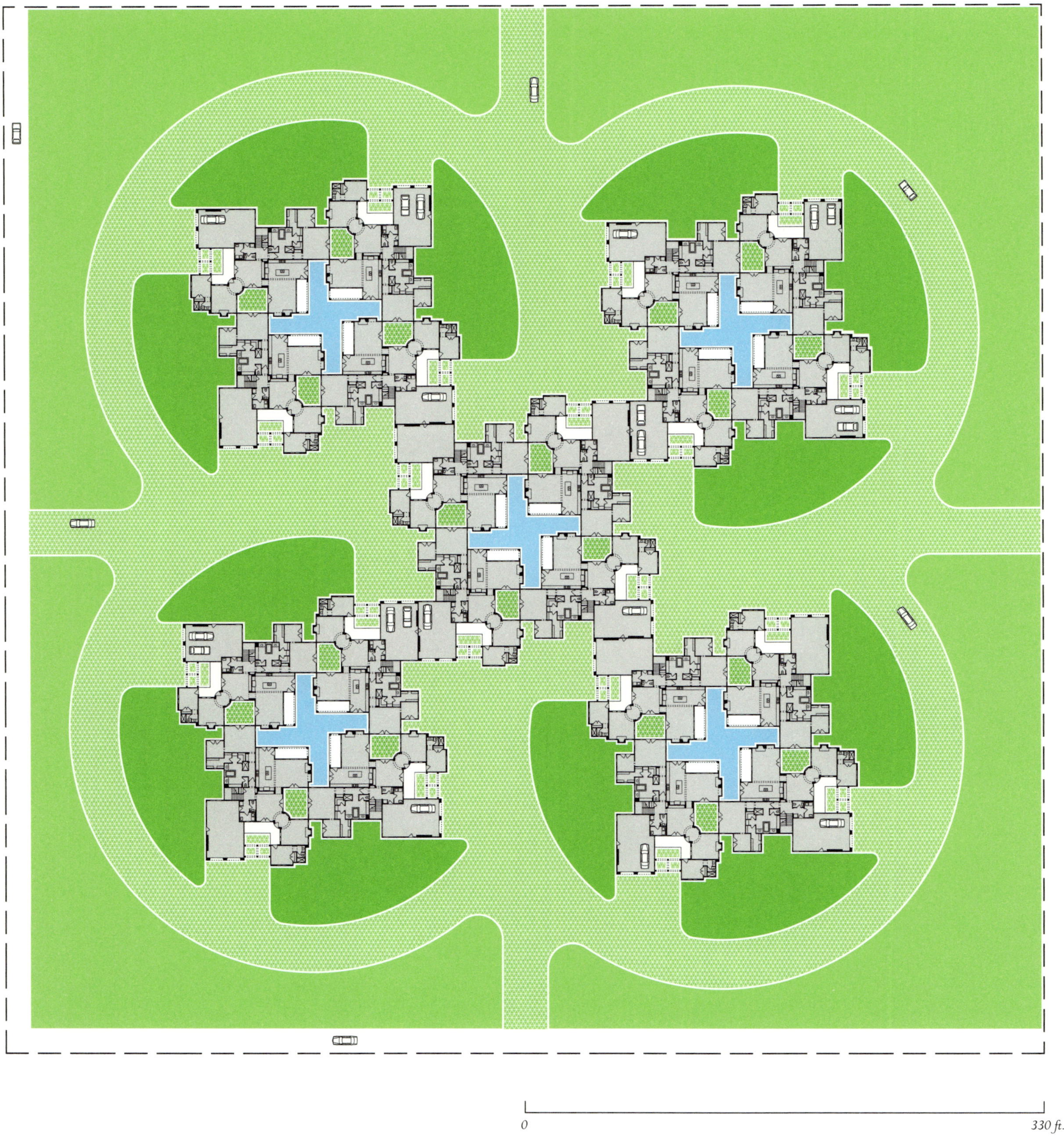

Atypical Plans

SW 1/4 NE 1/4 Section 32

20 Houses
122,440 Square Feet
100 Bedrooms
100 Full Bathrooms
20 Half Bathrooms

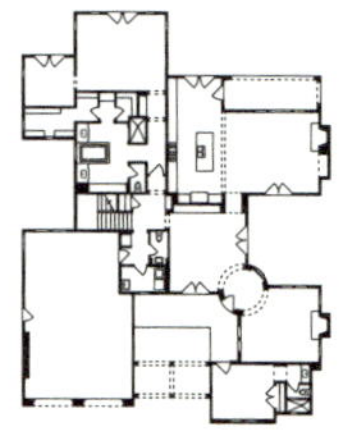

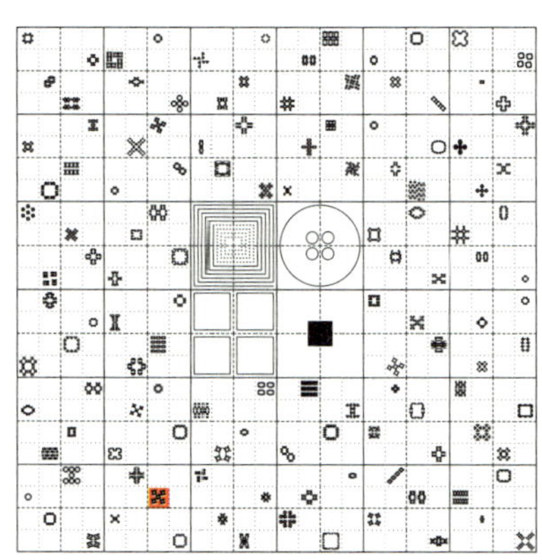

Standard Pacific Homes, Residence 1H, 6122 sq. ft., California

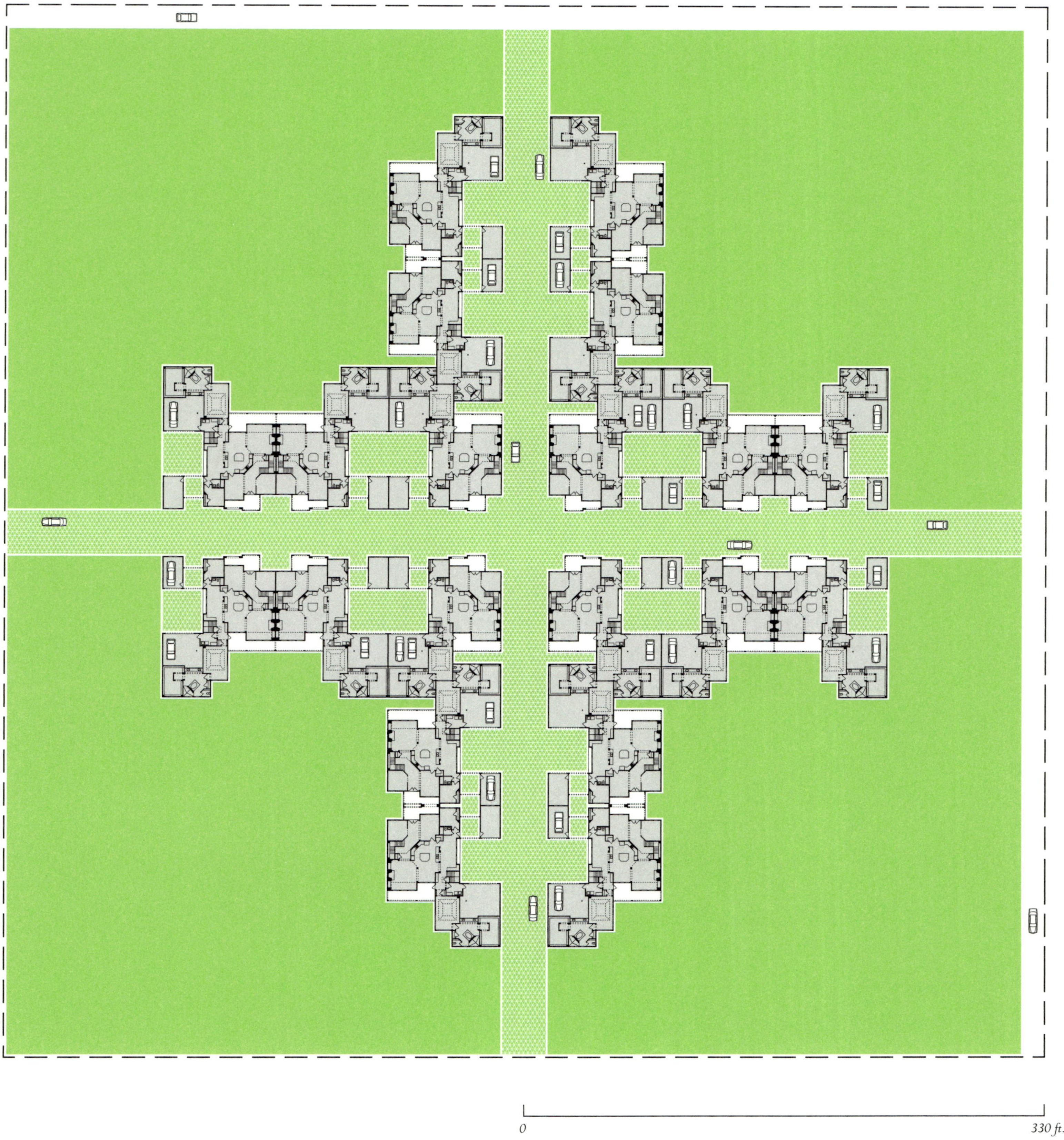

Eupepsia Farms

NE 1/4 NW 1/4 Section 32

20 Houses
113,120 Square Feet
100 Bedrooms
100 Full Bathrooms
20 Half Bathrooms

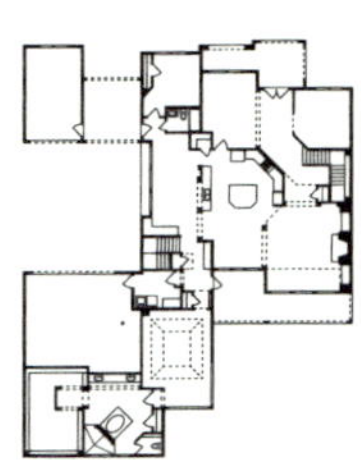

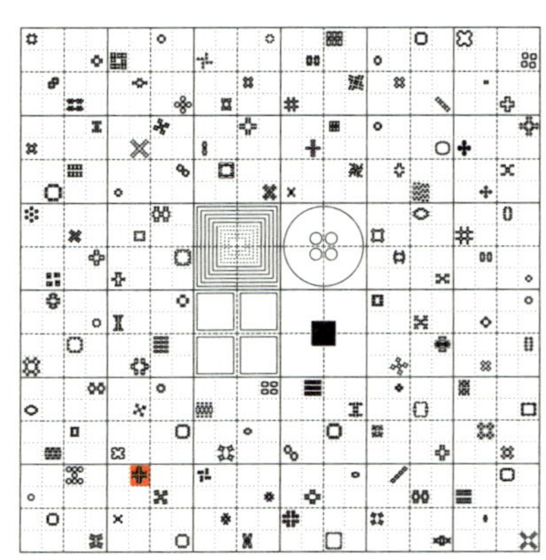

David Weekley Homes, McKeon, 5656 sq. ft., Texas

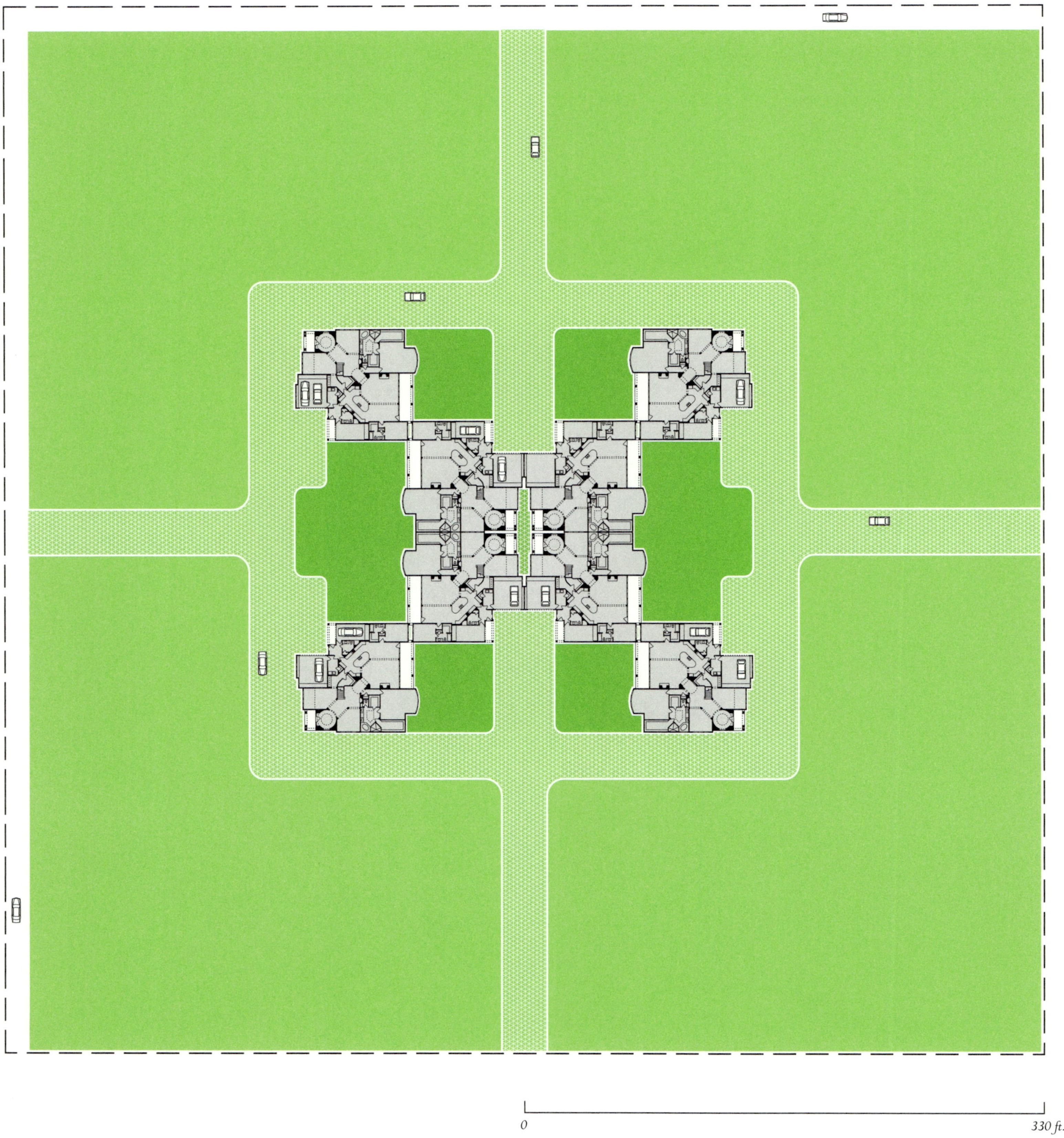

The Reserve at Freedomland
NW 1/4 SW 1/4 Section 32

8 Houses
56,008 Square Feet
48 Bedrooms
40 Full Bathrooms
8 Half Bathrooms

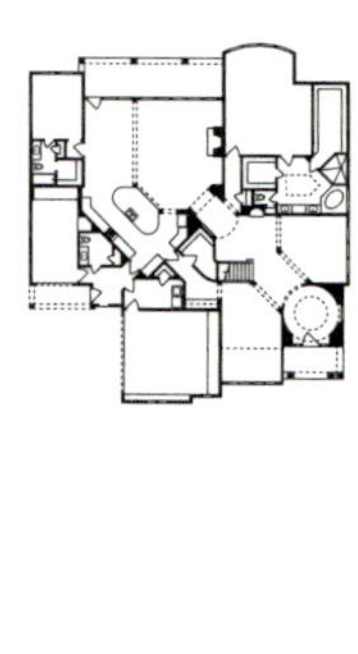

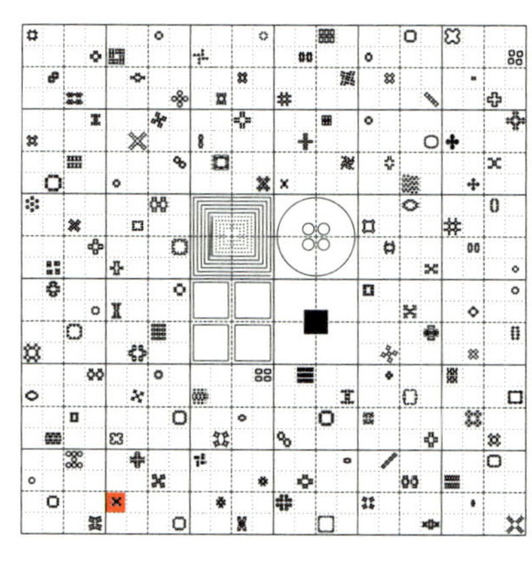

Perry Homes, Plan 7001W, 7001 sq. ft., Texas

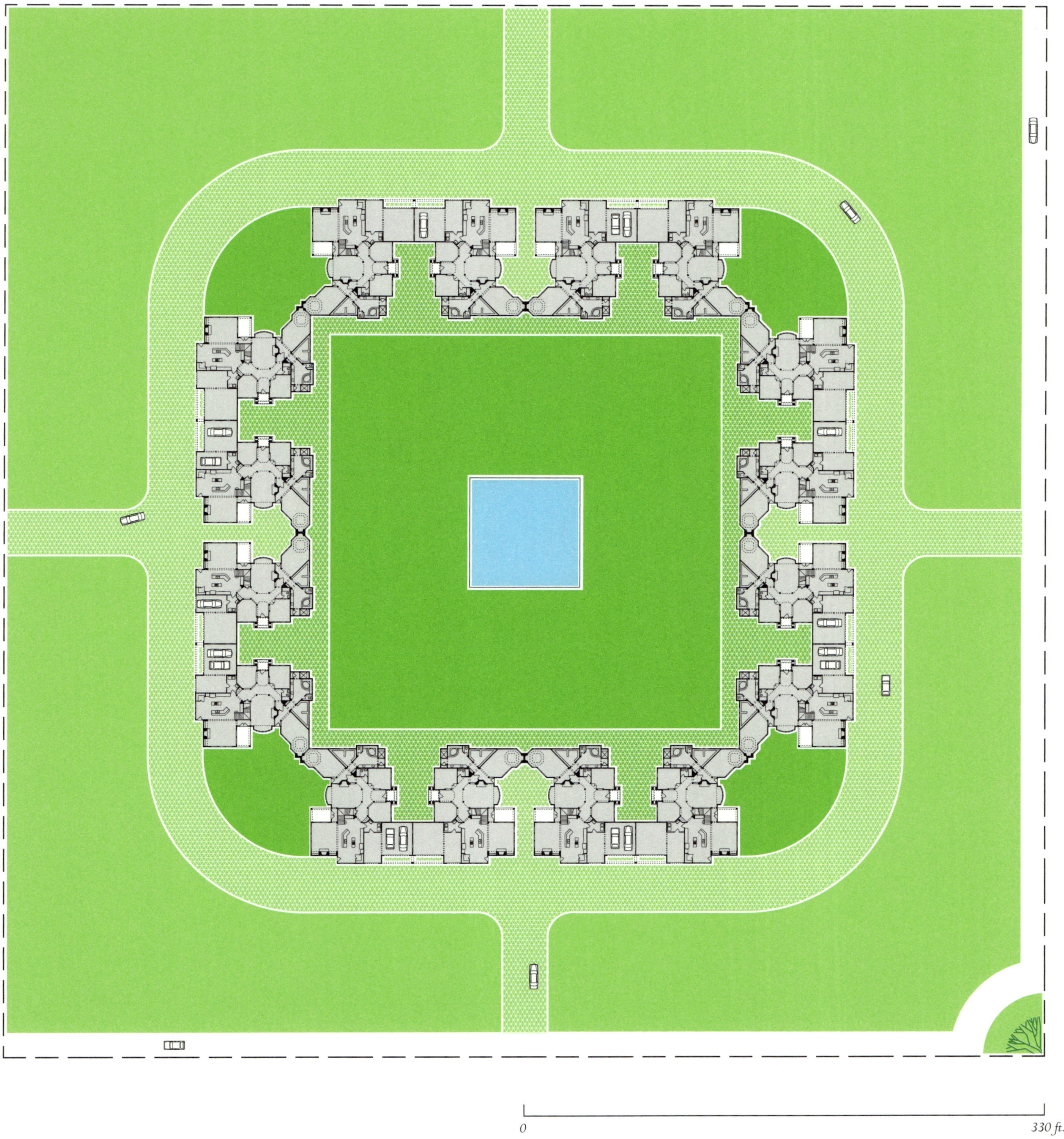

Linda Court

SE 1/4 SE 1/4 Section 32

16 Houses
68,560 Square Feet
64–80 Bedrooms
64 Full Bathrooms
16 Half Bathrooms

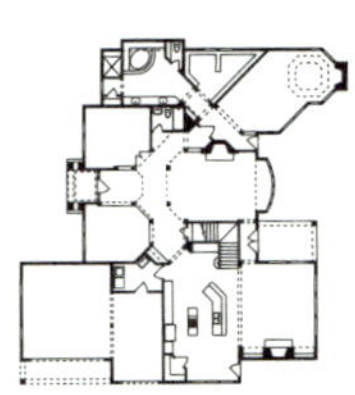

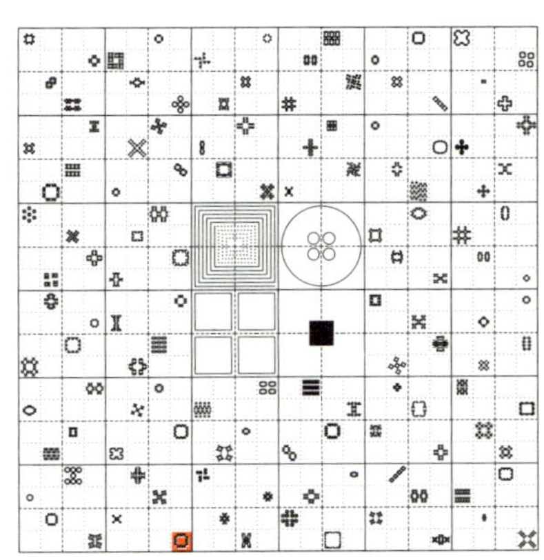

David Weekley Homes, The Lynnhaven, 4285 sq. ft., Texas

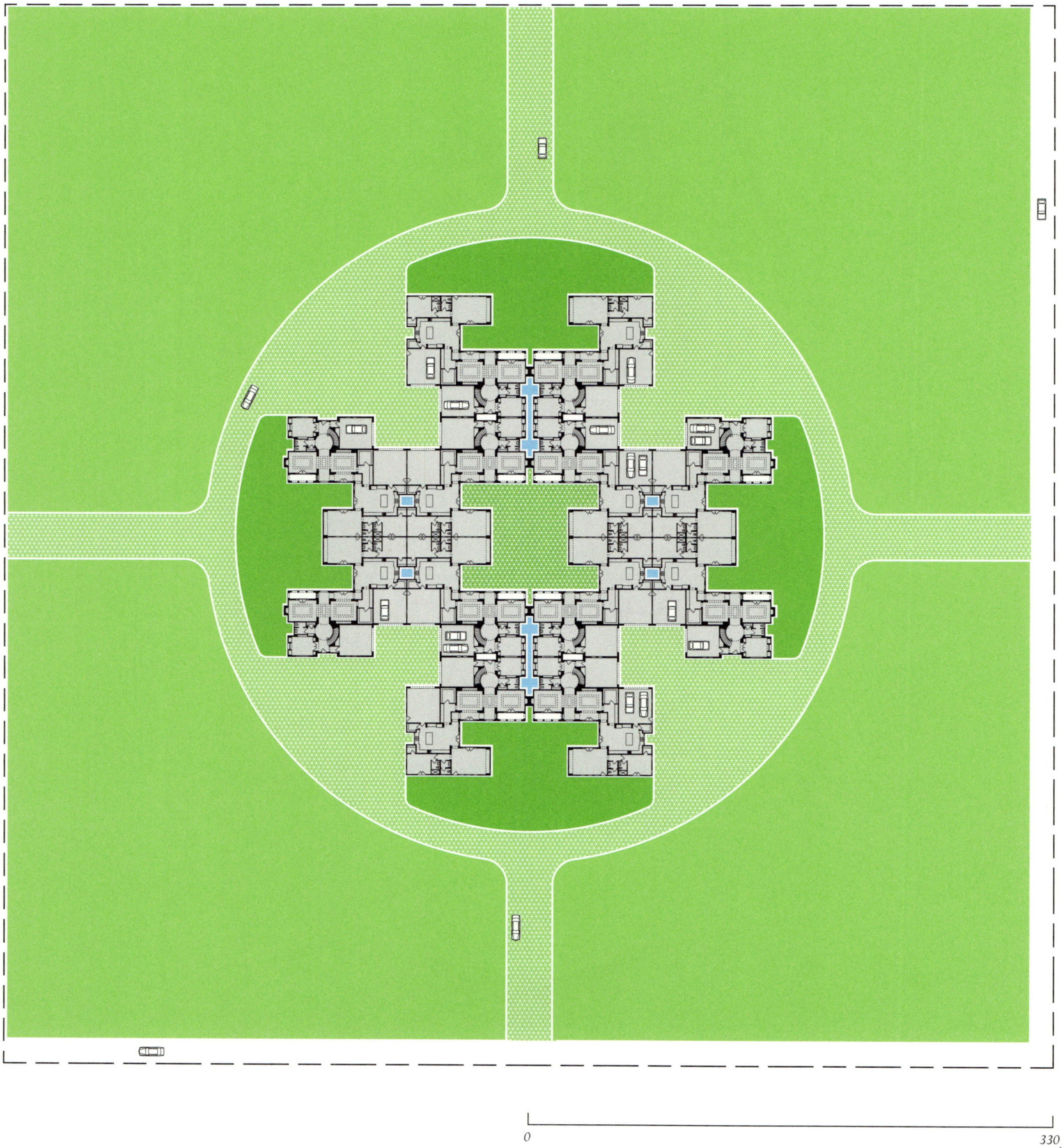

Topolobampo

SE 1/4 NE 1/4 Section 33

12 Houses
78,696 Square Feet
60 Bedrooms
60 Full Bathrooms
24 Half Bathrooms

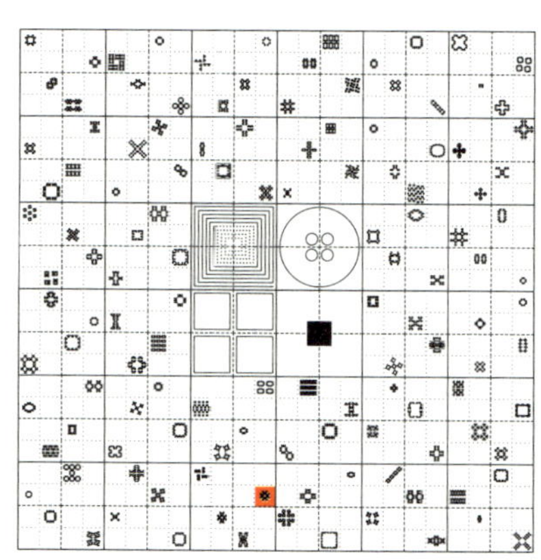

KB Home, The Stratford, 6558 sq. ft., California

Citizen Farmers near Monticello Manor Homes, Freedomland
after *The Return of the Reapers,* 1886
Henry Herbert La Thangue

Monticello Manor Homes

NW 1/4 NW 1/4 Section 33

16 Houses
85,200 Square Feet
64 Bedrooms
64 Full Bathrooms
32 Half Bathrooms

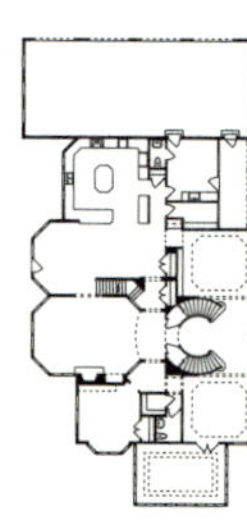

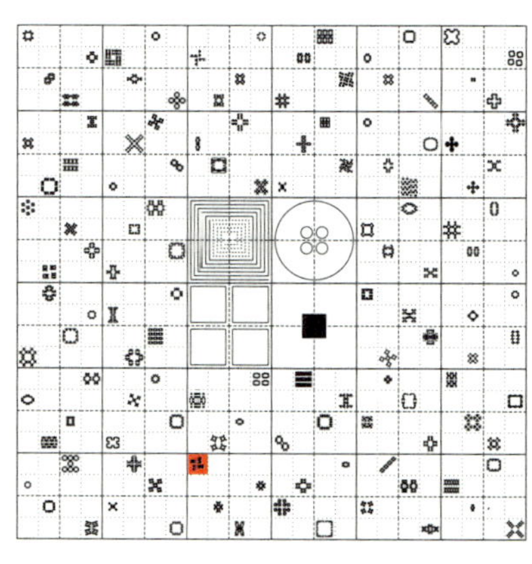

K. Hovnanian Homes, The Tara, 5325 sq. ft., Maryland

Wilson Estates at Outterbridge Park
NE 1/4 SW 1/4 Section 33

12 Houses
72,000 Square Feet
60 Bedrooms
60 Full Bathrooms
12Half Bathrooms

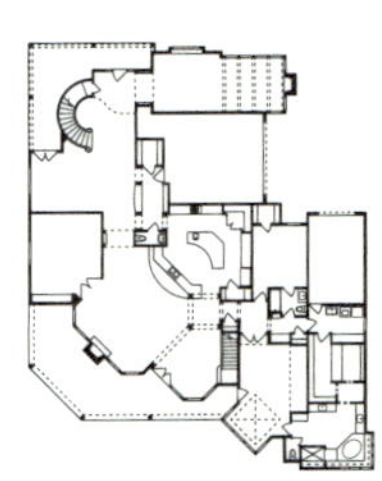

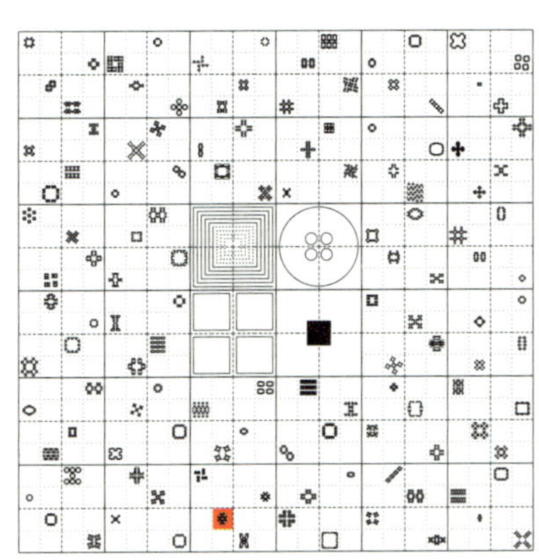

Meritage Homes, The Chalet, 6000 sq. ft., Texas

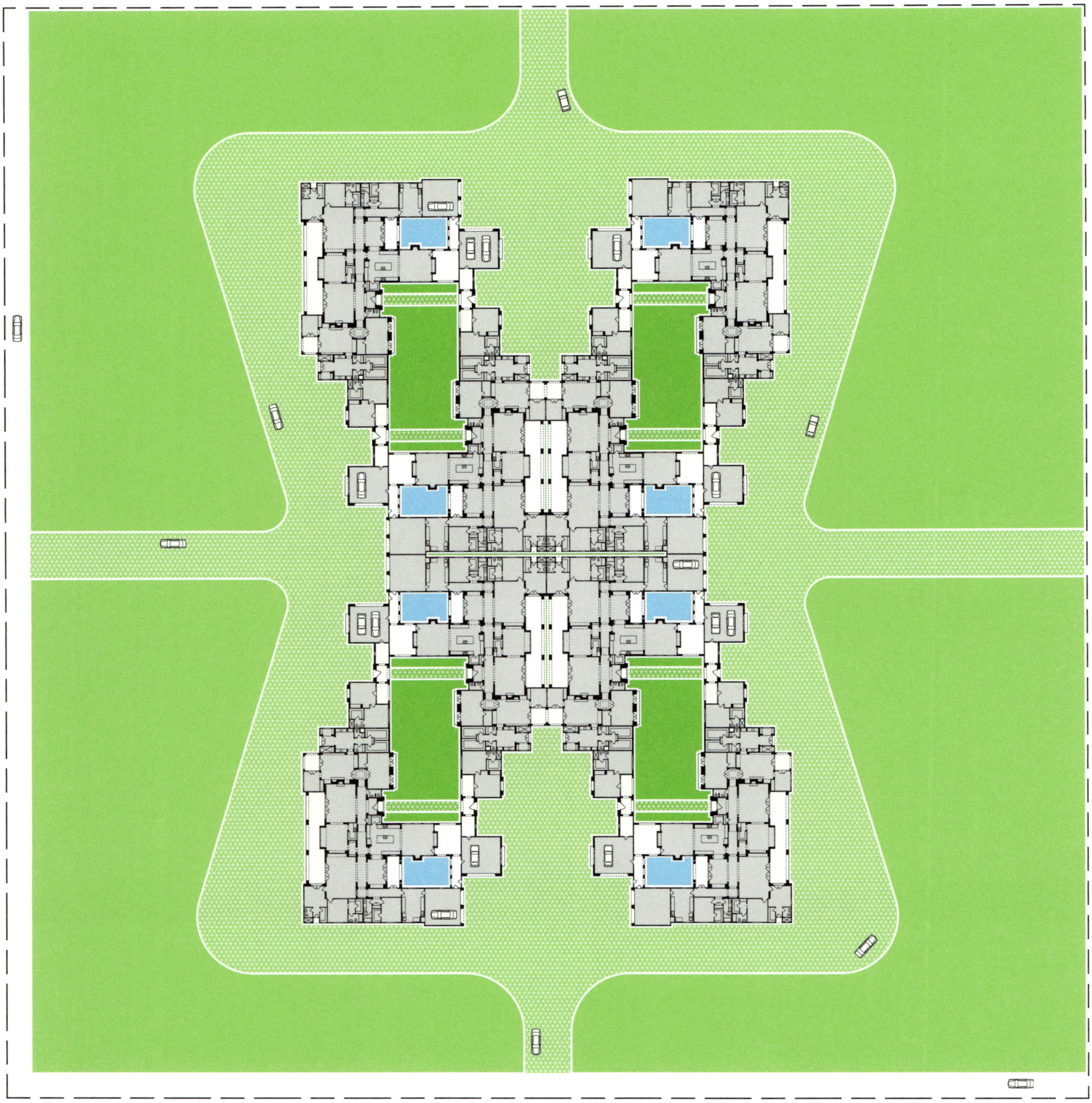

Fort Goodwill

SW 1/4 SE 1/4 Section 33

8 Houses
48,800 Square Feet
40–48 Bedrooms
40–48 Full Bathrooms
8 Half Bathrooms

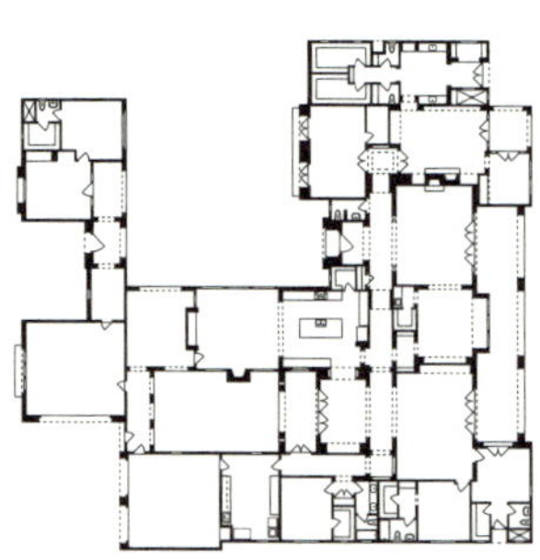

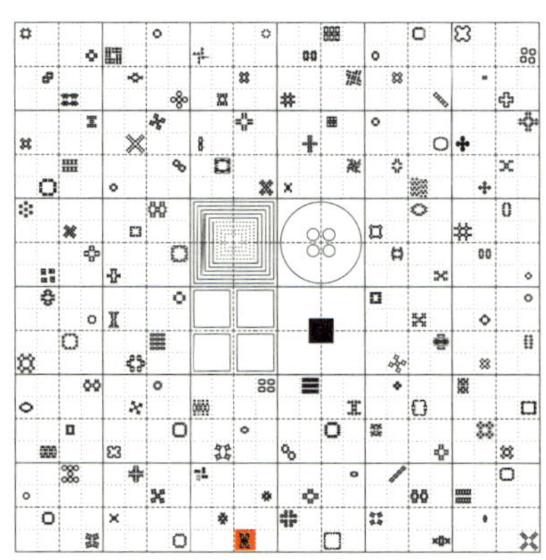

Toll Brothers, The Terreno, 6100 sq. ft., Arizona

Hay Harvest at The Colony, Freedomland
after *Hay Harvest*, circa 1880s
Laszlo Pataky von Sospatak

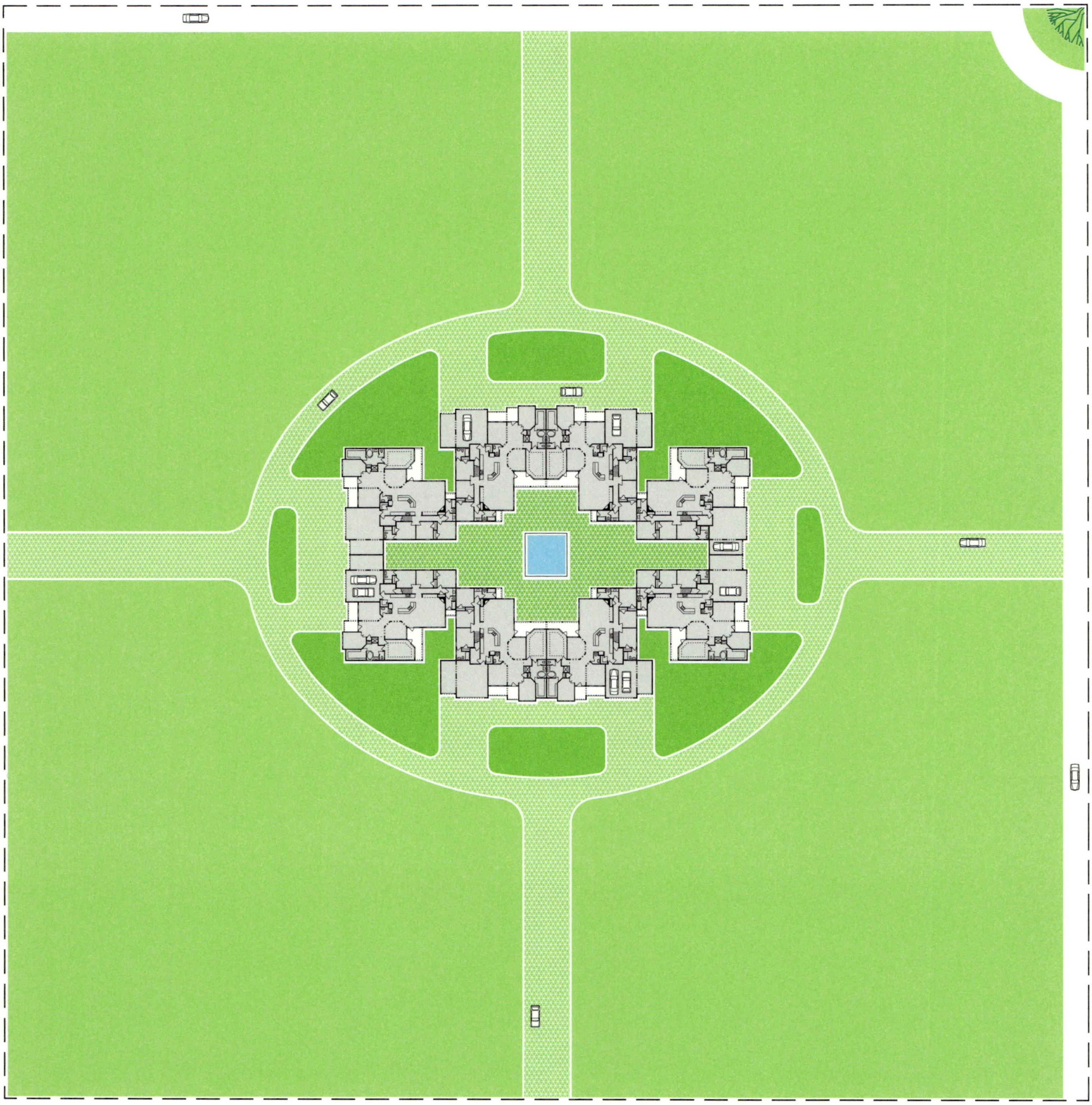

0 330 ft.

The Colony

NE 1/4 NE 1/4 Section 34

8 Houses
29,128 Square Feet
32 Bedrooms
24 Full Bathrooms
8 Half Bathrooms

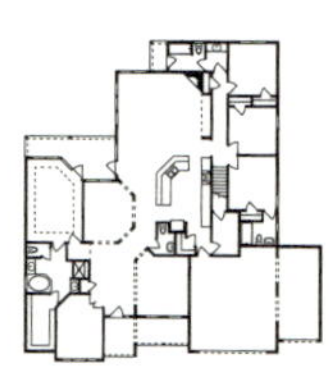

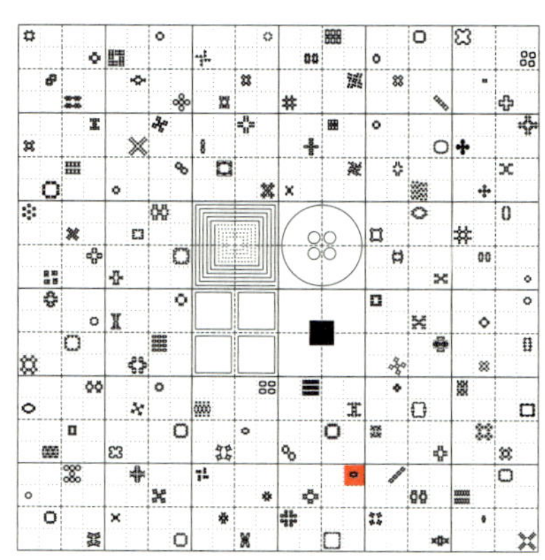

Pulte Homes, Monet, 3641 sq. ft., Texas

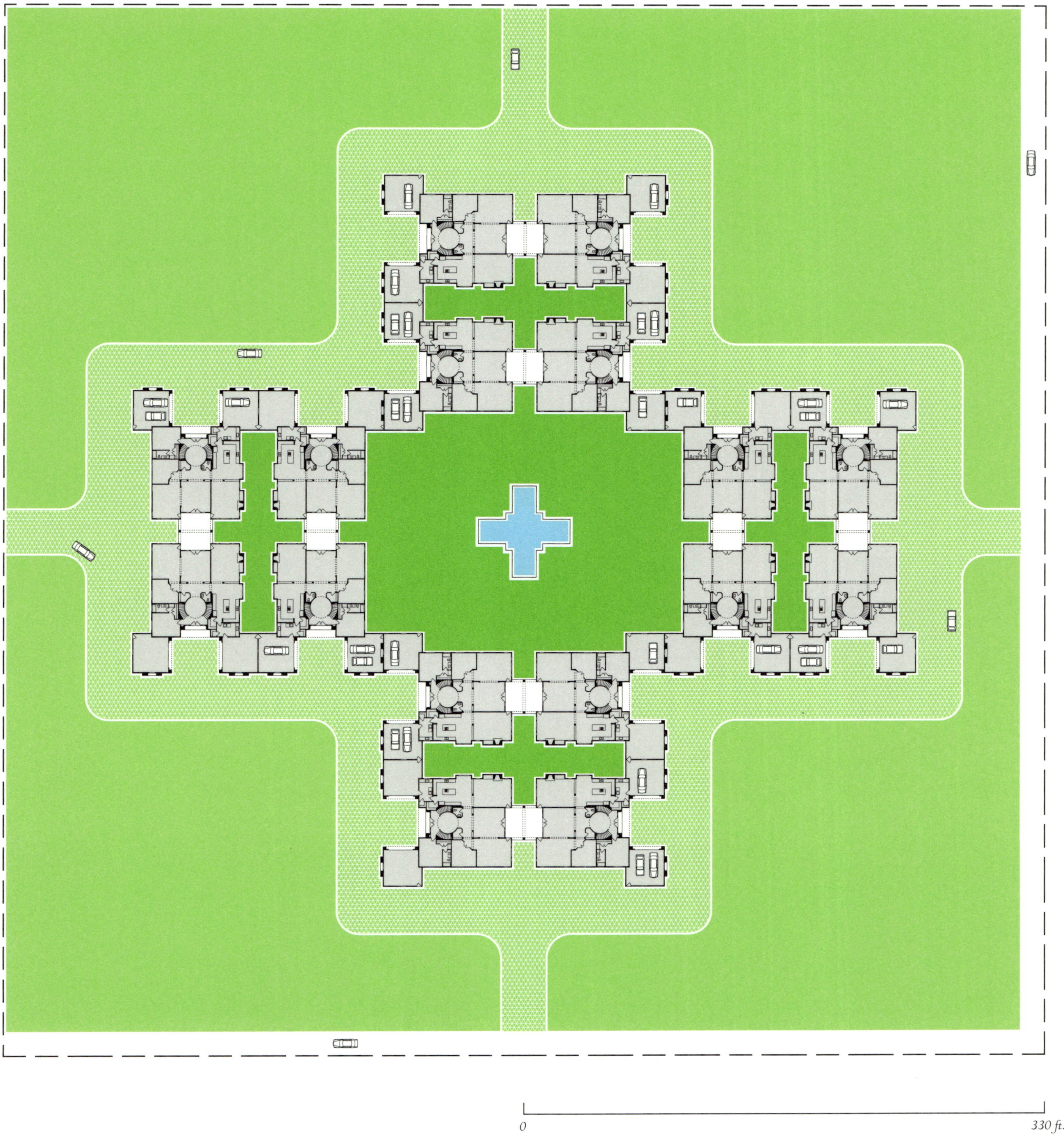

The Sanctuary

SE 1/4 NW 1/4 Section 34

16 Houses
82,000 Square Feet
64–80 Bedrooms
64 Full Bathrooms
16 Half Bathrooms

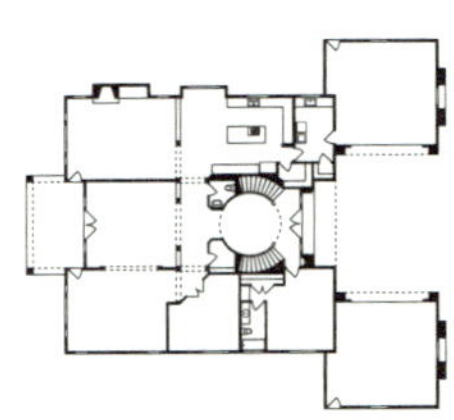

Toll Brothers, The Mirador, 5125 sq. ft., Arizona

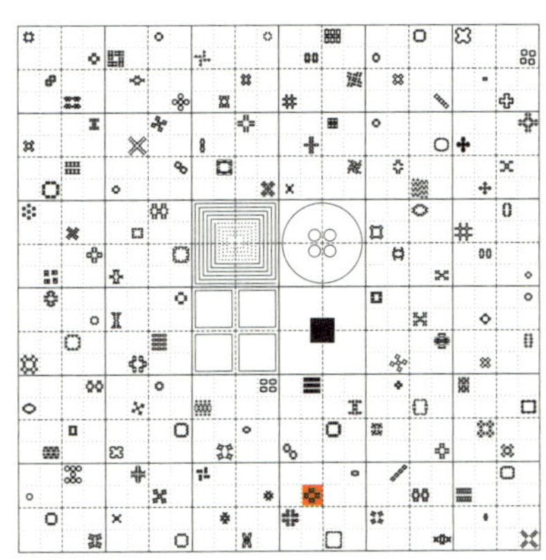

Shangri-La

NW 1/4 SW 1/4 Section 34

48 Houses
177,744 Square Feet
144 Bedrooms
96 Full Bathrooms
48 Half Bathrooms

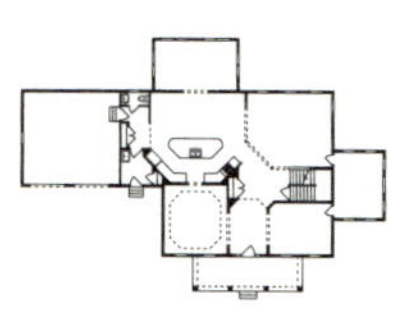

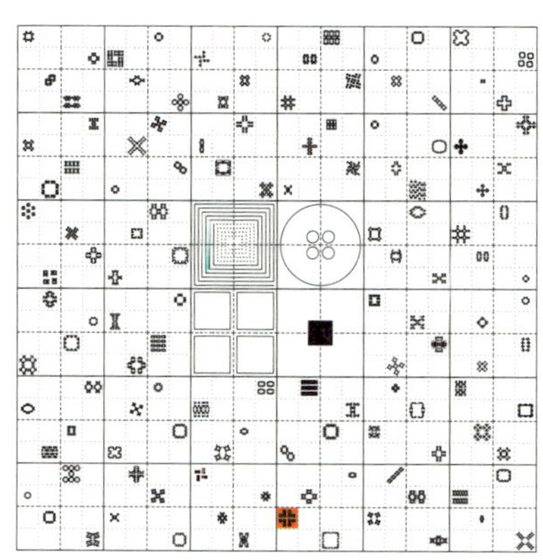

Ryland Homes, The Wye, 3703 sq. ft., Delaware

There is but one mode by which man can possess in perpetuity all the happiness which his nature is capable of enjoying,—that is by the union and co-operation of all for the benefit of each.

—Robert Owen, *The Social System,* 1826.

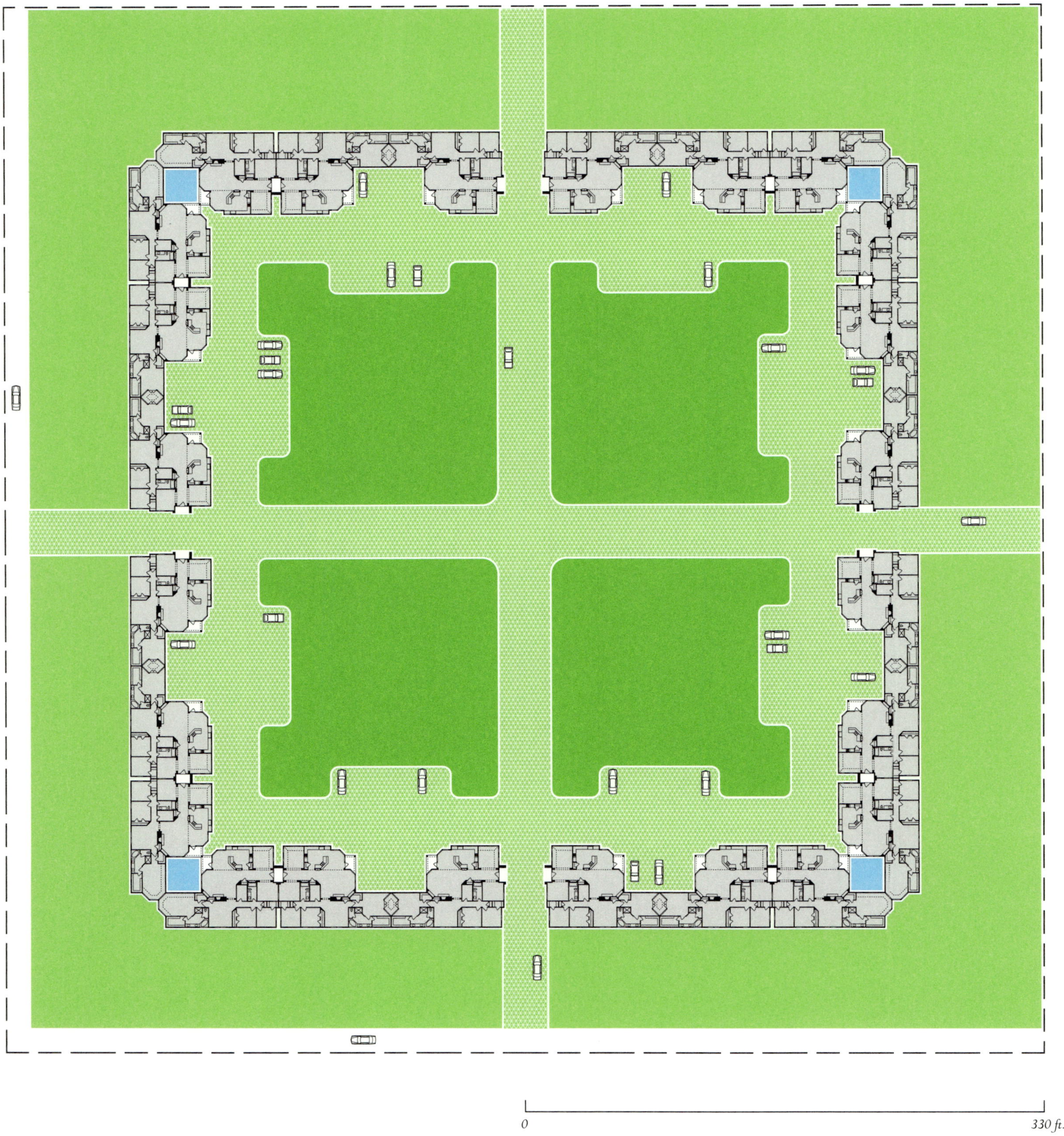

Really New Harmony

SW 1/4 SE 1/4 Section 34

24 Houses
58,128 Square Feet
72–96 Bedrooms
48 Full Bathrooms
0 Half Bathrooms

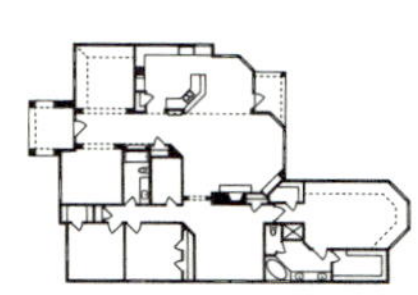

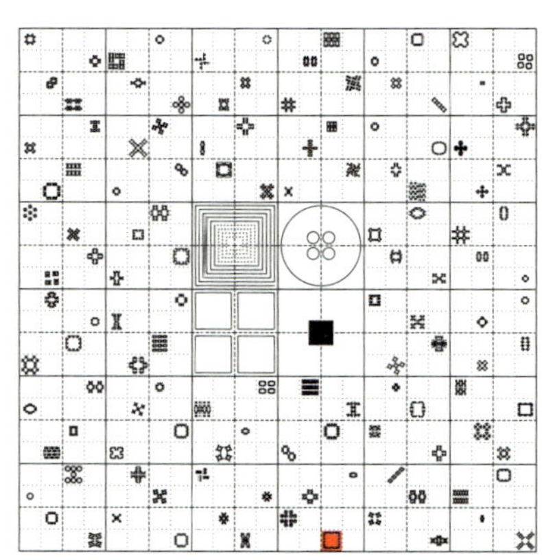

Beazer Homes, The Muirfield, 2422 sq. ft., Texas

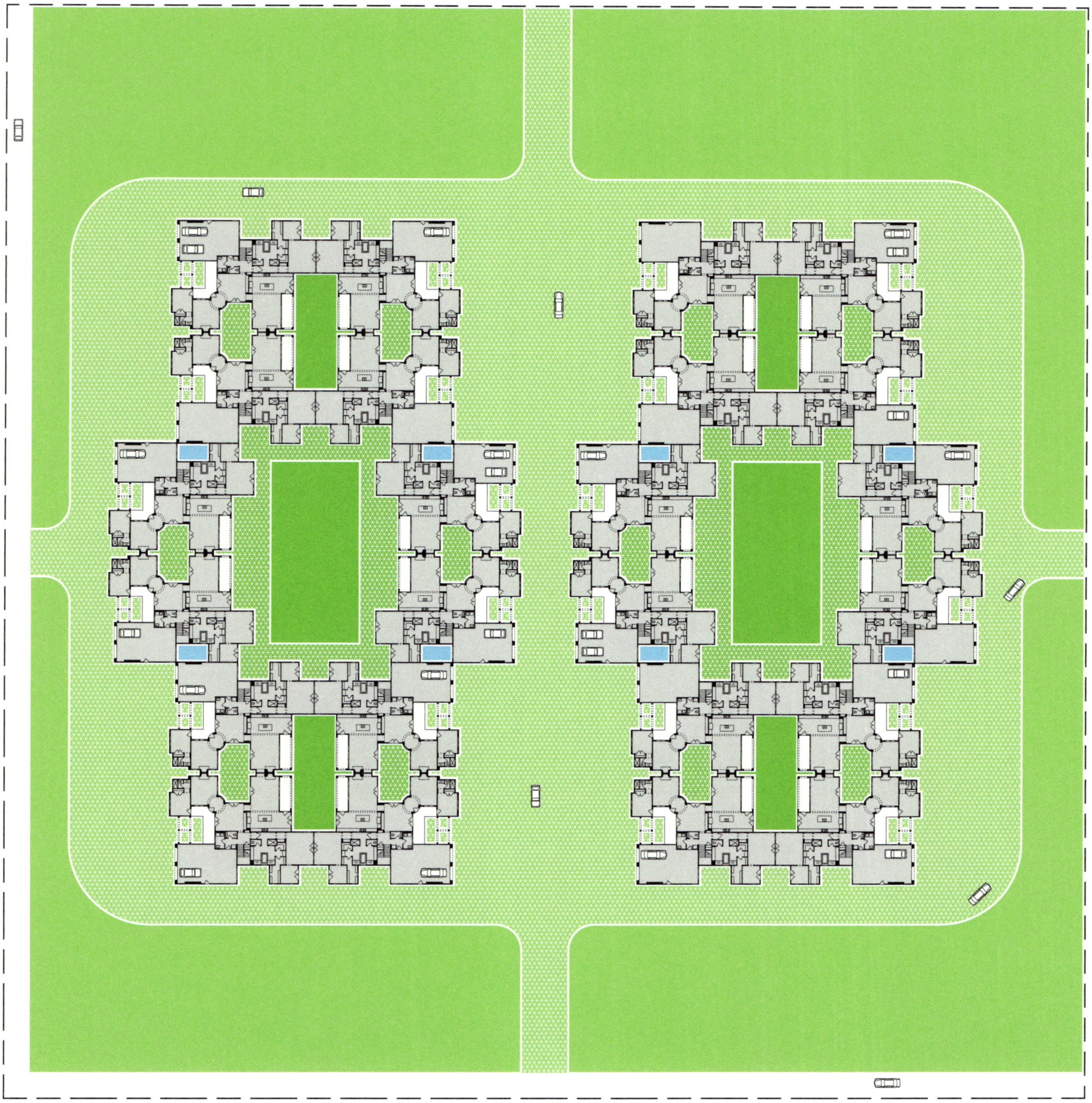

Leroy's

SW 1/4 NE 1/4 Section 35

24 Houses
146,928 Square Feet
120 Bedrooms
120 Full Bathrooms
24 Half Bathrooms

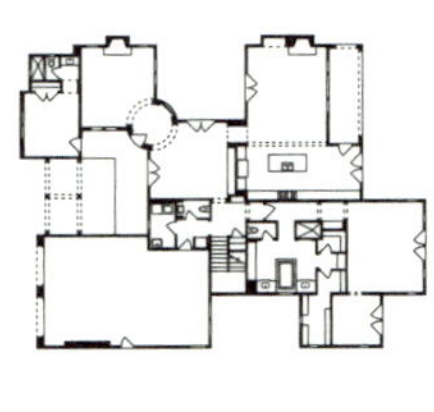

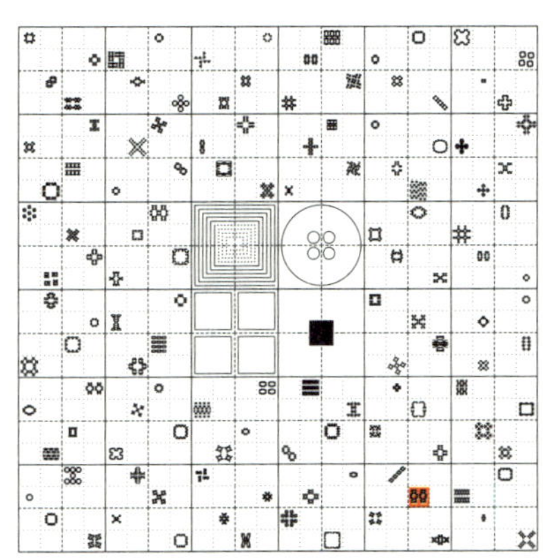

Standard Pacific Homes, Residence 1H, 6122 sq. ft., California

Palats Soren

NE 1/4 NW 1/4 Section 35

16 Houses
74,000 Square Feet
64 Bedrooms
64 Full Bathrooms
32 Half Bathrooms

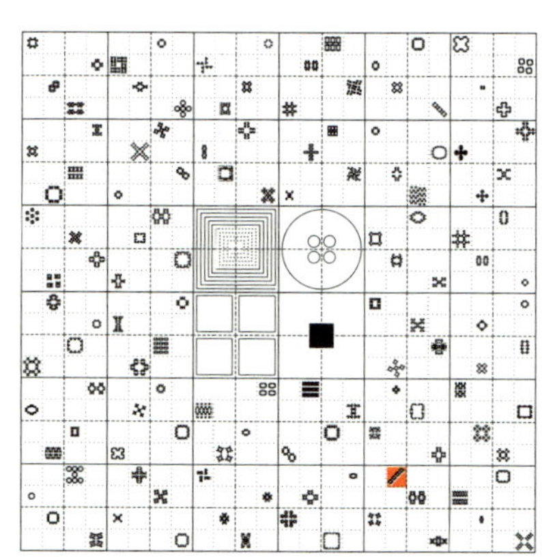

Shea Homes, Plan 2 at Maravilla, 4625 sq. ft., California

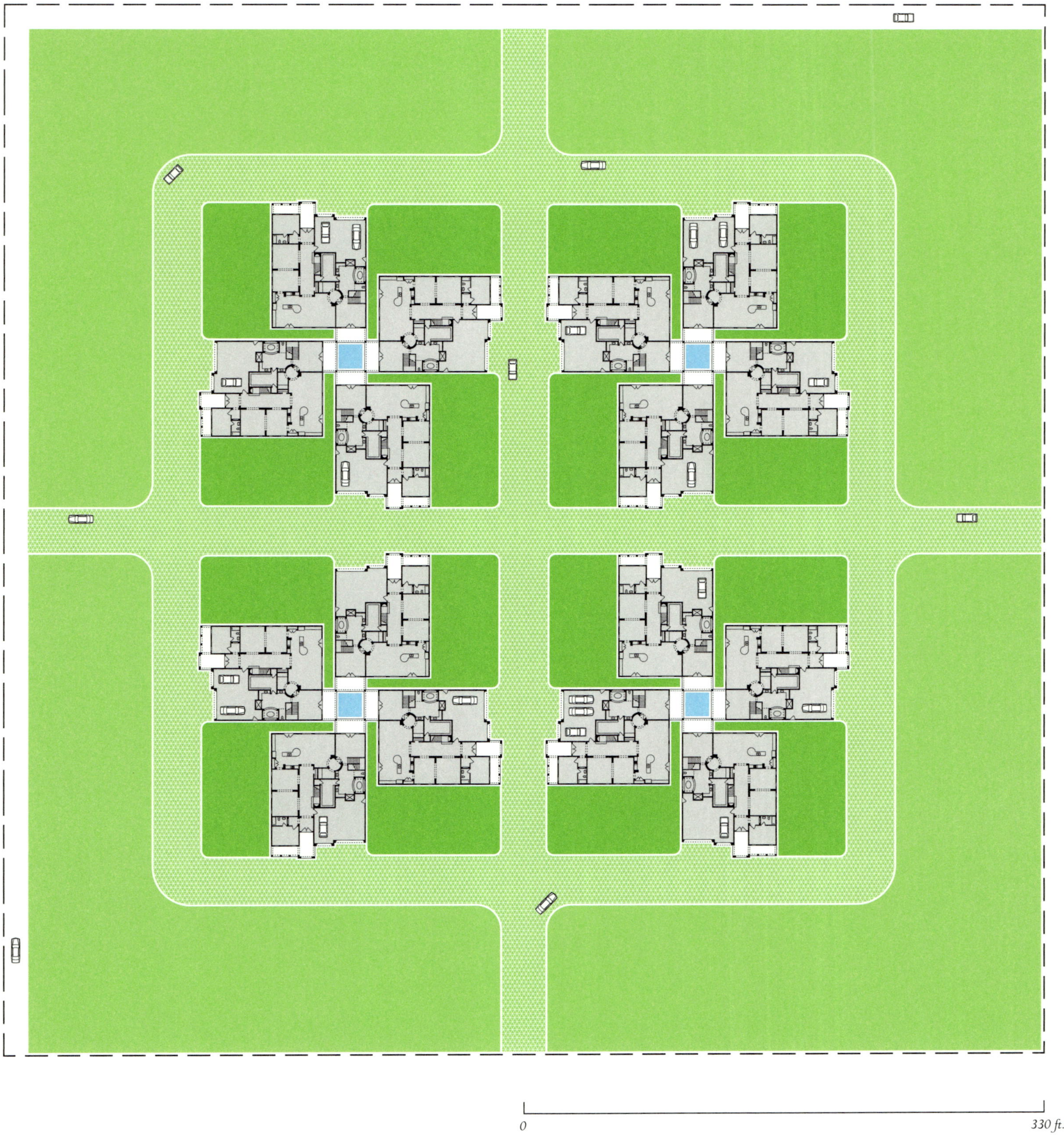

Village Green Preservation Villas

NW 1/4 SW 1/4 Section 35

16 Houses
76,000 Square Feet
96–112 Bedrooms
64 Full Bathrooms
16 Half Bathrooms

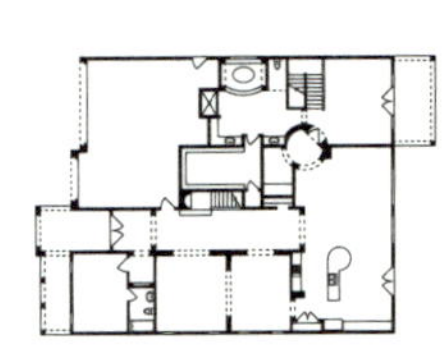

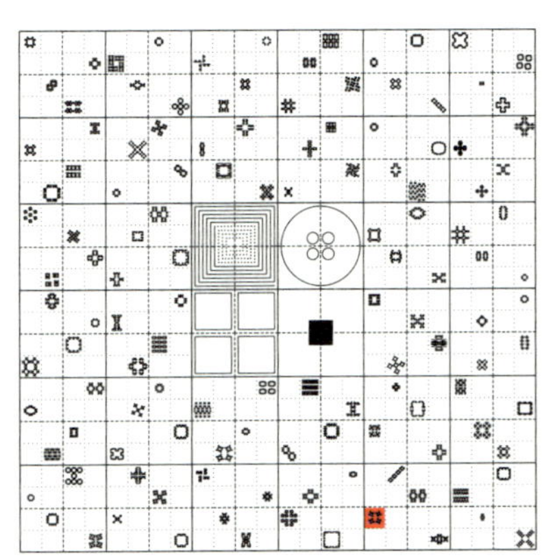

Richmond American Homes, Picasso, 4750 sq. ft., Arizona

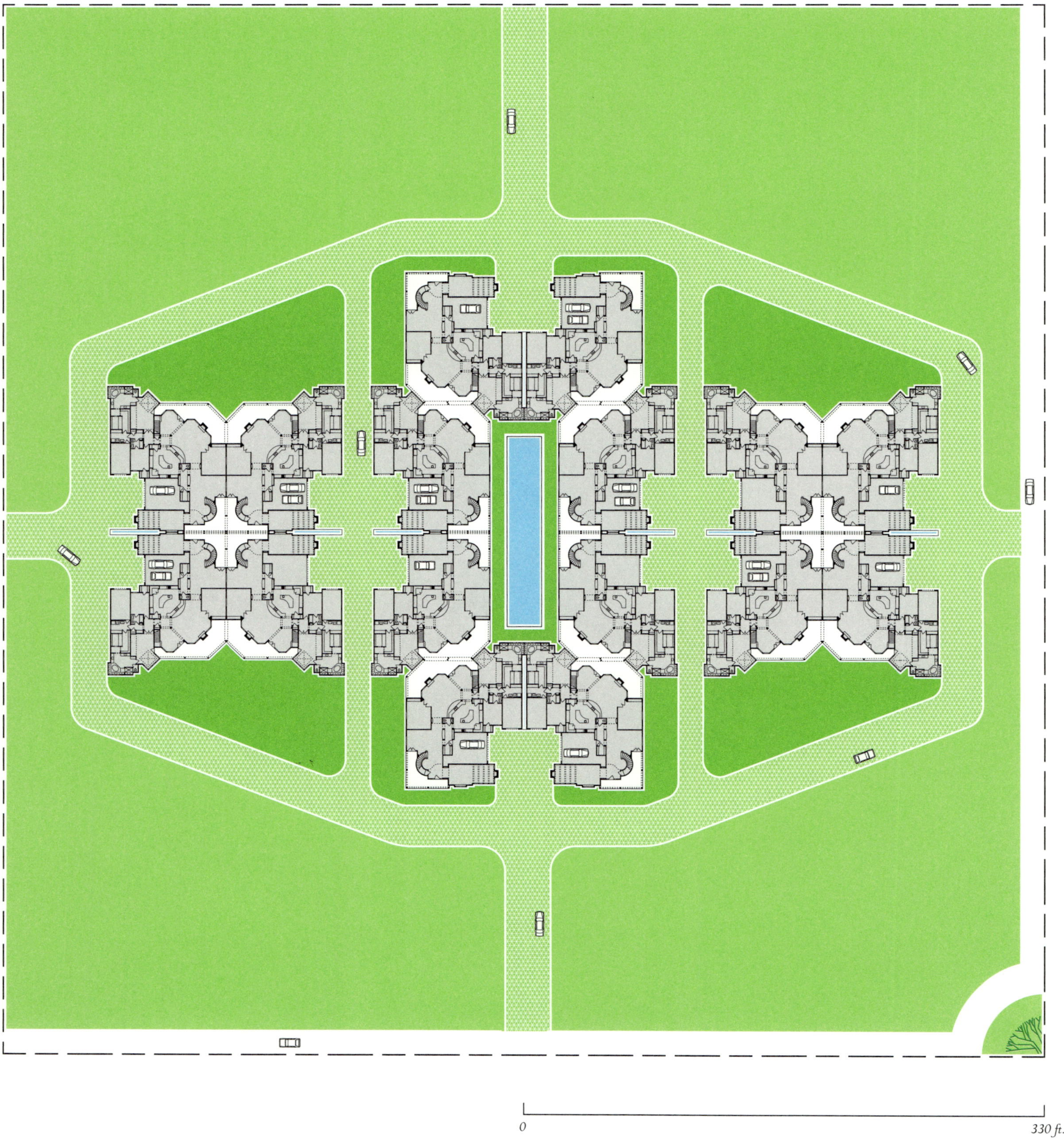

Pleiades Prospect
SE 1/4 SE 1/4 Section 35

16 Houses
96,000 Square Feet
80 Bedrooms
80 Full Bathrooms
16 Half Bathrooms

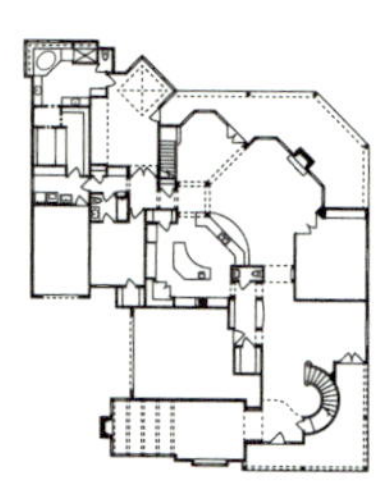

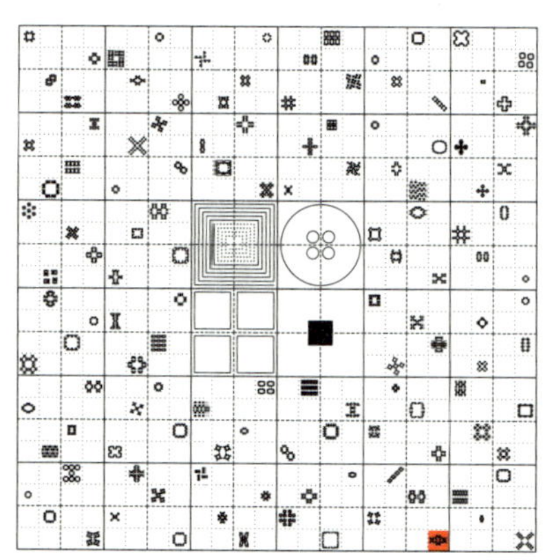

Meritage Homes, The Chalet, 6000 sq. ft., Texas

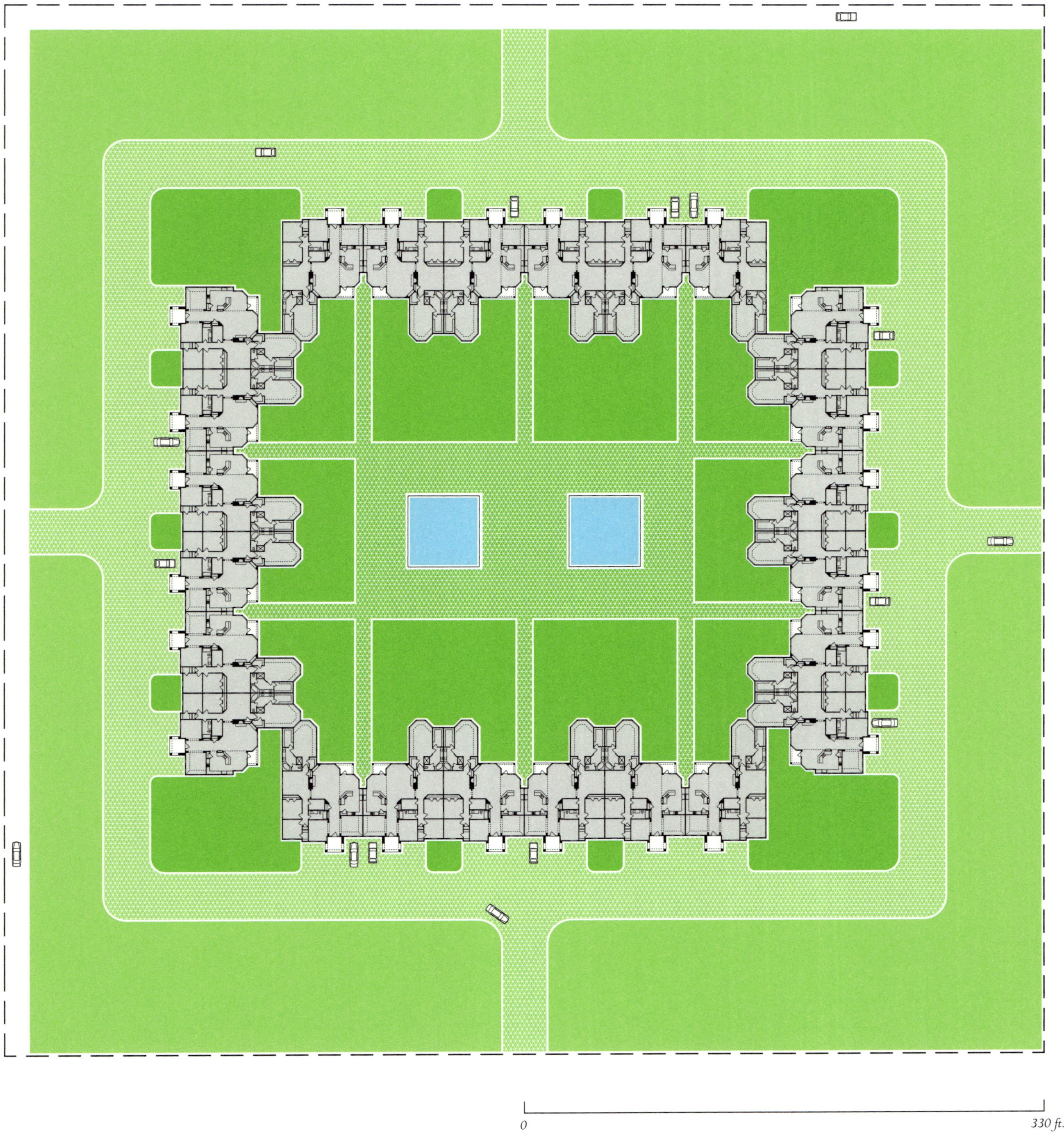

Parallelogram Park

NW 1/4 NE 1/4 Section 36

24 Houses
58,128 Square Feet
72–96 Bedrooms
48 Full Bathrooms
0 Half Bathrooms

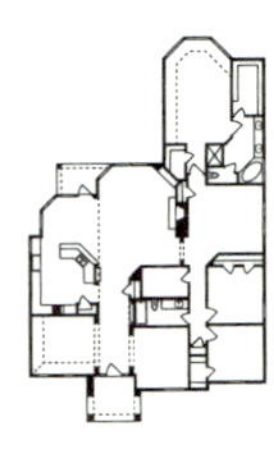

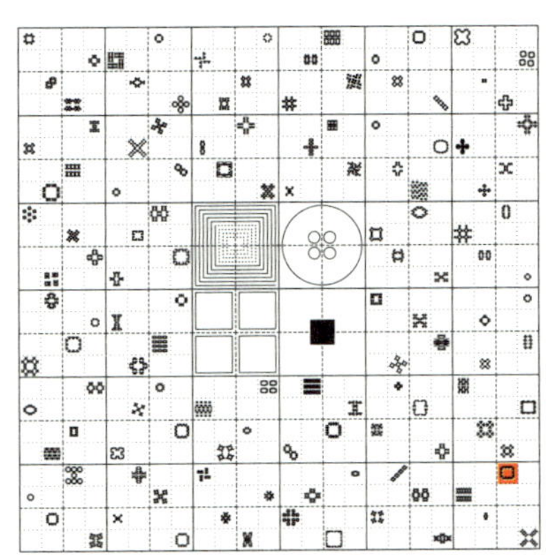

Beazer Homes, The Muirfield, 2422 sq. ft., Texas

The Architects of Freedomland
after *A Group of Danish Artists in Rome*, 1837
Constantin Hansen

I view great cities as pestilential to the morals, the health and the liberties of man. True, they nourish some of the elegant arts; but the useful ones can thrive elsewhere; and less perfection in the others, with more health, virtue and freedom, would be my choice.

—Thomas Jefferson, from a letter to Benjamin Rush, 1800.

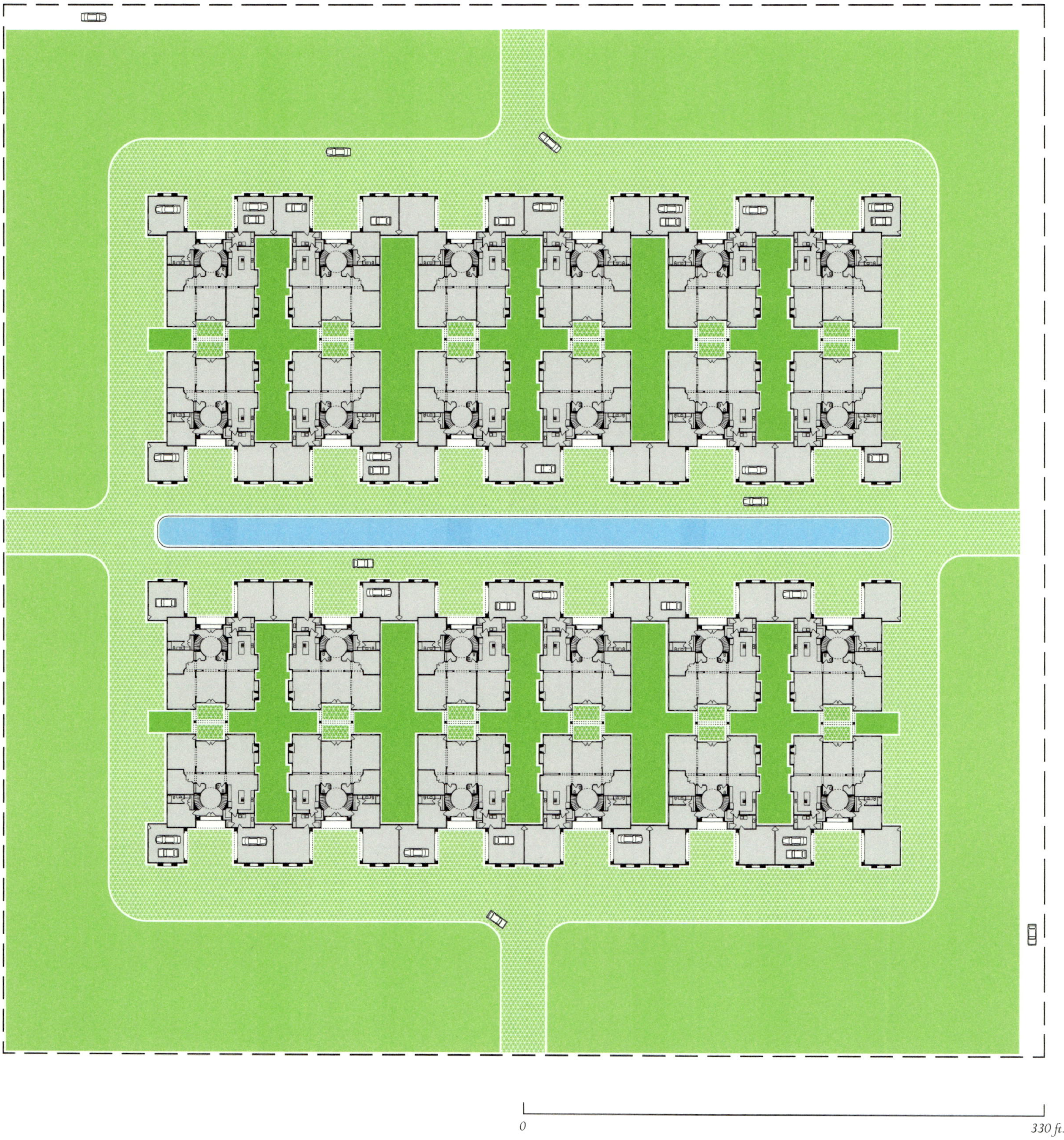

Animal Farm

SW 1/4 NW 1/4 Section 36

24 Houses
123,000 Square Feet
96–120 Bedrooms
96 Full Bathrooms
24 Half Bathrooms

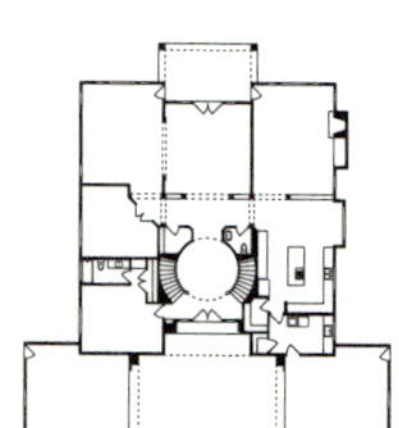

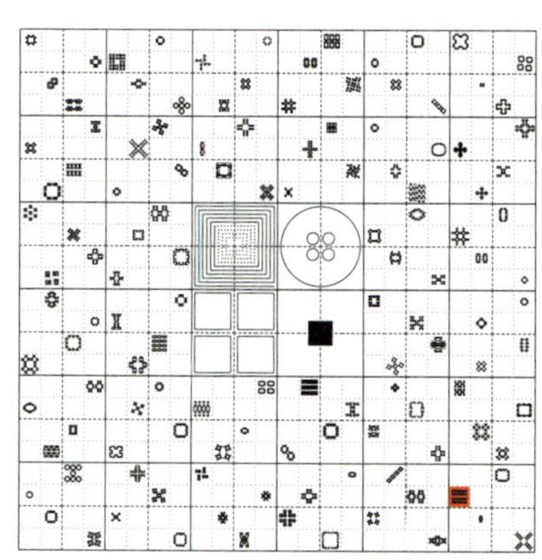

Toll Brothers, The Mirador, 5125 sq. ft., Arizona

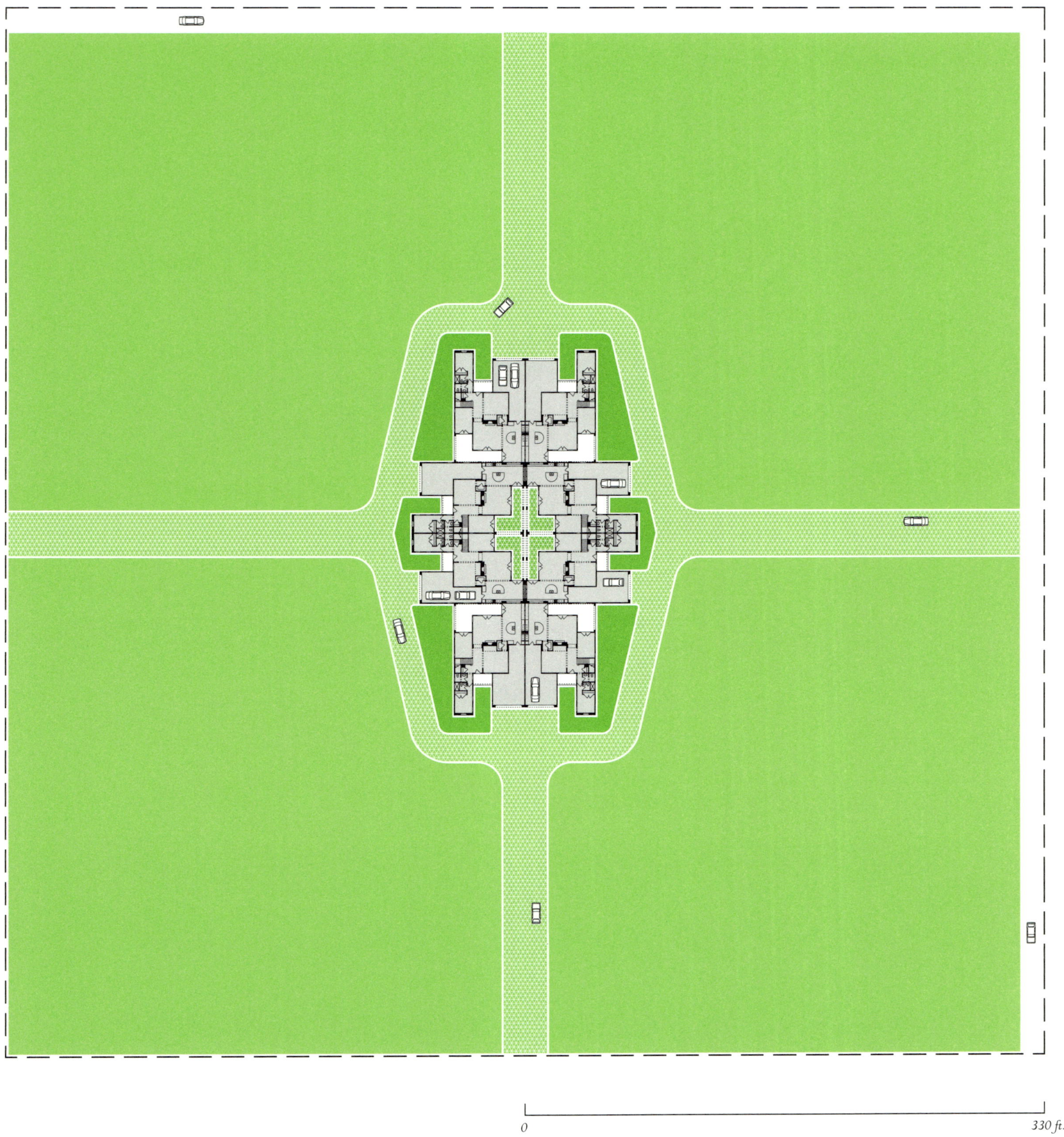

Cockaigne Hall

NE 1/4 SW 1/4 Section 36

8 Houses
31,136 Square Feet
40 Bedrooms
32 Full Bathrooms
8 Half Bathrooms

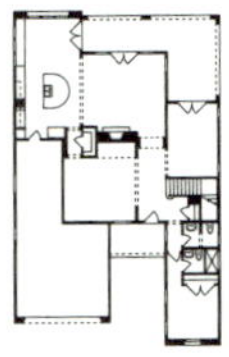

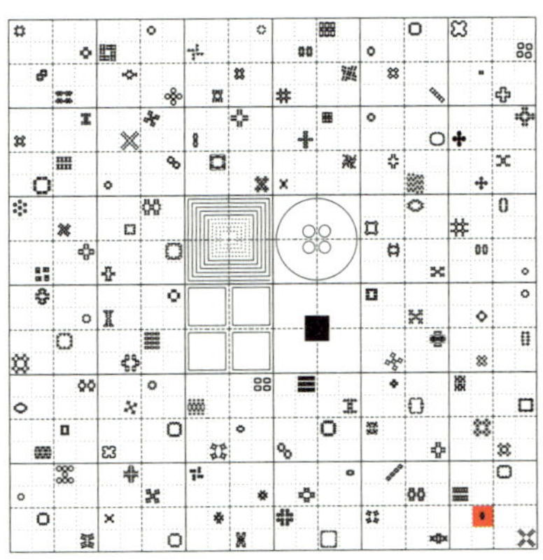

Shea Homes, Plan 4 at Vista Vallerta, 3892 sq. ft., California

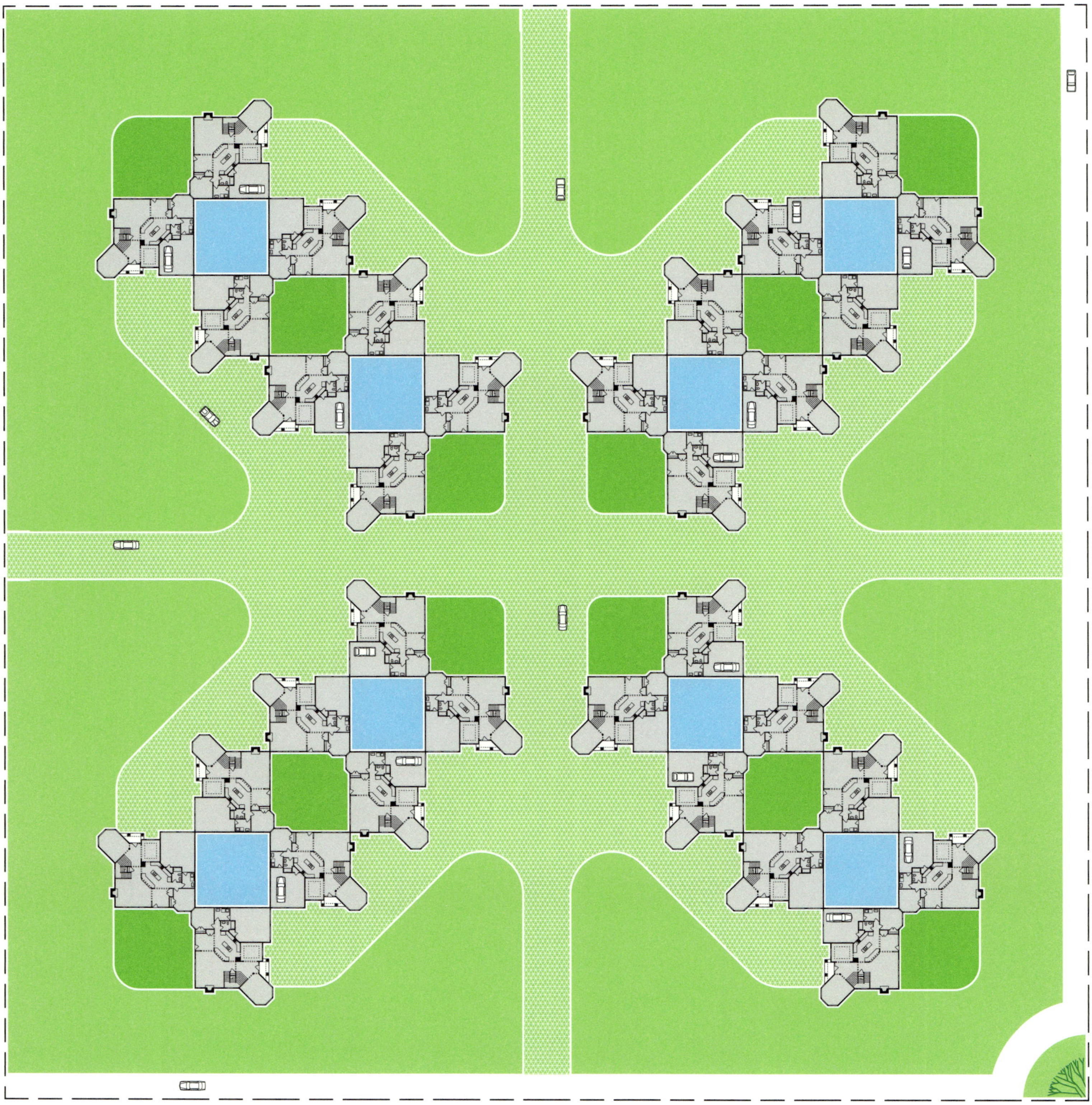

La Ville Radieuse

SE 1/4 SE 1/4 Section 36

32 Houses
107,520 Square Feet
128 Bedrooms
96 Full Bathrooms
0 Half Bathrooms

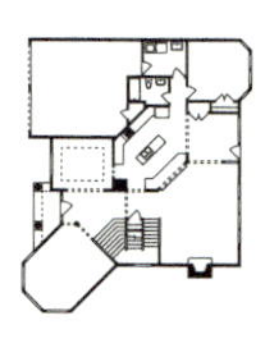

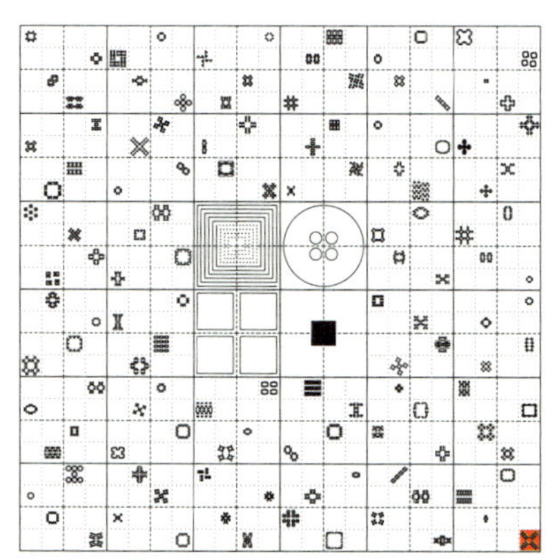

Centex Homes, The Wellington, 3360 sq. ft., Georgia

A View of Life in Freedomland
after *Vue Perspective, Lavoir et École rurale de Meilliand,* 1804
Claude-Nicolas Ledoux

AN APPENDIX

CONTAINING DOCUMENTS PERTINENT TO THE ORIGINS

OF

FREEDOMLAND

INCLUDING

"ATYPICAL PLANS,"

"SUPERMODEL HOMES,"

"SIX TYPICAL PLANS"

&

"NOTES ON FREEDOMLAND"

The Homes of Freedomland

(Presented in order of their appearance in the plan, beginning with Section 1)

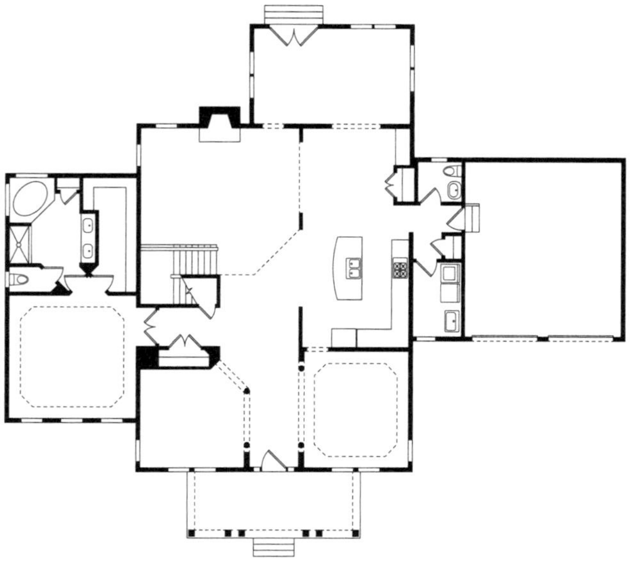

Ryland Homes, The Parson, 3584 sq. ft., Delaware
Sections 1, 7, 14, 28 & 29

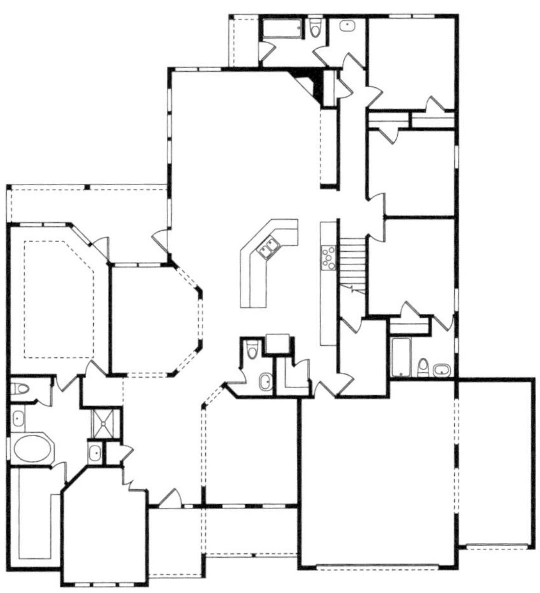

0 20 ft.

Pulte Homes, The Monet, 3641 sq. ft., Texas
Sections 1, 4, 7, 24, 30 & 34

[A]Typical Plan[s]

"Typical Plan," a self-described "meditation" on the American office building, was written by Rem Koolhaas in 1993 and published in *S,M,L,XL*. "[A]Typical Plan[s]," a post-bubble revision, shifts the focus to the American house.

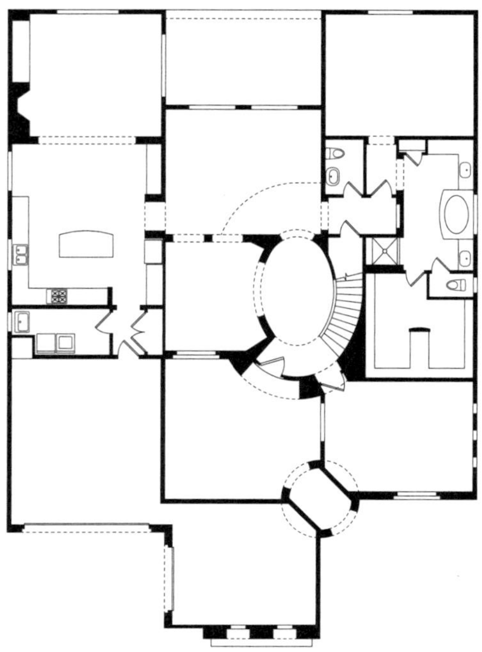

Del Webb, Mirasol, 4063 sq. ft., Arizona
Sections 1, 3, 8 & 18

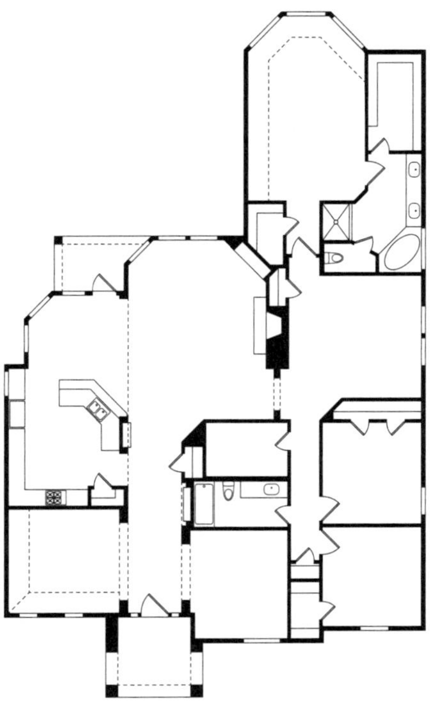

0 20 ft.

Beazer Homes, The Muirfield, 2422 sq. ft., Texas
Sections 1, 5, 6, 10, 34 & 36

[A]Typical Plan[s] ~~is~~ are an American ~~invention~~ fabrication. ~~It is~~ They are ~~zero~~ 360-degree architecture, architecture ~~stripped of all traces of uniqueness and specificity~~ drunk on an excess of space and resources. ~~It~~ They belong~~s~~ to the New World.

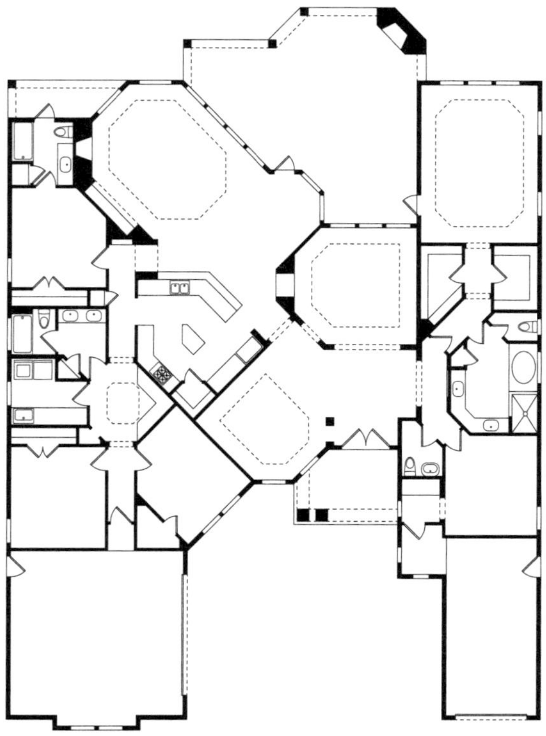

Ryland Homes, The Suffolk, 3223 sq. ft., Florida
Sections 2, 11, 25, 27 & 30

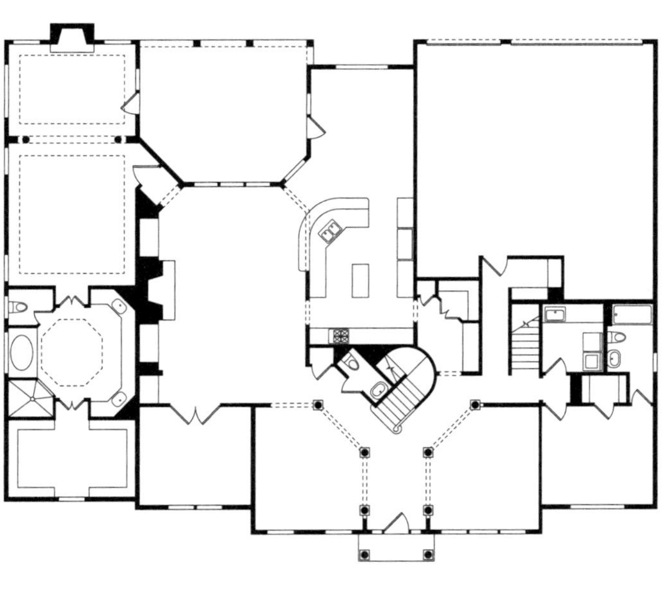

0 20 *ft.*

Beazer Homes, Versailles, 5571 sq. ft., Tennessee
Sections 2, 10 & 30

The notion of the atypical plan is ~~therapeutic~~ disconcerting; it is the Beginning and the End of Architectural History, which is nothing but the hysterical fetishization of the proto-~~a~~typical plan. [A]Typical Plan[s] ~~is a segment~~ are fragments of an ~~un~~acknowledged utopia, ~~the~~ promises of a glorious architectural past and a post-architectural future.

Just as *The Man Without Qualities* haunts European literature, "the plan with~~out~~ surplus qualities" is the great ~~quest~~ achievement of American homebuilding.

From the ~~late~~ mid 19th century to the early ~~1970s~~ 21st century, there is an "American century" (and a half) in which [A]Typical Plan[s] ~~is~~ developed from the ~~primitive loft type~~ English country house (ruthless creation of ~~floor~~ luxurious domestic spaces of retreat through the sheer multiplication of ~~a given site~~ rooms) via early masterpieces of ~~*smooth*~~ multiplied *space* like the ~~RCA Building (1933)~~ Alden House (1879)—its ~~escalators~~ serially distinct rooms linked by broad doorways, its ~~elevators~~ bays and turrets, the ~~Zen-like serenity of its office suites~~ rambling expanse of its porches—to provisional culminations such as ~~the Exxon Building (1971)~~ Charles Moore's Klotz House (1969) and ~~the World Trade Center (1972-73)~~ Robert A. M. Stern's Westchester House (1974–76). Together they represent evidence of the discovery and subsequent mastery of a *new*, soon to be endlessly multiplied and publicly traded, *architecture* ~~(often proclaimed but never realized at the scale of Typical Plan)~~.

The horizontally sprawling, many-gabled, multi-turreted, and porch-encrusted Alden House is one of the first landmarks of the Shingle style. It was built by McKim, Mead & Bigelow on Lloyd's Neck on the north shore of Long Island.

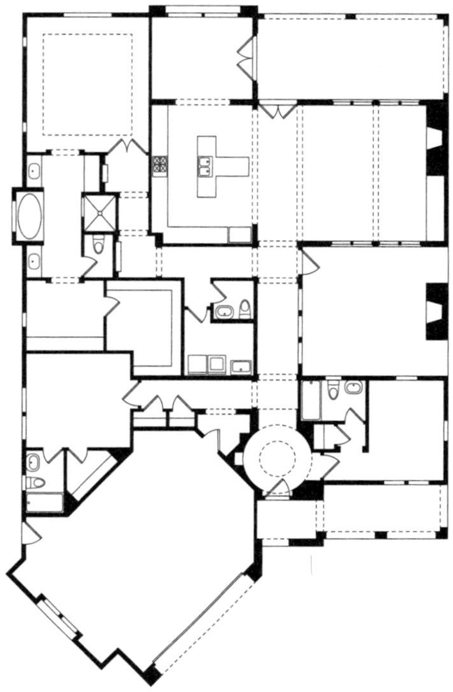

Maracay Homes, Plan 2011 - Angelico, 2688 sq. ft., Arizona
Sections 2, 4 & 6

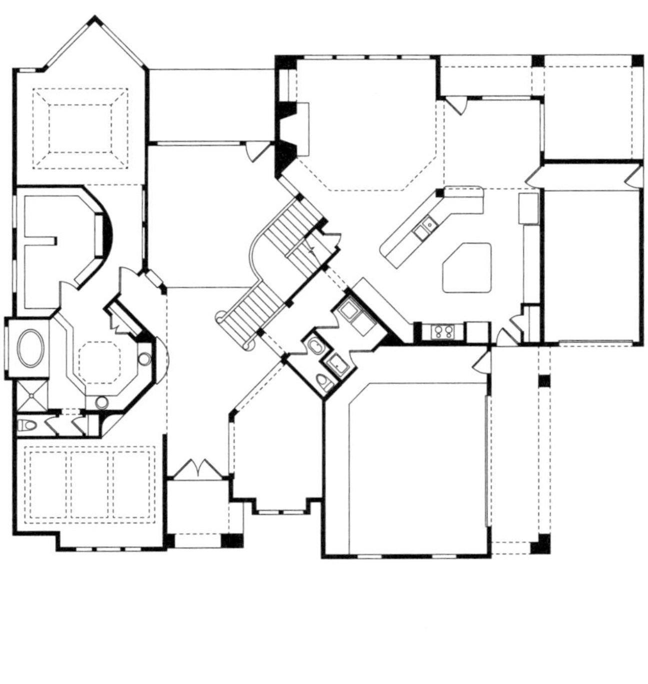

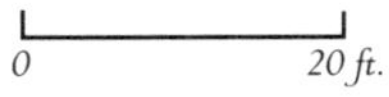

David Weekley Homes, The Kramer, 4460 sq. ft., Texas
Sections 2, 8, 19, 23 & 31

The ambition of [A]Typical Plan[s] is to create new territories for the ~~smooth~~ pleasurable, and profitable, unfolding of ~~new~~ old processes, in this case, idealized accommodations for ~~business~~ domestic activities in an "ownership society." But what is ~~business~~ domesticity? Supposedly the most primitive and circumscribed program, it is actually the most ~~formless~~ modern and mutable. ~~Business~~ Domesticity makes ~~no~~ conflicting demands. The architects of [A]Typical Plan[s] ~~understood~~ understand the secret of the business of domesticity: the ~~office building~~ house represents the first totally ~~abstract~~ absorptive program—it ~~does not~~ demands a particular, but not a specific, architecture, its ~~only~~ function is to ~~let~~ both distinguish its occupants' *exist*ence and signal their market participation. ~~Business~~ Dwelling can invade *any* architecture, domesticity cannot. ~~Out of this indeterminacy~~ Within this financially determined framework [A]Typical Plan[s] generate~~s~~ marketable character.

In a speech delivered on December 16, 2003, President George W. Bush first articulated his vision of an "ownership society," saying: "This Administration will constantly strive to promote an ownership society in America. We want more people owning their own home. It is in our national interest that more people own their own home. After all, if you own your own home, you have a vital stake in the future of our country."

~~Raymond Hood~~ Vincent Scully, one of its ~~inventors~~ greatest chroniclers, defined the atypical plan, and the dreams attached to it, with ~~tautological~~ bravura: "~~The plan is of primary importance, because on the floor are performed all the activities of the human occupants~~ The massing has now become complex and voluminous; the interior, around its great fireplaces, is no longer a colonial box but a varied landscape of its own. It opens up at several levels and pushes out to porches, green-shadowed pavilions of permissive relaxation, of summer-stock assignations among cane chairs and the gliders, middle-class heaven, somnolent with novels."

Vincent Scully, *American Architecture and Urbanism*. New York: Praeger Publishers, Inc. 1969, p. 116.

([A]Typical Plan[s] provide~~s the~~ multiple physical and financial platforms ~~of~~ for the demise of 20th-century market democracy.)

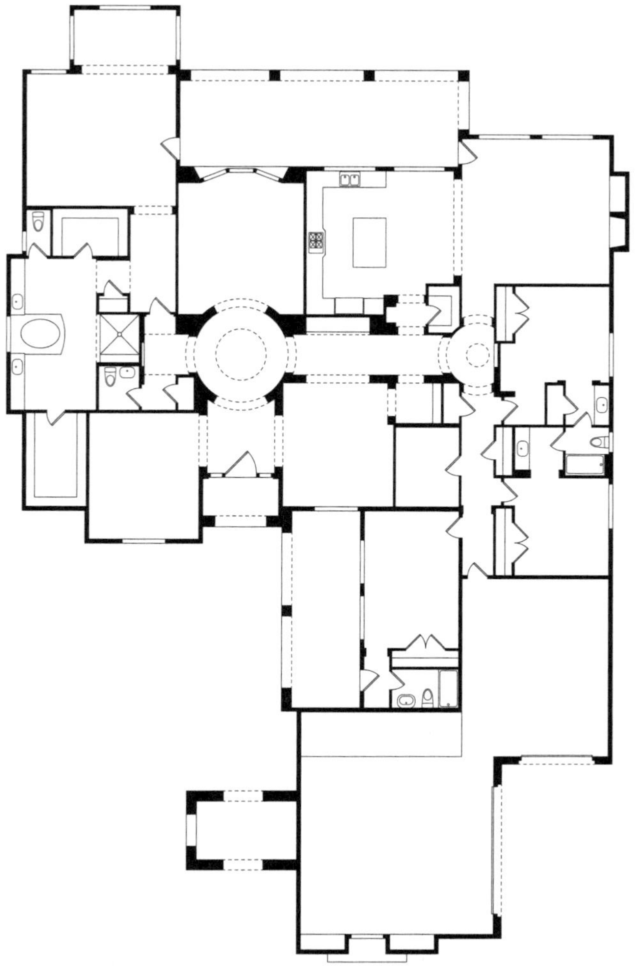

Meritage Homes, Residence 4 at Mirabel, 4217 sq. ft., Arizona
Sections 3, 14 & 24

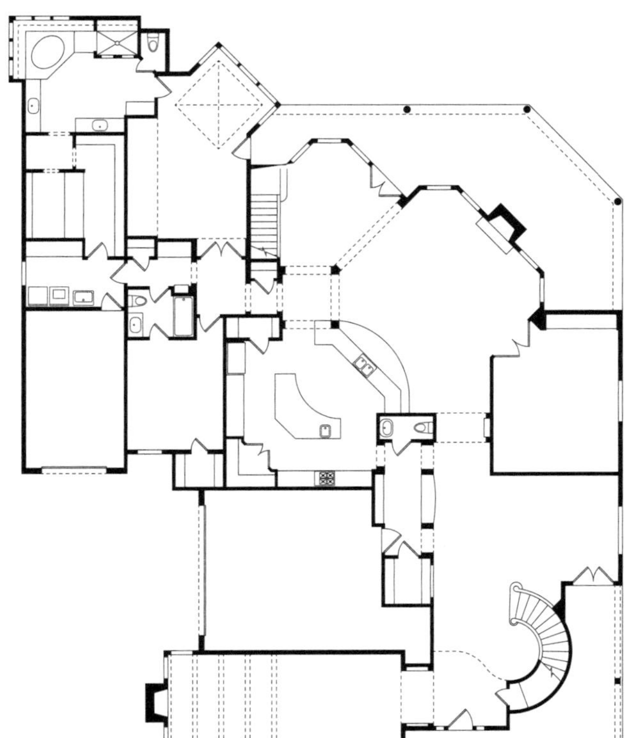

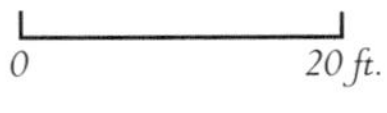

Meritage Homes, The Chalet, 6000 sq. ft., Texas
Sections 3, 18, 33 & 35

[A]Typical Plan[s] ~~is~~ are ~~an~~ architecture of the ~~rectangle~~ not simply rectilinear; any ~~other~~ accumulation of shapes makes ~~it~~ them atypical—even ~~the~~ squares. ~~It is~~ They are ~~the~~ products of a (new) world where sites, physical and financial, are made, not found. At ~~its~~ their best, ~~it~~ they acquire~~s~~ a ~~Platonic neutrality~~ formless iconicity; ~~it~~ they represent~~s~~ the point where ~~pragmatism~~ the home, through sheer economic irrationality and spatial inefficiency, assumes an almost mystical status.

[A]Typical Plan[s] ~~is~~ are ~~minimalism~~ maximalism for the masses; already latent in the first ~~brutally~~ exuberantly non-utilitarian explorations, by the end of the era of [A]Typical Plan[s], i.e., ~~the sixties~~ NOW, the non-utilitarian is refined as a sensuous science of coordination—oversized columns ~~grids~~, massive multi-layered facades ~~modules~~, coffered ceilings, marble tiles, accent lighting, luxurious bathroom fixtures, ~~partitions,~~ abundant electrical outlets, hardwood flooring, artfully staged furniture, tasteful color schemes, central air-conditioning ~~grills~~—that transcends the practical to emerge in a rarified existential domain of ~~*pure*~~ guilt-free ~~*objectivity*~~ subjectivity.

You can never only *be* in [A]Typical Plan[s], ~~not~~ you can only act, sleep, eat, make love, and, hopefully, refinance.

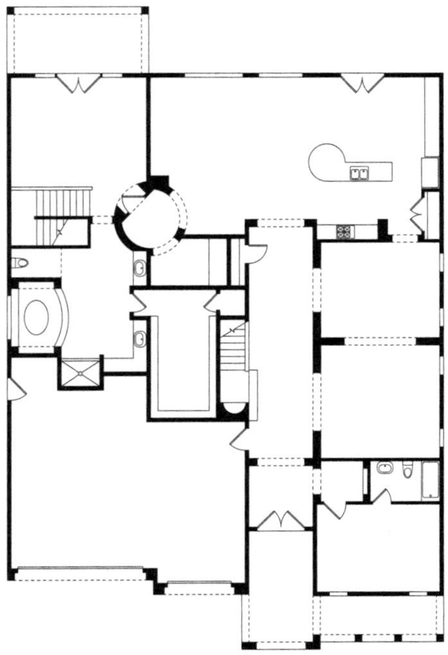

Richmond American Homes, Picasso, 4750 sq. ft., Arizona
Sections 3, 8 & 35

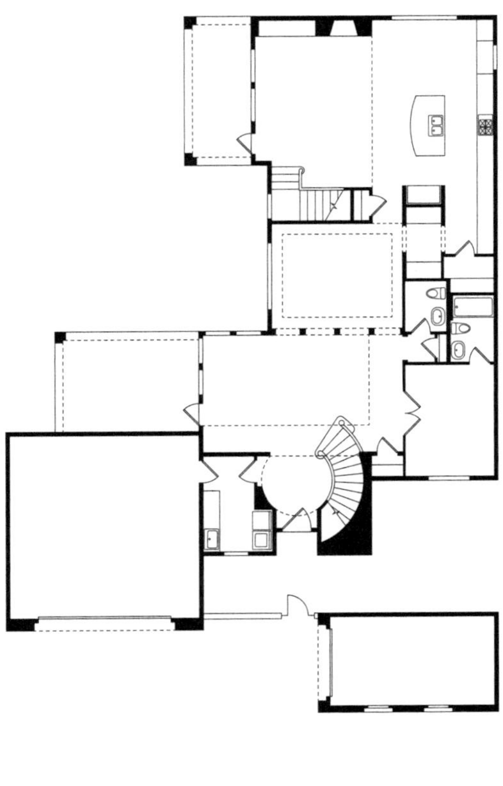

Pulte Homes, The Provence, 3800 sq. ft., Nevada
Sections 4, 7, 12, 19, 23, 25 & 27

[A]Typical Plan[s] ~~is~~ are deep, wide, and sprawling. ~~It has~~ They have evolved beyond the naive humanist assumption that contact with the exterior—so-called reality—is a necessary condition for human happiness, for survival. (If that is true, why build at all? And anyway, aren't the disadvantages of the exterior, disadvantages which the multiplication of [A]Typical Plan[s] helped produce—ozone-depleted, carbo-charged, globally heated—by now well established?)

~~Air conditioning~~ Mortgage-backed securities (and mortgage interest deductions), which ~~is~~ are the *sine qua non* of [A]Typical Plan[s], impose~~s~~ a regime of ~~sharing~~ speculation (~~air~~ money) that defines invisible communities, not quite homogenous segments of a~~n~~ ~~air~~ market-borne collective ~~aligned in more powerful wholes like the iron molecules that form a magnetic field~~ channeled, via a complicated calculus, through Real Estate Mortgage Investment Conduits.

"A Real Estate Mortgage Investment Conduit (REMIC) is an . . . investment vehicle that is used to pool mortgage loans and issue mortgage-backed securities . . . Similar to collateralized mortgage obligations, REMICs piece together mortgages into pools based on risk and issue bonds or other securities to investors." http://www.investopedia.com/terms/r/real-estate-mortgage-investment-conduit-remic.asp#ixzz3z1xrFa2o

Heroically, the egoless architects of [A]Typical Plan[s] effortlessly deliver~~s a~~ generic worlds ~~laundered~~ of pure ego.

[A]Typical Plan[s] ~~is~~ are ~~Western~~ American. There ~~is~~ are no equivalents in any other culture. ~~It is~~ They are the ~~stamp~~ residue of modern~~ity~~ capitalism itself. In the ever-increasing dimension from ~~skin~~ income to ~~core~~ debt—the hidden potential of ~~depth~~ credit—~~it~~ they proclaim~~s~~ the superiority of the luxury of the artificial to the poverty of the real which remains, whether admitted or not, the true credo of ~~Western~~ American civilization, the source of its universal attraction.

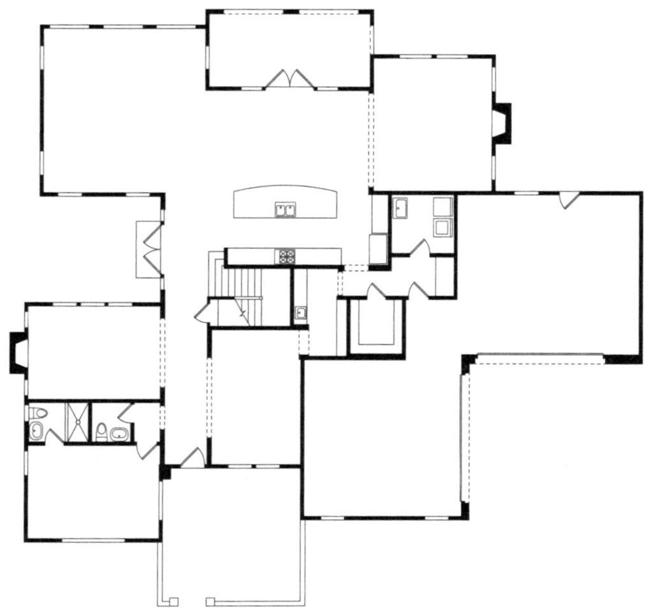

Shea Homes, Plan 2 at Maravilla, 4625 sq. ft., California
Sections 4, 9, 11, 13, 25, 28 & 35

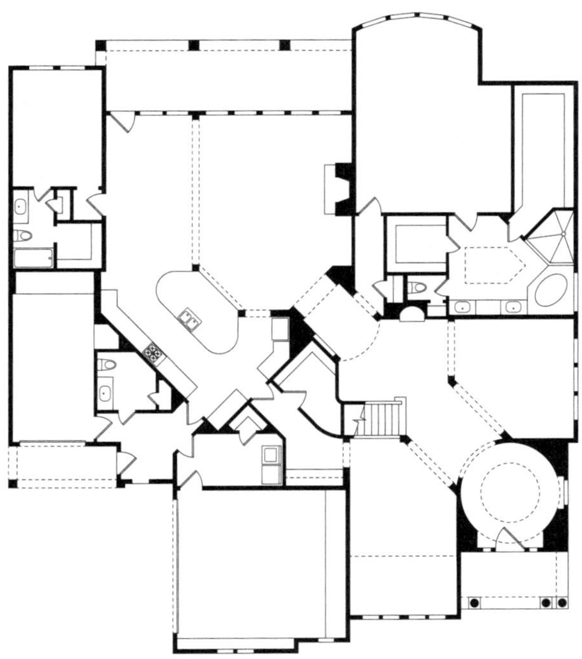

0 20 *ft.*

Perry Homes, Plan 7001W, 7001 sq. ft., Texas
Sections 5, 13 & 32

[A]Typical Plan[s] ~~knows~~ have learned what ~~European~~ architecture ~~will~~ can never ~~learn~~ admit: that ~~modular~~ the coordination of matter and desire is at most *postponed failure*, a temporary rollback of the frontiers of (economic) chaos.

[A]Typical Plan[s] ~~is~~ are not gridded, not ~~in the~~ absolute, ~~clumsy manner of~~ their rambling inelegance runs counter to European Platonics (a moralistic system to measure misfit and thus create unhappiness)~~,~~. ~~but on~~ On the contrary, through the development of anti-ideological devices: *a metaphysics of slack* that gives an aura of ~~crispness~~ dignified authority to even the most severely conflicted ~~geometrical~~ formal and stylistic coexistences, they bestow~~ing~~ the appearance of ~~modular~~ decorous conquest on the essentially messy, reasserting ~~orthogonality~~ formality from the most comprised givens.

[A]Typical Plan[s] ~~is~~ are not neutral, ~~not~~ but they are strangely anonymous. ~~It is a~~ They are places of isolated worship. More ~~austere~~ voluminous than ~~a Cistercian monastery~~ baroque churches, ~~it~~ they ~~accommodates~~ provide infinitely greater ~~numbers~~ space per congregant, ~~a~~ private 20th-century ~~church~~ chapels with~~out~~ a shared doctrine of ever-increasing equity. Although the dominant emphasis of [A]Typical Plan[s] is on ~~abstraction~~ representation, there is plumbing, elaborately deployed. ~~It doesn't~~ Rather than deny those residual features that make humans animals still, they celebrate every bowel movement, every bath.

Ingenious architectural arrangements of miniature~~, very understandable labyrinths~~ symmetries and coordinated sight lines organize the visual traffic, ~~between the~~ creating exalted realms ~~and the~~ out of normally impure zones ~~of~~ in the typical [A]Typical Plan. These spaces—~~restrooms, urinals, pantries, service stairs, trucking bays~~ master bathrooms, kitchens—are the highly visible sanctuaries for all those primitive aspects upon whose ~~ex~~*inclusion* the correct unfolding of the business of pleasurable domesticity depends.

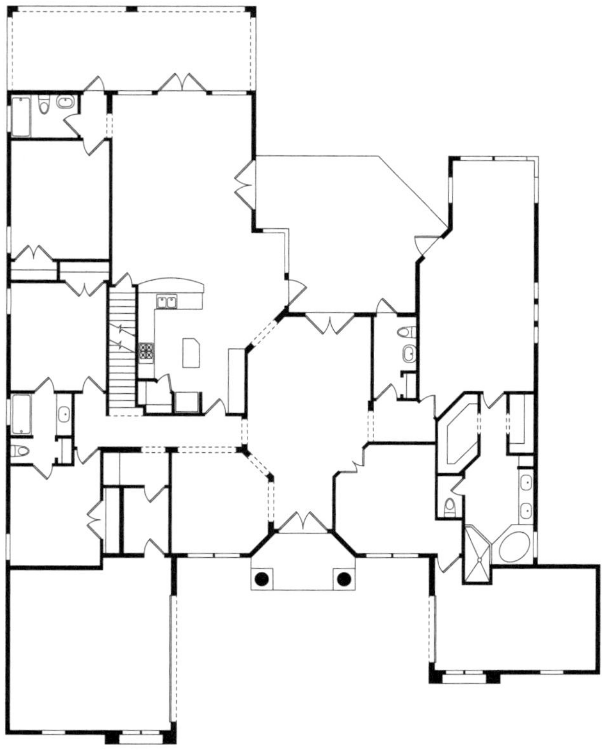

Ryland Homes, Charleston II, 3475 sq. ft., Florida
Sections 5, 17 & 26

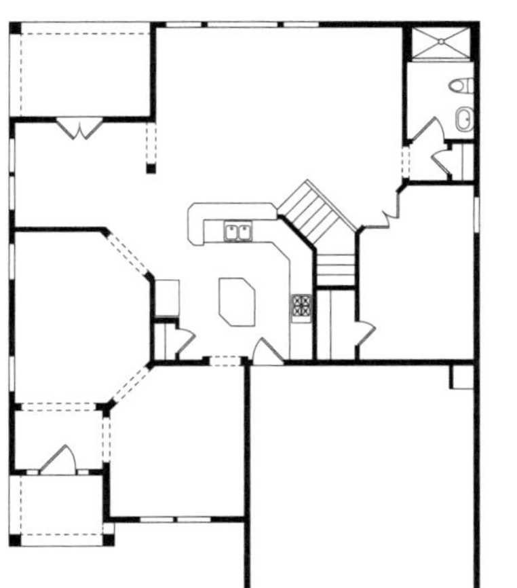

Beazer Homes, Terrace, 3015 sq. ft., Nevada
Sections 5 & 31

[A]Typical Plan[s] ~~is~~ are to the ~~office population~~ resident what ~~graph paper~~ the stage set is to the ~~mathematical curve~~ actor. ~~Its neutrality records~~ Their familiarity facilitates performance, event, ~~flow,~~ exchange, ~~accumulation, deduction,~~ appearance, disappearance, ~~mutation, fluctuation,~~ failure, ~~oscillation, deformation~~ success. [A]Typical Plan[s] ~~is~~ are relentlessly enabling, ennobling *background.*

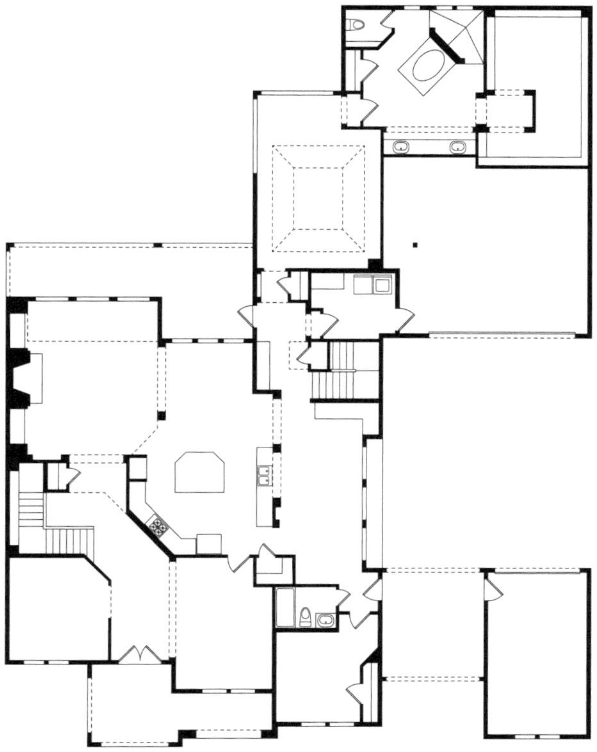

David Weekley Homes, McKeon, 5656 sq. ft., Texas
Sections 6, 10, 20, 26 & 32

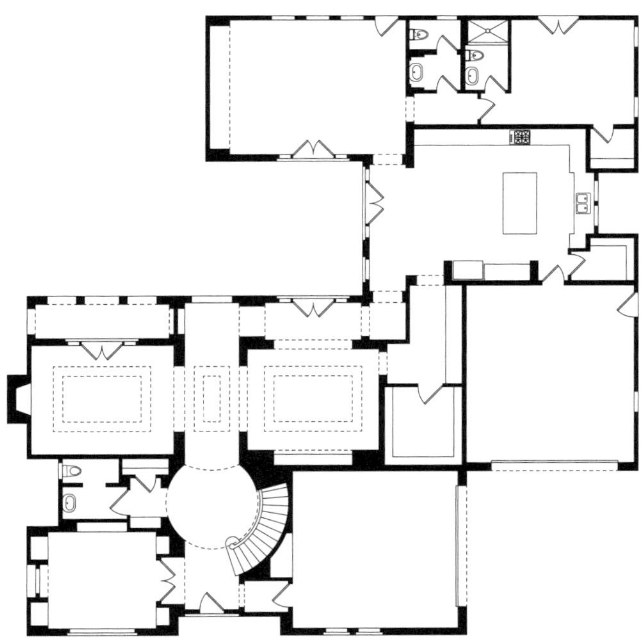

0 20 *ft.*

KB Home, The Stratford, 6558 sq. ft., California
Sections 6, 14, 20 & 33

[A]Typical Plan[s] ~~implies~~ demand *repetition*—~~it~~ each instance is the *n*th plan: to be atypical, there must be many—and articulated *indeterminacy:* to be atypical, ~~it~~ each must be ~~sufficiently~~ conspicuously undefined. ~~It presumes~~ They require the presence of many other~~s~~ somewhat similar plans, but at the same time suggest~~s~~ that each plan is unique and that their exact number is of no importance.

[A]Typical Plan[s] x n = ~~a building~~ the suburban metropolis (hardly a reason to study architecture~~!~~, but perhaps a reason to study economics): ~~floors~~ houses strung together by ~~elevators~~ roads of incomprehensible smoothness and equations of incomprehensible complexity, each discreet ~~'ting' of arrival~~ welcome mat and Wall Street transaction part of a never-ending addition.

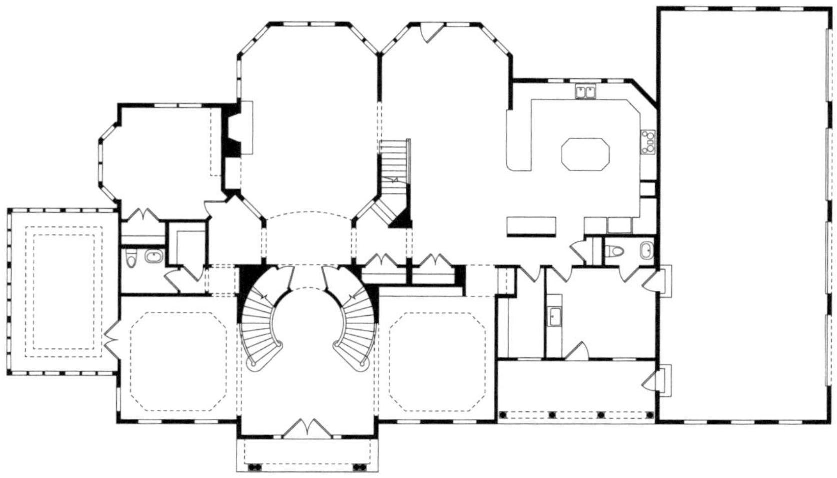

K. Hovnanian Homes, The Tara, 5325 sq. ft., Maryland
Sections 7, 26 & 33

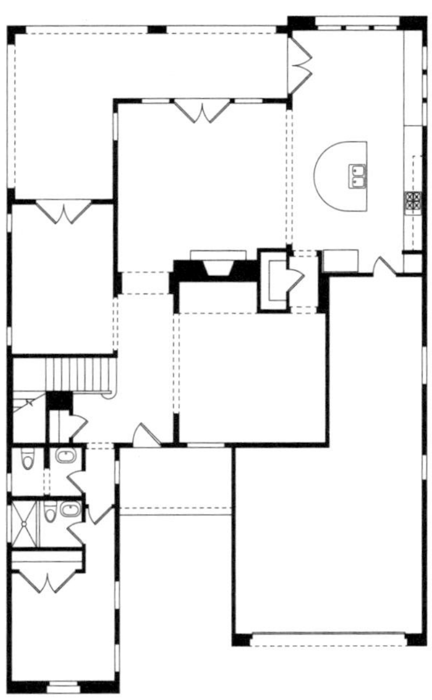

0 20 *ft.*

Shea Homes, Plan 4 at Vista Vallerta, 3892 sq. ft., California
Sections 8, 9, 24, 29 & 36

[A]Typical Plan[s] threaten~~s~~ the myth of the architect as demiurge, enlightened source of ~~unlimited supplies of uniqueness~~ order and discipline.

As in the scene of a crime, the removal of all signs of the perpetrator characterizes the true atypical plan; its authors form an avant-garde of ~~architects~~ developers as *erasers*. Its unsung, and unnamed, designers—~~Bunshaft, Harrison and Abramovitz, Emery Roth~~ laboring anonymously for the Toll Brothers, D.R. Horton, KB Home, and a host of others—represent vanishing acts so successful that ~~they are now completely forgotten~~ it is as if they had never appeared. These architects ~~were able to create~~ transform comfort into luxury, creating aleatory playgrounds (interior Elysian fields accessible in anyone's lifetime), i.e., ~~perfection~~ the American Dream in quantities—trillions of acres—that ~~have become, 25 years later, literally~~ are no longer unimaginable.

Securely entrenched in the domain of philistinism, [A]Typical Plan[s] ~~actually has~~ have ~~hidden~~ obvious affinities with other popular arts: the ~~positioning of its cores on the floor~~ sampling of familiar yet distorted references has a ~~*supramatist* tension~~ focus-grouped quality; it is the equivalent of ~~atonal~~ manufactured pop music, serial~~ity~~ television, ~~concrete~~ greeting card poetry, assembly line art ~~brut~~; it is architecture as ~~mantra~~ affirmation.

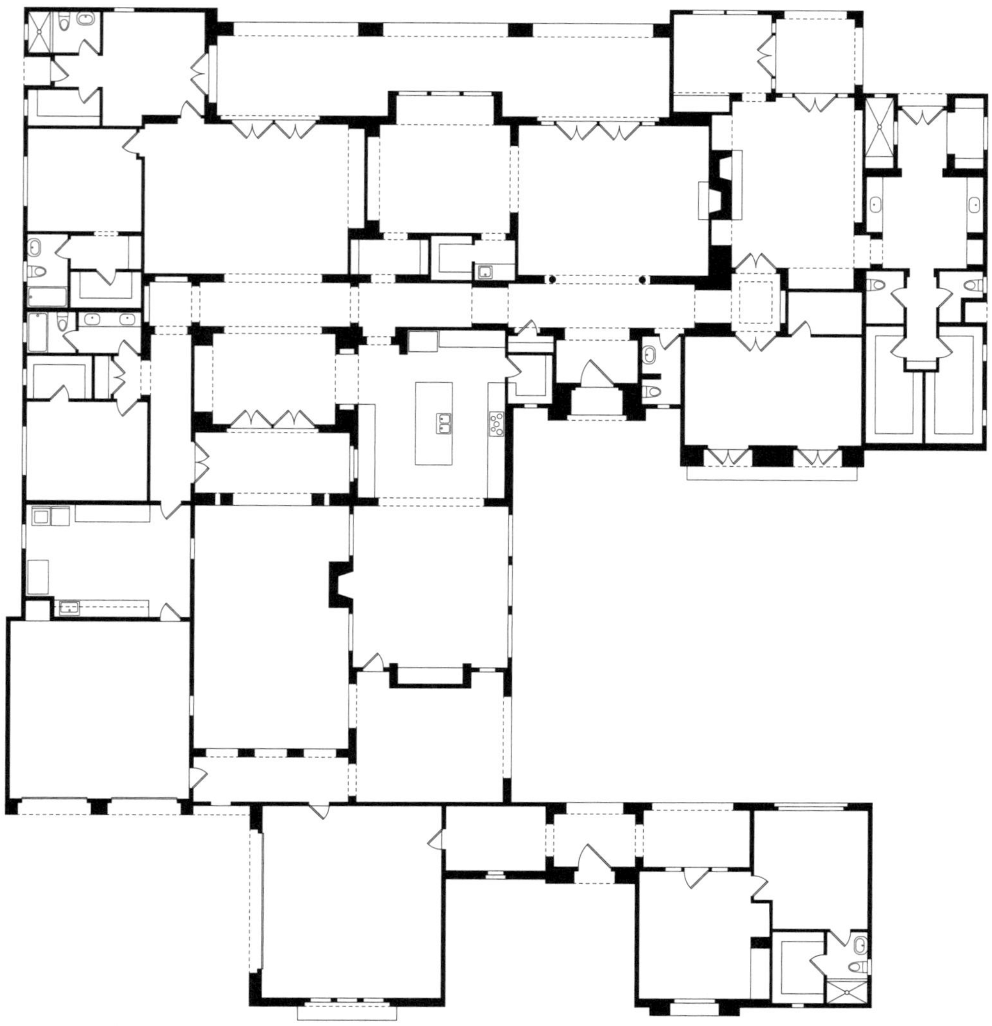

Toll Brothers, The Terreno, 6100 sq. ft., Arizona
Sections 9, 23 & 33

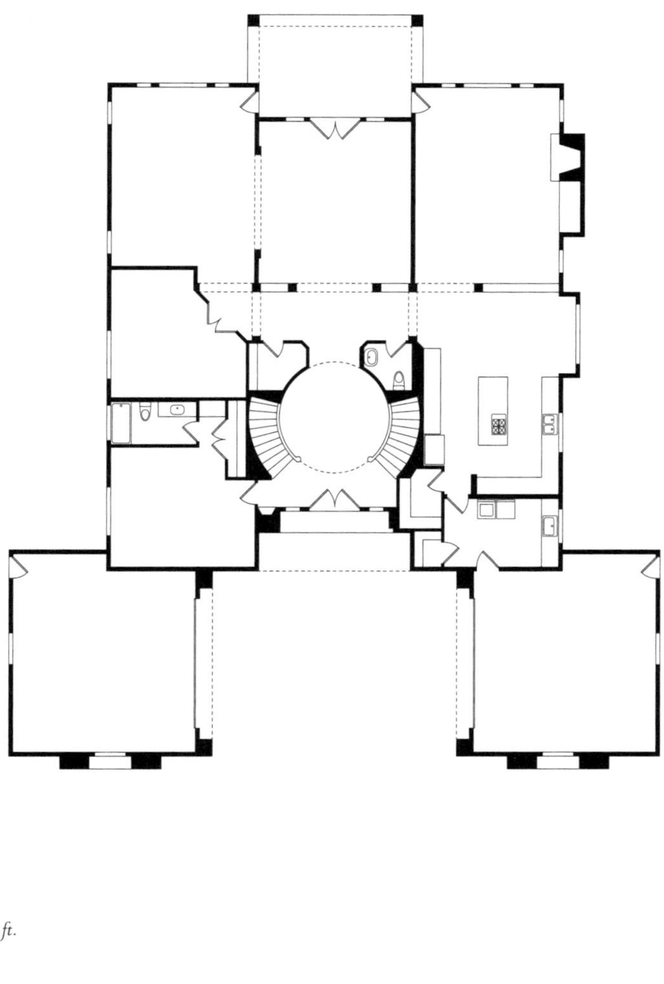

Toll Brothers, The Mirador, 5125 sq. ft., Arizona
Sections 9, 12, 29, 34 & 36

[A]Typical Plan[s] ~~is~~ are as ~~empty~~ full as possible: ~~a~~ of floor level changes, ~~a core~~ of layered views, ~~a~~ of volume pressurizing an irregular perimeter, and of a ~~mini~~ maximum of ~~columns~~ materials. All other architecture is about ~~inclusion and accommodation~~ reason and consistency, ~~incident and event~~ order and security; [A]Typical Plan[s] ~~is~~ are about ~~exclusion, evacuation, non-event~~ passion, the soothing of insecurities.

Architecture is monstrous in the way in which each choice leads to the reduction of possibility. It implies a regime of either/or decisions often claustrophobic, even for the architect. All other architecture preempts the future; [A]Typical Plan[s]—by making ~~*no*~~ *any* choice~~s~~ viable—~~postpones~~ deny it entirely, ~~keeps it open~~ along with any real sense of the past, keeping us forever in the present.

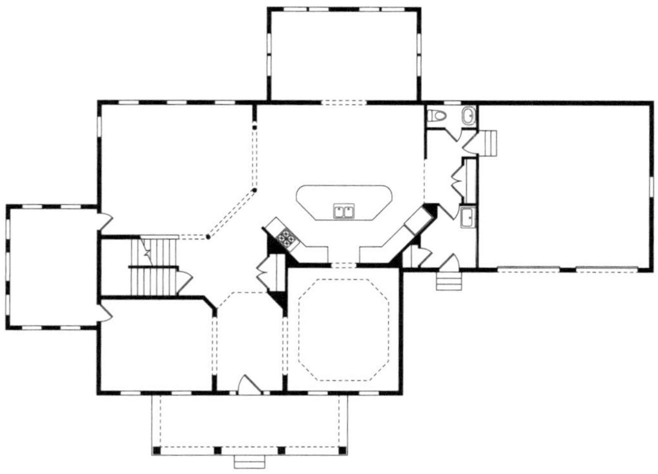

Ryland Homes, The Wye, 3703 sq. ft., Delaware
Sections 10, 12, 18, 20 & 34

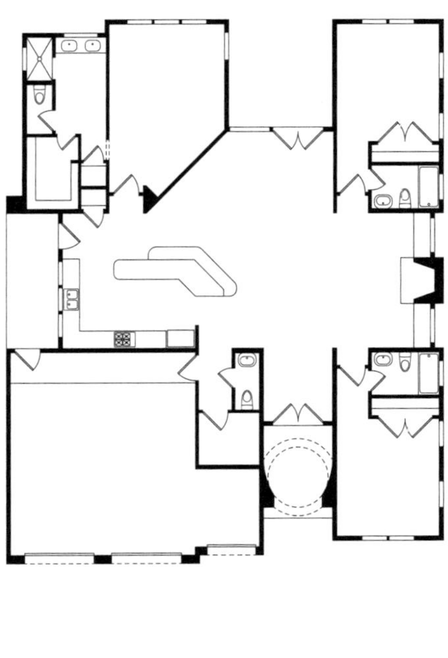

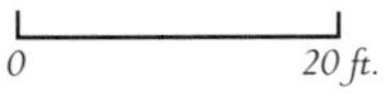

Avatar Homes, Valderama, 2087 sq. ft., Arizona
Sections 11, 14 & 27

The cumulative effect of all this ~~vacancy~~ fullness—this systemic ~~lack of~~ commitment to volume—is, paradoxically, low-density. The typical American ~~downtown~~ city is a brute accumulation of [A]Typical Plans, a ~~*massif*~~ vast plain of incrementally planned indetermination, hollowness as ~~core~~ field.

Could the ~~office building~~ speculative house be the most radical typology? A kind of ~~reverse~~ omnitype defined by all the qualities its ~~does *not* have~~ occupants aspire to? As the ~~major new~~ most delivered program of the late modern age, its effect is ~~one of deprogramming~~ totalizing. [A]Typical Plan[s] ~~is~~ are the ~~initial~~ latest mutation in a chain that has revolutionized the urban condition. Concentrations of [A]Typical Plan[s] have produced the ~~skyscraper~~ subdivision: ~~monolith~~ picturesque cluster; accumulations of ~~skyscrapers~~ subdivisions, the only "new" urban condition: ~~downtown~~ exurbs, defined by sheer quantity of low-density, high-calorie matter rather than as a specific formal configuration. The ~~center~~ periphery is ~~no longer unique but~~ now universal, ~~no longer a~~ an everyplace ~~but a condition~~ defined by likeminded (in)difference. Practically immune to local variation, [A]Typical Plan[s] ~~has~~ have made the city unrecognizable, an unidentifiable object. [A]Typical Plan[s] ~~is~~ are a quantum leap that provokes a conceptual leap: an ~~*absence*~~ *abundance* of content in quantities that overwhelm, or simply preempt, intellectual speculation.

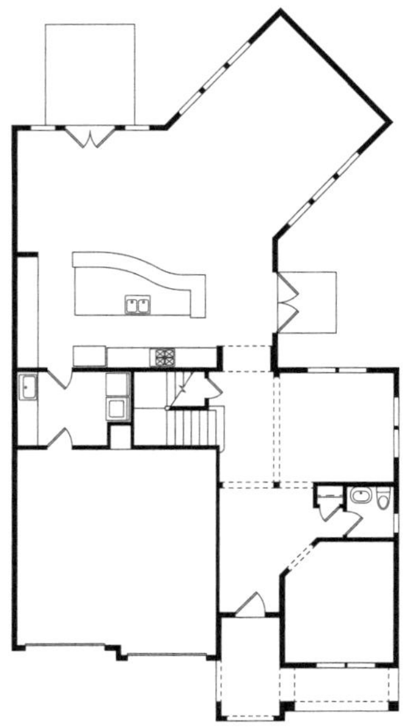

KB Home, Garden Plan 3238, 3238 sq. ft., California
Sections 11 & 28

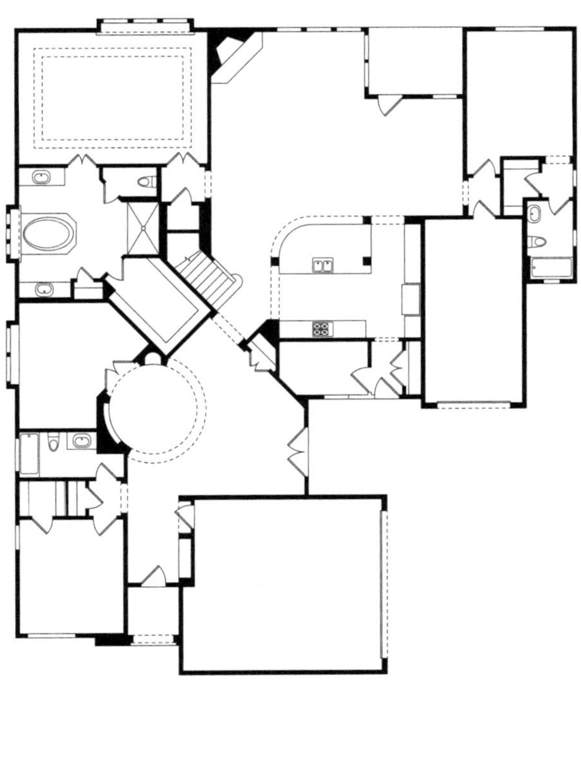

K. Hovnanian Homes, Bellvue VIII, 3043 sq. ft., Texas
Sections 12, 17 & 25

Warren Buffet, in his 2009 letter to shareholders and apropos of the 2008 finanical collapse, wrote: "Investors should be skeptical of . . . models [c]onstructed by a nerdy-sounding priesthood using esoteric terms such as beta, gamma, sigma and the like, these models tend to look impressive . . . Our advice: Beware of geeks bearing formulas."

What ~~insecurity~~ delusion triggered the ~~crisis~~ spread of [A]Typical Plan[s]? Where did the ~~rot~~ sprawl start? Was it ~~its~~ their very apotheosis that turned ~~neutrality~~ houses into ~~anonymity~~ real estate, dwelling into gambling?

Did ~~the~~ plans with~~out~~ surplus qualities create men with~~out qualities~~ outsized appetites? ~~Was~~ Were the spaces of [A]Typical Plan[s] the incubators of the ~~man in the gray flannel suit~~ faithful followers of "geeks bearing formulas"?

Suddenly, the ~~graph~~ actor blamed the ~~graph paper~~ set for ~~its~~ his lack of character.

~~It was as if~~ If Typical Plan ~~created the castrated white-collar caricature, suppressed family photos, frowned on the fern, resisted the personal debris that now—20 years later—~~ accommodated inconspicuous production, [A]Typical Plan[s] celebrate conspicuous consumption. They make~~s~~ most ~~offices ghastly repositories of~~ houses into individual trophies, ~~packed~~ filling the city with the alarming assertions of millions of environmentally disconnected yet financially interdependent individual mini-ecologies.

~~An e~~Environments that seemingly demanded ~~nothing~~ little and ~~gave everything~~ promised everything ~~was~~ were suddenly seen as ~~an~~ infernal machines for stripping identity (and wealth).

~~Nietzsche~~ Tony Robbins lost out to ~~Sociology~~ Economics 101.

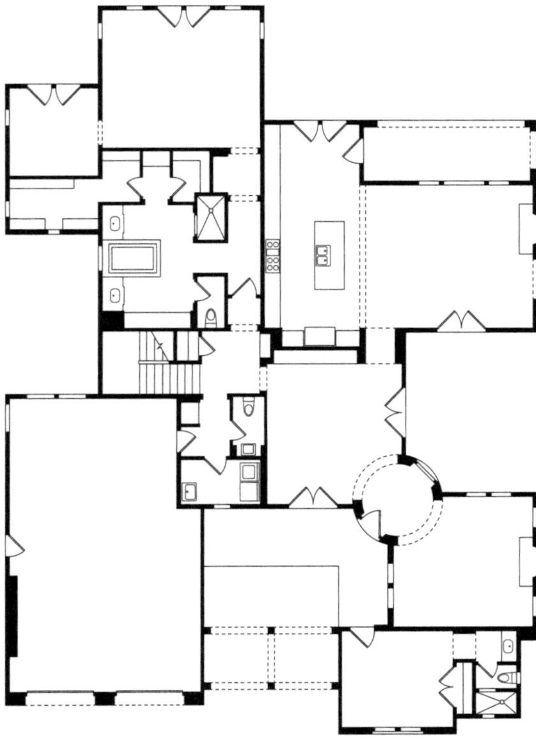

Standard Pacific Homes, Residence 1H, 4719 sq. ft., California
Sections 13, 19, 30, 32 & 35

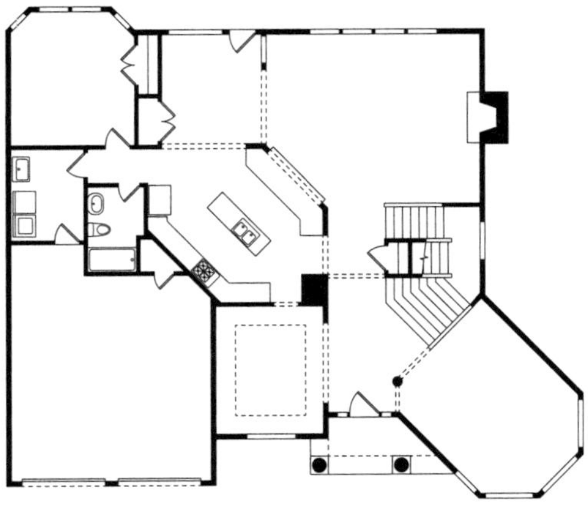

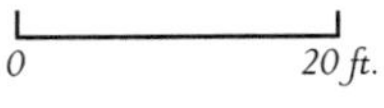

Centex Homes, The Wellington, 3360 sq. ft., Georgia
Section 13, 31 & 6

The Narkomfin building, an experimental Constructivist housing structure, was completed in 1930.

Habitat, an experiment in the production of dense urban dwelling environments, was built as the Candadian Pavilion for Expo '67.

In ~~Europe~~ modern architecture, ~~there~~ are there ~~no~~ only Typical Plans~~.~~?

In the teens and twenties, ~~European~~ architects fantasized about ~~offices~~ dwellings. In ~~1921~~ 1914, ~~Mies~~ Corb imagined the ultimate ~~a~~typical plan in the ~~Friedrichstrasse~~ Maison Domino; in 1929, ~~Ivan Leodinov~~ Moisei Ginzburg and Ignati Milinis ~~proposed~~ built the first ~~office~~ dwelling slab for Moscow, a ~~House of Industry~~ communal house for workers. Its rectangles were conceived as a socialist proto-Typical Plan~~s~~: ~~a parallel zone~~ two perpendicular blocks ~~re~~introduced the workers to the full paraphernalia of ~~daily~~ a new collective domestic life—~~pools~~ a communal dining hall, ~~tanning beds~~ a sports hall, ~~clublike arrangements~~ a library, ~~small dormitories~~ transitional "living units"—to create an ~~compressed~~ expanded experimental ~~24-hour cycle~~ super-house ~~not of business-life, but~~ of Soviet ~~life-business~~ lifestyle. In ~~1970~~ 1967, ~~Archizoom~~ Moshe Safdie ~~interpreted~~ deployed Typical Plans in Montréal as the terminal dwelling condition of (Western) civilization, a utopian mountain of ~~the~~ normalized modules.

Since then, the one ~~really new~~ architectural subject ~~this~~ the 20th century ~~has introduced~~ delivered en masse has been endlessly denigrated in the name of ideology—its occupants "slaves," its environment "faceless," its accumulations "ugly." ~~Europe~~ Architecture has suffered from a catastrophic failure to ~~accommodate~~ participate in the production of—to ~~"think"~~ "perform"—the one typology whose ~~emergence~~ proliferation was ~~architecturally~~ economically and urbanistically ~~irresistible~~ inevitable. [A]Typical Plan[s] ~~has~~ have been ~~forced underground,~~ condemned to the status of ~~parasite~~ a cancer—devouring larger and larger sections of ~~historical substance~~ land, invading whole ~~centers~~ ecologies—~~or~~ no longer only exiled to the periphery, they returned with a vengeance to consume the city itself.

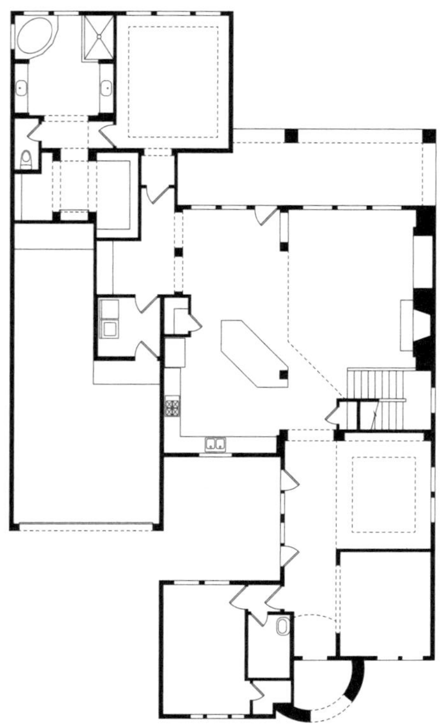

David Weekley Homes, The Palladio, 3708 sq. ft., Texas
Sections 17, 26 & 29

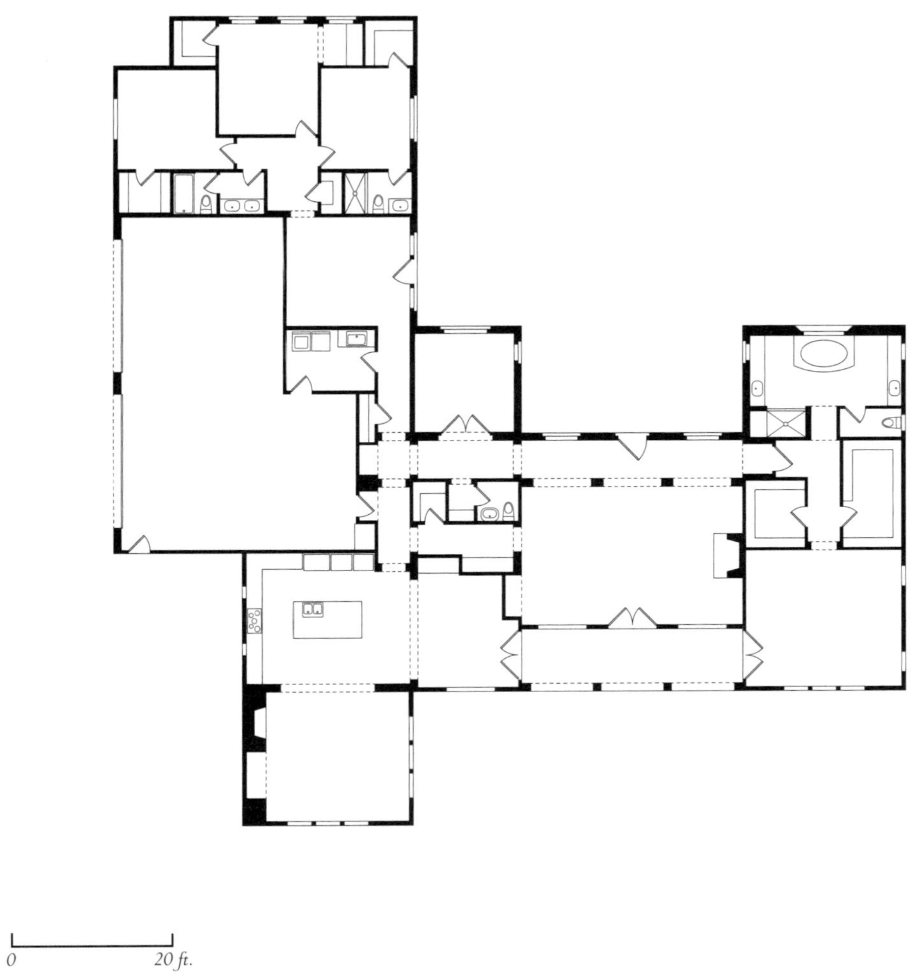

Pulte Homes, The Appaloosa, 4176 sq. ft., California
Sections 17, 28 & 31

For ~~offices~~ houses, ~~Europe~~ America multiplies ~~a~~ typical plans atypically, using a model known since the Renaissance: ~~a corridor with rooms on both sides~~ the villa or manor house. (Is there a connection between the notorious ~~absenteeism~~ individualism of the ~~Western European office~~ American population and its sacred cow, the detached private ~~cell~~ residence?)

The ~~European office~~ American house is ~~thin~~ fat, as ~~thin~~ fat as its ~~more historic~~ ground-blanketing cumulative substance is thin. The ~~European~~ American needs ~~daylight~~ status and ~~air~~ space, even though a simple extrapolation of the square ~~meters~~ feet involved reveals that this need will destroy the very ~~décor~~ resources that reassure~~s~~ him of his ~~historical status~~ manifest destiny.

Where the ~~American office~~ European "minimum dwelling" assembles a critical mass, the ~~European office~~ American house ~~dismantles~~ inflates it, simply because the things that happen in a~~n office~~ house are supposed to be ~~"bad"~~ "good"; we like our ~~badness~~ goodness in ~~small~~ big doses.

There is something almost insane and masochistic about the quantity of utterly inferior substance that is generated in the ~~Old~~ New World—in the name of ~~identity~~ achievement, even.

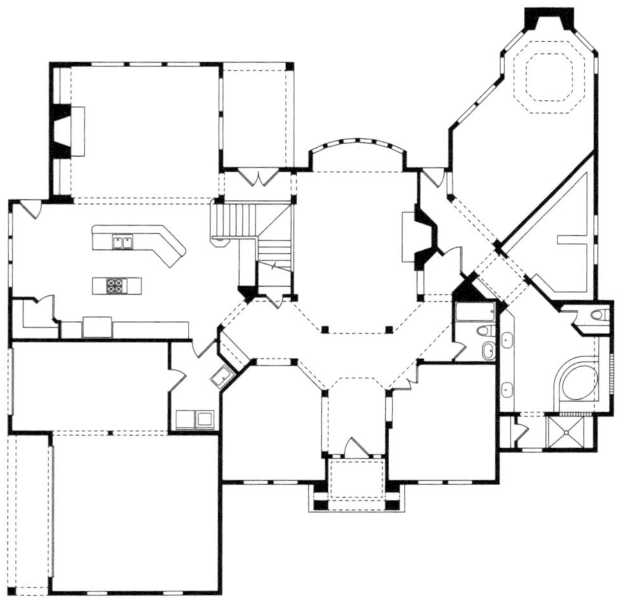

David Weekley Homes, The Lynnhaven, 4285 sq. ft., Texas
Sections 18, 23 & 32

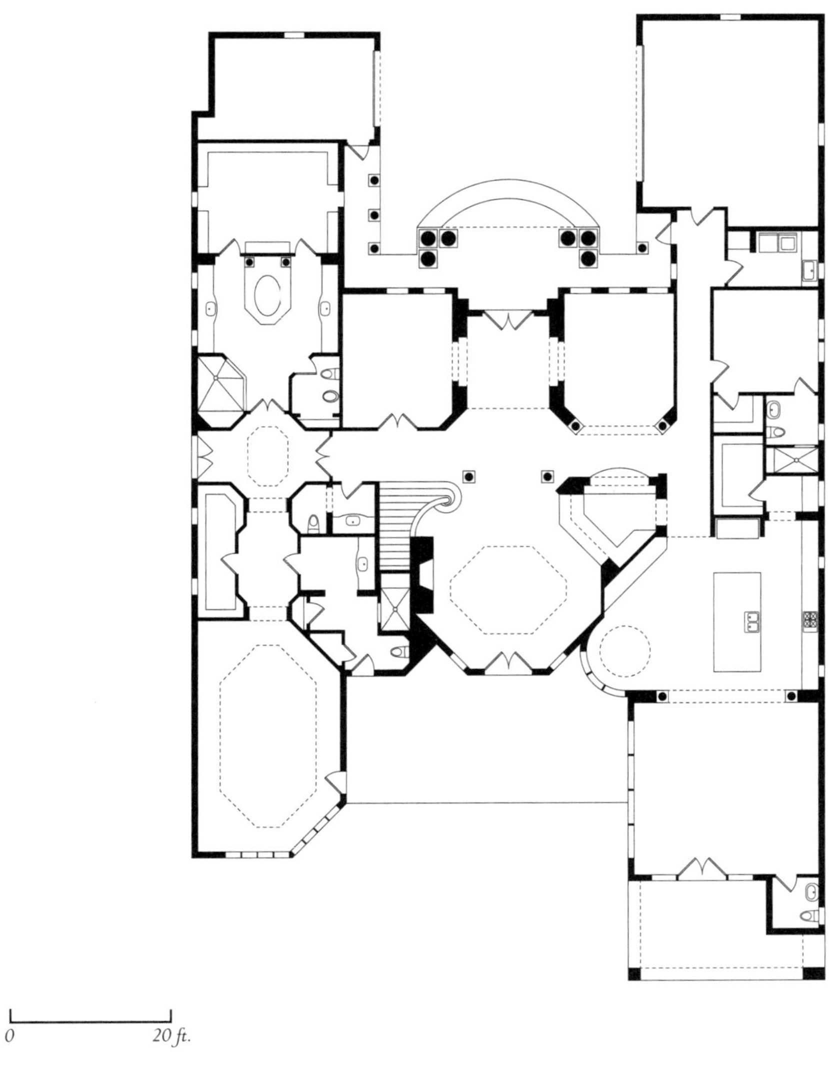

Taylor Morrison Homes, Casa del Playa, 7905 sq. ft., Florida
Sections 19, 20, 24 & 27

Morgan Bank is an attempt at a typical plan in Europe. It is a loft building—a block of Typical Plans. Because it is projected in Amsterdam and within Berlage's famous extension—a fragile composition of axes, coherences, coordinations, controls—it undergoes a minimum of adaptation to perform certain urbanistic duties: a negative corner of two high walls defines an important Berlage plaza and the entrance—a slit that communicates as little as possible about the interior; a roof patio consolidates the "not-office" program—cafeteria, meeting rooms, etc. Otherwise the building is simply abstract office space, its dimensions chosen to enable a maximum of permutations, introducing, in Holland, unusual (and ultimately unwelcome) depth. The raised floor distributes homogeneous conditions of services across the entire surface. Columns give minimal interference. The single "feature" is a glass staircase that connects all floors.

Since the project is in Europe, a height limit was imposed. The proportion typical/atypical plan is itself atypical: a typically European 50/50 split.

If Typical Plans promise the dream of a mass-produced collective dwelling, [A]Typical Plan[s] deliver the reality of a mass-customized collective debt.

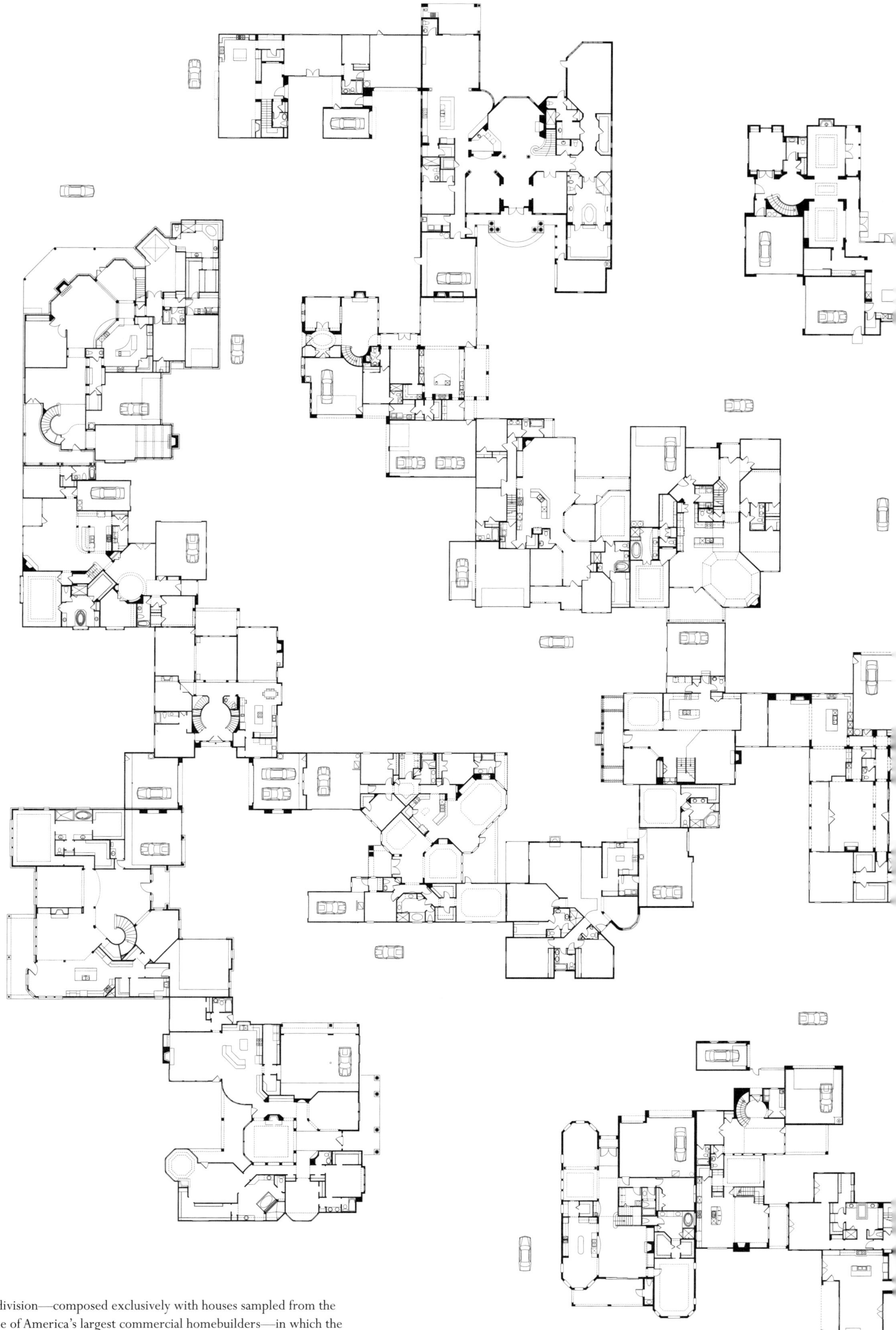

Alison's Acres

Study for a mat subdivision—composed exclusively with houses sampled from the plan catalogs of some of America's largest commercial homebuilders—in which the hidden and generally unacknowledged interdependencies that bind Amercian houses together are manifest in the overall arrangement.

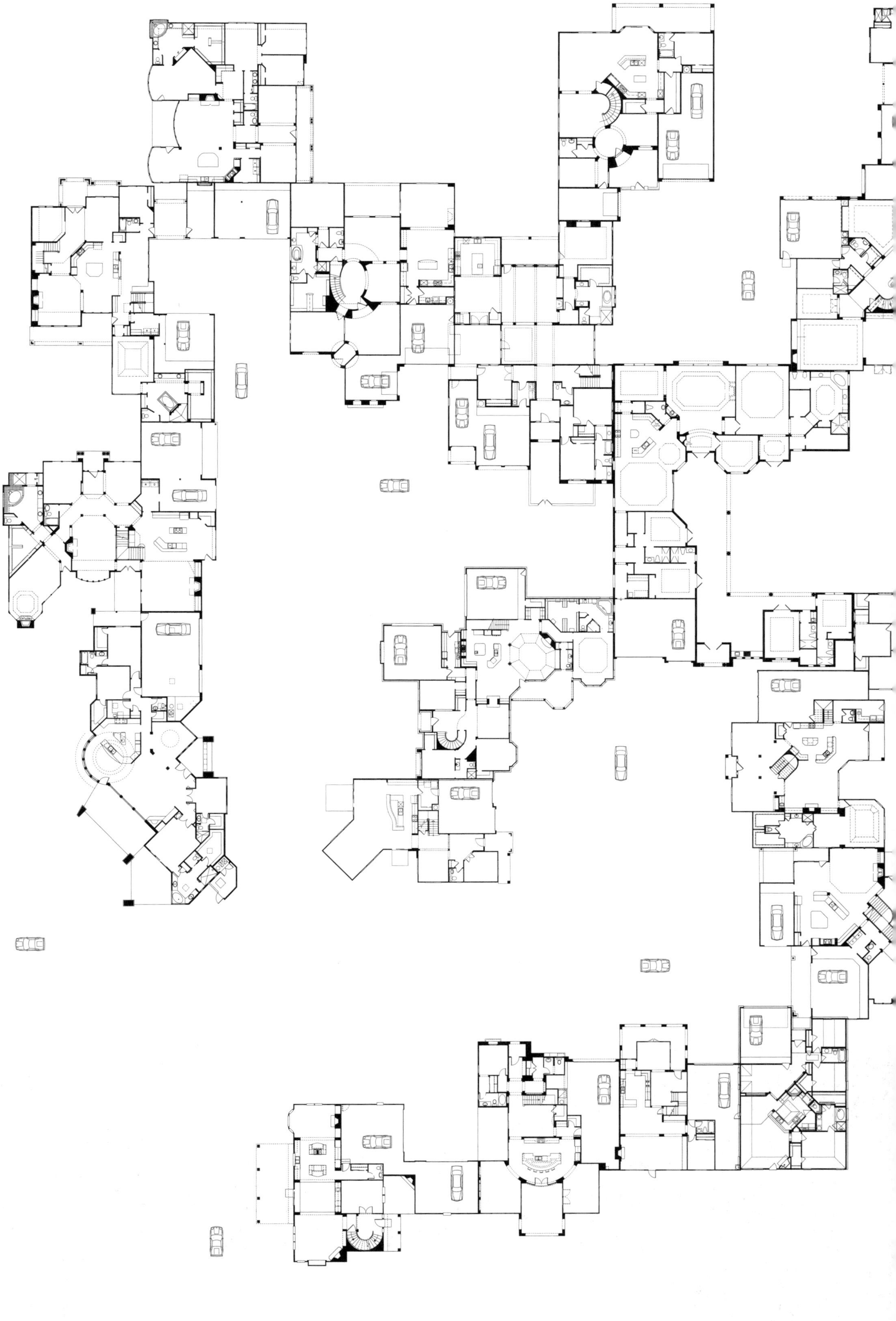

The Winchester The Collingsworth

SuperModel Homes™

David Weekley Court at David Weekley New Home Center™, Houston, Texas

The Wilkins

We offer homes and lifestyles . . .[1]

On Highway 290, in northwest Houston, superstores offer "everyday low prices" for everything needed to stock the average American home and fuel the average American lifestyle. Walmart, Home Depot, Target, Academy Sports and Outdoor, and others populate a big-box landscape of high volumes and deep discounts. In 1997, a new player entered the big-box game. David Weekley Homes™ opened the David Weekley New Home Center™, a 17,000-square-foot superstore.[2] This "one-stop home shop" turned the superstore concept inside out: selling not household goods but the houses themselves.

David Weekley™ positions his superstore of houses to be a category killer like its big-box neighbors. The New Home Center™ capitalizes on big-box innovations, adding personal service to consumer choice and competitive prices. "Designed to service the needs of customers from start to finish,"[3] it incorporates almost every conceivable component of the home-buying process: a map room of Weekley communities, on-site model homes, a showroom of finishes and fixtures, and even a mortgage and title company to assist in financing and closing the deal. This combination of service and selection generates an atmosphere of

1. New Home Marketing Company (http://www.newhomeswichita.com/)
2. Since then, Weekley has opened additional "Design Centers" in metropolitan markets across the country.
3. Quotes used in this essay are taken from promotional material found online at www.davidweekleyhomes.com

exclusivity by offering a seemingly customized experience.

Homebuyers can choose from over 100 floor plans and, through consultation with a Weekley designer, "personalize their home [in one of over thirty different subdivisions] with hundreds of design options . . . and thousands of decorator selections."[4] After selecting a home plan, buyers meet their designer to finalize finishes and fixtures and are assigned a Personal Builder™ who supervises construction of their "custom" home. The buyer can check construction status daily via a personal, password-protected "Homebuyer" website.

In the "Build on Your Lot" program, a critical component of the New Home Center™, buyers can even choose to build their David Weekley™ home anywhere in Houston. Weekley—the largest private homebuilder in the US—sells almost 1,000 homes per year in the city. That volume creates an economy of scale that allows Weekley to compete across multiple sales brackets throughout the city.[5] More importantly, it creates an economic position that allows the builder to work on individual, scattered lots. The necessary economies of scale, previously available only in large subdivisions where houses are constructed in a factory-like manner, are now distributed lot-by-lot across Houston. Essentially, every neighborhood becomes a potential David Weekley™ subdivision.

Marketing offers the consumer an entire philosophy of living at the New Home Center™. The homes are presented as the product of "over 20 years of research into how people live." LifeDesign™, as Weekley's residential ethos is trademarked, is, according to sales literature, "an art, a science, a unique ingredient in each home we build that enhances its value." LifeDesign™ spins David Weekley™ products out of the ordinary cycles of suburban marketing and into the world of custom construction, "ensuring that your home will live as well as it looks." The sales experience transforms a more or less typical suburban home into an "innovative design," achieved through "incomparable choice" with "inspired service." The buyer is not just purchasing a house, but a perfectly crafted, and carefully marketed, lifestyle.

Marketing as Planning

Marketing is everything—and not just at David Weekley Homes™. It shapes both our products and our relationships to products. It effectively and efficiently transforms our world through formulas that combine consumers and producers in complex socio-economic equations, determining not only the style of individuals' lives but the appearance and performance of their collective environment—the city—as well. As everything is reduced to a marketable product, it becomes increasingly difficult to distinguish any values not directly related to increased financial return. In cities, the results are clear: Collective, civic interests—cultural, social, or environmental—are swept under by waves of private development, immune to any values save the bottom line.

This is not to say that other values disappear. In fact, they're touted, espoused, and of course, capitalized upon every day. You can't market anything—save perhaps stocks or bonds—by transparently presenting its effect on the producer's profits. Added, apparently market-free values—patriotism, family, Main Street Americana, neighborliness—provide the necessary camouflage to shepherd products safely to market. All manner of goods and services, from pharmaceuticals to cities, are commonly clothed in co-opted value systems that construct visions of the good life, free from everyday struggles.

Cities—as marketplaces, the traditional domain of marketing—are now literally constructed through marketing. Planning is dead. And not just in Houston, notorious for its lack of zoning, but frankly no better or worse than any other sprawling American metropolis. Notwithstanding the popularity of lifestyle magazines that sell visions of jet-set urbanity in plush, sexed-up environs, the suburban dream and its attendant value structure still drives most current marketing. Since the Second World War, the private, bucolic realm of the single-family home set among like-minded neighbors has symbolized comfort, success, and security in an otherwise unstable (and presumably unsightly) world. That suburban image, once limited to a city's edges, increasingly invades all territories, both rural and urban. The suburban product world now shapes virtually all private development (for the most part, the only game in town), turning every place, except perhaps Manhattan, into a suburb. For the marketer as for the consumer, the suburban sylvan ideal displaces a dirty urban reality.

Never mind that as cities expand our parents' suburban becomes our urban, as ours will most likely be our children's. In Houston, arguably the country's most suburban city, recent private development has reconceived the older, more urban core—including yesterday's suburbs—as a new territory ripe for suburban colonization. In the constant search for new fields of operation, private developers are now backfilling the Inner Loop with development products and lifestyles

4. The apparently wide spectrum of choice can be frustrating, however, as distinctions between offerings is often somewhat minimal. When I visited the New Home Center I saw an obviously overwhelmed young woman burying her head in her hands, as she and her husband faced a wall of not-quite-the-same bathroom fixtures.

5. (http://www.davidweekleyhomes.com/search.asp) Searching the David WeekleyTM database online, one finds houses available from a more modest, 1,500-square-foot, $229,990 house to grander, custom-built, 6,000-square-foot houses with a price of over 1 million dollars.

born on its outer shores. The small city lots are stuffed with oversized McMansions or multiple townhouses boasting suburban-scaled interiors; candy-colored strip centers complete with synthetic stucco pediments and plenty of paving are placed along every busy street. Even when new typologies for housing are introduced or rediscovered—townhouses, lofts, or apartments over retail—they are clothed in the neo-traditional garb of their suburban cousins and often exhibit the same negligent behavior in regard to the public realm. Adjoining townhouses huddle in gated, insular enclaves or line block after block with a continuous wall of garage doors facing the street. As development seeks new shelf space in the Inner Loop, the complex mixture of buildings and programs that defines a vibrant urban setting is replaced with the bland homogeneity of the newest exurban subdivisions and strips.

Writing about Houston in 1978, British architecture and design critic Reyner Banham noted that the city "has no native-grown culture with which to explain itself to the world. It has no history to explain itself to itself even."[6] An enthusiastic observer of American building culture and cities, Banham, in a one-day tour of the city, astutely observed the "open game" of land values, combined with the lack of any geographic impediments or zoning, which, then as now, drives the speculative production in this city. But he missed the game's importance: It is the culture with which Houstonians explain themselves to themselves. Ever since the Allen brothers gambled on the marketability of a bend in Buffalo Bayou, Houston's "native-grown culture" has been real-estate speculation—and marketing.

6. Reyner Banham, "Collect $2,000,000," in *New Society*, June 15, 1978, p. 608.

Big-Box Urbanism

Marketing-as-planning structures Houston as a vast retail environment—not just a city of big boxes but the city as a big box. Walmart, not only the world's largest retailer but also the world's largest company, constantly manipulates its floor stock in response to real-time demographic profiling. As customers check out, their purchases are correlated item by item with other purchases made in every other store in the system. Armed with that information, Walmart adjusts the distribution of its products both globally and locally. In a similar manner, but without benefit of management, real-estate product in Houston is constantly repositioned for better market performance. The city's streets—its shelves—are constantly restocked. New product replaces old, as suburban settings are displayed for sale throughout the city.

Real estate products in Houston and other major cities are increasingly similar. That sameness has its uses. Mortgage banking and real estate development protocols demand a certain level of design uniformity to best guarantee the maximum market share available. Mortgages are traded as commodities, and a uniform product makes mortgage transfer easier. If each house were deeply different, then something other than a spreadsheet would be required to assess and communicate its market value as covered by the mortgage.

Design distinctions offer no competitive advantage in the housing market. A unique product, however innovative or intelligent, introduces an unacceptable level of financial risk for developers and banks alike. Success sells, and difference is dangerous. With design reduced to replicating previous successes, the question becomes how to distinguish an undistinguished housing product.

As all real estate products—houses, townhouses, subdivisions, retail centers—become more generic, it becomes harder for a builder to gain a competitive edge. Better product placement (exclusivity) or discount pricing (economy) offer advantages, but both tend to reduce the potential size of the market. It is possible, however, to offer an essentially generic product under the guise of exclusivity, and to offer the appearance of distinction with the assurance of affordability.

That, of course, is the magic of David Weekley's big box.

SuperModel Homes

Behind the New Home Center™ on David Weekley Court sit three "Idea Homes" that demonstrate "just how David Weekley's designs become buyers' dreams." Each home is styled—or, more precisely, life-styled—to show the advantages attained in purchasing a Weekley Home. The smallest, the Wilkins, is relatively modest by current Houston standards: one story, two baths, three bedrooms plus FlexSpace℠—a Weekley, service-marked term for space-we-don't-know-what-to-do-with-yet. The Wilkins' not-so-subtle French theme in blue and yellow carries through to the color-coordinated socks and shirts hanging to dry in the laundry room. In the kitchen, prints of Parisian street scenes line the walls, and a cookbook called *Backroad Bistros, Farmhouse Fare* lies open near a wicker breadbasket overflowing with baguettes.

The Wilkins is not the smallest plan in David Weekley's arsenal. In fact, at approximately 2,200 square feet, it's almost 600 square feet larger than something called the

Eastdale. But the Wilkins is clearly the starter house in the Idea Homes trio.

The furnishings and household belongings suggest that the home's fictional family is a young couple with an infant and a toddler. The smallest bedroom is furnished as a nursery. Stuffed animals fill the crib, and a changing table is stocked with Huggies. The second bedroom, a little girl's, houses "Patsy's Puppet Playhouse," with the puppet actors hung from the theater's ceiling and an audience of dolls on the bed. The FlexSpace℠ is certainly the young father's domain—at least until another child comes along. The room is outfitted with fishing poles, nets, aquatic taxidermy, and fishing-related prints. On the desk sits a small flat-screen computer by Props™, an electronics company that apparently reduces overhead by dispensing with circuitry.

The master bedroom (or "owner's retreat," as it is known in most current residential developers' plans) is least distinguished by any character traits except, of course, a taste for the good life. A food tray with a plastic fruit-and-croissant breakfast sits on the king-size bed. Clearly, this is just the beginning for the Wilkins family. Available for between $152,000 and $212,000, depending on location, the house is the first step in a three-tiered rise to the top of the home market.

The second model on the David Weekley Court, the Collingsworth, measures almost 2,900 square feet. It costs anywhere from a modest $194,000 for the "Urban" model from the "Build on Your Lot" program to a location up-charged $485,000 Custom Classic™ at Cole's Crossing, described as "an exit from the fast lane . . . where the milkman still delivers." (In fact, buyers receive six months of free milk delivery.) A step up from the Wilkins, this house introduces the increasingly popular "children's retreat" between Bedrooms Two and Three. It's described as "a special place just for the kids, where they can do their homework, play games or watch TV while mom and dad enjoy some quiet time with a movie or reading by the family room fire." The room holds an easel and several board games, along with a colorful array of kid-friendly furniture.

The display model corresponds perfectly with the idealized life of Weekley's literature. The kids in this house, the second rung on the ladder to domestic bliss, are slightly older than those at the Wilkins and are starting to display personality traits with their bedroom furnishings. The young girl in Bedroom Three is still obsessed with dolls (an antique baby carriage sits in her room), while the young boy in Bedroom Two is in the midst of a politically correct cowboys-and-Indians phase. (His wallpaper shows an integrated Southwestern camp with teepees and a chuck wagon.) Apparently the boy also dreams of growing up to be David Weekley™. On his desk, beside a tomahawk and beneath a Buffalo Bill poster, sits a Props™ computer with a sales report displayed on its frozen screen. According to the report, Props™ provides a critical sales advantage to the home seller; for the past four quarters, sales of model homes with Props™ electronics have outperformed those without.

The Collingsworth's FlexSpace℠ is an optional attic room complete with dormers. Perhaps the cowboy-loving son chose its saloon furnishings: swingin' doors, saddle barstools, cowboy boots, a full-sized John Wayne cardboard placard, and cartoon cowboy wall covering. Several resin-filled, foam-topped beer mugs and a few bowls of stale popcorn sit next to unplayed hands at the poker table. It's as if a neutron bomb has erased all the occupants without disturbing their domestic dreams.

By now, you feel as though you're spying on strangely perfect Stepford families. In several rooms, embroidered pillows sport epigrams like, "If you want the best seat in the house, move the dog," "My favorite thing to make for dinner is reservations," and of course, "I may have my faults but being wrong is not one of them." The unseen Weekley set decorator seems to be asking, "How could anyone who lives this well be wrong?"

The Collingsworths may not be wrong, but they're not as right as their neighbors: The Winchester measures 3,400 square feet and is priced as low as $227,000 on your own "Urban" lot. The biggest of the three Idea Homes, the Winchester still ranks a significant notch below the biggest, the most expensive of the David Weekley Homes™. (The Kramer, for instance, measures 4,500 square feet, and is available at Cole's Crossing for about $500,000.) But among the three "Idea Homes," the Winchester represents the top of the ladder, the ultimate in the three-steps-to-success, David Weekley New Home Center™ supermodel series.

As you enter the Winchester, a flat, stiff butler, cut out of wood and painted to resemble a servant from Masterpiece Theatre, greets you. He stands in the foyer, holding a serving tray with four crystal brandy snifters. With this aristocratic flourish, the scene is set.

A dinner party is about to take place. To the left of the foyer, the table is carefully set, and delicious-looking (albeit artificial) desserts are lined up on the sideboard. To the right, dark-stained wood wainscoting and built-in bookcases line the walls of the library, which features an antique drop-front writing desk and a crystal decanter filled with *faux* Scotch. Curiously, Leon Uris's *Armageddon* claims a prominent place on the bookshelf. Has David Weekley™ imagined the neutron-bomb scenario as well?

As in the other homes, the kitchen is the picture of good, healthy living. Several plastic artichokes waiting to be prepared sit on the cutting board, fresh herbs dry on a rack, and a can of Ghirardelli coffee sits on the counter. A cornucopia overflows with wheat on the island next to the range.

On the other side of the spacious family room, the owner's retreat is finished in nineteenth-century French neo-classical style. The wallpaper shows a classical frieze, and carefully framed beaux arts prints hang on the walls. A breakfast tray rests on the ottoman, complete with a fresh bowl of plastic strawberries, a plastic croissant—from the Wilkins bakery, perhaps?—and an empty coffee cup. A photo on the dresser shows smiling grandparents with three teenaged children. Through a corner window, a person relaxing in the sitting area could look out onto . . . an overflowing dumpster in the parking lot next door. The trash is conspicuously out of place in this perfect world. For a moment, the illusion is broken.

The three upstairs bedrooms surround the requisite children's retreat. This retreat is clearly the domain of teenagers. The board game Clue (It was the butler in the foyer with the brandy snifter!) is hidden in the closet. Commanding far more attention, a book-shelf/desk unit along the wall displays what must be the complete Props™ product line—a computer, stereo, and television.

The kids' bedrooms in the Winchester are the most fully developed spaces in the Idea Homes. These children are ambitious and hard working, with clearly defined dreams and ambitions. Bedroom Four is the romantic traveler's room with model bi-planes, sailing ships, and hot-air balloons, accompanied by Victorian-era painted wooden figures. In the closet, two leather suitcases await duty.

Bedroom Number 2 (if only the occupants had names!) is home to the future archaeologist. Prehistoric-looking models of insects, a book on fossils, a globe, and an African drum sit among rattan furniture. Mosquito netting drapes the canopy bed, and a *Raiders of the Lost Ark* poster hangs next to the door.

The last room, Bedroom Number 3 at the front of the house, belongs to a young woman obsessed with architecture. She appears little interested in the teenage trappings that so annoy adults; only a few desultory clippings of heartthrobs and a homecoming ribbon are displayed on a small tack board. This young woman focuses mainly on her goals. A large wire model of the Eiffel Tower stands next to the bed. Framed photographs of classical details hang on the walls, along with a surrealist montage of the interior of a Gothic cathedral overlaid on an Atget-like urban street scene. A slipcover on the chair at the drafting table matches a patterned, Frank Lloyd Wright-inspired bedspread. The shelves are stocked with books on architecture (along with, oddly, a copy of *Mommy Dearest*): Assorted Frank Lloyd Wright volumes keep company with a book of late-twentieth-century skyscrapers, a technical drafting book, and Diana Agrest's *Architecture from Without*. A drawing tube sits on the shelf in the closet, and nosy shoppers who open the drawer next to the desk find a collection of drafting supplies.

More than any other room in the Idea Homes at David Weekley's New Home Center™, this last one—filled with architectural ambition—is the most strongly themed. Moving through the homes on David Weekley Court, it is obvious how carefully the domestic environment is crafted to articulate a progression through three stages in the life of a successful family. But this last room—the end of all the family's striving?—is confusing. Why is this fictional young woman obsessed with architecture, when architecture is so clearly not the issue in Weekley's world? Why not medicine? Or law?

Because, as the British artist Richard Hamilton once observed, "Design is a sales weapon."[7] The designer himself is a marketing aid, Hamilton argued; the fact that someone thought about the design of a product is more valuable to sales than the product itself. And David Weekley wields his "sales weapon" well, capitalizing on architecture's cultural cachet more than architects do.

Weekley distinguishes his product from other speculative residential construction with a marketing campaign that emphasizes the company's design intelligence and sensitivity at every turn. With typical immodesty, the website states: "LifeDesign™ blends the fundamentals of design, architecture, engineering, physics, psychology, and sociology to create a home that looks better—and lives better—than all the rest." And at the New Home Center™, architecture, a symbol of success and one of market capitalism's ultimate luxury goods, is made available in a retail format—the big box superstore—familiar to every American shopper.

7. Richard Hamilton, "Persuading Image" (1959), from idem, *Collected Words: 1953-1982*. London: Thames and Hudson 1982, p. 135.

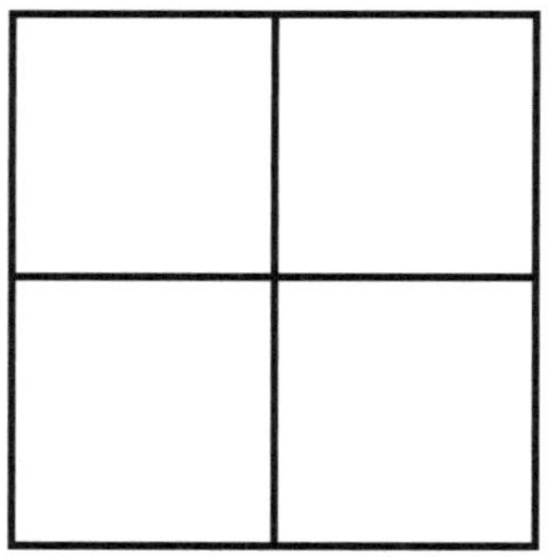

Foursquare

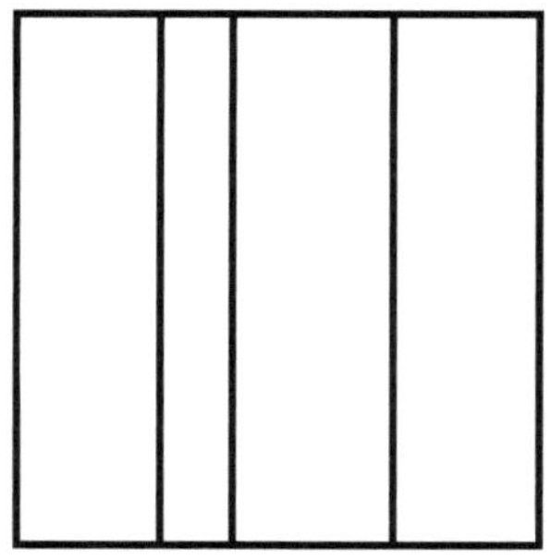

Laminar

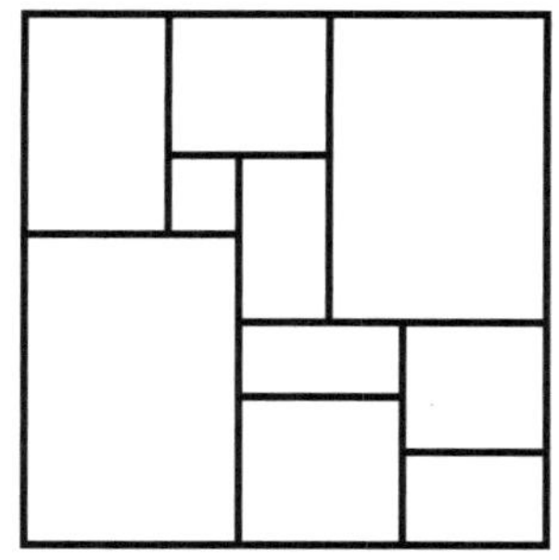

Cellular

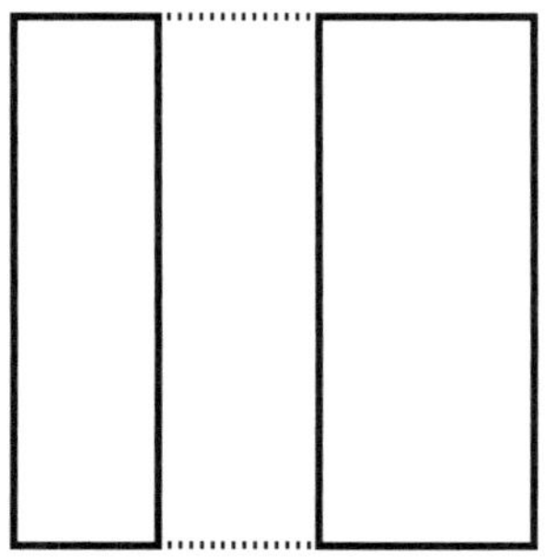

Bisected

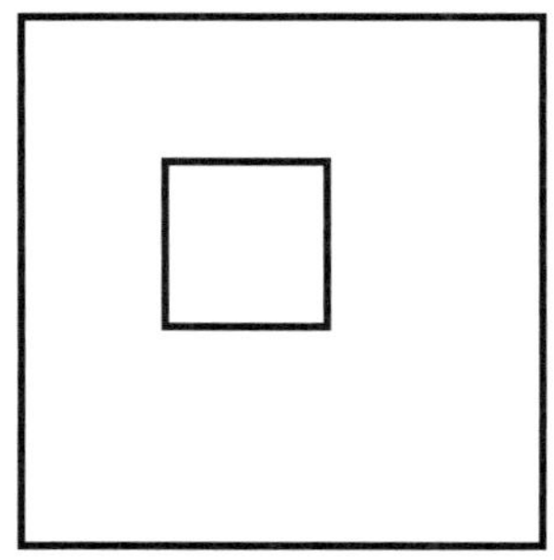

Nuclear

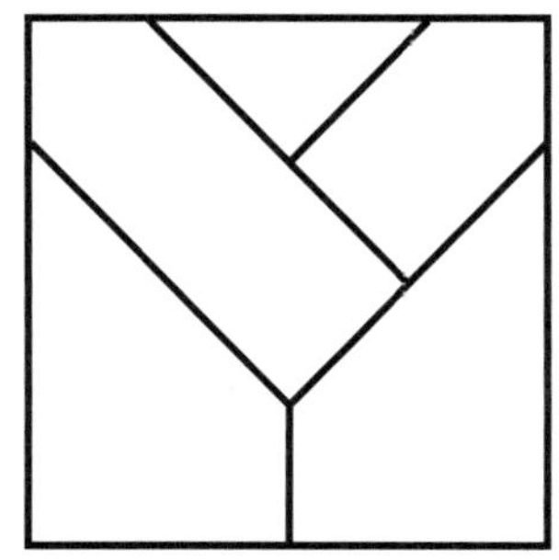

Branching

Six Typical Plans

The suburban single-family house, more than any other object, is the primary symbol of success in America. It is the preeminent representation of its owners' aspirations; it functions to construct individual identity and register personal achievement. To own a home is to live the Dream.[1]

American homebuilders have long capitalized on this equation, which binds that house as an object to the Dream as a concept. Over the course of the most recent housing boom, the catalog of available models exploded as builders sought ever more elaborate ways of engendering desire for their products. These products, the primary building blocks of the contemporary suburban metropolis, are carefully calibrated weapons of commerce that connect with, and simultaneously create, the domestic expectations of consumers. While it might seem difficult to categorize these products as architecture, to dismiss them out of hand—at a time when much architectural research is dedicated to redressing the ills of the suburban environment—is to disconnect architecture from a live current of contemporary culture. So, rather than reject these models wholesale, it seems necessary to identify and utilize the actionable intelligence embedded in them. This requires that we see these houses as architecture and assess them as such.

"Six Typical Plans" is the result of just such an assessment; it is an investigation into the organizational logics that lie behind the speculative house's seemingly normative facade. The result of a comparative analysis of nearly 1,000 house plans, it identifies a series of architectural strategies that govern the design of the models deployed by American homebuilders.

The individual plan, as used in the marketing material of a homebuilder, maps out an idea of domesticity, of a possible lifestyle for the prospective homebuyer. Many plans, when analyzed critically, offer evidence of an underlying set of six distinct plan types that form the core of the homebuilder's arsenal and allow them to deliver different levels of design to a diverse array of homebuyers. Two of these types, Foursquare and Laminar, are essentially variations of long-used production house types. The other four types—Cellular, Bisected, Nuclear, and Branching—all betray some relationship to the simpler Foursquare and Laminar organizational techniques and offer evidence of the builders' carefully considered reorganizations and amplifications of familiar domestic arrangements.[2] These primary organizational arrangements are complimented by the knowing and considered use of an array of design techniques, including the thickening of surfaces, the exploitation of diagonal lines of sight and movement, the scenographic layering of spaces, and the deployment of distinct room shapes and profiles. Thus, while only six basic types define the canon of the contemporary American production house, an innumerable number of variations, or models, allow that house to be marketed as a customized product, providing a sense of distinctive luxury to each buyer, regardless of income level.

1. "I do believe in the American Dream. I believe there is such a thing as the American Dream. . . . Owning a home is a part of that dream; it just is. Right here in America, if you own your own home, you're realizing the American Dream." President George W. Bush,from Remarks at St. Paul AME Church in Atlanta, Georgia, June 17, 2002

2. These houses are everywhere: there are Nuclear versions haunting the deserts of the southwest, Bisected homes roaming the edges of cities from New York to Atlanta to Minneapolis, and Branching plans reproducing and running wild across the prairies of Texas and the forests of the southeast.

A Tree of Types

Six primary plan types—Foursquare, Laminar, Cellular, Nuclear, Bisected, and Branching—lie behind the wide variety of floor plans offered by contemporary American homebuilders. These types define a core set of organizational arrangements that guide the planning and design of a majority of American houses. While the plans of some houses are near-perfect examples of pure types, most incorporate properties from more than one type, as the types themselves exhibit qualities of morphological transformation. In this regard, a path can be traced from the simplest type, the Foursquare, to the more complex types, noting the organizational similarities and fundamental transformations along the way. It is interesting to note that the average price per square foot increases proportionally as the houses become both larger and more complex. This suggests that the cost of housing today is a function not only of size but also of design.

Cellular plans are organized as a system of room-to-room associations. This gives an equivalence to the spaces that is exemplified by the two-axis symmetry of the Foursquare. The Cellular is an order more complex than the Foursquare but is structured by similar principles.

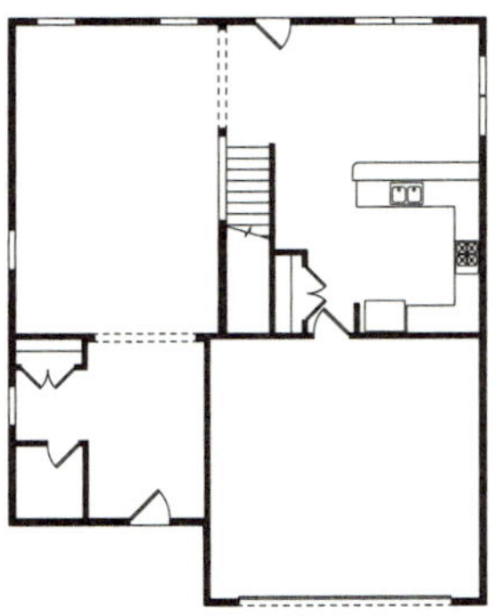

Foursquare
Average price per square foot: $119

The Foursquare becomes the Laminar in two distinct ways: either by elongation or widening. When elongated, the plan is stretched out as rooms are added behind the first four spaces, thereby producing two long bars side by side. The process of widening occurs by adding spaces to the sides of the house, producing a plan composed of three or more layers.

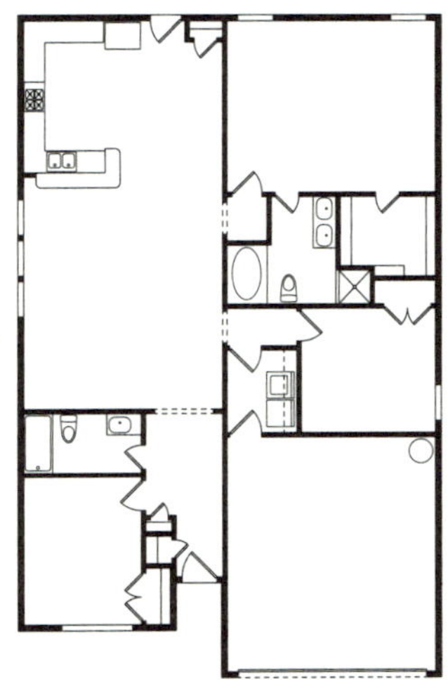

Laminar (Deep)
Average price per square foot: $140

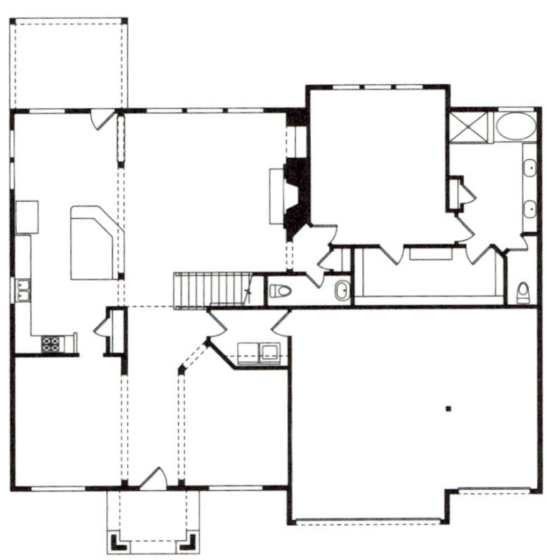

Laminar (Wide)
Average price per square foot: $140

Bisected plans are organized in a layered manner similar to the Laminar type, but with a formal symmetry composed of an entry hall flanked by two—often only approximately—equal wings. The central axis typically ends in a large living space.

Nuclear plans are often similar to Cellular plans but are distinguished by a type-defining central space. This is often an exterior courtyard, particularly in the Sun Belt states, but is sometimes a central kitchen or living room that serves as a hub around which the other residential functions orbit.

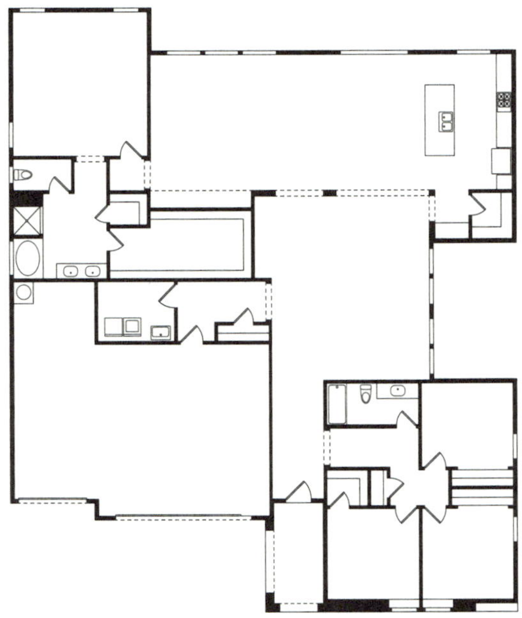

Cellular
Average price per square foot: $152

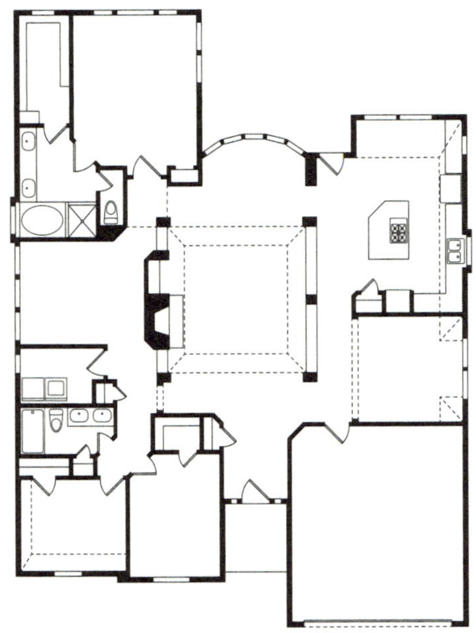

Nuclear
Average price per square foot: $171

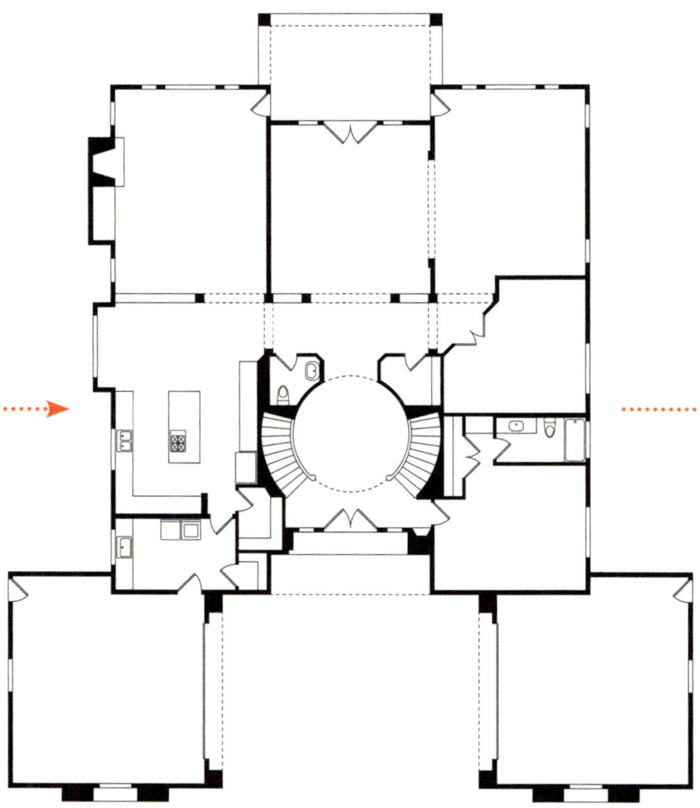

Bisected
Average price per square foot: $187

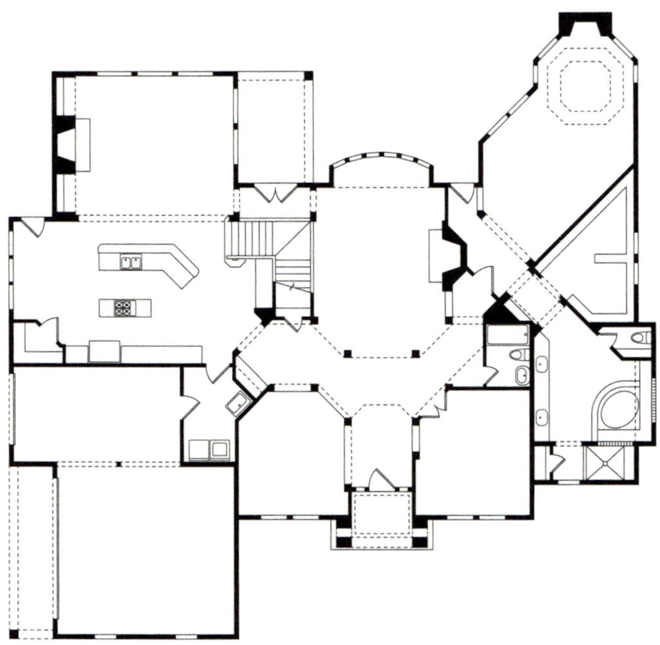

Branching
Average price per square foot: $198

The forking paths in the circulation of Branching houses are a further development of the hall-based strategies found in the Bisected type. The Branching method is frequently used in wider houses to formally connect spaces as the plan spreads laterally. The diagonal lines also accentuate the perception of scale.

0 20 ft.

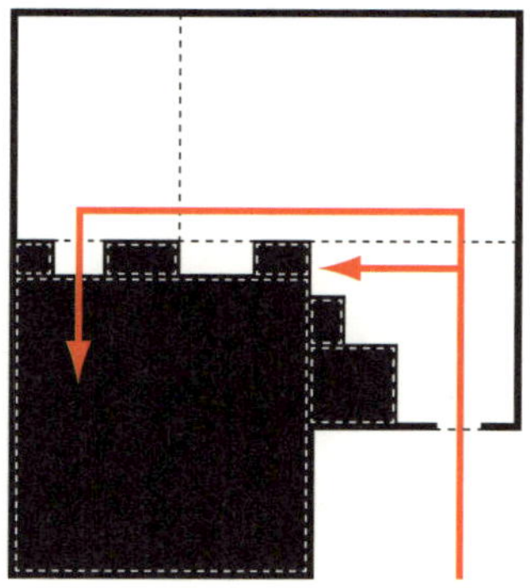

KB Home, Plan 1806, 1806 sq. ft., Georgia

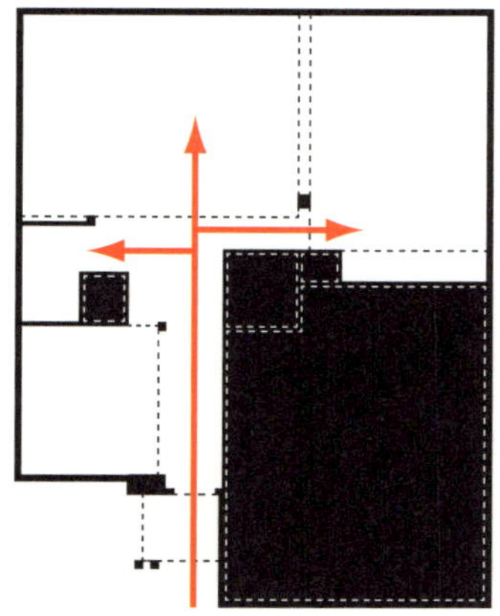

David Weekley Homes, The Stormwood, 2000sq. ft., Georgia

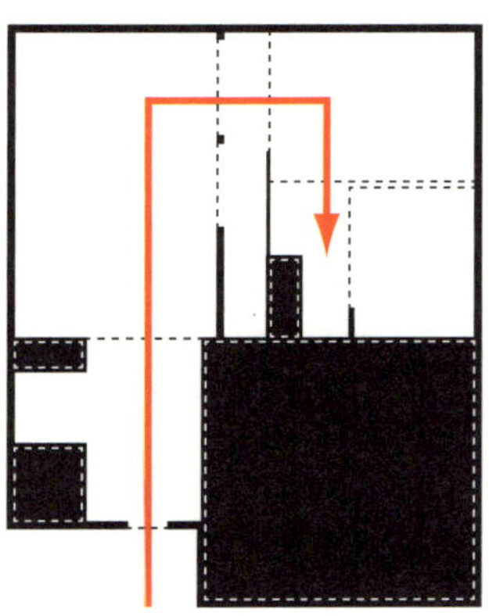

Beazer Homes, Hartford, 2392 sq. ft., Indiana

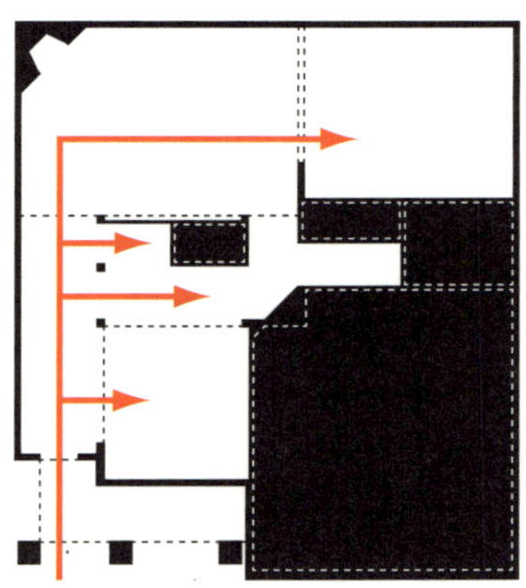

Ryland Homes, The Prescott, 2005 sq. ft., Georgia

Foursquare Plans

Foursquare plans, typically of modest size and often compact, tend towards a two-floor arrangement with roughly centered entrances. Clear descendants of the traditional foursquare home, these plans are defined by spaces of relatively equal size grouped two by two in a more or less square formation, as shown here in The Hartford from Beazer Homes and in KB Home's modestly sized (and named) Plan 1806.
In most contemporary interpretations one of the quadrants is a garage. Often, an element usually found only in larger, more "formal" homes—such as the dining room in Ryland Homes' The Prescott—will be nested into one of the quadrants. Other elements, such as the oversized entry columns on The Prescott, are often added to the simple Foursquare type to give it a greater sense of stature. A Foursquare organization can be read in some plans even as the house begins to swell and grow. The Conrad from David Weekley exhibits a super-Foursquare order but is beginning to resemble something more akin to a Laminar, or even Cellular, arrangement.

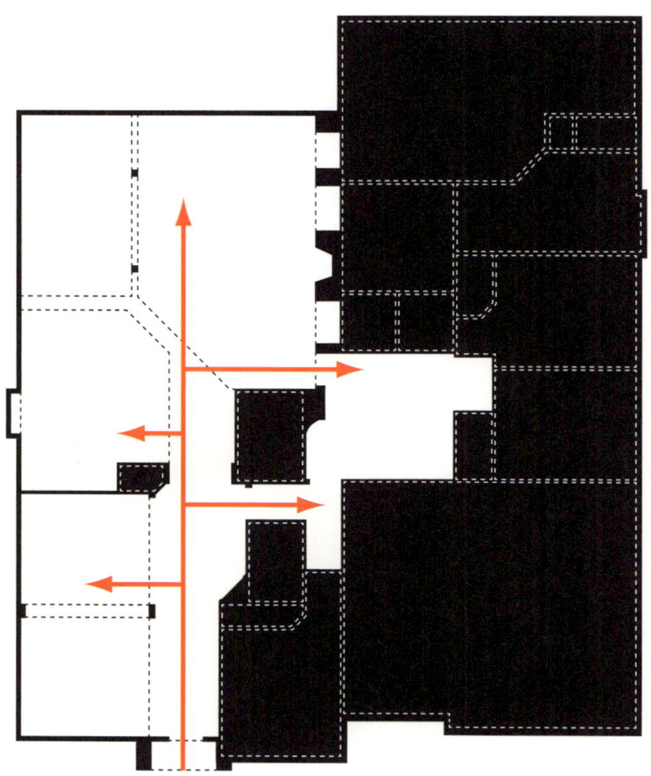

David Weekley Homes, The Conrad, 3180sq. ft., Texas

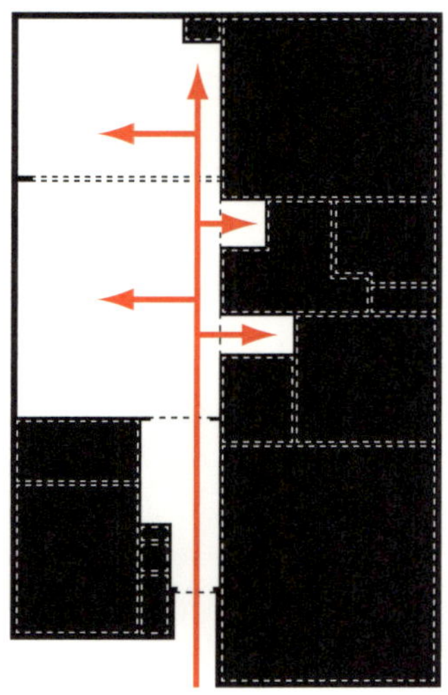

Beazer Homes, The Adams, 1539 sq. ft., South Carolina

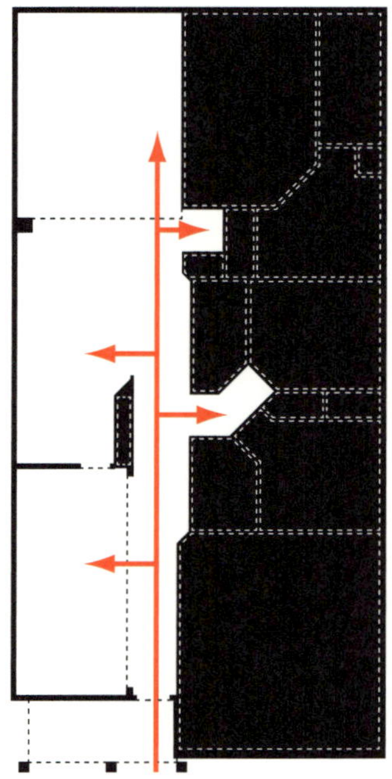

David Weekley Homes, The Benjamin, 1906 sq. ft., Texas

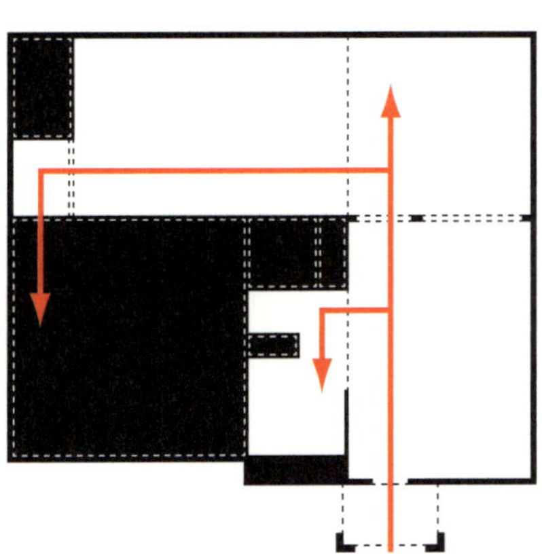

KB Home, Plan 2808, 2808 sq. ft., Florida

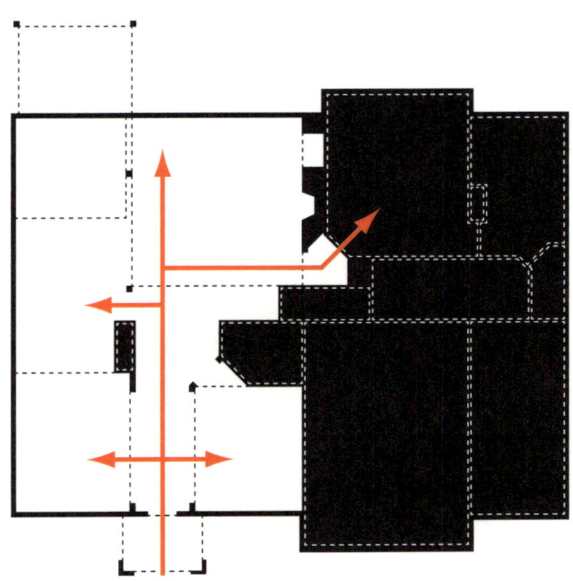

David Weekley Homes, The Paulette, 3562 sq. ft., Texas

Laminar Plans

One of the most commonly utilized types, Laminar plans use a layered formation of rooms and spaces to create linear organizational strips. The layers can be quite regular with only the simplest internal subdivision and cross-grain circulation servicing connections across and between bands. The clearest examples of this type simply extend the bays of the Foursquare either vertically, as in The Adams from Beazer Homes, or horizontally as in Plan 2808 from KB Home. Two- and three-bay versions of this type have limited circulation between the strips, thereby creating more distinct zones (e.g., master bedroom and children's rooms) within each band. Laminar plans are often quite simple, taking the form of just two bands with a clear linear boundary dividing them and a narrow cleft denoting the entry. Other Laminar schemes are more complex in terms of the number of layers, sometimes reading—as in David Weekley's The Paulette—as a classic center hall colonial with layers added to one side to accommodate the garage, and in this case, the increasingly common extra-large "owner's retreat." Supersized Laminar plans, such as The Mayfair from Toll Brothers, tend to grow laterally, adding band after band as the number of public rooms (and garages) accumulates in the more high-end houses. With its accretion of rooms, this plan also suggests the next of the six types: the Cellular.

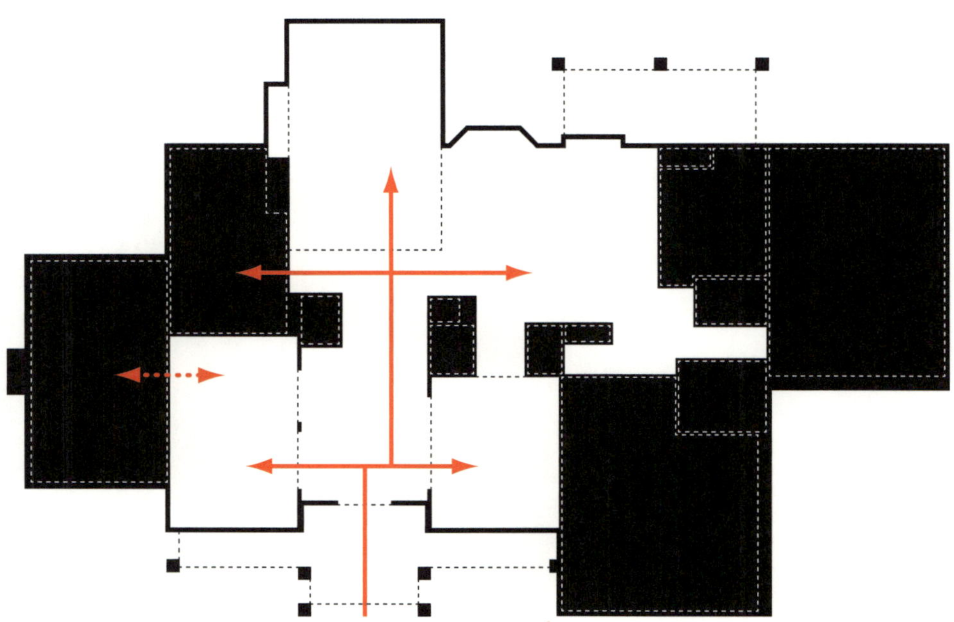

Toll Brothers, The Mayfair, 5257 sq. ft., California

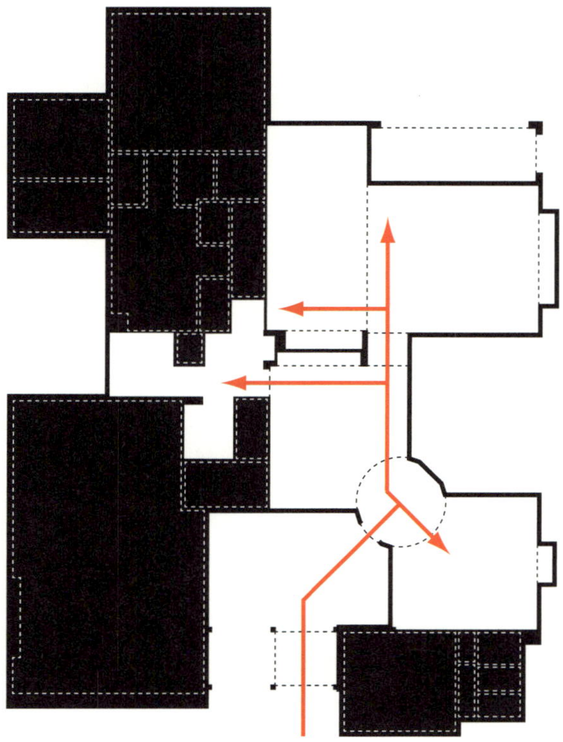

Standard Pacific Homes, Residence 1H, 4719 sq. ft., California

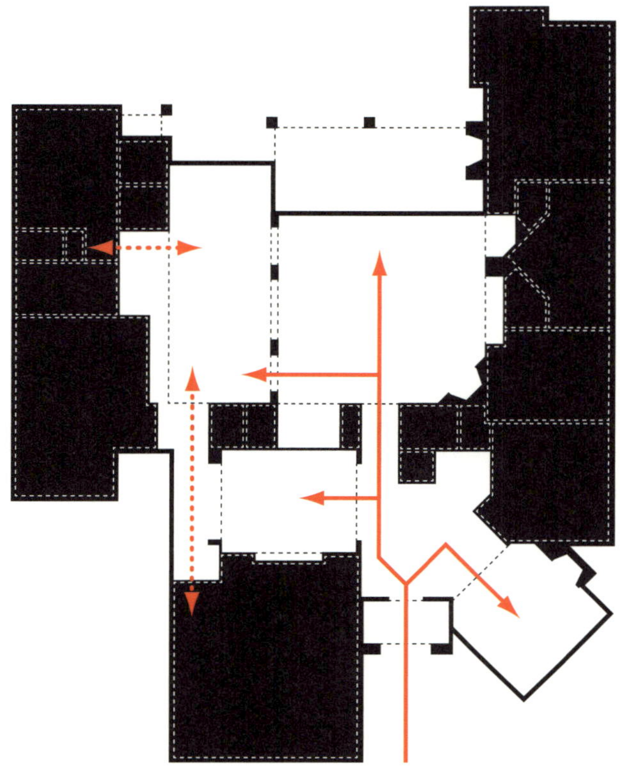

David Weekley Homes, Plan 5278, 4806 sq. ft., Texas

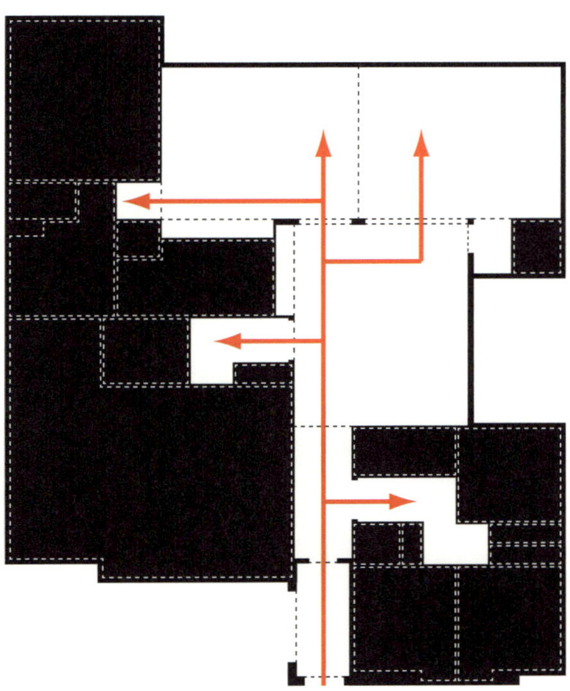

KB Home, Plan Five, 2729 sq. ft., California

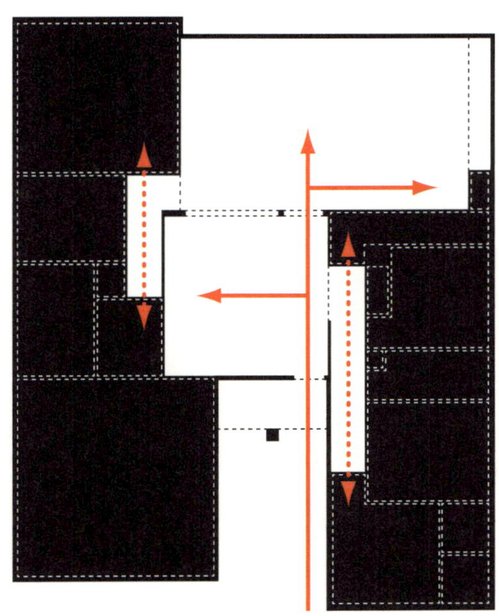

KB Home, Maidstone, 2126 sq. ft., Colorado

Cellular Plans

Cellular plans are built from more or less irregular clusters of rooms and other spaces that are lined up along hallways or joined directly one to another with no immediately perceptible overall order. Sprawling or compact, this scheme can produce the appearance of rooms piled on top of rooms, in which hierarchies between programs and spaces are obscured. In its more compact form, the cellular type can be used to create fairly efficient plans. Still, Cellular schemes are more typically found in large plans with many rooms, a loose or figural envelope, and drifting and disjointed circulation paths, such as David Weekley's Plan 5278 or the Toll Brothers' St Michel, both in Texas.

These plans almost never rely on symmetry—and rarely on any overt formal planning strategy—yet they often still produce expected programmatic adjacencies. In fact, while it is an obviously unique type, primarily due to the loose, room-by-room planning techniques; Cellular plans often incorporate familiar elements from the other categories. Toll Brothers' massive St. Michel plan betrays traces of Laminar logic. KB Home's Maidstone anticipates the characteristics of Bisected schemes (a long entry hall that ends in a large family room) and is beginning to suggest a Nuclear organization centered loosely on what is referred to as a "flex space" just inside the front entry.

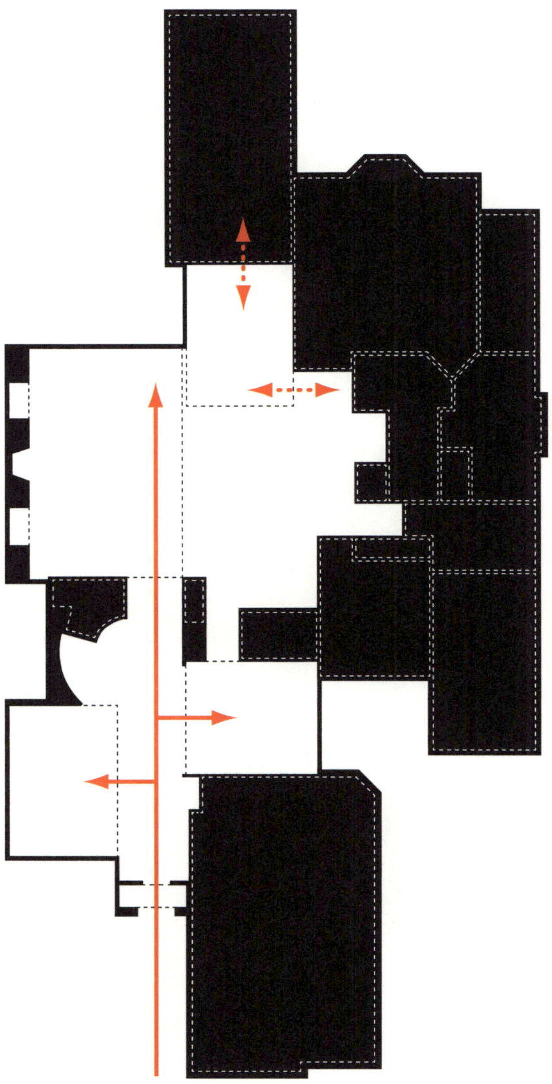

Toll Brothers, St. Michel, 5000 sq. ft., Texas

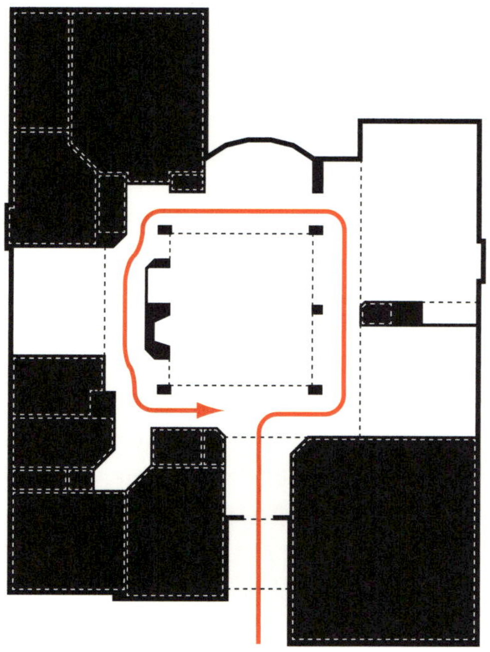

David Weekley Homes, The Wilkins, 2400 sq. ft., Texas

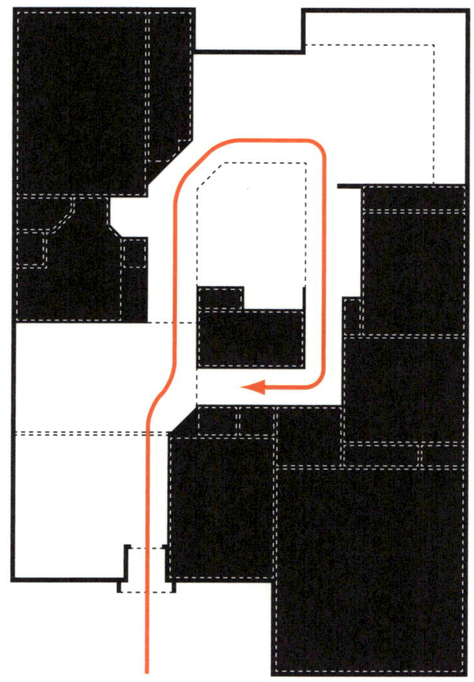

Beazer Homes, Reno, 2200 sq. ft., Texas

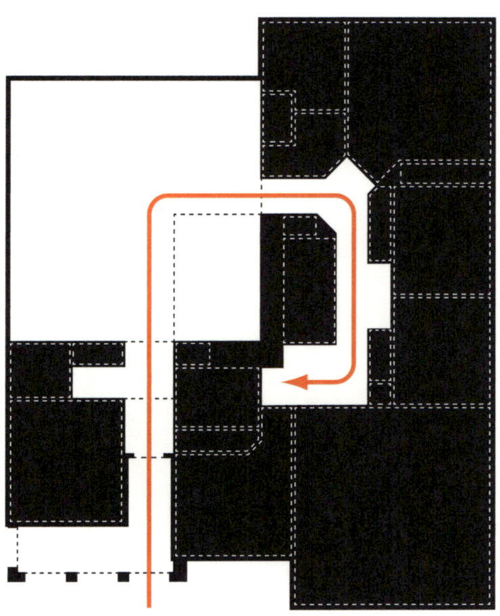

KB Home, Plan One, 2187 sq. ft., California

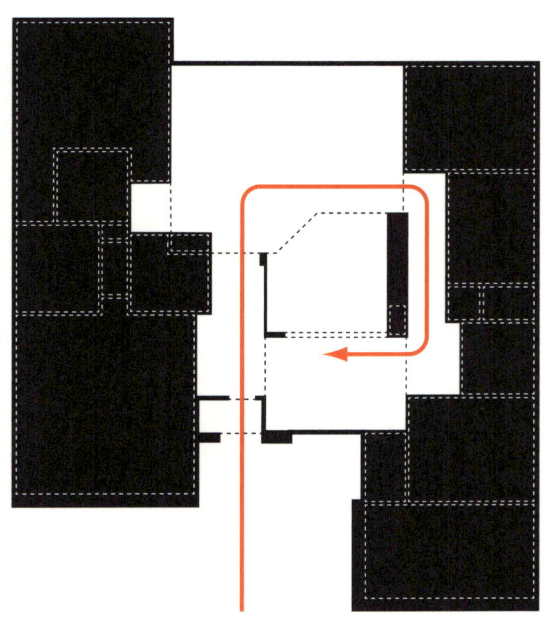

KB Home, Plan Three, 2414 sq. ft., California

Nuclear Plans

Nuclear plans, while often displaying traces of underlying Laminar and Bisected organizations, are characterized by a central space like a kitchen, living room, or courtyard around which the other spaces in the house orbit. This central space is often entirely enveloped by circulation space. The Wilkins from David Weekley closely approximates the Nuclear diagram in its pure form. In this plan, a central element—the main living room—is surrounded by a perfect ring of circulation to which all of the other spaces in the house are more or less directly attached. In another David Weekley home, The Crawford, the central space is the kitchen. It is again surrounded by a ring of circulation, but in this instance it opens only to the family room at the back of the house. The bedrooms, each in their own corner, orbit this space. KB Home's Plan One is similar, but the ring of circulation is incomplete, creating a kind of domestic cul-de-sac of bedrooms.

In Plan Three, also from KB Home, the circulation ring wraps around the kitchen and connects back through an open dining nook at the front of the house. This scheme further demonstrates the kind of blurring that occurs between and across plan types. It is in many ways a Bisected plan in which the central axis has been displaced by the nucleus of the kitchen.

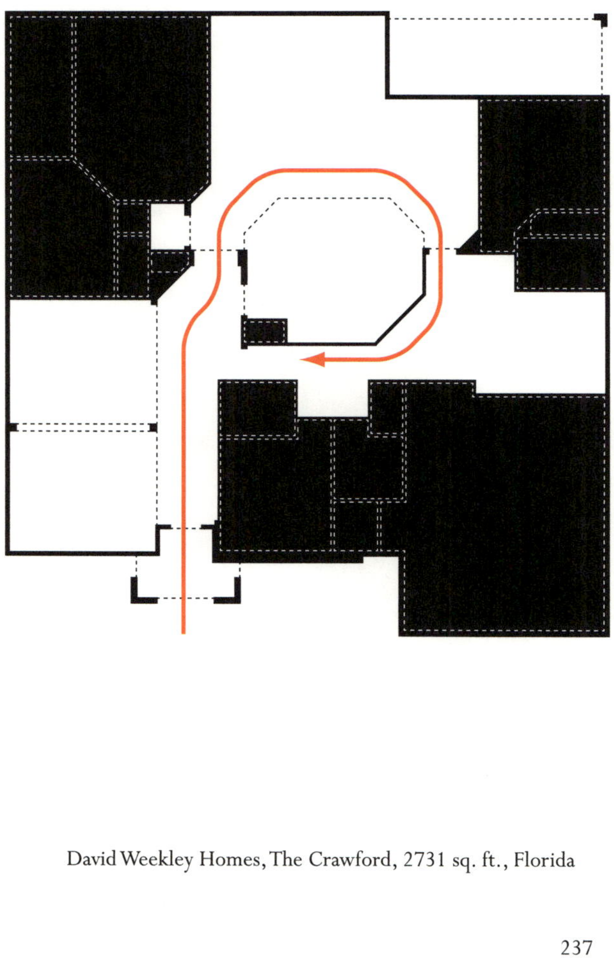

David Weekley Homes, The Crawford, 2731 sq. ft., Florida

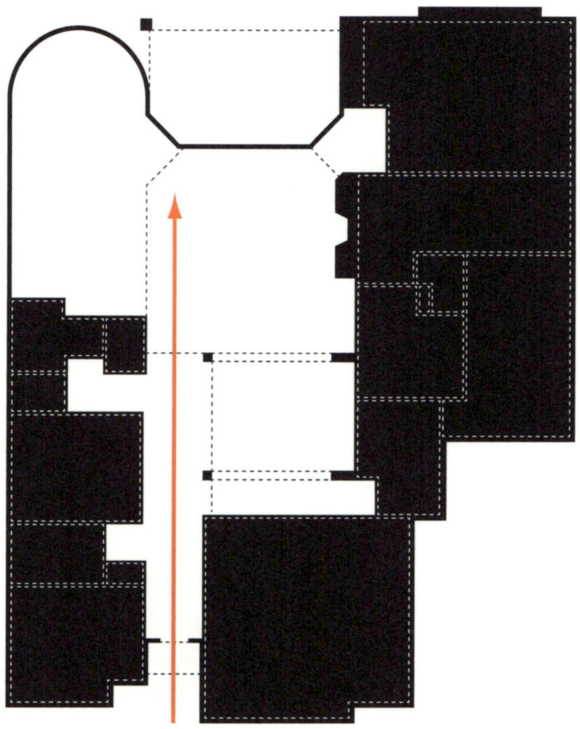

K. Hovnanian Homes, Benbrook III,4841 sq. ft., Texas

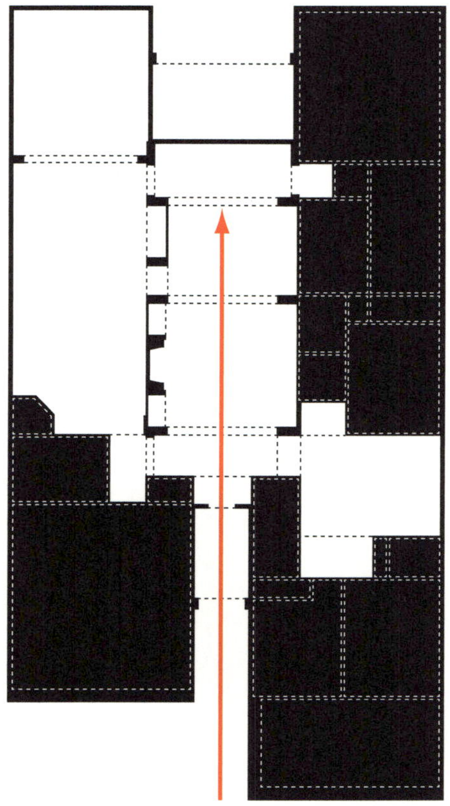

Meritage Homes, Ocotillo, 3039 sq. ft., Arizona

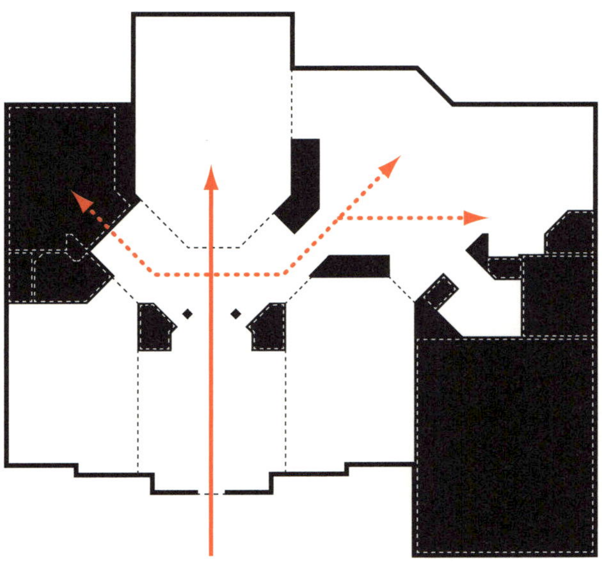

NV Homes, The Monticello, 4923 sq. ft., Virgina

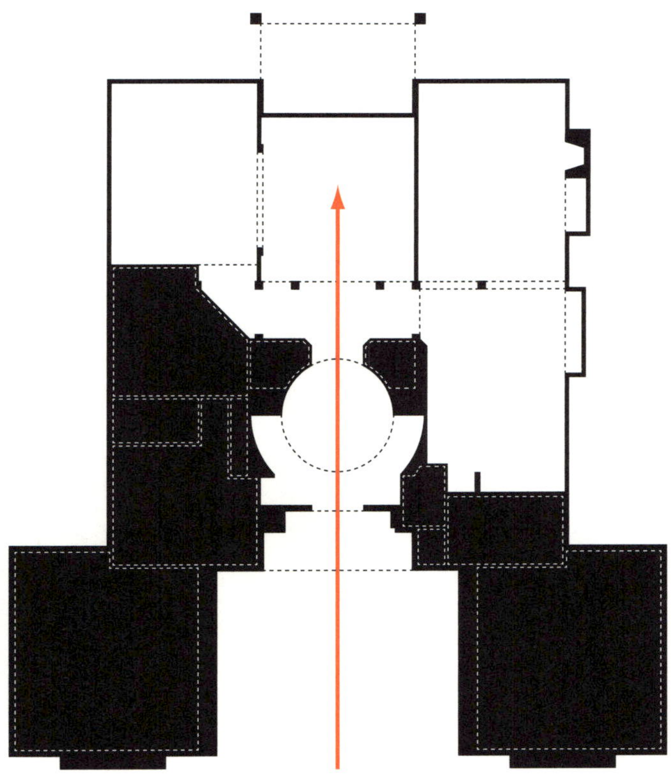

Toll Brothers, The Mirador, 5125 sq. ft., Arizona

Bisected Plans

In Bisected plans the axis through the entrance and a dominant central living space defines the main organizational structure of the house. The most classical of the six types, it frequently produces symmetrical or near-symmetrical arrangements. Often the Bisected plan uses symmetry and inflated proportions, both outside and in, to generate a feeling of luxury and wealth. Toll Brothers' The Mirador, with ambitions towards Palladian grandeur, uses two symmetrically arranged two-car garages to frame a grand formal entry.

Other versions of the Bisected plan, such as Meritage Homes' Octillo, lack the grand formal gestures of The Mirador while retaining the organizational principle of rooms and spaces split by a clear axial connection from the front entry to a rear public room. Often Laminar in their basic layout, these plans frequently have a relatively compact perimeter.

Single-story Bisected plans, like Maracay Homes' Plan 2042, sometimes employ a cross axis of major rooms to further subdivide the plan into distinct enclaves. Versions of the Bisected type, like K. Hovnanian's Benbrook III can appear nearly Cellular in their planning but are differentiated by the clear separation of a central space for circulation and gathering purposes.

Finally, Bisected plans can begin to express qualities of the sixth type, the Branching plan. The Monticello from NV Homes shows the clear central axis from front to back that characterizes the Bisected type, but because of its wide Laminar structure, a dedicated layer of circulation is added that branches off from the main axis to serve the house's other public spaces.

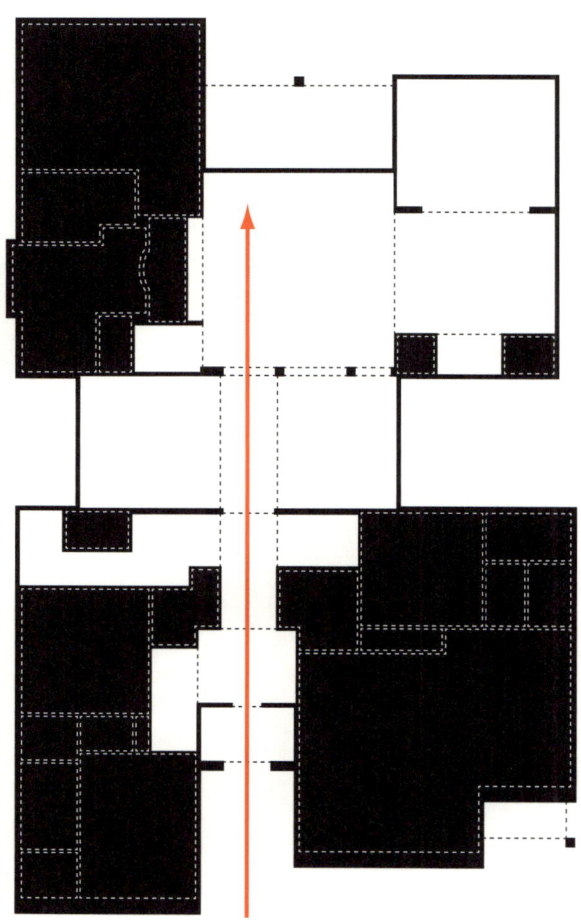

Maracay Homes, The Perugino, 4669 sq. ft., Arizona

0 20 ft.

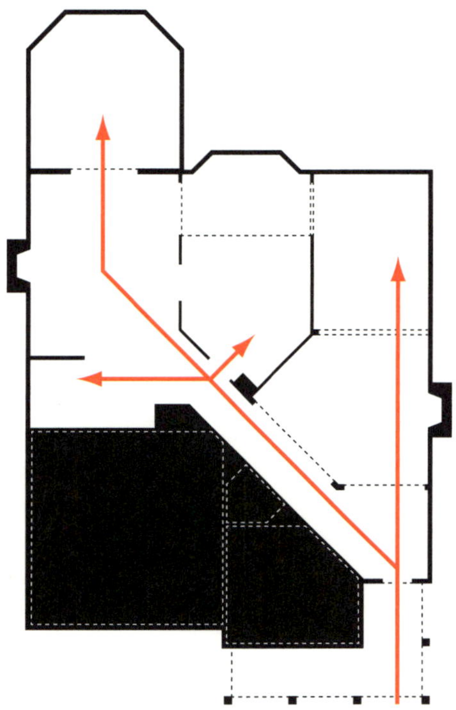

Beazer Homes, The Franklin, 3206 sq. ft., Maryland

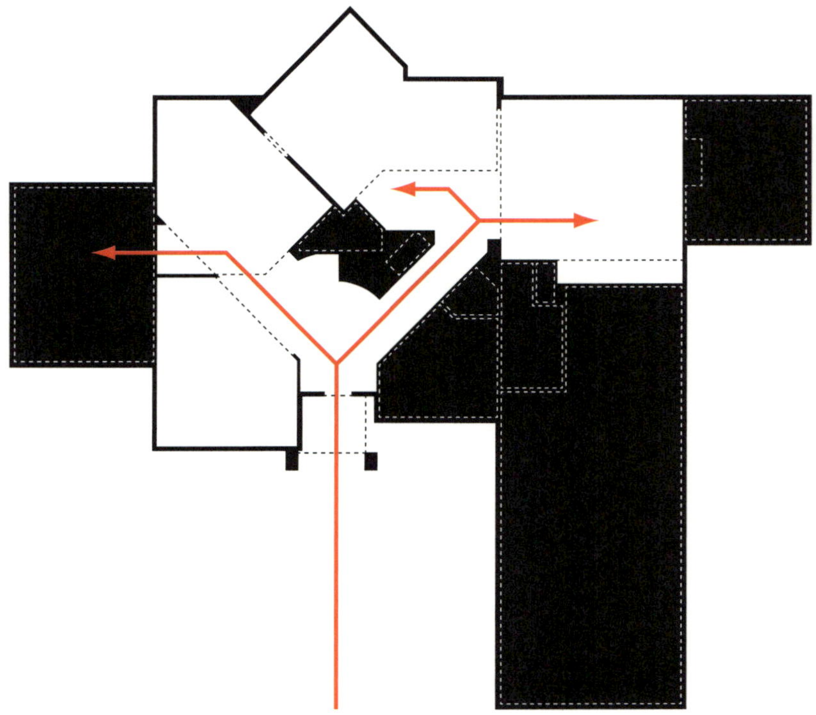

Toll Brothers, The Silverton, 4035 sq. ft., Colorado

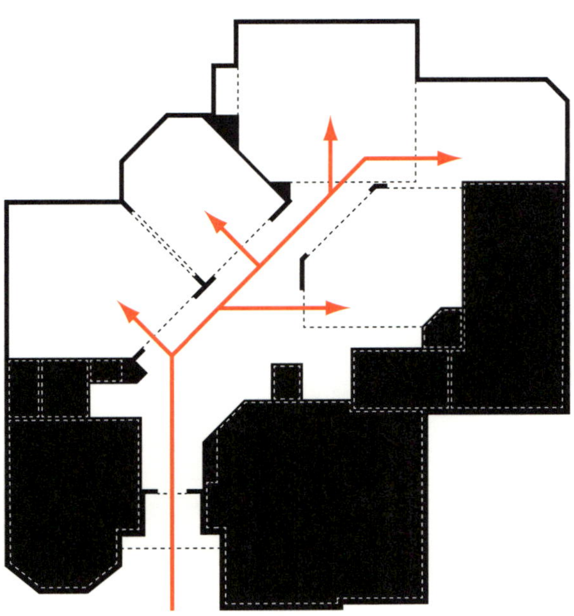

Centex Homes, Shenandoah, 3434 sq. ft., Georgia

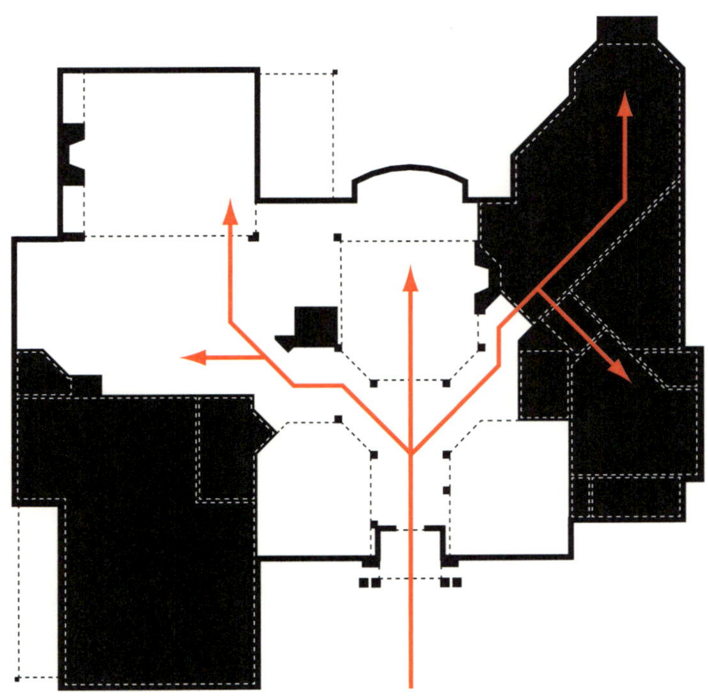

David Weekley Homes, The Lynnhaven, 4923 sq. ft., Texas

Branching Plans

All Branching plans share the distinguishing feature of a tree of branching circulation routes that originate at the entry to the house. This arrangement accentuates lines of sight and movement, which exaggerates perceived dimensions and dramatizes the relationships between spaces. In smaller, more compact houses, this effect is even more pronounced, as in Beazer Homes' The Franklin, where a diagonal path from the entrance at the front to the family room at the back creates a longer line of sight, amplifying the apparent scale of the house.

Branching plans often combine properties of the Bisected type—a dominant central entrance hall—with sprawling iterations of the Cellular or Laminar types, deploying diagonal lines of circulation to stitch the rooms of the house together as the plan grows deeper (Centex Homes' Shenandoah) or wider (Toll Brothers' The Silvertron).

The bifurcating, diagonal circulation routes in this type commonly produce highly figured plans, like David Weekley's The Lynnhaven, composed of distinctly shaped rooms with chamfered corners, projecting bays, and layered spatial sequences. The oblique paths often also result in rooms rotated against the regular, orthogonal geometry of the house as can be seen in The Silverton plan from Toll Brothers. These rotations and internal embellishments often result in figured and irregular building envelopes as can be seen in all of the plans shown here,

While most builders have plans based on this scheme, it is used to the greatest effect by David Weekley, the master of the Branching plan, whose complex, layered plans—such as The Lynnhaven and The Kramer—incorporate multiple forking paths, dissolved spatial boundaries, and contoured room profiles.

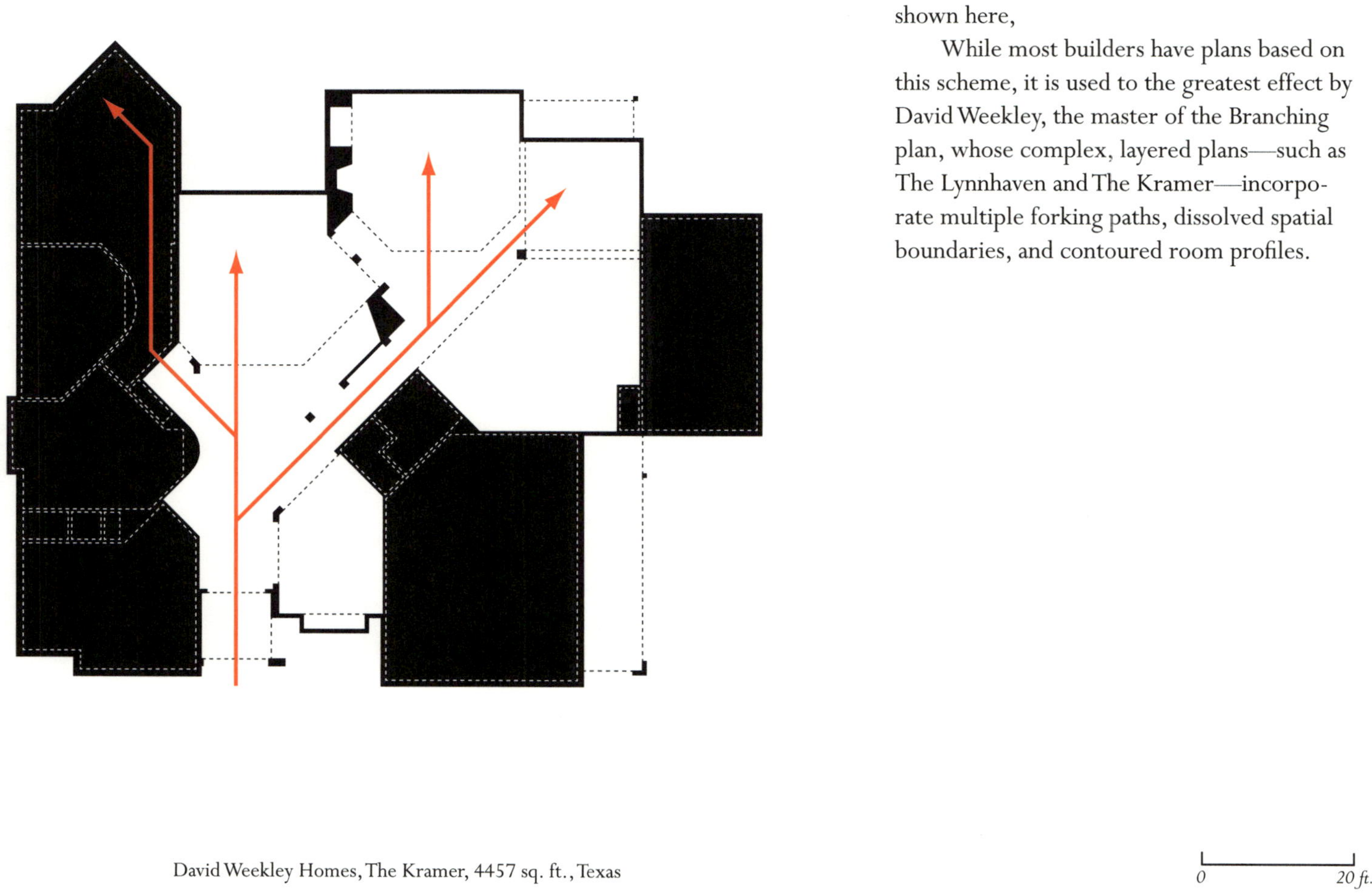

David Weekley Homes, The Kramer, 4457 sq. ft., Texas

The Architect
after *The Misanthrope*, 1568
Pieter Bruegel the Elder

Notes on Freedomland

Constituting opinions and remarks on the nature and context of the work

1 The notes hereto subjoined, contain sundry remarks upon the foregoing Designs; and as far as they go, and may happen to meet with the reader's approbation, they may be looked upon as so many architectural Maxims or Aphorisms: but previous thereto, I hope I shall stand excused, if by way of relaxation, from the dry exercise of measuring plans, I indulge in a few Miscellaneous observations and reflections, just as they happen to rise in my mind. The reader will, perhaps, now and then, be led a little from the point; but when that happens, it is hoped, the step or two he may take out of the main path, may lead him to some thing, not totally uninteresting, or unconnected with the matter in hand, although, perhaps, not always entirely original.[1]

2 He who borrows an idea . . . and so accommodates it to his own work, that it makes a part of it, with no seam or joining appearing, can hardly be charged with plagiarism. . . . But an artist should not be contented with this only; he should enter into a competition with his original, and endeavor to improve what he is appropriating to his own work. Such imitation is . . . a perpetual exercise of the mind, a continual invention.[2] Nothing can come of nothing; he who has laid up no materials can produce no combinations.[3]

3 Like the combination of sounds, which is capable of producing new music to infinity, design and invention in Architecture . . . are in little danger of being exhausted by the most acute and persevering genius that ever did, or ever will exist. Many treatises have contained nothing more than a different arrangement of the same materials, and the very best have still left an ample field for the unlimited excursions of taste and fancy.[4]

4 Over the length and breadth of this country are scattered cities and villages by thousands, and public and private edifices innumerable; and yet we may fairly say, there are the buildings, but where is the architecture? There is the matter, but where is the manner? There is the opportunity, but where is the agreeable result? . . . Why is there comparatively so little beauty in American buildings?[5]

5 In a country like this, where the printing-press accompanies each stride that is made into new localities, and where every step is marked by a building of some sort, it seems inconsistent that there should be but little popular literature on architectural matters; yet such is undoubtedly the fact, and although Americans are certainly diligent readers and energetic builders, their habit of reading has scarcely had so much influence for good on their habit of building.[6] Without recourse to a book of designs, the builder must in his own plans be necessarily tame and uniform, his edifices will be but a copy of each other, and that which he intended for an improvement, may, in reality, be a deformity.[7]

6 There is no discrimination in the present style of Architecture: every kind of Structure meets with similar treatment.[8]

7 It may not, perhaps, be quite improper to intimate, that the plans here offered to the public were taken up at a venture, from a large parcel of others of the same species.[9] In the[m] I have endeavoured to lay before the public a variety of [Designs] suitable to persons in genteel life . . . and applicable for size and expense to many situations on an extensive estate. The [Designs] are calculated for those persons whose liberal minds may lead them to accommodate their . . . dependents with dwellings, and at the same time to embellish their domains with a variety of picturesque buildings, which shall be both ornamental and useful.[10] As I have been particularly careful in compiling the designs, to render them very clear and intelligible to gentlemen and workmen, they cannot fail being found striking and useful, many of the designs being entirely out of the common style of building.[11]

8 [In] a speculative profession, if we restrict and fetter our conceptions by arbitrary rules, we block up the pleasing and attractive avenues to our improvement within the limits of the most narrow confines, and thereby check the efforts of genius, which can never produce masterpieces unless it is at liberty to indulge in the flights of imagination.[12] [Still] I have endeavored steadily to keep in view the fact that Homes are needed, and that the urgency of the want must not be met by the offering of whimsical and unreal fancies.[13]

9 The domestic architecture of a people should be the natural outgrowth of its character, institutions, customs, and habits, modified by the climate and scenery in the midst of which it is built up. . . . We should have a style, or perhaps several styles, peculiar to ourselves; and no doubt we shall have them in due time. . . . In the meantime, we must borrow and modify as best we may.[14]

10 Every Man's proper Mansion House and Home, being the Theater of his Hospitality, the Seate of Selfe-Frution, the Comfortablest part of his owne Life, the Noblest of his Sonnes Inheritance, a kinde of private Princedom; Nay, to the Possessors thereof, an Epitomie of the whole World: may well deserve by these attributes, according to the degree of the Master, to be decently and delightfully adorned.[15] It is necessary, above all things, to remember that houses are made to live in, and the convenience of their inmates is the first thing to be considered; after that, ornament may be added.[16] [For] in the habitations of Man it is proper and necessary to combine the *utile* with the *dulce*.[17]

11 If happiness is anywhere to be found, it is surely in a country house, agreeably sited, far from the cares of business, the tumult of the cities, and the vices of overpopulous communities. In such peaceable dwellings the sweetest repose may be enjoyed, and the joys of study savored without distraction; there, the delights of friendship are unconstrained; the soul is exalted by the magnificent spectacle of nature.[18] The love of a country life seems to be innate in the human breast: man seeks the large and populous city from necessity.[19] [But] in the country, the gentleman is at full liberty to do just as he pleases, and . . . the architect has a full scope to display his genius and talents. . . . No wonder then to find gentlemen whose employments and business lies in the city are so desirous of a villa, or country seat, a few miles out of town.[20]

12 Such is the superiority of rural occupations and pleasures, that commerce, large societies, or crowded cities, may be justly reckoned unnatural. . . . Large cities, from their very nature, are scenes of continual activity. . . . In the country, however, it is otherwise: there, a gentleman may live with his family upon his own estate, free from the intrusion, bustle, and discord, which prevail in public cities.[21] A city is a camp that has become stagnant and which grows by accretion. A city is a camp that has ceased to march, a community that has called a halt.[22] Such life is unnatural and injurious, simply because it is artificial. If, then, we would leave the city, not for fashion, but for prudence; if we would really recuperate our strength and energies, we must seek the repose of a genuine country home.[23]

13 A homestead . . . naturally suggests a place somewhat isolated and independent, rather than a residence on the street of a country town or village: it should be complete in itself, liberal in extent, and free from all intrusions—in fine, a little principality.[4] This [then] was the American Dream: a sanctuary on the earth for individual man: a condition in which he could be free not only of the old established closed-corporation hierarchies of arbitrary power which had oppressed him as a mass, but free of that mass into which the hierarchies of church and state had compressed and held him individually thralled and individually impotent.[25]

14 [But s]omething happened to the Dream.[25] [Consider] Happy Valley and the remarkable infelicity of its title. Generous as [Americans] are in the use of adjectives, this passe[s] into the domain of irony.[27] Our prevailing rural architecture is discordant in appearance; it may be added, that it is also uncouth, out of keeping with correct rules, and, ofttimes offensive

to the eye of any lover of rural harmony.[28] In this country, where . . . [w]e believe in the bettering influence of beautiful . . . country houses—in the improvement of human nature necessarily resulting to all classes, from the possession of lovely gardens and fruitful orchards[29] [t]oo many glaring instances of impropriety of situation are to be met with in the environs of the metropolis; [particularly] among regular Buildings near the suburbs.[30]

15 Upon the mere numerical preponderance of the suburban house in the domestic architecture of the United States there can be no manner of doubt. The majority of ordinary middle-class Americans live in suburban houses. . . . Every large American city is fringed with a larger or smaller stretch of two or three-story houses, built for the most part of wood upon lots of varying size, but alike in the fundamental fact of being individual and detached structures.[31] The lack of taste perceptible all over the country in small buildings is a decided bar to healthy, social enjoyments; it is a weakness that affects the whole bone and muscle of the body politic; . . . inexpensive grace ought habitually to be the distinctive marks of every habitation in which a free American dwells.[32]

16 American house-building of the last . . . years is out of joint.[33] The structures too many of us now inhabit . . . are inconvenient, absurd, and out of all harmony of purpose.[34] Almost every man, possessed of a competency, is naturally desirous of a residence in the Country, and in prosecuting a search for a suitable dwelling, often meets with a variety of disappointments.[35] It has been the fate of many . . . in a circumstance of this kind, to have been counteracted in their designs by ignorant and tasteless [speculators], and not unfrequently obliged to sacrifice their own sublimer conceptions to the bad taste, the prejudice, or the obstinacy of contemporaries, by which their design has been spoiled and disfigured, so as to exhibit the above derangements.[36]

17 The manufactured house is set in the midst of a manufactured environment. The quality of this environment calls for satire rather than description.[37] What real want can such a place ever fulfill? It is neither city nor country, nor can it ever supply the place of either.[38] [In regards to these] mean and sawed-off little fragments of the expansive surface of the earth, it is well to point out, however imperfectly, how detrimental . . . is this policy of stinginess in dealing out slices of land.[39] It was not fields and space that were thought of in the preparation of these miserable country homes . . . but a diminutive house, a diminutive garden of a few square yards, and in this isolation it was pretended that there had been found a safeguard for all domestic virtues![40]

18 The suburbs, take them how you will, are not Paradise and can never now be made so.[41] We formed the habit of using the land, not as a home, a permanent seat of culture, but as a means to something else—principally as a means to the temporary advantages of profitable speculation and exploitation.[42] When a modern town begins to sprawl its squalor or its suburban gentility out into the fields, what desecration of scenery follows! Most people feel this without realizing the cause very fully. But if we look for it, we shall find that modern suburbs specially offend in coming between the town and the country. . . . For between lie . . . acres of ill-assorted villas, each set in a scrap of so-called landscape garden.[43]

19 [This leaves] us with a heavy burden—not merely blasted and disorderly landscapes, but the habit of tolerating and producing blasted and disorderly landscapes.[44] The present scheme is petering out; it has run its tether. . . . Our America, in the form it held hitherto, is no more booked for continuance than are the other institutions of that prehistoric era before the [collapse]. The best thing we can say about our Constitution is that it provides the machinery for its own annulment. I suppose that Alexander Hamilton let loose more currents of greed . . . than any other man now inhabiting the kingdoms of the dead.[45]

20 Society is a false harmony—a gamut out of tune—from which men persist in drawing false and discordant sounds, when it is but putting the notes into order, and they will immediately form a series of harmonious and melodious tones.[46]

21 Man is not put in this world for himself alone. It is impossible for any one man to make himself happy or useful. His duty is to give to society, at least, an equivalent for what society has given him. . . . Ideas, talents, accomplishments, and skill are as much the product and the outcome of the community in which they have been fostered and obtained as the unearned increment from land is the outcome of the coming together of people in city life.[47]

22 Human society and the beauty of nature are meant to be enjoyed together. The two magnets must be made one. . . . The town is the symbol of society. . . . The country is the . . . source of all health, all wealth, all knowledge. But its fullness of joy and wisdom has not revealed itself to man. Nor can it ever, so long as this unholy, unnatural separation of society and nature endures. Town and country must be married, and out of this joyous union will spring a new hope, a new life, a new civilization.[48]

23 It is not good for either town or country to live alone. We may have all that is best in both, and steer clear of the bad points of each.[49] The garden-city experience . . . offers a striking contrast to lonely country life on the one hand, and crowded city life on the other, striking a happy medium in which the advantages of both are nicely blended and their drawbacks largely avoided.[50] [It is a] rural metropolis: a municipality of milk and honey. In this natural form of state, the farm articulates with the marketplace; so that countryman and townsman are not two separate classes, but the same man is both.[51]

24 The prospects of architecture are not divorced from the prospects of the community. If man is created, as the legends say, in the image of the gods, his buildings are done in the image of his own mind and institutions.[52] Architecture has always reflected the condition of the society in which it flourished, being great in times of organisation, and deteriorating in times of disintegration. Recently it has very clearly represented the inordinate desire for individual independence. Society is, however, now realising very fast that this independence is no end in itself, and is only good in that it sets free the individuals to form new relationships based on mutual association.[53]

25 The law of Association discovered by Fourier is a continuation of the Newtonian calculation upon Attraction—it is applying to the social world, the Newtonian theory upon the equilibrium of the Earth.[54]

26 Association is the Social Destiny of Man—is the true and natural system of Society . . . and will, when established upon earth, secure to him that happiness for which he has so long sought in vain.[55] An Association is an assemblage of persons . . . united voluntarily for the purpose of prosecuting with order and unity the various branches of Industry, Art and Science, in which they engage; and of directing their efforts, energies and talents in the best way for the Happiness and Elevation of the whole.[56]

27 In Association the building of the home ceases to be at the mercy of the ignorance and lack of means of the individual; for that which isolated resources cannot accomplish becomes possible when those resources are combined. Constructed with a view to unity of purpose and interests, the homes, like the people, approach each other, stand solidly together, and form a vast pile in which all the resources of the builder's art contribute to best answer the needs of families and individuals.[57]

28 Houses built in [groups] are not only attended with less expense in their erection than when detached, but[58] when judiciously grouped together in large masses, whether in clusters . . . or other dwellings of greater magnitude, contribute to exhibit the most striking and picturesque effects.[59]

29 If we wish to picture to ourselves in imagination an Association established and in operation, we must imagine spreading out before us a fine Domain,[60] . . . a square of land, on which shall be erected a large mansion,[61] . . . a palace which Fourier calls a Phalanstery, the home of all the associates. Poor and rich there enjoy commodious and salubrious lodgings, according to the means and tastes of each.[61] The [palace], rising in the midst of the finely cultivated fields and gardens of the Domain, would present a beautiful spectacle of architectural Unity, in comparison with which our present little and isolated constructions would appear most insignificant and discordant.[63]

30 This, then, is . . . what may be fairly termed A Magnificent Palace, containing within itself the advantages of A Metropolis, A University, and A Country Residence, without any of their disadvantages, and situated within A Beautiful Park . . . placing within the reach of its inhabitants . . . arrangements far superior to any now known, . . . [nor] yet possessed by the most favoured individuals in any age or country.[64] In these great palaces every family and every inmate is provided with the strictest privacy as well as the conveniences of association, and the dignity and magnificence of habitation which could be attained in large buildings only.[65] No palace of any King was ever so grand, so healthful, so convenient, and so elevating to the life and character of its occupants. The Mansion may be ornamented to any degree.[66]

31 When the earth shall be covered with Phalanxes, the poorest . . . will then enjoy eight hundred thousand palaces, much more agreeable than those of Paris or Rome.[67]

32 In this New World, the inhabitants will attain a state of existence, in which a spirit of charity and affection will pervade the whole human race; man will become . . . happy amidst a race of superior beings. The knowledge which he will thus acquire, of himself and of nature, will induce and enable him, through his self-interest, or desire for happiness, to form such superior external arrangements as will place him within a terrestrial paradise.[68] The numerous evils of the present densely crowded centers as well as the lonely country abodes would thus be entirely removed, so that the fullest benefits and conveniences of both city and country would then be right at the door of every Modern Paradiser.[69]

33 This motor, brought to a successful issue, is the key which will unlock the treasure house of the lower man, so that the New . . . may be a surety; not what the world calls a beautiful dream, but an actually materialized inspiration for man's unfoldment.[70]

34 [Such a] Model City will be a constant delight to its residents and visitors, and an example to the world for centuries to come, so that in time all the progressive and ambitious people in the world will be living in Model Cities, Towns and Villages, and the present cities and towns will be abandoned as useless and worthless.[71]

35 We want a little originality. What made the American republic so interesting to democratic European observers a century ago was its originality. Men moved forward on a new road.[72]

36 There's a certain American spirit about bigger, better, more.[73] Disregard what you may have heard about how hard times may usher in an era of restraint . . . [Americans] . . . always want bigger.[74] It should [also] always be remembered that there are two great principles at the bottom of our national character, which the apostle of taste in the most benighted, graceless village may safely count upon. One of these is the principle of imitation, which will never allow a Yankee to be outdone by his neighbors; and the other, the principle of progress, which will not allow him to stand still when he discovers that his neighbor has really made an improvement.[75] For Americans are the most quickly imitative people in the world; and when their imitativeness has a standard to copy, which makes an appeal to their sense of excellence, good effects follow with astonishing rapidity.[76]

37 Modellers of towns, creators of order in the countryside. They are responsible before the . . . future, for the direction of human enterprise. At the threshold of the house they install a vigilant guardian: the conditions of nature. On their coming, the revolution will be accomplished.[77]

38 Although I am for the Revolution in principle, I haven't done much about it lately in a practical way. So in order not to think about this distressing situation I thought about the palace. . . . The palace exists; we have only to get there—that is, walk hard enough. That is a beautiful idea of which I have always been very fond. The truth is that the palace does not exist but the serfs do.[78]

39 This book [then] is not the idle creation of an uncontrolled imagination, but the outcome of earnest, sober reflection, and of a profound scientific investigation . . . [into] the existing economic and social order.[79] Some will say I have overwrought the theme,[80] [and] it will perhaps be objected, "Thus have numberless reformers spoken and written, since the days of Sir Thomas More; and what has been proposed to mankind as a panacea for all suffering has always proved to be Utopian."[81] [But] I have not invented; I have recorded.[82] If, after reading my book, [the reader] should not have attained to the firm conviction that the realisation of this new order—apart, of course, from unimportant details—is absolutely inevitable, then I must be content to be placed in the same category as More, Fourier, Cabet, and the rest who have mistaken their desires for sober reality.[83]

40 Fiction is about creating foolishness and practical difficulties and allowing them to tangle and fester until they are beyond repair.[84]

1. Jose Mac Packe, A Bricklayer's Assistant (pseudonym of James Peacock), *OIKIΔIA, or, Nutshells: Being Ichnographic Distributions for Small Villas; Chiefly upon Œconomical Principles. In Seven Classes with Occasional Remarks.* London: C. Dilly 1785, pp. 51–52.
2. Joshua Reynolds, "A Discourse, Delivered … December 10, 1774," in *Seven Discourses Delivered to the Royal Academy by the President.* London: T. Cadell 1778, p. 236.
3. Joshua Reynolds, "A Discourse, Delivered … December 11, 1769," in *Seven Discourses Delivered to the Royal Academy by the President.* London: T. Cadell 1778, p. 36.
4. James Lewis, *Original Designs in Architecture: Consisting of Plans, Elevations, and Sections for Villas, Mansions, Town-Houses, &c.* London: Printed for the Author 1780, p. 1.
5. Calvert Vaux, *Village and Cottage Architecture. A Series of Designs Prepared for Execution in the United States.* New York: Harper & Brothers, Publishers 1867, pp. 25–26.
6. Ibid., p. 44.
7. S.H. Brooks, *Designs for Cottage and Villa Architecture; Containing Plans, Elevations, Sections, Perspective Views, and Details, for the Erection of Cottages and Villas.* London: Thomas Kelly 1839, pp. iii–iv.
8. James Malton, *An Essay on British Cottage Architecture: Being An Attempt to perpetuate on Principle, that peculiar mode of Building, which was originally the effect of Chance.* London: Hookham and Carpenter 1798, p. 10.
9. Mac Packe, *OIKIΔIA, or, Nutshells,* p. 4.
10. R. Lugar, *Architectural Sketches, for Cottages, Rural Dwellings, and Villas, in the Grecian, Gothic, and Fancy Styles, with Plans; Suitable to Persons of Genteel Life and Moderate Fortune.* London: J. Taylor, The Architectural Library 1815, p. 1.
11. John Crunden, *Convenient and Ornamental Architecture, Consisting of Original Designs, for Plans, Elevations, and Sections: Beginning with the Farm House, and Regularly ascending to the most grand and magnificent Villa; Calculated both for Town and Country, and to suit all Persons in every Station of Life.* London: J. Taylor, The Architectural Library 1797, pp. iii–iv.
12. Richard Elsam, *An Essay on Rural Architecture, Illustrated with Original and Œconomical Designs; Being an Attempt, also to Refute, By Analogy, the Principles of Mr. James Malton's Essay on "British Cottage Architecture," Supported by Several Designs: to which are Added, Rural Retreats and Villas, in the Gothic, Castle, Roman, and Grecian Styles of Architecture.* London: The Philanthropic Society 1803, p. 41.
13. Gervase Wheeler, *Homes for the People, in Suburb and Country; The Villa, The Mansion, and the Cottage, Adapted to American Climate and Wants.* New York: Geo. E. Woodward 1868, p. iv.
14. Daniel Harrison Jacques, *The House, a Manual of Rural Architecture, or, How to Build Country Houses and Out-buildings.* New York: Geo. E. Woodward 1866, pp. 25–26.
15. Henry Wotton, *The Elements of Architecture.* London: Printed for the Author 1624, p. 82.
16. Edward Shaw, *Rural Architecture: Consisting of Classic Dwelling, Doric Ionic, Corinthian and Gothic.* Boston: James B. Dow 1843, p. 63.
17. John Plaw, *Sketches for Country Houses, Villas, and Rural Dwellings; Calculated for Persons of Moderate Income, and for Comfortable Retirement.* London: J. Taylor, The Architectural Library 1800, p. 3.
18. Jean-Nicolas-Louis Durand, *Précis des leçons d'architecture données à l'École Royae Polytechnique,* 2 vols (Paris: the author, 1802–1805). English translation: *Précis of the Lectures on Architecture: with Graphic Portion of the Lectures on Architecture,* trans. by David Britt, with introduction by Antoine Picon, Los Angeles: The Getty Research Institute 2000, pp. 173–174.
19. Edmund Bartell, *Hints for Picturesque Improvements in Ornamented Cottages, and Their Scenery: Including Some Observations on the Labourer and His Cottage.* London: J. Taylor, Architectural Library 1804, p. vi.
20. Elsam, *An Essay on Rural Architecture,* p. 19.
21. John Claudius Loudon, *A Treatise on the Forming, Improving, and Managing of Country Residences … Vol. I.* London: Longman, Hurst, Rees, and Orme 1806, pp. 4–6.
22. Henry Ford, "The Modern City: A Pestiferous Growth," in *Ford Ideals: Being a selection from Mr. Ford's Page in the Dearborn Independent.* Dearborn, MI: The Dearborn Publishing Company 1922, p. 154.
23. Henry Holly, *Holly's Country Seats.* New York: D. Appleton and Company1863, p. 22.
24. Ibid., p. 23.
25. William Faulkner, "On Privacy: the American Dream: what happened to it," in *Harper's Magazine* July 1955, p. 34.
26. Ibid., p. 34.
27. Bret Harte, "Neighborhoods I Have Moved From," in *Mrs. Skagg's Husband and Other Sketches.* Boston: James R. Osgood and Company 1874, p. 254.
28. Lewis Allen, *Rural Architecture. Being a Complete Description of Farm Houses, Cottages and Out Buildings.* New York: C.M. Saxton 1863, p. 14.
29. A.J. Downing, "Moral Influence of Good Houses" (February 1848), in *Rural Essays.* New York : Leavitt and Allen 1854, p. 210.
30. W.F. Pocock, *Architectural Designs for Rustic Cottages, Picturesque Dwellings, Villas, &c.* London: J. Taylor, The Architectural Library 1807, p. 19.
31. "The Contemporary Suburban Residence," in *Architectural Record,* Vol XI no. 3. January 1902, p. 69.
32. Vaux, *Village and Cottage Architecture,* p. 48.
33. Allen, *Rural Architecture,* p. 20.
34. Ibid., p. 19.
35. Mac Packe, *OIKIΔIA, or, Nutshells,* p. 52.
36. Richard Brown, *Domestic Architecture: Containing a History of the Science, and the Principles of Designing Public Buildings, Private Dwelling-Houses, Country Mansions, and Suburban Villas.* London: George Virtue 1841, p. 81.
37. Lewis Mumford, *Sticks and Stones: a Study of American Architecture and Civilization.* New York: Boni and Liveright, Inc. 1924, p. 186.
38. H.A. Caparn, "Parallelogram Park—Suburban Life by the Square Mile," in *The Craftsman,* Volume 10, 1906, p. 770.
39. Ibid., p. 773.
40. M. Godin, "Stray Social Ideas," in *Social Solutions,* Translated by Marie Howland, New York: John W. Lovell Company 1886, p. 85.
41. J.E. Panton, *Suburban Residences and How to Circumvent Them.* London: Ward & Downey Limited 1896, pp. 1–2.
42. Mumford, *Sticks and Stones,* p. 202.
43. Raymond Unwin, "Building and Natural Beauty," in *The Art of Building a Home,* by Barry Parker and Raymond Unwin. London: Longmans, Green & Co. 1901, pp. 83–84.
44. Mumford, *Sticks and Stones,* p. 203.
45. Bouck White, *The Free City: A Book of Neighborhood.* New York: Moffat, Yard & Company 1919, p. 1.
46. Madame Gatti de Gamond, *The Phalanstery; or, Attractive Industry and Moral Harmony.* Translated by "An English Lady," London: Whittaker & Co. 1841, p. 8.
47. Albert K. Owen, *Pacific City Studies.* Boston 1892 (print produced for the author), pp. 16–17.
48. Ebenezer Howard, *Garden Cities of Tomorrow (Being the Second Edition of "To-morrow: A Peaceful Path to Real Reform").* London: Swan, Sonnenschein and Co., Ltd. 1902, pp. 17–18.
49. William Arthur, *Our Home City.* Omaha: Printed for the Author 1911, pp. 9–10.
50. William E. Smythe "Social Life of the Garden City," in *City Homes on Country Lanes: Philosophy and Practice of the Home-In-A-Garden.* New York: The MacMillan Company 1921, p. 171.
51. White, *The Free City,* pp. 24–25.
52. Mumford, *Sticks and Stones,* p. 187.
53. Raymond Unwin, "Co-operation in Building," in *The Art of Building a Home,* by Barry Parker and Raymond Unwin. London: Longmans, Green & Co. 1901, pp. 107–108.
54. Gatti de Gamond, *The Phalanstery,* p. 9.
55. Albert Brisbane, *Association; or, A Concise Exposition of the Practical Part of Fourier's Social Science.* New York: Greeley & McElrath 1843, p. 3.
56. Ibid., p. 3.
57. Godin, "Social Solutions," p. 49.
58. James Thomson, *Retreats: a Series of Designs, Consisting of Plans and Elevations for Cottages, Villas, and Ornamental Buildings.* London: J. Taylor, Architectural Library 1827, p. 10.
59. Elsam, *An Essay on Rural Architecture,* p. 3.
60. Brisbane, *Association,* p. 16.
61. Gatti de Gamond, *The Phalanstery,* p. 21.
62. M. Godin, "Fourier and Association," in *Social Solutions,* translated by Marie Howland. New York: John W. Lovell Company 1886, p. 50.
63. Brisbane, *Association,* p. 16.
64. Robert Owen, *A Development of the Principles and Plans on which to Establish Self-Supporting Home Colonies.* London: Home Colonization Society 1841, p. 40.
65. C. W. Wooldridge, *Perfecting the Earth: A Piece of Possible History.* Cleveland: Utopia Publishing Company 1902, p. 182.
66. Henry Olerich, *Modern Paradise: An Outline or Story of How Some of the Cultured People will Probably Live, Work and Organize in the Near Future.* Omaha: Equality Publishing Company 1915, p. 49.
67. Gatti de Gamond, *The Phalanstery,* pp. 27–28.
68. Robert Owen, *The Book of the New Moral World, Containing The Rational System of Society, Founded on Demonstrable Facts, Developing the Constitution and Laws of Human Nature and of Society.* London: Effingham Wilson 1836, pp. xiv–xx.
69. Olerich, *Modern Paradise,* p. 153.
70. Charles W. Caryl, *New Era: Presenting the Plans for The New Era Union To Help Develop and Utilize the Best Resources of this Country.* Denver 1897 (print produced for the author), p. 52.
71. Ibid., p. 118.
72. William Arthur, *A Well-Ordered Household or The Ideal City Containing Plans and Specifications for a Proposed Model City.* Omaha 1905 (print produced for the author), p. 6.
73. Kira McCarron, Toll Brothers' chief marketing officer, quoted in "Master Overbuilder" by Andrew Rice, in Portfolio.com, October 2008, http://www.portfolio.com/executives/features/2008/09/18 Toll-Brothers-Chief-on-Housing-Slump?print=true
74. Jeff Canarelli, V.P. for Sales, American West quoted in "Building Is Booming in a City of Empty Houses" by David Streitfeld, in *The New York Times,* May 15, 2010, http://www.nytimes.com/2010/05/16/business/16builder.html?_r=0
75. A.J. Downing, "On the Improvement of Country Villages," in *Rural Essays.* New York: Leavitt and Allen 1854, pp. 230–231.
76. "The Contemporary Suburban Residence," p. 80.
77. Le Corbusier and François De Pierrefeu, *The Home of Man.* London: The Architectural Press 1948, p. 132.
78. Donald Barthelme, "The Palace," in *The Teachings of Don B.,* New York: Vintage Books 1992, pp. 24–25.
79. Dr. Theodor Hertzka, *Freeland: A Social Anticipation,* translated by Arthur Ransom. London: Chatto and Windis 1891, p. 442.
80. White, *The Free City,* p. 314.
81. Hertzka, *Freeland,* p. 442.
82. White, *The Free City,* p. 314.
83. Hertzka, *Freeland,* p. 443.
84. Larissa MacFarquhar, "The Dead are Real," in *The New Yorker,* October 15, 2012, http://www.newyorker.com/magazine/2012/10/15/the-dead-are-real

An Afterword

by Albert Pope

Anthropologists claim that societies are reflected in the things they make, that objects function as irrefutable material evidence of both the outermost ambitions and the innermost fears of the cultures that produced them. According to this view, the way objects are constructed, and the manner in which they are interrelated and set upon the earth, encodes a legible social order—a way of being in the world—that can be read back as a comprehensive "material culture." This legibility holds for all artifacts of all cultures in all human settlements, regardless of whether those settlements take the form of a primitive village, a factory town, or an outpost of imperial Rome.

It follows that we, too, should be able to see ourselves writ large in the objects and environments that we produce today. We should literally see our own visage whenever we look at a shopping mall, a golf course, an office park, an airport, or a tract of mass housing. That we rarely do is unfortunate—as is the fact that, when we do turn the anthropological gaze upon ourselves, we rarely think of the urbanism that has grown like weeds over the last five decades. Instead, what we routinely choose to recognize and regard as "the city" is the city that our ancestors built prior to the Second World War: the pre-modern grids of anthropomorphically scaled blocks and streets that make up our urban cores. When we think of the city, we think of Manhattan or Brooklyn—slightly remodeled to be sure, but not enough to ruin the illusion that the nineteenth-century city is our own.

The upshot of this misrecognition is that we designate everything we have built in the past half-century as "sub"-urban—as a literal subclass of what we deem to be actually and properly urban—and calm ourselves by retreating into the cities of the past and repeating an essentialist mantra: "once a city, always a city, from antiquity to the present day." Through a feat of synchronic thinking, we seek to put the city outside of or beyond history (especially recent history), and to regard urbanism as an affair of streets and blocks regardless of who built it, or when or why it was built.

Meanwhile, our actual urban production—our "sub"-urbanism—grows in greater and greater proportion to the ancestral urbanism to which we cling until all that we regard as legitimate is just a tiny fraction of the urban world. And this fraction is gentrifying so fast that soon all that will remain of urban debate are the manners of the privileged few and the tourists who come to ogle them. Projects like the High Line in Manhattan and the boutique towers it gives rise to cannot be classified as urban innovation; rather, they are analogous to the installation of a new plasma screen in your grandparents' living room. Our values are not reflected in the outmoded urban environments of the nineteenth century, but in the material culture that we ourselves have produced in the twentieth and twenty-first.

Our continuing fetishization of traditional urbanism impedes any real and progressive reforms, limiting our urban ambitions to street furniture, stoplights, bike lanes, and boutique towers. To address our most pressing urban problems—rampant gentrification, ruinous carbon pollution, acute housing shortages, absurd commuting times—requires that we look in good faith at the urbanism that we actually make. To state the obvious, the problem is not simply in our "sub"-urbanism itself; the problem is in our failure to acknowledge and embrace it as a function of our own worldview. Absent this understanding, we remain helpless in the face of problems we cannot even recognize, let alone solve.

Our urban forms, and the lifeworld they create, are always tied to the economic order that produced them. The global consumer economy that emerged following the Second World War is unique in the history of the world, bearing little relation to economies that preceded it. This Great Acceleration, as it is referred to in economic and environmental circles, underwrote an entirely new mode of urbanization largely antithetical to its predecessors—a mode characterized by a shift from a continuous grid-based urbanism (whose unit of aggregation is the city block) to a discontinuous spine-based "sub"-urbanism (whose unit of aggregation is the subdivision, the office park, and the commercial mall) that by now accounts for roughly 75% of the built environment.

Over the years our attempts to reconcile the workings of our economy with a desirable, or even survivable, urban form have proven inadequate. They are crumbling today under the weight of scientific evidence we can no longer afford to ignore or deny. We are extracting resources and emitting toxic by-products at rates that are calamitous and that if left unchecked will change the planet beyond all recognition in mere decades. It should be clear by now that the ruinous material culture that we have produced over the past half-century cannot take us into the future.

The clusterfuck that falls under the rubric of climate change bears witness to the pressing need to experiment with the production of urban superstructures—a contemporary material culture—that are tied to the fates of the Great Acceleration and capable of prioritizing human existence. To return to the anthropological gaze, our identity, such as it exists, is manifest in the objects produced in the service of a mass consumer economy and integrated into a landscape routinely referred to as "sub"-urban "sprawl." These objects, and the world they create, constitute—because they concretize, in form and space, our own social and environmental relationships, not those of our grandparents—a legitimate point of departure for the production of a reformed material culture.

In this regard, we cannot continue to approach urbanism as a matter of window dressing, of sprucing up antiquated urban models that are so remote from the economic and environmental realities of the present as to be comical. We must instead develop models that are capable of redirecting a consumer economy that has run off the rails, an economy whose scale and complexity cannot be shoved into either a rural or urban nineteenth-century template.

But how do we tame this beast? Surely not with a righteous nostalgia for urban settings based on economic systems that bear no resemblance to our own. Which, finally, brings me to the subject of Keith Krumwiede's Freedomland.

Freedomland sounds like the kind of name a right-wing zealot would give to a nativist-inspired New Town built in the imaginary heart of (red state) America. In fact, just such a zealot, talk radio personality Glenn Beck, did precisely this in 2013 with a New Urbanist development that he called "Independence USA." Like all New Urbanist proposals, it employs a nostalgia for Brooklyn filtered through the equally nostalgic ideals of the English Garden City movement. In the Garden City, the agricultural village became the model, if not the very ideal, of urban industrial reform. Despite the passage of more than a century, it remarkably remains the predominant model of urban development in North America and, even more remarkably, is the envy of the world. And while it does directly reflect our own social and environmental values—a high level of social individuation combined with a direct relation to idealized natural settings—it is a model that, in its inefficiencies and wastefulness, has zero chance of taking us through what is shaping up to be a perilous century.

Attempts to reroute the Great Acceleration by referencing an agrarian economy seem absurd at face value. But not too long ago the idea of emulating small-scale, agrarian settlements was not as far-fetched as it now seems. Regionalism, that great grail of twentieth-century urbanism, was intended to provide a modernist bridge back to the rural world. The dreams of Lewis Mumford, Frank Lloyd Wright, and Ludwig Hilberseimer were grounded, after a fashion, in the economic substructure of the time. Anticipating the coming of the Great Acceleration and correctly recognizing the ability for capital to decentralize and disperse into the landscape, the regional ideal was quickly overrun by the reality of the new consumer economy. The dream of the "Fourth Migration"—a balanced distribution of the metropolitan populations across a bountiful continental expanse—was brutally translated into endless tracts of mass housing. The regional ideal has long since died in the midst of corporate monocultures, feedlots the size of large cities, atavistic red state politics, and an enormous cloud of methamphetamine smoke. Still, in spite of its abject failure, regionalism remains of great value as one of the first attempts to articulate a modern, environmentally based urban culture.

While the regional ideal and the Garden City were pressed into the service of giving form to the new, postwar economic order over the latter half of the past century, more recently the references have shifted increasingly towards the urban—to Barcelona and Brooklyn—as a preference for gardens has come to be challenged by a preference for streets. In the end, it doesn't matter; neither the garden nor the street has been able to produce a viable urbanism capable of harnessing the forces of the Great Acceleration.

In that context, Freedomland arrives on the scene with the intention of turning the anthropological gaze back upon ourselves. Offering an extravagant, sardonic reflection upon the "sub"-urbanism that we have long disdained but continue to construct, Freedomland attempts to open our eyes to the urban production by which we are defined. It reminds us of the crucial relationship that binds an economic structure to a material culture, engaging as it does the suburban development that we have been producing for more than half a century.

Turning the anthropological gaze upon ourselves is tricky; it must be done with skill, with humor, and with compassion, all combined with an explicit critical agenda. Freedomland reminds us that a Smallville, USA and a walkable Brooklyn are both outmoded, last-century paradigms that were built upon modes of economic production remote from those of the Great Acceleration. Beautiful as they once were, today they constitute distractions from the work at hand. Freedomland avoids these distractions, forcing us to look directly at the sites of contemporary urban construction as the point of departure for our badly needed urban reforms.

Yet Freedomland also reminds us that, in their failure, the deployment of the agrarian village and gridiron city constitute progress, in that their basic ideals endure despite the monstrous compromises they undergo in the process of being realized. Through their concrete expression, we learn that a subdivision is not a "town," or that while you can try to make a copy of Brooklyn in the middle of an exurban parking lot, it will lose everything that made it desirable in the first place. But such failures do not mean that the references, however diminished, are without value. We still recall the importance of Brooklyn's social fabric and Smallville's intimate connections to the natural world.

In drawing its vocabulary from the grotesquerie of contemporary mass housing tracts, Freedomland more than mimics the status quo: It reveals our urban values with new and even unforeseen clarity. It exposes values that require our cities to provide a high degree of individual autonomy aided by rapid mobility. It demonstrates that this mobility must provide direct connections, not only within the urban environment but also to the openness and space of refined natural settings, and further, that we are no longer satisfied to just visit such settings; we should be able to live in their midst. And while all of these social and environmental interactions have been delivered cheaply by the urbanism of global consumerism for over fifty years, their appearance in Freedomland reveals them, once again, as a point of departure for serious urban reforms.

Freedomland does this with a beautiful allusion to a nearly forgotten chapter of modern urban history. Departing from the world as we find it, Freedomland deviates from the specific patterns of suburban aggregation that provide its inspiration. At the heart of the book are the so-called housing estates, for which there are 128 plan drawings, made up of thirty-two typical, true-to-life developer plans that are filtered through six organizational types. According to Krumwiede, these estates range in scale and configuration from "villages to villas." While the detached dwellings of Smallville provide the unit of aggregation, the patterns of aggregation are radically altered. In fact, to my mind, there are no villages in Freedomland, only villas of varying degrees of compaction. And just as villages have been historically mediated by the Garden City movement, villas have been mediated by what is historically known as the "phalanstery"—a radical experiment in communal organization invented by Charles Fourier in the early nineteenth century. It is in this deviation that Freedomland does the work of excavating our latent ideals. Lurking beneath the compromises of our mass housing tracts, Freedomland locates an enduring collective ideal that is directly tied to the logic of the Jeffersonian vision. In delivering this vision, Freedomland invents "Another America," a thought experiment where we are asked to imagine what the city would look like today if the collective spirit of Charles Fourier's phalanstery had won out over Ebenezer Howard's "town."

The small American town is as much a figment of Sarah Palin's imagination as Brooklyn is a figment of Lena Dunham's imagination. While both make for great entertainment, neither will provide the substance through which we can take on the destructive economic practices that drive suburban production today. We were once, even recently, proud of the cities we made, so proud that we fled the sclerotic corpse of our ancestors' urbanism, which we now so exclusively celebrate, for planned communities, anchored by malls and awash in nature. Rather than disparage the choices made by the vast majority of the population, "we" must, above all, recover some measure of faith in our own urban production. We must finally and fully turn our backs on Smallville and Brooklyn in order to face the challenges of the Great Acceleration. In order to be effective in this mission, we must get beyond our beautiful yet futile upgrades to an urban system that carries way too much legacy code.

The power of Freedomland stems directly from the fact that we routinely fail to see ourselves in the cities that we make. The more reluctant we are to embrace our own urban production, the more disturbing (and more moving) Freedomland becomes. By sleight of hand, Krumwiede tweaks the conventions of our own Arcadian idyll to reveal what Megalopolis really is, and has been for a half-century: mass housing. Throwing the entire absurdity of our so-called "way of life" back into our faces makes Freedomland—no less a polemical statement than No-Stop City—the most highly charged political document to come from within the discipline since the late 1960s. For by now, contemporary urbanism is so long collapsed under the weight of its own contradictions, the only response is the absurd.

Any path to meaningful urban reform, driven either by class inequity, environmental decline, or simply a reaffirmation of our "right to the city," will remain ineffectual if it is predicated on outmoded urban traditions. Instead, reform must issue from the underlying logic of our economic system and the urban values that, to date, it ineptly materializes. These latent values—represented in the very substance of Freedomland—are the key to tempering the economic maelstrom that has brought us to this moment. Before any reconstruction can take hold in the present, a detour through Freedomland is necessary.

While the present may seem so little to work with, it contains enough: a "shadow of the future" in the sense articulated by Henri Lefebvre four decades ago. As a final word on Freedomland, I would like to quote the passage in full:

> *The city historically constructed is no longer lived and is no longer understood practically. It is only an object of cultural consumption for tourists, for aestheticism, avid for spectacles and the picturesque. Even for those who seek to understand it with warmth, it is gone. Yet, the urban remains in a state of dispersed and alienated actuality, as kernel and virtuality. What the eyes and analysis perceive on the ground can at best pass for the shadow of the future object in the light of a rising sun. It is impossible to envisage the reconstitution of the old city, only the construction of a new one on new foundations, on another scale and in other conditions, in another society. The prescription is: there cannot be a going back (towards the traditional city), nor a headlong flight, towards a colossal and shapeless agglomeration. In other words, for what concerns the city the object of science is not given. The past, the present, the possible cannot be separated.*
>
> —Henri Lefebvre, *Writings on Cities,* page 148, 1968.

New Homes for America

A very short architectural story

Working feverishly through the night on her new assignment, the architect shuffled through The Company's catalog of home plans, searching for the perfect profiles, the right balance of expression and order, internal embellishment and external massing. Huddled over the machine, she made copy after copy, mirroring the plans as she went, clipping away a bit here or a chunk there, and then matching it to its inverted neighbor. She was on a deadline. Her employer wanted something new, something bigger and better—for all those empty nesters whose grown children with children were returning, all those new, expanded families—but not something too new. "Work with what we have," they told her. "We know how to build these things."

She remembered laughing derisively under her breath when the HR rep, reading aloud from the latest sales brochure, described LifeDesign^{SM} to the new recruits: "Remember, you're not just designing houses, you're designing lives. Because as the boss says, 'LifeDesign^{SM} blends the fundamentals of design, architecture, engineering, physics, psychology, and sociology to create a home that looks better—and lives better—than all the rest.'" At the time it sounded absolutely absurd, but now, she got it. And now, as her houses grew ever longer and more elaborate, she laughed aloud with uncontrollable glee as she imagined the fantastic new lives that would unfold along their length.

As day broke, she stood up and stepped back from the table, exhausted. She surveyed her creations, and she was happy. Then it struck her: Her houses needed names. The Company always named their plans. And they always used names that, through association, lent an air of sophistication or gravitas to their products. There were the plans named after Italian cities—The Vicenza, The Roma, The Pisa, The Milano—or famous artists (or architects)—The Picasso, The Renoir, The Van Gogh, The Palladio—or the Founding Fathers—The Washington, The Hamilton, The Franklin, The Jefferson. The names rarely had anything to do with the actual design—though occasionally a design resembling Mount Vernon might be called The Mount Vernon.

She realized that she wanted her houses to have names that were meaningful, names with history, names that spoke to her wild aspirations for the lives of those who would eat and drink, and laugh and cry, and love and hate in them. Then it came to her.

At the design meeting later that morning, she presented the fruits of her labor: The Buckingham, The Ledoux, The Fourier, and The Owen. She could tell by the look on her boss' face that she wasn't going to be around much longer.

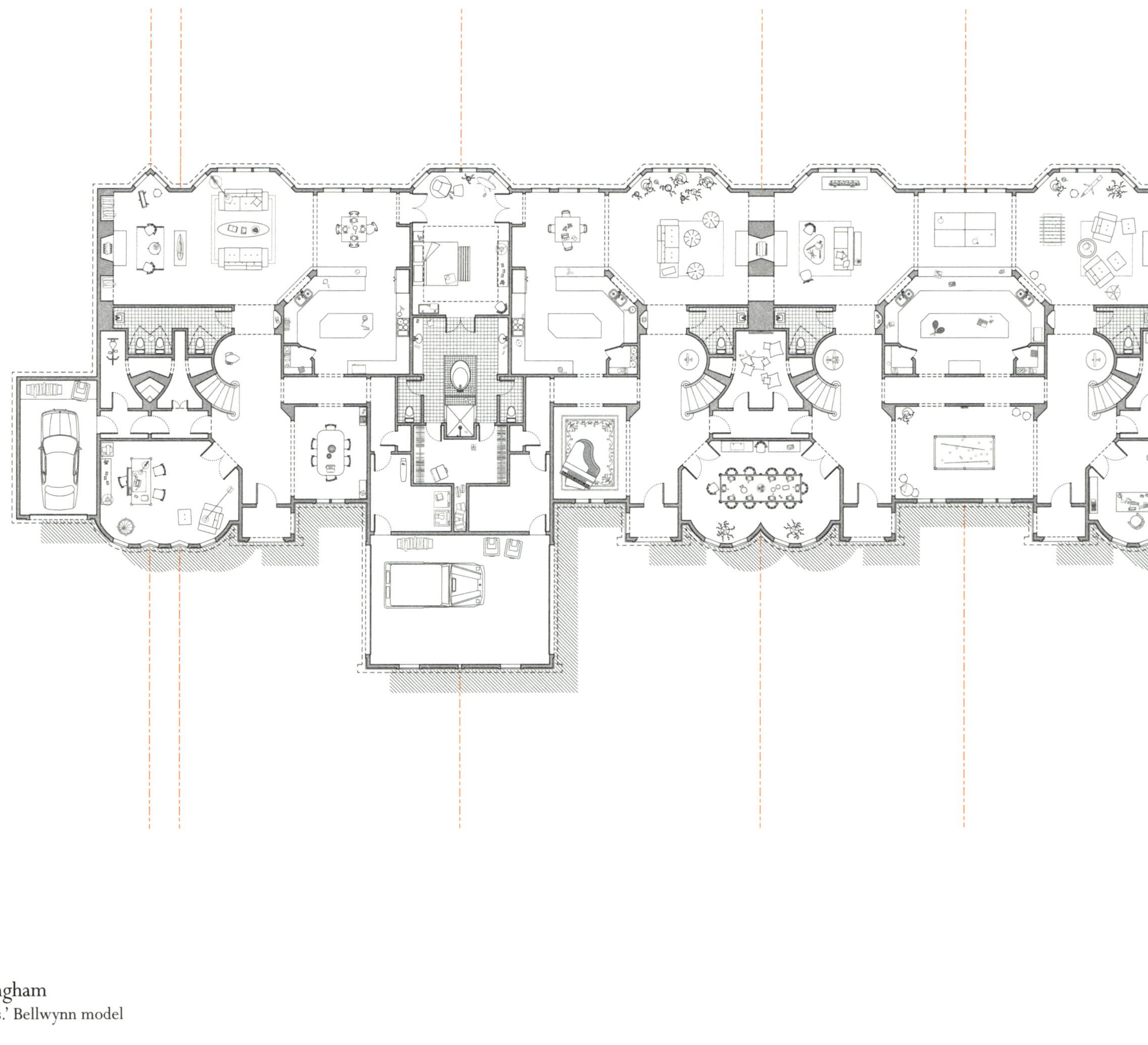

The Buckingham
after Toll Bros.' Bellwynn model

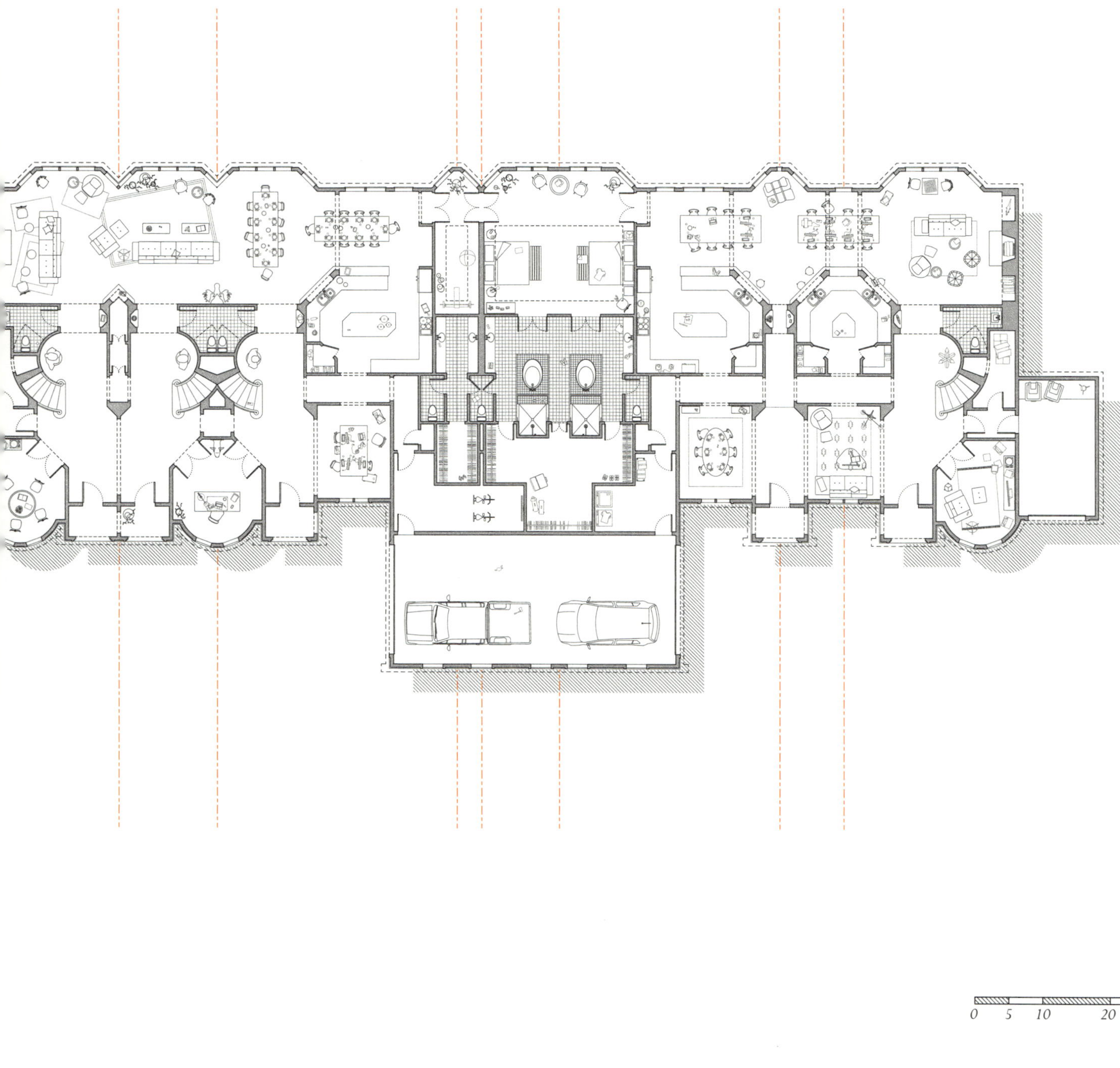

0 5 10 20 40 ft.

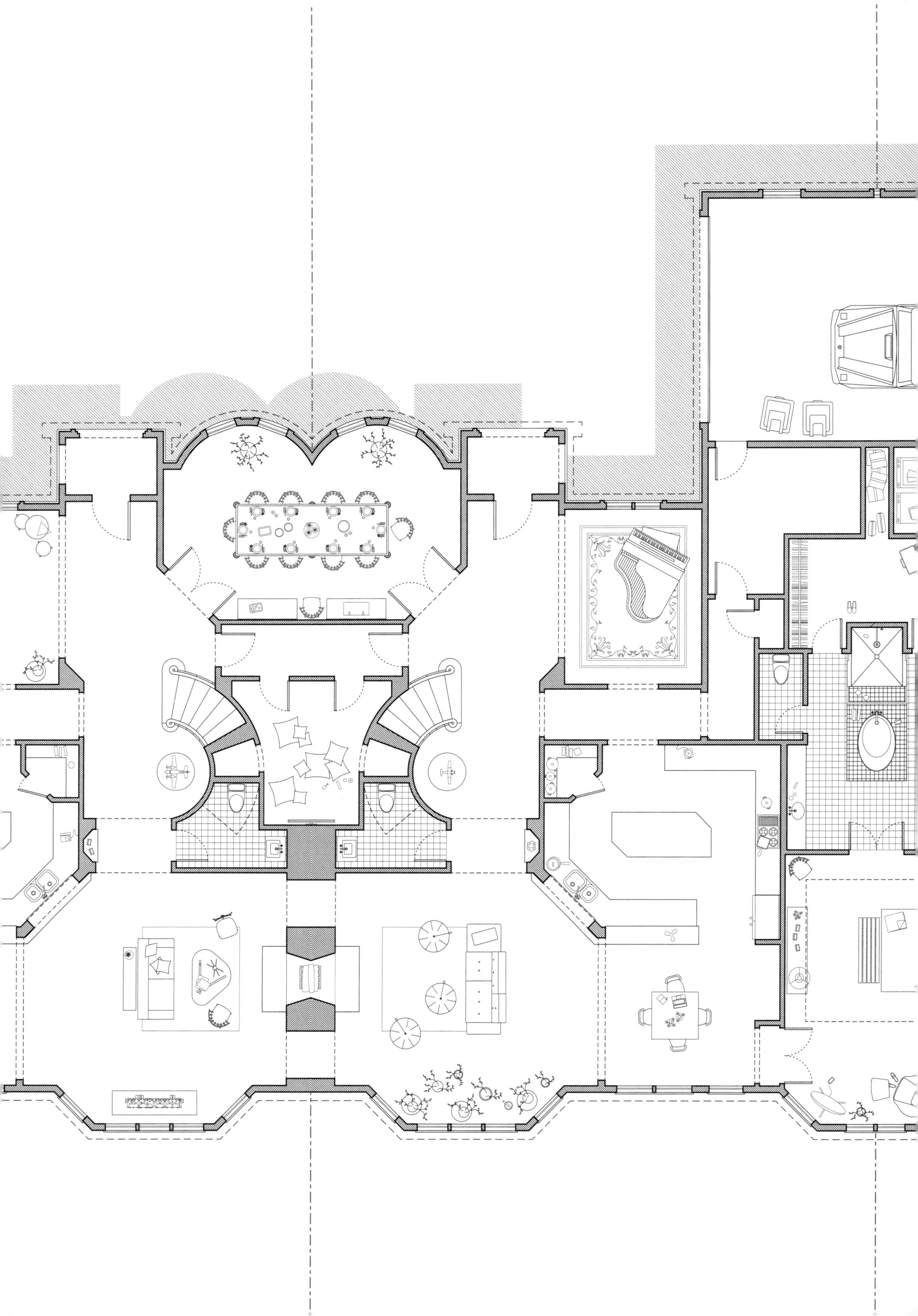

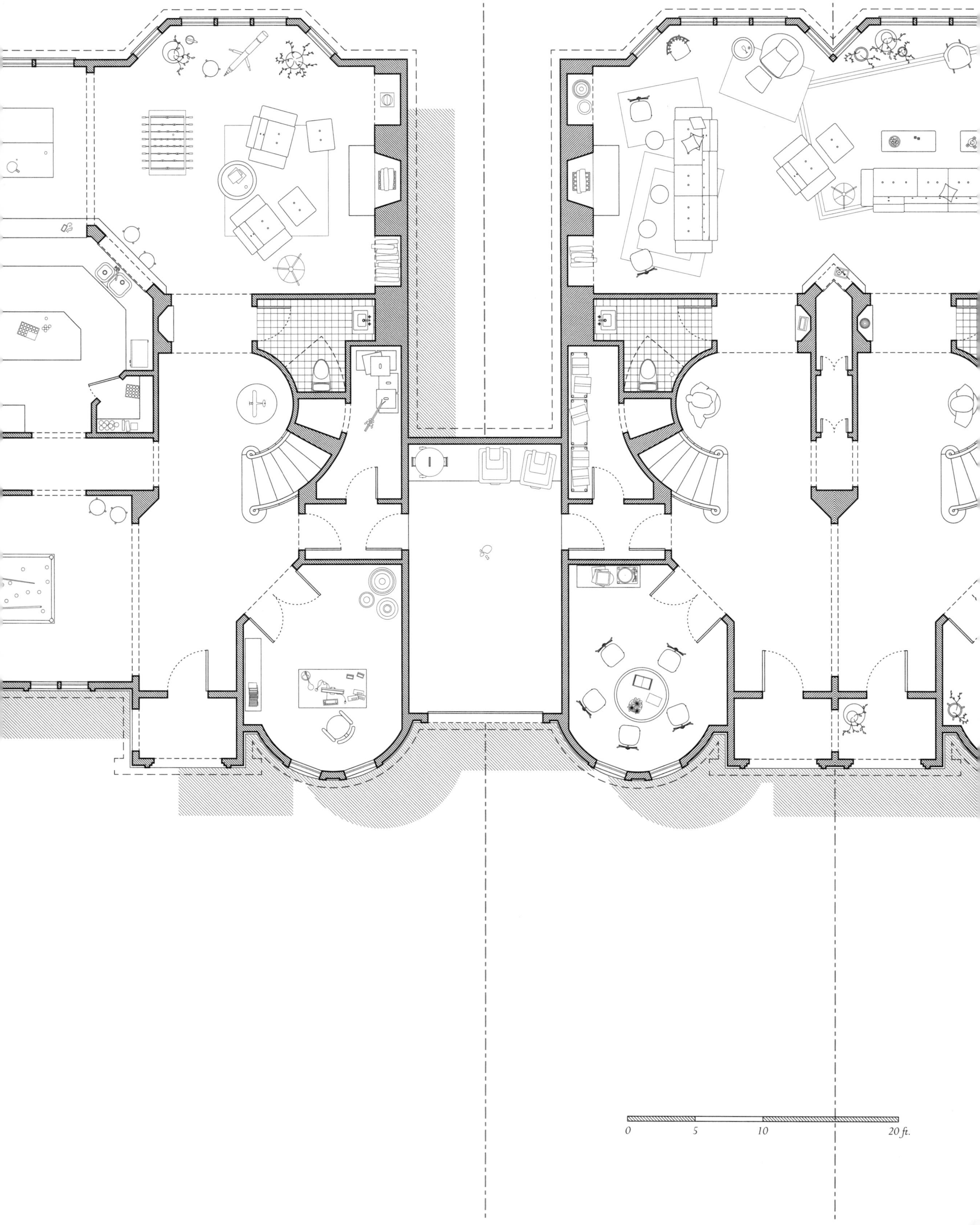
0
5
10
20 ft.

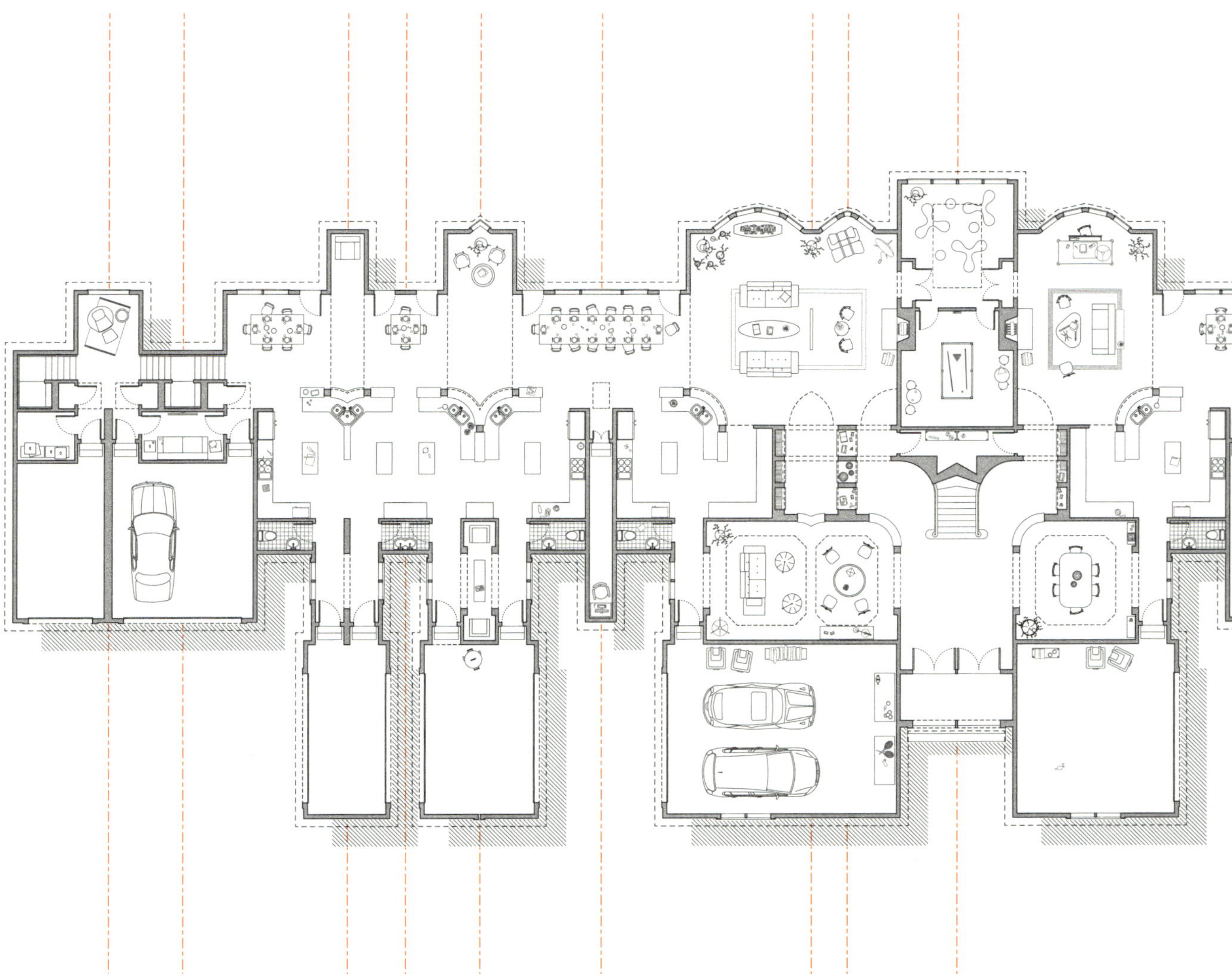

The Ledoux
after Toll Bros.' Magnolia model

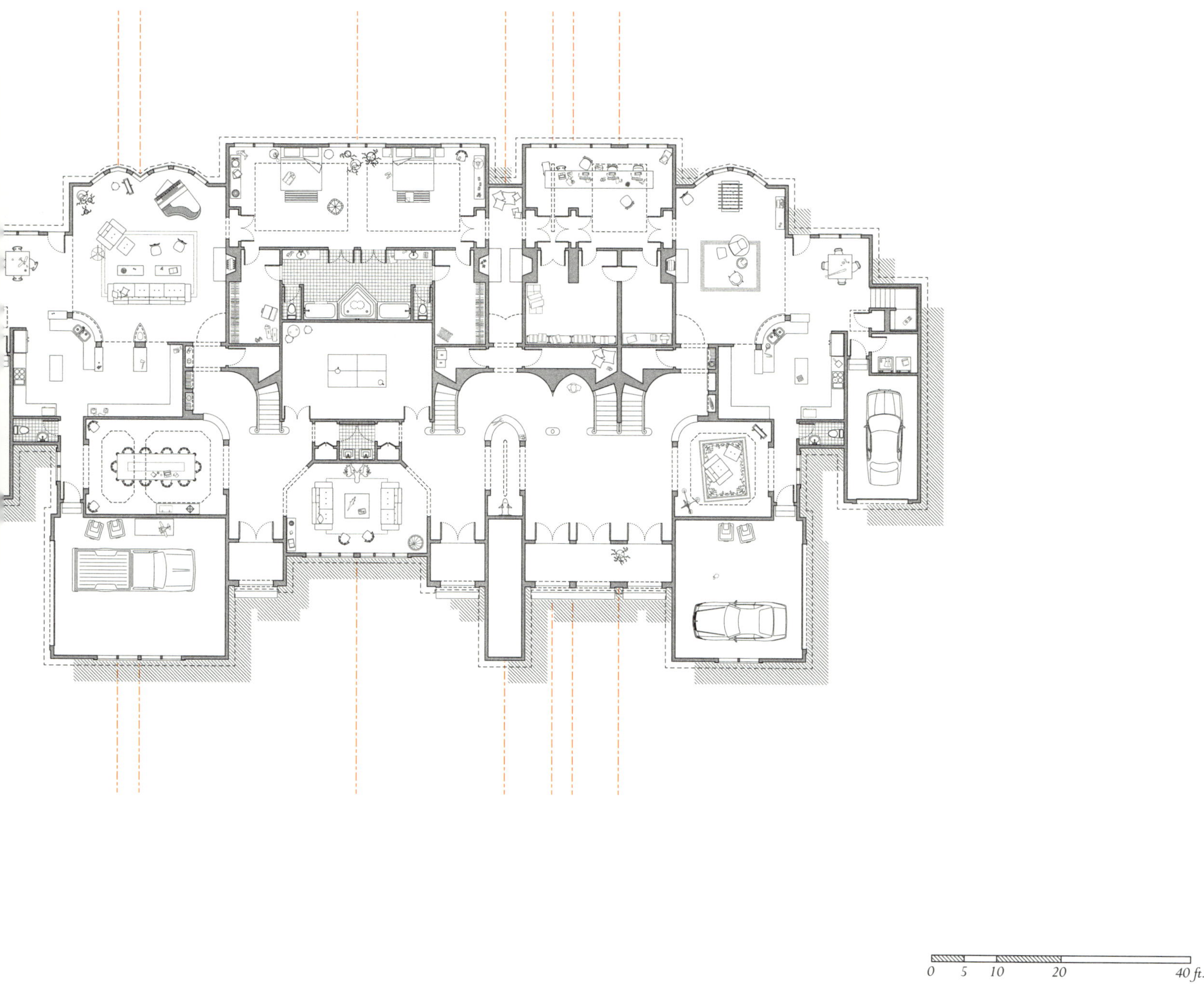
0 5 10 20 40 ft.

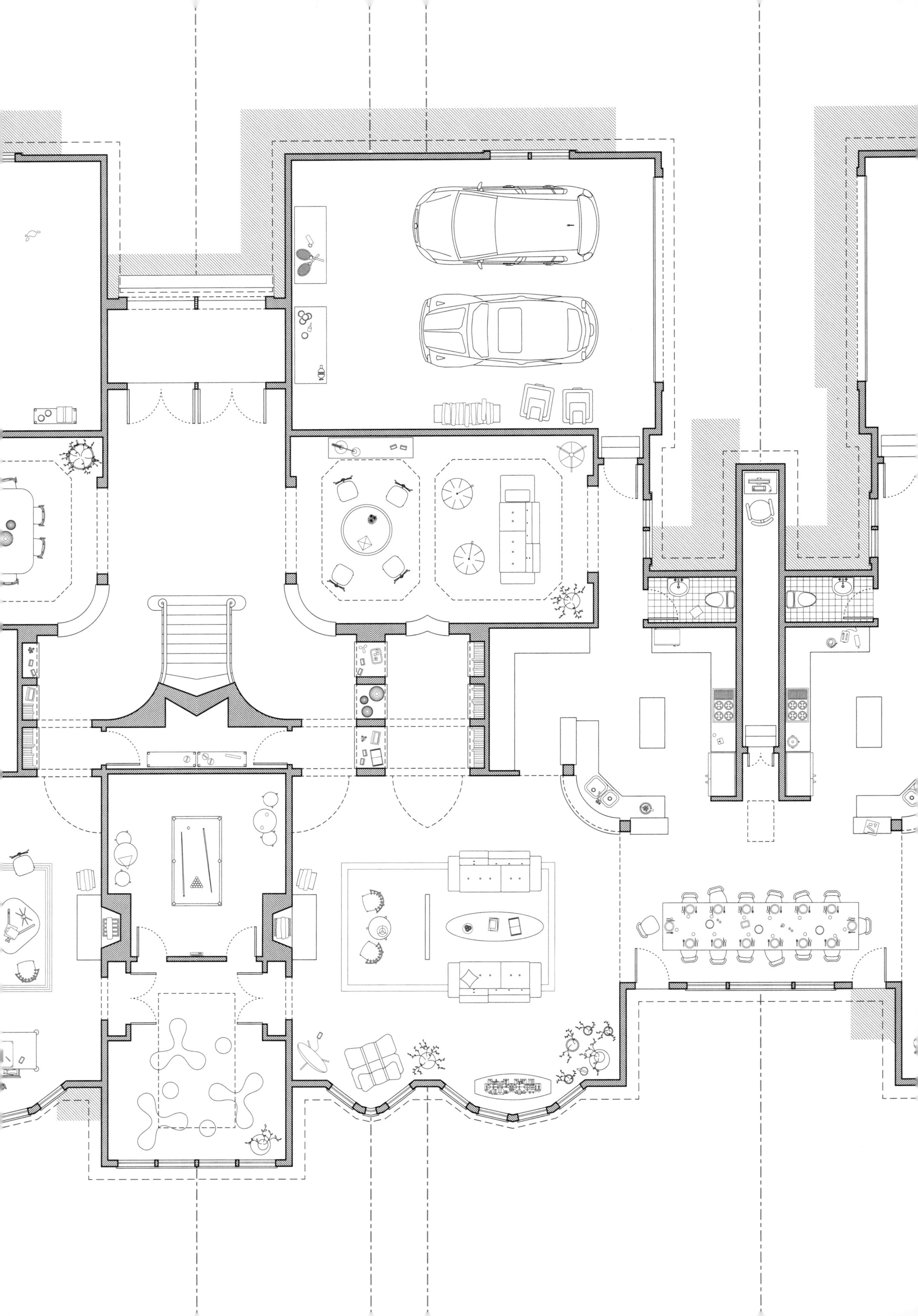

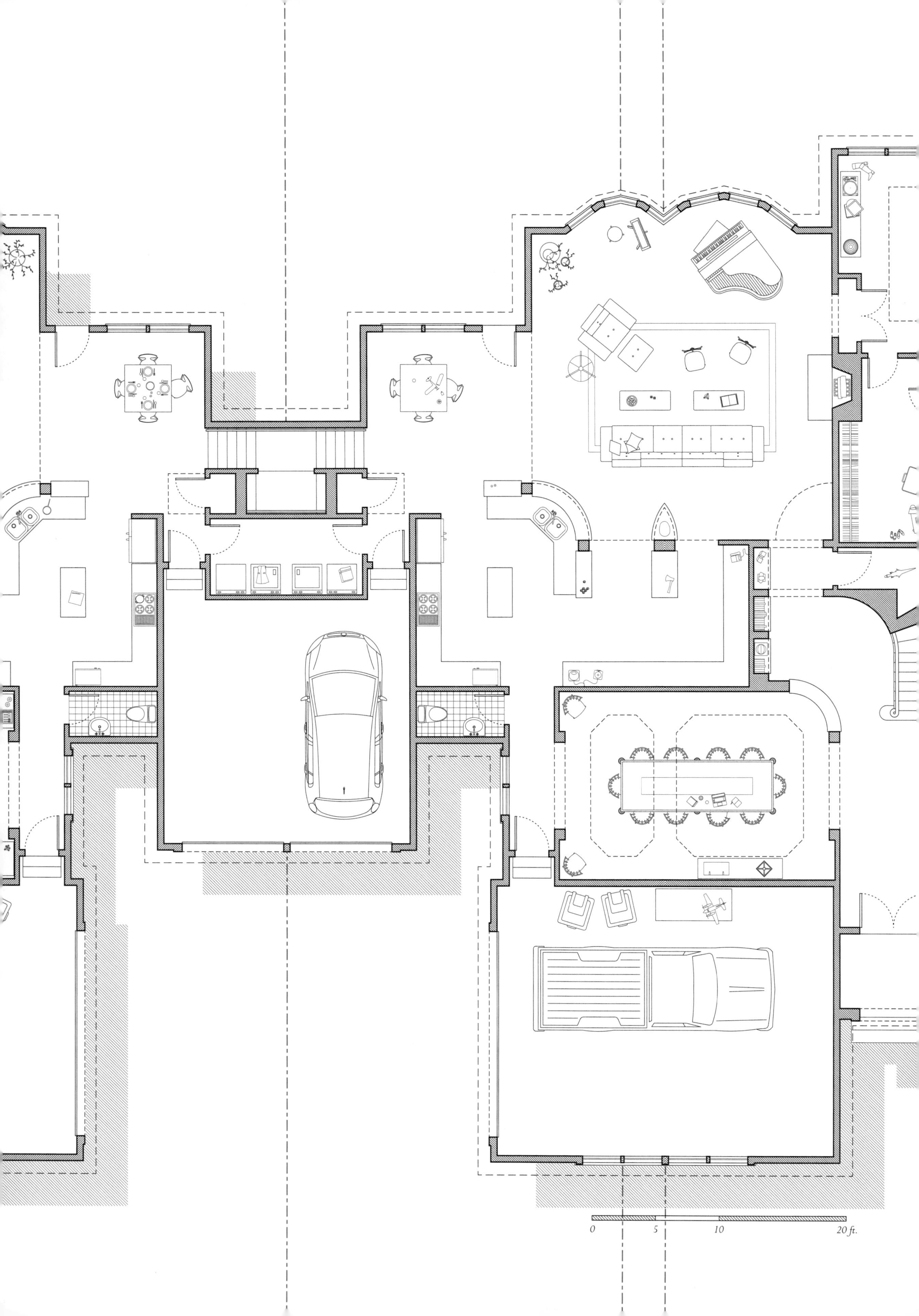
0
5
10
20 ft.

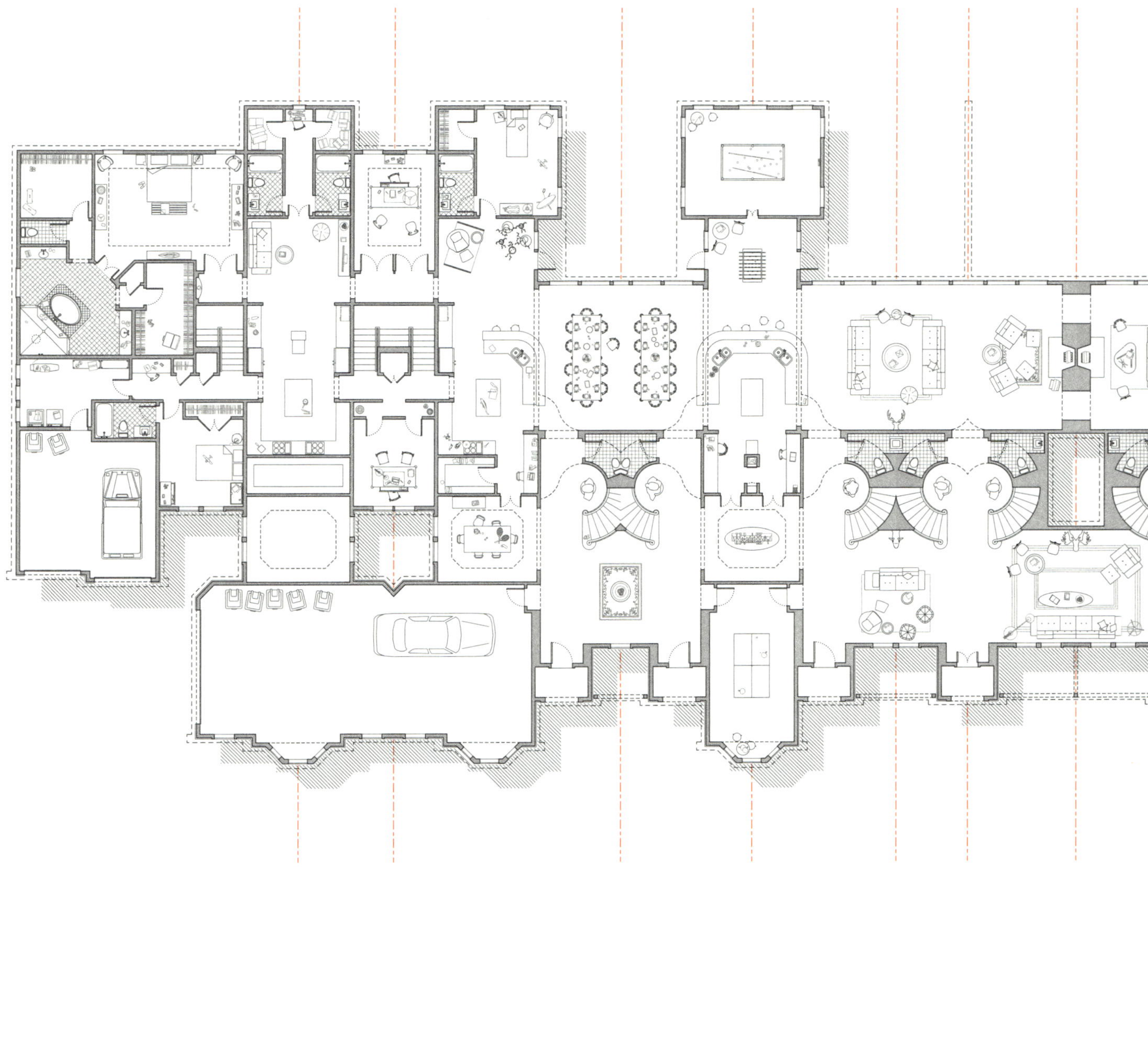

The Fourier
after Toll Bros.' St. Paul model

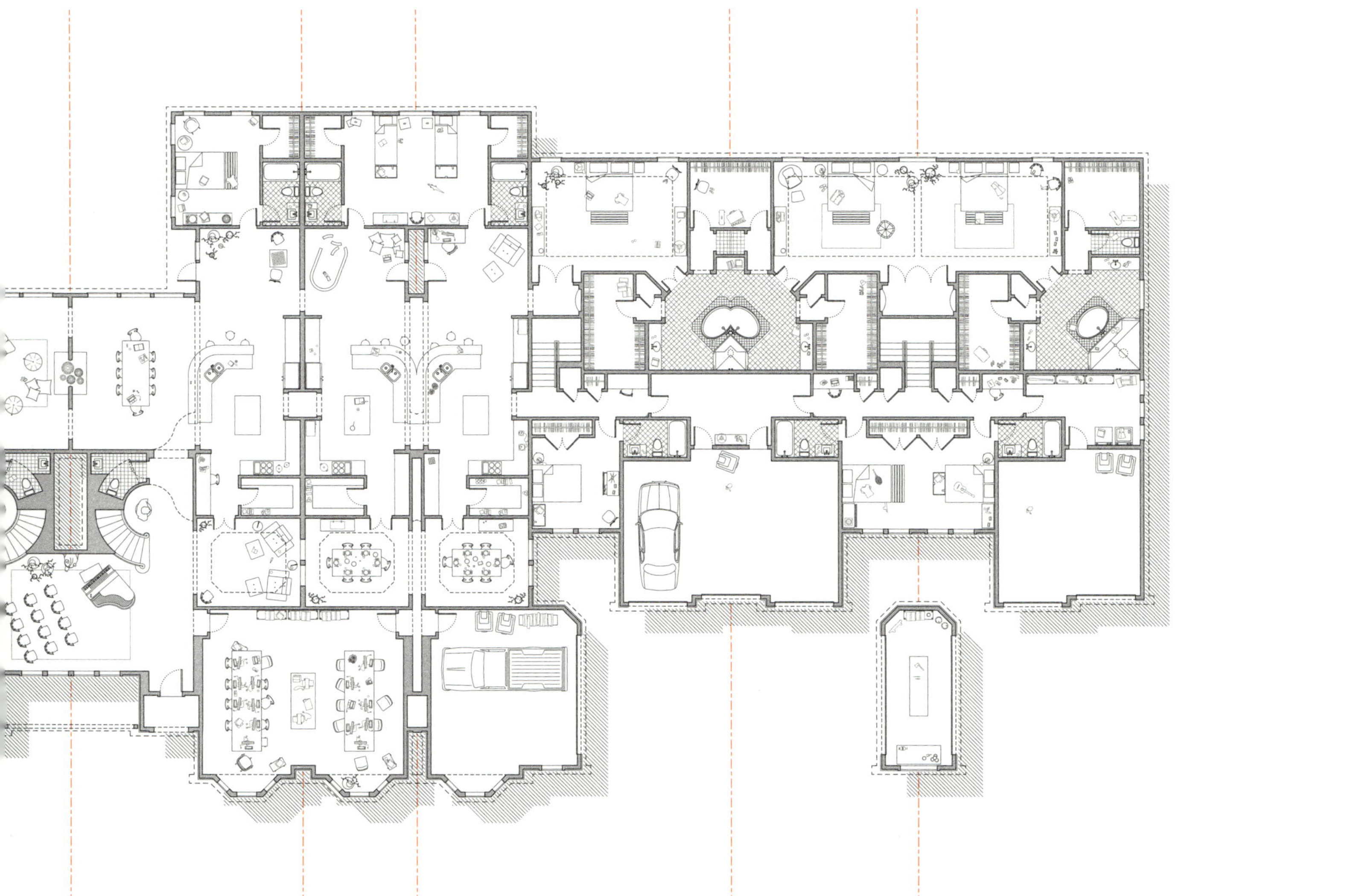
0 5 10 20 40 ft.

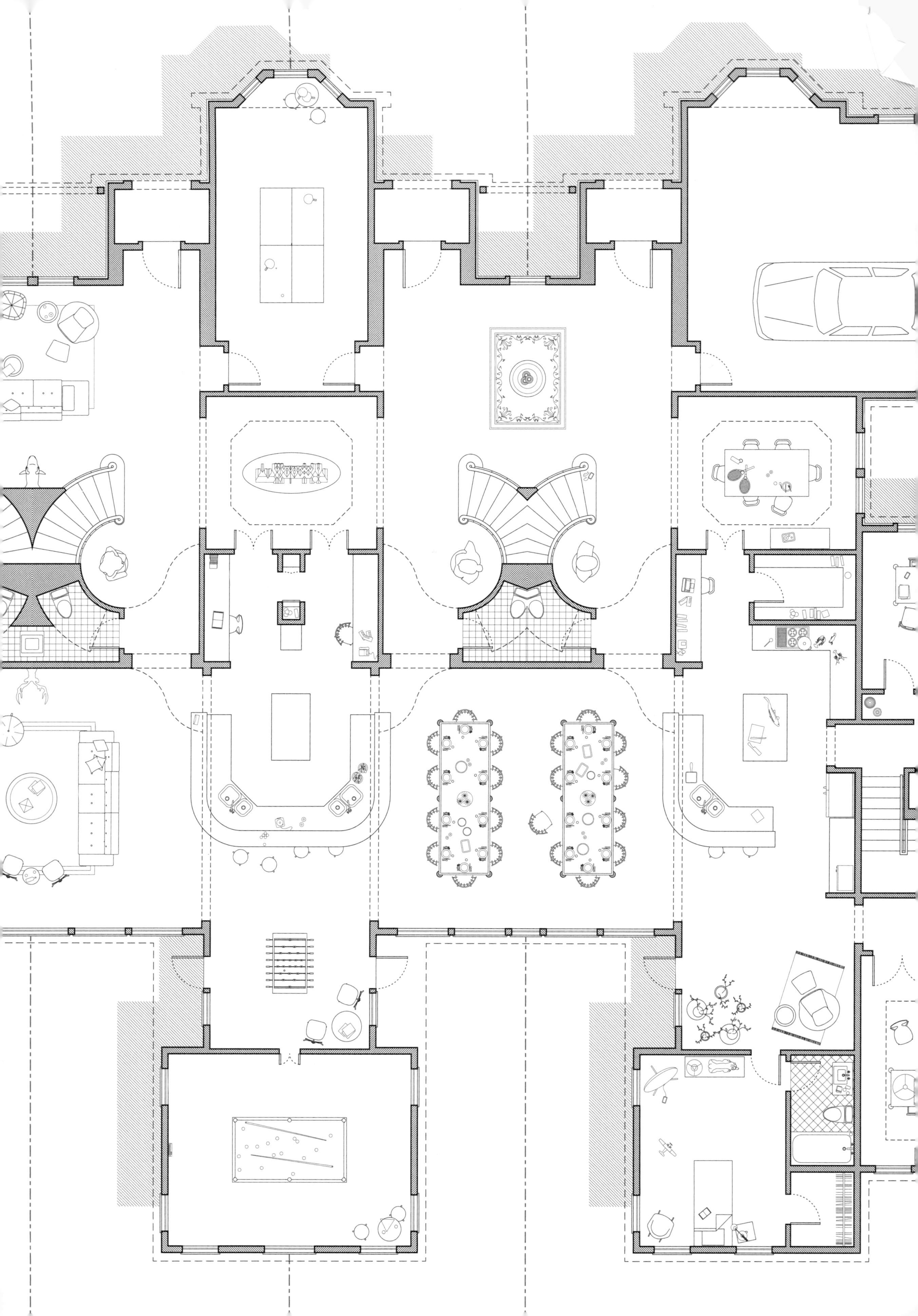

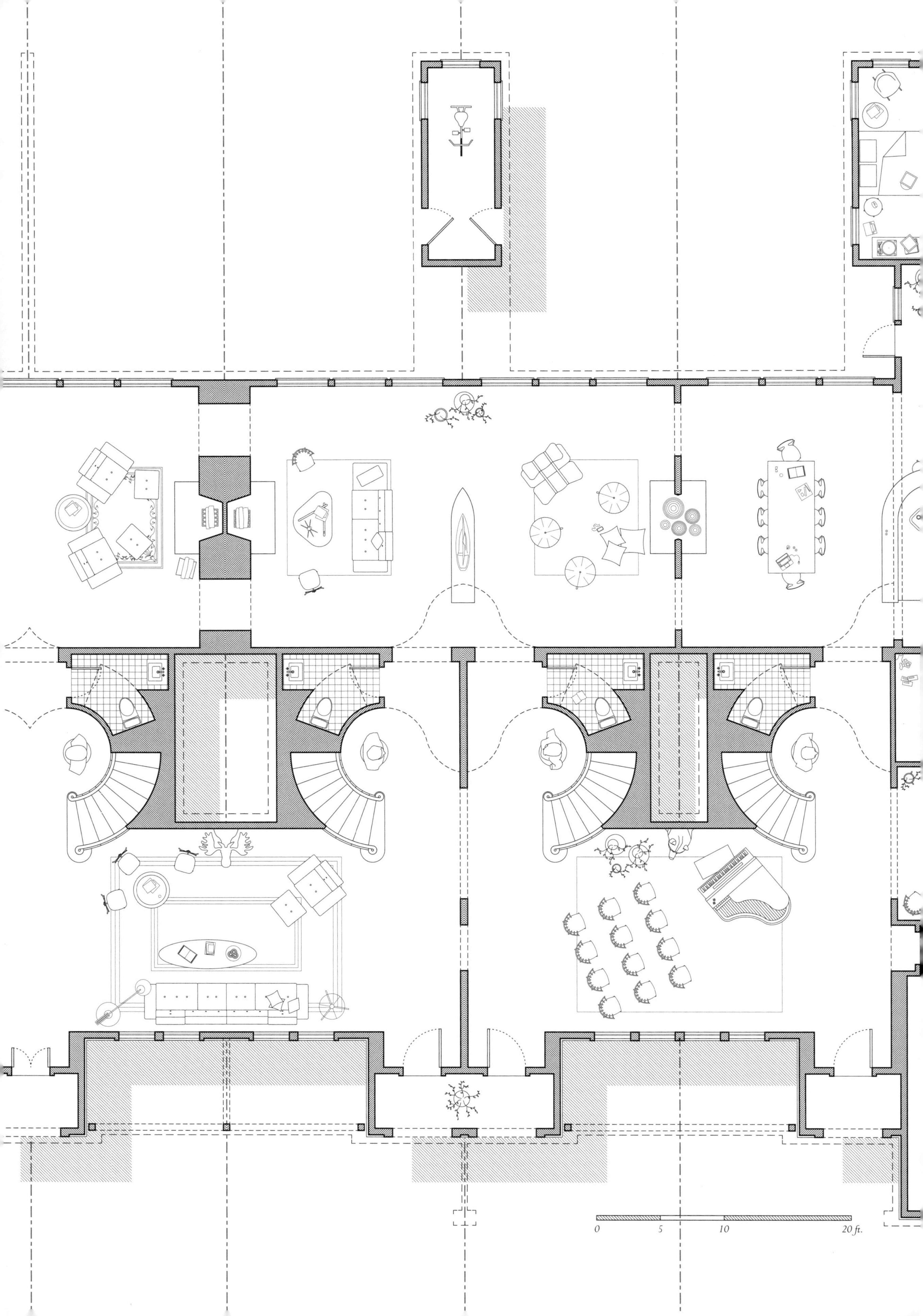
0
5
10
20 ft.

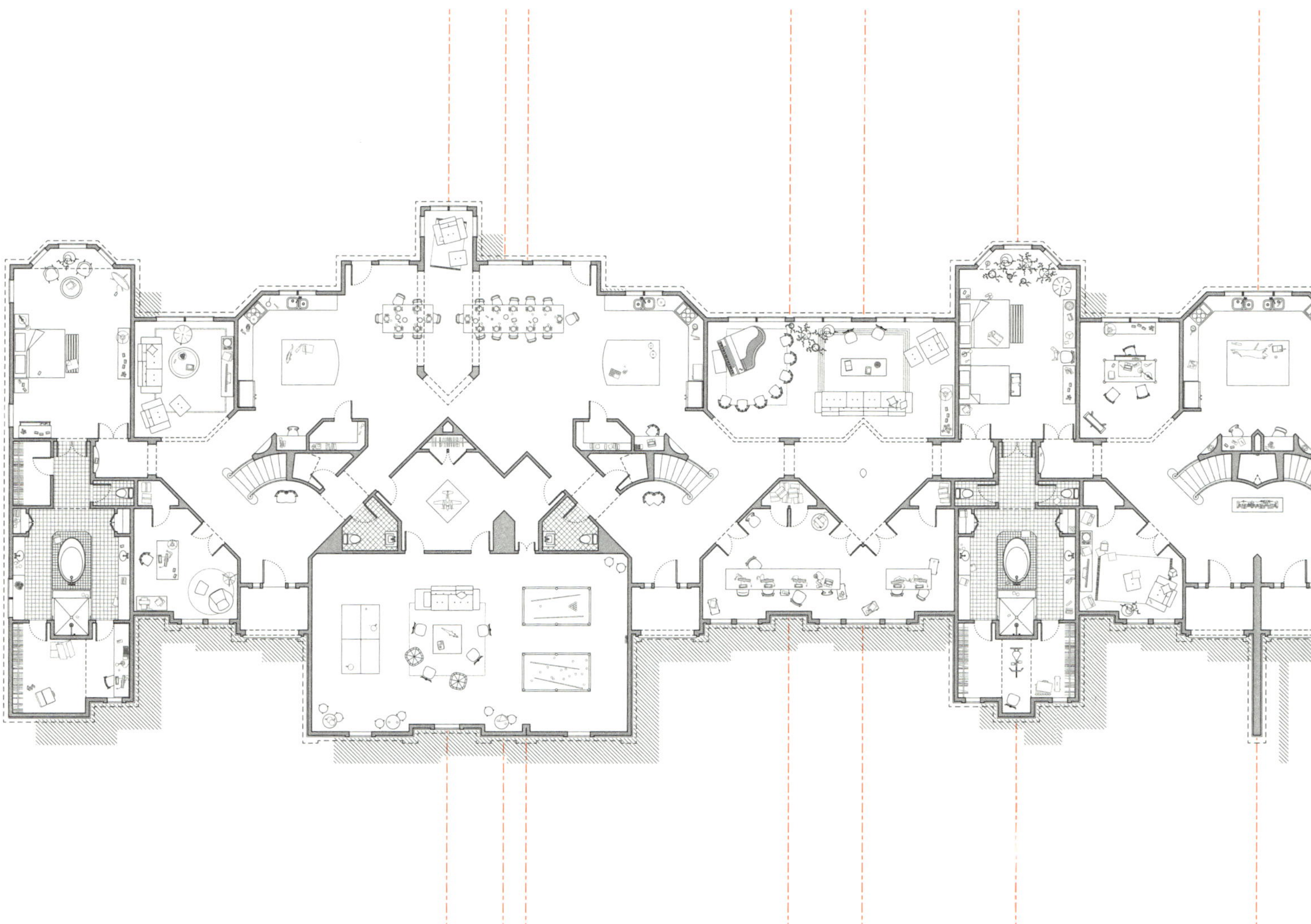

The Owen

after Toll Bros.' Cartengena model

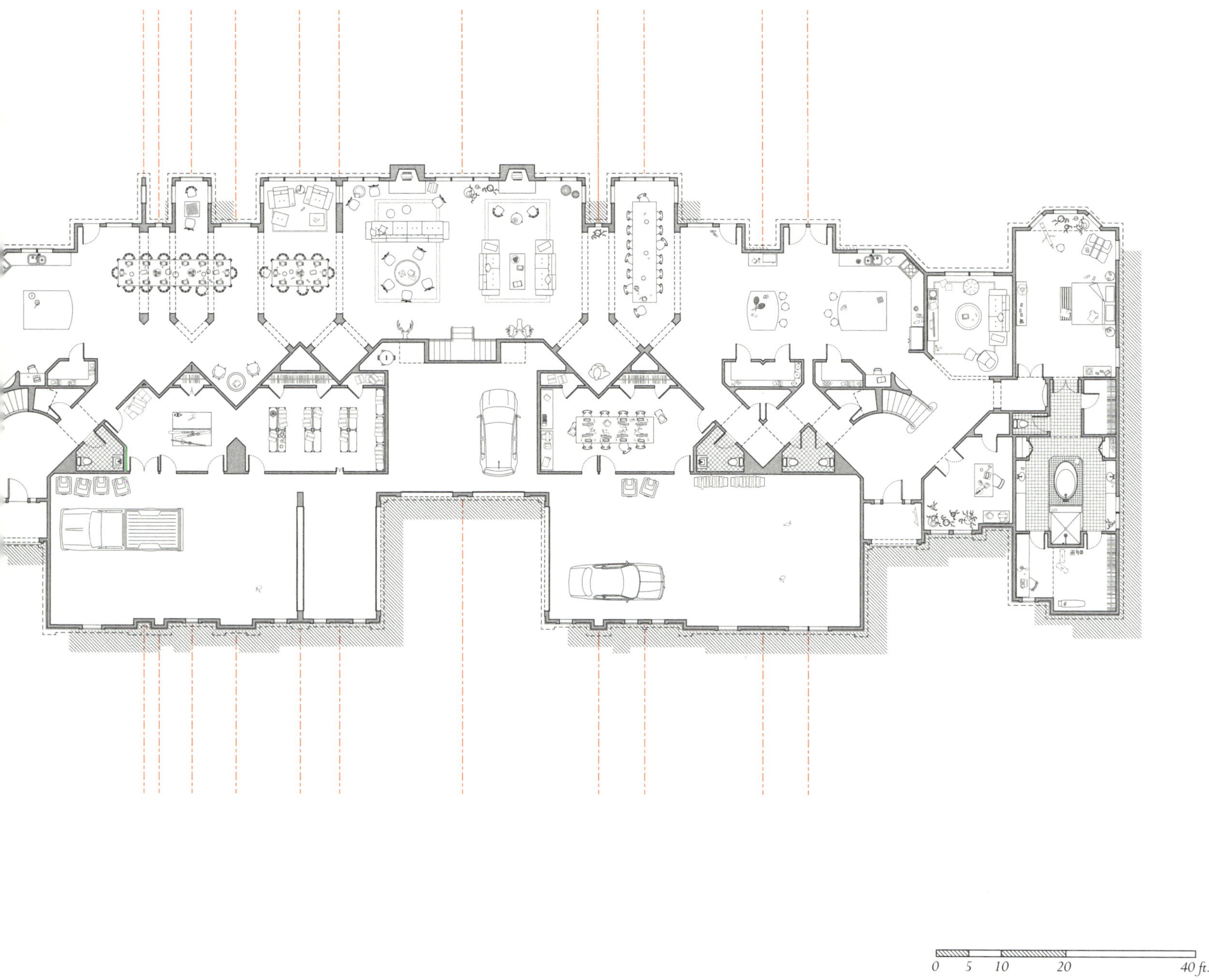

0 5 10 20 40 ft.

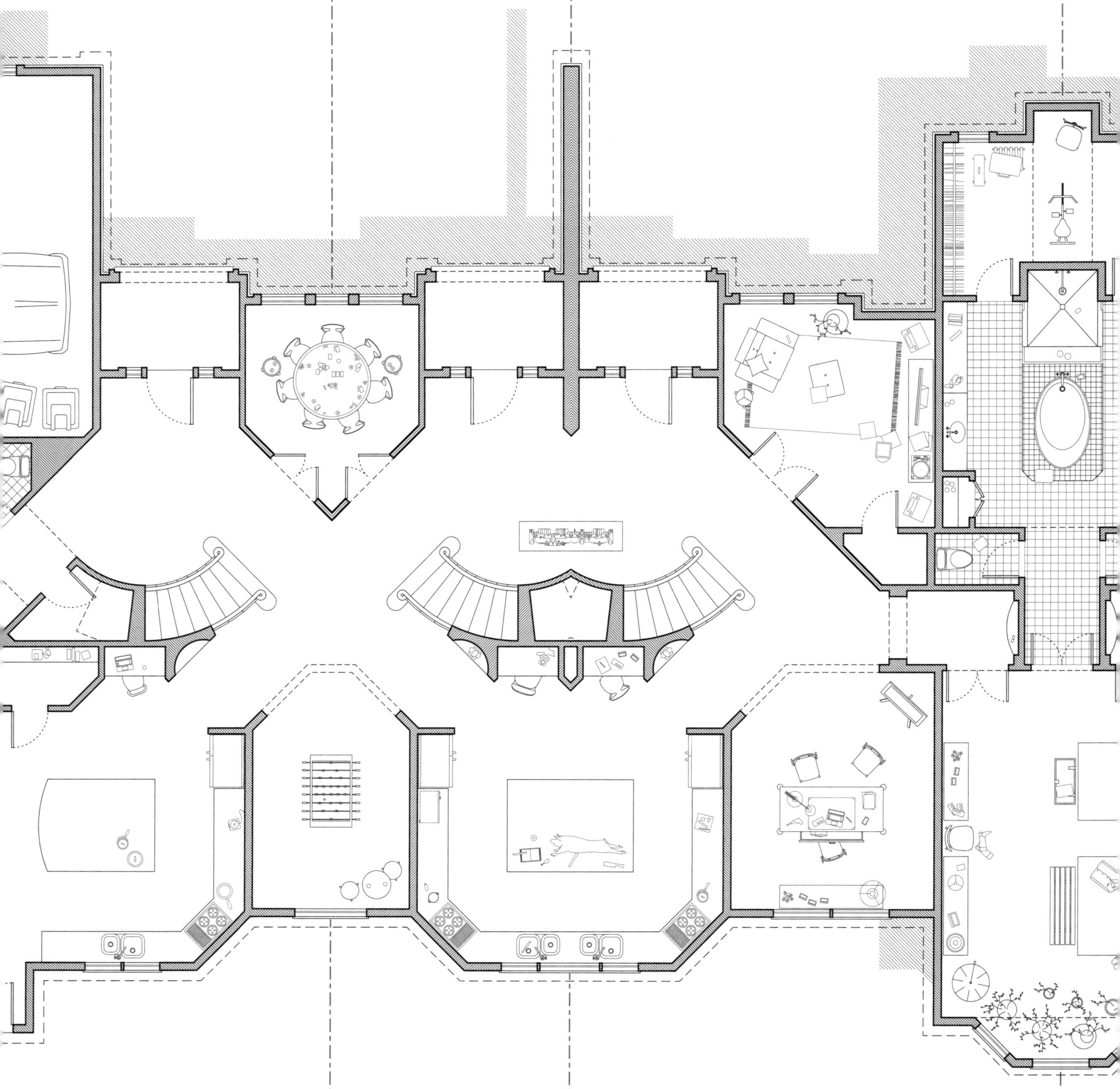

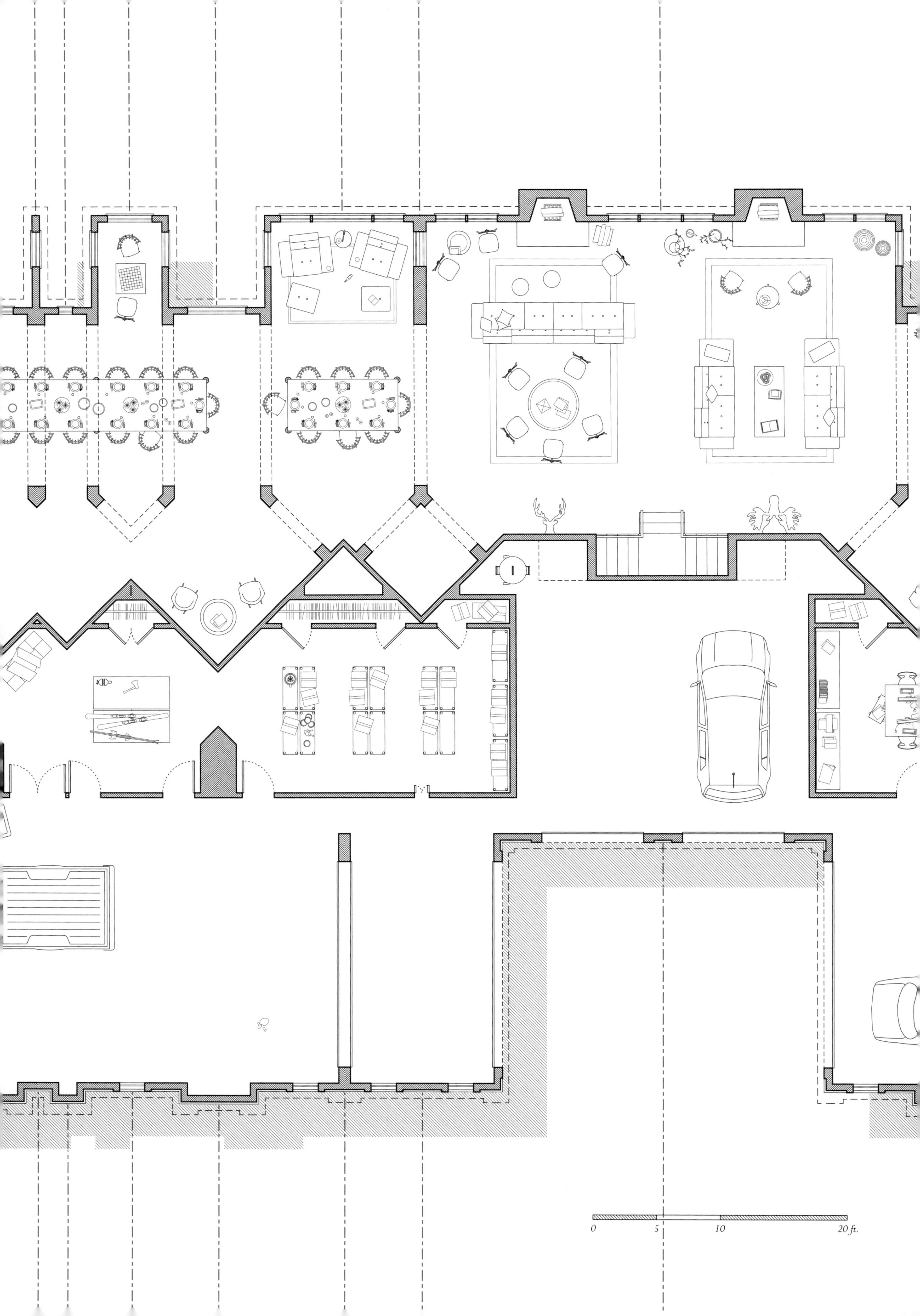
0
5
10
20 ft.

Imprint

Atlas of Another America
An Architectural Fiction

Concept
Keith Krumwiede

Graphic Design
Keith Krumwiede
with the advice of Luke Bulman

Drawings
Keith Krumwiede
assisted by Andrew Bruno, Nicholas McDermott, and John Vogt

Proofreading
Lisa Schons

Typesetting
Tina Henderson
Keith Krumwiede

Lithography, Printing, and Binding
DZA Druckerei zu Altenburg GmbH, Thuringia

[A]Typical Plan[s]
previously published in *Perspecta 43: Taboo*

SuperModel Homes
previously published in *Cite: The Architecture and Design Review of Houston,* no. 54

Selections from Freedomland
previously published in *306090: Making a Case* and *Praxis: True Stories*

Park Books AG
Niederdorfstrasse 54
8001 Zurich
Switzerland

www.park-books.com

ISBN 978-3-03860-002-2

Acknowledgments

This book owes its existence to the generous support, encouragement, and advice of the following:

Emily Abruzzo, Stan Allen, Gerald Bodziak, Jack Brough, Andrew Bruno, Luke Bulman, Daniel Claro, McLain Clutter, Martina Decker, Seher Erdogan, Britt Eversole, Fabrizio Gallanti, Lisa Gray, Jason Griffiths, Chris Grimley, Jacqui Hawkins, Adam Hayes, Francisca Insulza, Lauren Kern, Parsa Khalili, Mark Kroeckel, Michael Kubo, Jesse LeCavalier, Lars Lerup, Nicholas McDermott, Cornelia Mechler, Maria Hurtado de Mendoza, Ana Miljacki, Michael Mostoller, Dung Ngo, Mark Pasnik, Albert Pope, Amrita Raja, Matt Roman, Lisa Schons, Robert A.M. Stern, Jesse Vogler, John Vogt, Alejandro Zaera-Polo, and Mimi Zeiger

The research for "Six Typical Plans" was supported by an
A. Whitney Griswold Faculty Research Grant at Yale University.

for
Soren

In recognition for their support of the first public exhibition of Freedomland, the following were granted naming rights to an estate:

Sunil Bald – Bald Bend
Patrick Bellew – Bellew Green
Kent Bloomer – Bloomersbury
Jack Brough – Brough of Birsay
Brennan Buck – Bastide de Buck
Tom Buresh – Ville d'Anelle
Kevin Daly – CityLAB Center for Practical Utopias
Trattie Davies – Davies Lawn and Tennis Club
Richard DeFlumeri – Du Flumadon
Cemre Durusoy – Durusoy Landing
Martin Finio – Finio Farms
Mark Foster Gage – Gage's Glorious Gay Gardens
Elizabeth Gessel – Gessel Manor
Elijah Huge – Huge Acres
Maria de Ibanez de Sendadiano – Rancho Riata
Linda Jarvin and Marco Lubrano – Palazzo del Popolo di Otto Totti
Makram El Kadi – Bayt el Kadi
Terry Kern – Palais Kern
Suzie Kern – Estate del Suzanne
Parsa Khalili – Wazeone Woods
Emily Kirkland and Luke Bulman – The Villas at Pek Park
Michael Kubo – Kubo Verde
Jared Levy – Levy's Landing
Andrew Lyon – Lyon's Gate at Freedomland
Nick McDermott – Maison Très McDermott
David Martin – Martin-Hall-in-the-Meadows
Ed Mitchell – Hopeloos Stad
Lee Moreau and Ana Miljacki – Smiley's Acres
Alan Organschi – Acri Anonimi
Ben Pell – Pellitshker Plotz
Emmanuel Petit – La Grande Place des Petit
Noah Riley – Riley's Safe House
Matthew Roman and Jacqui Hawkins – Atria Romano Accipitris
Pam Samuels – Samuelsville
Blair Satterfield – Satter Fields
Fred Scharmen – Scharmen's Overlook
Ingrid Schoenlank – Pleiades Prospect
Matt Seltzer – Seltzer Springs
Mary Springer – Marigold Springs
Robert A.M. Stern – RAMSALAND
Marc Swackhamer – Swackhamer Grange
James Michael Tate – Estate of Mind
Jessica Varner – Via Varner
M.O. Wilson – Wilson Estates at Outterbridge Park
Michael Young – Les Joie des Jeunes
Mimi Zeiger – La Quinta de Zeiger

L'Abri de la Bourgeoisie
after *L'Abri du Pauvre,* 1804
Claude-Nicolas Ledoux